Analysable Real-Time Systems Programmed in Ada

Alan Burns and Andy Wellings

University of York

The rights of Alan Burns and Andy Wellings to be identified as authors of this work have been asserted to them in accordance with the Copyright Design and Patents Act 1988.

All rights are reserved. No part of this publication may be reproduced, stored in a retrieval system or transmitted in any form or by any means, electronic, mechanical, photocopying, recording or otherwise, without prior permission of Alan Burns and Andy Wellings.

Material in the book has been updated and extended from

Real-Time Systems and Programming Languages
Ada, Real-Time Java and C/Real-Time POSIX
Fourth Edition, Addison Wesley
2009

©Alan Burns and Andy Wellings, 2016
ISBN-13: 978-1530265503
ISBN-10: 1530265509

Contents

Preface   **xi**

I INTRODUCTION   1

1 Introduction to real-time systems   1
1.1 Definition of a real-time system 1
1.2 Examples of real-time systems 4
1.3 Characteristics of real-time systems 10
1.4 Development cycle for real-time systems 16
Summary 21

2 Real-time principles   23
2.1 Specifying timing requirements 23
2.2 Temporal scopes 24
2.3 Specifying temporal scopes and activities 27
2.4 A real-time programming model 30
Summary 34

3 Reliability and fault tolerance   35
3.1 Reliability, failure and faults 36
3.2 Failure modes 39
3.3 Fault prevention and fault tolerance 41
3.4 N-version programming 45
3.5 Software dynamic redundancy 49
3.6 The recovery block approach to software fault tolerance 55
3.7 Dynamic redundancy and exceptions 59
3.8 Fault tolerance and the real-time programming model 60
3.9 Measuring and predicting the reliability of software 62
3.10 Safety, reliability and dependability 63
Summary 64

II SCHEDULING THEORY FOR REAL-TIME SYSTEMS   67

4 Scheduling real-time systems   69
  4.1 The cyclic executive approach 70
  4.2 Task-based scheduling 71
  4.3 Rate monotonic priority assignment 74
  4.4 Utilization-based schedulability tests for FPS 75
  4.5 Worst-case execution time 79
  Summary 81

5 Response-Time Analysis for Fixed Priority Scheduling (FPS)   83
  5.1 Independent periodic tasks 83
  5.2 Sporadic and aperiodic tasks 87
  5.3 Task systems with constrained deadlines ($D < T$) 89
  5.4 Task interactions and blocking 91
  5.5 Priority ceiling protocols 95
  Summary 99

6 Earliest Deadline First (EDF) Scheduling   101
  6.1 Utilization-based schedulability tests for EDF 101
  6.2 Utilization-based schedulability tests for LLF 103
  6.3 Processor demand criteria for EDF 103
  6.4 The QPA test 107
  6.5 Blocking and EDF 108
  6.6 Deadline-floor protocol 108
  6.7 Aperiodic tasks and EDF execution-time servers 109
  Summary 110

7 Advanced analysis techniques   111
  7.1 Release jitter 111
  7.2 Arbitrary deadlines 113
  7.3 Cooperative scheduling 114
  7.4 Fault tolerance 116
  7.5 Incorporating offsets 117
  7.6 Priority assignment 119
  7.7 Execution-time servers 121
  7.8 Scheduling for power-aware systems 122
  7.9 Incorporating system overheads 123
  Summary 128

8 Mixed criticality, multiprocessor and open systems   131
  8.1 Mixed criticality systems (MCS) 132
  8.2 Multiprocessor systems 138
  8.3 Partitioned and global placement 138
  8.4 Scheduling the network 142
  8.5 Mutual exclusion on multiprocessor platforms 143
  8.6 Open systems 144

Summary 146

III DEVELOPING REAL-TIME SYSTEMS IN ADA 149

9 The Ada programming language 151
9.1 Languages for programming real-time systems 152
9.2 An introduction to Ada 155
9.3 Overview of Ada 156
9.4 Programming in the large 170
9.5 Aspects and attributes 187
Summary 187

10 Concurrent programming 191
10.1 Motivation 191
10.2 Processes and tasks/threads 192
10.3 Concurrent execution 196
10.4 Task representation 200
10.5 Concurrent execution in Ada 202
10.6 Multiprocessor and distributed systems 209
10.7 A simple embedded system 213
10.8 Language-supported versus operating-system-supported concurrency . . . 219
Summary 220

11 Shared variable-based synchronization and communication 223
11.1 Mutual exclusion and condition synchronization 224
11.2 Coordinated sections 225
11.3 Busy waiting 227
11.4 Suspend and resume 231
11.5 Semaphores 233
11.6 Conditional critical regions 241
11.7 Monitors 242
11.8 Protected objects in Ada 245
11.9 Shared memory multiprocessors 260
11.10 Simple embedded system revisited 262
Summary 264

12 Resource control 267
12.1 Resource management 268
12.2 Expressive power and ease of use 268
12.3 The requeue facility 277
12.4 Real-time solutions to the resource control problem 281
12.5 Resource control and security 284
12.6 Resource usage 285
12.7 Deadlock 286
Summary 287

13 Real-time facilities — 289
- 13.1 The notion of time — 289
- 13.2 Access to a clock — 291
- 13.3 Delaying a task — 296
- 13.4 Programming timeouts — 298
- Summary — 300

14 Programming real-time abstractions — 301
- 14.1 Real-time tasks — 302
- 14.2 Programming periodic activities — 302
- 14.3 Programming aperiodic and sporadic activities — 303
- 14.4 The role of real-time events and their handlers — 306
- 14.5 Controlling input and output jitter — 308
- 14.6 The Ravenscar profile — 314
- 14.7 Simple embedded system revisited — 319
- Summary — 320

15 Programming schedulable systems — 323
- 15.1 Programming cyclic executives — 324
- 15.2 Programming preemptive priority-based systems — 325
- 15.3 Ada and fixed priority scheduling — 325
- 15.4 Dynamic priorities and other Ada facilities — 328
- 15.5 Programming EDF systems — 329
- 15.6 Mixed scheduling — 338
- 15.7 Scheduling and the Ravenscar profile — 340
- 15.8 Simple embedded system revisited — 340
- Summary — 341

16 Low-level programming — 343
- 16.1 Hardware input/output mechanisms — 343
- 16.2 Language requirements — 350
- 16.3 Programming devices in Ada — 352
- 16.4 Scheduling device drivers — 362
- 16.5 Memory management — 364
- Summary — 367

17 Exceptions and exception handling — 369
- 17.1 Exception handling in older real-time languages — 370
- 17.2 Modern exception handling — 372
- 17.3 Exception handling in Ada — 379
- 17.4 Recovery blocks and exceptions — 387
- 17.5 The real-time impact of exception handling — 390
- Summary — 390

18 Atomic actions, concurrent processes and reliability — 393
- 18.1 Atomic actions — 394
- 18.2 Atomic actions in Ada — 398

	18.3 Recoverable atomic actions	401
	18.4 Asynchronous notification	405
	18.5 Asynchronous notification in Ada	408
	18.6 Atomic actions and scheduling analysis	424
	Summary	425

19 Tolerating timing faults 427
    19.1 Dynamic redundancy and timing faults 427
    19.2 Deadline miss detection 430
    19.3 Overrun of worst-case execution time 432
    19.4 Overrun of sporadic events 434
    19.5 Overrun of resource usage 438
    19.6 Damage confinement 439
    19.7 Error recovery 446
    Summary 453

IV CONCLUSIONS 455

20 Mine control case study 457
    20.1 Mine drainage 457
    20.2 The HRT-HOOD design method 462
    20.3 The logical architecture design 463
    20.4 The physical architecture design 467
    20.5 Translation to Ada 471
    20.6 Fault tolerance and distribution 489
    Summary 491

21 Conclusions 493
    21.1 Future challenges 494

References 497

Index 503

List of Programs

10.1 The `Ada.Task_Identification` package. 207
10.2 The `Ada.Task_Termination` package. 208
10.3 The `System.Multiprocessors` package. 212
10.4 The `System.Multiprocessor.Dispatching_Domains` package. 212

11.1 The `Ada.Synchronous_Task_Control` package. 232
11.2 The `Ada.Synchronous_Barriers` package. 257

13.1 The `Ada.Calendar` package. 294
13.2 The `Ada.Real_Time` package 295

14.1 The `Ada.Real_Time.Timing_Events` package. 307

15.1 The `Ada.Dynamic_Priorities` package. 328
15.2 The `Ada.Asynchronous_Task_Control` package. 329
15.3 The `Ada.Dispatching.EDF` package. 330

16.1 The `Ada.Interrupts` package. 358
16.2 The `Ada.Interrupts.Names` package. 359
16.3 The `System.Storage_Pools` package. 366

17.1 The `Standard` package. 373
17.2 The `Ada.Exceptions` pacakge. 380

19.1 An abridged version of the `Ada.Execution_Time` package. 433
19.2 The `Ada.Execution_Time.Timers` package. 435
19.3 The `Ada.Execution_Time.Interrupts` package. 437
19.4 The `Ada.Execution_Time` package's support for interrupts. . . . 437
19.5 The `Ada.Execution_Time.Group_Budgets` package. 441

x   LIST OF PROGRAMS

Preface

In 1981, a software error caused a stationary robot to move suddenly and with impressive speed to the edge of its operational area. A nearby worker was crushed to death.
 This is just one example of the hazards of embedded real-time systems. Since 1981, there have been many more accidents involving equipment controlled by computers. What these sobering examples illustrate is that there is a need to take a system-wide view of embedded systems. Indeed it can be argued that there is the requirement for real-time systems to be recognised as a distinct engineering discipline. This book is a contribution towards the development of this discipline. It cannot, of course, cover all the topics that are apposite to the study of real-time systems engineering; it does, however, present a comprehensive description and assessment of the means of analysing real-time systems, and the programming languages and operating system primitives used in this domain. Particular emphasis is placed on language primitives and their role in the production of reliable, predicable, safe and dependable software.

Audience

The book is aimed at Final Year and Masters students in Computer Science and related disciplines. It has also been written with the professional software engineer, and real-time systems engineer, in mind. Readers are assumed to have knowledge of sequential programming languages and some prior experience of languages such as C, Java and Ada, and to be familiar with the basic tenets of software engineering. The material presented reflects the content of courses developed over a number of years by the authors at various universities and for industry. These courses specifically address real-time systems and programming languages.

Structure and content

The book is organised into four Parts. In the first part there are three chapters. Chapter 1 provides an extended introduction. The characteristics and requirements of real-time systems are presented, then an overview of the design of such systems is given. Design is

xii   PREFACE

not the primary focus of this book; nevertheless, it is important to discuss implementation within an appropriate context. Chapter 2 then describes a set of principles that are central to representing the timing requirements of real-time systems. This is followed in Chapter 3 by an introduction to further principles that underlying reliability and fault tolerance.

Part II is focussed on scheduling and timing analysis. It contains five chapter that cover various aspects of the analysis that can be used to determine the worst-case temporal behaviour of a real-time system. Topics covered in these chapters are cyclic executive construction, fixed-priority scheduling, EDF (Earliest Deadline First) scheduling, priority ceiling protocols for predictable synchronisation, analysis of more flexible model of computation, mixed criticality systems and systems implemented upon multi-processor platforms.

Part III then looks at how real-time systems can be programmed in the Ada programming language. Future versions of the book may have separate Part IIIs dedicated to other languages, such as Java. Here we concentrate on the language that arguably has the most features of relevance to the domain on real-time and fault tolerant programming. An introduction to Ada is provided in Chapter 9. In the next ten chapters a systematic description and evaluation of Ada is provided. Topics covered include tasking (concurrency), inter-task communication via the use of protected objects, how to access time via various clock abstractions, programming real-time and schedulable systems, low-level programming for device driving and interrupt handling, exception handling, resource control, atomic actions, and the programming of fault-tolerant real-time systems.

Part IV starts with a chapter containing a case study. An example from a mine control system is used. Inevitably a single scaled down study cannot illustrate all the issues covered in the previous chapters; in particular factors such as size and complexity are not addressed. Nevertheless, the case study does cover many important aspects of real-time systems. Conclusions are presented in Chapter 21.

Changes from the previous book: Real-Time Systems and Programming Languages

The current book represents a complete re-write of our previous book which had itself gone through four editions. In this new book we provide more material on analysis and address the issue of programming real-time systems by the use of just a single language. Our aim is to provide a coherent coverage of the topic that can be taught within a course of, say, thirty lectures backed up by problem classes and programming exercises (including a bare-board embedded marble sorter).

We would like to thank all the students that have attended our courses at the University of York. They have provided invaluable assistance in the development of the material presented in this book. We also wish to repeat our thanks to those who helped us with the four editions of our previous book.

Teaching Aids

This text is supported by further material available via the following website:

```
http://www.cs.york.ac.uk/rts/ARTSbook.html
```

Overhead projection foil layouts are available for many parts of the book. Teachers/lecturers who make use of this book are invited to contribute to these web pages.

Real-Time Systems Research at York

Alan Burns and Andy Wellings are members of the Real-Time Systems Research Group in the Department of Computer Science at the University of York (UK). This group undertakes research into all aspects of the design, implementation and analysis of real-time systems.

Specifically, the group is addressing: formal and structured methods for development, scheduling theories, reuse, language design, kernel design, communication protocols, distributed and parallel architectures, mixed criticality systems, FPGA platforms and program code analysis. The aim of the group is to undertake fundamental research, and to bring into engineering practice modern techniques, methods and tools. Areas of application of our work include space and avionic systems, engine controllers, vehicle control and multi-media systems. Further information about the group's activities can be found via:

```
http://www.cs.york.ac.uk/rts/
```

Alan Burns & Andy Wellings

September 2016

Part I

INTRODUCTION

Chapter 1
Introduction to real-time systems

1.1 Definition of a real-time system
1.2 Examples of real-time systems
1.3 Characteristics of real-time systems
1.4 Development cycle for real-time systems
Summary

As computers become smaller, faster, more reliable and cheaper, so their range of application widens. Built initially as equation solvers, their influence has extended into all walks of life, from washing machines to air traffic control. One of the fastest expanding areas of computer exploitation is that involving applications whose prime function is *not* that of information processing, but which nevertheless require information processing in order to carry out their prime function. A microprocessor-controlled washing machine is a good example of such a system. Here, the prime function is to wash clothes; however, depending on the type of clothes to be washed, different 'wash programs' must be executed. These types of computer applications are generically called **real-time** or **embedded**. It has been estimated that 99% of the worldwide production of microprocessors is used in embedded systems. These embedded systems place particular requirements on the computer languages needed to program them, as they have different characteristics from the more traditional information processing systems. One of the key differences is that embedded systems have time constraints that must be guaranteed by the implementation to be met. Hence, they must be analysable for their response times.

This book is concerned with how to implement analysable embedded computer systems in the Ada programming language.

1.1 Definition of a real-time system

Before proceeding further, it is worth trying to define the phrase 'real-time system' more precisely. There are many interpretations of the exact nature of a real-time system; how-

2 INTRODUCTION TO REAL-TIME SYSTEMS

ever, they all have in common the notion of response time – the time taken for the system to generate output from some associated input. The *Oxford Dictionary of Computing* gives the following definition of a real-time system:

> Any system in which the time at which output is produced is significant. This is usually because the input corresponds to some movement in the physical world, and the output has to relate to that same movement. The lag from input time to output time must be sufficiently small for acceptable timeliness.

Here, the word 'timeliness' is taken in the context of the total system. For example, in a missile guidance system, output is required within a few milliseconds, whereas in a computer-controlled car assembly line, the response may be required only within a second. To illustrate the various ways in which 'real-time' systems are defined, two further definitions will be given. Young [82] defines a real-time system to be:

> any information processing activity or system which has to respond to externally generated input stimuli within a finite and specified period.

Another definition is [68]:

> A real-time system is a system that is required to react to stimuli from the environment (including the passage of physical time) within time intervals dictated by the environment.

In their most general sense, all these definitions cover a very wide range of computer activities. For example, an operating system like Windows may be considered real-time in that when a user enters a command he or she will expect a response within a few seconds. Fortunately, it is usually not a disaster if the response is not forthcoming. These types of system can be distinguished from those where *failure* to respond can be considered just as bad as a wrong response. Indeed, for some, it is this aspect that distinguishes a real-time system from others where response time is important but not crucial. Consequently, *the correctness of a real-time system depends not only on the logical result of the computation, but also on the time at which the results are produced.* Practitioners in the field of real-time computer system design often distinguish between **hard** and **soft** real-time systems. Hard real-time systems are those where it is absolutely imperative that responses occur within the specified deadline. Soft real-time systems are those where response times are important but the system will still function correctly if deadlines are occasionally missed. Soft systems can themselves be distinguished from interactive ones in which there are no explicit deadlines. For example, the flight control system of a combat aircraft is a hard real-time system because a missed deadline could lead to a catastrophic failure, whereas a data acquisition system for a process control application is soft, as it may be defined to sample an input sensor at regular intervals but to tolerate intermittent delays. Of course, many systems will have both hard and soft real-time subsystems. Indeed, some services may have both a soft and a hard deadline. For example, a response to some warning event may have a soft deadline of 50 ms (for an optimally efficient reaction) and a hard deadline of 200 ms (to guarantee that no damage to equipment or personnel takes place). Between 50 ms and 200 ms, the 'value' (or utility) of the output decreases.

DEFINITION OF A REAL-TIME SYSTEM 3

As these definitions and examples illustrate, the use of the term 'soft' does not imply a single type of requirement, but incorporates a number of different properties. For example:

- the deadline can be missed occasionally (typically with an upper limit of misses within a defined interval)
- the service can occasionally be delivered late (again, with an upper limit on tardiness)

A deadline that can be missed occasionally, but in which there is no benefit from late delivery, is called **firm**. In some real-time systems, optional firm components may be given probabilistic requirements (for example, a hard service must produce an output every 300 ms; at least 80% of the time this output will be produced by a firm component, X; on other occasions, a hard, but functionally much simpler component, Y, will be used).

In this book, the term 'real-time system' is used to mean both soft and hard real-time. Where discussion is concerned specifically with hard real-time systems, the term 'hard real-time' will be used explicitly.

In a hard or soft real-time system, the computer is usually interfaced directly to some physical equipment and is dedicated to monitoring or controlling the operation of that equipment. A key feature of all these applications is the role of the computer as an information processing component within a larger engineering system. It is for this reason that such applications have become known as **embedded computer systems**.

Another means of classifying the role that time has in real-time systems is to distinguish between **reactive systems** and **time-aware systems**. Time-aware systems make explicit references to the time frame of the enclosing environment. For example, if a bank safe's doors are to be locked from midnight to nine o'clock in the morning then these absolute time values must be available to the system. By comparison, a reactive system is typically concerned with relative times: an output has to be produced within 50ms of an associated input. The key requirement of a reactive system is that it 'keeps up with the environment'; that is it must always be able to process input data before new data arrives. Often reactive systems are also control systems and hence they need to be synchronized with their environment. In particular, input sampling and output signaling must be done very regularly with controlled variability – there is a need to bound what is called **input jitter** and **output jitter**.

In order for reactive systems to 'keep up with its environment' they are often structured to be **time-triggered**. Here all computation activities are **periodic** in that they have a defined cycle time, for example 50ms, and are released for execution by an internal clock. The alternative to time-triggered is **event-triggered** in which the environment explicitly controls (perhaps via an interrupt) the release for execution of some software activity. These activities are termed **aperiodic** or, if there is a bound on how often the releasing event can occur in any time interval, **sporadic activities**. Many systems will contain periodic and sporadic activities. However, some design approaches restrict the software architecture so that there are only time-triggered activities; 'events' must be polled for (that is, examined via a periodic activity).

Again, in this book a broad definition of 'real-time system' is assumed. The term is taken to include reactive and time-aware systems that may have both time-triggered

4   INTRODUCTION TO REAL-TIME SYSTEMS

and event-triggered invocations of work. Periodic, aperiodic and sporadic activities are all likely to be present in the same system.

1.2 Examples of real-time systems

Having defined what is meant by a real-time systems, some examples of their use are now given.

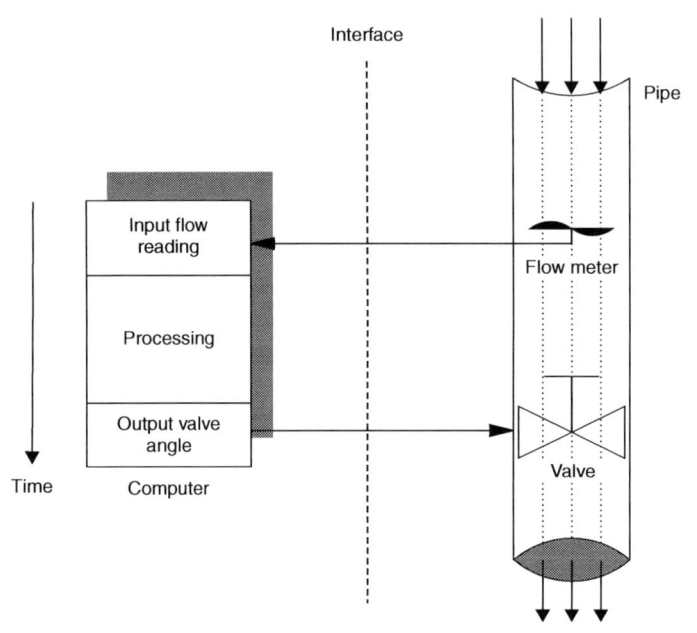

Figure 1.1: A fluid control system.

1.2.1 Process control

The first use of a computer as a component in a larger engineering system occurred in the process control industry in the early 1960s. Nowadays, the use of microprocessors is the norm. Consider the simple example shown in Figure 1.1, where the computer performs a single activity: that of ensuring an even flow of liquid in a pipe by controlling a valve. On detecting an increase in flow, the computer must respond by altering the valve angle; this response must occur within a finite period if the equipment at the receiving end of the pipe is not to become overloaded. Note that the actual response may involve quite a complex computation in order to calculate the new valve angle.

This example shows just one component of a larger control system. Figure 1.2 illustrates the role of a real-time computer embedded in a complete process control environment. The computer interacts with the equipment using sensors and actuators. A valve is an example of an actuator, and a temperature or pressure transducer is an example of a sensor. (A transducer is a device that generates an electrical signal that is proportional to the physical quantity being measured.) The computer controls the operation of the sensors

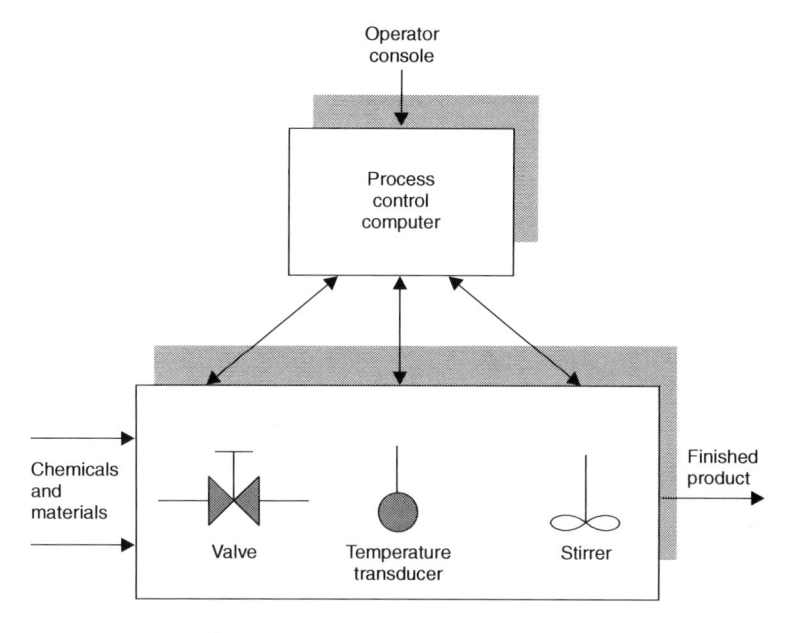

Figure 1.2: A process control system.

and actuators to ensure that the correct plant operations are performed at the appropriate times. Where necessary, analogue to digital (and digital to analogue) converters must be inserted between the controlled process and the computer.

1.2.2 Manufacturing

The use of computers in manufacturing has become essential in order that production costs can be kept low and productivity increased. Computers have enabled the integration of the entire manufacturing process from product design to fabrication. It is in the area of production control that embedded systems are best illustrated. Figure 1.3 diagrammatically represents the role of the production control computer in the manufacturing process. The physical system consists of a variety of mechanical devices – such as machine tools, manipulators and conveyor belts – all of which need to be controlled and coordinated by the computer.

A modern manufacturing control systems will employ a wide range of robots. These will again need to be controlled and coordinated, but they are also autonomous real-time systems in their own right. They have large numbers of sensors (for example proximity indicators), many moving parts that need controlling and often vision subsystems that require considerable computational power. When mobile robots and humans operate in the same physical space then there are considerable safety issues that dictate that at least part of the robots functions are hard real-time.

6   INTRODUCTION TO REAL-TIME SYSTEMS

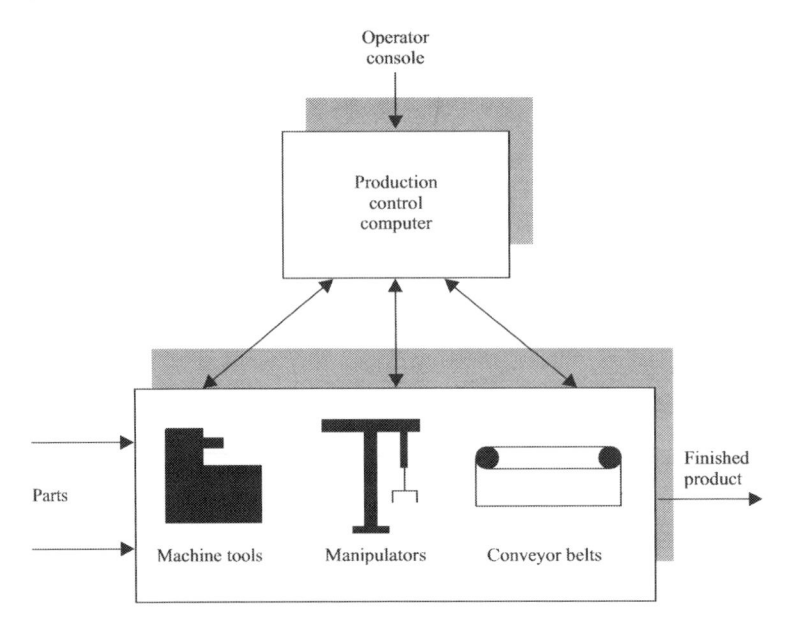

Figure 1.3: A production control system.

1.2.3 Communication, command and control

Although **communication, command and control** is a military term, there is a wide range of disparate applications which exhibit similar characteristics; for example, airline seat reservation, medical facilities for automatic patient care, air traffic control, remote bank accounting and large-scale manufacturing plants. Each of these time-aware systems consists of a complex set of policies, information gathering devices and administrative procedures which enable decisions to be supported, and provide the means by which they can be implemented. Often, the information gathering devices and the instruments required for implementing decisions are distributed over a wide geographical area. Figure 1.4 diagrammatically represents such a system.

1.2.4 A typical embedded real-time system

In each of the examples shown above, the computer is interfaced directly to physical equipment in the real world, and is reacting to changes in this environment. In order to control these real-world devices, the computer will need to sample the measurement devices at regular intervals (i.e. periodic activities); a real-time clock is therefore required. Usually, there is also an operator's console to allow for manual intervention. The human operator is kept constantly informed of the state of the system by displays of various types, including graphical ones.

The system will also keep records of its state changes in a database, which can be interrogated by the operators, either for a post mortem (in the case of a system crash), or to provide information for administrative purposes. Indeed, this information is increasingly

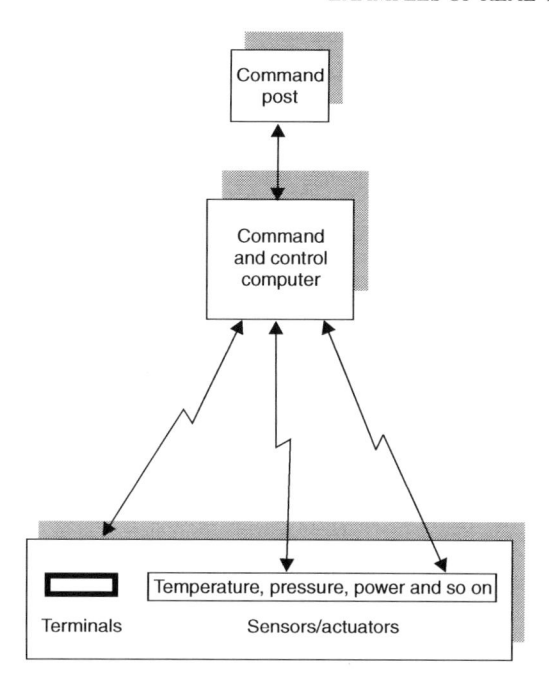

Figure 1.4: A command and control system.

being used to support decision making in the day-to-day running of systems. For example, in the chemical and process industries, plant monitoring is essential for maximizing economic advantages rather than simply maximizing production. Decisions concerning production at one plant may have serious repercussions for other plants at remote sites, particularly when the products of one process are being used as raw material for another.

A typical large embedded real-time computer system can, therefore, be represented by Figure 1.5. The software which controls the operations of the system can be written in modules which reflect the physical nature of the environment. Usually there will be a module which contains the algorithms necessary for physically controlling the devices; a module responsible for recording the system's state changes (perhaps in the Cloud); a module to retrieve and display those changes; and a module to interact with the operator.

1.2.5 Multi-media systems

Entertainment systems such as radios, televisions, stereo systems, video systems and games of various kinds are all real-time systems in which the temporal requirements are determined by the perception and cognition of human users. There are clear requirements on visual frame rates, sound/picture synchronization and response times (to, for example, joystick movements) that must be satisfied if the quality of the human experience is not to be noticeably compromised. Multi-media systems in which many of these entertainment media are integrated with each other and with services such as phone communications, internet searches, email interactions, news updates, and the streaming of audio and video

8   INTRODUCTION TO REAL-TIME SYSTEMS

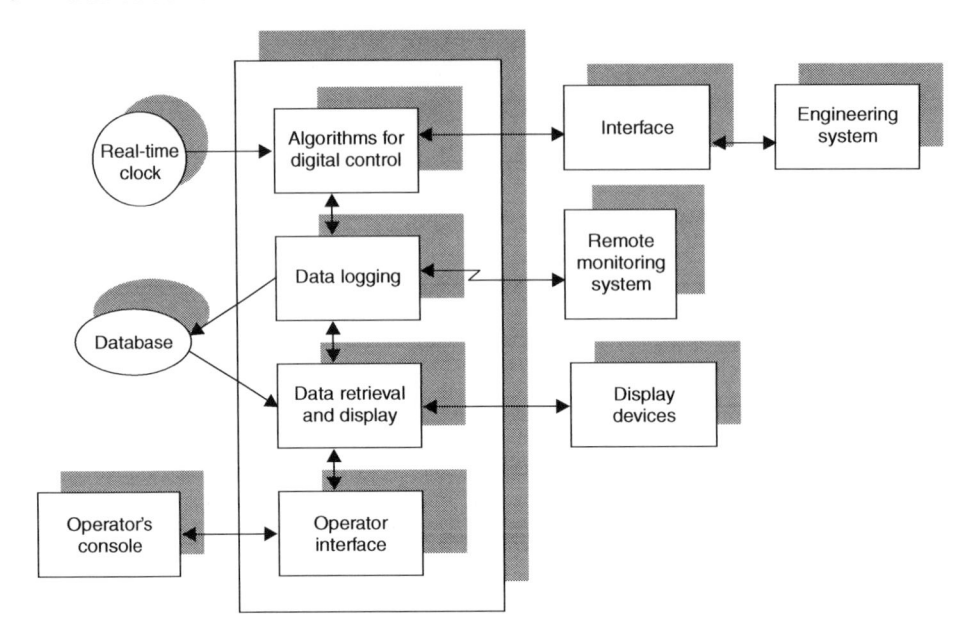

Figure 1.5: A typical embedded system.

content from remote servers, pose significant challenges for developers. There is an economic imperative to manufacture these systems at minimum cost, but the quality of the user experience must be maintained – and this means that the temporal requirements have to be central to the development process. From the design of special purpose on-chip units (for example, video decoders) to the choice of communication subsystems and the implementation of the software control components, the need to manipulate significant volumes of digital data within tight timing deadlines is the key engineering challenge.

The development of these home-based multi-media systems is one noticeable application area for real-time systems. But such fixed systems are not the only commodities under development. There is an increasing need to allow devices to be mobile whilst still linked to communication services. The mobile phone has evolved into a general purpose essential accessory that supports most of the technologies of the fixed system together with new emerging services such as providing a means of paying for goods in shops, an aid to personal security and/or surveillance and of course a camera and general purpose recording device. The one single defining property of all mobile systems is that they are indeed *mobile* – they rely on batteries for power. And batteries have finite life which adds to the challenges of developing these complex real-time systems.

1.2.6   Cyber-physical systems

A relatively new application area for real-time systems comes from the linking of digital information systems, such as that furnished by the internet, and real-time data collection typified by networks of sensors. This coupling of what is usually called the cyber world with the physical world has naturally led to the term **cyber-physical systems**. An example of a cyber-physical service is an adaptive navigation aid. Here there is a link between a detailed digitalised (and static) road map and traffic flow information that is being sensed at key locations on the roads. This traffic information is clearly real-time and dynamic. The navigational aid can potentially use sophisticated traffic flow models to predict future problems and advise as to the least congested route. This advice will diminish in usefulness as the data on which it is based becomes stale. Hence the need to update the advice as new data becomes available.

Cyber-physical systems may operate over wide areas, perhaps even globally, involve many computational elements and communication services, and have access to enormous volumes of real-time data. In the traffic system, consider the quantity of data generated if all junctions on all roads in Europe (or the USA or China) are sensing traffic flow (in all directions) and feeding this data into the internet. The sensing component of the cyber-physical system may be quite simple, for example a temperature sensor, or be a significant entity in its own right, such as a camera permanently viewing some scene. The local sensory system must, in this case, decide whether raw data or a processed (simpler) form of the data is fed into the digital world.

A cyber-physical system is likely to have real-time requirements that range from the millisecond level for the sensing activity to minutes or even hours for the applications that are built upon the amalgamation of the dynamic and static data. It should be clear to all readers, who have presumably spent time 'on the net', that the current internet with its simple protocols and architecture cannot guarantee real-time behaviour. Future enhancements (or alternatives) to the internet are, however, likely to respond to the challenges of cyber-physical systems and provide QoS (Quality of Service) that does provide real-time guarantees – even if the guarantees are not absolute (hard) they will have a high probability of being met.

An example of an advanced cyber-physical system that most readers will have direct experience of is a modern car. Automotive systems have grown in complexity over recent years to the extent that a high proportion of a car's cost relates to the on-board software it contains. Over 100 million lines of code is typical on a high-end vehicle. This is distributed over a range on individual ECUs (Engine Control Units). Each ECU, of which there might be over 40 in every new car, has control over some aspects of the car's behaviour. So breaking, engine control, cruse control, steering support, collision avoidance, automatic parking, lighting, door locking, window control, environment control, entertainment etc are all under the control of an ECU. And these ECU's and their associated sensors and actuators are linked by one or more real-time communication networks called CAN (Controller Area Network).

As car manufacturers move towards ever increasing automation, driver support systems will increase in sophistication. For many in the industry the ultimate aim is to produce driver-less cars. With the need for intelligent sensors and reliable and safe vehicle control, the size of the on-board software will increase by a further order of magnitude. Predictable real-time performance will be needed for much of this software; and multiprocessor ECUs will be needed to support the processing load. At the same time the commercial imperative to produce efficient, cost-effective and affordable cars will mean that well engineered solutions will be needed that are not wasteful in their use of computing and communication resources.

1.3 Characteristics of real-time systems

A real-time system possesses many special characteristics (either inherent or imposed) which are identified in the following sections. Clearly, not all real-time systems will exhibit all these characteristics; however, any general purpose language which is to be used for the effective programming of real-time systems must have facilities that support these characteristics. Furthermore, any analysis techniques will need to be capable of modelling these facilities.

1.3.1 Real-time control facilities

Response time is crucial in any embedded system. Unfortunately, it is very difficult to design and implement systems which will guarantee that the appropriate output will be generated at the appropriate times under all possible conditions. To do this, and make full use of all computing resources at all times is often impossible. For this reason, real-time systems are usually constructed using processors with considerable spare capacity, thereby ensuring that 'worst-case behaviour' does not produce any unwelcome delays during critical periods of the systems' operations.

Given adequate processing power, language and run-time support are required to enable the programmer to:

- specify times at which actions are to be performed,
- specify times by which actions are to be completed,
- support repeating (periodic or aperiodic) work,
- control (i.e. bound) the jitter on input and output operations,
- respond to situations where not all of the timing requirements can be met,
- respond to situations where the timing requirements are changed dynamically.

These are called real-time control facilities. They enable the program to synchronize with time itself. For example, with direct digital control algorithms it is necessary to sample readings from sensors at certain periods of the day, for example, 2 p.m., 3 p.m. and so on, or at regular intervals, for instance, every 5 seconds (with control systems, sample rates can vary from a few hundred hertz to several hundred megahertz). As a result of these readings, other actions will need to be performed. In an electricity power station, it is necessary at 6 p.m. on Monday to Friday each week to increase the supply of electricity to domestic consumers. This is in response to the peak in demand caused by families returning home from work, turning on lights, cooking dinner and so on. In recent years in the UK, the demand for domestic electricity reaches a peak immediately after high profile sporting events, when millions of viewers leave their living rooms, turn on lights in the kitchen and switch on the kettle in order to make a cup of tea or coffee.

An example of a dynamic change to the timing requirements of a system can be found in an aircraft flight control system. If an aircraft has experienced depressurization, there is an immediate need for all computing resources to be given over to handling the emergency. More normally, the move from taxiing to taking off to climbing and then to cruising all involve changes to the basic operation of the flight control system. These changes, which are known generally as **mode changes**, also have consequences for the temporal characteristics of the executing software.

In order to meet response time constraints, it is necessary for a system's behaviour to be predictable. The means by which worst-case response times can be minimised and calculated are the focus of the chapters in Part II in this book. The chapters in Part III consider the facilities and techniques used to obtain predictable program behaviour.

1.3.2 Extremely reliable and safe

The more society relinquishes control of its vital functions to computers, the more imperative it becomes that those computers do not fail. The failure of a system involved in automatic fund transfer between banks can lead to millions of dollars being lost irretrievably; a faulty component in electricity generation could result in the failure of a vital life-support system in an intensive care unit; and the premature shutdown of a chemical plant could cause expensive damage to equipment or environmental harm. These somewhat dramatic examples illustrate that computer hardware and software must be reliable and safe. Even in hostile environments, such as those found in military applications, it must be possible to design and implement systems that will fail only in a controlled way. Furthermore, where operator interaction is required, care must be taken in the design of the interface in order to minimize the possibility of human error.

The sheer size and complexity of real-time systems exacerbates the reliability problem; not only must expected difficulties inherent in the application be taken into account, but also those introduced by faulty software design.

In Chapter 3, the problems of producing reliable and safe software will be considered in general. The facilities that languages have introduced to cope with both expected and unexpected error conditions are examined in Part III.

1.3.3 Concurrent control of separate system components

An embedded system will tend to consist of computers and several coexisting external elements with which the computer programs must interact simultaneously. It is the very nature of these external real-world elements that they exist in parallel. In our typical embedded computer example, the program has to interact with an engineering system (which will consist of many parallel activities such as robots, conveyor belts, sensors, actuators and so on), the computer's display devices, the operator's console, the database and the real-time clock. Fortunately, the speed of a modern computer is such that usually these actions may be carried out in sequence but give the illusion of being simultaneous. In some embedded systems, however, this may not be the case, for example where the data is to be collected and processed at various geographically distributed sites, or where the response time of the individual components cannot be met by a single computer. In these cases, it is necessary to consider distributed and multiprocessor embedded systems.

A major problem associated with the production of software for systems which exhibit concurrency is how to express that concurrency in the structure of the program. One

12 INTRODUCTION TO REAL-TIME SYSTEMS

approach is to leave it all up to the programmer who must construct his/her system so that it involves the cyclic execution of a program sequence to handle the various concurrent tasks. There are several reasons, however, why this is inadvisable:

- it complicates the programmer's already difficult task and involves him or her in considerations of structures which are irrelevant to the control of the tasks in hand;
- the resulting programs are more obscure and inelegant;
- it makes proving program correctness more difficult;
- it makes decomposition of the problem more complex;
- parallel execution of the program on more than one processor is much more difficult to achieve;
- the placement of code to deal with faults is more problematic.

Older real-time programming languages, for example, RTL/2 and Coral 66, relied on operating system support for concurrency; and C is usually associated with Unix, Linux or POSIX. However, the more modern languages, such as Ada, C# and Java (and the most recent versions of C and C++) have direct support for general concurrent programming.

Although concurrency is a fundamental characteristic of real-time systems, different types of systems need different facilities. For reactive control systems with hard timing constraints, but relatively straightforward behaviour, it is sufficient to constrain each concurrent activity to be of the form:

```
input data
perform required computations with no external interactions
output data
```

For more complicated systems, the input and output activities cannot be separated from the computational part. Only during the computation activity itself will it be possible to determine the external data that is needed (for example from another activity, a shared database or from some interface into the environment).

Predicting the response-time of systems consisting of many concurrent entities executing on one or more computers is inevitably more difficult than dealing with purely sequential code. Nevertheless, the run-time flexibility it facilitates makes it easier to use hardware resources efficiently and hence to bound system response times so that deadlines are met.

In the chapters of Part III, the Ada model of concurrent programming using shared data is considered in detail. Attention is also focused on achieving reliable communication and synchronization between concurrent processes in the presence of design errors.

1.3.4 Low-level programming

The nature of embedded systems requires the computer components to interact with the external world. They need to monitor sensors and control actuators for a wide variety of real-world devices. These devices interface to the computer via input and output registers, and their operational requirements are device- and computer-dependent. Devices may also generate interrupts to signal to the processor that certain operations have been performed or that error conditions have arisen.

In the past, interfacing to devices has either been left under the control of the operating system, or has required the application programmer to resort to assembly language inserts to control and manipulate the registers and interrupts. Nowadays, because of the variety of devices and the time-critical nature of their associated interactions, their control must often be direct, and not through a layer of operating system functions. Furthermore, reliability requirements argue against the use of low-level programming languages.

Since real-time systems are time-critical, efficiency of implementation will be more important than in other systems. It is interesting that one of the main benefits of using a high-level language is that it enables the programmer to abstract away from implementation details, and to concentrate on solving the problem at hand. Unfortunately, the embedded computer systems programmer cannot afford this luxury. He or she must be constantly concerned with the cost of using particular language features. For example, if a response to some input is required within a microsecond there is no point in using a language feature whose execution takes a millisecond!

It was noted earlier that a significant class of embedded systems are now mobile and rely on batteries for power. Efficient implementation can reduce the load on the processor, and memory, and lead to lowering of processor speed and the subsequent reduction in battery usage. Typically, halving of processor speed leads to a quadrupling of the life of the battery.

In Chapter 16, the facilities provided by Ada that enable the specification of device registers and interrupt control will be considered. The role of the execution environment in providing efficient and predictable implementations will also be examined.

1.3.5 Support for numerical computation

As was noted earlier, many real-time systems involve the control of some engineering activity. Figure 1.6 exemplifies a simple control system. The controlled entity, the plant, has a vector of output variables, y, that change over time, hence $y(t)$. These outputs are compared with the desired (or reference) signal $r(t)$ to produce an error signal, $e(t)$. The controller uses this error vector to change the input variables to the plant, $u(t)$. For a very simple system, the controller can be an analogue device working on a continuous signal. Figure 1.6 illustrates a feedback controller. This is the most common form, but feed-forward controllers are also used.

In order to calculate what changes must be made to the input variables, so that a desirable effect on the output vector takes place, it is necessary to have a mathematical model of the plant. The derivation of these models is the concern of the distinct discipline of control theory. Often a plant is modeled as a set of first-order differential equations. These link the output of the system with the internal state of the plant and its input variables. Changing the output of the plant involves solving these equations to give required input values. Most physical systems exhibit inertia, so that change is not instantaneous. A real-time requirement to move to a new set point within a fixed time period will add to the complexity of the manipulations needed, both to the mathematical model and to the phys-

14   INTRODUCTION TO REAL-TIME SYSTEMS

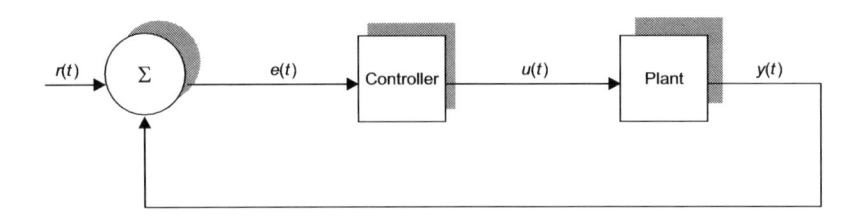

Figure 1.6: A simple controller.

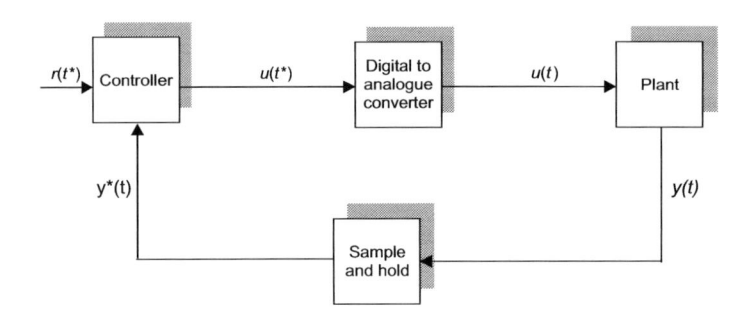

Figure 1.7: A simple computerised controller.

ical system. The fact that, in reality, linear first-order equations are only an approximation to the actual characteristics of the system also presents complications.

Because of these difficulties, the complexity of the model, and the number of distinct (but not independent) inputs and outputs, most controllers are implemented as digital computers. The introduction of a digital component into the system changes the nature of the control cycle. Figure 1.7 is an adaptation of the earlier model. Items marked with a '*' are now discrete values; the sample and hold operation being carried out by an analogue-to-digital converter, which is under the direct control of the computer.

Within the computer, the differential equations can be solved by numerical techniques, although the algorithms themselves need to be adapted to take into account the fact that plant outputs are now being sampled. The design of control algorithms is a topic outside the scope of this book; the implementation of these algorithms is, however, of direct concern. They can be mathematically complex and require a high degree of precision. A fundamental requirement of a real-time programming language, therefore, is the ability to manipulate real or floating-point numbers. Fortunately most engineering languages do provide the necessary abstractions in this area. There are standards for floating-point arithmetic that fully specify the required output of floating point computations even when there are overflows, underflow etc.

1.3.6 Large and complex

It is often said that most of the problems associated with developing software are those related to size and complexity. Writing small programs present no significant problems as they can be designed, coded, maintained and understood by a single person. If that person leaves the company or institution using the software, then someone else can learn the program in a relatively short period of time. Indeed, for these programs, there is an *art* or *craft* to their construction and *small is beautiful*.

Unfortunately, not all software exhibits this most desirable characteristic of smallness. Lehman and Belady [53], in attempting to characterize large systems, reject the simple and perhaps intuitive notion that largeness is simply proportional to the number of instructions, lines of code, modules comprising a program, or algorithmic complexity. Instead, they relate largeness to **variety**, and the degree of largeness to the amount of variety. Traditional indicators, such as number of instructions and development effort are, therefore, just symptoms of variety.

> The variety is that of needs and activities in the real world and their reflection in a program. But the real world is continuously changing. It is evolving. So too are, therefore, the needs and activities of society. Thus large programs, like all complex systems, must continuously evolve [53].

Embedded systems by their definition must respond to real-world events. The variety associated with these events must be catered for; the programs will, therefore, tend to exhibit the undesirable property of largeness. Inherent in the above definition of variety is the notion of **continuous change**. The cost of redesigning or rewriting software to respond to the continuously changing requirements of the real world is prohibitive. Therefore, real-time systems undergo constant maintenance and enhancements during their lifetimes. They must be extensible.

Although real-time software is often complex, features provided by real-time languages and environments enable these complex systems to be broken down into smaller components which can be managed effectively. The use of abstract data types, classes and objects, generic components, APIs and interfaces, and separate compilation are all language features that engineering languages provide to manage this software complexity. These issues are discussed further in Part III.

1.3.7 Structure of the book

The characteristics of real-time systems outlined in these short sections introduce the topics that are covered in this book.

The overarching requirement of all real-time systems is that they support real-time control facilities and that response times can be guaranteed to be within the required time

16   INTRODUCTION TO REAL-TIME SYSTEMS

constraints. Programs that are not well-structured, or have unpredictable control flow paths, cannot form part of a system that needs to be analysable. For this reason, real-time programs must conform to a structure that facilitates analysability. Chapter 2 discusses this programming model.

Real-time systems are often control systems and, therefore, interact with the environment. As a consequence, they must be reliable and safe. In Chapter 3 the problems of producing reliable and safe software will be considered in general. The facilities that languages have introduced to cope with both expected and unexpected error conditions are examined in Part III.

In order to predict how a real-time program will perform it is necessary to understand how the concurrent tasks are scheduled for execution on the underlying platform, and the impact of any synchronization constraints of shared resources has on this schedule. This is the topic of schedulability analysis. The timing properties of a program can only be determined if the programming model has an associated schedulability analysis technique. Part II considers in detail the techniques that can be used for both single processor and multiprocessor platforms. In one sense, the chapters in Part II provide the scheduling theory that underpins the development of analysable real-time systems. The remainder of the book (Part III) considers how this theory can be put into practice using the Ada programming language.

In Chapters 10, 11 and 12, various models of concurrent programming are discussed and the Ada model is considered in detail. Attention is then focused, in the following two chapters, on achieving reliable communication and synchronization between concurrent processes in the presence of design errors. Support for real-time control and real-time programming abstractions is discussed in Chapters 13 and 14. The Ravenscar Ada subset is introduced. In Chapter 15, the language facilities that assist in the scheduling of time critical operations is covered. In Chapter 16, the facilities provided by real-time programming languages which enable the specification of device registers and interrupt control are considered, along with the role of the execution environment in providing efficient and predictable implementations.

In Chapter 3 and then again in Chapter 17, the problems of producing reliable and safe software will be considered along with the facilities that languages have introduced to cope with both expected and unexpected error conditions. The issue is examined further in Chapter 18. The techniques used to detect and recover from timing failures are considered in Chapter 19.

The remainder of this introductory chapter outlines a number of other important issues whose detailed consideration is nevertheless beyond the scope this book. In particular the development cycle (i.e. requirements specification, design, implementation and testing) is introduced and a number of general language topics are summarised. These discussions provide the backdrop to the detailed treatments in the following chapters and help deal with the size and complexity problems inherent in the development of most real-time systems.

1.4   Development cycle for real-time systems

Clearly, the most important stage in the development of any real-time system is the generation of a consistent design that satisfies an authoritative specification of requirements.

In this, real-time systems are no different from other computer applications, although their overall scale often generates quite fundamental design problems. The discipline of software engineering is now widely accepted as the focus for the development of methods, tools and techniques aimed at ensuring that the software production process is manageable, and that reliable and correct programs are constructed. It is assumed here that readers are familiar with the basic tenets of software engineering and consideration is thus restricted to the particular problems and requirements furnished by real-time embedded systems. Even within this restriction, it is not possible to give a comprehensive account of the many design methodologies proposed. Issues of design *per se* are not the main focus of attention in this book. Rather, the investigation of how Ada allows designs to be realised, is the central theme. Although almost all design approaches are top-down, they are built upon an understanding of what is feasible at lower levels. In essence, all design methods involve a series of transformations from the initial statement of requirements to the executing code. This section gives a brief overview of some of the typical stages that are passed through on this route, that is:

- requirements specification – during which an authoritative specification of the system's required functional and meta-functional behaviour is produced;

- architectural design – during which a top-level description of the proposed system is developed;

- detailed design – during which the complete system design is specified;

- coding – during which the system is implemented;

- testing – during which the efficacy of the system is tested.

As different activities are isolated, notations are required that enable each stage to be documented. Transformations from one stage to another are, therefore, nothing more than translations from one notation to another. For example, a compiler produces executable code from source code that is expressed in a programming language. Unfortunately, other translations (further up the design hierarchy) are less well defined; usually because the notations employed are too vague and imprecise, and cannot fully capture the semantics of the requirements or of the design.

Linked to notations are the models that can be expressed in these languages. The current emphasis on development approaches is focused on what is called **model driven architectures** (MDA). Here formal notations are used to develop models of the systems that can then be subject to verification. Techniques such as model-checking and mechanical proof are used to increase the designer's confidence that the systems once fully implemented will behave as expected in both the functional and temporal domains. Advocates of the MDA approach argue that it will be possible to automatically generate the executable code of the implementation from these higher-level models. This may well be the right approach in the future for relatively straightforward systems. However, the current state of these MDA approaches is not sufficiently advanced for general real-time systems to be developed by code-generation techniques alone. Hence in this book the focus is on the abstractions and facilities provided by the Ada programming language.

1.4.1 Requirement specification

Almost all computing projects start with an informal description of what is desired. This should then be followed by an extensive analysis of requirements. It is at this stage that the functionality of the system is defined. In terms of specific real-time factors, the temporal behaviour of the system should be made explicit, as should the reliability requirements and the desired behaviour of the software in the event of component failure. The requirements phase will also define which acceptance tests should apply to the software.

In addition to the system itself, it is necessary to build a model of the environment of the application. It is a characteristic of real-time systems that they have important interactions with their environment. Hence such issues as maximum rate of interrupts, maximum number of dynamic external objects (for example, aeroplanes in an air traffic control system) and failure modes are all important.

The analysis phase provides an authoritative specification of requirements. It is from this that the design will emerge. There is no more critical phase in the software life cycle, and yet natural language documents are still the normal notation for this specification. Nevertheless, formal methods can be applied to these specifications and are increasing being required in safety-critical applications.

1.4.2 Design activities

The design of a large embedded system cannot be undertaken in one exercise. It must be structured in some way. To manage the development of complex real-time systems, two complementary approaches are often used: decomposition and abstraction. Together, they form the basis of most software engineering methods. Decomposition, as its name suggests, involves the systematic breakdown of the complex system into smaller and smaller parts until components are isolated that can be understood and engineered by individuals or small groups. At each level of decomposition, there should be an appropriate level of description and a method of documenting (expressing) this description. Abstraction enables the consideration of detail, particularly that appertaining to implementation, to be postponed. This allows a simplified view of the system and of the objects contained within it to be taken, which nevertheless still contains the essential properties and features. The use of abstraction and decomposition pervades the entire engineering process and has influenced the design of real-time programming languages and associated software design methods.

If a formal notation is used for the requirement specification then top-level designs may use the same notation and can thus be proven to meet the specification. Many structured notations are, however, advocated to either fill out the top-level design or to replace the formal notation altogether. Indeed, a structured top-level design may, in effect, be the authoritative specification of requirements.

The hierarchical development of software leads to the specification and subsequent development of program subcomponents. The needs of abstraction dictate that these subcomponents should have well-defined roles, and clear and unambiguous inter-connections and interfaces. If the specification of the entire software system can be verified just in terms of the specification of the immediate subcomponents then decomposition is said to be **compositional**. This is an important property when formally analysing programs.

Sequential programs are particularly amenable to compositional methods, and a number of techniques have been used to encapsulate and represent subcomponents. Simula introduced the significant **class** construct. More recently *object-oriented* languages, such as C++, Java and Eiffel, have emerged to build upon the class construct. Ada uses a combinations of packages, type extensions and interfaces to support object-oriented programming.

Objects, while providing an abstract interface, require extra facilities if they are to be used in a concurrent environment. Typically, this involves the addition of some form of task (thread/process). The *task* abstraction is, therefore, the abstraction on which this book will focus. In Chapter 10, the notion of an Ada task is introduced, Chapter 11 then considers shared-variable based task interaction.

Both object and task abstractions are important in the design and implementation of reliable embedded systems. These forms of encapsulation lead to the use of modules with well-defined (and abstract) interfaces. From the definition of modules, more sizeable *components* can be defined that may even be re-usable in subsequent designs. But how should a large system be decomposed into components and modules? To a large extent, the answer to this question lies at the heart of all software design activities. Cohesion and coupling are two metrics that are often used to describe the relationships between entities within a design (in the following, the term 'module' is used for a distinct software entity).

Cohesion is concerned with how well a module holds together – its internal strength. Allworth and Zobel [2] give six measures of cohesion that range from the very poor to the strong:

- **coincidental** – elements of the module are not linked other than in a very superficial way, for example, written in the same month;
- **logical** – elements of the module are related in terms of the overall system, but not in terms of the actual software; for example all output device drivers;
- **temporal** – elements of the module are executed at similar times; for example, start-up routines;
- **procedural** – elements of the module are used together in the same section of the program; for example, user interface components;
- **communicational** (*sic*) – elements of the module work on the same data structure, for example, algorithms used to analyse an input signal;
- **functional** – elements of the module work together to contribute to the performance of a single system function; for example, the provision of a distributed file system.

Coupling, by comparison, is a measure of the interdependence of program modules. If two modules pass control information between them, they are said to possess high (or tight) coupling. Alternatively, the coupling is loose if only data is communicated. Another way of looking at coupling is to consider how easy it would be to remove a module (from a completed system) and replace it with an alternative one.

Within all design methods, a good decomposition is one that has strong cohesion and loose coupling. This principle is equally true in sequential and concurrent programming domains.

It was noted earlier that most real-time practitioners advocate the use of object and task (process) abstractions. Formal techniques do exist that enable concurrent time-constrained systems to be specified and analysed. Nevertheless, these techniques are not yet sufficiently mature to constitute 'tried and tested' design methods. Rather, the real-time industry uses, at best, structured methods and software engineering approaches that are applicable to all information processing systems. They do not give specific support to the real-time domain, and they lack the richness that is needed if the full power of implementation languages is to be exploited.

1.4.3 Testing and simulation

With the high reliability requirements that are the essence of most real-time systems, it is clear that testing must be extremely stringent. A comprehensive strategy for testing involves many techniques, most of which are applicable to all software products. It is, therefore, assumed that the reader is familiar with these techniques.

The difficulty with real-time concurrent programs is that the most intractable system errors are usually the result of subtle interactions between tasks. Often the errors are also time dependent and will only manifest themselves in rarely entered states. Murphy's Law dictates that these rare states are also crucially important and only occur when the controlled system is, in some sense, critical.

Testing is, of course, not restricted to the final assembled system. The decomposition incorporated in the design and manifest within program modules (including tasks) forms a natural architecture for component testing. Of particular importance (and difficulty) within real-time systems is that not only must correct behaviour in a correct environment be tested, but dependable behaviour in an arbitrarily incorrect environment must be catered for. All error recovery paths must be exercised and the effects of simultaneous errors investigated.

To assist in any complex testing activity, a realistic test bed presents many attractions. For software, such a test environment is called a simulator.

A simulator is a program which imitates the actions of the engineering system in which the real-time software is embedded. It simulates the generation of interrupts and performs other I/O actions in real-time. Using a simulator, abnormal as well as 'normal' system behaviour can be created. Even when the final system has been completed, certain error states may only be safely experimented with via a simulator. The meltdown of a nuclear reactor is an obvious, if somewhat extreme, example.

Simulators are able to reproduce accurately the sequence of events expected in the real system. In addition, they can repeat experiments in a way that is usually impossible in a live operation. However, to faithfully recreate simultaneous actions it may be necessary to have a very powerful computational platform. And even then with very complicated applications it may not be possible to build an appropriate emulation of the system.

Simulators are clearly non-trivial and expensive systems to develop. They may even require special hardware. In the NASA Space Shuttle project, the simulators cost more than the real-time software itself. This money turned out to be well spent, with many system errors being found during hours of simulator 'flight'.

1.4.4 Postscript

In many ways, this discussion on design issues has been a divergent one. It has introduced more problem areas and engineering issues than can possibly be tackled in just one book. This broad sweep across the 'design process' is aimed at setting the rest of the book in context. By now focusing on scheduling theory, language issues and programming activities, the reader will be able to understand the 'end product' of design, and judge to what extent current methodologies, techniques and tools are appropriate.

Summary

In this chapter, a real-time system has been defined as

> any information processing activity or system which has to respond to externally generated input stimuli within a finite and specified delay.

Two main classes of such systems have been identified: hard real-time systems, where it is absolutely imperative that responses occur within the specified deadline; and soft real-time systems, where response times are important, but the system will still function correctly if deadlines are occasionally missed. Various types of real-time systems have been introduced including reactive systems and time-aware systems, also time-triggered and event-triggered systems.

The basic characteristics of a general real-time or embedded computer system have been considered. They are:

- real-time control,
- concurrent control of separate system components,
- low-level programming,
- support for numerical computation,
- largeness and complexity,
- extreme reliability and safety.

The main aspects associated with the term 'real-time' that have been introduced in this chapter are illustrated in Figure 1.8.

This chapter has also outlined the major stages involved in the design and implementation of real-time systems. These include requirements specification, systems design, detailed design, coding and testing. The high reliability requirements of real-time systems dictate that, wherever possible, rigorous methods should be employed.

Predictable implementation, which is the primary focus of attention in this book, necessitates the use of a programming language. Early real-time languages lacked the expressive power to deal adequately with this application domain. More recent languages have attempted to incorporate concurrency and error-handling facilities. A discussion of these features, in the context of Ada, is contained in the chapters of Part III.

22 INTRODUCTION TO REAL-TIME SYSTEMS

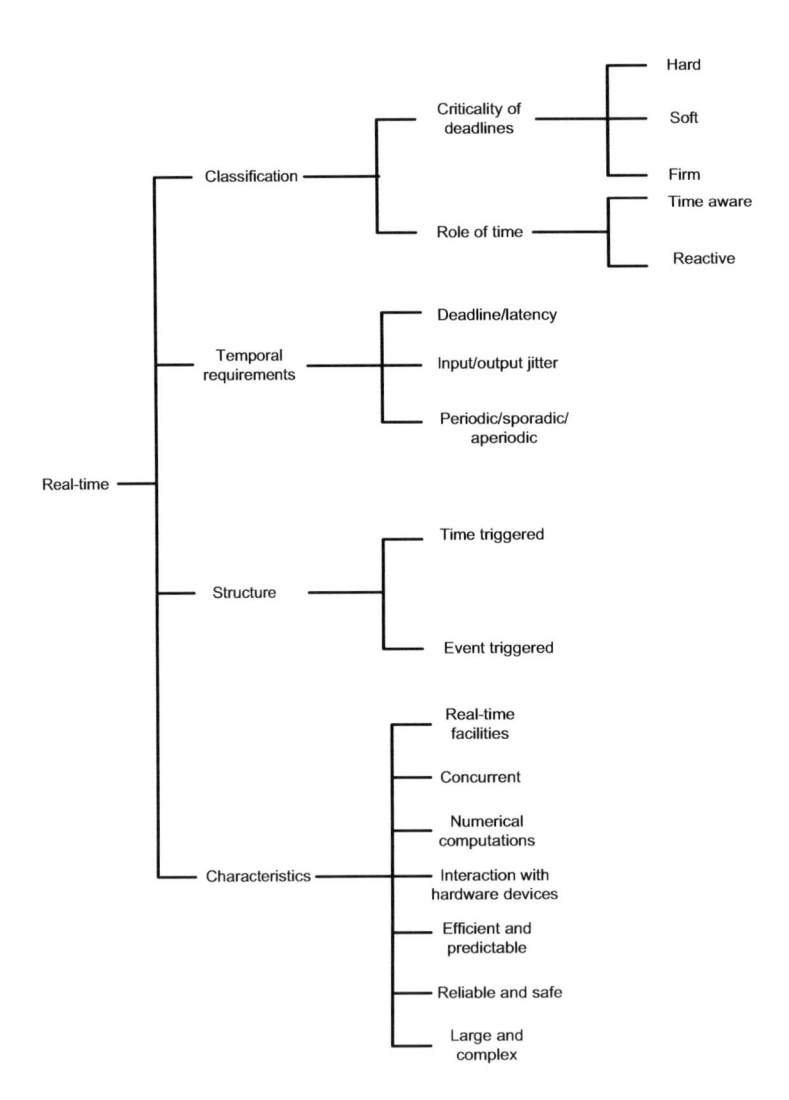

Figure 1.8: Aspects of real-time systems.

Chapter 2
Real-time principles

2.1 Specifying timing requirements
2.2 Temporal scopes
2.3 Specifying temporal scopes and activities
2.4 A real-time programming model
Summary

In Chapter 1, it was noted that a language for programming embedded systems requires facilities for real-time control. Indeed, the term 'real-time' has been used as a synonym for this class of system. There are essentially two activities that any real-time language must enable.

(1) The representation of timing requirements; for example, enabling the specifying of rates of execution and deadlines.
(2) The scheduling of concurrent activities to satisfy timing requirements.

This chapter is largely concerned with the former. The material in Part II considers ways of scheduling systems such that the worst-case temporal behaviour can be predicted, and hence timing requirements ratified.

2.1 Specifying timing requirements

For most real-time systems, it is not sufficient for the software to be logically correct; the programs must also satisfy timing constraints determined by the underlying physical system. Unfortunately, existing practices in the engineering of large real-time systems are, in general, still rather *ad hoc*. Often, a logically correct system is specified, designed and constructed (perhaps as a prototype) and then tested to see if it meets its timing requirements. If it does not, then various fine tunings and rewrites ensue. The result is a system that may be difficult to understand and expensive to maintain and upgrade. A more systematic treatment of time is required.

Work on a more rigorous approach to this aspect of real-time systems has followed two largely distinct paths. One direction of development has concerned the use of formally defined language semantics and timing requirements, together with notations and logics that enable temporal properties to be represented and analysed. The other path has focused on the performance of real-time systems in terms of the feasibility of scheduling the required workload on the available resources (processors, networks and so on).

In this book, attention is focused mainly on the latter work. The reasons for this are three-fold. Firstly, the formal techniques are not yet mature enough to reason about large complex real-time systems. Secondly, there is little reported experience of the use of these techniques in actual real-time systems. Finally, to include a full discussion of such methods would involve a substantial amount of material that is outside the scope of this book. This is not meant to imply that this area is irrelevant to real-time systems. The understanding of, for example, formal techniques based on CSP, temporal logics, real-time logics, model checking and specification techniques that incorporate notions of time, is becoming increasingly important.

The success of model checking in verifying functional properties has been extended into the real-time domain. A system is modelled as a collection of Timed Automata (that is, finite state machines with clocks) and then model checking is used to 'prove' that undesirable states cannot be reached or that desirable states will be entered before some internal clock has reached a critical time (deadline). The latter property is known as **bounded liveliness**. Although the explorations undertaken by model checking are subject to state explosion, a number of tools are now available that can tackle problems of a reasonable size. The technique is likely to become standard industrial practice over the coming years.

The verification of a real-time system can usefully be interpreted as requiring a two-stage process:

(1) Verifying requirements/designs – given an infinitely fast reliable computer, are the temporal requirements coherent and consistent; that is, have they the potential to be satisfied?
(2) Verifying the implementation – with a finite set of (possible unreliable) hardware resources, can the temporal requirements be satisfied?

As indicated above, (1) may require formal reasoning (and/or model checking) to verify that necessary temporal (and causal) orderings are satisfied. For example, if event A must be completed before event B, but is dependent on some event C that occurs after B, then (no matter how fast the processor) it will never be possible to satisfy these requirements. Early recognition of this difficulty is therefore essential. The second issue (implementation verification) is the topic of the chapters of Part II. The remainder of this chapter will concentrate on how temporal requirements can actually be represented in programming languages.

2.2 Temporal scopes

To facilitate the specification of the various timing constraints found in real-time applications, the notion of **temporal scopes** is introduced. Such scopes identify a collection of statements with an associated timing constraint. The possible attributes of a temporal scope are illustrated in Figure 2.1, and include:

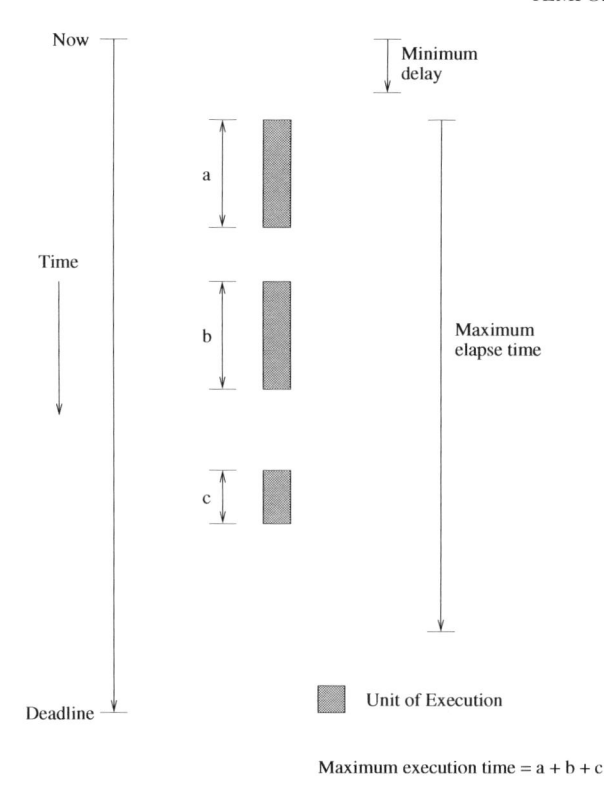

Figure 2.1: Temporal scopes.

(1) deadline – the time by which the execution of a temporal scope must be finished;
(2) minimum delay – the minimum amount of time that must elapse before the start of execution of a temporal scope;
(3) maximum execution time – of a temporal scope;
(4) maximum elapse time – of a temporal scope.

Temporal scopes with combinations of these attributes are also possible. And, for some timing constraints, a combination of sequentially executed temporal scopes is necessary. For example, consider a simple control action that reads a sensor, computes a new setting and outputs this setting via an actuator. To get fine control over when the sensor is read, an initial temporal scope with a tight deadline is needed. The output is produced in a second temporal scope which has a minimum delay equal to the first scope's deadline but a later deadline — see code examples below (Section 2.3). As noted in Chapter 1, variation of when a sensor is read is called **input jitter**. If there is a need to also control **output jitter** then a third temporal scope could be added which has a long 'minimum delay' and a short time interval before its deadline.

Temporal scopes can themselves be described as being either **periodic** or **aperiodic**. Typically, periodic temporal scopes sample data or execute a control loop and have defined deadlines that must be met. Aperiodic, or **sporadic**, temporal scopes usually arise from asynchronous events outside the embedded computer. These scopes have specified response times associated with them.

In general, aperiodic temporal scopes are viewed as being activated randomly, following, for example, a Poisson distribution. Such a distribution allows for bursts of arrivals of external events, but does not preclude any possible concentration of aperiodic activity. It is, therefore, not possible to do worst-case analysis (there is a non-zero probability of any number of aperiodic events occurring within a given time). To allow worst-case calculations to be made, a minimum period between any two aperiodic events (from the same source) is often defined. If this is the case, the activity involved is said to be **sporadic**. In this book, the term 'aperiodic' is used for the general case and 'sporadic' is reserved for situations where a minimum delay between subsequent executions is needed.

In many real-time languages, temporal scopes are, in effect, associated with the tasks that embody them. Tasks can be described as periodic, aperiodic or sporadic depending on the properties of their internal temporal scope. Most of the timing attributes given in the above list can thus be satisfied by:

(1) running periodic tasks at the correct rate,

(2) running sporadic tasks when required,

(3) running aperiodic tasks when possible, and

(4) completing all tasks by their deadline.

The problem of satisfying timing constraints thus becomes one of scheduling tasks to meet deadlines, or **deadline scheduling**.

Although all computer systems strive to be efficient, and many are described as real-time, further classification is needed to deal adequately with the different levels of importance that time has within applications. As noted in the Introduction, a system is said to be **hard** real-time if it has deadlines that cannot be missed or else the system fails. By comparison, a system is **soft** if the application is tolerant of missed deadlines. A system is merely **interactive** if it does not have specified deadlines but strives for 'adequate response times'. To give a little more precision, a task with a soft deadline may still deliver its service late – the system will still draw some value from the tardy service. A non-hard task that has a fixed rigid deadline (that is, a tardy service is useless/valueless) is said to be **firm**.

The distinction between hard, firm and soft real-time becomes somewhat blurred in fault-tolerant systems. Nevertheless, it is usually appropriate to use the term 'hard' if a specific error recovery (or fail safe) routine is triggered by a missed deadline, and firm/soft if the nature of the application is tolerant of the occasional missed deadline or deadlines that are not missed by much.

Within the classification of hard real-time systems there may be a distinction made between different levels of criticality; there may be, for example, safety-critical, mission-critical (business-critical) and performance-critical deadlines. Such **mixed-criticality systems** give rise to challenging scheduling problems which will be discussed in Chapter 8. Finally, note that many real-time systems will have hard deadlines of different criticality and, additionally, some deadlines which are soft or firm.

2.3 Specifying temporal scopes and activities

The internal structures of the common forms of activities identified above are now considered. In particular, the repeating loop that is at the heart of all real-time tasks is explored. As noted earlier, many real-time tasks embed a control loop which reads from the environment via hardware sensors, updates its internal state, computes the required output values and writes these to the environment via one or more actuators:

```
loop
  read from sensors (in)
  out := G(S,in)
  S := F(S,in)
  write to actuators (out)
end loop
```

Within this pseudo code, a number of parameters are employed. The variable S is an arbitrary complex data structure representing internal state (history), and F and G are arbitrary complex software functions. Also the in and out variables are sufficient to capture the interactions with the environment via the sensors and actuators of which there may be just one of either or a large family of both. The functions F and G are represented as being distinct, but may of course involve shared components.

The rate of change of the physical entity being monitored (e.g. temperature or speed) will determine how often it must be sampled. For example, in an anti-skid braking system it is necessary to determine the speed of rotation of the wheel. In general, control theory (sampling theory) requires that samples are taken very regularly. So there is a sampling frequency and a bound on the variability on when samples are taken. As noted earlier, the latter is called the **input jitter**.

A control loop may be specified to execute with a frequency of, say, 50 times per second. This is expressed in Hertz (cycles per second). More usual, in the real-time world, the period of the loop is specified, say 20ms. So the periodic control loop is executed every 20ms. The period of the control loop is represented by the symbol, T. Input jitter is usually expressed as a bound on the time of the sensor readings; so a control loop with a period of 20ms may require that inputs are taken within 2ms. This is encoded as:

```
loop every 20ms
  read from sensors (in) within 2ms
  out := G(S,in)
  S := F(S,in)
  write to actuators (out)
end loop
```

The function G must take into account, and therefore know, the time it takes to produce the system's output after reading the inputs. Hence the control loop must complete its outputs within a defined time interval from when the inputs are taken. This is usually expressed as a deadline from the start of the loop until completion of the output operations, e.g. 15ms:

28   REAL-TIME PRINCIPLES

```
loop every 20ms
  read from sensors (in) within 2ms
  out := G(S,in)
  S := F(S,in)
  write to actuators (out) within 15ms
end loop
```

The relative deadline of this loop, and therefore of the task that contains it, is usually represented by the symbol, D.

There are three possible relationships between the period of an activity and it relative deadline. If, as illustrated in the code above, the deadline is less than period then it said to be **constrained**. Alternatively, for many activities it is sufficient for one iteration of the control loop to complete before the next begins; here deadline is equal to period, and the deadline is termed **implicit**. Finally, if there is no constraint on the deadline, and it can indeed be greater than the period then the deadline is said to be **arbitrary**.

Simple control loops often have just implicit deadlines. Other activities, such as warning signals occur rarely but have short deadlines when they do – here the deadline is constrained. These are the two most common forms of deadline. A deadline greater than period is used when there is more uneven behaviour. Messages may arrive at a processor in bursts; it is not possible to deal with each message before the next one arrives, so they are queued. The activity that deals with these messages must, on average, complete one execution before being released again. But when dealing with a burst of messages, it will run 'late'. If it had an implicit deadline then some deadlines would be missed. However, if the length of the bursty behaviour is bounded, it is possible to define a deadline that is greater than period which will always be satisfied.

For some systems there may also be a constraint on the output being produced too early. This is defined as a bound on the output jitter. So, for example, an output may be required by 15ms but not before 12ms:

```
loop every 20ms
  read from sensors (in) within 2ms
  out := G(S,in)
  S := F(S,in)
  write to actuators (out) after 12ms within 15ms
end loop
```

As the control loop may contain significant computational activities (interactions with the sensors and actuators, and the functions G and F) there is a need to know how long it would take for these to be completed, even if the code is executed in total isolation. The worst-case execution time (**WCET**) of the control loop is denoted by the symbol, C. It follows that $C \leq T$, and indeed $C \leq D$. Note C is a function of the application's code and the hardware platform, whereas T and D are properties solely of the application.

As well as being time-triggered, systems can also be event-triggered. Here an event in the environment triggers some computation (typically called the **event handler**). For example, user input with a cruise control system or rapid deceleration requiring the release of the air-bag. And each time this event occurs, the computation must be executed (though perhaps not for the same air-bag). The event may bring with it input data (or the handler may need to access some sensors):

```
loop
  wait for event (in)
  out := G(S,in)
  S := F(S,in)
  write to actuators (out)
end loop
```

There will be a deadline on completion of the outputs (relative to the time of the event). This deadline is again represented by the symbol, D. In order to bound the impact of the event handling there must be a bound on how often the event can be fired. The simplest bound is to say there is a minimum time interval between events. This is the constraint implied by a sporadic event.

An example of a sporadic event is the interrupt that is generated by the full rotation of a car wheel. As the car goes faster then events come more frequently. But if the car has a maximum speed then the minimum time bound between events is defined.

The time bound is also called the 'period' of the sporadic (as usually the worst-case behaviour of a sporadic is when it executes as rapidly as possible, as if it were periodic), and is again denoted by the symbol T. So the code for a sporadic activity that executes at most every half second but has a deadline of 10ms from the arrival of the event is as follows:

```
loop at most every 500ms
  wait for event (in)
  out := G(S,in)
  S := F(S,in)
  write to actuators (out) within 10ms
end loop
```

Events that cannot be given a minimum arrival interval are aperiodic. They must be constrained by some other means. Typically the amount of computation time they are allowed is constrained. In the following the aperiodic is allowed, by definition, a maximum of 10ms of CPU time per 50ms. If the aperiodic is within the budget defined then it has a deadline that should be satisfied:

```
loop with (10ms every 50ms)
  wait for event (in)
  S := F(S,in)
  out := G(S,in)
  write to actuators (out) within 30ms
end loop
```

If the aperiodic event occurs too frequently for the budget that has been assigned then either the events are queued to be dealt with later (potentially after their deadline) or they are lost/discarded. Clearly aperiodic activities cannot be crucial to the correct behaviour of a real-time application.

The above description has focused on events that arise from the program's environment. But there are also internal events that are raised in one activity (or the underlying operating systems) and handled in another activity. An example here would be an alarm event sent when a fault is identified such as a deadline been missed (see next chapter).

30 REAL-TIME PRINCIPLES

Communication and Synchronization

The final topic to address in this section is communication. Interactions between activities will be needed in almost all meaningful applications. Typically, concurrent tasks can interact safely by either some form of protected shared data (using, for example, semaphores, monitors or protected objects) or by using some form of message passing. All of these features lead to the possibility of a task being suspended until some necessary future event has occurred (for example, waiting to gain a lock on a semaphore, or entry to a monitor, or until some other task is in a position to receive or send a message).

The structure (sometimes called **software architecture**) of a multi-tasking program needs to define how tasks interact. One approach, which attempts to minimise interactions during execution, only allows tasks to interact with other tasks at the start and end of their activities. That is, at the start they read any required data (that has been produced by other tasks), they then execute, and finally they produce data for other tasks. In effect, the task interacts with other tasks in the same way as it interacts with the program's environment. So, for example:

```
loop every 20ms
   read data produced by other tasks
   read from sensors (in) within 2ms
   out := G(S,in)
   S := F(S,in)
   write to actuators (out)
   write data for other tasks
end loop
```

Here the data could be send from task to task via asynchronous message passing or by the use of shared variables. However the G and F functions do not communicate, either directly or indirectly, with other tasks. With this approach the behaviour of the tasks is usually constrained so that the tasks that produce the shared data do not execute at the same time as the tasks that read the data. The shared variables therefore do not need to be protected.

The alternative structure is to allow G and F to contained references to shared state (e.g. data used by more than one task). Now the data must be protected. But this protection must not lead to close coupling between the tasks especially if they run at different times and have different deadlines.

2.4 A real-time programming model

The above descriptions have identified patterns for real-time activities. These were based on the idea of temporal scopes, i.e. code sequences that have temporal constraints. From this a real-time programming model can be defined that:

(1) is implementable with existing programming languages and real-time operating systems, and

(2) is analysable with existing scheduling and timing analysis.

A REAL-TIME PROGRAMMING MODEL   31

The existing scheduling and timing analysis will be covered in the chapters of Part II. Here, the focus is on the necessary programming abstractions.

First the programming language must be concurrent. Tasks (or threads) must be dispatched at run-time in a predictable way that is in keeping with the requirements of the analysis. For most of the activities defined above, a single task per activity is needed. In addition to the abstractions required for normal programming, real-time programming requires two further primitives **delay** and **deadline**. A delay statement will suspend a task until it is time for it to continue; a deadline statement will indicate that the task must reach this point in its code no later than the time specified. So for example a period task (with no jitter requirements) will have the form:

```
task Task_Periodic
  ...
begin
  release_time := some computed start time
  relative_deadline := some static value
  period := some static value
  loop
    delay until (release_time)
      ... code of temporal score
    deadline (release_time + relative_deadline)
    release_time := release_time + period
  end
end
```

where `period` represents the iteration time (e.g. 20ms, with `relative_deadline` having, say, the value 15ms).

The 'delay' primitive is relatively easy to implement, a clock and a suspension mechanism will allow the task to 'wait' until real-time has caught up. The deadline statement is, however, of a different kind. It can give an indication of a task's urgency and it can trigger error recovery if the deadline is not met, but it cannot force the hardware (or the compiler) to execute (or deliver) code in such a manner that it is guaranteed to 'to be quick enough'. *Rather it is the analysis that verifies that the implementation will indeed meet all its deadlines.*

A sporadic task has a similar form:

```
task Task_Sporadic
  ...
begin
  relative_deadline := some static value
  loop
    wait until release_event
      ... code of temporal score
    deadline (release_event_time + relative_deadline)
  end
end
```

The release event may have originated from the environment, and been transmitted to the real-time code as an interrupt. The programming model must, therefore, incorporate whatever is needed to handle interrupts. More generally, the exchange of data with input

32 REAL-TIME PRINCIPLES

and output hardware devices will require a range for low-level programming facilities.

If aperiodic activities are to be supported then some form of budget enforcement will be needed at run-time. And, as indicated in the last section, shared state between tasks must be protected by some mechanism such as a monitor.

The final issue to address in the programming model is the requirements that arise from input and output jitter requirements. Recall that the control loop to be supported has the form:

```
loop every 20ms
  read from sensors (in) within 2ms
  out := G(S,in)
  S := F(S,in)
  write to actuators (out) after 12ms within 15ms
end loop
```

This could be implemented in a single task by appropriate use of the delay and deadline primitives:

```
task Task_Periodic_With_Jitter
   ...
begin
  release_time   := some computed start time
  loop
    delay until (release_time)
      ... first temporal score, undertake inputs
    deadline (release_time + 2ms)
      ... second temporal score, compute out and S
    delay until (release_time + 12ms)
      ... third temporal scope, undertake outputs
    deadline (release_time + 15ms)
    next release := next release + 20ms
  end
end
```

The input activities of this task takes place in the 1st temporal scope and hence the deadline at the end of this scope regulates the maximum input jitter for the task. The input data may already be available in buffers for the task, or the task may need to read input registers in the sensor's device interface. The 2nd temporal scope incorporates whatever computations are needed to calculate the task's output values and update the task's state (this may include interacting with other tasks). The 3rd scope is concerned with the output action. Here the delay statement is important; it is measured from the beginning of the loop and constrains the time before the output can be produced by the task. The deadline on this final temporal scope places an upper bound on the time of the output phase.

Although it would be possible to incorporate this sequence into a single task, scheduling analysis (see the chapters in Part II) places restrictions on the structure of a task. Specifically, a task must only have one delay statement (at the beginning of the execution sequence) and one deadline (at the end). So, three tasks are necessary and would take the following form:

A REAL-TIME PROGRAMMING MODEL

```
task Task_Periodic_With_Jitter_PartA
  release_time : time
  ...
begin
  release_time  := some computed start time
  loop
    delay until (release_time)
      ... undertake inputs, store in X
    deadline (release_time + 2ms)
    release_time := release_time + 20ms
  end
end


task Task_Periodic_With_Jitter_PartB
  release_time : time
  ...
begin
  release_time  := same computed start time
  loop
    delay until (release_time + 2ms)
      ... read X and compute out and S
    deadline (release_time + 12ms)
    release_time := release_time + 20ms
  end
end


task Task_Periodic_With_Jitter_PartC
  release_time : time
  ...
begin
  release_time  := same computed start time
  loop
    delay until (release_time + 12ms)
      ... read out and undertake outputs
    deadline (release_time + 15ms)
    release_time := release_time + 20ms
  end
end
```

Note the three tasks are never active at the same time; this comes from them sharing the same 'start time' although all three tasks have their own `release_time` variable. Data is passed from one task to the next. Also note that the deadline on the second task is not fixed, it could be later than release time + 15 as long as the third task is delayed until the deadline time of the second. It is said to be a **derived deadline**, as it is not fixed by the requirements of the application.

The real-time programming model presented in this section is quite restrictive, and will not be adequate to express all of the application requirements identified in Chapter 1. In particular, real-time systems must be able to tolerate faults. This topic is covered in detail in the next Chapter, which will also revisit the programming model (in Section 3.8) and propose some additions.

Summary

For real-time systems, it is not sufficient for the software to be logically correct; the programs must also satisfy timing constraints. Unfortunately, existing practices in the engineering of large real-time systems are, in general, still rather *ad hoc*. To facilitate the specification of timing constraints and requirements, it is useful to introduce the notion of temporal scopes and activities. To recapitulate:

- Real-time systems have periodic, sporadic and aperiodic activities.
- All of these activities have deadlines (D).
- Periodic and sporadic activities have periods (T).
- Aperiodic activities have their run-time behaviour monitored and restricted.
- All activities have worst-case computational requirements (C).
- Control activities may have further constraints on input jitter and sometimes output jitter.

Temporal scopes and activities can be combined and embedded in tasks that are required to execute in accordance with their timing constraints. A real-time programming model must therefore:

- Support the concurrent execution of tasks/threads.
- Support delay and deadline primitives.
- Support low level programming, including interrupt handling.
- Support resource monitoring and budget control.
- Support some form of safe communication mechanism for data sharing between tasks.

The defining feature of a real-time system is the existence of deadlines and the challenge in specifying and building real-time systems is for them to deliver predictable behaviour in both the functional and temporal domain. The deadlines themselves are usually specified relative to the period of the system's tasks, in particular:

- If $D = T$ then the deadline is said to be implicit.
- If $D < T$ then the deadline is said to be constrained.
- If D is unconstrained and hence $D > T$ is possible then the deadline is said to be arbitrary.

Chapter 3
Reliability and fault tolerance

3.1 Reliability, failure and faults
3.2 Failure modes
3.3 Fault prevention and fault tolerance
3.4 N-version programming
3.5 Software dynamic redundancy
3.6 The recovery block approach to software fault tolerance
3.7 Dynamic redundancy and exceptions
3.8 Fault tolerance and the real-time programming model
3.9 Measuring and predicting the reliability of software
3.10 Safety, reliability and dependability
Summary

Although the presence of deadlines is the defining property of real-time systems, reliability and safety requirements are also usually much more stringent for real-time and embedded systems than for other computer systems. For example, if an application which computes the solution to some scientific problem fails then it may be reasonable to abort the program, as only computer time has been lost. However, in the case of an embedded system, this may not be an acceptable action. A process control computer, for instance, responsible for the operation of a large gas furnace, cannot afford to close down the furnace as soon as a fault occurs. Instead, it must try to provide a degraded service and prevent a costly shutdown operation. More importantly, real-time computer systems may endanger human lives if they abandon control of their application. An embedded computer controlling a nuclear reactor must not let the reactor run out of control, as this may result in a core meltdown and an emission of radiation. A military avionics system should at least allow the pilot to eject before permitting the plane to crash!

It is now widely accepted that the society in which we live is totally dependent on the use of computer-based systems to support its vital functions. It is, therefore, imperative that these systems do not fail. Without wishing to define precisely what is meant by a system failure or a fault (at the moment), there are, in general, four sources of faults which can result in an embedded system failure.

(1) Inadequate specification. It has been suggested that the great majority of

software faults stem from inadequate specification [54]. Included in this category are those faults that stem from misunderstanding the interactions between the program and the environment.

(2) Faults introduced from design errors in software components.

(3) Faults introduced by failure of one or more hardware components of the embedded system (including processors).

(4) Faults introduced by transient or permanent interference in the supporting communication subsystem.

It is these last three types of fault which impinge on the analysis and programming language used in the implementation of an embedded system. The errors introduced by design faults are, in general, unanticipated (in terms of their consequences), whereas those from processor and network failure are, in some senses, predictable. One of the main requirements, therefore, for any real-time programming language, is that it must facilitate the construction of highly dependable systems. In this chapter, some of the general design techniques that can be used to improve the overall reliability of embedded computer systems are considered. Part III (Chapter 17) will show how **exception handling** facilities can be used to help implement some of these design philosophies, particularly those based on **fault tolerance**.

3.1 Reliability, failure and faults

Before proceeding, more precise definitions of reliability, failures and faults are necessary. Randell et al. [69] define the **reliability** of a system to be

> a measure of the success with which the system conforms to some authoritative specification of its behaviour.

Ideally, this specification should be complete, consistent, comprehensible and unambiguous. It should also be noted that the *response times* of the system are an important part of the specification. The above definition of reliability can now be used to define a system **failure**. Again, quoting from Randell et al.

> When the behaviour of a system deviates from that which is specified for it, this is called a failure.

Section 3.9 will deal with the metrics of reliability; for the time being, *highly reliable* will be considered synonymous with a *low failure rate*.

The alert reader will have noticed that our definitions, so far, have been concerned with the *behaviour* of a system; that is, its *external* appearance. Failures result from unexpected problems internal to the system which eventually manifest themselves in the system's external behaviour. These problems are called **errors** and their mechanical or

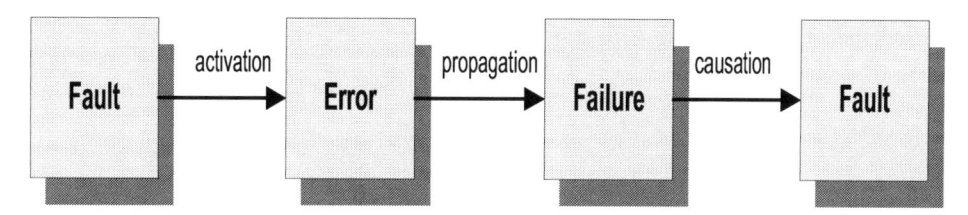

Figure 3.1: Fault, error, failure, fault chain.

algorithmic cause are termed **faults**. A faulty component of a system is, therefore, a component which, under a particular set of circumstances during the lifetime of the system, will result in an error. Viewed in terms of state transitions, a system can be considered as a number of *external* and *internal* states. An external state which is not specified in the behaviour of the system is regarded as a failure of the system. The system itself consists of a number of components, each with their own states, all of which contribute to the system's external behaviour. The combined states of these components are termed the internal state of the system. An internal state which is not specified is called an error and the component which produced the illegal state transition is said to be faulty.

A fault is **active** when it produces an error, until this point it is **dormant**. Once produced, the error can be transformed into other errors via the computational progress as it propagates through the system. Eventually, the error manifests itself at the boundaries on the system causing a service delivery to fail [8].

Of course, a system is usually composed of components; each of these may be considered as a system in its own right. Hence a failure in one system will lead to a fault in another which will result in an error and potential failure of that system. This in turn will introduce a fault into any surrounding system and so on (as illustrated in Figure 3.1).

There are many different classifications of fault types depending on the aspect of interest. For example, whether they are created during development or during operation, whether they are intentionally or accidentally created, whether they are hardware or software in origin etc. From a real-time perspective, the duration of the fault is one of the most important aspects. Three types of fault can be distinguished.

(1) **Transient faults** A transient fault occurs at a particular time, remains in the system for some period and then disappears. It will initially be dormant but can become active at any time. Examples of such faults occur in hardware components which have an adverse reaction to some external interference, such as electrical fields or radioactivity. After the disturbance disappears so does the fault (although not necessarily the induced error). Many faults in communication systems are transient.

(2) **Permanent faults** Permanent faults start at a particular time and remain in the system until they are repaired; for example, a broken wire or a software design error.

(3) **Intermittent faults** These are transient faults that occur from time to time. An example is a hardware component that is heat sensitive, it works for a time, stops working, cools down and then starts to work again.

Software faults are usually called **bugs** and it can be notoriously difficult to isolate and identify them. Over the years, particular types of bugs have been given names in an informal classification. Originally two types of software bugs were identified [40]:[1]

- Bohrbugs – These bugs are reproducible and usually identifiable. Hence they can easily be removed during testing. If they cannot be removed, then design diversity techniques can be employed during operation (see Section 3.4).
- Heisenbugs – These are software bugs that only activate under certain rare circumstances. A good example is code shared between concurrent tasks that is not properly synchronized. Only when two tasks happen to execute the code concurrently will the fault activate and even then the error may propagate a long way from its source until it is detected. Because of this, they often disappear when investigated – hence their name.

A particular type of Heisenbug is one that results from "software aging" [63]. In one sense, software can be thought of as not deteriorating with age (unlike hardware). Whilst this is true, faults can remain dormant for a long time, and only become active after significant continual use of the software. These faults are normally related to resources: for example in a dynamic application where memory is constantly allocated and freed, a fault that doesn't free unused memory will result in a **memory leak**. If this is small, the program may run for a significant period of time before memory becomes exhausted.

A good example of the effects of software aging can be found with the use of the US Patriot Missile Defence System in the Gulf War in 1991 (see GAO/IMTEC-92-26 Patriot Missile Software Problem at http://www.fas.org/spp/starwars/gao/im92026.htm). The Patriot system was originally designed for mobile operations in Europe. The design assumed that it would only operate for a few hours at one location. During the Gulf war it was used continuously for many hours. Its main battery could last for 100 hours. After the Patriot's radar detects an airborne object that has the characteristics of a Scud missile, the range gate (an electronic detection device within the radar system) calculates an area in the air space where the system should next look for the detected missile. The range gate filters out information about airborne objects outside its calculated area and only processes the information needed for tracking, targeting, and intercepting Scuds. Finding an object within the calculated range gate area confirms that it is a Scud missile. In February 1991, a Patriot missile defense system failed to track and intercept an incoming Scud. This Scud subsequently hit an Army barracks, killing 28 people.

The reason for the failure of the Patriots systems is explained by considering the range gate's prediction software, which used the Scud's velocity and the time of the last radar detection. Time is kept continuously by the system's internal clock in tenths of seconds held as an integer variable. The longer the system has been running, the larger the number representing time. To predict where the Scud will next appear, both time and velocity must be expressed as floating point numbers. The registers in the Patriot computer are only 24 bits long, and the conversion of time results in a loss of precision causing a

---

[1] The names come from analogies with Physics. The assertion that most production software bugs are ephemeral – Heisenbugs that go away when you look at them – is well known to systems programmers. Bohrbugs, like the Bohr atom, are solid, and easily detected by standard techniques.

Hours	Seconds	Calculated Time (Seconds)	Inaccuracy (Seconds)	Approximate Shift In Range Gate (Metres)
0	0	0	0	0
1	3600	3599.9966	.0034	7
8	28800	28799.9725	.0025	55
20	72000	71999.9313	.0687	137
48	172800	172799.8352	.1648	330
72	259200	259199.7528	.2472	494
100	360000	359999.6667	.3433	687

Table 3.1: Effect of extended run time on Patriot operation.

less accurate time calculation. The effect of this inaccuracy on the range gate's calculation is directly proportional to the target's velocity and the length of time the system has been running. Consequently, performing the conversion after the Patriot has been running continuously for extended periods causes the range gate to shift away from the center of the target, making it less likely that the target missile will be successfully intercepted. Table 3.1 (taken from http://www.fas.org/spp/starwars/gao/im92026.htm) shows the effect of these inaccuracy. After 20 hours, the target becomes outside the range gate. As with all software aging problems, restarting the system (in this case before 20 hours of continual operational time) would clear the problem.

To create reliable systems, all types of fault must be prevented from causing erroneous system behaviour (that is failure). The difficulty this presents is compounded by the indirect use of computers in the *construction* of safety-critical systems. For example, in 1979 an error was discovered in a program used to design nuclear reactors and their supporting cooling systems. The fault that this caused in the reactor design had not been found during installation tests as it concerned the strength and structural support of pipes and valves. The program had supposedly guaranteed the attainment of earthquake safety standards in operating reactors. The discovery of the bug led to the shutting down of five nuclear power plants [54].

3.2 Failure modes

A system can fail in many different ways. A designer who is using system X to implement another system, Y, usually makes some assumptions about X's expected failure modes. If X fails differently from that which was expected then system Y may fail as a result.

A system provides services. It is, therefore, possible to classify a system's failure modes according to the impact they have on the services it delivers. Two general domains of failure modes can be identified:

- Value failure – the value associated with the service is in error;
- Time failure – the service is delivered at the wrong time.

Combinations of value and timing failures are often termed **arbitrary**.

40   RELIABILITY AND FAULT TOLERANCE

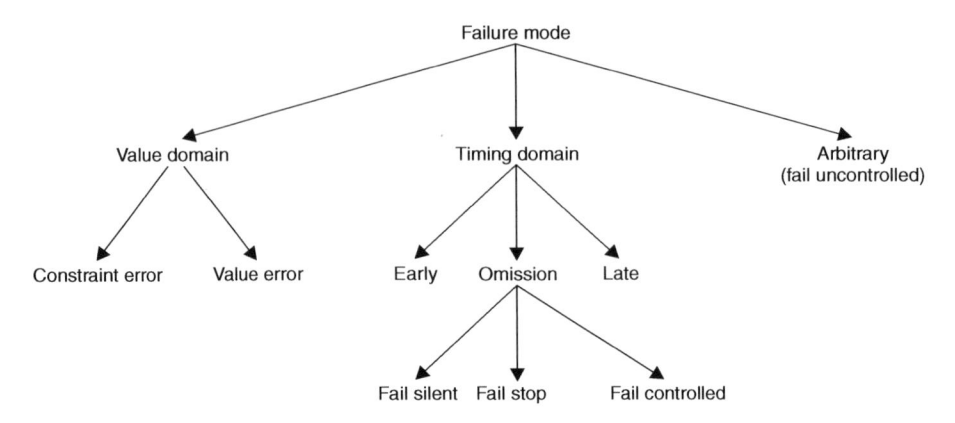

Figure 3.2: Failure mode classification.

In general, a value error might still be within the correct range of values or be outside the range expected from the service. The latter is equivalent to a type error in programming languages and is called a **constraint error**. It is usually easy to recognize this class of failure but its consequence can still be devastating. (Witness the cause of the Arianne 5 disaster where an exception was caused during execution of a data conversion from 64-bit floating point to 16-bit signed integer value. The floating point number which was converted had a value greater than what could be represented by a 16-bit signed integer – see "ARIANE 5, Flight 501 Failure, Report by the Inquiry Board" at http://sunnyday.mit.edu/accidents/Ariane5accidentreport.html.)

Failures in the time domain can result in the service being delivered:

- too early – the service is delivered earlier than required
- too late – the service is delivered later than required (often called a **performance error** or deadline miss)
- infinitely late – the service is never delivered (often called an **omission failure**).

One further failure mode should be identified, which is where a service is delivered which is not expected. This is often called a **commission** or **impromptu** failure. It is, of course, often difficult to distinguish between a failure in both the value and the time domain from an commission failure followed by an omission failure. Figure 3.2 illustrates the failure mode classification.

Given the above classification of failure modes, it is now possible to make some assumptions about how a system might fail:

- **Fail uncontrolled** – a system which can produce arbitrary errors in both the value and the time domains (including impromptu errors).
- **Fail late** – a system which produces correct services in the value domain but may suffer from a 'late' timing error.
- **Fail silent** – a system which produces correct services in both the value and time domains until it fails; the only failure possible is an omission failure and when this

occurs all following services will also suffer omission failures.
- **Fail stop** – a system which has all the properties of fail silent, but also permits other systems to detect that it has entered the fail-silent state.
- **Fail controlled** – a system which fails in a specified controlled manner.
- **Fail never** – a system which always produces correct services in both the value and the time domain.

Other assumptions and classifications are clearly possible, but the above list will suffice for this book.

3.3 Fault prevention and fault tolerance

Two approaches that can help designers improve the reliability of their systems can be distinguished [3]. The first is known as **fault prevention**; this attempts to eliminate any possibility of faults creeping into a system before it goes operational. The second is **fault tolerance**; this enables a system to continue functioning even in the presence of faults. Both approaches attempt to produce systems which have well-defined failure modes.

3.3.1 Fault prevention

There are two stages to fault prevention: **fault avoidance** and **fault removal**.

Fault avoidance attempts to limit the introduction of potentially faulty components during the construction of the system. For hardware this may entail [69]:

- the use of the most reliable components within the given cost and performance constraints;
- the use of thoroughly-refined techniques for the interconnection of components and the assembly of subsystems;
- packaging the hardware to screen out expected forms of interference.

The software components of large embedded systems are nowadays much more complex than their hardware counterparts. It is virtually impossible in all cases to write fault-free programs. However the quality of software can be improved by:

- rigorous, if not formal, specification of requirements (for example, using B or Z);
- the use of proven design methodologies (for example, those based on UML, such as Real-Time UML [34]);
- the use of analysis tools to verify key program properties (such as model checkers or proof checkers to ensure multitask programs are free from deadlock);
- the use of languages with facilities for data abstraction and modularity (for example, Ada or Java);

- the use of software engineering tools to help manipulate software components and thereby manage complexity (for example, configuration management tools such as SVN).

In spite of fault avoidance techniques, faults will inevitably be present in the system after its construction. In particular, there may be design errors in both hardware and software components. The second stage of fault prevention, therefore, is *fault removal*. This normally consists of procedures for finding and then removing the causes of errors. Although techniques such as design reviews, program verification, and code inspections may be used, emphasis is usually placed on system testing. Unfortunately, system testing can never be exhaustive and remove all potential faults. In particular, the following problems exist.

- A test can only be used to show the presence of faults, not their absence.
- It is sometimes impossible to test under realistic conditions – one of the major causes for concern over the American Strategic Defense Initiative (SDI)[2] was the impossibility of testing any system realistically except under battle conditions. Most tests are done with the system in simulation mode and it is difficult to guarantee that the simulation is accurate. The last French nuclear testing at Mururao in the Pacific during 1995 was allegedly to allow data to be collected so that future tests would not be necessary but could be simulated accurately.
- Errors that have been introduced at the requirements stage of the system's development may not manifest themselves until the system goes operational. For example, in the design of the F18 aircraft an erroneous assumption was made concerning the length of time taken to release a wing-mounted missile. The problem was discovered only during operation when the missile failed to separate from the launcher after ignition, causing the aircraft to go violently out of control [54].

In spite of all the testing and verification techniques, hardware components will fail; the fault prevention approach will, therefore, be unsuccessful when either the frequency or duration of repair times are unacceptable, or the system is inaccessible for maintenance and repair activities. An extreme example of the latter is the crewless spacecraft Voyager.

3.3.2 Fault tolerance

Because of the inevitable limitations of the fault prevention approach, designers of embedded systems must consider the use of fault tolerance. Of course, this does not mean that attempts at preventing faulty systems from becoming operational should be abandoned. However, this book will focus on fault tolerance rather than fault prevention.

Several different levels of fault tolerance can be provided by a system.

- **Full fault tolerance** – the system continues to operate in the presence of faults, albeit for a limited period, with no significant loss of functionality or performance.

---

[2]This was proposed by President Reagan in the 1980s. Its goal was to use ground-based and space-based systems to protect the US from attacks by ballistic missiles. It was never fully developed or deployed.

FAULT PREVENTION AND FAULT TOLERANCE 43

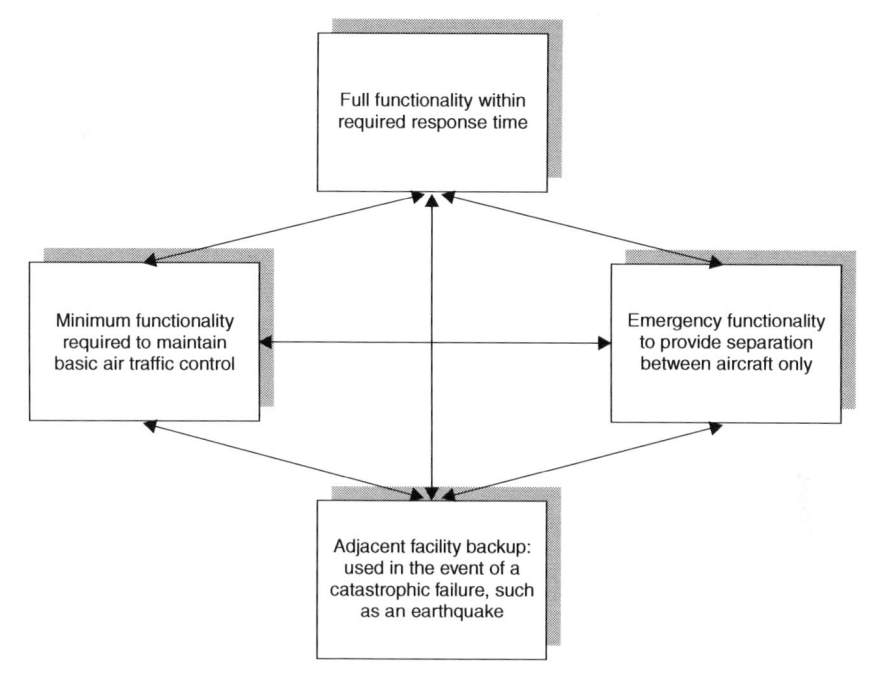

Figure 3.3: Graceful degradation and recovery in an air traffic control system.

[Diagram showing four boxes connected by arrows:
- Full functionality within required response time
- Minimum functionality required to maintain basic air traffic control
- Emergency functionality to provide separation between aircraft only
- Adjacent facility backup: used in the event of a catastrophic failure, such as an earthquake]

- **Graceful degradation** (or fail soft) – the system continues to operate in the presence of errors, accepting a partial degradation of functionality or performance during recovery or repair.
- **Fail safe** – the system maintains its integrity while accepting a temporary halt in its operation.

The level of fault tolerance required will depend on the application. Although in theory most safety-critical systems require full fault tolerance, in practice many settle for graceful degradation. In particular, those systems which can suffer physical damage, such as combat aircraft, may provide several degrees of graceful degradation. Also, with highly complex applications which have to operate on a continuous basis (they have *high availability* requirements) graceful degradation is a necessity, as full fault tolerance is not achievable for indefinite periods. For example, the Federal Aviation Administration's Advanced Automation System, which provides automated services to both *en route* and terminal air traffic controllers throughout the USA, has three levels of graceful degradation for its area control computer couplers [7]. This is illustrated in Figure 3.3.

In some situations, it may simply be necessary to shut down the system in a safe state. These fail-safe systems attempt to limit the amount of damage caused by a failure. For example, the A310 Airbus's slat and flap control computers, on detecting an error on landing, restore the system to a safe state and then shut down. In this situation, a safe state is having both wings with the same settings; only asymmetric settings are hazardous in landing [61].

44   RELIABILITY AND FAULT TOLERANCE

Early approaches to the design of fault-tolerant systems made three assumptions:

(1) the algorithms of the system have been correctly designed,
(2) all possible failure modes of the components are known,
(3) all possible interactions between the system and the environment have been foreseen.

However, the increasing complexity of computer software and the introduction of multicore hardware components mean that it is no longer possible to make these assumptions (if it ever was). Consequently, both anticipated and unanticipated faults must be catered for. The latter include both hardware and software design faults.

3.3.3 Redundancy

All techniques for achieving fault tolerance rely on extra elements introduced into the system to detect and recover from faults. These components are redundant in the sense that they are not required for the system's normal mode of operation. This is often called **protective redundancy**. The aim of fault tolerance is to minimize redundancy while maximising the reliability provided, subject to the cost, size and power constraints of the system. Care must be taken in structuring fault-tolerant systems because the added components inevitably increase the complexity of the overall system. This itself can lead to *less* reliable systems. For example, the first launch of the Space Shuttle was aborted because of a synchronization difficulty with the replicated computer systems [37]. To help reduce problems associated with the interaction between redundant components, it is therefore advisable to separate out the fault-tolerant components from the rest of the system.

There are several different classifications of redundancy, depending on which system components are under consideration and which terminology is being used. Software fault tolerance is the main focus of this chapter and therefore only passing reference will be made to hardware redundancy techniques. For hardware, Anderson and Lee [3] distinguish between *static* (or masking) and *dynamic* redundancy. With static redundancy, redundant components are used inside a system (or subsystem) to hide the effects of faults. An example of static redundancy is **Triple Modular Redundancy** (TMR). TMR consists of three identical subcomponents and majority voting circuits. The circuits compare the output of all the components, and if one differs from the other two that output is masked out. The assumption here is that the fault is not due to a common aspect of the subcomponents (such as a design error), but is either transient or due to component deterioration. Clearly, to mask faults from more than one component requires more redundancy. The general term **N Modular Redundancy** (NMR) is therefore used to characterise this approach.

Dynamic redundancy is the redundancy supplied inside a component which indicates explicitly or implicitly that the output is in error. It therefore provides an *error detection* facility rather than an error-masking facility; recovery must be provided by another component. Examples of dynamic redundancy are checksums on communication transmissions and parity bits on memories.

For fault tolerance of software design errors, two general approaches can be identified. The first is analogous to hardware masking redundancy and is called N-version programming. The second is based on error detection and recovery; it is analogous to dynamic redundancy in the sense that the recovery procedures are brought into action only after an error has been detected.

3.4 N-version programming

The success of hardware TMR and NMR have motivated a similar approach to software fault tolerance. Here, the approach is used to focus on detecting design faults. In fact, this approach (which is now known as N-version programming) was first advocated by Babbage in 1837 [67]:

> When the formula is very complicated, it may be algebraically arranged for computation in two or more distinct ways, and two or more sets of cards may be made. If the same constants are now employed with each set, and if under these circumstances the results agree, we may then be quite secure of the accuracy of them all.

N-version programming is defined as the independent generation of N (where N is greater than or equal to 2) functionally equivalent programs from the same initial specification [28]. The independent generation of N programs means that N individuals or groups produce the required N versions of the software *without interaction* (for this reason N-version programming is often called **design diversity**). Once designed and written, the programs execute concurrently with the same inputs and their results are compared by a **driver task**. In principle, the results should be identical, but in practice there may be some difference, in which case the consensus result, assuming there is one, is taken to be correct.

N-version programming is based on the assumptions that a program can be completely, consistently and unambiguously specified, and that programs which have been developed independently will fail independently. That is, there is no relationship between the faults in one version and the faults in another. This assumption may be invalidated if each version is written in the same programming language, because errors associated with the implementation of the language may be common between versions. Consequently, different programming languages and different development environments should be used. Alternatively, if the same language is used, compilers and support environments from different manufacturers should be employed. Furthermore, in either case, to protect against physical faults, the N versions must be distributed to separate machines which have fault-tolerant communication lines. On the Boeing 777 flight control system, a single Ada program was produced but three different processors and three distinct compilers were used to obtain diversity.

The N-version program is controlled by a driver task which is responsible for

- invoking each of the versions,
- waiting for the versions to complete,
- comparing and acting on the results.

So far it has been implicitly assumed that the programs or tasks run to completion before the results are compared, but for embedded systems this often will not be the case; such

46 RELIABILITY AND FAULT TOLERANCE

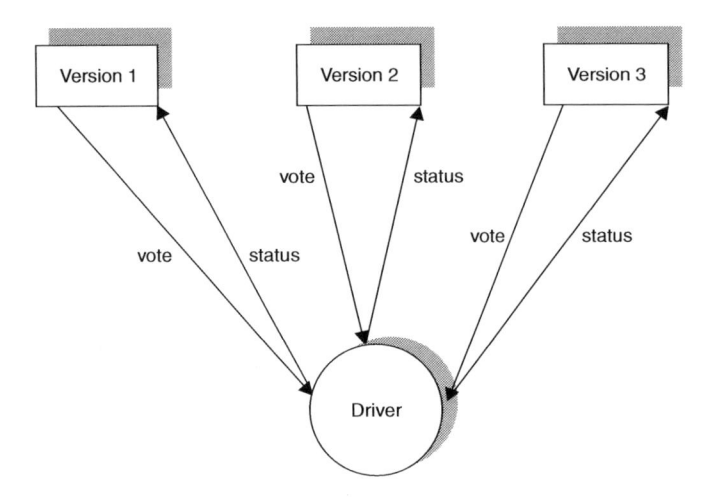

Figure 3.4: N-version programming.

tasks may never complete. The driver and N versions must, therefore, communicate during the course of their executions.

It follows that these versions, although independent, must interact with the driver program. This interaction is specified in the requirements for the versions. It consists of three components [28]:

(1) comparison vectors,
(2) comparison status indicators,
(3) comparison points.

How the versions communicate and synchronize with the driver will depend on the programming language used and its model of concurrency (see Chapters 10 and 11). If different languages are used for different versions, then a real-time operating system will usually provide the means of communication and synchronization. The relationship between the N versions and the driver for an N = 3 version system is shown diagrammatically in Figure 3.4.

Comparison vectors are the data structures which represent the outputs, or votes, produced by the versions plus any attributes associated with their calculation; these must be compared by the driver. For example, in an air traffic control system, if the values being compared are the positions of aircraft, an attribute may indicate whether the values were the result of a recent radar reading or calculated on the basis of older readings.

The comparison status indicators are communicated from the driver to the versions; they indicate the actions that each version must perform as a result of the driver's comparison. Such actions will depend on the outcome of the comparison: whether the votes agreed and whether they were delivered on time. Possible outcomes include:

- continuation,
- termination of one or more versions,

- continuation after changing one or more votes to the majority value.

The comparison points are the points in the versions where they must communicate their votes to the driver task. As Hecht and Hecht [43] point out, an important design decision is the frequency with which the comparisons are made. This is the **granularity** of the fault tolerance provision. Fault tolerance of large granularity, that is, infrequent comparisons, will minimize the performance penalties inherent in the comparison strategies and permit a large measure of independence in the version design. However, a large granularity will probably produce a wide divergence in the results obtained because of the greater number of steps carried out between comparisons. The problems of vote comparison or voting (as it is often called) are considered in the next subsection. Fault tolerance of a fine granularity requires commonality of program structures at a detailed level, and therefore reduces the degree of independence between versions.

3.4.1 Vote comparison

Crucial to N-version programming is the efficiency and the ease with which the driver program can compare votes and decide whether there is any disagreement. For applications which manipulate text or perform integer arithmetic there will normally be a single correct result; the driver can easily compare votes from different versions and choose the majority decision.

Unfortunately, not all results are of an exact nature. In particular, where votes require the calculation of floating point numbers, it will be unlikely that different versions will produce exactly the same result. This might be due to the inexact hardware representation of real numbers or the data sensitivity of a particular algorithm. The techniques used for comparing these types of results are called **inexact voting**. One simple technique is to conduct a range check using a previous estimation or a median value taken from all N results. However, it can be difficult to find a general inexact voting approach.

Another difficulty associated with finite-precision arithmetic is the so-called **consistent comparison problem** [17]. This trouble occurs when an application has to perform a comparison based on a finite value given in the specification; the result of the comparison then determines the course of action to be taken. As an example, consider a process control system which monitors temperature and pressure sensors and then takes appropriate actions according to their values to ensure the integrity of the system. Suppose that when either of these readings passes a threshold value some corrective course of action must be taken. Now consider a 3-version software system (V_1, V_2, V_3) each of which must read both sensors, decide on some action and then vote on the outcome (there is no communication between the versions until they vote). As a result of finite-precision arithmetic, each version will calculate different values (say T_1, T_2, T_3 for the temperature sensor and P_1, P_2, P_3 for the pressure sensor). Assuming that the threshold value for temperature is T_{th} and for pressure P_{th}, the consistent comparison problem occurs when both readings are around their threshold values.

The situation might occur where T_1 and T_2 are just below T_{th} and T_3 just above; consequently V_1 and V_2 will follow their normal execution paths and V_3 will take some corrective action. Now if versions V_1 and V_2 proceed to another comparison point, this time

48   RELIABILITY AND FAULT TOLERANCE

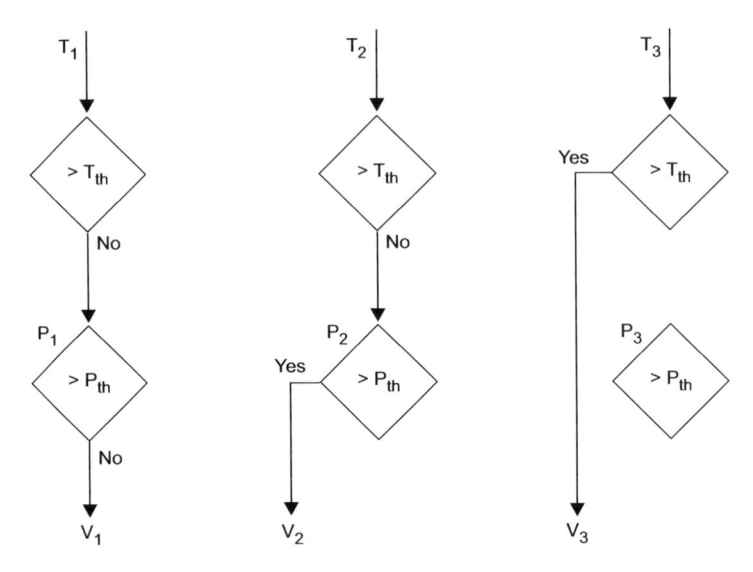

Figure 3.5: Consistent comparison problem with three versions.

with the pressure sensor, then it is possible that P_1 could be just below and P_2 just above P_{th}. The overall result will be that all three versions will have followed different execution paths, and therefore produce different results, each of which is valid. This process is represented diagrammatically in Figure 3.5.

At first sight, it might seem appropriate to use inexact comparison techniques and assume that the values are equal if they differ by a tolerance Δ, but as Brilliant et al. [17] point out, the problem reappears when the values are close to the threshold value $\pm\Delta$.

Still further problems exist with vote comparison when multiple solutions to the same problem naturally exist. For example, a quadratic equation may have more than one solution. Once again disagreement is possible, even though no fault has occurred [3].

3.4.2   Principal issues in N-version programming

It has been shown that the success of N-version programming depends on several issues, which are now briefly reviewed.

(1) **Initial specification** – It has been suggested that the great majority of software faults stem from inadequate specification [54]. Current techniques are a long way from producing complete, consistent, comprehensible and unambiguous specifications, although formal specification methods are proving a fruitful line of research. Clearly a specification error will manifest itself in all N versions of the implementation.

(2) **Independence of design effort** – Some experiments [48, 9, 18, 35, 42] have been undertaken to test the hypothesis that independently produced software will display distinct failures; however, they produce conflicting results. Knight et al. [48] have shown that for a particular problem with a thoroughly refined specification, the hy-

pothesis had to be rejected at the far from adequate 99% confidence level. In contrast, Avizienis et al.[9] found that it was very rare for identical faults to be found in two versions of a six-version system. In comparing their results and those produced by Knight et al., they concluded that the problem addressed by Knight et al. had limited potential for diversity, the programming process was rather informally formulated, testing was limited, and the acceptance test was totally inadequate according to common industrial standards. Avizienis et al. claim that the rigorous application of the N-version programming paradigm would have led to the elimination of all of the errors reported by Knight et al. before the acceptance of the system. However, there is concern that where part of a specification is complex this will inevitably lead to a lack of understanding of the requirements by all the independent teams. If these requirements also refer to rarely occurring input data, then common design errors may not be caught during system testing. In more recent years, studies by Hatton [42] found that a three-version system is still around 5 to 9 times more reliable than a single-version high-quality system.

(3) **Adequate budget** – With most embedded systems, the predominant cost is software. A three-version system will therefore almost triple the budget requirement and cause problems for maintenance personnel. In a competitive environment, it is unlikely that a potential contractor will propose an N-version technique unless it is mandatory. Furthermore, it is unclear whether a more reliable system would be produced if the resources potentially available for constructing N versions were instead used to produce a single version.

It has also been shown that in some instances it is difficult to find inexact voting algorithms, and that unless care is taken with the consistent comparison problem, votes will differ even in the absence of faults.

Although N-version programming may have a role in producing reliable software it should be used with care and in conjunction with other techniques; for example, those discussed below.

3.5 Software dynamic redundancy

N-version programming is the software equivalent of static or masking redundancy, where faults inside a component are hidden from the outside. It is static because each version of the software has a fixed relationship with every other version and the driver; and because it operates whether or not faults have occurred. With **dynamic** redundancy, the redundant components only come into operation *when* an error has been detected.

This technique of fault tolerance has four constituent phases [3].

(1) **Error detection** – Most faults will eventually manifest themselves in the form of an error; no fault tolerance scheme can be utilised until that error is detected.

(2) **Damage confinement and assessment** – When an error has been detected, it must be decided to what extent the system has been corrupted (this is often called **error diagnosis**). The delay between a fault occurring and the manifestation of the as-

sociated error means that erroneous information could have spread throughout the system.

(3) **Error recovery** – This is one of the most important aspects of fault tolerance. Error recovery techniques should aim to transform the corrupted system into a state from which it can continue its normal operation (perhaps with degraded functionality).

(4) **Fault treatment and continued service** – An error is a symptom of a fault; although the damage may have been repaired, the fault may still exist, and therefore the error may recur unless some form of maintenance is undertaken.

Although these four phases of fault tolerance are discussed under software dynamic redundancy techniques, they can clearly be applied to N-version programming. As Anderson and Lee [3] have noted: error detection is provided by the driver which does the vote checking; damage assessment is not required because the versions are independent; error recovery involves discarding the results in error, and fault treatment is simply ignoring the version determined to have produced the erroneous value. However, if all versions have produced differing votes then error detection takes place, but there are *no* recovery facilities.

The next sections briefly cover the above phases of fault tolerance. For a fuller discussion, the reader is referred to the book by Anderson and Lee [3].

3.5.1 Error detection

The effectiveness of any fault tolerant system depends on the effectiveness of its error detection techniques. Two classes of error detection techniques can be identified.

- **Environmental detection**. These are the errors which are detected in the environment in which the program executes. They include those that are detected by the hardware, such as 'illegal instruction executed', 'arithmetic overflow' and 'protection violation'. They also include errors detected by the run-time support system for the real-time programming language; for example, 'array bounds error', 'null pointer referenced' and 'value out of range'. These type of error will be considered in the context of the Ada programming language in Chapter 17.
- **Application detection**. These are the errors that are detected by the application itself. The majority of techniques that can be used by the application fall into the following broad categories.
    - **Replication checks**. It has been shown that N-version programming can be used to tolerate software faults and that the technique can be used to provide error detection (by using two-version redundancy).
    - **Timing checks**. Two types of timing check can be identified. The first involves a **watchdog timer** task that, if not reset within a certain period by a component, assumes that the component is in error. The software component must continually reset the timer to indicate that it is functioning correctly.
    In embedded systems, where timely responses are important, a second type of check is required. These enable the detection of faults associated with missed

deadlines. Where deadline scheduling is performed by the underlying runtime support system, the detection of missed deadlines can be considered to be part of the environment. For example, with the Real-Time Specification for Java it is the real-time JVM that detects deadline misses. However, an Ada programmer must detect such errors in the application code. The issue of tolerating timing faults is covered in detailed in Chapter 19.

Of course, timing checks do *not* ensure that a component is functioning correctly, only that it is functioning on time! Time checks should therefore be used in conjunction with other error detection techniques.

- **Reversal checks**. These are feasible in components where there is a one-to-one (isomorphic) relationship between the input and the output. Such a check takes the output, calculates what the input should be, and then compares the value with the actual input. For example, for a component which finds the square root of a number, the reversal check is simply to square the output and compare it with the input. (Note that inexact comparison techniques may have to be used when dealing with floating point numbers.)

- **Coding checks**. Coding checks are used to test for the corruption of data. They are based on redundant information contained within the data. For example, a value (checksum) may be calculated and sent with the actual data to be transmitted over a communication network. When the data is received, the value can be recalculated and compared with the checksum.

- **Reasonableness checks**. These are based on knowledge of the internal design and construction of the system. They check that the state of data or value of an object is reasonable, based on its intended use. Typically with modern real-time languages, much of the information necessary to perform these checks can be supplied by programmers, as type information associated with data objects. For example, in Ada integer objects which are constrained to be within certain values can be represented by subtypes of integers which have explicit ranges. Range violation can then be detected by the run-time support system.

  Sometimes explicit reasonableness checks are included in software components; these are commonly called **assertions** and take a logical expression which evaluates at run-time to true if no error is detected.

- **Structural checks**. Structural checks are used to check the integrity of data objects such as lists or queues. They might consist of counts of the number of elements in the object, redundant pointers, or extra status information.

- **Dynamic reasonableness checks**. With output emitted from some digital controllers, there is usually a relationship between any two consecutive outputs. Hence an error can be assumed if a new output is too different from the previous value.

Note that many of the above techniques may be applied also at the hardware level and therefore may result in 'environmental errors'.

52 RELIABILITY AND FAULT TOLERANCE

3.5.2 Damage confinement and assessment

As there can be some delay between a fault occurring and an error being detected, it is necessary to assess any damage that may have occurred. While the type of error that was detected will give the error handling routine some idea of the damage, erroneous information could have spread throughout the system and into its environment. Thus damage assessment will be closely related to the damage confinement precautions that were taken by the system's designers. Damage confinement is concerned with structuring the system so as to minimize the damage caused by a faulty component. It is also known as **firewalling**.

There are two techniques that can be used for structuring systems which will aid damage confinement: **modular decomposition** and **atomic actions**. With modular decomposition the emphasis is simply that the system should be broken down into components where each component is represented by one or more modules. Interaction between components then occurs through well-defined interfaces, and the internal details of the modules are hidden and not directly accessible from the outside. This makes it more difficult for an error in one component to be indiscriminately passed to another.

Modular decomposition provides a *static* structure to the software system in that most of that structure is lost at run-time. Equally important to damage confinement is the *dynamic* structure of the system as it facilitates reasoning about the run-time behaviour of the software. One important dynamic structuring technique is based on the use of atomic actions.

The activity of a component is said to be atomic if there are *no* interactions between the activity and the system for the duration of the action. That is, to the rest of the system an atomic action appears to be *indivisible* and takes place *instantaneously*. No information can be passed from within the atomic action to the rest of the system and vice versa. Atomic actions are often called **transactions** or **atomic transactions**. They are used to move the system from one consistent state to another and constrain the flow of information between components. Where two or more components share a resource then damage confinement will involve constraining access to that resource. The implementation of this aspect of atomic actions, using the communication and synchronization primitives found in Ada, will be considered in Chapter 18.

Other techniques which attempt to restrict access to resources are based on **protection mechanisms**, some of which may be supported by hardware. For example, each resource may have one or more modes of operation each with an associated access list (for example, read, write and execute). An activity of a component, or task, will also have an associated mode. Every time a task accesses a resource, the intended operation can be compared against its **access permissions** and, if necessary, access is denied.

In the time domain, damage confinement techniques focus on resource reservation techniques. Budgets can be given to tasks that can be policed at run-time. This topic is covered in detail in Chapter 19.

3.5.3 Error recovery

Once an error situation has been detected and the damage assessed, error recovery procedures must be initiated. This is probably one of the most important phase of any fault-tolerance technique. It must transform an erroneous system state into one which can continue its normal operation, although perhaps with a degraded service. Two approaches to error recovery have been proposed: **forward** and **backward** recovery.

Forward error recovery attempts to continue from an erroneous state by making selective corrections to the system state. For embedded systems, this may involve making safe any aspect of the controlled environment which may be hazardous or damaged because of the failure. Although forward error recovery can be efficient, it is system specific and depends on accurate predictions of the location and cause of errors (that is, damage assessment). Examples of forward recovery techniques include redundant pointers in data structures and the use of self-correcting codes, such as Hamming Codes. An abort, or asynchronous exception, facility may also be required during the recovery action if more than one task is involved in providing the service when the error occurred.

Backward error recovery relies on restoring the system to a safe state previous to that in which the error occurred. An alternative section of the program is then executed. This has the same functionality as the fault-producing section, but uses a different algorithm. As with N-version programming, it is hoped that this alternative approach will *not* result in the same fault recurring. The point to which a task is restored is called a **recovery point** and the act of establishing it is usually termed **checkpointing**. To establish a recovery point, it is necessary to save appropriate system state information at run-time.

State restoration has the advantage that the erroneous state has been cleared and that it does not rely on finding the location or cause of the fault. Backward error recovery can therefore be used to recover from unanticipated faults including design errors. However, its disadvantage is that it cannot undo any effects that the fault may have had in the environment of the embedded system; it is difficult to undo a missile launch, for example. Furthermore, backward error recovery can be time-consuming in execution, which may preclude its use in some real-time applications. For instance, operations involving sensor information may be time dependent, therefore costly state restoration techniques may simply not be feasible. Consequently, to improve performance **incremental checkpointing** approaches have been considered. The **recovery cache** is an example of such a system [3]. Other approaches include audit trails or logs; in these cases, the underlying support system must undo the effects of the task by reversing the actions indicated in the log.

With concurrent tasks that interact with each other, state restoration is not as simple as so far portrayed. Consider two tasks depicted in Figure 3.6. Task T_1 establishes recovery points R_{11}, R_{12} and R_{13}. Task T_2 establishes recovery points R_{21} and R_{22}. Also, the two tasks communicate and synchronize their actions via IPC_1, IPC_2, IPC_3 and IPC_4. The abbreviation IPC is used to indicate Inter-Process Communication.

If T_1 detects an error at time T_e then it is simply rolled back to recovery point R_{13}. However, consider the case where T_2 detects an error at T_e. If T_2 is rolled back to R_{22} then it must undo the communication IPC_4 with T_1; this requires T_1 to be rolled back to R_{12}. But if this is done, T_2 must be rolled back to R_{21} to undo communication IPC_3, and so on. The result will be that both tasks will be rolled back to the beginning of their interaction with each other. In many cases, this may be equivalent to aborting both tasks! This phenomenon is known as the **domino effect**.

Obviously, if the two tasks do not interact with each other then there will be no domino effect. When more than two tasks interact, the possibility of the effect occurring increases. In this case, consistent recovery points must be designed into the system so that an error detected in one task will not result in a total rollback of all the tasks with which

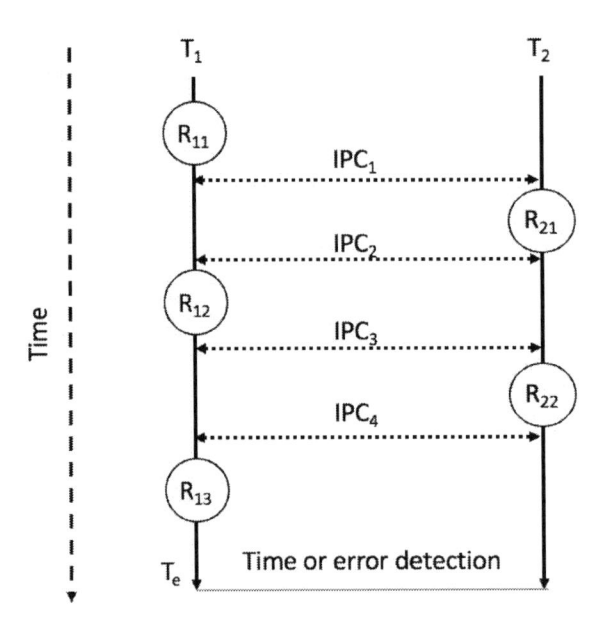

Figure 3.6: The domino effect.

it interacts; instead, the tasks can be restarted from a consistent set of recovery points. These **recovery lines**, as they are often called, are closely linked with the notion of atomic actions, introduced earlier in this chapter. The issue of error recovery in concurrent tasks will be revisited in Chapter 18. For the remainder of this chapter, sequential systems only will be considered.

The concepts of forward and backward error recovery have been introduced; each has its advantages and disadvantages. Not only do embedded systems have to be able to recover from unanticipated errors but they also must be able to respond in finite time; they may therefore require *both* forward and backward error recovery techniques.

3.5.4 Fault treatment and continued service

An error is a manifestation of a fault, and although the error recovery phase may have returned the system to an error-free state, the error may recur. Therefore the final phase of fault tolerance is to eradicate the fault from the system so that normal service can be continued.

The automatic treatment of faults is difficult to implement and tends to be system-specific. Consequently, some systems make no provision for fault treatment, assuming that all faults are transient; others assume that error recovery techniques are sufficiently powerful to cope with recurring faults.

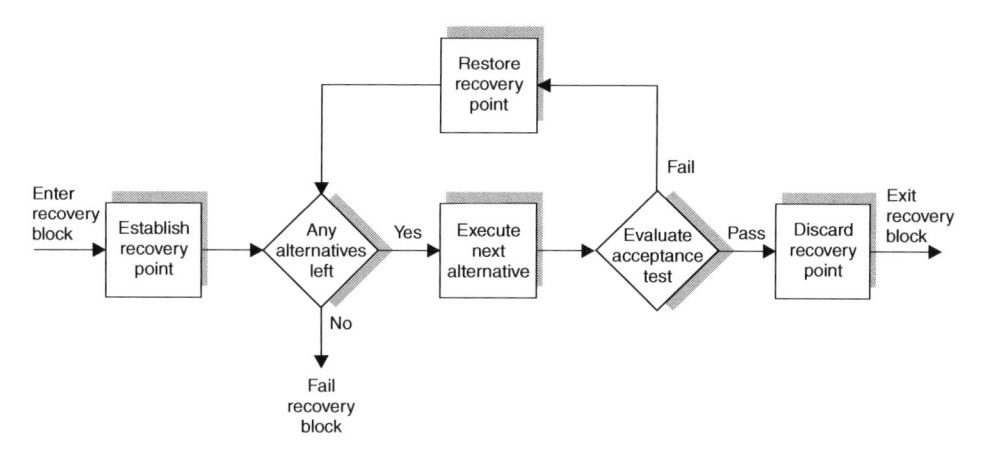

Figure 3.7: Recovery block mechanism.

Fault treatment can be divided into two stages: fault location and system repair. Error detection techniques can help to trace the fault to a component. For a hardware component this may be accurate enough and the component can simply be replaced. A software fault can be removed in a new version of the code. However, in most non-stop applications it will be necessary to modify the program while it is executing. This presents a significant technical problem, but will not be considered further here.

3.6 The recovery block approach to software fault tolerance

Recovery blocks [46] are **blocks** in the normal programming language sense except that, at the entrance to the block is an automatic **recovery point** and at the exit an **acceptance test**. The acceptance test is used to test that the system is in an acceptable state after the execution of the block (or **primary module** as it is often called). The failure of the acceptance test results in the program being restored to the recovery point at the beginning of the block and an **alternative module** being executed. If the alternative module also fails the acceptance test then again the program is restored to the recovery point and yet another module is executed, and so on. If all modules fail then the block fails and recovery must take place at a higher level. The execution of a recovery block is illustrated in Figure 3.7.

In terms of the four phases of software fault tolerance: error detection is achieved by the acceptance test, damage assessment is not needed as backward error recovery is assumed to clear all erroneous states, and fault treatment is achieved by use of a stand-by spare.

Although no commercially available real-time programming language has language features for exploiting recovery blocks, some experimental systems have been developed [73, 65]. A possible syntax for recovery blocks is illustrated below

```
ensure <acceptance test>
by
  <primary module>
```

56 RELIABILITY AND FAULT TOLERANCE

```
else by
  <alternative module>
else by
  <alternative module>
  ...
else by
  <alternative module>
else error
```

Like ordinary blocks, recovery blocks can be nested. If a block in a nested recovery block fails its acceptance tests and all its alternatives also fail, then the outer level recovery point will be restored and an alternative module to that block executed.

To show the use of recovery blocks, the various methods used to find the numerical solution of a system of differential equations are considered. As such methods do not give exact solutions, but are subject to various errors, it may be found that some approaches will perform better for certain classes of equations than for others. Unfortunately, methods which give accurate results across a wide range of equations are expensive to implement (in terms of the time needed to complete the method's execution). For example, an **explicit Kutta** method will be more efficient than an **implicit Kutta** method. However, it will only give an acceptable error tolerance for particular problems. There is a class of equations called **stiff** equations whose solution using an explicit Kutta leads to an accumulation of rounding errors; the more expensive implicit Kutta method can more adequately deal with this problem. The following illustrates an approach using recovery blocks which enables the cheaper method to be employed for non-stiff equations but which does not fail when stiff equations are given.

```
ensure rounding_error_within_acceptable_tolerance
by
  Explicit Kutta Method
else by
  Implicit Kutta Method
else error
```

In this example, the cheaper explicit method is usually used; however, when it fails the more expensive implicit method is employed. Although this error is anticipated, this approach also gives tolerance to an error in the design of the explicit algorithm. If the algorithm itself is in error and the acceptance test is general enough to detect both types of error result, the implicit algorithm will be used. When the acceptance test cannot be made general enough, nested recovery blocks can be used. In the following, full design redundancy is provided; at the same time the cheaper algorithm is always used if possible.

```
ensure rounding_error_within_acceptable_tolerance
by
  ensure sensible_value
  by
    Explicit Kutta Method
  else by
    Predictor-Corrector K-step Method
  else error
else by
```

```
  ensure sensible_value
  by
    Implicit Kutta Method
  else by
    Variable Order K-Step Method
  else error
else error
```

In the above, two explicit methods are given; when both methods fail to produce a sensible result, the implicit Kutta method is executed. The implicit Kutta method will, of course, also be executed if the value produced by the explicit methods is sensible but not within the required tolerance. Only if all four methods fail will the equations remain unsolved.

The recovery block could have been nested the other way around as shown below. In this case, different behaviour will occur when a non-sensible result is also not within acceptable tolerance. In the first case, after executing the explicit Kutta algorithm, the Predictor Corrector method would be attempted. In the second, the implicit Kutta algorithm would be executed.

```
ensure sensible_value
by
  ensure rounding_error_within_acceptable_margin
  by
    Explicit Kutta Method
  else by
    Implicit Kutta Method
  else error
else by
  ensure rounding_error_within_acceptable_margin
  by
    Predictor-Corrector K-step Method
  else by
    Variable Order K-Step Method
  else error
else error
```

3.6.1 The acceptance test

The acceptance test provides the error detection mechanism which then enables the redundancy in the system to be exploited. The design of the acceptance test is crucial to the efficacy of the recovery block scheme. As with all error detection mechanisms, there is a trade-off between providing comprehensive acceptance tests and keeping the overhead this entails to a minimum, so that normal fault-free execution is affected as little as possible. Note that the term used is **acceptance** not **correctness**; this allows a component to provide a degraded service.

All the error detection techniques discussed in Section 3.5.1 can be used to form the acceptance tests. However, care must be taken in their design as a faulty acceptance test may lead to residual errors going undetected.

3.6.2 A comparison between N-version programming and recovery blocks

Two approaches to providing fault-tolerant software have been described: N-version programming and recovery blocks. They clearly share some aspects of their basic philosophy, and yet at the same time they are quite different. This section briefly reviews and compares the two.

- **Static versus dynamic redundancy**

    N-version programming is based on static redundancy; all versions run in parallel irrespective of whether or not a fault occurs. In contrast, recovery blocks are dynamic in that alternative modules only execute when an error has been detected.

- **Associated overheads**

    Both N-version programming and recovery blocks incur extra development cost, as both require alternative algorithms to be developed. In addition, for N-version programming, the driver task must be designed and recovery blocks require the design of the acceptance test.

    At run-time, N-version programming in general requires N times the resources of a single version. Although recovery blocks only require a single set of resources at any one time, the establishment of recovery points and the task of state restoration is expensive. However, it is possible to provide hardware support for the establishment of recovery points [52], and state restoration is only required when a fault occurs.

- **Diversity of design** Both approaches exploit diversity in design to achieve tolerance of unanticipated errors. Both are, therefore, susceptible to errors that originate from the requirements specification.

- **Error detection**

    N-version programming uses vote comparison to detect errors whereas recovery blocks use an acceptance test. Where exact or inexact voting is possible there is probably less associated overhead than with acceptance tests. However, where it is difficult to find an inexact voting technique, where multiple solutions exist or where there is a consistent comparison problem, acceptance tests may provide more flexibility.

- **Atomicity**

    Backward error recovery is criticised because it cannot undo any damage which may have occurred in the environment. N-version programming avoids this problem because all versions are assumed not to interfere with each other: they are atomic. This requires each version to communicate with the driver task rather than directly with the environment. However, it is entirely possible to structure a program such that unrecoverable operations do not appear in recovery blocks.

It perhaps should be stressed that although N-version programming and recovery blocks have been described as competing approaches, they also can be considered as complementary ones. For example, there is nothing to stop a designer using recovery blocks within each version of an N-version system.

3.7 Dynamic redundancy and exceptions

In this section, a framework for implementing software fault tolerance is introduced which is based on dynamic redundancy and the notion of exceptions and exception handlers.

So far in this chapter, the term 'error' has been used to indicate the manifestation of a fault, where a fault is a deviation from the specification of a component. These errors can be either anticipated, as in the case of an out of range sensor reading due to hardware malfunction, or unanticipated, as in the case of a design error in the component. An **exception** can be defined as the occurrence of an error. Bringing an exception condition to the attention of the invoker of the operation which caused the exception, is called **raising** (or **signalling** or **throwing**) the exception and the invoker's response is called **handling** (or **catching**) the exception. Exception handling can be considered a *forward error recovery* mechanism, as when an exception has been raised the system is not rolled back to a previous state; instead, control is passed to the handler so that recovery procedures can be initiated.

Although an exception has been defined as the occurrence of an error, there is some controversy as to the true nature of exceptions and when they should be used. For example, consider a software component or module which maintains a compiler symbol table. One of the operations it provides is to look up a symbol. This has two possible outcomes: *symbol present* and *symbol absent*. Either outcome is an anticipated response *and* may or may not represent an error condition. If the *lookup* operation is used to determine the interpretation of a symbol in a program body, *symbol absent* corresponds to 'undeclared identifier', which is an error condition. If, however, the *lookup* operation is used during the declaration process, the outcome *symbol absent* is probably the normal case and *symbol present*, that is 'duplicate definition', the exception. What constitutes an error, therefore, depends on the context in which the event occurs. However, in either of the above cases it could be argued that the error is not an error of the symbol table component or of the compiler, in that either outcome is an anticipated result and forms part of the functionality of the symbol table module. Therefore neither outcome should be represented as an exception.

Exception-handling facilities were *not* incorporated into programming languages to cater for programmer design errors; however, it will be shown in Part III (Section 17.4) how they can be used to do just that. The original motivation for exceptions came from the requirement to handle abnormal conditions arising in the environment in which a program executes. These exceptions could be termed rare events in the functioning of the environment, and it may or may not be possible to recover from them within the program. A faulty valve or a temperature alarm might cause an exception. These are rare events which, given enough time, might well occur and must be tolerated.

Despite the above, exceptions and their handlers will inevitably be used as a general-purpose error-handling mechanism. To conclude, exceptions and exception handling can be used to:

- cope with abnormal conditions arising in the environment,
- enable program design faults to be tolerated,
- provide a general-purpose error-detection and recovery facility.

60 RELIABILITY AND FAULT TOLERANCE

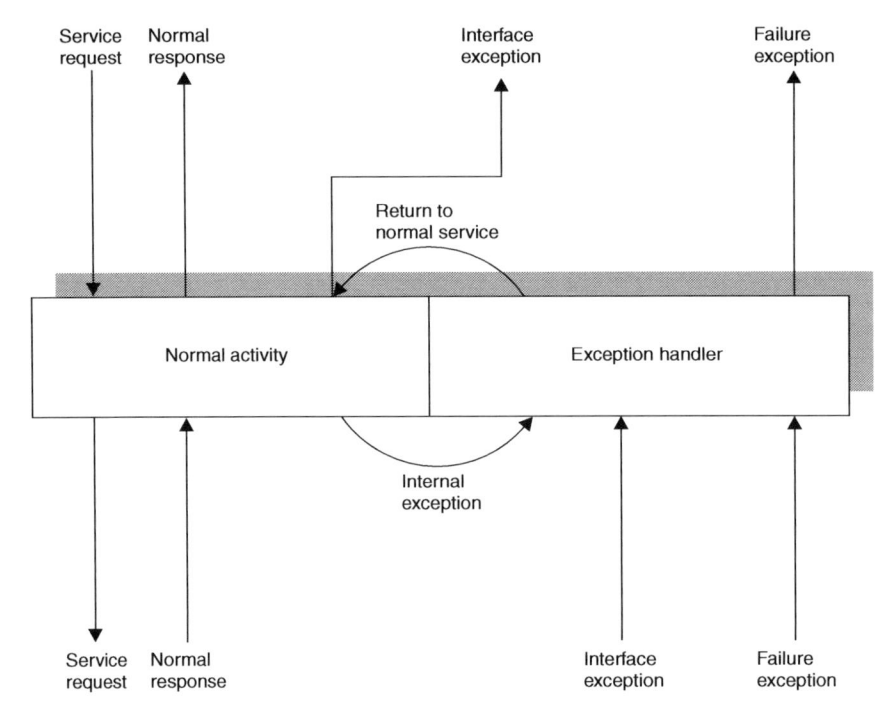

Figure 3.8: An ideal fault-tolerant component.

Exceptions are considered in more detail in Chapter 17.

Ideal fault-tolerant system components

Figure 3.8 shows the ideal component from which to build fault-tolerant systems [3]. The component accepts service requests and, if necessary, calls upon the services of other components before yielding a response. This may be a normal response or an exception response. Two types of fault can occur in the ideal component: those due to an illegal service request, called **interface exceptions**, and those due to a malfunction in the component itself, or in the components required to service the original request. Where the component cannot tolerate these faults, either by forward or backward error recovery, it raises **failure exceptions** in the calling component. Before raising any exceptions, the component must return itself to a consistent state, if possible, in order that it may service any future request.

3.8 Fault tolerance and the real-time programming model

Having now introduced the main approaches to fault tolerance it is possible to link these schemes with the timing issues addressed in the previous chapter. Recall from the previous chapter that the code for a simple periodic task (as an example) has the following form:

FAULT TOLERANCE AND THE REAL-TIME PROGRAMMING MODEL 61

```
loop every 20ms
  read from sensors (in)
  out := G(S,in)
  S := F(S,in)
  write to actuators (out) within 15ms
end loop
```

This periodic task executes every 20ms and has a deadline of 15ms each time it executes. The main functionality of the task is embedded in the functions G and F.

If fault tolerance is now considered, two issues must be addressed. First, the functions may need to include code for error detection and recovery. And second, the missing of the designated deadline is a failure of the task and may need recovery code.

Functions G and F may be enhanced to include active replication, recovery blocks or exception handlers. All these additions will add to the size of the code and the time it will take to execute. As time is obviously an issue for real-time systems, there needs to be a bound on the extra execution time that will result from error detection and recovery. No system can continue to meet its deadlines if faced with an arbitrary number of errors.

To give an upper bound on this extra execution time a **fault model** is introduced. The role of the fault model is to define the number and type of errors that must be tolerated by the system without the system missing any deadlines. So if the system is behaving within its fault model, all deadlines are guaranteed, but outside the fault model then a new failure (a deadline miss) may be unavoidable.

A missed deadline cannot, of course, be resolved by backward error recovery; time cannot be reversed. So for timing faults it is usual to use forward error recovery. Here actions are taken to minimise the consequences of the deadline miss. For some situations, the sensible action is just to allow the code to continue executing and then deal with the impact of late delivery. But for other conditions, the deadline miss is evidence of other faults; indeed the code may be in an indefinite loop and will never finish. Here the actions of the task must be abandoned. The code outline becomes:

```
loop every 20ms
  read from sensors (in)
  out := G*(S,in)
  S := F*(S,in)
  write to actuators (out) within 15ms
    action-on-deadline-miss within 1ms
  abort after 18ms
    action-on-abort within 2ms
end loop
```

where G* and F* are the fault tolerant versions of the task's code, `action-on-deadline-miss` is the code to be executed if the activity fails to complete by its deadline, and `action-on-abort` is the code to be executed in the event of code abandonment.

With this example each iteration of the task should complete within 15ms. If this fails to occur then 3 further milliseconds are allowed. Even if the activity completes within this extra margin the fact that a deadline has been missed may lead to an action being executed. This action will itself have a deadline. After 18ms (from the start) the task is aborted and the recovery code executed. This recovery code similarly has a deadline of 2ms. Overall, unless there are further problems with the extra code this task will always complete within 20ms.

In the previous chapter, the notions of hard and soft deadlines were introduced. A hard deadline is one that must be met (or else the system is deemed to have failed). Once we move to fault tolerant systems then this definition of a hard deadline needs to be qualified. In the above example, the deadline of 15ms may well still be hard, in that the system is designed so that it is guaranteed to be met. But errors, of intensity beyond that allowed by the fault model, can undermine this guarantee. Error recovery, be that graceful degradation or the movement of the system to a safe state, may inevitable mean that even hard deadlines are compromised.

3.9 Measuring and predicting the reliability of software

Reliability metrics for hardware components have long been established. Traditionally, each component is regarded as a representative of a population of identical members whose reliability is estimated from the proportion of a sample that fail during a specified interval of time, e.g. during testing. Software reliability prediction and measurement, however, is not as well an established discipline. It was ignored for many years by those industries requiring extremely reliable systems because software is assumed not to deteriorate with use; software was regarded as either correct or incorrect – a binary property.

Also, in the past, particular software components were used once only, in the systems for which they were originally intended; consequently, although any errors found during testing were removed, this did not lead to the development of more reliable components which could be used elsewhere. This can be contrasted with hardware components, which are mass produced; any errors found in the design can be corrected, making the next batch more reliable.

The view that software is either correct or not correct is still commonly held. If it is not correct, program testing or program proving will indicate the location of faults which can then be corrected. This chapter has tried to illustrate that the traditional approach of software testing, although indispensable, can never ensure that programs are fault-free, especially with very large and complicated systems where there may be residual specification or design errors. Furthermore, in spite of the continual advances made in the field of proof of correctness, the application of these techniques to non-trivial systems, particularly those involving the concept of time, is still beyond the *"state of the art"*. Indeed it may always be beyond the capability of such techniques due to the tendency to make systems and programs ever larger and more complex.

It is for all these reasons that methods of improving reliability through the use of redundancy have been advocated. Unfortunately, even with this approach, it cannot be guaranteed that systems containing software will not fail. It is therefore essential that techniques for assessing software reliability are developed.

As hardware is deemed to be subject to *random* failures it is natural to use a probabilistic approach for reliability assessment. It is perhaps less clear why *systematic* software failures should be characterised similarly. Although systematic in nature, the process by which any particular demand on the system will give rise to a failure is essentially non-deterministic [55]. Software reliability can therefore be considered as *the probability that a given program will operate correctly in a specified environment for a specified length of time.*

Several models have been proposed which attempt to estimate software reliability. These can be broadly classified as [38]

- software reliability growth models,
- statistical models.

Growth models attempt to predict the reliability of a program on the basis of its error history (e.g. when faults are identified and repaired). Other statistical models attempt to estimate the reliability of a program by determining its success or failure response to a random sample of test cases, without correcting any errors found. Unfortunately, Littlewood and Strigini [56] have argued that testing alone can only provide effective evidence for reliability estimates of at best 10^{-4} (that is 10^{-4} failures per hour of operation). This should be compared with the often quoted reliability requirement of 10^{-9} for avionics systems. To increase the assessment of reliability by an order of magnitude to 10^{-5} would required the observation of 460,000 hours (over 50 years) of fault-free operation [55].

To estimate the reliability of N-version components is even more difficult as the level of correlation between the versions is, as indicated earlier, very difficult to estimate. Even strong advocates of the approach would not argue that two 10^{-4} versions would combine to give a 10^{-8} service.

3.10 Safety, reliability and dependability

Safety can be defined as *freedom from those conditions that can cause death, injury, occupational illness, damage to (or loss of) equipment (or property), or environmental harm* [54]. However, as this definition would consider most systems which have an element of risk associated with their use as unsafe, software safety is often considered in terms of **mishaps** [54]. A mishap is an **unplanned event** or **series of events** that can result in death, injury, occupational illness, damage to (or loss of) equipment (or property), or environmental harm.

Although reliability and safety are often considered as synonymous, there is a difference in their emphasis. Reliability has been defined as a measure of the success with which a system conforms to some authoritative specification of its behaviour. This is usually expressed in terms of probability. Safety, however, is the probability that conditions that can lead to mishaps do not occur *whether or not the intended function is performed*. These two definitions can conflict with each other. For example, measures which increase the likelihood of a weapon firing when required may well increase the possibility of its accidental detonation. In many ways, the only safe aeroplane is one that never takes off; however, it is not very reliable. Nevertheless, any system (or subsystem) whose primary role is to provide safety must itself be *sufficiently* reliable. For example, a secondary Nuclear Reactor Protection System (NRPS) is only required to act when other systems have failed. It provided additional safety and hence is of value if its own reliability is assessed as being no more than 10^{-4} failures per demand. The primary NRPS may be assessed to

64   RELIABILITY AND FAULT TOLERANCE

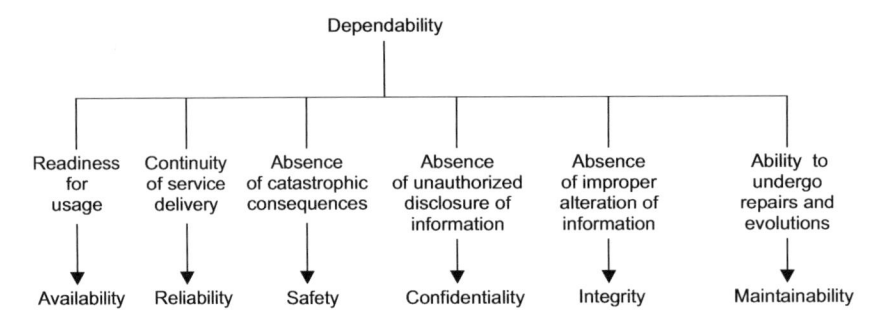

```
                          Dependability
     ┌─────────┬──────────┬──────────┬──────────┬─────────┐
 Readiness  Continuity  Absence    Absence    Absence   Ability to
   for     of service  of catastrophic of unauthorized of improper  undergo
  usage     delivery  consequences  disclosure of  alteration of  repairs and
                                   information   information   evolutions
     │         │          │          │          │          │
     ▼         ▼          ▼          ▼          ▼          ▼
 Availability Reliability Safety  Confidentiality Integrity Maintainability
```

Figure 3.9: Aspects of dependability.

have reliability of only 10^{-3}; as long as the primary and secondary systems are independent this provides an overall reliability of at least 10^{-7}. Plant safety is only compromised if these two systems fail *and* the plant controller itself suffers a 'meltdown' failure – an exceedingly rare event in itself.

As with reliability, to ensure the safety requirements of an embedded system, system safety analysis must be performed throughout all stages of its life cycle development. It is beyond the scope of this book to enter into details of safety analysis.

Dependability

The dependability of a system is that property of the system which allows reliance to be justifiably placed on the service it delivers. Dependability, therefore, includes as special cases the notions of reliability, safety and security [51]. Figure 3.9, based on that given by Laprie [51], illustrates these and other aspects of dependability (where security is viewed in terms of integrity and confidentiality). In this figure, the term 'reliability' is used as a measure of the continuous delivery of a proper service; (un)availability is a measure of the frequency of periods of improper service.

Dependability itself can be described in terms of three components [51].

- *threats* – circumstances causing or resulting in non-dependability;
- *means* – the methods, tools and solutions required to deliver a dependable service with the required confidence;
- *attributes* – the way and measures by which the quality of a dependable service can be appraised.

Figure 3.10 summarizes the concept of dependability in terms of these three components.

Summary

This chapter has identified reliability as a major requirement for any real-time system. The reliability of a system has been defined as a measure of the success

SAFETY, RELIABILITY AND DEPENDABILITY   65

```
Dependability ─┬─ Attributes ─┬─ Availability
               │              ├─ Reliability
               │              ├─ Safety
               │              ├─ Confidentiality
               │              ├─ Integrity
               │              └─ Maintainability
               │
               ├─ Means ──────┬─ Fault prevention
               │              ├─ Fault tolerance
               │              ├─ Fault removal
               │              └─ Fault forecasting
               │
               └─ Threats ────┬─ Faults
                              ├─ Errors
                              └─ Failures
```

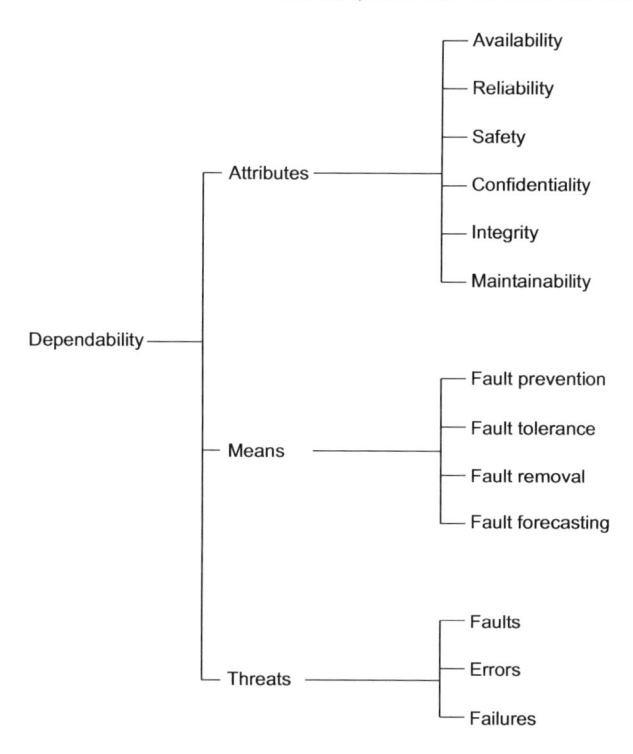

Figure 3.10: Dependability terminology.

with which the system conforms to some authoritative specification of its behaviour. When the behaviour of a system deviates from that which is specified for it, this is called a failure. Failures result from faults. Faults can be accidentally or intentionally introduced into a system. They can be transient, permanent or intermittent.

There are two approaches to system design that help ensure that potential faults do not cause system failure: fault prevention and fault tolerance. Fault prevention consists of fault avoidance and fault removal. Fault tolerance involves the introduction of redundant components into a system so that faults can be detected and tolerated. In general, a system will provide either full fault tolerance, graceful degradation or fail-safe behaviour.

Two general approaches to software fault tolerance have been discussed: N-version programming (static redundancy) and dynamic redundancy using forward and backward error recovery. N-version programming is defined as the independent generation of N (2 or more) functionally equivalent programs from the same initial specification. Once designed and written, the programs execute concurrently with the same inputs and their results are compared. In principle, the results should be identical, but in practice there may be some difference, in which case the consensus result, assuming there is one, is taken to be correct. N-version programming is based on the assumptions that a program can be completely, consistently and unambiguously specified, and that programs which have been developed independently will fail independently. These assumptions may not always be valid, and although N-version programming may have a role in producing reliable software it should be used with care and in conjunction with techniques based on dynamic redundancy.

Dynamic redundancy techniques have four constituent phases: error detection, damage confinement and assessment, error recovery, and fault treatment and continued service. One of the most important phases is error recovery for which two approaches have been proposed: backward and forward. With backward error recovery, it is necessary for communicating tasks to reach consistent recovery points to avoid the domino effect. For sequential systems, the recovery block has been introduced as an appropriate language concept for expressing backward error recovery. Recovery blocks are blocks in the normal programming language sense except that at the entrance to the block is an automatic recovery point and at the exit an acceptance test. The acceptance test is used to test that the system is in an acceptable state after the execution of the primary module. The failure of the acceptance test results in the program being restored to the recovery point at the beginning of the block and an alternative module being executed. If the alternative module also fails the acceptance test, the program is restored to the recovery point again and yet another module is executed, and so on. If all modules fail then the block fails.

Although forward error recovery is system-specific, exception handling has been identified as an appropriate framework for its implementation. The concept of an ideal fault tolerant component was introduced which used exceptions. Timing faults, e.g. the missing of a specified deadline links reliability and real-time behaviour. Not only must some form of error recovery be scheduled if a deadline is missed, but the error recovery itself may have a deadline imposed upon it.

Finally, the notions of software safety and dependability were introduced.

Part II

SCHEDULING THEORY FOR REAL-TIME SYSTEMS

Chapter 4
Scheduling real-time systems

4.1 The cyclic executive approach
4.2 Task-based scheduling
4.3 Rate monotonic priority assignment
4.4 Utilization-based schedulability tests for fixed priority scheduling
4.5 Work-case execution time
Summary

In a concurrent program it is not necessary to specify the exact order in which tasks execute. Synchronization primitives are used to enforce local ordering constraints, such as mutual exclusion, but the general behaviour of a program exhibits significant non-determinism. If the program is correct then its functional outputs will be the same regardless of internal behaviour or implementation details. For example, five independent tasks can be executed non-preemptively in 120 different ways on a single processor. With a multiprocessor system or preemptive behaviour, there are infinitely more interleavings.

While the program's outputs will be identical with all these possible interleavings, the timing behaviour will vary considerably. If one of the five tasks has a tight deadline then perhaps only interleavings in which it is executed first will meet the program's temporal requirements. A real-time system needs to restrict the non-determinism found within concurrent systems. This activity is known as **scheduling**. In general, a scheduling scheme provides two features:

- An algorithm for ordering the use of system resources (in particular the CPUs).
- A means of predicting the worst-case behaviour of the system when the scheduling algorithm is applied.

The predictions can then be used to confirm that the temporal requirements of the system are satisfied.

A scheduling scheme can be **static** (if the predictions are undertaken before execution) or **dynamic** (if run-time decisions are used). The chapters in Part II will concentrate mainly on static schemes. Most attention will be given to preemptive priority-based scheduling on a single processor system. Here, tasks are assigned

70   SCHEDULING REAL-TIME SYSTEMS

priorities such that at all times the task with the highest priority is executing (if it is not delayed or otherwise suspended). A scheduling scheme will therefore involve a priority assignment algorithm and a schedulability test. Other scheduling approaches, such as EDF (Earliest Deadline First) are also introduced in this chapter. The first approach to be review, however, will be the traditional scheme involving the production of a cyclic executive.

4.1 The cyclic executive approach

With a fixed set of purely periodic tasks it is possible to lay out a complete schedule such that the repeated execution of this schedule will cause all tasks to run at their correct rate. The cyclic executive is, essentially, a table of procedure calls, where each procedure represents part of the code for a 'task'. The complete table is known as the **major cycle**; it typically consists of a number of **minor cycles** each of fixed duration. So, for example, four minor cycles of 25 ms duration would make up a 100 ms major cycle. During execution, a clock interrupt every 25 ms will enable the scheduler to loop through the four minor cycles. Table 4.1 provides a task set that can be implemented via a simple four-slot major cycle on a single processor. A possible mapping onto the cyclic executive is shown in Figure 4.1, which illustrates the job that the processor is executing at any particular time.

Task	Period, T	Computation time, C
a	25	10
b	25	8
c	50	5
d	50	4
e	100	2

Table 4.1: Cyclic executive task set.

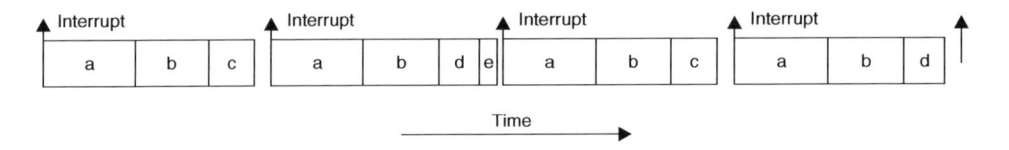

Figure 4.1: Time-line for task set.

Even this simple example illustrates some important features of this approach:

- No actual tasks exist at run-time; each minor cycle is just a sequence of procedure calls.
- There may be times between the minor cycles during which the processor is idle.

- The procedures share a common address space and can thus pass data between themselves. This data does not need to be protected (via a semaphore, for example) because concurrent access is not possible.
- All 'task' periods must be a multiple of the minor cycle time.

This final property represents one of the major drawbacks of the cyclic executive approach; others include:

- the difficulty of incorporating sporadic tasks;
- the difficulty of incorporating tasks with long periods; the major cycle time is the maximum period that can be accommodated without secondary schedules (that is, a procedure in a major cycle that will call a secondary procedure every N major cycles);
- the difficulty of actually constructing the cyclic executive;
- any 'task' with a sizable computation time will need to be split into a fixed number of fixed sized procedures (this may cut across the structure of the code from a software engineering perspective, and hence may be error-prone; it must also be the case that data shared with other tasks must be contained within a single slice).

If it is possible to construct a cyclic executive then no further schedulability test is needed (the scheme is 'proof by construction'). However, for systems with high utilization, the building of the executive is problematic. An analogy with the classical bin packing problem can be made. With that problem, items of varying sizes (in just one dimension) have to be placed in the minimum number of bins such that no bin is over-full. The bin packing problem is known to be NP-hard and hence is computationally infeasible for sizable problems (a typical realistic system will contain perhaps 40 minor cycles and 400 entries). Heuristic sub-optimal schemes must therefore be used. However, the application of optimal ILP (Integer Linear Programming) solvers to the problem of laying out a cyclic schedule has recently been shown to be effective.

Although for simple periodic systems the cyclic executive will remain an appropriate implementation strategy, a more flexible and accommodating approach is furnished by the task-based scheduling schemes. These approaches will therefore be the focus in the remainder of this chapter.

4.2 Task-based scheduling

With the cyclic executive approach, at run-time, only a sequence of procedure calls are executed. The notion of task (thread) is not preserved during execution. An alternative approach is to support task execution directly (as is the norm in general-purpose operating systems) and to determine which task should execute at any one time by the use of one or more scheduling attributes. With this approach, a task is deemed to be in one of a number of *states* (assuming no intertask communication):

- runnable,

- suspended waiting for a timing event – appropriate for periodic tasks,
- suspended waiting for a non-timing event – appropriate for sporadic tasks.

4.2.1 Scheduling approaches

There are, in general, a large number of different scheduling approaches. In this book we will consider four.

- Fixed-Priority Scheduling (FPS) – this is the most widely used approach and is the main focus of this and the following chapter. Each task has a fixed, **static**, priority which is computed pre-run-time. The runnable tasks are executed in the order determined by their priority. *In real-time systems, the 'priority' of a task is derived from its temporal requirements, not its importance to the correct functioning of the system or its integrity or criticality.*
- Earliest Deadline First (EDF) Scheduling. Here the runnable tasks are executed in the order determined by the absolute deadlines of the tasks; the next task to run is the one with the shortest (nearest) deadline. Although it is usual to know the relative deadlines of each task (e.g. 25 ms after release), the absolute deadlines are computed at run-time, and hence the scheme is described as **task dynamic and job static** – i.e. each invocation of the task (each job) has a difference absolute deadline, but once a job is released it retains the same deadline.
- Least Laxity First (LLF), Here the runnable tasks are executed in the order determined by the slack (laxity) of the tasks. The next task to run is the one with the shortest laxity (absolute deadline minus work to do). So a task with a deadline of 12 o'clock with 3 hours work to do, is executed before one with deadline of 11.00 o'clock and 1 hour of work to do. With LLF the laxity of a job changes as time progresses. Hence the scheme is both **task dynamic and job dynamic**.
- Value-Based Scheduling (VBS). If a system can become overloaded (current utilization greater than 100%) then the use of simple static priorities or deadlines is not sufficient; a more **adaptive** scheme is needed. This often takes the form of assigning a *value* to each task and employing an online value-based scheduling algorithm to decide which task to run next.

As indicated earlier, the bulk of this and the next chapter is concerned with FPS as it is supported by various real-time languages and operating system standards. The use of EDF is also important and some consideration of its analytical basis is given in Chapter 6. LLF in also addressed in that chapter. A short description of the use of VBS is given in Chapter 8.

4.2.2 Scheduling characteristics

There are a number of important characteristics that can be ascribed to a scheduling test. The two most important are **sufficiency** and **necessity**:

- A schedulability test is defined to be **sufficient** if a positive outcome guarantees that all deadlines are always met.
- A test can also be labeled as **necessary** if failure of the test will indeed lead to a deadline miss at some point during the execution of the system.

A **sufficient and necessary** test is **exact** and hence is, in some sense, optimal; a sufficient but not necessary test is pessimistic, but for many situations an exact test is intractable. From an engineering point of view, a tractable sufficient test with low pessimism is ideal.

A scheduling test is usually applied to the worst-case behavioural description of the application. A system is schedulable with respect to a specified scheduling policy if it will meet all its timing requirements when executed on its target platform with that scheduling policy. A scheduling test is said to be **sustainable** if it correctly predicts that a schedulable system will remain schedulable when its operational parameters 'improve' – for example if a system is schedulable it should remain so even if some of its tasks have their periods or deadlines increased, or their resource requirement reduced; or if the application is moved to a faster processor.

One scheduling test (ST1) is said to **dominate** another test (ST2) if all task sets deemed schedulable by ST2 are also deemed schedulable by ST1 *and* there exists at least one task set that is correctly passed by ST1 but fails ST2. It follows that all exact tests dominate all sufficient only tests.

4.2.3 Preemption and non-preemption

With priority-based scheduling, a high-priority task may be released during the execution of a lower priority one. In a **preemptive** scheme, there will be an immediate switch to the higher-priority task. Alternatively, with **non-preemption**, the lower-priority task will be allowed to complete before the other executes. In general, preemptive schemes enable higher-priority tasks to be more reactive, and hence they are preferred. Between the extremes of preemption and non-preemption, there are alternative strategies that allow a lower priority task to continue to execute for a bounded time (but not necessarily to completion). These schemes are known as **deferred preemption** or **cooperative dispatching**. These will be considered again in Section 7.3. Before then, dispatching will be assumed to be preemptive. Schemes such as EDF and VBS can also take on preemptive or non-preemptive forms.

4.2.4 Simple task model

An arbitrarily complex concurrent program cannot easily be analysed to predict its worst-case behaviour. Hence it is necessary to impose some restrictions on the structure of real-time concurrent programs. This section will present a very simple model in order to describe some standard scheduling schemes. The model is generalised in later chapters. The basic model has the following characteristics:

- The application is assumed to consist of a fixed set of tasks.

- All tasks are periodic, with known periods.
- All tasks are completely independent of each other.
- All system's overheads, context-switching times and so on are ignored (that is, assumed to have zero cost).
- All tasks have deadlines equal to their periods (that is, each task must complete before it is next released, its deadline is implicit).
- All tasks have fixed worst-case execution times and execute preemptively.
- No task contains any internal suspension points (e.g. an internal delay statement or a blocking I/O request).
- All tasks execute on a single processor (CPU).
- All tasks are of equal value/importance/criticality.

One consequence of the task's independence is that it can be assumed that at some point in time all tasks will be released together. This represents the maximum load on the processor and is known as a **critical instant**[1] (and is often taken to be time 0). Table 4.2 gives a standard set of notations for task characteristics.

Notation	Description
B	Worst-case blocking time for the task (if applicable)
C	Worst-case computation time (WCET) of the task
D	Deadline of the task
I	The interference time of the task
J	Release jitter of the task
N	Number of tasks in the system
P	Priority assigned to the task (if applicable)
R	Worst-case response time of the task
T	Minimum time between task releases (task period)
U	The utilization of each task (equal to C/T)
$a - z$	The name of a task

Table 4.2: Standard notation.

Each task is assumed to give rise to a (potentially) unbounded series of executions. Each execution is known as an **invocation** or **release** of the task. A single task invocation is also known as a **job**.

4.3 Rate monotonic priority assignment

With the straightforward model outlined above, there exists a simple optimal priority assignment scheme for fixed priority scheduling (FPS) known as **rate monotonic** priority

---

[1] The critical instant is, by definition, the worst-case alignment of task releases. For simple tasking models it occurs when all tasks are released at the same time, but there are task models where this is not the case.

assignment. Each task is assigned a (unique) priority based on its period: the shorter the period, the higher the priority (that is, for two tasks i and j, $T_i < T_j \Rightarrow P_i > P_j$). This assignment is optimal in the sense that if any task set can be scheduled (using preemptive priority-based scheduling) with a fixed-priority assignment scheme, then the given task set can also be scheduled with a rate monotonic assignment scheme. Table 4.3 illustrates a five task set and shows what the relative priorities must be for optimal temporal behaviour. Note that priorities are represented by integers, and that the higher the integer, the greater the priority. Care must be taken when reading other books and papers on priority-based scheduling, as often priorities are ordered the other way; that is, priority 1 is the highest. In this book, *priority 1 is the lowest*, as this is the normal usage in most programming languages and operating systems.

Task	Period, T	Priority, P
a	25	5
b	60	3
c	42	4
d	105	1
e	75	2

Table 4.3: Example of priority assignment.

4.4 Utilization-based schedulability tests for FPS

This section describes a very simple schedulability test for FPS which, although not exact, is attractive because of its simplicity.

Liu and Layland in 1973 [57] showed that by considering only the utilization of the task set, a test for schedulability can be obtained (when the rate monotonic priority ordering is used). If the following condition is true then all N tasks will meet their deadlines (note that the summation calculates the total utilization of the task set):

$$\sum_{i=1}^{N} \left(\frac{C_i}{T_i} \right) \leq N(2^{1/N} - 1) \tag{4.1}$$

Table 4.4 shows the utilization bound (as a percentage) for small values of N. For large N, the bound asymptotically approaches 0.693. Hence any task set with a combined utilization of less than 69.3% will always be schedulable by a preemptive priority-based scheduling scheme, with priorities assigned by the rate monotonic algorithm.

Three simple examples will now be given to illustrate the use of this test. In these examples, the units (absolute magnitudes) of the time values are not defined. As long as all the values (Ts, Cs and so on) are in the same units, the tests can be applied. So in these (and later examples), the unit of time is just considered to be a *tick* of some notional time base.

SCHEDULING REAL-TIME SYSTEMS

N	Utilization bound
1	100.0%
2	82.8%
3	78.0%
4	75.7%
5	74.3%
10	71.8%

Table 4.4: Utilization bounds.

Table 4.5 contains three tasks that have been allocated priorities via the rate monotonic algorithm (hence task c has the highest priority and task a the lowest). Their combined utilization is 0.82 (or 82%). This is above the threshold for three tasks (0.78), and hence this task set fails the utilization test.

Task	Period, T	Computation time, C	Priority, P	Utilization, U
a	50	12	1	0.24
b	40	10	2	0.25
c	30	10	3	0.33

Table 4.5: Task set A.

The actual behaviour of this task set can be illustrated by drawing out a **time-line**. Figure 4.2 shows how the three tasks would execute if they all started their executions at time 0. Note that, at time 50, task a has consumed only 10 ticks of execution, whereas it needed 12, and hence it has missed its first deadline.

Time-lines are a useful way of illustrating execution patterns. For illustration, Figure 4.2 is drawn as a **Gantt chart** in Figure 4.3.

The second example is contained in Table 4.6. Now the combined utilization is 0.775, which is below the bound, and hence this task set is guaranteed to meet all its deadlines. If a time-line for this set is drawn, all deadlines would be satisfied.

Task	Period, T	Computation time, C	Priority, P	Utilization, U
a	80	32	1	0.400
b	40	5	2	0.125
c	16	4	3	0.250

Table 4.6: Task set B.

Although cumbersome, time-lines can be used to test for schedulability. But how far must the line be drawn before one can conclude that the future holds no surprises? For task sets that share a common release time, it can be shown that a time-line equal to the size of the longest period is sufficient. If all tasks meet their first deadline then they will meet all future ones.

UTILIZATION-BASED SCHEDULABILITY TESTS FOR FPS   77

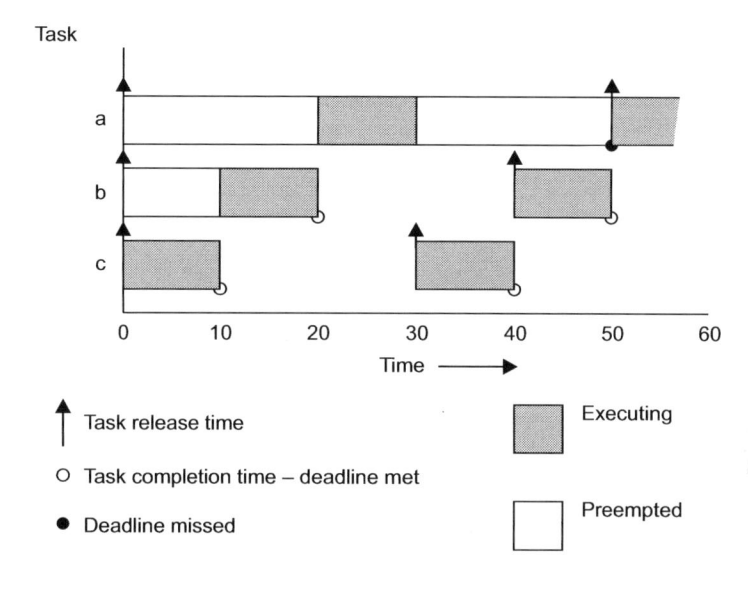

Figure 4.2: Time-line for task set A.

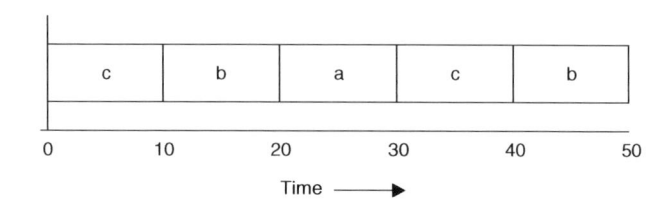

Figure 4.3: Gantt chart for task set A.

A final example in given in Table 4.7. This is again a three-task system, but the combined utility is now 100%, so it clearly fails the test. At run-time however, the behaviour seems correct, all deadlines are met up to time 80 (see Figure 4.4). Hence the task set fails the test, but at run-time does not miss a deadline. Therefore, the test is sufficient but not necessary. If a task set passes the test, it *will* meet all deadlines; if it fails the test, it *may* or *may not* fail at run-time.

A final point to note about this utilization-based test is that it only supplies a simple yes/no answer. It does not give any indication of the actual worst-case response times of the tasks. This is remedied in the response time approach described in the next chapter.

Task	Period, T	Computation time, C	Priority, P	Utilization, U
a	80	40	1	0.50
b	40	10	2	0.25
c	20	5	3	0.25

Table 4.7: Task set C.

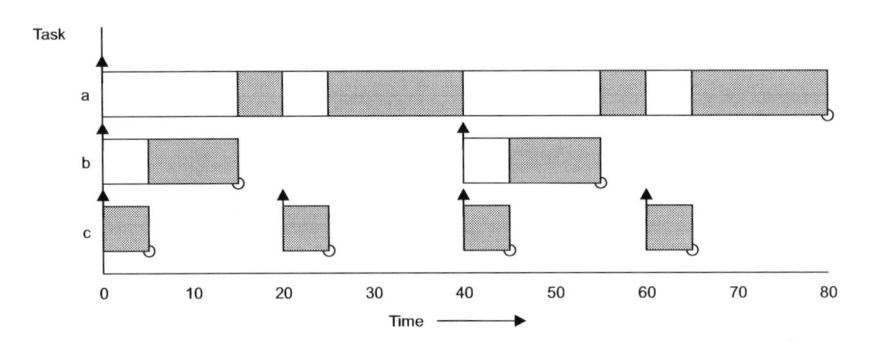

Figure 4.4: Time-line for task set C.

Improved utilization-based tests for FPS

Since the publication of the Lui and Layland utilization bound, a number of improvements have been developed. Here two alternative schemes are considered. First a simple re-interpretation of equation 4.1 can be employed. Rather than the N standing for the number of tasks, it can be defined to be the number of distinct task families in the application. A family of tasks have periods that are multiples of a common value (for example 8, 16, 64 and 128).

Consider the task sets defined earlier. For task set B (Table 4.6) there are 3 tasks but only 2 families (the 80 and 40 periods imply a single family). So the bound for this system is now 0.828 (not 0.78). The utilization of task set B is 0.775 so is below both bounds. However, if the period of task c is shortened to 14 (from 16) then the utilization of the task set rises to 0.81 (approximately) – this is above the Lui and Layland bound for three tasks but below the new bound and hence this new task set is correctly deemed schedulable by this new test. The two tasks can be transformed into a single task because task a that needs 32 in 80 is equivalent to a task that needs 16 in 40. It can be added to task b that needs 5 in 40 to give a combined requirement of 21 in 40.

For task set C (see Table 4.7) there is an even more impressive improvement. Now there is only one family (as the periods are 80, 40 and 20). So the utilization bound is 1.0 and hence this system is schedulable by this test. Although this result shows the effectiveness of this approach there is a drawback with this test – it appears not to be sustainable. Consider a minor change to the characteristics of this task set; let the period of task A move from 80 to 81. This alteration should make the system easier to schedule, a period has been extended and hence the overall utilization has been reduce (though only by a small amount, from 1 to 0.994). But the move from 80 to 81 results in there now being two families and not just one, so the bound drops from 1 to 0.82. The new system cannot be proven to be schedulable by this test (although it clearly is if the original task set was schedulable). So although the test does not seem to be sustainable it actually is — a task set that passes the test will remain schedulable if periods are increased or computations times decreased.

Another improved utilization-based test was developed by Bini et al [14] and has a different form.

$$\prod_{i=1}^{N}\left(\frac{C_i}{T_i}+1\right) \leq 2 \qquad (4.2)$$

To give a simple example of the use of this formulation consider again task set B (Table 4.6) with the minor modification that the period of task a is now 76 (rather than 80). The total utilization of this new system is 0.796 which is above the bound for 3 tasks, and hence schedulability is unproven. Note there are now three families so no improvement from the other approach. Applying equation (4.2):

$$1.421 * 1.125 * 1.25 = 1.998 < 2$$

indicates that the system is schedulable by this test, and indeed, a time-line for this revised task set would show that all deadlines have been met.

4.5 Worst-case execution time

In most of the scheduling approaches described so far (that is, cyclic executives, FPS, EDF and LLF), it is assumed that the worst-case execution time of each task is known. This is the maximum any task invocation/release (i.e. job) could require.

Worst-case execution time estimation (represented by the symbol C but also known by the acronym WCET) can be obtained by either measurement or analysis. The problem with measurement is that it is difficult to be sure when the worst case has been observed. The drawback of analysis is that an effective model of the processor (including caches, pipelines, branch prediction, out-of-order execution, memory wait states and so on) must be available.

Most analysis techniques involve two distinct activities. The first takes the task and decomposes its code into a directed graph of **basic blocks**. These basic blocks represent straight-line code. The second component of the analysis takes the machine code corresponding to a basic block and uses the processor model to estimate its worst-case execution time.

Once the times for all the basic blocks are known, the directed graph can be collapsed. For example, a simple choice construct between two basic blocks will be collapsed to a single value (that is, the largest of the two values for the alternative blocks). Loops are collapsed using knowledge about maximum bounds.

More sophisticated graph reduction techniques can be used if sufficient semantic information is available. To give just a simple example of this, consider the following code:

```
for I in 1.. 10 loop

  if Cond then
    -- basic block of cost 100
  else
    -- basic block of cost 10
  end if;

end loop;
```

With no further information, the total 'cost' of this construct would be 10×100 + the cost of the loop construct itself, giving a total of, say, 1005 time units. It may, however, be possible to deduce (via static analysis of the code) that the condition Cond can only be true on at most three occasions. Hence a less pessimistic cost value would be 375 time units.

Other relationships within the code may reduce the number of feasible paths by eliminating those that cannot possibly occur; for instance, when the 'if' branch in one conditional statement precludes a later 'else' branch. Techniques that undertake this sort of semantic analysis usually require annotations to be added to the code. The graph reduction task can then make use of tools such as ILP (Integer Linear Programming) to produce a tight estimate of worst-case execution time. They can also advise on the input data needed to drive the program down the path that gives rise to this estimation.

Clearly, if a task is to be analysed for its worst-case execution time, the code itself needs to be restricted. For example, all loops and recursion must be bounded, otherwise it would be impossible to predict offline when the code terminates. Furthermore, the code generated by the compiler must also be analysable.

The biggest challenge facing worst-case execution time analysis comes from the use of modern processors with multicores, on-chip caches, pipelines, branch predictors and so on. All of these features aim to reduce *average* execution time, but their impact on *worst-case* behaviour can be hard to predict. If one ignores these features the resulting estimates can be very pessimistic, but to include them is not always straightforward. One approach is to assume non-preemptive execution, and hence all the benefits from caching and so on can be taken into account. At a later phase of the analysis, the number of actual preemptions is calculated and a penalty applied for the resulting cache misses and pipeline refills.

To model in detail the temporal behaviour of a modern processor is non-trivial and may need proprietary information that can be hard or impossible to obtain. For real-time systems one is left with the choice of either using simpler (but less powerful) processor architectures or to put more effort into measurement. Given that all high-integrity real-time systems will be subject to considerable testing, an approach that combines testing and measurement for code units (basic blocks) but path analysis for complete components seems appropriate with today's technology.

This brief discussion has only addressed a few of the issues involved with WCET estimation. A comprehensive coverage would double the size of this part of the book.

Summary

A scheduling scheme has two facets: it defines an algorithm for resource sharing; and a means of predicting the worst-case behaviour of an application when that form of resource sharing is used.

Many current periodic real-time systems are implemented using a cyclic executive. With this approach, the application code must be packed into a fixed number of 'minor cycles' such that the cyclic execution of the sequence of minor cycles (called a 'major cycle') will enable all system deadlines to be met. Although an effective implementation strategy for small systems, there are a number of drawbacks with this cyclic approach.

- The packing of the minor cycles becomes increasingly difficult as the system grows.
- Sporadic activities are difficult to accommodate.
- Tasks with long periods (that is, longer than the major cycle) are supported inefficiently.
- Tasks with large computation times must be split up so that they can be packed into a series of minor cycles.
- The structure of the cyclic executive makes it very difficult to alter to accommodate changing requirements.

Because of these difficulties, this chapter has focused on the use of more dynamic scheduling schemes. Fixed priority, earliest deadline first, least laxity and value-based scheduling approaches were introduced. And a simple task model was defined on which utilization-based tests of schedulability for fixed priority scheduling were employed.

Tasks themselves are defined to be either preemptive or non-preemptive; with deferred preemption being a third intermediately alternative. Scheduling tests are characterised as being either sufficient or necessary (or exact if they are both). They may also be sustainable.

The chapter concluded by briefly considering the important topic of estimating the worst-case execution time of tasks.

Chapter 5
Response-Time Analysis for Fixed Priority Scheduling (FPS)

5.1 Independent periodic tasks
5.2 Sporadic and aperiodic tasks
5.3 Task systems with constrained deadlines $(D < T)$
5.4 Task interactions and blocking
5.5 Priority ceiling protocols
Summary

The utilization-based tests for FPS have two significant drawbacks: they are not exact, and they are not really applicable to a more general task model. This chapter provides a different form of test for single processor systems. The test is in two stages. First, an analytical approach is used to predict the worst-case response time (R) of each task. These values are then compared, trivially, with the task deadlines. This requires each task to be analysed individually.

This chapter also motivates the need for priority inheritance protocols to control the temporal interference (priority inversion) that inevitably arises when tasks share (protected) data and other system resources. The priority ceiling protocols are then described as they provide the standard means of limiting priority inversion and providing a deadlock free means of inter-task sharing.

5.1 Independent periodic tasks

For the highest-priority task, its worst-case response time will equal its own computation time (that is, $R = C$). Other tasks will suffer **interference** from higher-priority tasks; this is the time spent executing higher-priority tasks when a low-priority task is runnable. So for a general task i:

$$R_i = C_i + I_i \tag{5.1}$$

where I_i is the maximum interference that task i can experience in any time interval $[t, t+R_i)$.[1] The maximum interference obviously occurs when all higher-priority tasks are

---
[1] Note that as a discrete time model is used in this analysis, all time intervals must be closed at the beginning

released at the same time as task i (that is, at a critical instant). Without loss of generality, it can be assumed that all tasks are released at time 0. Consider one task (j) of higher priority than i. Within the interval $[0, R_i)$, it will be released a number of times (at least one). A simple expression for this number of releases is obtained using a ceiling function:

$$Number\_Of\_Releases = \left\lceil \frac{R_i}{T_j} \right\rceil$$

The ceiling function ($\lceil \ \rceil$) gives the smallest integer greater than the fractional number on which it acts. So the ceiling of 1/3 is 1, of 6/5 is 2, and of 6/3 is 2. The definitions of the ceilings of negative values need not be considered. Later in this book floor functions are employed ($\lfloor \ \rfloor$), they compute the largest integer smaller than the fractional part; therefore the floor of 1/3 is 0, of 6/5 is 1 and of 6/3 is again 2.

So, if R_i is 15 and T_j is 6 then there are 3 releases of task j (at times 0, 6 and 12). Each release of task j will impose an interference of C_j. Hence

$$Maximum\_Interference = \left\lceil \frac{R_i}{T_j} \right\rceil C_j$$

If $C_j = 2$ then in the interval $[0, 15)$ there are 6 units of interference. Each task of higher priority is interfering with task i, and hence:

$$I_i = \sum_{j \in hp(i)} \left\lceil \frac{R_i}{T_j} \right\rceil C_j$$

where $hp(i)$ is the set of higher-priority tasks (than i). Substituting this value back into equation (5.1) gives:

$$R_i = C_i + \sum_{j \in hp(i)} \left\lceil \frac{R_i}{T_j} \right\rceil C_j \tag{5.2}$$

Although the formulation of the interference equation is exact, the actual amount of interference is unknown as R_i is unknown (it is the value being calculated). Equation (5.2) has R_i on both sides, but is difficult to solve due to the ceiling functions. It is an example of a fixed-point equation. In general, there will be many values of R_i that form solutions to equation (5.2). The smallest (positive) such value of R_i represents the worst-case response time for the task. The simplest way of solving equation (5.2) is to form a **recurrence relationship**:

$$w_i^{n+1} = C_i + \sum_{j \in hp(i)} \left\lceil \frac{w_i^n}{T_j} \right\rceil C_j \tag{5.3}$$

(denoted by '[') and open at the end (denoted by a ')'). Thus a task can complete executing on the same tick as a higher-priority task is released.

INDEPENDENT PERIODIC TASKS

The set of values $\{w_i^0, w_i^1, w_i^2, ..., w_i^n, ...\}$ is, clearly, monotonically non-decreasing. When $w_i^n = w_i^{n+1}$, the solution to the equation has been found. If $w_i^0 < R_i$ then w_i^n is the smallest solution and hence is the value required. If the equation does not have a solution then the w values will continue to rise (this will occur for a low-priority task if the full task set has a utilization greater than 100%). Once the w_i^n values get bigger than the task's period, T, it can be assumed that the task will not meet its deadline. The starting value for the process, w_i^0, must not be greater than the final (unknown) solution R_i. As $R_i \geq C_i$, a safe starting point is C_i – there are however more efficient starting values.

The above analysis gives rise to the following algorithm for calculation response times:

```
for i in 1..N loop -- for each task in turn
  n := 0
  wⁿᵢ := Cᵢ
  loop
    calculate new wⁿ⁺¹ᵢ from equation (5.3)
    if wⁿ⁺¹ᵢ = wⁿᵢ then
      Rᵢ := wⁿᵢ
      exit value found
    end if
    if wⁿ⁺¹ᵢ > Tᵢ then
      exit value not found
    end if
    n := n + 1
  end loop
end loop
```

By implication, if a response time is found it will be no greater than T_i, and hence less than or equal to D_i, its deadline (remember with the simple task model $D_i = T_i$).

In the above discussion, w_i has been used merely as a mathematical entity for solving a fixed-point equation. It is, however, possible to get an intuition for w_i from the problem domain. Consider the point of release of task i. From that point, until the task completes, the processor will be executing tasks with priority P_i or higher. The processor is said to be executing a P_i-**busy period**. Consider w_i to be a time window that is moving down the busy period. At time 0 (the notional release time of task i), all higher priority tasks are assumed to have also been released, and hence

$$w_i^1 = C_i + \sum_{j \in hp(i)} C_j$$

This will be the end of the busy period unless some higher-priority task is released a second time. If it is, then the window will need to be pushed out further. This continues with the window expanding and, as a result, more computation time falling into the window. If this continues indefinitely then the busy period is unbounded (that is, there is no solution). However, if at any point, an expanding window does not suffer an extra 'hit' from a higher-priority task then the busy period has been completed, and the size of the busy period is the response time of the task. To illustrate how the response time analysis is used, consider task set D given in Table 5.1.

RESPONSE-TIME ANALYSIS FOR FIXED PRIORITY SCHEDULING (FPS)

Task	Period, T	Computation time, C	Priority, P
a	7	3	3
b	12	3	2
c	20	5	1

Table 5.1: Task set D.

The highest-priority task, a, will have a response time equal to its computation time (for example, $R_a = 3$). The next task will need to have its response time calculated. Let w_b^0 equal the computation time of task b, which is 3. Equation (5.3) is used to derive the next value of w:

$$w_b^1 = 3 + \left\lceil \frac{3}{7} \right\rceil 3$$

that is, $w_b^1 = 6$. This value now balances the equation ($w_b^2 = w_b^1 = 6$) and the response time of task b has been found (that is, $R_b = 6$).

The final task will give rise to the following calculations:

$$w_c^0 = 5$$

$$w_c^1 = 5 + \left\lceil \frac{5}{7} \right\rceil 3 + \left\lceil \frac{5}{12} \right\rceil 3 = 11$$

$$w_c^2 = 5 + \left\lceil \frac{11}{7} \right\rceil 3 + \left\lceil \frac{11}{12} \right\rceil 3 = 14$$

$$w_c^3 = 5 + \left\lceil \frac{14}{7} \right\rceil 3 + \left\lceil \frac{14}{12} \right\rceil 3 = 17$$

$$w_c^4 = 5 + \left\lceil \frac{17}{7} \right\rceil 3 + \left\lceil \frac{17}{12} \right\rceil 3 = 20$$

$$w_c^5 = 5 + \left\lceil \frac{20}{7} \right\rceil 3 + \left\lceil \frac{20}{12} \right\rceil 3 = 20$$

Hence R_c has a worst-case response time of 20, which means that it will just meet its deadline. This behaviour is illustrated in the Gantt chart shown in Figure 5.1.

Consider again the task set C (given in Table 4.7). This set failed the simple utilization-based test but was observed to meet all its deadlines up to time 80. Table 5.2 shows the response times calculated by the above method for this collection. Note that all tasks are now predicted to complete before, or at, their deadlines.

The response time calculations have the advantage that they are sufficient and necessary – if the task set passes the test they will meet all their deadlines; if they fail the test, then, at run-time, a task will miss its deadline (unless the computation time estimations,

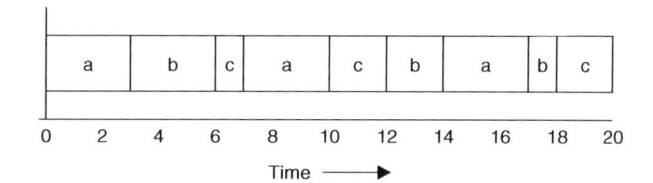

Figure 5.1: Gantt chart for task set D.

Task	Period, T	Computation time, C	Priority, P	Response time, R
a	80	40	1	80
b	40	10	2	15
c	20	5	3	5

Table 5.2: Response time for task set C.

the Cs, themselves turn out to be pessimistic). As these tests are superior to the utilization-based ones, this chapter will concentrate on extending the applicability of the response time method.

5.2 Sporadic and aperiodic tasks

To expand the simple model of the previous chapter to include sporadic (and aperiodic) task requirements, the value T is interpreted as the minimum (or average) inter-arrival interval. A sporadic task with a T value of 20ms is guaranteed not to arrive more than once in any 20ms interval. In reality, it may arrive much less frequently than once every 20ms, but the response time test will ensure that the maximum rate can be sustained (if the test is passed).

The other requirement that the inclusion of sporadic tasks demands concerns the definition of the deadline. The simple model assumes that $D = T$. For sporadic tasks, this is unreasonable. Often a sporadic is used to encapsulate an error-handling routine or to respond to a warning signal. The fault model of the system may state that the error routine will be invoked very infrequently – but when it is, it is urgent and hence it has a short deadline. Our model must therefore distinguish between D and T, and allow $D < T$. Indeed, for many periodic tasks, it is also required to allow the application to define deadline values less than period.

An inspection of the response time algorithm for fixed priority scheduling, described in Section 5.1 reveals that:

- it works perfectly for values of D less than T as long as the stopping criterion becomes $w_i^{n+1} > D_i$,
- it works perfectly well with any priority ordering – $hp(i)$ always gives the set of higher-priority tasks.

Although some priority orderings are better than others, the test will provide the worst-case response times for the given priority ordering. In Section 5.3, an optimal priority ordering for $D < T$ is defined (and proved). A later section will consider an extended algorithm and optimal priority ordering for the general case of $D < T, D = T$ or $D > T$ (i.e. arbitrary deadlines).

5.2.1 Hard and soft tasks

For sporadic tasks, average and maximum arrival frequencies may be defined. Unfortunately, in many situations the worst-case figure is considerably higher than the average. Interrupts often arrive in bursts and an abnormal sensor reading may lead to significant additional computation. It follows that determining schedulability with worst-case figures may lead to very low processor utilizations being observed in the actual running system. As a guideline for the minimum requirement, the following two rules should always be complied with:

- Rule 1 – all tasks should be schedulable using average execution times and average arrival rates.
- Rule 2 – all hard real-time tasks should be schedulable using worst-case execution times and worst-case arrival rates of all tasks (including soft).

A consequent of Rule 1 is that there may be situations in which it is not possible to meet all current deadlines. This condition is known as a **transient overload**; Rule 2, however, ensures that no hard real-time task will miss its deadline. If Rule 2 gives rise to unacceptably low utilizations for 'normal execution', direct action should be taken to try and reduce the worst-case execution times (or arrival rates).

5.2.2 Aperiodic tasks and fixed priority execution-time servers

One simple way of scheduling aperiodic tasks, within a priority-based scheme, is to run such tasks at priorities below the priorities assigned to hard tasks. In effect, the aperiodic tasks run as background activities, and therefore cannot steal, in a preemptive system, resources from the hard tasks. Although a safe scheme, this does not provide adequate support to soft tasks which will often miss their deadlines if they only run as background activities. To improve the situation for soft tasks, a **server** (or execution-time server) can be employed. Servers protect the tasking resources needed by hard tasks, but otherwise allow soft tasks to run as soon as possible.

Since they were first introduced in 1987, a number of server methods have been defined. Here only two will be considered: the Deferrable Server (DS) and the Sporadic Server (SS).

With the DS, an analysis is undertaken (using, for example, the response time approach) that enables a new task to be introduced at the highest priority.[2] This task, the

---

[2]Servers at other priorities are possible, but the description is more straightforward if the server is given a

server, thus has a period, T_s and a capacity C_s. These values are chosen so that all the hard tasks in the system remain schedulable even if the aperiodic load is such that the server repeatedly executes with its maximum capacity (i.e. with period T_s and execution time C_s). At run-time, whenever an aperiodic task arrives, and there is capacity available, it starts executing immediately and continues until either it finishes or the capacity is exhausted. In the latter case, the aperiodic task is suspended (or transferred to a background priority). With the DS model, the capacity is replenished every T_s time units.

The operation of the SS differs from DS in its replenishment policy. With SS, if a task arrives at time t and uses c capacity then the server has this c capacity replenished T_s time units after t. In general, SS can furnish higher capacity than DS but has increased implementation overheads; DS and SS can be analysed using response time analysis (see Section 7.7).

As all servers limit the capacity that is available to aperiodic soft tasks, they can also be used to ensure that sporadic tasks do not execute more often than expected. If a sporadic task with interarrival interval of T_i and worst-case execution time of C_i is implemented not directly as a task, but via a server with $T_s = T_i$ and $C_s = C_i$, then its impact (interference) on lower-priority tasks is bounded even if the sporadic task arrives too quickly (which would be an error condition).

All servers (DS, SS and others) can be described as *bandwidth preserving* in that they attempt to

- make CPU resources available immediately to aperiodic tasks (if there is a capacity);
- retain the capacity for as long as possible if there are currently no aperiodic tasks (by allowing the hard tasks to execute).

Another bandwidth preserving scheme, which often performs better than the server techniques, is **dual-priority scheduling**. Here, the range of priorities is split into three bands: high, medium and low. All aperiodic tasks run in the middle band. Hard tasks, when they are released, run in the low band, but they are promoted to the top band in time to meet their deadlines. Hence in the first stage of execution they will give way to aperiodic activities (but will execute if there is no such activity). In the second phase they will move to a higher priority and then have precedence over the aperiodic work. In the high band, priorities are assigned according to the deadline monotonic approach (see below). Promotion to this band occurs at time $D - R$. However, to implement the dual-priority scheme requires a dynamic priority provision.

5.3 Task systems with constrained deadlines ($D < T$)

In the above discussion on sporadic tasks is was argued that, in general, it must be possible for a task to define a deadline that is less than its inter-arrival interval (or period). It was also noted earlier that for $D = T$ the rate monotonic priority ordering is optimal for a fixed priority scheme. For $D < T$ a similar formulation could be defined – the deadline

---

higher priority than all the hard tasks.

monotonic priority ordering (DMPO). Here, the fixed priority of a task is inversely proportional to its relative deadline: $(D_i < D_j \Rightarrow P_i > P_j)$. Table 5.3 gives the appropriate priority assignments for a simple task set. It also includes the worst-case response time – as calculated by the algorithm in Section 5.1. Note that a rate monotonic priority ordering would not schedule these tasks.

Task	Period, T	Deadline, D	Computation time, C	Priority, P	Response time, R
a	20	5	3	4	3
b	15	7	3	3	6
c	10	10	4	2	10
d	20	20	3	1	20

Table 5.3: Example task set for DMPO.

In the following subsection, the optimality of DMPO is proven. Given this result and the direct applicability of response time analysis to this task model, it is clear that fixed priority scheduling can adequately deal with this more general set of scheduling requirements.

Proof that DMPO is optimal

Deadline monotonic priority ordering (DMPO) is optimal if any task set, Q, that is schedulable by priority scheme, W, is also schedulable by DMPO. The proof of optimality of DMPO will involve transforming the priorities of Q (as assigned by W) until the ordering is DMPO. Each step of the transformation will preserve schedulability.

Let i and j be two tasks (with adjacent priorities) in Q such that under W: $P_i > P_j$ and $D_i > D_j$. Define scheme W' to be identical to W except that tasks i and j are swapped. Consider the schedulability of Q under W':

- All tasks with priorities greater than P_i will be unaffected by this change to lower-priority tasks.
- All tasks with priorities lower than P_j will be unaffected. They will all experience the same interference from i and j.
- Task j, which was schedulable under W, now has a higher priority, suffers less interference, and hence must be schedulable under W'.

All that is left is the need to show that task i, which has had its priority lowered, is still schedulable.

Under W, $R_j \leq D_j$, $D_j < D_i$ and $D_i \leq T_i$ and hence task i only interferes once during the execution of j.

Once the tasks have been switched, the new response time of i becomes equal to the old response time of j. This is true because under both priority orderings $C_j + C_i$ amount of computation time has been completed with the same level of interference from

TASK INTERACTIONS AND BLOCKING

higher-priority tasks. Task j was released only once during R_j, and hence interferes only once during the execution of i under **W′**. It follows that:

$$R'_i = R_j \leq D_j < D_i$$

It can be concluded that task i is schedulable after the switch.

Priority scheme W' can now be transformed (to W'') by choosing two more tasks 'that are in the wrong order for DMPO' and switching them. Each such switch preserves schedulability. Eventually there will be no more tasks to switch; the ordering will be exactly that required by DMPO and the task set will still be schedulable. Hence, DMPO is optimal.

Note that for the special case of $D = T$, the above proof can be used to show that, in this circumstance, rate monotonic ordering is also optimal.

5.4 Task interactions and blocking

One of the simplistic assumptions embodied in the system model, described in the previous chapter, is the need for tasks to be independent. This is clearly unreasonable, as task interaction will be needed in almost all meaningful applications. In Chapter 11, it is noted that tasks can interact safely by either some form of protected shared data (using, for example, semaphores, monitors or protected objects) or directly (using some form of rendezvous). All of these language features lead to the possibility of a task being suspended until some necessary future event has occurred (for example, waiting to gain a lock on a semaphore, or entry to a monitor). In general, synchronous communication leads to more pessimistic analysis as it is harder to define the real worst case when there are many dependencies between task executions. The following analysis is therefore more accurate when related to asynchronous communication where tasks exchange data via protected shared resources. The majority of the material in the next two sections is concerned with fixed-priority scheduling. The issue of task interactions and EDF scheduling will be considered in a later chapter.

If a task is suspended waiting for a lower-priority task to complete some required computation then the priority model is, in some sense, being undermined. In an ideal world, such **priority inversion** (that is, a high-priority task having to wait for a lower-priority task) should not exist. However, it cannot, in general, be totally eliminated. Nevertheless, its adverse effects can be minimised. If a task is waiting for a lower-priority task, it is said to be **blocked**. In order to test for schedulability, blocking must be bounded and measurable; it should also be small.

To illustrate an extreme example of priority inversion, consider the executions of four periodic tasks: a, b, c and d. Assume they have been assigned priorities according to the deadline monotonic scheme, so that the priority of task d is the highest and that of task a the lowest. Further, assume that tasks d and a (and tasks d and c) share a critical section (resource), denoted by the symbol Q (and V), protected by mutual exclusion. Table 5.4 gives the details of the four tasks and their execution sequences; in this table 'E' represents a single tick of execution time and 'Q' (or 'V') represent an execution tick with access to the Q (or V) critical section. Thus task c executes for four ticks; the middle two while it has access to critical section V.

Task	Priority	Execution sequence	Release time
a	1	EQQQQE	0
b	2	EE	2
c	3	EVVE	2
d	4	EEQVE	4

Table 5.4: Execution sequences.

Figure 5.2 illustrates the execution sequence for the start times given in the table. Task a is released first, executes and locks the critical section, Q. It is then preempted by the release of task c which executes for one tick, locks V and is then preempted by the release of task d. The higher-priority task then executes until it also wishes to lock the critical section, Q; it must then be suspended (as the section is already locked by a). At this point, c will regain the processor and continue. Once it has terminated, b will commence and run for its entitlement. Only when b has completed will a be able to execute again; it will then complete its use of the Q and allow d to continue and complete. With this behaviour, d finishes at time 16, and therefore has a response time of 12; c has a value of 6, b a value of 8, and a a value of 17.

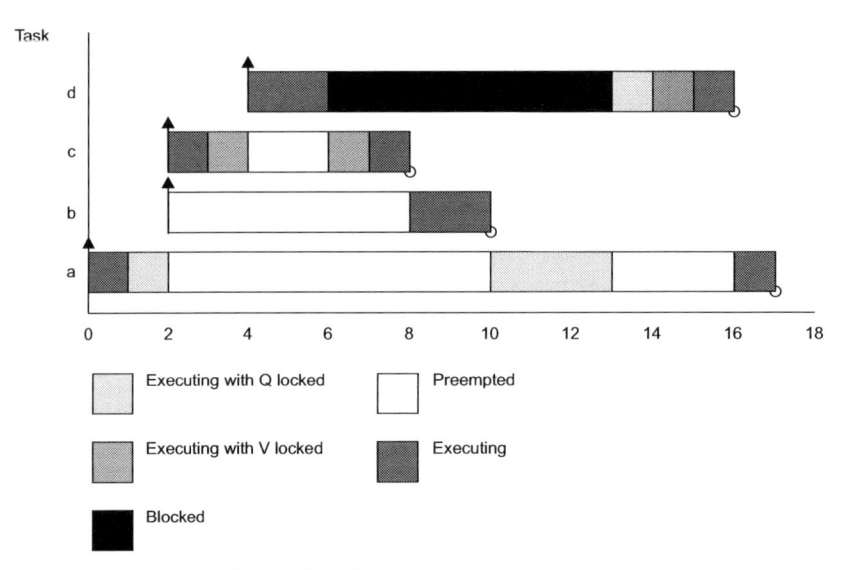

Figure 5.2: Example of priority inversion.

An inspection of Figure 5.2 shows that task d suffers considerable priority inversion. Not only is it blocked by task a but also by tasks b and c. Some blocking is inevitable; if the integrity of the critical section (and hence the shared data) is to be maintained then a must run in preference to d (while it has the lock). But the blocking of d by tasks c and b is unproductive and will severely affect the schedulability of the system (as the blocking on task d is excessive).

Priority inversion is not just a theoretical problem, real systems have been known to fail due to this phenomena. A much publicised.[3] case was that of the NASA Mars Pathfinder. Although the Sojourner rover successfully survived the bouncy landing on Mars and was able to collect meteorological data, the spacecraft initially experienced a series of total system resets resulting in lost data. Tasks on the Pathfinder spacecraft were executed as fixed priority threads. The high priority data bus management thread and a low priority meteorological data gathering thread shared an 'information bus' protected by a mutex. A communications thread ran with medium priority. At run-time, the release pattern of the threads was such that the high priority thread was waiting for the mutex to be release on the information bus, but the lower priority thread which was using the bus and hence held the mutex lock could not make progress as it was preempted by the relatively long running medium priority thread. This resulted in a watchdog timer being triggered as the urgent high priority data bus thread was missing its deadline. The watchdog initiated a total system reset. The situation then repeated itself again and again. The solution to this problem, once it was identified (which was not easy), was to turned on **priority inheritance** that was fortunately supported by the spacecraft's operating system.

With priority inheritance, a task's priority is no longer static; if a task p is suspended waiting for task q to undertake some computation then the priority of q becomes equal to the priority of p (if it was lower to start with). In the example given a above, task a will be given the priority of task d and will, therefore, run in preference to task c and task b. This is illustrated in Figure 5.3. Note as a consequence of this algorithm, task b will now suffer blocking even though it does not use a shared object. Also note that task d now has a second block, but its response time has been reduced to 9. With the Mars Pathfinder example, once priority inheritance was turned on, the lower priority thread inherited the data bus thread's priority and thus ran in preference to the medium priority thread.

With this simple inheritance rule, the priority of a task is the maximum of its own default priority and the priorities of all the other tasks that are at that time dependent upon it.

In general, inheritance of priority is not restricted to a single step. If task d is waiting for task c, but c cannot deal with d because it is waiting for task b then b as well as c is given d's priority.

In the design of a real-time language, priority inheritance is of paramount importance. To have the most effective model, however, implies that the concurrency model should have a particular form. With standard semaphores and condition variables, there is no direct link between the act of becoming suspended and the identity of the task that will reverse this action. Inheritance is therefore not easily implemented and requires run-time support.

Sha et al. [72] show that with a priority inheritance protocol, there is a bound on the number of times a task can be blocked by lower priority tasks. If a task has m critical sections that can lead to it being blocked then the maximum number of times it can be

---

[3] See http://research.microsoft.com/en-us/um/people/mbj/Mars_Pathfinder/Mars_Pathfinder.html

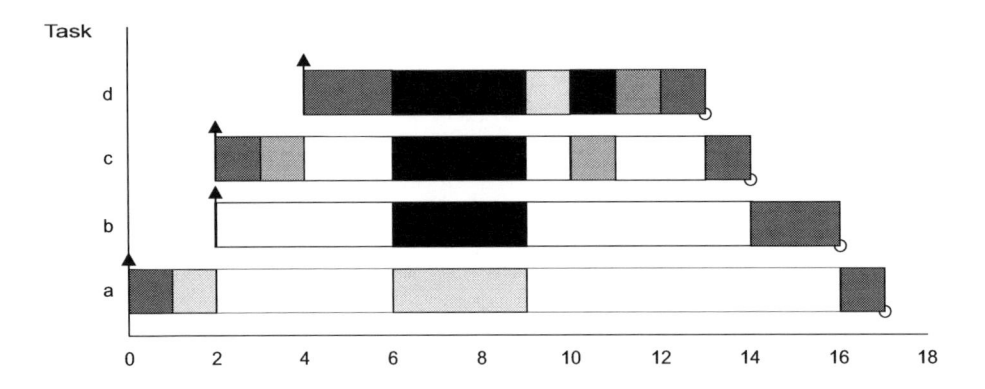

Figure 5.3: Example of priority inheritance.

blocked is m. That is, in the worst case, each critical section will be locked by a lower-priority task (this is what happened in Figure 5.3). If there are only n ($n < m$) lower-priority tasks then this maximum can be further reduced (to n).

If B_i is the maximum blocking time that task i can suffer then for this simple priority inheritance model, a formula for calculating B can easily be found. Let K be the number of critical sections (resources) in the system. Equation (5.4) thus provides an upper bound on B.

$$B_i = \sum_{k=1}^{K} usage(k,i) C(k) \tag{5.4}$$

where $usage$ is a 0/1 function: $usage(k,i) = 1$ if resource k is used by at least one task with a priority less than P_i, and at least one task with a priority greater or equal to P_i. Otherwise it gives the result 0. $C(k)$ is the worst-case execution time of the k critical section. Nested resources are not accommodated by this simple formulae, they require the $usage$ function to track resources that use other resources.

This algorithm is not optimal for this inheritance protocol. Firstly, it assumes a single cost for using the resource, it does not try and differentiate between the cost of each task's use of the resource. Secondly, it adds up the blocking from each resource, but this can only happen if each such resource is used by a different lower priority process. This may not be possible for a particular application. For example, if all k resources are only used by one lower priority task then there would be just one term to include in the equation for B. Nevertheless, the equation serves to illustrate the factors that need to be taken into account when calculating B. In Section 5.5, better inheritance protocols will be described and an improved formulae for B will be given.

Response time calculations and blocking

Given that a value for B has been obtained, the response time algorithm can be modified to take the blocking factor into account:[4]

$$R = C + B + I$$

that is,

$$R_i = C_i + B_i + \sum_{j \in hp(i)} \left\lceil \frac{R_i}{T_j} \right\rceil C_j \qquad (5.5)$$

which can again be solved by constructing a recurrence relationship:

$$w_i^{n+1} = C_i + B_i + \sum_{j \in hp(i)} \left\lceil \frac{w_i^n}{T_j} \right\rceil C_j \qquad (5.6)$$

Note that this formulation may now be pessimistic (that is, not necessarily sufficient and necessary). Whether a task actually suffers its maximum blocking will depend upon task phasings. For example, if all tasks are periodic and all have the same period then no preemption will take place and hence no priority inversion will occur. However, in general, equation (5.5) represents an effective scheduling test for real-time systems containing cooperating tasks.

5.5 Priority ceiling protocols

While the standard inheritance protocol gives an upper bound on the number of blocks a high-priority task can encounter, this bound can still lead to an unacceptably pessimistic worst-case calculation. This is compounded by the possibility of chains of blocks developing (transitive blocking), that is, task c being blocked by task b which is blocked by task a and so on. As shared data is a system resource, from a resource management point of view not only should blocking be minimised, but failure conditions such as deadlock should be eliminated. All of the above issues are addressed by the ceiling priority protocols [72]; two of which will be considered in this chapter: the **original ceiling priority protocol** and the **immediate ceiling priority protocol**. The original protocol (OCPP) will be described first, followed by the somewhat more straightforward immediate variant (ICPP). When either of these protocols are used on a single-processor system:

- a high-priority task can be blocked *at most once* during its execution by lower-priority tasks;
- deadlocks are prevented;
- transitive blocking is prevented; and

---
[4]Blocking can also be incorporated into the utilization-based tests, but now each task must be considered individually.

- mutual exclusive access to resources is ensured (by the protocol itself).

The ceiling protocols can best be described in terms of resources protected by critical sections. In essence, the protocol ensures that if a resource is locked, by task a say, and could lead to the blocking of a higher-priority task (b), then no other resource that could block b is allowed to be locked by any task other that a. A task can therefore be delayed by not only attempting to lock a previously locked resource but also when the lock could lead to multiple blocking on higher-priority tasks.

5.5.1 Original ceiling priority protocol

The original protocol takes the following form.

(1) Each task has a static default priority assigned (perhaps by the deadline monotonic scheme).
(2) Each resource has a static ceiling value defined, this is the maximum priority of the tasks that use it.
(3) A task has a dynamic priority that is the maximum of its own static priority and any it inherits due to it blocking higher-priority tasks.
(4) A task can only lock a resource if its dynamic priority is higher than the ceiling of any currently locked resource (excluding any that it has already locked itself).

The locking of a first system resource is allowed. The effect of the protocol is to ensure that a second resource can only be locked if there does not exist a higher-priority task that uses both resources. Consequently, the maximum amount of time a task can be blocked is equal to the execution time of the longest critical section in any of the lower-priority tasks that are accessed by higher-priority tasks; that is, equation (5.4) becomes:

$$B_i = \max_{k=1}^{K} usage(k,i) C(k) \tag{5.7}$$

The benefit of the ceiling protocol is that a high-priority task can only be blocked once (per activation) by any lower-priority task. The cost of this result is that more tasks will experience this block.

Not all the features of the algorithm can be illustrated by a single example, but the execution sequence shown in Figure 5.4 does give a good indication of how the algorithm works and provides a comparison with the earlier approaches (that is, this figure illustrates the same task sequence used in Figures 5.3 and 5.2).

In Figure 5.4, task a again locks the first critical section, as no other resources have been locked. It is again preempted by task c, but now the attempt by c to lock the second section (V) is not successful as its priority (3) is not higher than the current ceiling (which is 4, as Q is locked and is used by task d). At time 3, a is blocking c, and hence runs with its priority at the level 3, thereby blocking b. The higher-priority task, d, preempts a at time 4, but is subsequently blocked when it attempts to access Q. Hence a will continue

PRIORITY CEILING PROTOCOLS

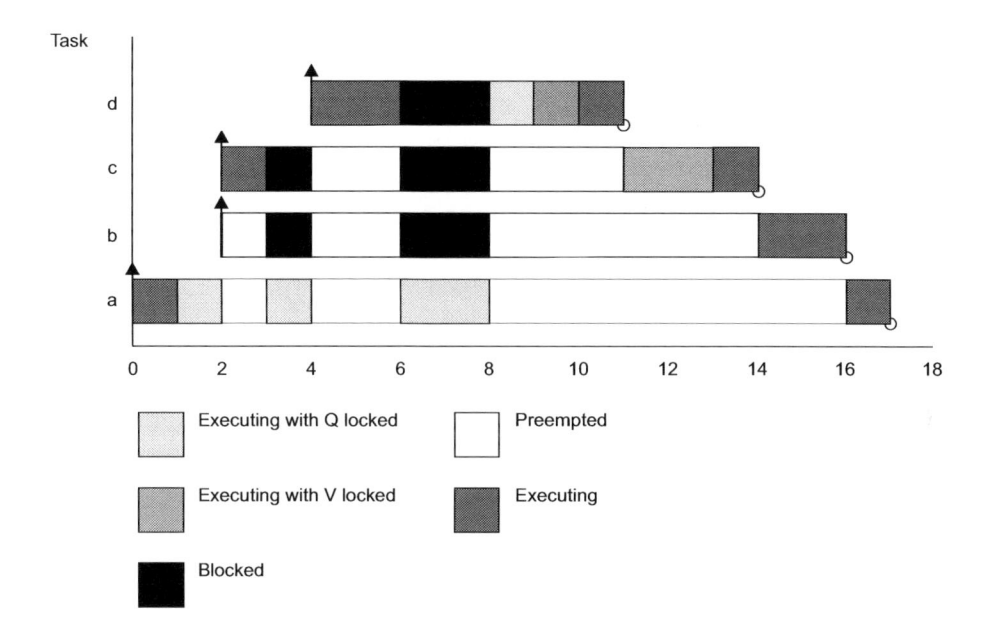

Figure 5.4: Example of priority inheritance – OCPP.

(with priority 4) until it releases its lock on Q and has its priority drop back to 1. Now, d can continue until it completes (with a response time of 7, i.e. 11 - 4).

The priority ceiling protocols ensure that a task is only blocked once during each invocation. Figure 5.4, however, appears to show task b (and task c) suffering two blocks. What is actually happening is that a single block is being broken in two by the preemption of task d. Equation (5.7) determines that all tasks (apart from task a) will suffer a maximum single block of 4. Figure 5.4 shows that for this particular execution sequence task c and task b actually suffer a block of 3 and task d a block of only 2.

5.5.2 Immediate ceiling priority protocol

The immediate ceiling priority algorithm (ICPP) takes a more straightforward approach and raises the priority of a task as soon as it locks a resource (rather than only when it is actually blocking a higher-priority task). The protocol is thus defined as follows.

- Each task has a static default priority assigned (perhaps by the deadline monotonic scheme).
- Each resource has a static ceiling value defined, this is the maximum priority of the tasks that use it.

- A task has a dynamic priority that is the maximum of its own static priority and the ceiling values of any resources it has locked.

As a consequence of this final rule, a task will only suffer a block at the very beginning of its execution. Once the task starts actually executing, all the resources it needs must be free; if they were not, then some task would have an equal or higher priority and the task's execution would be postponed.

The same task set used in earlier illustrations can now be executed under ICPP (see Figure 5.5).

Task a having locked Q at time 1, runs for the next 4 ticks with priority 4. Hence neither task b, task c nor task d can begin. Once a unlocks Q (and has its priority reduced), the other tasks execute in priority order. Note that all blocking is before actual execution and that d's response time is now only 6. This is somewhat misleading, however, as the worst-case blocking time for the two protocols is the same (see equation (5.7)).

Although the worst-case behaviour of the two ceiling schemes is identical (from a scheduling view point), there are some points of difference:

- ICCP is easier to implement than the original (OCPP) as blocking relationships need not be monitored.
- ICPP leads to less context switches as blocking is prior to first execution.
- ICPP requires more priority movements as this happens with all resource usages; OCPP changes priority only if an actual block has occurred.

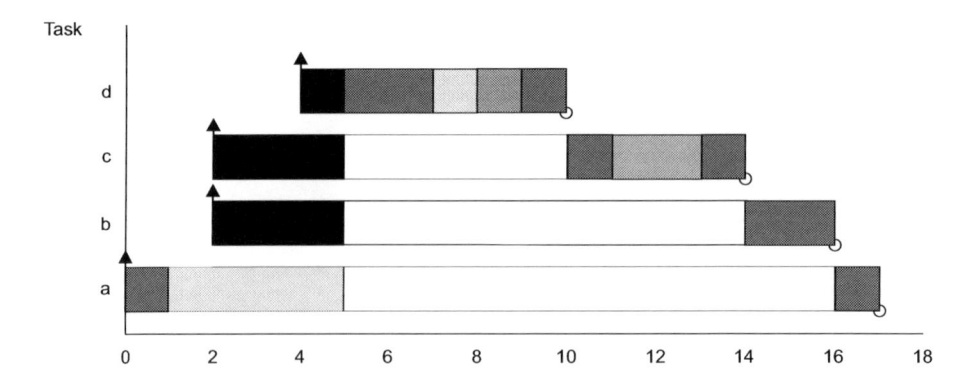

Figure 5.5: Example of priority inheritance – ICPP.

Finally, note that ICPP is called the Priority Protect Protocol in Real-Time POSIX and the Priority Ceiling Emulation in Real-Time Java.

5.5.3 Ceiling protocols, mutual exclusion and deadlock

Although the above algorithms for the two ceiling protocols were defined in terms of locks on resources, it must be emphasised that the protocols themselves rather than some other synchronization primitive provides the mutual exclusion access to the resource (at least on a single processor system and assuming the tasks do not suspend whilst holding a lock). Consider ICPP; if a task has access to some resource then it will be running with the ceiling value. No other task that uses that resource can have a higher priority, and hence the executing task will either execute unimpeded while using the resource, or, if it is preempted, the new task will not use this particular resource. Either way, mutual exclusion is ensured.

The other major property of the ceiling protocols (again for single-processor systems and non self suspension) is that they are deadlock-free. The ceiling protocols are a form of deadlock prevention. If a task holds one resource while claiming another, then the ceiling of the second resource cannot be lower than the ceiling of the first. Indeed, if two resources are used in different orders (by different tasks) then their ceilings must be identical. As one task is not preempted by another with merely the same priority, it follows that once a task has gained access to a resource then all other resources will be free when needed. There is no possibility of circular waits, and deadlock is prevented.

Summary

This chapter has introduced Response-Time Analysis (RTA) which is now the standard way on analysing fixed priority real-time systems. RTA is an exact method for the simple task model presented in the previous chapter. It remains exact when one of the constraints of this model is weakened, namely the deadline of a task is allowed to be less than the task's period; it is *constrained* rather than *implicit*. This flexibility allows sporadic as well as periodic tasks to be supported.

The other restriction of the simple task model to be removed in this chapter is the requirement for tasks to be independent. Normal programs exchange or share data, and hence some form of support for intertask synchronization is needed.

Programming primitives such as a monitor provide mutual exclusive access to shared data, but they can give rise to priority inversion unless some form of priority inheritance is used. Two particular protocols were described in detail in this chapter: 'original ceiling priority inheritance' and 'immediate ceiling priority inheritance'. They both have the properties (on a single processor) that they prevent deadlock, restricting blocking to a single instance and deliver mutual exclusion without any further operating system's lock.

Also considered in this chapter are aperiodic tasks that require constraints to be imposed if they are to co-exist with periodic and sporadic tasks. Execution-time servers, such as the deferrable and sporadic servers, are one means of restricting the CPU time given to aperiodic tasks.

Chapter 6
Earliest Deadline First (EDF) Scheduling

6.1 Utilization-based scheduling tests for EDF
6.2 Utilization-based scheduling tests for LLF
6.3 Processor demand criteria for EDF
6.4 The QPA test
6.5 Blocking and EDF
6.6 Deadline-floor protocol
6.7 Aperiodic tasks and EDF execution-time servers
Summary

Fixed priority scheduling (FPS) is undoubtedly the most popular scheduling approach available to the implementers of real-time systems. However, as discussed in Chapter 2, it is not the only approach studied in the real-time scheduling community. This chapter focuses on an alternative approach, Earliest Deadline First (EDF), that has a number of properties that makes it as important as FPS. Unfortunately, it is currently less supported by languages and operating systems. For this reason EDF analysis is not covered here to the same level of detail afforded to FPS analysis.

The principle property of EDF scheduling is that all executing tasks have absolute deadlines by which they should finish, and the scheduler always chooses the task with the most immediate (i.e. earliest) deadline. Recall that all real-time tasks are defined to have a static relative deadline (denoted by the symbol D); their absolute deadline is computed as 'release time + relative deadline'. So each time a task is released (i.e. each job of the task) it will have a new absolute deadline but will retain the same relative deadline.

6.1 Utilization-based schedulability tests for EDF

Not only did the seminal paper of Liu and Layland [57] introduce a utilization-based test for fixed priority scheduling but it also gave one for EDF. The following equation is for the simple task model introduced in Section 4.2.4 — in particular, $D = T$ for all tasks, and a single processor platform.

$$\sum_{i=1}^{N}\left(\frac{C_i}{T_i}\right) \leq 1 \qquad (6.1)$$

Clearly this is a much simpler test than the corresponding test for FPS (equation (4.1)). As long as the utilization of the task set is less than the total capacity of the processor then all deadlines will be met (for the simple task model). In this sense EDF is superior to FPS; it can always schedule any task set that FPS can, but not all task sets that are passed by the EDF test can be scheduled using fixed priorities. EDF is therefore said to **dominate** FPS. One can also see that EDF is *exact* (necessary and sufficient) and is indeed *optimal* as it can schedule task sets with 100% processor utilisation, and obviously that is the best any scheme can achieve. The test is obviously *sustainable* as utilization will only reduce if task periods are increased or worst-case execution times decreased.

Given this advantage it is reasonable to ask why EDF is not the preferred task-based scheduling method? The reason is that FPS has a number of advantages over EDF:

- FPS is easier to implement, as the scheduling attribute (*priority*) is static; EDF is dynamic and hence requires a more complex run-time system which will have higher overhead.

- It is easier to incorporate tasks without deadlines into FPS (by merely assigning them a priority); giving a task an arbitrary deadline is more artificial.

- The deadline attribute is not the only parameter of importance; again it is easier to incorporate other factors into the notion of priority than it is into the notion of deadline. For example, the criticality of the task.

- During overload situations (which may be a fault condition), the behaviour of FPS is more predictable (the lower priority tasks are those that will miss their deadlines first); EDF is unpredictable under overload and can experience a domino effect in which a large number of tasks miss deadlines.

- The utilization-based test, for the simple model, is misleading as it is necessary and sufficient for EDF but only sufficient for FPS. Hence higher utilizations can, in general, be achieved for FPS.

Notwithstanding this final point, EDF does have an advantage over FPS because of its higher utilization. Indeed, it is easy to show that if a task set, with restrictions such as deadline equal to period removed, is schedulable by any scheme then it will also be schedulable by EDF. The proof of this property follows the pattern used for proving that deadline monotonic priority ordering is optimal (see Section 5.3). Starting with the feasible schedule it is always possible to transform the schedule to one that becomes identical with the one EDF would produce – and at each transformation schedulability is preserved.

As noted above, the schedulability test defined in equation (6.1) is exact for the simple task model. If deadline is now allowed to be less than period ($D < T$) then a simple sufficient utilization-based test can be derived:

$$\sum_{i=1}^{N} \left(\frac{C_i}{D_i}\right) \leq 1 \tag{6.2}$$

To obtain an exact test, PDA must be used (see Section 6.3).

6.2 Utilization-based schedulability tests for LLF

In Chapter 4 the LLF (Least Laxity First) scheduling scheme was introduced. Here the next task to be executed is always the one that has the minimum slack. Interestingly the scheduling test represented by equation (6.1) is also applicable to LLF. So a utilization bound of 1.0 applies and hence LLF is also an *optimal* scheme.

Although both EDF and LLF are optimal schemes (for a single processor) there are some important differences between them. With EDF two jobs (invocations from two tasks) have a static relationship in terms of the scheduler. If job j_1 has an earlier deadline than job j_2 then it will run earlier. The absolute deadlines of the two jobs do not change, so neither does their relative urgency. This is however not the case with LLF. Here the executing job keeps the same 'laxity' but the non-executing task has its 'laxity' reduced until it becomes the more urgent task and it will then preempt the executing task. Later the situation will reverse and the jobs will oscillate it terms of their claim to the processor.

To illustrate this behaviour, consider two jobs (j_1 and j_2) released at time 0; one with C_1=10 and absolute deadline of 20, the other with C_2=8 and absolute deadline of 16. So the two jobs have, initially, laxity of 10 and 8 respectively; hence j_2 executes. After two units of execution, j_1 has it laxity reduced to 8 (as there are 18 units of time before the deadline of 20, and 10 units of execution are required); whereas j_2 has unchanged laxity (it needs 6 in 14, so still 8). Now both jobs have the same laxity, if j_2 executes for any more time, j_1 will have the least laxity and so must preempt. The two jobs will then swap backwards and forwards as they progress towards completion. An activity that can be described as thrashing.

It follows form this observation that the statement that LLF is optimal is predicated on the assumption that run-time overheads (e.g. the cost of context switching) are ignored. Once the overheads are taken into account then LLF become a less attractive proposition. However, LLF can be used with a threshold to prevent thrashing by only context switching when the laxity difference become greater than the threshold. But now the optimal bound represented by equation (6.1) no longer applies.

6.3 Processor demand criteria for EDF

One of the disadvantages of the EDF scheme is that the worst-case response time for each task does not occur when all tasks are released at a critical instant. In this situation only tasks with a shorter relative deadline will interfere. But later there may exist a position in which all (or at least more) tasks have a shorter absolute deadline. In situations where the simple utilization-based test cannot be applied (for example when there is release jitter or when deadlines are shorter then periods) then a more sophisticated scheduling test must be used. In FPS this takes the form of response-time analysis (calculate the worst-case response time for each task and then check that this is less than the related deadline). For EDF this approach can again be used, but it is much more complicated to calculate these response time values and hence it will not be described here. There is however an alternative scheme that checks for schedulability directly rather than via response times. This method, called PDA (**Processor Demand Analysis**) or PDC (**Processor Demand Criteria**), is defined as follows.

Assuming a system starts at time 0 and all tasks arrive at their maximum frequency. At any future time, t, it is possible to calculate the load on the system, $h(t)$. This is the amount of work that must be completed before t. In other words all jobs that had absolute deadlines before (or at) t. It is easy to give a formulae for $h(t)$ (this time using floor functions rather then the ceiling functions used with RTA):

$$h(t) = \sum_{i=1}^{N} \left\lfloor \frac{t + T_i - D_i}{T_i} \right\rfloor C_i \qquad (6.3)$$

where N is the number of tasks in the system[1].

To motivate this formula, consider a single task with $T = 5$, $D = 3$ and $C = 1$, and two possible values of t: $t1 = 12$ and $t2 = 14$. Figure 6.1 illustrates these parameters. The third deadline of the task is at 13 and hence is after $t1$ so $h(t1)$ for this task should be 2 (from two jobs). But at $t2 = 14$ another job of the task must be completed and so $h(t2) = 3$. To compute these values easily, $T - D$ is added to t; if this results in a value after the next period then the floor function in equation (6.3) will correctly add an extra C to the total. So, in the example, $T - D = 2$, $t1 + 2 = 14$ and hence $\lfloor 14/5 \rfloor = 2$. But $t2 + 2 = 16$ and so $\lfloor 16/5 \rfloor = 3$.

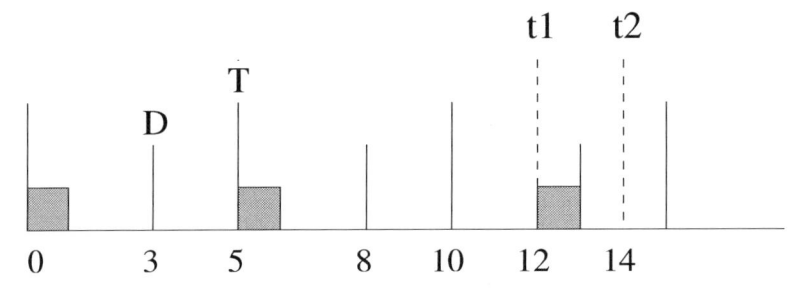

Figure 6.1: PDA example.

The requirement for schedulability is that the load must never exceed the time available to satisfy that level of load:

$$\forall t > 0 \ \ h(t) \leq t \qquad (6.4)$$

---

[1] This formulae is only valid for $D \leq T$, in the more general case of arbitrary deadlines the floor function must be capped so as to never give a negative value.

PDA involves applying this equation to a limited number of t values. The number of points is limited by two factors:

- only values of t that correspond to deadlines of tasks need be checked, and
- there is an upper bound (L) on the values of t that must be checked – this means that an unschedulable system will have $h(t) > t$ for some value of $t < L$.

The first reduction comes from the fact that $h(t)$ is constant between deadlines and hence the worst case occurs at a deadline. It follows that only values of t corresponding to an actual deadline needs to be checked.

The second factor concerns the size of the interval that must be checked. In the literature there are a number of schemes defined for computing this upper-bound (which is usually represented by the symbol L). Two formulas are given below. The first formulae comes from the need to check at least the first deadline of each task, and a bound based on utilization (the derivation of all the equations given in the section can be found in the literature [58, 25]).

$$L_a = \max\left\{D_1, ..., D_N, \frac{\sum_{i=1}^{N}(T_i - D_i)C_i/T_i}{1 - U}\right\} \qquad (6.5)$$

where U is again the total utilisation of the task set; note L_a is not defined for $U=1$, in this case the following must be used.

The second formulae is derived from the busy period of the system (that is, the time from start-up at time 0 to the first null or background tick where no task is executing – at this time, by definition, the load has been satisfied). This is easily obtained from a recurrence relation similar to that used in FPS:

$$w^0 = \sum_{i=1}^{N} C_i$$

$$w^{j+1} = \sum_{i=1}^{N} \left\lceil \frac{w^j}{T_i} \right\rceil C_i$$

When $w^{j+1} = w^j$ then this is the end of the busy period and $L_b = w^j$. Note this busy period is bounded if the utilization of the task set is not greater then 1 (so this is always checked first).

To obtain the least upper-bound, the simple minimum of these two values is used:

$$L = \min(L_a, L_b) \qquad (6.6)$$

To give an example of the derivation of these bounds, consider the three task system depicted in Table 6.1. The utilization of this task set is 0.92. The computed values of L_a and L_b are 30.15 and 15 respectively; hence the least upper bound is 15.

These values are obtained as follows. First the L_a bound which is defined by equation (6.5). The maximum relative deadline is 14. The second term requires three values to be

106 EARLIEST DEADLINE FIRST (EDF) SCHEDULING

Task	T	D	C
a	4	4	1
b	15	10	3
c	17	14	8

Table 6.1: A task set for EDF.

added together and then divided by 1-U (i.e. 0.08). As the first task has $T=D$ it does not contribute, the other two are

$$(15 - 10) * 3/15 \; + \; (17 - 14) * 8/17$$

which reduces to

$$1 \; + \; 24/17$$

and then the full value of L_a comes from

$$L_a \;=\; \max\left\{14, \frac{2.411}{0.08}\right\} \;=\; 30.15$$

Note that the value of L_a does not have to be an integer. If L_a did determine the value of L (i.e. $L_a > L_b$) then its value would be rounded up to the next highest integer.

The value of L_b is equivalent to calculating the response-time of task c if it were given the lowest priority. So

$$w^0 \;=\; \sum_{i=1}^{3} C_i \;=\; 12$$

$$w^1 = \left\lceil \frac{12}{4} \right\rceil 1 + \left\lceil \frac{12}{15} \right\rceil 3 + \left\lceil \frac{12}{17} \right\rceil 8 = 14$$

$$w^2 = \left\lceil \frac{14}{4} \right\rceil 1 + \left\lceil \frac{14}{15} \right\rceil 3 + \left\lceil \frac{14}{17} \right\rceil 8 = 15$$

$$w^3 = \left\lceil \frac{15}{4} \right\rceil 1 + \left\lceil \frac{15}{15} \right\rceil 3 + \left\lceil \frac{15}{17} \right\rceil 8 = 15$$

and hence $L_b=15$.

In the time period from 0 to 15 there are five deadlines to check – Task a at times 4, 8 and 12; Task b at time 10; and Task c at time 14. At all of these points equation (6.4) is satisfied and the system is determined to be schedulable. For example $h(15)$ is 14 and $h(12)$ is 6.

Note if this task set is analysed by the sufficient test (given by equation (6.2)) then it is deemed unschedulable (as the sum of the C/D terms is greater then 1).

If the example is now modified to increase the computation time of b to 4 then the utilization is still acceptable (0.987) but it is not schedulable. At time 14, $h(t)$ has the value 15, so $h(14) > 14$.

6.4 The QPA test

For non-trivial systems, the upper bound, L, on the duration over which the PDA test must be applied can be large and the number of deadlines between 0 and L that need to be checked becomes excessive. Fortunately, an efficient scheme has recently been developed that can significantly reduce the number of time points that need to be tested. This scheme, known as QPA (Quick Processor demand Analysis) [84], exploits the following property: rather than progress from 0 to L checking each deadline, QPA starts at L and moves backwards towards 0 checking only a necessary subset of the deadlines.

Let $h(L) = s$. If $s > L$ then the system is unschedulable. If this is not the case ($s \leq L$) then $h(t) < t$ for all values of t: $s < t < L$. Hence there is no need to check the deadlines within the interval $s..L$. To verify this property assume (in order to construct a counterexample) a value t within the range has $h(t) > t$. Now $t > s$, so $h(t) > s$. Also $h(t) < h(L)$ as $t < L$ (the function h is monotonic in t). We must conclude that $s > L$ which contradicts the assumption that $s < L$.

Having jumped from L back to $h(L)$, the procedure is repeated from $h(L)$ to $h(h(L))$ etc, at each step the essential test of $h(t) < t$ is undertaken. Of course if $h(t) = t$ then no progress can be made and it is necessary to force progress by moving from t $(= h(t))$ to t-1 (or to the largest absolute deadline (d) in the system such as $d < t$).

The QPA test looks at only a small fraction of the number of points that would need to be analysed if all deadlines were checked. An example of the approach is as follows. Six tasks have the characteristics given in Table 6.2. The utilization of this task set is 0.918. The value of L is 59 and there are 25 deadlines that need to be checked in this interval using PDA (at times 4, 6, 8, 10, 12, 14, 16, 20, 22, 24, 27, 28, 30, 32, 36, 38, 40, 41, 42, 44, 48, 50, 52, 56, 57)

Task	T	D	C
a	4	4	1
b	8	6	1
c	10	10	1
d	12	8	2
e	15	12	2
f	21	20	3

Table 6.2: A task set for EDF.

Applying QPA results in just 13 points that need to be considered, these correspond to the following values of t: 59, 53, 46, 43, 40, 33, 29, 24, 21, 19, 12, 9, 5 and 1. Both tests agree (of course) on the schedulability of this task set.

In general QPA typically requires only 1% of the effort of the original processor demand analysis scheme.

6.5 Blocking and EDF

When considering shared resources and blocking, there is a direct analogy between EDF and FPS. Where FPS suffers *priority inversion*, EDF suffers *deadline inversion*. This is when a task requires a resource that is currently locked by another task with a longer deadline. Not surprisingly inheritance and ceiling protocols have been developed for EDF, but as with earlier comparisons, the EDF schemes are somewhat more complex.

As priorities are static, it is easy to determine which tasks can block the task currently being analysed. With EDF, this relationship is dynamic; it depends on which tasks (with longer deadlines) are active when the task is released. And this varies from one release to the next throughout the system's execution.

Probably the currently best known scheme for EDF is Baker's **Stack Resource Policy** (SRP) [10]. This works in a very similar way to the immediate ceiling priority protocol (ICPP) for FPS (indeed SRP influenced the development of ICPP). Each task, under SRP, is assigned a **preemption level**. *Preemption levels reflect the relative deadlines of the tasks, the shorter the deadline the higher the preemption level;* so they actually designate the static priority of the task as assigned by the deadline monotonic scheme. At run-time, resources are given ceiling values based on the maximum preemption level of the tasks that use the resource.

> *When a task is released, it can only preempt the currently executing task if its absolute deadline is shorter and its preemption level is higher than the highest ceiling of the currently locked resources.*

The result of applying this protocol is identical to applying ICPP (on a single processor). Tasks suffer only a single block (it is as they are released), deadlocks are prevented and a simple formulae is available for calculating the blocking time which is represented by the term B. The blocking term, once calculated, can be incorporated into PDA and QPA:

$$\forall t > 0 \quad \sum_{i=1}^{N} \left\lfloor \frac{t + T_i - D_i}{T_i} \right\rfloor C_i + B \leq t \tag{6.7}$$

6.6 Deadline-floor protocol

Even the above brief description of SRP should indicate that is it not a straightforward protocol and that its implementation may indeed be complex and have a relatively high overhead. Tasks need to be queued according to their absolute deadlines and, separately, their preemption level. It is perhaps one of the reasons that EDF has not been more widely applied; real-time operating systems and languages have not supported SRP.

More recently, a new protocol (based on an old idea of deadline inheritance) has been developed that is more intuitive and is easier to implement. Recall the basic properties of the immediate ceiling priority protocol for FPS.

- All shared resources have a priority ceiling defined which is the maximum priority of any task that uses the resource.
- Whenever a task accesses a shared resource, its priority is raised to the ceiling of that resource.
- As a result, accesses to shared resources are serialised (i.e mutual exclusive access to the resource is ensured).

The key behaviour is obtained by the property that if a task with access to a resource is preempted then the newly executing task cannot access that resource (to preempt its priority must be higher than the ceiling of the resource, so it cannot use the resource).

The new protocol, called **deadline-floor protocol** (DFP) [21] is a direct analogy to the ICPP:

- All shared resources have a deadline defined which is the minimum relative deadline of any task that uses the resource (hence the name deadline-floor protocol).
- Whenever a task accesses a shared resource, its absolute deadline is reduce to reflect the deadline floor of the resource.
- As a result, accesses to shared resources are serialised (i.e mutual exclusive access to the resource is ensured).

The basic protocol works as follows. Assume a task with absolute deadline a accesses a resource with deadline floor df at time t. If $t + df < a$ then the task's absolute deadline is temporarily reduce to $t + df$. When it leaves the resource its absolute deadline will return to a. Alternatively if $t + df \geq a$ then no change is made to the task's absolute deadline.

As with ICPP, if a task with access to a resource is preempted then the newly executing task cannot access that resource. The newly released task must be released after t (say at time s). If it preempts then $s+$ its relative deadline must be less than $t + df$. It follows that its relative deadline must be less than the deadline floor of the resource and so it cannot use the resource.

To implement DFP, it is necessary to have access to a clock that can record the time when the resource request is made. At all times the run-time system must order executable tasks according to their absolute deadline. There are a number of efficient way of doing this. It is, therefore, likely that DFP will become the standard way of supporting shared resources in EDF scheduled systems.

6.7 Aperiodic tasks and EDF execution-time servers

Following the development of bandwidth preserving server technology for fixed priority systems, most of the common approaches have been reinterpreted within the context of dynamic EDF systems. For example, there is a Dynamic Sporadic Server and a Dynamic Deferrable Server. Whereas the static schemes need a priority to be assigned (which is done pre-run-time), the dynamic versions need to compute a deadline each time the server needs to execute.

In addition to these common forms of servers there are also a number that are EDF-specific. These take the form of virtual (but slow) processors that can guarantee C in T. So an aperiodic task that requires to execute for $3C$ will be guaranteed to complete in $3T$ if the server has no other work to do. To find more about EDF servers and EDF scheduling in general, the reader is referred to the books by Liu [58] and Buttazzo [25].

Summary

Following fixed priority scheduling, the next significant scheduling approach is EDF – here the task with the shortest (earliest) deadline is the one to execute first. EDF has the advantage that it optimally allocates the processor. If an application cannot be scheduled on a single processor by EDF then it cannot be scheduled by any other approach. For simple systems with $D = T$ then a very simple and exact utilization-based test can be used to check schedulability. When $D \leq T$ then Processor Demand Analysis has to be undertaken. An efficient approach to this form of analysis called QPA was introduced and illustrated by examples.

This chapter has also considered protocols to reduce blocking, and execution-time servers that work specifically with EDF. The equivalent of the priority-inheritance protocol for EDF is the deadline-floor protocol (DFP). This also ensures that blocking is minimised and that deadlock-free execution is guaranteed.

The combination of QPA analysis, DFP for blocking and bandwidth preserving servers for aperiodic work means that EDF-based approaches are now a realistic means of supporting real-time systems. In Part III of this book the facilities available to program EDF-scheduled task sets will be considered.

Chapter 7
Advanced analysis techniques

7.1 Release jitter
7.2 Arbitrary deadlines
7.3 Cooperative scheduling
7.4 Fault tolerance
7.5 Incorporating offsets
7.6 Priority assignment
7.7 Execution-time servers
7.8 Scheduling for power-aware systems
7.9 Incorporating system overheads
Summary

It was noted earlier that the model outlined in Section 4.2.4 was too simplistic for practical use. In the context of fixed priority based scheduling, three important restrictions have already been removed:

- Deadlines can be less than period ($D < T$).
- Sporadic and aperiodic tasks, as well as periodic tasks, can be supported.
- Task interactions are possible, with the resulting blocking being factored into the response time equations.

Within this chapter, several further generalizations will be given. The chapter will also look at a number of other issues including a general-purpose priority assignment algorithm. The chapter will conclude by showing how the inevitable overheads associated with implementing a scheduler can be taken into account within the scheduling analysis itself.

7.1 Release jitter

In the simple model, all tasks are assumed to be periodic and to be released with perfect periodicity; that is, if task l has period T_l then it is released with exactly that frequency. Sporadic tasks are incorporated into the model by assuming that their minimum inter-arrival interval is T. This is not, however, always a realistic assumption. Consider a sporadic task s being released by a periodic task l (on another processor). The period of the first task is T_l and the sporadic task will have the same rate, but it is incorrect to assume

112   ADVANCED ANALYSIS TECHNIQUES

that the maximum load (interference) s exerts on low-priority tasks can be represented in equations (5.2) or (5.3) as a periodic task with period $T_s = T_l$.

To understand why this is insufficient, consider two consecutive executions of task l. Assume that the event that releases task s occurs at the very end of the periodic task's execution. On the first execution of task l, assume that the task does not complete until its latest possible time, that is, R_l. However, on the next invocation assume there is no interference on task l so it completes within C_l. As this value could be arbitrarily small, let it equal zero. The two executions of the sporadic task are not separated by T_l but by $T_l - R_l$. Figure 7.1 illustrates this behaviour for T_l equal to 20, R_l equal to 15 and minimum C_l equal to 1 (that is, two releases of the sporadic task within 6 time units). Note that this phenomenon is of interest only if task l is remote. If this was not the case then the variations in the release of task s would be accounted for by the standard equations, where a critical instant can be assumed between the releaser and the released.

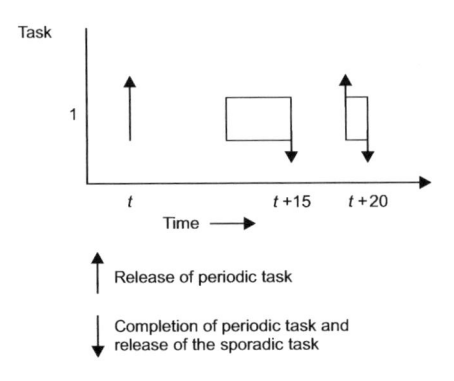

Figure 7.1: Releases of sporadic tasks.

To capture correctly the interference sporadic tasks have upon other tasks, the recurrence relationship must be modified. The maximum variation in a task's release is termed its **release jitter** (and is represented by J). For example, in the above, task s would have a jitter value of 15. In terms of its maximum impact on lower-priority tasks, this sporadic task will be released at time 0, 5, 25, 45 and so on. That is, at times 0, $T - J$, $2T - J$, $3T - J$, and so on. Examination of the derivation of the schedulability equation implies that task i will suffer one interference from task s if R_i is between 0 and $T - J$, that is $R_i \in [0, T - J)$, two if $R_i \in [T - J, 2T - J)$, three if $R_i \in [2T - J, 3T - J)$ and so on. A slight rearrangement of these conditions shows a single hit if $R_i + J \in [0, T)$, a double hit if $R_i + J \in [T, 2T)$ and so on. This can be represented in the same form as the previous response time equations as follows [5]:

$$R_i = B_i + C_i + \sum_{j \in hp(i)} \left\lceil \frac{R_i + J_j}{T_j} \right\rceil C_j \tag{7.1}$$

In general, periodic tasks do not suffer release jitter. An implementation may, however, restrict the granularity of the system timer (which releases periodic tasks). In this situation, a periodic task may also suffer release jitter. For example, a T value of 10 but a system granularity of 8 will imply a jitter value of 6 – at time 16 the periodic task will be released for its time '10' invocation. If response time (now denoted as $R_i^{periodic}$) is to be measured relative to the real release time then the jitter value must be added to that previously calculated:

$$R_i^{periodic} = R_i + J_i \qquad (7.2)$$

If this new value is greater than T_i then the following analysis must be used.

7.2 Arbitrary deadlines

In the analysis developed so far, the scheduling model has assumed that a task must complete its execution before it is next released (i.e. $D \leq T$). For most systems this is a valid assumption. But there are situations in which a more relaxed model is required. Consider a data streaming application in which a periodic producer task can sometimes execute beyond (i.e. overrun) its period due to the volume of data that needs to be processed. To facilitate this behaviour a buffer is placed between the producer and consumer. At the start of the application's execution the buffer is filled and then the periodic consumer task starts executing. As long as the average response-time of the producer task is no worse than its period, and its worst-case behaviour is known then the size of the buffer can be computed. The consumer task will always find data available when it accesses the buffer and it will therefore execute reliably. There is an increase in the end-to-end latency of the streaming system but the temporal properties are guaranteed.

To cater for situations where D_i (and hence potentially R_i) can be greater than T_i, the analysis must again be adapted. When deadline is less than (or equal) to period, it is necessary to consider only a single release of each task. The critical instant, when all higher-priority tasks are released at the same time, represents the maximum interference and hence the response time following a release at the critical instant must be the worst case. However, when deadline is greater than period, a number of releases must be considered. *The following assumes that the release of a task will be delayed until any previous releases of the same task have completed.*

If a task executes into the next period then both releases must be analysed to see which gives rise to the longest response time. Moreover, if the second release is not completed before a third occurs than this new release must also be considered, and so on.

For each potentially overlapping release, a separate window $w(q)$ is defined, where q is just an integer identifying a particular window (that is, $q = 0, 1, 2, ...$). Equation (5.3) can be extended to have the following form (ignoring release jitter) [77] :

$$w_i^{n+1}(q) = B_i + (q+1)C_i + \sum_{j \in hp(i)} \left\lceil \frac{w_i^n(q)}{T_j} \right\rceil C_j \qquad (7.3)$$

so with q equal to 2, three releases of the task will occur in the window. For each value

114 ADVANCED ANALYSIS TECHNIQUES

of q, a stable value of $w(q)$ can be found by iteration – as in equation (5.3). The response time is then given as

$$R_i(q) = w_i^n(q) - qT_i \tag{7.4}$$

for example, with $q = 2$ the task started $2T_i$ into the window and hence the response time is the size of the window minus $2T_i$.

The number of releases that need to be considered is bounded by the lowest value of q for which the following relation is true:

$$R_i(q) \leq T_i \tag{7.5}$$

At this point, the task completes before the next release and hence subsequent windows do not overlap. The worst-case response time is then the maximum value found for each q:

$$R_i = \max_{q=0,1,2,\ldots} R_i(q) \tag{7.6}$$

Note that for $D \leq T$, the relation in equation (7.5) is true for $q = 0$ (if the task can be guaranteed), in which case equations (7.3) and (7.4) simplify back to the original equations. If any $R > D$, then the task is not schedulable.

When this arbitrary deadline formulation is combined with the effect of release jitter, two alterations to the above analysis must be made. First, as before, the interference factor must be increased if any higher priority tasks suffers release jitter:

$$w_i^{n+1}(q) = B_i + (q+1)C_i + \sum_{j \in hp(i)} \left\lceil \frac{w_i^n(q) + J_j}{T_j} \right\rceil C_j \tag{7.7}$$

The other change involves the task itself. If it can suffer release jitter then two consecutive windows could overlap if response time plus jitter is greater than period. To accommodate this, equation (7.4) must be altered:

$$R_i(q) = w_i^n(q) - qT_i + J_i \tag{7.8}$$

The final issue to note when considering arbitrary deadlines is priority assignment. The simple deadline-monotonic assignment algorithm is no longer optimal. This issue is returned to in Section 7.6 where an optimal scheme for a number of more general task models is defined.

7.3 Cooperative scheduling

The models described above have all required true preemptive dispatching. In this section, an alternative scheme is outlined (the use of deferred preemption). This has a number of advantages, but can still be analysed by the scheduling technique based on response-time analysis. In equation (5.5), for example, there is a blocking term B that accounts for the time a lower-priority task may be executing while a higher-priority task is runnable. In the application domain, this may be caused by the existence of data that is shared (under mutual exclusion) by tasks of different priority. Blocking can, however, also be caused by the run-time system or kernel. Many systems will have the non-preemptable context switch as the longest blocking time (for example, the release of a higher-priority task being delayed by the time it takes to context switch to a lower-priority task – even though an immediate context switch to the higher-priority task will then ensue).

One of the advantages of using the immediate ceiling priority protocol (to calculate and bound B) is that blocking is not cumulative. A task cannot be blocked both by an application task and a kernel routine – only one could actually be happening when the higher-priority task is released.

Cooperative scheduling exploits this non-cumulative property by increasing the situation in which blocking can occur. Let B_{MAX} be the maximum blocking time in the system (using a conventional approach). The application code is then split into non-preemptive blocks, the execution times of which are bounded by B_{MAX}. At the end of each of these blocks, the application code offers a 'de-scheduling' request to the kernel. If a high-priority task is now runnable the kernel will instigate a context switch; if not, the currently running task will continue into the next non-preemptive block.

The normal execution of the application code is thus totally cooperative. A task will continue to execute until it offers to de-schedule. Hence, as long as any critical section is fully contained between de-scheduling calls, mutual exclusion is assured. This method does, therefore, require the careful placement of de-scheduling calls.

To give some level of protection over corrupted (or incorrect) software, a kernel could use an asynchronous signal, or abort, to remove the application task if any non-preemptive block lasts longer than B_{MAX}.

The use of deferred preemption has two important advantages. It may increase the schedulability of the system, and it can lead to lower values of C. In the solution of equation (5.2), as the value of w is being extended, new releases of higher-priority tasks are possible that will further increase the value of w. With deferred preemption, no interference can occur during the last block of execution. Let F_i be the execution time of the final block, such that when the task has consumed $C_i - F_i$ time units, the last block has (just) started. equation (5.2) is now solved for $C_i - F_i$ rather than C_i:

$$w_i^{n+1} = B_{MAX} + C_i - F_i + \sum_{j \in hp(i)} \left\lceil \frac{w_i^n}{T_j} \right\rceil C_j \qquad (7.9)$$

The value of B_{MAX} can be computed as the largest value of $C_i - F_i$ within any lower priority task.

When this converges (that is, $w_i^{n+1} = w_i^n$), the response time is given by:

$$R_i = w_i^n + F_i \qquad (7.10)$$

In effect, the last block of the task has executed with a higher priority (the highest) than the rest of the tasks.

This straightforward use of response-time analysis is however misleading and may in certain circumstances lead to errors – that is, the analysis is not sufficient. Consider as

116   ADVANCED ANALYSIS TECHNIQUES

a simple example a two task system with each task having deadline equal to period. The first task has a period of 6 and a computation time of 2 which is executed as a single non-preemptive block. The other task has a period of 8 and an execution time of 6 split into two 3 unit blocks. The longer period for this task means that it has the lower priority. The first task has a blocking term of 3 which, with its own computation time of 2, gives a response time of 5. The second task is first analysed to see when it first block will complete. This has a computation time of 3 and suffers 2 units of interference and so w_i^n converges simple to the value 5. To this is added the F_i value of 3 to give an overall response time of 8. This appears to imply that the system is schedulable. But this is impossible – the overall utilization of these two tasks is greater than 1 (1/3 + 3/4) which is indisputable evidence of unschedulability.

So why does the analysis fail on this example? There is a constraint on using equations (7.9) and (7.10) that is hidden and this example highlights the problem because it does not satisfy this constraint. For these equations to apply, the worst-case response time for each task *with preemption* must be less than the task's period. If this is not the case then it is possible for the second (or third ...) release of the task to be the worst. If releases overlap in this way then the analysis used in the previous section for deadline greater than period must be used.

For the example, the preemptive worst-case response time is 10 (two interferences plus execution time of 6) which is greater than 8 and hence the second release must be analysed. The easiest method for computing this is to look at the worst case response-time of a task made up of two serial executions. Now this new task has a computation time of 12 made up of four 3 unit blocks. Applying equations (7.9) and (7.10) gives a value of w_i^n of 15; when the final 3 is added in this gives a response-time of 18 which breaks the deadline value of 16 (for the second invocation).

It must be emphasised that for most systems with utilization not greater than 1, releases will not overlap and the straightforward use of these equations will provide the correct result – but the constraint must always be checked.

The other advantage of deferred preemption comes from predicting more accurately the execution times of a task's non-preemptable basic blocks. As discussed in Section 4.5, modern processors have caches, prefetch queues and pipelines that all significantly reduce the execution times of straight-line code. Typically, simple estimations of worst-case execution time are forced to ignore these advantages and obtain very pessimistic results because preemption will invalidate caches and pipelines. Knowledge of non-preemption can be used to predict the speed-up that will occur in practice. However, if the cost of postponing a context switch is high, this will militate against these advantages.

Safety-critical systems may prefer to use cooperative scheduling as programs have more deterministic execution. This facilitates testing procedures as arbitrary preemptions cannot occur. The downside of the approach is that the application must have "reschedule" commands inserted at the correct positions within the code.

7.4   Fault tolerance

As noted in Chapter 3, fault tolerance via either forward or backward error recovery always results in extra computation. This could be an exception handler or a recovery block. In a real-time fault tolerant system, deadlines should still be met even when a certain level of fault activations occur (i.e. errors are generated). This level of fault tolerance is know as the **fault model**. If C_i^f is the extra computation time that results from an error in task i, then the response time equation can easily be changed.

$$R_i = B_i + C_i + \sum_{j \in hp(i)} \left\lceil \frac{R_i}{T_j} \right\rceil C_j + \max_{k \in hep(i)} C_k^f \qquad (7.11)$$

where $hep(i)$ is the set of tasks with a priority equal or higher than i. Note, that $hep(i)$ is needed so as to include task i itself.

Here, the fault model defines a maximum of one fault and there is an assumption that a task will execute its recovery action at the same priority as its ordinary computation. Equation (7.11) is easily changed to increase the number of allowed faults (F):

$$R_i = B_i + C_i + \sum_{j \in hp(i)} \left\lceil \frac{R_i}{T_j} \right\rceil C_j + \max_{k \in hep(i)} F C_k^f \qquad (7.12)$$

Indeed, a system can be analysed for increasing values of F to see how many faults (arriving in a burst) can be tolerated. Alternatively, the fault model may indicate a minimum arrival interval for faults, in this case the equation becomes:

$$R_i = B_i + C_i + \sum_{j \in hp(i)} \left\lceil \frac{R_i}{T_j} \right\rceil C_j + \max_{k \in hep(i)} \left(\left\lceil \frac{R_i}{T_f} \right\rceil C_k^f \right) \qquad (7.13)$$

where T_f is the minimum inter-arrival time between faults.

In equations (7.12) and (7.13), the assumption is made that in the worst case, the fault will always occur in the task that has the longest recovery time.

7.5 Incorporating offsets

In the scheduling analysis presented so far in this book, it has been assumed that all tasks share a common release time. This critical instant is when all tasks are released simultaneously (this is usually taken to occur at time 0). For fixed priority scheduling, this is a safe assumption; if all tasks meet their timing requirements when released together then they will always be schedulable. There are, however, sets of periodic tasks that can benefit from explicitly choosing their release times so that they do not share a common release. This may result in improved schedulability. One task is said to have an **offset** with respect to the others. Consider for illustration the three tasks defined in Table 7.1.

If a common release is assumed then task a has response time of 4, task b has a response time of 8, but the third task has a worst-case response time of 16, which is beyond its deadline. For task c the interference from task b is sufficient to force a further interference from a, and this is crucial. However, if task c is given an offset (O) of 10 (that is, retain the same period and relative deadline, but have its first release at time 10) then it

118   ADVANCED ANALYSIS TECHNIQUES

Task	T	D	C
a	8	5	4
b	20	10	4
c	20	12	4

Table 7.1: Example of a task set.

Task	T	D	C	O	R
a	8	5	4	0	4
b	20	10	4	0	8
c	20	12	4	10	8

Table 7.2: Response time analysis of the task set.

will never execute at the same time as b. The result is a schedulable task set – see Table 7.2.

Unfortunately, task sets with arbitrary offsets are not amenable to analysis. It is a strongly NP-hard problem to choose offsets so that a task set is optimally schedulable. Indeed, it is far from trivial to even check if a set of tasks with offsets share a common release time[1].

Notwithstanding this theoretical result, there are task sets that can be analysed in a relatively straightforward (although not necessarily optimal) way. In most realistic systems, task periods are not arbitrary but are likely to be related to one another. As in the example just illustrated, two tasks have a common period. In these situations it is ease to give one an offset (of $T/2$) and to analyse the resulting system using a transformation technique that removes the offset – and hence simple critical instant analysis applies. In the example, tasks b and c (c having the offset of 10) are replaced by a single notional task with period 10, computation time 4, deadline 10 but no offset. This notional task has two important properties.

- If it is schedulable (when sharing a common release with all other tasks), the two real task will meet their deadlines when one is given the half period offset.

- If all lower priority tasks are schedulable when suffering interference from the notional task (and all other high-priority tasks), they will remain schedulable when the notional task is replaced by the two real tasks (one with the offset).

These properties follow from the observation that the notional task always uses more (or equal) CPU time than the two real task. Table 7.3 shows the analysis that would apply to the transformed task set. The notional task is given the name 'n' in this table.

More generally the parameters of the notional task are calculated from the real tasks a and b as follows:

---

[1] One interesting result is that a task set with co-prime periods will always have a common release no matter what offsets are chosen.

Task	T	D	C	O	R
a	8	5	4	0	4
n	10	10	4	0	8

Table 7.3: Response time analysis of the transformed task set.

$$T_n = T_a/2 \quad (or\ T_b/2\ as\ T_a = T_b)$$
$$C_n = Max(C_a, C_b)$$
$$D_n = Min(D_a, D_b)$$
$$P_n = Max(P_a, P_b)$$

where P denotes priority.

Clearly, what is possible for two tasks is also applicable to three or more tasks. A fuller description of these techniques is given by Bate and Burns [13]. In summary, although arbitrary offsets are effectively impossible to analyse, the judicious use of offsets and the transformation technique can return the analysis problem to one of a simple task set that shares a common release. All the analysis given in earlier sections of this chapter, therefore, applies.

In Chapter 2, offsets are used to control input and output jitter. Typically the input and output activities involve much less computation time than the 'middle' task that implement whatever algorithms are necessary to convert the input value to an output setting. To analyse this program structure it is acceptable to ignore offsets. As noted earlier a system that is schedulable when offsets are ignored remains schedulable when they are added to the implementation scheme.

7.6 Priority assignment

The formulation given for arbitrary deadlines has the property that no simple algorithm (such as rate or deadline monotonic) gives the optimal priority ordering. In this section, a theorem and algorithm for assigning priorities in arbitrary situations is given [6]. The theorem considers the behaviour of the lowest priority task:

Theorem *If task p is assigned the lowest priority and is feasible, then, if a feasible priority ordering exists for the complete task set, an ordering exists with task p assigned the lowest priority.*

The proof of this theorem comes from considering the schedulability equations – for example, equation (7.3). If a task has the lowest priority, it suffers interference from all higher-priority tasks. This interference is not dependent upon the actual ordering of these higher priorities. Hence if any task is schedulable at the bottom value it can be assigned that place, and all that is required is to assign the other $N - 1$ priorities. Fortunately, the theorem can be reapplied to the reduced task set. Hence through successive reapplication,

120   ADVANCED ANALYSIS TECHNIQUES

a complete priority ordering is obtained (if one exists). No backtracking through previous priority allocations is necessary.

The following code in Ada implements the priority assignment algorithm;[2] Set is an array of tasks that is notionally ordered by priority; Set(N) being the highest priority, Set(1) being the lowest. The procedure Task_Test tests to see whether task K is feasible at that place in the array. The double loop works by first swapping tasks into the lowest position until a feasible result is found, this task is then fixed at that position. The next priority position is then considered. If at any time the inner loop fails to find a feasible task, the whole procedure is abandoned. Note that a concise algorithm is possible if an extra swap is undertaken.

```
procedure Assign_Pri (Set : in out Task_Set; N : Natural;
                      Ok  : out Boolean) is
begin
  for K in 1..N loop
    for Next in K..N loop
      Swap(Set, K, Next);
      Task_Test(Set, K, Ok);
      exit when Ok;
    end loop;
    exit when not Ok;   -- failed to find a schedulable task
  end loop;
end Assign_Pri;
```

If the test of feasibility is exact (necessary and sufficient) then the priority ordering is optimal. Thus for arbitrary deadlines (without blocking), an optimal ordering is found. Where there is blocking, the priority ceiling protocols ensure that the blocking is relatively small and, therefore, the above algorithm produces adequate near optimal results.

Insufficient priorities

In all of the analysis presented in this book it has been assumed that each task has a distinct priority. Unfortunately it is not always possible to accommodate this 'one priority per task' ideal. If there are insufficient priorities then two or more tasks must share the same priority. Fortunately, to check the schedulability of shared priority tasks requires only a minor modification to the response-time test. Consider the basis equation (5.2) derived earlier in this chapter, it has a summation over all the higher priority tasks. If tasks share priorities then this summation must be over all equal or higher priority tasks:

$$R_i = C_i + \sum_{j \in hep(i)} \left\lceil \frac{R_i}{T_j} \right\rceil C_j \qquad (7.14)$$

where $hep(i)$ is the set of higher, or equal priority tasks (than i).

So, if tasks a and b share priority i then a assumes it is getting interference from b and b assumes it is getting interference from a. Clearly if a and b are schedulable when

---
[2]This algorithm has become known as *Audsley's algorithm*.

they share priority i then they will remain schedulable if they are assigned distinct but adjacent priorities. The converse is however not true.

One way to reduce the number of priority levels required for a specific system is to first make sure the system is schedulable with distinct priorities. Then, starting from the lowest priority, tasks are grouped together until the addition of an extra task breaks schedulability. A new group is then started with this task, and the process continues until all tasks are in groups (though some groups may contain only a single task). A minor variant of the priority assignment algorithm given above can easily implement this scheme.

Reducing the number of priority levels inevitable reduces schedulability. However, tests have shown that 92% of systems that are schedulable with distinct priorities will remain schedulable if only 32 levels are available. For 128 priority values this rises to 99%. The programming language Ada requires a minimum of 31 distinct priorities, for Real-Time POSIX the minimum is 32 and for Real-Time Java the minimum is 28.

7.7 Execution-time servers

Next in this description of fixed priority scheduling the topic of execution-time servers will be briefly reconsidered. As applications and hardware platforms become more complicated it is useful to employ a virtual resource layer between the set of applications and the processor (or processors) they execute on. An execution-time server guarantees both a certain level of service and ensures that no more resource is allocated than is implied by the 'service contract'. So, for example, two multi-threaded applications may co-exist on the one processor. One application receives 4ms every 10ms, the other 6ms. These levels are guaranteed and policed. The first application will definitely get 4ms but it will not be allocated more than 4ms in a 10ms interval even if it has runnable high priority tasks.

There have been a number of execution-time servers proposed for FPS (see Section 5.2.2). Here three common ones are described: the **periodic server**, the **deferrable server** and the **sporadic server**. The simple periodic server has a budget (capacity) and a replenishment period. Following replenishment, client tasks can execute until either the budget is exhausted or there are no longer any runnable client tasks. The server is then suspended until the next replenishment time. The deferrable server is similar except that the budget remains available even after clients have been satisfied – a client arriving late will be serviced if there is budget available. Both Periodic and Deferrable servers are replenished periodically and the budget still available at replenishment is lost. The Sporadic server behaves a little differently. The budget remains indefinitely until it is used. When a client arrives (at time t, say) it can use up the available budget which is then replenished at time t + the replenishment period of the server.

A complete system can contain a number of servers of these three types. The Periodic server is ideally suited for supporting periodic tasks, the Sporadic server is exactly what is required for sporadic tasks and the Deferrable server is a good match for handling aperiodic work. In the latter case, aperiodic tasks can be handled quickly if there is budget available – but once this is exhausted then the aperiodic tasks will not be serviced and hence an unbounded load on the server will have no detrimental effects on other parts of the system.

Scheduling these three server types on a fixed priority system is relatively straightforward. Each server, of whichever type, is allocated a distinct priority. Response-time analysis is then used to verify that all servers can guarantee their budget and replenishment period. Fortunately Periodic and Sporadic servers behave exactly the same as periodic tasks and hence the straightforward analysis for these servers is directly applicable. For Deferrable servers, the worst-case impact such a server can have on lower priority tasks occurs when its budget is used at the very end of one period and then again at the start of the next. Conveniently this behaviour is identical to a periodic task suffering release jitter and hence can be analysed using the formulation given in Section 7.1 with the jitter term been given by: $J_i = T_i - C_i$.

It follows from this brief discussion that the schedulability test for a task running on a server involves two steps; first to verify that the server's parameters are valid and second that the response-time of the task on that server is bounded by the task's deadline. To compute the worst-case response time for a task executing on a server can be done in a number of ways. For example, a server that guarantees 2ms every 10ms is equivalent to a processor running at 1/5 of its original speed. If all task computation times are multiplied by 5 then standard response time analysis can be applied (using these new C values)[3]. A similar approach is taken with variable speed processors – an example of this analysis is given in the next section.

7.8 Scheduling for power-aware systems

All of the scheduling tests presented in this chapter have the common form of: given a set of execution time requirements (the Cs), will all the tasks complete by their deadlines (the Ds)? This assumes a fixed speed processor (or processors) so that the worst-case execution times values can be obtained prior to attempting the system-wide scheduling analysis. There are however variable speed processors that can give rise to a difference scheduling question – at what speed must the processor execute in order for the tasks to be schedulable?

Variable speed resources are typically found in **power-aware** applications. That is in embedded systems that are powered from batteries. Examples of such systems are those that run on mobile devices and nodes in a sensor net. All battery-based systems have the need to preserve energy and thereby extend their operational life or periods between recharges.

To save power, the voltage to the processor is reduced with the result that it runs slower. But the saving is non-linear. Halving the speed of a processor may quadruple its life. Some processor have variable speed, others support just a finite set of speed settings. From the point of view of the scheduling analysis, the verification problem now has two stages:

- With the processor running at its maximum speed (Max), is the system schedulable – this is a standard test.

---

[3] With this example, the computed response times may need to have the value 8 added to take into account the 'dead time' before the sever can respond to requests from its client tasks. That is, in the worst-case when a task arrives it is just too late to receive immediate attention as the current budget has been used up by other tasks. So it arrives just as 2ms have been allocated, so must wait a further 8ms before there is anymore budget to use; it then get 2ms every 10ms. However, if the server is not shared between client tasks this dead time can be ignored.

- If the system is schedulable, by what maximum factor k can all the C values be increased so that the system remains schedulable?

There is no simple way to compute k, rather it needs to be found by a branch and bound search. Consider the fixed priority example given in Table 7.4 where the C values are those that are appropriate for the maximum speed of the processor.

Task	T	D	C
a	70	70	5
b	120	100	7
c	200	200	11

Table 7.4: Example task set with maximum speed.

This is clearly schedulable using RTA ($R_a = 5$, $R_b = 12$ and $R_c = 23$). If k is given the value 10 (i.e. execution times are now 50, 70 and 110) then the utilization is greater than 1 so the system is clearly unschedulable. So k must lie between 1 and 10. Using, for illustration, only integer values for k, the value 6 could be tried next (result unschedulable) then 4 (schedulable) and then 5. The results for $k = 5$ are shown in Table 7.5. Note the response time for task c is just on its deadline (200), any increase in any C parameter would cause this task to become unschedulable. Hence $k = 5$ is the optimum value and it is possible to conclude that the task set is schedulable on a processor with speed (of at least) $Max/5$.

Task	T	D	C	R
a	70	70	25	25
b	120	100	35	60
c	200	200	55	200

Table 7.5: Example task set with reduced speed.

This discussion has focused on statically fixing the processor speed so that all deadlines are (just) met. In more dynamic systems where the work load fluctuates at run-time it is possible to change the processor's speed whilst continuing to execute the application. For all variable speed processors there is a cost (overhead) in making changes to the processor's speed, these overheads need to be taken into account. It is also necessary to take into account the impact on memory performance and I/O devices — savings in processing cost may not lead to overall system economy.

7.9 Incorporating system overheads

In all the analysis presented so far the overheads of actually implementing the multi-tasking system software have been ignored. Clearly for a real system this is not acceptable and hence the scheduling equations need to be expanded to include terms for the overhead

124   ADVANCED ANALYSIS TECHNIQUES

factors. The following characteristics are typical of many operating system kernels or language run-times.

- The cost of a context switch between tasks is not negligible and may not be a single value. The cost of a context switch to a higher-priority periodic task (following, for example, a clock interrupt) may be higher than a context switch from a task to a lower-priority task (at the end of the high-priority task's execution). For systems with a large number of periodic tasks, an additional cost will be incurred for manipulating the delay queue (for periodic tasks when they execute, say, an Ada 'delay until' statement).
- All context switch operations are non preemptive.
- The cost of handling an interrupt (other than the clock) and releasing an application sporadic task is not insignificant. Furthermore, for DMA (Direct Memory Access) and channel-program controlled devices (see Chapter 16), the impact of shared-memory access can have a non-trivial impact on worst-case performance – such devices are best avoided in hard real-time systems.
- A clock interrupt (say every 10ms) could result in periodic tasks being moved from a delay queue to the dispatch/ready queue. The costs for this operation varies depending on the number of tasks to be moved.

In addition to the above, the scheduling analysis must take into account the features of the underlying hardware, such as the impact of the cache and processor pipelines.

7.9.1 Modeling non-trivial context switch times

Most scheduling models ignore context switch times. This approach is, however, too simplistic if the total cost of the context switches is not trivial when compared with the application's own code. Figure 7.2 illustrates a number of significant events in the execution of a typical periodic task.

A – the clock interrupt that designates the notional time at which the task should start (assuming no release jitter or non-preemptive delay – if the interrupts were disabled due to the operation of the context switch then the clock handler would have its execution delayed; this is taken into account in the scheduling equations by the blocking factor B).

B – the earliest time that the clock handler can complete, this signifies the start of the context switch to the task (assume it is the highest priority runnable task)

C – the actual start of the execution of the task

D – the completion of the task (the task may be preempted a number of times between C and D)

E – the completion of the context switch away from the task

A' – the next release of the task

INCORPORATING SYSTEM OVERHEADS 125

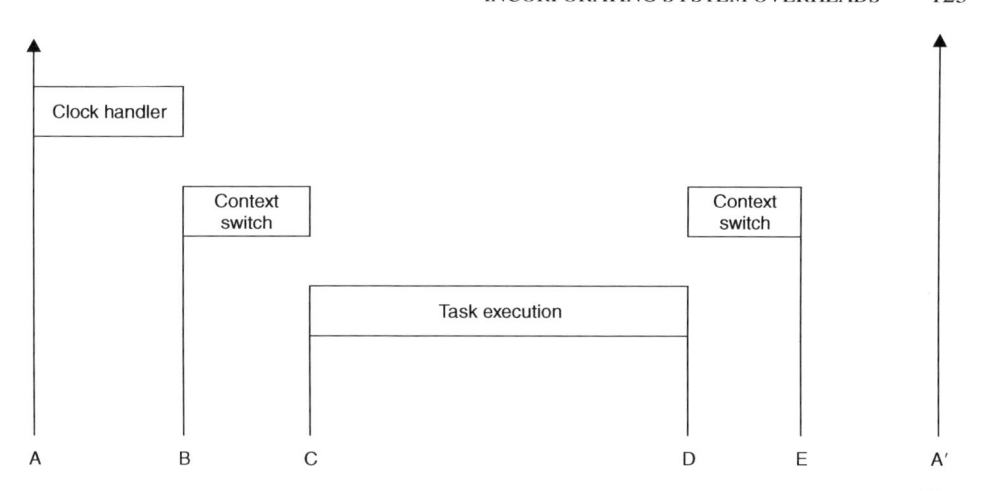

Figure 7.2: Overheads when executing tasks.

The typical requirement for this task is that it completes before its next release (that is, D < A′), or before some deadline prior to its next release. Either way, D is the significant time, not E. Another form of requirement puts a bound on the time between the start of execution and termination (that is, D–C). This occurs when the first action is an input and the last an output (and there is a deadline requirement between the two). While these factors affect the meaning of the task's own deadline (and hence its response time) they do not affect the interference this task has on lower-priority tasks; here the full cost of both context switches counts. Recall that the basic scheduling equation (5.5) has the form:

$$R_i = C_i + B_i + \sum_{j \in hp(i)} \left\lceil \frac{R_i}{T_j} \right\rceil C_j$$

This now becomes (for periodic tasks only):

$$R_i = CS^1 + C_i + B_i + \sum_{j \in hp(i)} \left\lceil \frac{R_i}{T_j} \right\rceil (CS^1 + CS^2 + C_j) \tag{7.15}$$

where CS^1 is the cost of the initial context switch (to the task) and CS^2 is the cost of the context switch away from each task at the end of its execution. The cost of putting the task into the delay queue (if it is periodic) is incorporated into C_i. Note that in practice this value may depend on the size of the queue; a maximum value would need to be incorporated into C_i.

This measure of the response time is from point B in Figure 7.2. To measure from point C, the first CS^1 term is removed. To measure from point A (the notional true release time of the task) requires the clock behaviour to be measured (see Section 7.9.3).

For multiprocessor systems the context switch itself may be more complicated if global placement is used as tasks may need to migrate from one processor to another. This will add to the context switch overhead and will make the prediction of worst-cases execution time (WCET) more difficult as the cache may not be shared between all the processors.

7.9.2 Modeling sporadic tasks

For sporadic tasks released by other sporadic tasks, or by periodic tasks, equation (7.15) is a valid model of behaviour. However, the computation time for the task, C_i, must include the overheads of blocking on the agent that controls its release.

When sporadic tasks are released by an interrupt, priority inversion can occur. Even if the sporadic has a low priority (due to it having a long deadline) the interrupt itself will be executed at a high hardware priority level. Let Γs be the set of sporadic tasks released by interrupts. Each interrupt source will be assumed to have the same arrival characteristics as the sporadic that it releases. The additional interference these interrupt handlers have on each application task is given by:

$$\sum_{k \in \Gamma s} \left\lceil \frac{R_i}{T_k} \right\rceil IH$$

where IH is the cost of handling the interrupt (and returning to the running task, having released the sporadic task). Equation (7.15) now becomes:

$$R_i = CS^1 + C_i + B_i + \sum_{j \in hp(i)} \left\lceil \frac{R_i}{T_j} \right\rceil (CS^1 + CS^2 + C_j)$$
$$+ \sum_{k \in \Gamma s} \left\lceil \frac{R_i}{T_k} \right\rceil IH \qquad (7.16)$$

This representation assumes that all interrupt handlers give rise to the same cost; if this is not the case then IH must be defined for each k.

Within Ada, timing events are also used to release sporadic tasks or to undertake short event-handling activities. As timing events are similar to interrupts they can be modelled in the above way.

7.9.3 Modelling the real-time clock handler

To support periodic tasks, the execution environment must have access to a real-time clock that will generate interrupts at appropriate times. An ideal system will use an interval timer, and will interrupt only when a periodic task needs to be released. The more common approach, however, is one in which the clock interrupts at a regular rate (say once every 10ms) and the handler must decide if none, one, or a number of periodic tasks must be released. The ideal approach can be modeled in an identical way to that introduced for sporadic tasks (see Section 7.9.2). With the regular clock method, it is necessary to develop a more detailed model as the execution times of the clock handler can vary considerably.

INCORPORATING SYSTEM OVERHEADS   127

Table 7.6 gives possible times for this handler (for a clock period of 10ms). Note that if the worst case was assumed to occur on all occasions over 10% of the processor would have to be assigned to the clock handler. Moreover, all this computation occurs at a high (highest) hardware priority level, and hence considerable priority inversion is occurring. For example, with the figures given in the table, at the LCM (least common multiple) of the 25 periodic tasks $1048\,\mu s$ of interference would be suffered by the highest priority application task that was released. If the task was released on its own then only $88\,\mu s$ would be suffered. The time interval is represented by B–A in Figure 7.2.

Queue state	Clock handling time, μs
No tasks on queue	16
Tasks on queue but none removed	24
One task removed	88
Two tasks removed	128
Twenty five tasks removed	1048

Table 7.6: Clock handling overheads.

In general, the cost of moving N periodic tasks from the delay queue to the dispatch queue can be represented by the following formulae:

$$C_{clk} = CT^c + CT^s + (N - 1)CT^m$$

Where CT^c is the constant cost (assuming there is always at least one task on the delay queue), CT^s is the cost of making a single move, and CT^m is the cost of each subsequent move. This model is appropriate due to the observation that the cost of moving just one task is often high when compared with the additional cost of moving extra tasks. With the kernel considered here, these costs were:

CT^c	24 μs
CT^s	64 μs
CT^m	40 μs

To reduce the pessimism of assuming that a computational cost of C_{clk} is consumed on each execution of the clock handler, this load can be spread over a number of clock ticks. This is valid if the shortest period of any application task, T_{min} is greater than the clock period, T_{clk}. Let M be defined by:

$$M = \left\lceil \frac{T_{min}}{T_{clk}} \right\rceil$$

If M is greater than 1 then the load from the clock handler can be spread over M executions. In this situation, the clock handler is modeled as a task with period T_{min} and computation time C'_{clk}:

$$C'_{clk} = M(CT^c + CT^s) + (N - M)CT^m$$

This assumes $M <= N$.

Equation (7.16) now becomes

$$R_i = CS^1 + C_i + B_i + \sum_{j \in hp(i)} \left\lceil \frac{R_i}{T_j} \right\rceil (CS^1 + CS^2 + C_j)$$

$$+ \sum_{k \in \Gamma s} \left\lceil \frac{R_i}{T_k} \right\rceil IH$$

$$+ \left\lceil \frac{R_i}{T_{min}} \right\rceil C'_{clk} \qquad (7.17)$$

To give further improvements (to the model) requires a more exact representation of the clock handlers actual execution. For example, using just CT^c and CT^s the following equation can easily be derived:

$$R_i = CS^1 + C_i + B_i + \sum_{j \in hp(i)} \left\lceil \frac{R_i}{T_j} \right\rceil (CS^1 + CS^2 + C_j)$$

$$+ \sum_{k \in \Gamma s} \left\lceil \frac{R_i}{T_k} \right\rceil IH + \left\lceil \frac{R_i}{T_{clk}} \right\rceil CT_c$$

$$+ \sum_{g \in \Gamma p} \left\lceil \frac{R_i}{T_g} \right\rceil CT_s$$

$$(7.18)$$

where Γp is the set of periodic tasks.

It is left as an exercise for the reader to incorporate the three-parameter model of clock handling.

Summary

This chapter has transformed the simple model introduced in earlier chapters to a multi-faceted model that can really address the features found in modern real-time systems. In particular this chapter has introduced:

- Release jitter – for tasks that arrive for execution periodically but may have some job releases delayed (as happens with the use of execution-time servers for aperiodic tasks).
- Arbitrary deadlines – although most tasks have implicit or constrained deadlines there are situations where is it useful to allow some tasks to have deadline greater than period; on average they must complete before their next job arrives, but in the worst-case they can buffer up a number of jobs.

- Cooperative scheduling – most real-time operating systems only support preemptive scheduling, but various levels of non-preemptive scheduling can be beneficial.
- Fault tolerance – to incorporate the extra computations required when errors are detected and recovery action taken.
- Offsets – for tasks with the same period, offsets can improve schedulability by ensuring that they are never released at the same time.
- Priority assignment – to obtain optimal priority ordering in the situations where simple schemes do not apply.
- Power-aware platforms – where benefit can be gained from running the processor as slow as possible whilst still guaranteeing that all deadlines are met.
- System overheads – the underlying real-time operating system cannot undertake instantaneous task management, the cost of their operations must be accounted for.

In addition to these characteristics there are many other task attributes that have been analysed in the fixed priority scheduling literature. For example, tasks with precedence, tasks that must meet N in M deadlines (e.g. 4 in 5) but not every deadline, and tasks that have a series of C values (called multiframes tasks). It is not necessary, however, to cover all these topics (and more) in order to complete this treatment of response-time analysis (RTA). The key property of RTA is that it is extendable and configurable. New characteristics can be easily accommodated into the theory.

The next chapter will address three further important properties of modern real-time systems: applications that have more than one level of criticality, multiprocessor hardware platforms, and open systems.

Chapter 8
Mixed criticality, multiprocessor and open systems

8.1 Mixed criticality systems (MCS)
8.2 Multiprocessor systems
8.3 Partitioned and global placement
8.4 Scheduling the network
8.5 Mutual exclusion on multiprocessor platforms
8.6 Open systems
Summary

All the analysis presented so far in this book has been concerned with the scheduling of concurrent tasks of the same criticality and importance, running on a single processor.

As applications become more complicated and integrated there is a need to address mixed criticality – that is, systems will be composed of components that have different needs in terms of fault-tolerance and availability. The level of guarantee needed, for example, with an automatic braking system in a car is higher than that needed for the optimal route planning software. Different levels of guarantee can influence how worst-case analysis of code is undertaken and can, therefore, effect scheduling.

As processors have become more powerful, the size and complexity of the applications that can fit on to a single processor has increased substantially. However, for a significant class of system, there is the need to move to a multiprocessor execution platform. This can take the form of a relatively simple dual processor or may involve a large multi-core chip. The processors may all be of an identical type (homogeneous) or may have quite different characteristics (heterogeneous). Also the links between the processors may be a shared memory bus or an independent network. Whatever the architecture, the scheduling problem for a multiprocessor system is significantly more complicated than the single processor case. Here three issues are addressed: the placement of tasks to processors, the scheduling of any shared network and the implementation of locks in shared-memory multiprocessor architectures.

Even within the same level of criticality, some applications (i.e. task sets) may be more important than others. Usually this is of no real consequence with hard real-time systems as all task are guaranteed to meet their deadlines. But in open soft real-time systems where new work arrives and an online admissions test must be applied then it is possible that not all work can be finished 'on time'. It follows that some means of deciding what tasks to include and which to abandoned must be employed. This is the final topic to be addressed in this part of the book.

8.1 Mixed criticality systems (MCS)

An increasingly important trend in the design of real-time and embedded systems is the integration of components with different levels of criticality onto a common hardware platform. At the same time, these platforms are migrating from single cores to multi-cores and, in the future, many-core architectures. **Criticality** is a designation of the level of assurance against failure needed for a system component. A mixed criticality system is one that has two or more distinct levels (for example safety critical, mission critical and low-critical). Perhaps up to five levels may be identified (see, for example, the IEC 61508, DO-178C, DO-254 and ISO 26262 standards). Typical names for the levels are ASILs (Automotive Safety and Integrity Levels), DALs (Design Assurance Levels) and SILs (Safety Integrity Levels).

Most of the complex embedded systems found in, for example, the automotive and avionics industries are evolving into mixed criticality systems in order to meet stringent non-functional requirements relating to cost, space, weight, heat generation and power consumption. Indeed the software standards in the European automotive industry (AUTOSAR) and in the avionics domain (ARINC) address mixed criticality issues; in the sense that they recognise that MCS must be supported on their platforms.

A key aspect of MCS is that system parameters, such as tasks' estimated worst-case execution times (WCETs), become dependent on the criticality level of the tasks. So the same code will have a higher WCET if it is defined to be safety-critical (as a higher level of assurance is required) than it would if it is just considered to be mission critical or indeed non-critical. This is due to the confidence that must be placed on the estimates of WCET. For safety-critical, as opposed to mission-critical, software a higher level of confidence is needed and hence a more conservative (larger) estimate is required for the WCET parameters.

A MCS is therefore composed of a collection of multi-task applications/components running on the same hardware. Each application, and hence each task, is allocated a criticality level, and may have more than one estimate of WCET (C). The simple fact that with MCS a task may have more than one C parameter significantly modifies/undermines many of the standard scheduling results that have been presented in previous chapters.

Consider as an example an Unmanned Aerial Vehicle (UAV). Its flight control software must be certified by a civil aviation authority (CAA) if it is to fly in open public air-space. Its key functional software (say, to control the surveying of a remote geographical area) is mission critical and must be signed off (passed fit for purpose) by the systems engineer. In addition there may be value-added software (e.g. optimal route planner, hardware health monitor etc.) that is not critical but improves the quality of the system. It can, therefore, fail without jeopardising the mission. Overall three levels of criticality are present in the UAV.

The verification of the software contained on the UAV will use techniques determined by the criticality level. For functional correctness:

- formal proof for the highest level;
- extensive (costly) testing for the middle level; and
- adequate (cost effective) testing for the lower level.

For timing, the main issue is how to do the WCET analysis:

- conservative static analysis for the highest levels;
- static path analysis plus basic block measurement for the middle level; and
- measurement for the lower levels – this could involve:
    - worst observed during testing + substantial safety margin,
    - worst observed during testing + small safety margin,
    - worst observed during testing,
    - average observed during testing.

Each of these techniques brings with it a different level of confidence and different actual estimates of WCET. All but the final three will probably deliver values that are greater than the real (unknown) worst-case execution time of the code. But the certification authorities require evidence and adequate 'safety margins'; hence for the highest levels of criticality the WCET estimates are likely to be *very* conservative (i.e. very pessimistic).

To incorporate mixed criticality we need to make a final modification to the task model. Each task is now assigned an integrity level, denoted by L, and has a worst-case execution time value per integrity level. So for the simple case of just two criticality levels:

$$L = \{High, Low\}$$

the single C parameter is replaced by $C(High)$ and $C(Low)$ with

$$C(High) \geq C(Low).$$

And the required schedulabilty constraint becomes (staying with just two criticality levels):

- All tasks with $L = High$ must be schedulable when they execute with $C(High)$ values, and
- All tasks must be schedulable when $C(Low)$ values are used.

One approach to scheduling mixed criticality systems is to partition the priority range so that all the higher criticality tasks have priorities greater than the lower criticality tasks. However, this can lead to very poor schedulability. The following consider three alternative ways that interleave priority levels and criticality to improve schedulability.

8.1.1 Method 1

This approach is due to Vestal and was proposed in 2007 [78]. Recall that the response-time equation for the simple task model is

$$R_i = C_i + \sum_{j \in hp(i)} \left\lceil \frac{R_i}{T_j} \right\rceil C_j$$

The Vestal approach modifies this equation to make it criticality aware:

$$R_i = C_i(L_i) + \sum_{j \in hp(i)} \left\lceil \frac{R_i}{T_j} \right\rceil C_j(L_i) \qquad (8.1)$$

where L_i is the criticality level of task i and the final term $C_j(L_i)$ is the worst-case execution time of task j at the criticality level of task i (the one being evaluated).

So if the task under consideration is of criticality $High$ then $C(High)$ values are used for all tasks; alternatively if the task under consideration is of criticality Low then $C(Low)$ values are used for all tasks. Consider the example given in Table 8.1 where the tasks are given in priority order (highest first).

Task	L	C(Low)	C(High)	D	T	P
a	Low	1	2	1	3	3
b	Low	1	2	10	10	2
c	High	-	20	X?	200	1

Table 8.1: Example mixed criticality task set.

Note there is no need to give a $C(Low)$ value for the lowest priority task as it does not interfere with any other task. The deadline for the high criticality task is not given, evaluation of this and the other methods will determine what value of X can be delivered.

Solving equation (8.1) for the first two tasks gives $R_a = 1$ and $R_b = 2$. For the third task:

$$R_c = 20 + \left\lceil \frac{R_c}{3} \right\rceil 2 + \left\lceil \frac{R_c}{10} \right\rceil 2$$

which has a solution of $R_c = 150$. Note that if L_b is changed form Low to $High$ then R_b would become 6 (this result is used below).

In the above example priorities were given. The optimal priority ordering is not however deadline monotonic. This is illustrated by a simple two task example given in Table 8.2.

If deadline monotonic priority ordering (DMPO) is used task a is given the highest priority, as a result task a is schedulable but task b is not. When considering the exectuion of task b the $High$ values must be used and so task a uses up all the processor, 2 in every 2, and task b will never execute.

Task	L	C(Low)	C(High)	D	T
a	Low	1	2	2	2
b	High	1	1	4	4

Table 8.2: Example mixed criticality task set.

However if the priorities are reversed then task b gets 1 in 4 and task a suffers an interference of 1 and hence can execute for its required 1 in 2.

Fortunately, although simple DMPO is not applicable, Audsley's priority assignment algorithm can be used (see Section 7.6). The task model has all the prerequisites for Audsley's algorithm; in particular response time is dependent on the set of higher priority tasks but not their relative priorities. Indeed all the methods described in this section are amenable to having their priorities assigned optimally by Audsley's algorithm.

The advantage of Vestal's method is that it can deliver schedulability when the simple task model cannot. It also has the advantage that no run-time monitoring is needed. But there is one crucial drawback with Method 1: all tasks must be analysed to gauge their worst-case execution time for each criticality level. For a $High$ criticality task, it is not too problematic to give an estimate of its $C(Low)$ value - indeed its $C(High)$ level could be used. But for a Low criticality task, the fact that is must also have a $C(High)$ estimate is a major (unnecessary) requirement. The cost of undertaking comprehensive static analyses of code is high, it should only be done to software that requires it (i.e. $High$ criticality tasks). To require all software of whatever integrity level to be analysed as if it were of the highest integrity level is prohibitively expensive. The next two methods do not suffer from this disadvantage, but they do require run-time monitoring.

A final point to emphasis about this approach is that if a $High$ criticality task executes for more than its $C(Low)$ value then it may induce a missed deadline on some lower priority Low criticality task. The $High$ criticality task will meets its deadline (as long as it does not execution for more than its $C(High)$ estimate) but the pre-condition for timely execution of the Low criticality tasks no longer holds. This property also applies to Method 2; but for Method 3 there is an even more dramatic impact on Low criticality tasks when a $High$ criticality task moved beyond it $C(Low)$ marker.

8.1.2 Method 2

A lower criticality task, say one with $L = Low$, has an estimate of worst-case execution, $C(Low)$ that is a valid bound that should be used for the scheduling analysis of this task. Moreover it should never execute for more than this value when it is interfering with lower priority but high integrity tasks. So it is reasonable to consider a Low criticality task executing for more than $C(Low)$ as an error. Moreover this is an error that should be caught and its impact minimised.

With run-time support in the form of execution-time monitoring or execution-time servers (e.g. periodic or sporadic servers), it is possible to catch a task which is about to execute beyond its $C(L)$ bound. At this point, the task can be de-scheduled, or at least be scheduled at a priority below all other tasks. As a result, it can never interfere for more than $C(L)$. This run-time monitoring has two advantages, its means that no task has to be evaluated at a higher criticality than it actually is, and an improvement in schedulability is obtained. The RTA equation becomes:

$$R_i = C_i(L_i) + \sum_{j \in hp(i)} \left\lceil \frac{R_i}{T_j} \right\rceil C_j(\min(L_i, L_j)) \qquad (8.2)$$

Only the last term has changed, but this can make a great difference in terms of schedulability. This term implies that if the task under consideration (task i) is of, for example, Low criticality then only $C(Low)$ values are used; but if it is of $High$ criticality then $C(High)$ is used for interfering $High$ criticality tasks, but only $C(Low)$ for interfering Low criticality tasks.

Task	L	C(Low)	C(High)	D	T	P
a	Low	1	-	1	3	3
b	High	-	2	10	10	2
c	High	-	20	X?	200	1

Table 8.3: Example mixed criticality task set.

If we return to the earlier example (see Table 8.3 - but note the criticality of task b has changed) we can again compute the response times. For task a, $R_a = 1$ again; R_b is now 3 (it was previously 6), and R_c is now the solution to:

$$R_c = 20 + \left\lceil \frac{R_c}{3} \right\rceil 1 + \left\lceil \frac{R_c}{10} \right\rceil 2$$

The reduction in assumed interference from R_a means that the solution to this equation is now 45; whereas for Method 1 it was 150.

8.1.3 Method 3

A further improvement in schedulability of mixed criticality systems can be obtained by extending the role of the run-time monitor. In Method 2, a Low criticality task is preventing from executing for more than $C(Low)$. If $High$ criticality tasks are also monitored (as they would be to see if they attempt to execute for more than $C(High)$) then it is possible to identify when such a task executes for more than its $C(Low)$ estimate. Now this task must continue to execute as it is of $High$ criticality, but it is reasonable to argue that the assumption upon which all Low criticality tasks were deemed schedulable has now been invalidated.

For Low criticality tasks, the basis for asserting schedulability is: *if all tasks execute for no more than $C(Low)$ then all their deadlines should be met*. So even when a $High$ criticality task executes for more than $C(Low)$ this axiom has been broken. This leads to a run-time scheme that abandons Low criticality tasks if a $High$ criticality task executes for more than $C(Low)$.

The mixed criticality real-time system is said to be behaving in low-crit (or normal) mode if all execution times are at or below $C(Low)$. If any tasks executes for more than $C(Low)$, a move to high-crit mode is made, and all Low criticality tasks are abandoned (or at least have their priorities reduced).

To take advantage of this scheme in the analysis, first the response-time ($R(Low)$) is computed for all Low criticality tasks in the low-crit mode (using $C(Low)$ values for all tasks) — these computed worst-case response times should all be no greater than the task's deadline for a potentially schedulable system.

Next the response-time ($R(Low)$) is computed for all $High$ criticality tasks in the low-crit mode; again using $C(Low)$ values.

Finally the the real response-time ($R(High)$) is calculated assuming that no Low criticality task executes after the mode change, but all $High$ criticality tasks execute with their maximum $C(High)$ values.

Returning to the example - and adding some necessary further parameters (see Table 8.4).

Task	L	C(Low)	C(High)	D	T	P
a	Low	1	-	1	3	3
b	$High$	1	2	10	10	2
c	$High$	10	20	X?	200	1

Table 8.4: Example mixed criticality task set.

Consider task c. First its response-time in low-crit mode is calculated by solving:

$$R_c(Low) = 10 + \left\lceil \frac{R_c}{3} \right\rceil 1 + \left\lceil \frac{R_c}{10} \right\rceil 1$$

this has the value 18.

Now $R_c(High)$ is computed by noting that task a cannot execute beyond 18 (or else task c would have completed in the low-crit mode). So the following equation must now be solved:

$$R_c(High) = 20 + \left\lceil \frac{18}{3} \right\rceil 1 + \left\lceil \frac{R_c}{10} \right\rceil 2$$

This converges on $R_c(High) = 34$.

Although only a single example has been given, the worst-case response times has significantly reduced through the methods. In the example, the response-time for Task c is reduced from 150, to 45 and then to 34. Depending on the deadline of the task, this could be significant.

Note even Method 3 is not exact. It is pessimistic to assume that task b is always executing with execution time of 2. To get tighter analysis, the worst-case time for the mode change must be known – but this is another example of an intractable problem and hence exact analysis is not possible.

Although much of the description of the three methods has assumed only two criticality levels, all three methods can be extended to more levels. The task model can also be extended to include blocking terms, release jitter etc. Versions of EDF scheduling that are criticality-aware also exist, as do schemes in which the T parameter as well as the C estimate is dependent on the required integrity of the task. Multiprocessor mixed criticality issues have also been addressed, but these are beyond the scope of this book. However single criticality (i.e the normal model) systems running on multiprocessor hardware is addressed and is the topic of the second part of this chapter.

8.2 Multiprocessor systems

As indicated in the introduction to this chapter, multiprocessor platforms are beginning to be common-place for many real-time embedded systems. Unfortunately, if tasks can migrate at run-time — which is called global scheduling, global dispatching or global placement — many of the results that have been derived for single processor systems are not applicable. For example, uniprocessor optimal schemes such as EDF and LLF (Least Laxity First) are no longer optimal once task migration can take place (this is illustrated in the next section). Moreover, RTA (Response-Time Analysis) is not easily applied to globally scheduled task set. This is due to a lack of a precise statement of where the critical instant is for an arbitrary set of tasks; it is not when all tasks are released at the same time as it is for the single processor case. In addition, the worst-case for a set of sporadic tasks may not be when they arrive at their maximum rate, which again makes it difficult to undertake exact analysis. Given these difficulties, RTA aims at providing only sufficient analysis, but even then there are further problems. The best analysis does not have an optimal priority assignment scheme; Audsley's algorithm is available, but only for inferior forms of analysis.

8.3 Partitioned and global placement

The first new issue that must be addressed with a multiprocessor platform is placement. This is the mapping of tasks to processors. Two fundamental schemes are possible: **global** and **partitioned**. As the names imply, a partitioned scheme is a pre run-time allocation; the dynamic global alternative allocates tasks as they become runnable, and even during execution a task may move from one processor to another. Both placement schemes have their advantages and disadvantages. The partitioned approach has the benefit of not requiring any run-time support and of being able to cater for certain types of systems that the global scheme has difficulty with. Consider a simple 3 task system that is to be implemented on two identical processors (see Table 8.5).

The total utilization of the system is 1.66 so it is capable of being scheduled (as $1.66 < 2$). A simple global placement scheme using either fixed priority or EDF would allocate a and b to the two processors. They would then execute until time 5. Now c can be placed on either processor as they are both free, but there are only 7 units of time left before the deadline at time 12. Hence c will fail to meet its deadline. Indeed as a and b are released again at time 10 then c will only execute for 5 units before its deadline.

The partitioned approach would allocate a and b to one processor (where they will completely utilise its capacity), leaving the other processor to c which can then easily meet

PARTITIONED AND GLOBAL PLACEMENT   139

Task	T	D	C
a	10	10	5
b	10	10	5
c	12	12	8

Table 8.5: Example task set.

its deadline. A different example, however, will show the benefits of the global scheme. Table 8.6 also has a three task / two processor configuration. No partitioned scheme can schedule this system. However a global scheme that starts with d and f for one tick and then executes d and e for the next eight ticks will be able to run f and e for the 10th tick and satisfy all requirements.

Task	T	D	C
d	10	10	9
e	10	10	9
f	10	10	2

Table 8.6: A further example task set.

The only way to fit this example into a partitioned scheme is to split f into two identical length parts. This artificial decomposition of a software model was criticised earlier within the context of cyclic executives and cannot be recommended. However, allowing f to migrate at run-time could enable the essentially partitioned approach to be more effective. This is the essence of the semi-partitioned approach which will be discussed later in this section.

The potential difficulty with global scheduling can be illustrated by an extreme example. Consider the 1001 tasks outlined in Table 8.7. Here the platform has 1000 processors, with the total utilization of the task set being under 2. And yet with either EDF or fixed priority scheduling with Deadline Monotonic Priority Assignment this task set is unschedulable.

Task	T	D	C
1-1000	1000	1000	1
1001	1002	1001	1001

Table 8.7: Extreme example.

This extreme behaviour, where a task set with relatively minuscule utilization is unschedulable, is known as the *Dhall effect* after the person who first illustrated it, in 1978 [30]. For many years this led to the view that global scheduling is never a useful approach to deploy. However, more recently it has been realised that what the Dhall effect is really demonstrating is that EDF and Deadline Monotonic Priority Ordering are poor approaches for global scheduling not that global scheduling itself is ineffective.

The challenge for the global scheme is to identify the optimal scheduling policy.

140   MIXED CRITICALITY, MULTIPROCESSOR AND OPEN SYSTEMS

For a single processor, EDF and LLF are optimal, but no optimal scheme is known for general task models executing on multiprocessor platforms. Not only are there no optimal schemes available, but what policies are available tend not to be sustainable – a schedulable system may become unschedulable if, for example, an extra processor is added. For these reasons, most current systems use a partitioned approach, which also has the advantage, as noted earlier, of run-time efficiency. Nevertheless for the future, global schemes have the potential to deliver better schedulability.

The main challenge for the partitioned approach is to generate a valid allocation. Once an allocation has been formed, it is straightforward to analyse each processor in turn using the analysis already available for single processors. Each processor can be scheduled via fixed priorities or EDF — it would even be possible to mix the schemes with EDF on some processors and fixed priorities on others. An allocation must not 'overfill' any processor and, hence, task mapping is similar to the classic bin-packing problem. Optimal schemes for large numbers of tasks and processors are, therefore, not possible — heuristics must be employed (see below).

Notwithstanding the lack of maturity in this area, it is possible to report some useful results. It was noted earlier in this book that single processor analysis started from a simple task model (in particular, tasks are independent and periodic, and have deadline equal to period). For uniprocessors, the model has been generalised significantly. But for multiprocessor scheduling, useful results are only really known for the simple task model. Here a number of such utilization-based results are stated.

(1) There is a global scheduling algorithm called *pfair* that is able to schedule any periodic system with utilization $\leq M$ on M identical processors [12]. However, schedules generated by the pfair algorithm tend to have a large number of preemptions, and tasks are frequently required to move from one processor to another.

(2) For FP scheduling with partitioned placement, the following utilization-based sufficient schedulability test has been derived for a first-fit (using decreasing task utilization) placement strategy [62]:

$$U \leq M(\sqrt{2} - 1) \tag{8.3}$$

(3) A sufficient utilization-based schedulability test is also known for EDF with partitioned first-fit placement. Let U_{max} denote the largest utilization of any task in the system: $U_{max} = \max_{i=1}^{N}\left(\frac{C_i}{T_i}\right)$. Letting β denote $\lfloor 1/U_{max} \rfloor$, this test is as follows [60]:

$$U \leq \frac{\beta M + 1}{\beta + 1} \tag{8.4}$$

(4) A sufficient schedulability test is known for global EDF [39], that depends only upon the utilization of the task system and U_{max}.

$$U \leq M - (M-1)U_{max} \tag{8.5}$$

(5) A variant of EDF with global placement, called fpEDF, has been proposed [11] that

(a) assigns greatest (fixed) priority to tasks with utilization $> \frac{1}{2}$ (if there are any such tasks), and

(b) schedules the remaining tasks according to EDF.

A couple of schedulability tests have been derived for fpEDF. One uses the utilization of the task system:

$$U \leq \left(\frac{M+1}{2}\right) \qquad (8.6)$$

Another, superior, test for fpEDF uses both the utilization of the system and the largest utilization of any task in the system:

$$U \leq \max\left[M - (M-1)U_{max}, \frac{M}{2} + U_{max}\right] \qquad (8.7)$$

(6) For fixed priority global scheduling, a priority assignment scheme called TkC has been shown to be effective for implicit deadline tasks and DkC for constrained deadline tasks. Here the priorities are related to period/deadline *and* computation time. So priorities are ordered according to $T - kC$ (or $D - kC$) where k is defined by

$$k = \frac{M - 1 + \sqrt{5M^2 - 6M + 1}}{2M} \qquad (8.8)$$

(7) A combination of LLF and EDF is used with the EDZL scheme; here tasks execute according to EDF until they have zero laxity, they then execute to completion. For constrained tasks with large M, the utilization bound is given as $U \leq 0.63M$.

A direct comparison between all these bounds would be misleading as the bounds are only sufficient. Tighter bounds are possible, indeed a number have been proposed in the literature for some of the above schemes. However, to illustrate the results that these tests produce, a couple of scenarios are defined and the tests applied. Case I has 10 processors ($M = 10$) with the highest utilization task having a capacity of 0.1. Case II has $M = 4$ and $U_{max} = 2/3$. Table 8.8 gives the maximum utilization that is guaranteed to lead to a schedulable system for each of the scheduling schemes. To compute the average 'per-processor' utilization these values need to be divided by M (which is 10 in the first scenario and 4 in the other).

Scheme	Case I	Case II
Partitioned FP (Eqn 8.3)	4.14	1.66
Partitioned EDF (Eqn 8.4)	9.18	2.50
Global EDF (Eqn 8.5)	9.10	2.00
fpEDF (Eqn 8.7)	9.10	2.67

Table 8.8: Utilization bounds.

For partitioned scheduling the usual heuristics for bin packing can be applied, so First Fit (FF), Best Fit (BF) and Worst Fit (WF). Of course, in the worst case, a set of M tasks each with a utilization of $0.5 + \Delta$ need M processors for arbitrary small Δ. However for lower utilization tasks there are some effective heuristics. For example with FF largest utilization first there are bounds of 0.63 for Rate Monotonic FPS and 0.82 for EDF.

As large tasks cause problems for the partitioned approach it is possible to employ a compromise between fully global and fully partitioned. In this **semi-partitioned** approach, most tasks are partitioned but a small number are split, with an initial part of the task executing on one processor and the final part executing on another.

Both FP and EDF schemes are possible. Typically $M-1$ tasks are split and therefore migrate from one processor to another at run-time. Consider a typical task defined by the usual parameters T, D and C. On its first processor it is given the highest priority (or shortest deadline) and is given a budget of C^* (with $C^* < C$). After executing for C^* the task migrates to a (statically defined) second processor where it must execute for $C - C^*$ with a new relative deadline of $D - C^*$. On completion the task returns to it original processor for its next release. The semi-partitioned scheme produces better schedulability than either the fully global or fully partitioned approaches.

Another approach which falls between the fully partitioned and global placement is **cluster-based** placement. With this approach, processors are split into clusters and tasks are assigned to clusters. Within a cluster tasks can migrate but not across clusters.

8.4 Scheduling the network

The next issue to consider is the communications infrastructure that links the different processors. For bus-based tightly coupled multiprocessors, the behaviour of multi-level caches makes worst-case execution time analysis even harder for these platforms. Heterogeneous processors and hierarchical multi-speed memories also adds significantly to these difficulties. With network based connections, the messages must themselves be scheduled if end-to-end data flows through the system are to be guaranteed. There are many different network protocols with some being more amenable to timing analysis than others. It is beyond the scope of this book to discuss these different protocols in detail, but three specific schemes are worth noting:

TDMA – here each processor is allocated a fixed time slot within a specified cycle during which tasks hosted on that processor can send messages.

CAN – here each message is given a fixed priority and the network supports priority-based arbitration.

Wormhole Routing – used on multi-core chips to supported managed communication between cores.

With TDMA, which is only really applicable to periodic tasks and static task allocation, no two processors ever wish to send messages at the same time. With CAN, competition can occur but priorities are used to order the messages. Being priority-based, standard response-time analysis is directly applicable to scheduling CAN. As a message cannot be preempted once it has started to be transmitted, the non-preemptive form of the analysis is the one employed with CAN (see Section 7.3). Where the parameter C is now the time needed to transmit the message.

The use of a network within a system opens up a number of issues as well as message scheduling. Unless the hardware architecture is fully connected, routing needs to be addressed. Static and dynamic route-finding are possible. Fault tolerance over message corruption is normally dealt with by the transmission protocol, but extra messages and perhaps alternative routes may be employed and these must be accommodated into the scheduling analysis.

On a multicore processor, shared busses are difficult to analyse and they do not scale to the large number of core that are currently being produced (or at least planned). A Network-on-Chip (NoC) is a simplified network that links each core. Messages are not subject to outside interference and hence corruption is not an issue (or is at the same level of likelihood as failures of the cores). Also, routing is usually statically predetermined with simple schemes such as X-Y routing being employed – here cores are given an address according to their position on the chip (e.g. 3,4). A message going, say, from (3,4) to (1,7) first travels along links and routers associated with cores (2,4) and (1,4) then it travels via the links and routers (1,5) and (1,6) to arrive at its destination (1, 7). Schemes such as X-Y routing have the additional benefit of being deadlock free.

There are a number of ways of passing messages through a NoC. The wormhole routing scheme uses a small buffer at each router. The message header has the address of the message's destination and it moves like a worm from source to this destination. Each message is said to be composed of a sequence of **flits**. So, for example, a message of length 20 flits moving from (3,4) to (1,7) would, when the header has reached (1.7), have a flit in (1,6), a flit in (1,5), a flit in (1,4), a flit in (2,4) and 15 further flits ready to move from (3,4).

With wormhole routing, each link can only pass one message at a time; it is in effect non-preemptive. But it is possible to map a number of **virtual links** onto one real link. Now, at each router, a choice can be made as to which virtual link to service. As a result, preemptive priority-based message passing can be supported. Hence, response-time analysis, using the form with release jitter (see Section 7.1), can be applied to wormhole routing.

8.5 Mutual exclusion on multiprocessor platforms

The final issue to address in this short review of the major problems involved in scheduling multiprocessor platforms is the provision of mutual exclusion over shared objects. In networked systems, these objects are typically controlled by a single thread so there are no new problems to solve, but for shared memory systems there is now the need to provide protection from true parallel access. The priority inheritance and priority ceiling protocols no longer work as they depend on an executing high priority task preventing a lower priority task from executing. This clearly will not occur if the lower priority task in on another processor. There are no simple equivalent protocols to those for single processors.

To implement mutual exclusion, in a multiprocessor shared memory system, usually requires locks that can be contended for globally. When a task holds such a lock it is usual to prevent it from being preempted locally (as this would further delay tasks on other processors waiting for the lock). When a lock is requested but not granted, the task will typically busy wait on the lock, waiting for it to become free – this is known as **spinning**. Obviously this spinning time will add to the task's execution time and, hence, has to be bounded if the task's interference on lower priority tasks is to be calculated. A system with many globally shared objects and nested usage patterns (i.e., accessing one object whilst holding the lock on others) will be harder to analyse and the analysis itself is likely to be pessimistic. Also error conditions such as deadlocks and livelocks are now possible whereas they were prevented by some of the single processor protocols.

Because of these difficulties with global locks, the use of lock-free algorithms are attractive. Here multiple copies of the shared object are supported and if necessary actions are repeated if conflicts over the copies have occurred. To give a simple example, consider an object that is read by many tasks but updated by only one. While the update is happening, all reads are made from an old copy of the object. Once the update is finished, a single flag is set to make the new copy available to future read operations. If the timing constraints on the system allow concurrent reads and writes then it must be acceptable for the read operation to get the old value – if it had arrived any earlier (or the writing task any later) then the old copy would have been the 'current' one.

Overall, multiprocessor systems whilst providing more computational power introduce a number of challenges for real-time systems. To move from scheduling a single resource to the coordination of multi-resources is a major one that requires a holistic approach to system scheduling. But the core of this approach will always be the management of each individual resource.

8.6 Open systems

The final topic to be addressed in this review of scheduling theory for real-time systems is open systems and its need for online analysis. All models so far employed have assumed the existence of a statically defined set of tasks that must be analysed before the system goes live to prove/demonstrate that all deadlines will be met once the system is indeed deployed. To undertake such analysis requires:

- arrival patterns of incoming work to be known and bounded (this leads to a fixed set of tasks with known periods or worst-case arrival intervals);
- bounded computation times; and
- a scheduling scheme that leads to predictable execution of the application tasks.

The chapters within Part II of this book has shown how fixed-priority scheduling (and to a certain extent, EDF) can provide a predictable execution environment.

With more general purpose platforms, there is an increasing need for systems to be open to new applications; to accept new tasks at run-time in a way that will not undermine the guarantees that have already been given to the currently running software. So a new application can always be rejected, but if it is accepted onto the platform then its tasks and the tasks of the remaining applications must be schedulable (or at least be terminated in a controlled way).

As open systems try to get the most from the available hardware (as future needs are not well defined), EDF is perhaps the best run-time algorithm to use for single processor (or partitioned multiprocessor) systems. But if the system becomes overloaded then EDF performs very badly. It is possible to get a cascade effect in which each task misses its deadline but uses sufficient resources to result in the next task also missing its deadline. To prevent this happening an online scheme has two mechanisms:

- an admissions control module that limits the number of tasks that are allowed to compete for the processors, and
- an EDF dispatching routine for those tasks that are admitted.

An ideal admissions algorithm prevents the processors getting overloaded so that the EDF routine works effectively.

Admission control can work at the level of the job or on a multi-tasking application. If at the level of the job then each time the task is released for execution it must pass the control test. This is clearly going to have significant overheads (see discussion below on best-effort scheduling). Alternatively, the open system only changes its behaviour when new applications arrive (or terminate). Now admission control must decide if the complete set of tasks associated with a newly arrived applications are to be admitted or not. If they are admitted then they execute as required (with no further test) until the application terminates (or is aborted due to the arrival of more important applications).

The admission algorithm must itself of course be efficient as it uses the same processing resource that the applications do. There is no point in running an exhaustive exact schedulability test if the advantage of the exact test is totally undermined by how long it took to deliberate on its decision. Rather, inexact but quick routines are needed. So although it is possible to undertake very fast Response-Time Analysis, utilization-based schemes may perform better overall.

If some applications are to be accepted while others are rejected then there must be some criteria for making this decision. Criticality is one much measure, but it would be expected that all critical software is statically guaranteed. Open systems are more concerned with non-critical, but still at least soft real-time task sets. To articulate the relative importance of a set of applications, the notion of **value** is employed. All applications are of the same level of criticality but have different values. As an ordinal scale, value can be classified as:

Static : the task always has the same value whenever it is released, or

Dynamic : the task's value can only be computed at the time the task is released (because it is dependent on either environmental factors or the current state of the system), or

Adaptive : here the dynamic nature of the system is such that the value of the task may change during its execution.

To assign static values (or to construct the algorithm and define the input parameters for the dynamic or adaptive schemes) requires the domain specialists to articulate their understanding of the desirable behaviour of the system. As with other areas of computing, knowledge elicitation is not without its problems. But these issues will not be considered here (see Burns et al. [23]).

An ordinal scale is capable of recording if application A is more important than application B; but it is insufficiently rich to ask questions such as 'is application A *and* application B more important that application C'. And to get the most from a value-based approach to scheduling, it must be possible to abort 'accepted' applications in order to make room for a new application of higher value.

One of the fundamental problems with online analysis is the trade-off that has to be made between the quality of the scheduling decision and the resources and time needed to make the decision. At one extreme, every time a new task arrives, the complete set of tasks could be subject to an exact test such as those described in this part of the book. If the task set is not schedulable, the lowest value task is dropped and the test repeated (until a schedulable set is obtained). This approach (which is known as **best-effort**) is optimal for static or dynamic value assignment – *but only if the overheads of the tests are ignored*. Once the overheads are factored in, the effectiveness of the approach is seriously compromised. In general, heuristics have to be used for online scheduling and it is unlikely that any single approach will work for all applications. This is still an active research area. It is clear, however, that what is required is not a single policy defined in a language or OS standard, but mechanisms from which applications can program their own schemes to meet their particular requirements.

The final topic to consider in this section is **hybrid systems** that contain both hard and dynamic components. It is likely that these will become the norm in many application areas. Even in essentially static systems, value-added computations, in the form of soft or firm tasks that improve the quality of the hard tasks, are an attractive way of structuring systems. In these circumstances, as was noted in Section 5.2.1, the hard tasks must be protected from any overload induced by the behaviour of the non-hard tasks. One way of achieving this is to use fixed priority scheduling for the hard tasks and execution-time servers for the remaining work. The servers can be executed at a given priority level, but can embody whatever admissions policy is desirable and service the incoming dynamic work using EDF.

Summary

In this chapter the final three scheduling topics have been covered. The newest area of research and deployment concerns mixed criticality. Here software components of different criticality are hosted on the same hardware platform. The behaviour of the lower critical tasks must not be able to induce failures in the higher critical tasks. And if there are insufficient resources, graceful degradation must ensure that the high critical tasks continue to meet their timing (and functional) requirements.

But the topic of mixed criticality is more than just multiple criticality. By recognising that key system parameters, such as estimates of the worst-case execution time of tasks, are criticality dependent it is possible to improve the schedulability of systems beyond what would be possible with just pure separation between tasks. This chapter has outlines some of the new fixed priority scheduling schemes that have been developed for mixed criticality systems. Although EDF-based scheduling was not addressed in this chapter, there are EDF-specific protocols that also deal with mixed criticality.

The second topic to be covered is multiprocessor scheduling as most hardware platforms are now at least dual core; and in the future highly parallel devices will become commonplace. The key new problem to address with multiprocessor systems is allocation (of tasks to processor/core and messages to busses or networks). Global and partitioned schemes have been described with the advantages and disadvantages of each illustrated by simple examples. Dhall's effect was also illustrated. The benefits of a semi-partitioned approach were outlined. Whilst global scheduling may in the future prove to be the best approach, current understanding and evidence from real systems implies that partitioned is the preferred scheme for today's real-time systems. And where partitioning fails, due to some large tasks, then the splitting of just a few tasks may be sufficient to deliver schedulability.

In addition to allocation, resource sharing be that objects in shared memory or communication media must also be managed appropriately if predictable behaviour is to be guaranteed. Issues concerned with these topics have also been covered in this chapter.

The third topic addressed was open systems which allow new task sets to be added to an existing executing system (and, of course, it allows existing task sets to naturally terminate or be aborted if more important work must be undertaken). To control the workload within a system an efficient admission control algorithm is needed that will ensure that the run-time scheduler is never overloaded. To accomplish this, it must be possible to reject some new applications and possibly to abort previously admitted ones. To control these decision some notion of important or value is needed. An overview of a value-based decision process was outlined.

To conclude this part of the book, the basic task model introduced in Chapter 4 will be revisited. It represented the set of restrictions needed in order to undertake simple scheduling analysis. The development of scheduling theory, as outlined in the descriptions given in this book, has allowed a much richer task model to be supported. This model can now support a wide range of application needs and can incorporate necessary practical issues. To summarise, the original model is repeated below with the advances *highlighted in italics*:

- The application is assumed to consist of a fixed set of tasks. *Offline static analysis will always need the set of tasks to be fixed and known prior to the system executing. However, online tests can deal with more open systems.*
- All tasks are periodic, with known periods. *Tasks can now be periodic, sporadic or aperiodic.*
- All tasks are completely independent of each other. *Tasks can now share data as long as it is protected by some appropriate protocol such as the immediate ceiling priority protocol.*
- All system's overheads, context-switching times and so on are ignored (that is, assumed to have zero cost). *Overheads can now be represented in the scheduling equations.*
- All tasks have deadlines equal to their periods (that is, each task must com-

plete before it is next released, its deadline is implicit). *Deadlines can now be less than, equal or greater then period.*
- All tasks have fixed worst-case execution times and execute preemptively. *Non-preemptive (and cooperative) execution is now possible, but estimates of worst-case execution time (WCET) are required for scheduling analysis to be undertaken, although for mixed criticality systems there may be more than one estimate of WCET. In addition, but not covered in this book, probabilistic estimates of WCET have been developed that aim to deal with the inherent uncertainty with these values.*
- No task contains any internal suspension points (e.g. an internal delay statement or a blocking I/O request). *This remains true, tasks that self-suspend present great difficulty for scheduling analysis.*
- All tasks execute on a single processor (CPU). *Multiprocessor executions are now open to analysis, both partitioned and global scheduling are supported.*
- All tasks are of equal value/importance/criticality. *Mixed criticality systems can now be analysed. And value can be used to control access to open systems.*

Part III

DEVELOPING REAL-TIME SYSTEMS IN ADA

Chapter 9
The Ada programming language

9.1 Languages for programming real-time systems
9.2 An introduction to Ada
9.3 Overview of Ada
9.4 Programming in the large
9.5 Aspects and attributes
Summary

Chapters 4 - 8 have presented the underlying scheduling theory upon which modern real-time systems are based. In order to produce analysable systems, designers must write programs that conform to the model outlined in Sections 2.4 and 3.8. Most programming languages are considered to be Turing-complete; this means that they are essentially equivalent in their ability to express solutions to computable problems. In practice, however, different languages are targeted at one or more different application domains, and provide programming abstractions that directly address common attributes of their associated domains. This makes the programmers' task of writing applications easier and leads to the construction of more reliable programs. Even in a "model-driven" development approach with automatic code generation, generating code in domain-specific languages facilitates more efficient and reliable code.

This chapters first reviews the programming languages that have been used in the real-time domain. The trend has been towards concurrent programming languages (such as Ada and Java), although sequential languages supported by a real-time operating systems are still important.

The focus of this book is the Ada programming language, which has concurrency supported directly through language syntax and predefined library packages. The language also provides facilities to supports real-time programming. Section 9.2 gives a brief introduction to Ada for those who have a good understanding of programming in languages like C++, C# and Java but perhaps lack direct Ada experience.

9.1 Languages for programming real-time systems

The development of implementation languages for real-time systems is a central theme of this book. Language design is still a very active research area. It is possible to identify three classes of programming languages which are, or have been, used in the development of real-time systems. These are assembly languages, sequential systems implementation languages and high-level concurrent languages. These types of languages will shortly be reviewed, but first some general language design criteria will be introduced.

9.1.1 General language design criteria

Although a real-time language may be designed primarily to meet the requirements of embedded computer system programming, its use is rarely limited to that area. Most real-time languages are also used as general-purpose systems implementation languages for applications such as compilers and operating systems.

There are several (sometimes conflicting) criteria for the basis of a real-time language design: security, readability, flexibility, simplicity, portability and efficiency. A similar list also appears in the original requirements for Ada.

Security

The security of a language design is a measure of the extent to which programming errors can be detected automatically by the compiler or language run-time support system. There is obviously a limit to the type and number of errors that can be detected by a language system; for example, errors in the programmer's logic cannot be detected automatically. A secure language must, therefore, be well structured and readable so that such errors can easily be spotted. The benefits of security include:

- the detection of errors much earlier in the development of a program – generating an overall reduction in cost;
- compile-time checks have no overheads at run-time – a program is executed much more often than it is compiled.

The disadvantage of security is that it may result in a more complicated language with an increase in compilation time and compiler complexity.

Readability

The readability of a language depends on a variety of factors including the appropriate choice of keywords, the ability to define types and the facilities for program modularization. The aim is to provide a language notation with sufficient clarity to enable the program to be understood by reading the program's text only, without resort to subsidiary flowcharts and written descriptions.

The benefits of good readability include:

- reduced documentation costs,
- increased security,
- increased maintainability.

The main disadvantage is that it usually increases the length of any given program.

Flexibility

A language must be sufficiently flexible to allow the programmer to express all the required operations in a straightforward and coherent fashion. Otherwise, as with older sequential languages, the programmer will often have to resort to operating system commands or machine code inserts to achieve the desired result.

Simplicity

Simplicity is a worthwhile aim of any design, be it of the international space station or a simple calculator. In programming languages, simplicity has the advantages of:

- minimizing the effort required to produce compilers,
- reducing the cost associated with programmer training,
- diminishing the possibility of making programming errors as a result of misinterpretation of the language features.

Flexibility and simplicity can also be related to the **expressive power** (the ability to express the solutions to a wide range of problems) and **usability** (ease of use) of the language.

Portability

A program, to a certain extent, should be independent of the hardware on which it executes. One of the main claims of Java is that programs are compiled once and run anywhere. For a real-time system, this is difficult to achieve (even with the advent of portable binary codes, such as Java Byte Code and the C# Common Intermediate Language) as a substantial part of any program will normally involve manipulation of hardware resources. However, a language must be capable of isolating the *machine-dependent* part of a program from the *machine-independent* part.

Efficiency

In a real-time system, response times must be guaranteed; therefore the language must allow efficient and predictable programs to be produced. Mechanisms which lead to unpredictable run-time overheads should be avoided. Obviously, efficiency requirements must be balanced against security, flexibility and readability requirements.

9.1.2 Assembly Languages

Initially, most real-time systems were programmed in the assembly language of the embedded computer. This was mainly because high-level programming languages were not well supported on most microcomputers and assembly language programming appeared to be the only way of achieving efficient implementations that could access hardware resources.

The main problem with the use of assembly languages is that they are machine-orientated rather than problem-orientated. The programmer can become encumbered with details which are unrelated to the algorithms being programmed, with the result that the algorithms themselves become obscure. This keeps development costs high and makes it very difficult to modify programs when errors are found or enhancements required.

Further difficulties arise because programs cannot be moved from one machine to another but must be rewritten. Also staff must be retrained if they are required to work with other machines.

9.1.3 Sequential systems implementation languages

As computers became more powerful, programming languages more mature, and compiler technology progressed, the advantages of writing real-time software in a high-level language outweighed the disadvantages. To cope with deficiencies in languages like FORTRAN, new languages were developed specifically for embedded programming. In the United States Air Force, for example, Jovial was in common use. In the UK, the Ministry of Defence standardised on Coral 66, and large industrial concerns like ICI standardised on RTL/2. Currently, the C and C++ programming languages are popular[1].

All these languages have one thing in common – they are sequential. They also tend to be weak in the facilities they provide for real-time control and reliability. As a result of these shortcomings, it is often necessary to rely on operating system support and assembly code inserts.

9.1.4 High-level concurrent programming languages

In spite of the increasing use of application-tailored languages, the production of computer software became progressively more difficult during the 1970s as computer-based systems became larger and more sophisticated. These problems grew to what became known as the *software crisis*. There are several symptoms of this crisis which have been recognised; unfortunately, many of these still occur with current large development projects:

- responsiveness – production systems which have been automated often do not meet users' needs;
- reliability – software is unreliable and will often fail to perform to its specification;
- cost – software costs are seldom predictable;
- modifiability – software maintenance is complex, costly and error prone;

---

[1] Although note that the most recent versions of these two languages now support concurrency.

- timeliness – software is often delivered late;
- transportability – software in one system is seldom used in another;
- efficiency – software development efforts do not make optimal use of the resources involved.

Perhaps one of the best illustrations of the impact of the software crisis can be found in the American Department of Defense's (DoD) search for a common high-order programming language for all its applications. As hardware prices began to fall during the 1970s, the DoD's attention was focused on the rising cost of its embedded software. It estimated that, in 1973, three thousand million dollars were spent on software alone. A survey of programming languages showed that at least 450 general-purpose programming languages and incompatible dialects were used in DoD embedded computer applications. An evaluation of existing languages occurred in 1976 against an emerging set of requirements. These evaluations resulted in four main conclusions:

(1) no current language was suitable,
(2) a single language was a desirable goal,
(3) the state-of-the-art of language design could meet the requirements,
(4) development should start from a suitable language base; those recommended were Pascal, PL/I and Algol 68.

The result was the birth of a new language in 1983 called Ada. In 1995, the language was updated to reflect 10 years of use and modern advances in programming language design. The same occurred in 2005, 2012 and 2015 when a number of key features were added to Ada.

Other older languages of note include PEARL, used extensively in Germany for process control applications, Mesa [81], used by Xerox in their office automation equipment, and CHILL [27] which was developed in response to CCITT requirements for programming telecommunication applications.

With the advent of the Internet, the Java programming language has become popular. Although initially not suitable for real-time programming, recently much effort has been dedicated to producing a real-time versions of Java called the Real-Time Specification for Java (RTSJ).

9.2 An introduction to Ada

Designing, implementing and maintaining software for large systems is a non-trivial exercise and one which is fraught with difficulties. These difficulties relate to the management of the software production process itself, as well as to the size and complexity of the software components. Ada is a mature general-purpose programming language that has been designed to address the needs of large-scale system development, especially in the embedded systems domain. A major aspect of the language is its support for concurrent and real-time programming.

156   THE ADA PROGRAMMING LANGUAGE

Ada has evolved over the last forty years from an object-based concurrent programming language into a flexible concurrent and distributed object-oriented language that is well suited for high-reliability, long-lived applications. It has been particularly successful in high-integrity areas such as air traffic control, space systems, railway signalling, and both the civil and military avionics domains. Ada success is due to a number of factors including the following.

- Hierarchical libraries and other facilities that support large-scale software development.
- Strong compile-time type checking.
- Safe object-oriented programming facilities.
- Language-level support for concurrent programming.
- A coherent approach to real-time systems development.
- High-performance implementations.
- Well-defined subsetting mechanisms, and in particular the SPARK and Ravenscar subsets for formal verification.

The development and standardisation of Ada have progressed through a number of definitions, the main ones being Ada 83, Ada 95, Ada 2005, Ada 2012 and Ada 2015. Ada attempts, successfully, to have the safety and portability of Java and the efficiency and flexibility of C/C++. It also has the advantage of being an international standard with clear well-defined semantics.

The reference manual for Ada (ARM) differentiates between the 'core' language and a number of annexes. Annexes do not add to the syntax of the language but give extra facilities and properties, typically by the introduction of language-defined library packages. For the focus of this book, the key elements of the reference manual are Chapter 9 which deals with tasking and the Real-Time Systems Annex (Annex D). In terms of presentation, this book does not draw a distinction between the core language and the annex-defined facilities. All are part of the Ada language.

9.3 Overview of Ada

In considering the features of high-level languages, it is useful to distinguish between those that aid the decomposition process and those that facilitate the programming of well-defined components. These two sets of features have been described as:

- support for programming in the large,
- support for programming in the small.

Programming in the small is a well-understood activity and will be discussed in this section. Section 9.4 is concerned with programming in the large and will address the more problematic issue of managing complex systems.

The overview presented here will itself assume some knowledge of programming, in a language like C or Java. Sufficient detail will be given to understand the example programs given later in the book. For a comprehensive introduction of the Ada, the reader must refer to books that provide a specialise introduction.

9.3.1 Lexical conventions

Programs are written once but read many times; it follows that the lexical style of the language syntax should appeal to the reader rather than the writer. One simple aid to readability is to use names that are meaningful. The form of a name can also be improved by the use of a separator. Ada allows a '_' to be included in identifiers. The following is an example identifier in Ada.

```
Example_Name_In_Ada
```

9.3.2 Overall style

Ada is a block structured language. A block consists of

(1) the declaration of objects that are local to that block (if there are no such objects then this declaration part may be omitted),

(2) a sequence of statements, and

(3) a collection of exception handlers (again this part may be omitted if empty).

A schema for such a block is:

```
declare
  <declarative part>
begin
  <sequence of statements>
exception
  <exception handlers>
end;
```

Exception handlers catch errors that have occurred in the block. They are considered in detail in Chapter 17.

An Ada block may be placed in the program wherever an ordinary statement may be written. They can thus be used hierarchically and support decomposition within a program unit. The following simple example illustrates how a new integer variable `Temp` is introduced to swap the values contained by the two integers A and B. Note, with Ada the variable name is given first followed by a colon followed by the type. This is in contrast to languages like C and Java, where the type name is given first and there is no colon. Note also that a comment in Ada starts with the double hyphen and goes on to the end of that line.

158   THE ADA PROGRAMMING LANGUAGE

```
declare
  Temp : Integer := A;   -- initial value given to
                         -- temporary variable
begin
  A := B;                -- := is the assignment operator
  B := Temp;
end;                     -- no exception part
```

9.3.3 Data types

In common with all high-level languages, Ada requires programs to manipulate objects that have been abstracted away from their actual hardware implementation. Programmers need not concern themselves about the representation or location of the entities that their programs manipulate. Moreover, by partitioning these entities into distinct types, the compiler can check for inconsistent usage, and thereby increase the security associated with using the language.

Ada allows the declaration of constants, types, variables, subprograms (procedures and functions) and packages. Subprograms are considered later in this section and packages are described in Section 9.4. The use of constants, types and variables is similar to that of most languages, except that they may occur in any order, provided that an object is declared before it is referenced.

Discrete types

Table 9.1 lists the predefined discrete types supported by Ada.

Integer
Short_Integer
Long_Integer
Boolean
Character
Wide_Character
Wide_Wide_Character

Table 9.1: Discrete types in Ada.

Ada is strongly typed (that is, assignments and expressions must involve objects of the same type), but explicit type conversions are supported.

Ada also allows the basic integer types to be signed or unsigned. The default is signed, but unsigned (or modular) types can be created. Although not required by the language, an Ada implementation may support Short_Integer and Long_Integer.

In addition to these predefined types, Ada allows for the definition of enumeration types. The following examples illustrate these points.

```
type Dimension is (Xplane,Yplane,Zplane);
type Map is (Xplane,Yplane);
Line,Force : Dimension;
Grid : Map;
begin
  Line := Xplane;
  Force := Dimension'Succ(Xplane);
  -- Force now has the value Yplane irrespective of the
  -- implementation technique

  Grid := Yplane;  -- the name 'Yplane' is unambiguous as
                   -- Grid is of type 'map'
  Grid := Line;  -- illegal - type clash
end;
```

Another facility that Ada supports is the use of subranges or subtypes to restrict the values of an object (of a particular base type). This allows for a closer association between objects in the program and the values, in the application domain, that could sensibly be taken by that object.

```
subtype Surface is Dimension range Xplane .. Yplane;
```

Note that Ada has predefined subtypes for positive and natural integers.

Importantly in Ada all types can be duplicated by defining a type to be a new version of a previous type:

```
type New_Int is new Integer;
type Projection is new Dimension range Xplane .. Yplane;
```

Whereas in Ada objects of a type and its subtypes can be mixed (in expressions), objects of a type and a derived type cannot. The two types are distinct:

```
declare
  D : Dimension;
  S : Surface;
  P : Projection;
begin
  D := S;  -- legal
  S := D;  -- legal but could cause run-time error if
           -- D has the value "Zplane"
  P := D;  -- illegal - type clash
  P := Projection(D); -- legal, explicit type conversion
end;
```

This provision (and its use) significantly increases the security of Ada programs.

Real numbers

Many real-time applications (for example, signal processing, simulation and process control) require numerical computation facilities beyond those provided by integer arithmetic. There is a general need to be able to manipulate *real* numbers, although the sophistication of the arithmetic required varies widely between applications. In essence, there are two distinct ways of representing real values within a high-level language:

(1) floating-point, and
(2) scaled integer.

Floating-point numbers are a finite approximation to real numbers and are applicable to computations in which exact results are not needed. A floating-point number is represented by three values: a mantissa, M, an exponent, E, and a radix, R. It has a value of the form $M \times R^E$. The radix is (implicitly) implementation-defined and usually has the value 2. As the mantissa is limited in length, the representation has limited precision. The divergence between a floating-point number and its corresponding 'real' value is related to the size of the number (it is said to have **relative error**).

The use of scaled integers is intended for exact numeric computation. A scaled integer is a product of an integer and a scale. With the appropriate choice of scale, any value can be catered for. Scaled integers offer an alternative to floating-point numbers when non-integer calculations are required. The scale, however, must be known at compile time; if the scale of a value is not available until execution, a floating-point representation must be used. Although scaled integers provide exact values, not all numbers in the mathematical domain can be represented exactly. For example, 1/3 cannot be viewed as a finite scaled decimal integer. The difference between a scaled integer and its 'real' value is its **absolute error**.

Scaled integers have the advantage (over floating-point) of dealing with exact numerical values and of making use of integer arithmetic. Floating-point operations require either special hardware (a floating-point unit) or complex software that will result in numerical operations being many times slower than the integer equivalent. Scaled integers are, however, more difficult to use, especially if expressions need to be evaluated that contain values with different scales.

Traditionally, languages have supported a single floating-point type (usually known as **real**) which has an implementation-dependent precision. Use of scaled integers has normally been left to the user (that is, the programmer had to implement scaled integer arithmetic using the system-defined integer type).

Ada uses the term Float for an implementation-dependent 'real' type. In addition to the predefined Float type, Ada provides the facilities for users to create both floating-point numbers with different precision and fixed point numbers. Fixed point numbers are implemented as scaled integers. The following are some examples of type definitions. To define a floating-point type requires a lower and upper bound, and a statement of the necessary precision (in decimal):

type New_Float **is digits** 10 **range** -1.0E18..1.0E18

A subtype of this type can restrict the range or the precision:

subtype Crude_Float **is** New_Float **digits** 2;
subtype Pos_New_Float **is** New_Float **range** 0.0..1000.0;

The statement of precision defines the minimum requirement, an implementation may give greater accuracy. If the minimum requirement cannot be accommodated, a compile-time error message is generated.

OVERVIEW OF ADA

Ada's fixed point numbers remove from the programmer the details of implementing the necessary scaled integer operators; these are predefined. To construct a fixed point type requires range information and an absolute error bound called **delta**. For example, the following type definition gives a delta of 0.05 or 1/20:

```
type Scaled_Int is delta 0.05 range -100.00..100.00
```

To represent all these decimal values (–100.00, –99.95, –99.90 ... 99.95, 100.00) requires a specific number of bits. This can easily be calculated. The nearest (but smaller) power of 2 to 1/20 is 1/32, which is 2^{-5}. Thus 5 bits are needed to provide the fraction part. The range –100.00..100.00 is contained within –128..128 which requires 8 bits (including a sign bit). In total, therefore, 13 bits are required:

```
sbbbbbbb.fffff
```

where s is the sign bit, b denotes an integer bit and f denotes a fractional bit. Clearly, this fixed-point type can easily be implemented on a 16 bit architecture.

Note again that although a fixed-point type represents, exactly, a range of binary fractions, not all decimal constants within the correct range will have an exact representation. For instance, decimal 5.1 will be held as 00000101.00011 (binary) or 5.09375 (decimal) in the fixed-point type defined above.

Structured data types

Ada support arrays and records. Arrays first and by example:

```
Max : Const Integer:= 10;
type Reading_T is array(0 .. Max-1) of Float;
Size : Const Integer:= Max - 1;
type Switches_T is array(0 .. Size, 0 .. Size) of Boolean;
Reading : Reading_T;
Switches : Switches_T;
```

Note that Ada uses round brackets for arrays, and that they can have any starting index, and be of any dimension.

The Ada record types are quite straightforward:

```
type Day_T is new Integer range 1 .. 31;
type Month_T is new Integer range 1 .. 12;
type Year_T is new Integer range 1900 .. 2050;
type Date_T is
  record
    Day : Day_T:= 1;
    Month : Month_T:= 1;
    Year : Year_T;
  end record;
```

The example shows how initial values can be given to some (but not necessarily all) fields of a record. The dot notation is used to address individual components and allow record component assignments. Ada also supports complete record assignments using record aggregates (array aggregates are also available):

```
D : Data
begin
  D.Year:= 1989;      -- dot notation
  -- D now has value 1-1-1989 due to
  -- initialization
  D := (3, 1, 1953);   -- complete assignment
  D := (Year => 1974, Day => 4, Month => 7);
     -- complete assignment using name notation
  ...
end;
```

The use of name notation in Ada improves readability and removes the errors that could otherwise be introduced by positional faults; for example, writing (1, 3, 1953) rather than (3, 1, 1953).

Ada also allows a record type to be extended with new fields. This is to facilitate object-oriented programming, which is discussed in Section 9.4.4.

Dynamic data types and pointers

There are many programming situations in which the exact size or organization of a collection of data objects cannot be predicted prior to the program's execution. Even though Ada supports variable length arrays, a flexible and dynamic data structure can only be achieved if a memory allocation facility is provided using reference, rather than direct, naming.

The implementation of dynamic data types represents a considerable overhead to the run-time support system for a language. For this reason, many real-time and embedded programs forbid the use of this facility.

In Ada, the term access type is used to denote a pointer; this is because Ada requires that all references to objects be checked to make sure they are still in existence. Much of this checking is done at compile time.

```
type Node;         -- incomplete declaration
type Ac is access Node;
type Node is
  record
     Value : Integer;
     Next : Ac;
  end record;
V : Integer;
A1 : Ac;
begin
  A1 := new(Node);   -- construct first node
  A1.Value := V;  -- the access variable is de-referenced
                  -- and the component identified
  A1.Next := null;  -- predefined
  ...
end;
```

The above program fragment illustrate the use of a 'new' facility for dynamically allocating an area of memory (from the heap). The Ada 'new' is an operator defined in the language; there is, however, no dispose operator, and no requirement for garbage collection. The language does allows (but does not require) all objects to be automatically collected when their related access type goes out of scope.

However, Ada does provides a generic procedure that removes storage from designated objects. This procedure (called `Unchecked_Deallocation`) does not check to see if there are outstanding references to the object. Hence, its use can undermine the referential integrity of a program.

Ada does not requires a garbage collector to be supported. This omission is not surprising as garbage collectors usually result in heavy and unpredictable overheads in execution time. These overheads may well be unacceptable in some real-time systems (see Section 16.5.1).

Ada allows references to be taken to static object or objects on the stack using the concept of an aliased types. Only aliased types can be referenced and the compiler will check to ensure that the access type and the aliased type have the same scope so that dangling pointers cannot occur at run-time:

```
Object : aliased Some_Type;
  -- aliased to say that it may be
  -- referenced by an access type

type General_Ptr is access all Some_Type;
  -- access all indicates that an access variable of this
  -- type can point to either static or dynamic objects

Gp : General_Ptr := Object'Access;
  -- assigns Object reference to Gp
```

A final form of access type definition allows a read-only restriction to be imposed on the use of accesses:

```
Object1 : aliased Some_Type;
Object2 : aliased constant Some_Type := ...;

type General_Ptr is access constant Some_Type;

Gp1 : General_Ptr := Object1'Access;
  -- Gp1 can now only read the value of Object1

Gp2 : General_Ptr := Object2'Access;
  -- Gp2 is a reference to a constant
```

9.3.4 Control structures

There is now common agreement on the control abstractions needed in a sequential programming language. These abstractions can be grouped together into three categories: sequences, decisions and loops. Each will be considered in turn. The necessary control structures for the concurrent parts of languages will be considered in Chapters 10.

Sequence structures

The sequential execution of statements is the normal activity of a (non-concurrent) programming language. The definition of a block in Ada (see Section 9.3.2) indicates that between 'begin' and 'end' there is a sequence of statements. Execution is required to follow this sequence. If a sequence is, in a particular circumstance, empty, Ada requires the explicit use of the `null` statement:

```
begin
  null;
end;
```

Decision structures

A decision structure provides a choice as to the route that execution takes from some point in a program sequence to a later point in that sequence. The decision as to which route is taken will depend upon the current values of relevant data objects. The important property of a decision control structure is that all routes eventually come back together. With such abstract control structures there is no need to use a `goto` statement, which often leads to programs that are difficult to test, read and maintain. Ada does provide such a statement, but it should be used sparingly.

The most common form of decision structure is the `if` statement. Although the requirements for such a structure are clear, earlier languages, such as Algol-60, suffered from a poor syntactical form which could lead to confusion. In particular, with a nested `if` construct, it was not clear to which `if` a trailing single `else` applied. Ada has a clear unambiguous structures. To illustrate, consider a simple problem; find out if $B/A > 10$ – checking first to make sure that A is not equal to zero. An Ada solution is given below; although the code has the shortcoming that the boolean variable `High` is not assigned a value if $A = 0$, the meaning of the program fragment is clear due to the explicit **end if** token:

```
if A /= 0 then
  if B/A > 10 then
    High := True;
  else
    High := False;
  end if;
end if;
```

Ada also supports two short-circuit control forms **and then** and **or else** which allow more concise expression of the above code.

To give another illustration, consider a multiway branch. The following example finds the number of digits in a positive integer variable `Number`. A maximum of 5 digits is assumed:

```
if Number < 10 then
  Num_Digits := 1;
else
  if Number < 100 then
```

```
    Num_Digits := 2;
  else
    if Number < 1000 then
      Num_Digits := 3;
    else
      if Number < 10000 then
        Num_Digits := 4;
      else
        Num_Digits := 5;
      end if;
    end if;
  end if;
end if;
```

This form, which is quite common, involves nesting on the **else** part and results in a trail of **end if**s at the end. To remove this clumsy structure, Ada provides an **elsif** statement. The above can therefore be written more concisely as:

```
if Number < 10 then
  Num_Digits := 1;
elsif Number < 100 then
  Num_Digits := 2;
elsif Number < 1000 then
  Num_Digits := 3;
elsif Number < 1000 then
  Num_Digits := 4;
else
  Num_Digits := 5;
end if;
```

The above is an example of a multiway branch constructed from a series of binary choices. In general, a multiway decision can be more explicitly stated and efficiently implemented using a **case** structure. To illustrate, consider a character (byte) value 'command' which is used to decide upon four possible actions:

```
case Command is
  when 'A' | 'a'    => Action1;       -- A or a
  when 't'          => Action2;
  when 'e'          => Action3;
  when 'x' .. 'z'   => Action4;       -- x, y or z
  when others       => null;          -- no action
end case;
```

Loop structures

A loop structure allows the programmer to specify that a statement, or collection of statements, is to be executed more than once. There are two distinct forms for constructing such loops:

(1) iteration, and
(2) recursion.

166   THE ADA PROGRAMMING LANGUAGE

The distinctive characteristic of iteration is that each execution of the loop is completed before the next is begun. With a recursive control structure, the first loop is interrupted to begin a second loop, which may be interrupted to begin a third loop and so on. At some point, loop n will be allowed to complete, this will then allow loop $n - 1$ to complete, then loop $n - 2$ and so on, until the first loop has also terminated. Recursion is usually implemented via recursive procedure calls. Attention here is focused on iteration.

Iteration comes in two forms: a loop in which the number of iterations is usually fixed prior to the execution of the loop construct; and a loop in which a test for completion is made during each iteration. The former is known generally as the **for** statement, the latter as the **while** statement. Most languages' **for** constructs also provide a counter that can be used to indicate which iteration is currently being executed.

The following example code illustrates the **for** construct; the code assigns into the first ten elements of array A the value of their position in the array:

```
for I in 0 .. 9 loop        -- I is defined by the loop
   A(I):= I;                -- I is read only in the loop
end loop;                   -- I is out of scope after the loop
```

Note that Ada has restricted the use of the loop variable.

The main variation with **while** statements concerns the point at which the test for exit from the loop is made. The most common form involves a test upon entry to the loop and subsequently before each iteration is made:

```
while <Boolean Expression> loop
   <Statements>
end loop;
```

Ada increases the flexibility of the construct by allowing control to pass out of the loop (that is, the loop to terminate) from any point within it:

```
loop
   .
   .
   exit when <Boolean Expression>;
   .
   .
end loop;
```

A common programming error is a loop that either does not terminate (when it is meant to) or terminates in the wrong state. Fortunately, formal methods of analysing loop structures are now well understood. They involve defining the pre- and post-conditions for the loop; the termination condition and the loop invariant. The loop invariant is a statement that is true at the end of each iteration but may not be true during the iteration. In essence, the analysis of the loop involves showing that the pre-condition will lead to loop termination and that, upon termination, the loop invariant will lead to a proof that the post-condition is satisfied. To facilitate the use of these formal approaches, exiting from the loop during an iteration is not advised. Where possible, the standard **while** construct is the best to use.

The final point to make about loops is that in real-time systems it is often required that a loop does not terminate. A control cycle will be expected to run indefinitely (that is, until the power is turned off). Although **while** True would facilitate such a loop, it

OVERVIEW OF ADA   167

may be inefficient and it does not capture the essence of an infinite loop. For this reason, Ada provides a simple loop structure:

loop
  <Statements>
end loop;

9.3.5 Subprograms

Even in the construction of a component or module, further decomposition is usually desirable. This is achieved by the use of procedures and functions; known collectively as *subprograms*.

Subprograms not only aid decomposition but also represent an important form of abstraction. They allow arbitrary complex computations to be defined and then invoked by the use of a simple identifier. This enables such components to be reused both within a program and between programs. The generality, and therefore usefulness, of subprograms is, of course, increased by the use of parameters.

Parameter-passing modes and mechanisms

A parameter is a form of communication; it is a data object being transferred between the subprogram user and the subprogram itself. There are a number of ways of describing the mechanisms used for this transfer of data. Firstly, one can consider the way parameters are transferred. From the invoker's point of view, there are three distinct modes of transfer.

(1) Data is passed into the subprogram.
(2) Data is passed out from the subprogram.
(3) Data is passed into the subprogram, is changed and is then passed out of the subprogram.

These three modes are often called: **in**, **out** and **in out**.

The second mechanism of describing the transfer is to consider the binding of the formal parameter of the subprogram and the actual parameter of the call. There are two general methods of interest here: a parameter may be bound by value or by reference. A parameter that is bound by value only has the value of the parameter communicated to the subprogram (often by copying into the subprogram's memory space); no information can return to the caller via such a parameter. When a parameter is bound by reference, any updates to that parameter from within the subprogram is defined to have an effect on the memory location of the actual parameter.

A final way of considering the parameter-passing mechanism is to examine the methods used by the implementation. The compiler must satisfy the semantics of the language, be these expressed in terms of modes or binding, but is otherwise free to implement a subprogram call as efficiently as possible. For example, a large array parameter that is 'pass by value' need not be copied if no assignments are made to elements of the array in the subprogram. A single pointer to the actual array will be more efficient but behaviourally equivalent. Similarly, a call by reference parameter may be implemented by a copy in and copy out algorithm.

Ada uses parameter modes to express the meaning of data transfer to and from a subprogram. For example, consider a procedure which returns the real roots (if they exist) of a quadratic equation.

```
procedure Quadratic (A, B, C : in Float;
                     R1, R2   : out Float;
                     Ok       : out Boolean);
```

An **in** parameter (which is the default) acts as a local constant within the subprogram – a value is assigned to the formal parameter upon entry to the procedure or function. Within the procedure, an **out** parameter can be written and read. A value is assigned to the calling parameter upon termination of the procedure. An 'in out' parameter acts as a variable in the procedure. Upon entry, a value is assigned to the formal parameter; upon termination of the procedure, the value attained is passed back to the calling (actual) parameter.

Procedures

The procedure bodies are quite straightforward and are illustrated by completing the 'quadratic' definitions given above. The procedure assumes that a `sqrt` function is in scope.

```
procedure Quadratic (A, B, C : in Float;
                     R1, R2 : out Float;
                     Ok : out Boolean) is
   Z : Float;
begin
   Z:= B*B - 4.0*A*C;
   if Z < 0.0 or A = 0.0 then
      Ok:= False;
      R1:= 0.0;       -- arbitrary values
      R2:= 0.0;
      return;         -- return from a procedure before
                      -- reaching logical end
   end if;
   Ok:= True;
   R1:= (-B + Sqrt(Z)) / (2.0*A);
   R2:= (-B - Sqrt(Z)) / (2.0*A);
end Quadratic;
```

The invoking of this procedure, merely involves naming the procedure and giving the appropriately typed parameters in parenthesis.

In addition to these basic features, there are two extra facilities available in Ada that improve readability. Consider an enumeration type `Setting` and an integer type that delineates 10 distinct valves:

```
type Setting is (Open, Closed);
type Valve is new Integer range 1 .. 10;
```

The following procedure specification gives a subprogram for changing the setting of one valve:

```
procedure Change_Setting (Valve_Number : Valve;
                          Position : Setting := Closed;
                          );
```

Note that one of the parameters has been given a default value. Calls to this procedure could take a number of forms:

```
Change_Setting(6, Open);       -- normal call
Change_Setting(3);             -- default value 'Closed' used
Change_Setting(Position => Open,
               Valve_Number => 9);   -- name notation
Change_Setting (Valve_Number => 4);  -- name notation and
                                     -- default value
```

Default values are useful if some of the parameters are nearly always given the same value. The use of name notation removes positional errors and increases readability.

Finally note, recursive (and mutually recursive) procedure calls are allowed in Ada.

Functions

Ada supports functions in a manner that is similar to procedures. Consider a simple example of a function that returns the smallest of two integer values:

```
function Minimum (X, Y : in Integer) return Integer is
begin
   return (if X > Y then Y else X);
end Minimum;
```

Ada allows functions to return any valid type including structured types.

The misuse of functions is a source of many errors within programs; the golden rule about functions is that they should not have side effects. An expression should mean what it says:

```
A := B + F(C)
```

The value of A becomes the value of B plus a value obtained from C by the application of the function F. In the execution of the above, only A should have its value changed.

Side effects can be introduced into the above expression in three ways.

(1) F could change the value of C as well as returning a value.

(2) F could change the value of B so that the expression has a different value if evaluated left to right as opposed to right to left.

(3) F could change the value of D, where D is any other variable in scope.

All such schemes should be avoided.

Subprogram pointers

Ada allows pointers to procedures and functions. For example, the following Ada type declaration (`Error_Report`) defines an access variable to a procedure which takes a string parameter. A procedure is then declared which has a parameter of this type, and a call is made to this procedure passing a pointer to the `Operator_Warning` procedure.

```
type Error_Report is access procedure (Reason: in String);

procedure Operator_Warning(Message: in String) is
begin
  -- inform Operator of error
end Operator_Warning;

procedure Complex_Calculation(Error_To : Error_Report; ... ) is
begin
  -- if error detected during the complex calculation
  Error_To("Giving Up");
end Complex_Calculation;

...
  Complex_Calculation(Operator_Warning'Access, ...);
...
```

Inline expansion

Although the use of subprograms is clearly beneficial in terms of decomposition, reuse and readability, for some real-time applications the overhead of implementing the actual call may be unacceptably high. One means of reducing the overhead is to substitute the code for the subprogram 'inline' whenever a call of that subprogram is made. This technique is known as **inline expansion** and has the advantage that it still allows the programmer to use subprograms but not to incur the run-time overhead. In Ada the programmer can, by use of the aspect `Inline`, request that inline expansion is used for the specified subprogram whenever possible.

9.4 Programming in the large

Decomposition and abstraction are the two most important methods that can be used to manage the complexity characteristic of large embedded systems. This complexity is due not just to the amount of code, but to the variety of activities and requirements that are commensurate with real world interaction. As was observed in Section 1.3.6, the real world is also subject to continuous change. Furthermore, the design, implementation and maintenance of software is often poorly managed and results in unsatisfactory products. This section considers those Ada language features that help to embody and support decomposition and the use of abstraction. These features are said to aid *programming in the large*.

The key structure that is missing from older languages is the module. A module can be described, informally, as a collection of logically related objects and operations.

The technique of isolating a system function within a module and providing a precise specification for the interface to the module is called **encapsulation**. Consequently, with a module structure, it is possible to support:

- information hiding,
- separate compilation,
- abstract data types.

In the following sections, the major motivations for a module structure are described. These needs are illustrated by examples coded in Ada. Ada supports modules explicitly in the form of **packages**.

Although the module allows encapsulation, it is essentially a static structuring mechanism and not part of the type model of a language.

9.4.1 Information hiding

In simple languages, all permanent variables have to be global. If two or more procedures wish to share data then that data must be visible to all other parts of the program. Even if a single procedure wishes to update some variable each time it is called, this variable must be declared outside the procedure, and therefore the possibility of misuse and error exists.

A module structure supports reduced visibility by allowing information to be hidden inside the module's 'body'. All module structures (of which there are many different models) allow the programmer to control access to module variables. To illustrate information hiding, consider the implementation of a FIFO dynamic queue. The interface of the queue manager (to the rest of the program) is via three procedures that allow elements to be added to or removed from the queue, and to provide a test for the queue being empty. It is not desirable that internal information about the queue (such as the queue pointer) should be visible outside the module. The following provides a package for this list structure. The main points to note are:

- An Ada package is always declared in two parts: a *specification* and a *body*. Only entities declared in the specification are visible externally.
- Ada uses 'open scope'. All identifiers visible at the point of the package declaration can be accessed within the package. There is no import list as in some languages, like Modula-2 and Java.
- All exported Ada identifiers are accessed from outside the package by quoting both the package name and the required identifier, for example, Queuemod.Empty.
- Only a single instance of the queue is supported; it is created in the package initialization section by calling Create.

```
package Queuemod is
  -- assume type Element is in scope
  function Empty return Boolean;
  procedure Insert (E : Element);
  procedure Remove (E : out Element);
end Queuemod;
```

172 THE ADA PROGRAMMING LANGUAGE

```ada
package body Queuemod is

  type Queue_Node_T;    -- forward declaration
  type Queue_Node_Ptr_T is access Queue_Node_T;

  type Queue_Node_T is
    record
      Contents : Element;
      Next : Queue_Node_Ptr_T;
    end record;

  type Queue_T is
    record
      Front : Queue_Node_Ptr_T;
      Back : Queue_Node_Ptr_T;
    end record;

  type Queue_Ptr_T is access Queue_T;

  Q : Queue_Ptr_T;

  procedure Create is
  begin
    Q := new Queue_T;
    Q.Front := null;  -- strictly not necessary as pointers
    Q.Back := null;   -- are always initialised to null
  end Create;

  function Empty return Boolean is
  begin
    return Q.Front = null;
  end Empty;

  procedure Insert(E : Element) is
    New_Node : Queue_Node_Ptr_T;
  begin
    New_Node := new Queue_Node_T;
    New_Node.Contents := E;
    New_Node.Next := null;
    if Empty then
      Q.Front := New_Node;
    else
      Q.Back.Next := New_Node;
    end if;
    Q.Back := New_Node;
  end Insert;

  procedure Remove(E : out Element) is
    Old_Node : Queue_Node_Ptr_T;
  begin
    Old_Node := Q.Front;
    E := Old_Node.Contents;
    Q.Front := Q.Front.Next;
```

```
    if Q.Front = null then
      Q.Back := null;
    end if;
    -- free up old_node, see Section \ref{generics}
  end Remove;
begin
  Create; -- create the queue
end Queuemod;
```

Both the specification and the body of a package must be placed within the same declarative part, although other entities may be defined between the two parts. In this way, two packages can call subprograms in each other without the need of forward declarations.

Any package can be used if it is in scope. To reduce the need for excessive naming, a 'use' statement is provided:

```
declare
  use Queuemod;
begin
  if not Empty then
    Remove(E);
  end if;
end;
```

The importance of the module construct to real-time programming cannot be overemphasised. However, as previously mentioned, modules are, typically, not first class language entities. Module types cannot be defined, pointers to modules cannot be created and so on. The issue of module types is closely tied to that of object-oriented programming, which is discussed in Section 9.4.4.

9.4.2 Separate compilation

If a program is constructed from modules, there are obvious advantages in having these modules compiled separately. Such a program is said to be compiled within the context of a library. Programmers can therefore concentrate on the current module but be able to construct, at least in part, the complete program so that their module can be tested. Once tested, and possibly authorised, the new unit can be added to the library in a precompiled form. As well as supporting project management, there are clearly resource savings if the entire program does not have to be recompiled for each minor edit.

In Ada, the package (module) specification and body, as outlined in the previous section, can be precompiled in a straightforward manner. If a library unit wishes to have access to any other library unit then it must indicate this, explicitly, using a **with clause**:

```
package Dispatcher is
  -- new visible objects
end Dispatcher;

with Queuemod;
package body Dispatcher is
  -- hidden objects
end Dispatcher;
```

174 THE ADA PROGRAMMING LANGUAGE

In this way, a hierarchy of dependencies between library units is constructed. The main program itself uses **with** clauses to gain access to the library units it requires.

An important feature of the Ada model is that the module specification and body are seen as distinct entities in the library. Obviously both must be present for the final program compilation. (To be completely accurate, some module specifications do not require a body; for example, if they only define types or variables.) During program development, however, a library may contain only specifications. These can be used to check the logical consistency of the program prior to the detailed implementation work. Within the context of project management, specifications may well be done by more senior staff. This is because the specification represents an interface between software modules. An error in such code is more serious than one within a package body, as a change to the specification requires all users of the module to be potentially changed and recompiled, whereas a change to a body requires only the body to be recompiled.

Separate compilation supports bottom-up programming. Library units are built up from other units until the final program can be coded. Bottom-up programming, within the context of top-down design, is quite acceptable, especially as it is bottom-up in terms of specifications (definitions), not implementations (bodies). Nevertheless, Ada has included a further feature of separate compilation that more directly supports top-down design. Within a program unit, a 'stub' can be left for inclusion later by using the **is separate** keywords. For example, the following schema shows how the procedure Convert can be left unimplemented until after the main program has been defined:

```
procedure Main is
  type Reading is ...
  type Control_Value is ...
  procedure Convert (R : Reading; Cv : out Control_Value)
          is separate;
begin
  loop
    Input (Rd);
    Convert(Rd, Cv);
    Output (Cv);
  end loop;
end;
```

Later the procedure body is added:

```
separate (Main)
procedure Convert (R : Reading; Cv : out Control_Value) is
  -- actual required code
end Convert;
```

In Ada, separate compilation is integrated into the language specification. Most importantly, the strong typing rules that would apply if the program was constructed as a single unit apply equally across library units.

9.4.3 Abstract data types

One of the major advantages of high-level languages is that programmers do not have to concern themselves with the physical representation of the data in the computer. From this separation comes the idea of data types. Abstract data types (ADT) are a further extension of this concept. To define an ADT, a module will name a new type and then give all the operations that can be applied to that type. The structure of the ADT is hidden within the module. Note that more than one instance of the type is now supported, and therefore a create routine is required in the interface of the module.

The facility for ADTs is complicated by the requirement for the separate compilation of a module specification from its body. As the structure of an ADT is meant to be hidden, the logical place for it to be defined is in the body. But then the compiler will not know the size of the type when it is compiling code which is using the specification. For this reason, Ada allows part of the implementation to appear in the specification but to be accessible only from the package body. This is called the **private** part of the specification.

Keeping with the queue example, for comparison, the Ada definition of an ADT for queue is as follows:

```
package Queuemod is
  type Queue is limited private;
  procedure Create (Q : in out Queue);
  function Empty (Q : Queue) return Boolean;
  procedure Insert (Q : in out Queue; E : Element);
  procedure Remove (Q : in out Queue; E : out Element);

private
    -- none of the following declarations are externally visible
  type Queuenode;
  type Queueptr is access Queuenode;
  type Queuenode is
    record
       Contents : Element;
       Next : Queueptr;
    end record;
  type Queue is
    record
       Front : Queueptr;
       Back : Queueptr;
    end record;
end Queuemod;

package body Queuemod is
   -- essentially the same as the original code
end Queuemod;
```

The keywords **limited private** mean that only those subprograms defined in this package can be applied to the type. A limited private type is, therefore, a true abstract data type. However, Ada recognizes that many ADTs need the assignment operator and tests for equality. Therefore, rather than have these be defined on all occasions that they are needed, a type can be declared as just **private**. If this is the case, then in addition to the defined subprograms, assignment and the equality test are available to the user. The following gives a common example of an ADT in Ada. It provides a package for complex arithmetic. Note that the subprograms defined with the type Complex take the form of overloaded operations and so allow 'normal' arithmetic expressions to be written:

176   THE ADA PROGRAMMING LANGUAGE

```ada
package Complex_Arithmetic is
  type Complex is private;
  function "+" (X,Y : Complex) return Complex;
  function "-" (X,Y : Complex) return Complex;
  function "*" (X,Y : Complex) return Complex;
  function "/" (X,Y : Complex) return Complex;
  function Comp (A,B : Float) return Complex;
  function Real_Part (X: Complex) return Float;
  function Imag_Part (X: Complex) return Float;
private
  type Complex is
    record
      Real_Part : Float;
      Imag_Part : Float;
    end record;
end Complex_Arithmetic;
```

9.4.4   Object-oriented programming

It has become fashionable to call variables of an ADT *objects* and to designate the programming paradigm that leads to their use *object-oriented programming* (OOP). There is, however, a stricter definition of an object abstraction that draws a useful distinction between objects and ADTs. In general, ADTs lack four properties that would make them suitable for object-oriented programming. They are

(1) type extensibility (inheritance),

(2) automatic object initialization (constructors),

(3) automatic object finalization (destructors),

(4) run-time dispatching of operations (polymorphism).

All of which are supported, in some form, by Ada. In the queue example given earlier, it was necessary to declare a queue variable and then call a create procedure to initialize it. Using OOP, this initialization (using a constructor routine) is done automatically on each queue object as it is declared. Similarly, as an object goes out of scope, a destructor procedure is executed.

Properties (2) and (3) are useful, but the significant concept in an object abstraction is extensibility. This enables a type to be defined as an extension of a previously defined type. The new type inherits the 'base' type but may include new fields and new operations. Once the type has been extended, run-time dispatching of operation is required to ensure the appropriate operation is called for a particular instance of the family of types.

It is beyond the scope of this book to address the full implications of object-oriented software development. However, it is necessary to have a good grasp of OOP principles in order to understand the facilities provided by Ada.

Ada supports object-oriented programming through two complementary mechanisms which provide type extensions and dynamic polymorphism: tagged types and class-wide types. Child packages and controlled types are also important features of the support that Ada provides.

Tagged types

In Ada, a new type can be *derived* from an old type and some of the properties of the type changed using subtyping. For example, the following declares a new type and a subtype called Setting which has the same properties as the Integer type but a restricted range. Setting and Integer are distinct and cannot be interchanged:

type Setting **is new** Integer **range** 1 .. 100;

New operations manipulating Setting can be defined; however, no new components can be added. Tagged types remove this restriction and allow extra components to be added to a type. Any type that might potentially be extended in this way must be declared as a **tagged** type. Because extending the type inevitably leads to the type becoming a record, only record types (or private types which are implemented as records) can be tagged. For example, consider the following type and a primitive operation:

```
type Coordinates is tagged
  record
    X : Float;
    Y : Float;
  end record;

procedure Plot(P: Coordinates);
```

This type can then be extended:

```
type Three_D is new Coordinates with
  record
    Z : Float;
  end record;

procedure Plot(P: Three_D); -- overrides the Plot subprogram
Point : Three_D := (X => 1.0, Y => 1.0, Z => 0.0);
```

All types derived in this way (including the original **root**) are said to belong to the same **class** hierarchy. When a type is extended, it automatically inherits any primitive operations (those defined with the type) available for the parent type.

The fields of the Three_D class in the above example are directly visible to users of the type. Ada also allows these attributes to be fully encapsulated by using private types:

```
package Coordinate_Class is
  type Coordinates is tagged private;

  procedure Plot(P: Coordinates);

  procedure Set_X(P: Coordinates; X: Float);
  function Get_X(P: Coordinates) return Float;
  -- similarly for Y
private
```

```ada
   type Coordinates is tagged
   record
      X : Float;
      Y : Float;
   end record;
end Coordinate_Class;
```

Other facilities include the notion of abstract tagged types and abstract primitive operations. Note that Ada supports only inheritance from a single parent, although an element of multiple inheritance can be achieved using interfaces.

Class-wide types

Tagged types provide the mechanism by which types can be extended incrementally. The result is that a programmer can create a hierarchy of related types. Other parts of the program may now wish to manipulate any member of that hierarchy for their own purposes without being too concerned which member it is processing at any one time. Ada is a strongly typed language, and therefore a mechanism is needed by which an object from any member of the hierarchy can be passed as a parameter. For example, a subprogram may wish to take a coordinate as a parameter without being too concerned whether it is a two-dimensional or three-dimensional one.

Class-wide programming is the technique which enables programs to be written which manipulate families of types. Associated with each tagged type, T, there is a type T'Class which comprises all the types which are in the family of types starting at T. Hence, the following subprogram will allow either a two-dimensional or three-dimensional coordinate to be passed.

```ada
procedure General_Plot(P : Coordinates'Class);
```

Any call to a primitive operation on a class-wide type will result in the correct operation for the actual type being called; a process known as **run-time dispatching**.

```ada
procedure General_Plot(P : Coordinates'Class) is
begin
   -- do some house keeping
   Plot(P);
   -- depending on the actual value of P, one of
   -- the defined Plot procedures will be called
end General_Plot;
```

Although run-time dispatching is a powerful mechanism, it does cause some problems for real-time systems. In particular, it is not possible to know from examining statically the code which operations are called. This makes static timing analysis difficult (see Section 4.5).

Child packages

The main motivation for child packages is to add more flexibility to the single-level packaging facility. Without them, changes to a package which resulted in modifications to the specification require recompilation of all clients using that package. This is at odds with object-oriented programming, which facilitates incremental changes. Furthermore, extending private tagged types is not feasible without further language additions, as access to data in private types can only be made from within the package body.

Consider the following example given in the previous section:

```
package Coordinate_Class is
  type Coordinates is tagged private;

  procedure Plot(P: Coordinates);

  procedure Set_X(P : Coordinates; X: Float);
  function Get_X(P : Coordinates) return Float;
  -- similarly for Y
private
  type Coordinates is tagged
  record
    X : Float;
    Y : Float;
  end record;
end Coordinate_Class;
```

To extend this class and have visibility of the parent data attributes would require the package to be edited.

Child packages allow direct access to the parents' private components without going through the parents' interfaces. Hence, the following code

```
package Coordinate_Class.Three_D is
  -- "." indicates that package Three_D is
  -- a child of Coordinate_Class

  type Three_D is new Coordinates with private;

  -- new primitive operations
  procedure Set_Z(P : Coordinates; Z: Float);
  function Get_Z(P : Coordinates) return Float;

  procedure Plot(P : Three_D); -- overrides the Plot subprogram
private
  type Three_D is new Coordinates with
  record
    Z : Float;
  end record;
end Coordinate_Class.Three_D;
```

allows the implementation of the new and overridden primitive operations to have access to the original class's data attributes.

Controlled types

Further support for object-oriented programming is provided by *controlled* types. With these types, it is possible to define subprograms that are called (automatically) when objects

180   THE ADA PROGRAMMING LANGUAGE

of the type:

- are created – *initialize*;
- cease to exist – *finalize*;
- are assigned a new value – *adjust*.

To gain access to these features, the type must be derived from Controlled, a predefined type declared in the library package Ada.Finalization, that is, it must be part of the Controlled class hierarchy. The package Ada.Finalization defines procedures for Initialize, Finalize and Adjust. When a type is derived from Controlled, these procedures may be overridden. As objects typically cease to exist when they go out of scope, the exiting of a block may involve a number of calls of Finalize.

9.4.5   Additional OOP features

Ada 95 introduced OOP into Ada. Ada 2005 and 2016 refined the model. This section provides a brief overview of these refinements. In particular:

- the prefix notation for object method calls,
- the role of interfaces in the derivation of tagged types and
- the difference between limited and non-limited interfaces.

The goal here is to provide enough understanding of the Ada 2005 OOP model so that the later material on using interfaces with Ada's task and protected types can be understood.

The prefix notation

In Ada, one way of representing an extensible object type (called a class in languages like Java) is shown below.

```
package Objects is
  type Object_Type is tagged private;

  procedure Op1(O : in out Object_Type; P : Parameter_Type);
  ... -- other operations

private
  type Object_Type is tagged
  record
    ... -- the type's attributes (instance variables)
  end record;
end Objects;
```

Instances of these are created in the usual way and the subprograms (methods) are called as shown below.

```
declare
  My_Object : Object_Type;  -- a new instance of the object type
  My_Parameter : Parameter_Type;
begin
   ...
   Op1(My_Object, My_Parameter);
      -- object passed as a parameter to the subprogram
   ...
end;
```

Ada 2005 still allows this style but also supports the following.

```
declare
  My_Object : Object_Type;
  My_Parameter : Parameter_Type;
begin
   ...
   My_Object.Op1(My_Parameter);
      -- object name prefixes the subprogram name
   ...
end;
```

This makes the program easier to understand and eases the transition for programmers used to other OOP languages such as C++ and Java.

The introduction of the prefix notion is more than just syntactic sugar. It eases the naming of methods when complex inheritance hierarchies are used, as there is no need to name all the associated packages in 'with' clauses.

Interfaces

An interface is a type that has no state. In Ada 95, it could be represented as an abstract tagged type without any components. For example, the following abstract type provides the interface needed to print an object. Any types that extend from this type must provide an implementation of the Print subprogram. Hence objects of all types in the hierarchy rooted in the Printable type can be printed. These can collectively be accessed by the Any_Printable type given below.

```
package Printable is
  type Printable_Interface is abstract tagged null record;
  procedure Print(X : in Printable_Interface) is abstract;

  type Any_Printable is access all Printable_Interface'Class;
end Printable;
```

Ada 95 did not allow multiple inheritance; therefore, it was not possible to have a derived type that can support multiple interfaces via the abstract tagged type mechanism. Ada 2005 solved this problem by introducing a language construct that is essentially an abstract tagged typed with null components. This is called an **interface**. All primitive operations on an interface type must be abstract or null – Ada 2005 has also introduced syntax for a null procedure: e.g. '**procedure** X (P: Parameter_Type) **is null;**'. This acts as shorthand for a procedure with a single enclosed null statement.

The above interface is represented in Ada 2005 as:

```ada
package Printable is
  type Printable_Interface is interface;
  procedure Print(X: in Printable_Interface) is abstract;

  type Any_Printable is access all Printable_Interface'Class;
end Printable;
```

Although the inspiration for Ada interfaces comes from the Java language, they cannot be used in exactly the same way as Java interfaces but should be thought of as abstract types. In particular, it is not possible to define an arbitrary method that takes as a parameter an interface (as it is in Java). The equivalent in Ada 2005 is to define the parameter type as a *class-wide type* or *class-wide access type* rooted at the Ada interface (as illustrated above with access types). Hence, Ada makes explicit what Java leaves as implicit.

For example, a Java-like comparable interface would be represented as:

```ada
package Comparable is
  type Comparable_Interface is interface;
  type Any_Comparable is access all Comparable_Interface'Class;
  function Compares(This: Comparable_Interface;
           To_That: in Comparable_Interface'Class)
           return Boolean is abstract;
end Comparable;
```

Here the first parameter to the `Compares` method is the controlling (dispatching) parameter. The second parameter represents the object to be compared with. The function returns true if the object components are equal in value.

Now consider an object that wants to support the above two interfaces (or *implement* them, as Java calls it). It simply declares a new tagged type from the two interface types and provides the primitive operations needed to support the interfaces.

```ada
with Printable; use Printable;
with Comparable; use Comparable;
package Printable_and_Comparable is
  type Object is new Printable_Interface and
                     Comparable_Interface with private;

  overriding procedure Print (This : Object);
  overriding function Compares (This : Object;
           To_That : Comparable_Interface'Class) return Boolean;
private
  type Object is new Printable_Interface and
                     Comparable_Interface with record
    X : Integer := 0;  -- say
  end record;
end Printable_and_Comparable;
```

The implementation is shown below:

```ada
with Ada.Text_IO; use Ada.Text_IO;
with Ada.Tags; use Ada.Tags;
package body Printable_and_Comparable is
```

```
   procedure Print (This : Object) is
   begin
      Put_Line (This.X'Img);
   end Print;

   function Compares (This : Object;
            To_That : Comparable_Interface'Class)
            return Boolean is
   begin
     return To_That in Object'Class and then
            This.X = Object(To_That).X;
   end Compares;
end Printable_and_Comparable;
```

Of course, if there is a pre-existing type that needs to become printable and comparable:

```
package My_Objects is
  type My_Object is tagged record
    X: Integer;
  end record;
end My_Objects;
```

It is possible to create a new tagged type that is derived from the My_Object tagged type that can now be printed and compared.

```
with Printable, Comparable, My_Objects;
use Printable, Comparable, My_Objects;
package My_Printable_And_Comparable_Objects is
  type My_Printable_And_Comparable_Object is new My_Object and
       Printable_Interface and Comparable_Interface with
       null record;
  overriding
  procedure Print(X: My_Printable_And_Comparable_Object);
  overriding
  function Compares(This: My_Printable_And_Comparable_Object;
                    To_That : in Comparable_Interface'Class)
                    return Boolean;
end My_Printable_And_Comparable_Objects;
```

Note that so far, equality is defined to be when an object has the same value in its X field, irrespective of whether it has other fields present or not. If equality was defined to be only for objects of the exact same type then the following would be needed.

```
function Alternative_Compares(This : Object;
         To_That : Comparable_Interface'Class)
         return Boolean is
begin
   return (To_That'Tag = Object'Tag and then
           This = Object(To_That));
end Alternative_Compares;
```

Formally, a tagged type can be derived from zero or one parent tagged type plus zero or more interface types. If a non-interface tagged type is present it must be the first in the list. Ada 2005 calls the other types **progenitors**. Hence interfaces themselves can be derived from other interfaces.

Limited interfaces

In Ada, a limited type is a type that does not support the assignment statement and has no predefined equality operator. Interfaces can be limited; they are, however, not limited by default. A non-limited interface has a predefined equality operator available, whereas a limited interface does not.

A new interface can be composed of a mixture of limited and non-limited interfaces but if any one of them is non-limited then the resulting interface must be specified as *non-limited*. This is because it must allow the equality and assignment operations implied by the non-limited interface. Similar rules apply to derived types that implement one or more interfaces. The resulting type must be non-limited if any of its associated interfaces are non-limited.

9.4.6 Reusability

Software production is an expensive business, with costs rising inexorably every year. One reason for the high costs is that software often seems to be constructed 'from scratch'. By comparison, the hardware engineer has a rich choice of well tried and tested components from which systems can be built. It has been a long held quest of software engineers to have a similar supply of software components.

Modern programming language techniques such as modular programming and object-oriented programming provide the foundations on which reusable software libraries can be constructed.

One inhibition to reusability is a strong typing model. With such a model, a module for sorting integers, for example, cannot be used for sorting floats or records even though the basic algorithms are identical. This type of restriction, although necessary for other reasons, severely restricts reusability. The designers of Ada have addressed this issue and have provided facilities that aids reuse without undermining the typing model. The facility is based on the concept of generics.

A **generic** is a template from which actual components can be **instantiated**. In essence, a generic will manipulate objects without regard to their type. An instantiation specifies an actual type. The language model ensures that any assumptions made about the type within the generic are checked against the type named in the instantiation. For example, a generic may assume that a **generic parameter** is of a discrete type. When an instantiation is made, the compiler will check that the specified type is indeed discrete.

A measure of a generic's reusability can be derived from the restrictions placed on the generic parameters. At one extreme, if the instantiated type has to be, for example, a one-dimensional array of an integer type, then the generic is not particularly reusable. Alternatively, if any type can be used at instantiation then a high level of reuse has been obtained.

The parameter model for Ada generics is comprehensive and will not be described in detail here; rather, a couple of examples will be given that have high reusability.

Generic parameters are defined in a way that specifies what operations are applied to them within the generic body. If no operations at all are applied then the parameters are said to be **limited private**. If only assignments and equality tests are performed then the parameters are **private**. Components with high reuse have limited private or private parameters. For a first example, consider the Queuemod package. As so far given, although an abstract data type for queue is provided, all such queues must only hold objects of type Element. There is, clearly, a need for a generic in which the type of the object being manipulated is a parameter. Within the package body for Queuemod, objects of type Element were only assigned in and out of queues. The parameter can therefore be private.

```ada
generic
  type Element is private;
package Queuemod_Template is
  type Queue is limited private;
  procedure Create (Q : in out Queue);
  function Empty (Q : Queue) return Boolean;
  procedure Insert (Q : in out Queue; E : Element);
  procedure Remove (Q : in out Queue; E : out Element);
private
  type Queuenode;
  type Queueptr is access Queuenode;
  type Queuenode is
    record
      Contents : Element;
      Next : Queueptr;
    end record;
  type Queue is
    record
      Front : Queueptr;
      Back : Queueptr;
    end record;
end Queuemod_Template;

package body Queuemod_Template is
  -- the same as before
end Queuemod_Template;
```

An instantiation of this generic creates an actual package:

```ada
declare
  package Integer_Queues is new Queuemod_Template(Integer);
  type Processid is
    record
      ...
    end record;
  package Process_Queues is new Queuemod_Template(Processid);
  Q1, Q2 : Integer_Queues.Queue;
  Pid : Process_Queues.Queue;
  P : Processid;
  use Integer_Queues;
```

```
  use Process_Queues;
begin
  Create(Q1);
  Create(Pid);
  ...
  Insert(Pid,P);
  ...
end;
```

Each of these packages defines an abstract data type for queue. But they are different as the element types are distinct.

The above discussion has concentrated upon generic parameters as types. Three other forms are available: constants, subprograms and packages. Buffers are often an important construct within real-time programs. They differ from queues in that they have a fixed size. The following shows the specification of a generic package for an abstract data type for buffers. Again, the element type is a generic parameter. In addition, the size of the buffer is a generic constant parameter; it has a default value of 32:

```
generic
  Size : Natural := 32;
  type Element is private;
package Buffer_Template is
  type Buffer is limited private;
  procedure Create(B : in out Buffer);
  function Empty(B : Buffer) return Boolean;
  procedure Place(B : in out Buffer; E : Element);
  procedure Take(B : in out Buffer; E : out Element);
private
  subtype Buffer_Range is Natural range 0..Size-1;
  type Buff is array(Buffer_Range) of Element;
  type Buffer is
    record
      Bf : Buff;
      Top : Buffer_Range := 0;
      Base: Buffer_Range := 0;
    end record;
end Buffer_Template;
```

An integer buffer of size 32 is instantiated as follows:

```
package Integer_Buffers is new Buffer_Template(Integer);
```

A buffer with 64 elements of some record type Rec is constructed with a similar instantiation:

```
package Rec_Buffers is new Buffer_Template(64,Rec);
```

As with parameters to subprograms, greater readability is furnished by using name association:

```
package Rec_Buffers is new Buffer_Template(Size => 64,
                                           Element => Rec);
```

An example of a generic subprogram parameter is given below. The generic package defines two procedures which both act upon an array of Elements. One procedure finds the largest Element; the other sorts the array. To implement these procedures it is necessary to compare any two Elements to see which is the greater. For scalar types the '>' operator is available; for general private types it is not. It follows that the generic package must import a '>' function.

```
generic
  Size : Natural;
  type Element is private;
  with function ">"(E1, E2 : Element) return Boolean;
package Array_Sort is
  type Vector is array(1..Size) of Element;
  procedure Sort(V : in out Vector);
  function Largest(V : Vector) return Element;
end Array_Sort;
```

The implementation of this generic is left as an exercise for the reader.

More sophisticated generic packages can be created by using packages (possibly themselves generic instantiations) as generic parameters. However, these will not be discussed, as they are not required for the material presented in the remaining chapters.

9.5 Aspects and attributes

As well as providing language keywords and predefined language packages, Ada also provides language-defined **aspects** and **attributes**. An aspect is a property of an entity (type, object, subprogram etc.) that can be specified by the program. An attribute is the property of an entity that can be queried by a program.

Aspects are introduced using a "with" clause after an entities declaration. For example, Ada allows programs to interface with components written in other languages. The following declaration tells the compiler that the Get_Time_In_Milliseconds function is a call to a C routine.

```
with Interfaces.C; use Interfaces.C;
function Get_Time_In_Milliseconds return int
  with Import => True, Convention => C, External_Name => "getTime";
```

Attributes are acquired using a ' notation in conjunction with the entity's name. For example, if My_Array is an object that is declared as follows:

```
type My_Arrays is array (1 .. 100) of Integer;
My_Array : My_Arrays;
```

the attribute My_Array'Last will return the value 100.

Both aspects and attributes are used extensively in the facilities employed for real-time programming.

Summary

In this chapter, the necessary language features for expressing algorithms and representing data structures for Ada have been given. To express algorithms, blocks and well-constructed loop and decision structures are needed. The `goto` statement is now totally discredited. To give a concrete realization of the distinct logical units found in most non-trivial modules, subprograms are also required. Procedure semantics are relatively uncontroversial (although different parameter-passing models exist), but functions are still problematic because of side effects.

The provision of a rich variety of data structures and the rules of typing are visible in Ada. Strong typing is now universally accepted as a necessary aid to the production of reliable code. The restrictions it imposes can lead to difficulties, but the provision of a controlled means of doing explicit type conversions removes these problems.

The data types themselves can be classified in a number of different ways. There is a clear division between scalar and structured data types. Scalar types can then be subdivided into discrete types (integer types and enumeration types) and real types. The structured data types can be classified in terms of three attributes: homogeneity, size and access method. A structured data type is said to be homogeneous if its subcomponents are all of the same type (for example, arrays). Alternatively, if the subcomponents can be of different types (for example, records) then the data structure is known as heterogeneous. The size attribute can be either fixed or variable. Records are fixed as are arrays in some languages. Dynamic data structures such as linked lists, trees or graphs are variable in size and are usually constructed by the programmer from a pointer (or reference) type and a memory allocator. Finally, there are several access methods for getting at the subcomponents of the structure. The two most important methods are direct and indirect. Direct access, as its name implies, allows the immediate referencing of a subcomponent (for example, an element of an array or a field of a record). Indirect access means that the addressing of a subcomponent may require a chain of accesses through other components. Most dynamic structures have only indirect access.

The attributes, homogeneity, size and access method, could theoretically give rise to at least eight different structures. In reality, the attributes are related (for example, a fixed size implies direct access) and only the following categories are necessary:

- arrays with arbitrary bounds and dimensions;
- records (or classes);
- pointers for constructing arbitrary dynamic data structures with indirect addressing.

Any language that provides appropriate control structures and all of these categories (as Ada does) is well able to support programming in the small.

Notwithstanding the discussion above, real-time languages may have to restrict the features available to the programmer. It is difficult, if not impossible, to make estimates of the time required to access dynamic data structures. Moreover, it is desirable to be able to guarantee before execution begins that there is sufficient memory available for the program. For this reason, dynamic arrays and pointers may need to be missing from the 'authorised' list of language features for real-time applications. Additionally, recursion and unbounded loop structures may need to be restricted.

In the evolution of programming languages, one of the most important constructs to have emerged is the module. This structure enables the complexity inherent in large real-time systems to be contained and managed. In particular, it supports

(1) information hiding
(2) separate compilation
(3) abstract data types

Ada has a static module structure. Ada uses 'open scope' so that all objects in scope at the declaration of a module are visible within it. Packages in Ada have well-defined specifications which act as the interface between the module and the rest of the program.

Separate compilation enables libraries of precompiled components to be constructed. This encourages reusability and provides a repository for project software. This repository must, however, be subject to appropriate project management so that issues such as version control do not become a source of unreliability.

The decomposition of a large program into modules or classes is the essence of programming in the large. It is, however, important that this decomposition process does lead to well-defined modules.

The use of abstract data types (ADTs), along with object-oriented programming mechanisms (inheritance and interfaces), provides one of the main tools that programmers can use to manage large software systems. Again it is the module (i.e., package) construct in Ada that enables ADTs to be built and used.

Languages that are strongly typed suffer from the restriction that modules cannot easily be reused as their behaviour is tied to the types of their parameters and subcomponents. This dependency is often more than is required. Ada's provision of a generic primitive is an attempt to improve the reusability of software. Generic packages and procedures can be defined which act as templates from which real code can be instantiated.

Chapter 10
Concurrent programming

10.1 Motivation
10.2 Processes and tasks/threads
10.3 Concurrent execution
10.4 Task representation
10.5 Concurrent execution in Ada
10.6 Multiprocessor and distributed systems
10.7 A simple embedded system
10.8 Language-supported versus operating-system-supported concurrency
Summary

Any language, natural or computer, has the dual property of enabling expression whilst at the same time limiting the framework within which that expressive power may be applied. If a language does not support a particular notion or concept, then those that use the language cannot apply that notion and may even be totally unaware of its existence. Early programming languages all shared the common property of being sequential languages. Programs written in those languages have a single thread of control. They start executing in some state and then proceed, by executing one statement at a time, until the program terminates. The path through the program may differ due to variations in input data, but for any particular execution of the program there is only one path.

A modern computer system will, by comparison, consist of one or more central processors and many I/O devices, all of which are operating in parallel. Sequential programs are unable to exploit fully the potential of these systems. Embedded computer systems must also deal with the inherent parallelism of the larger system. Any modern real-time programming language must, therefore, provide some facility for concurrent programming. This chapter provides some background on concurrency before exploring the facilities provided by Ada.

10.1 Motivation

Concurrent programming is the name given to the programming notations and techniques for expressing potential parallelism and solving the resulting synchronization and communication problems.

There are three main motivations for wanting to write concurrent programs.

(1) To model parallelism in the real world – Real-time and embedded programs have to control and interface with real-world entities (robots, conveyor belts, etc.) that are inherently parallel. Reflecting the parallel nature of the system in the structures of the program makes for a more readable, maintainable and reliable application.

(2) To fully utilize the processor – Modern processors run at speeds far in excess of the input and output devices with which they must interact. A sequential program that is waiting for I/O is unable to perform any other operation.

(3) To allow more than one processor to be used to solve a problem – A sequential program can only be executed by one processor (unless the compiler has transformed the program into a concurrent one). Modern hardware platforms consists of multiple processors to obtain more powerful execution environments. A concurrent program is able to exploit this true parallelism and obtain faster execution.

From a concurrency perspective, the implementation platform can be considered irrelevant. However, in some application areas the amount or presence of parallelism is critical to the success of the program. For example, in high performance computing there is a requirement to get maximum performance from the platform. Inevitably, creating many tasks adds overhead. Hence, there may be some advantages from limiting the number of concurrent activities to the numbers of CPUs, or rather writing the application so that the number of activities created at run time matches the number of processors available.

From a theoretical point of view, Amdahl's law gives the relationship between the expected speed-up of parallelising implementations of an algorithm. If P is the proportion of that algorithms code that can benefit from parallelization and N is the number of processors, the maximum speedup that can be achieved by using these N processors is

$$\frac{1}{(1-P) + \frac{P}{N}} \qquad (10.1)$$

In the limit, as N tends to infinity, the maximum speedup tends to $1/(1-P)$. Consequently, if only 50% of the algorithm is amenable to parallel execution, then the maximum possible speed up is only 2.

Of course, speedup is only one reason for the use of concurrent activities. Hence, even though the number of processors might be limited, there is still advantages to have more concurrent activities than processors. This, and the following two chapters, concentrate on the issues associated with general concurrent programming.

10.2 Processes and tasks/threads

Following the pioneering work of Dijkstra [32], a concurrent program is conventionally viewed as consisting of a collection of autonomous sequential processes, executing (logically) in parallel. Concurrent programming languages all incorporate, either explicitly or implicitly, the notion of process; each process itself has a single thread of control. All operating systems provide facilities for creating concurrent processes. Usually, each process

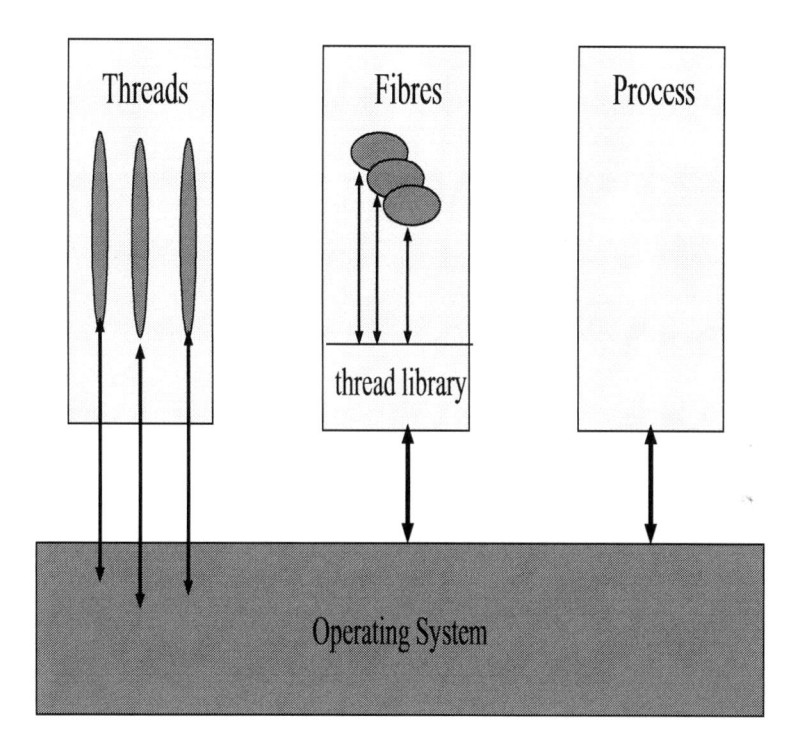

Figure 10.1: The relationship between processes, threads and fibers.

executes in its own virtual machine to avoid interference from other, unrelated, processes. Each process is, in effect, a single program. However, in recent years there has been a tendency to provide the facilities for processes to be created within programs.

Modern operating systems allow processes created within the same program to have unrestricted access to shared memory (such processes are called **threads** or **tasks**). Hence, in operating systems like those supporting the POSIX Application Programming Interface (API), it is necessary to distinguish the concurrency between programs (processes) from the concurrency within a program (threads/tasks). Often, there is also a distinction between threads which are visible to the operating system (often called *kernel-level* threads) and those that are supported solely by library routines (*library-level* threads). For example, Windows supports threads and **fibers**, the latter being invisible to the kernel. Figure 10.1, illustrates the relationship between these different concurrency abstractions. Hybrid models are also possible where a process can be allocated a maximum number of kernel-level threads and a thread library (or sometimes the kernel itself) is responsible for mapping the process's threads to the appropriate library or kernel-level threads.

> *In this book the term **task** will be used to represent a single thread of control. The term* process *will be used to indicate one or more tasks executing within its own shared memory context. With most concurrent programming languages,*

194   CONCURRENT PROGRAMMING

it is the task abstraction that is supported rather than the process abstraction.

Where a concurrent program is being executed on top of an operating system, its Run-Time Support System (RTSS) can either map the program's notion of a task onto the underlying operating system's notion of a thread, or it can make the program's notion of task invisible to the operating system (and in effect implement its own fibres library). Of course, in the latter case, the RTSS must ensure that all input/output operations are asynchronous, otherwise the whole concurrent program will block every time one of its tasks performs an operation requiring operating system support.

The actual implementation (that is, execution) of a collection of tasks usually takes one of three forms. Tasks can either:

(1) multiplex their executions on a single processor,
(2) multiplex their executions on a multiprocessor system where all processors have access to common shared memory (for example, a symmetric multiprocessor (SMP) system),
(3) multiplex their executions on several processors where there is no common shared memory (for example, a distributed system).

Hybrids of these three methods are also possible. For example, Non Uniform Memory Architectures (NUMA) where there may be a mixture of shared and non shared memory.

Only in cases (2) and (3) is there the possibility of true parallel execution of more than one task. The term **concurrent** indicates *potential* parallelism. Concurrent programming languages thus enable the programmer to express logically parallel activities without regard to their implementation.

The life of a task is illustrated, simply, in Figure 10.2. A task is created, moves into the state of initialization, proceeds to execution and termination. Note that some tasks may never terminate and that others, which fail during initialization, pass directly to termination without ever executing. After termination, a task goes to non-existing when it can no longer be accessed (as it has gone out of scope or been garbage collected). Clearly, the most important state for a task is executing; however, as processors are limited, not all tasks can be executing at once. Consequently, the term **executable** is used to indicate that the task could execute if there is a processor available.

From this consideration of a task, it is clear that the execution of a concurrent program is not as straightforward as the execution of a sequential program. Tasks must be created and terminated, and dispatched to and from the available processors. These activities are undertaken by the RTSS or Run-Time Kernel. The RTSS sits logically between the hardware (along with any provided operating system) and the application software. In reality, it may take one of a number of forms:

(1) A software structure programmed as part of the application (that is, as one component of the concurrent program). C and C++ programs often provide their own thread libraries that are tailored to their applications' requirements.
(2) A standard software system generated with the program object code by the compiler. This is normally the structure with Ada and Java programs.

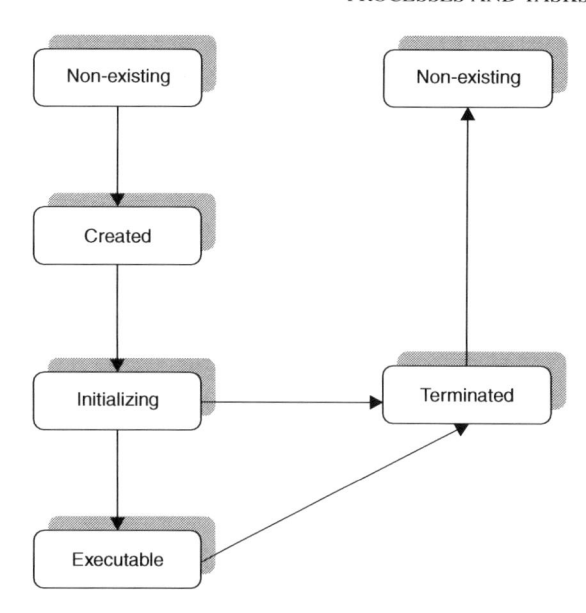

Figure 10.2: Simple state diagram for a task.

(3) A hardware structure microcoded into the processor for efficiency. For example, the aJile System's aJ-102 processor directly supports the execution of Java byte code.

The algorithm used for scheduling by an RTSS (or an operating system) to decide which task to execute next if there is more than one executable will affect the time behaviour of the program. However, for well-constructed programs, the logical behaviour of a program will not be dependent on the scheduling. From the program's point of view, the RTSS (or operating system) is assumed to schedule tasks *non-deterministically*. As discussed in Chapter 4, for real-time systems, the characteristics of the scheduling are significant.

10.2.1 Concurrent programming constructs

Although constructs for concurrent programming vary from one language (and operating system) to another, there are three fundamental facilities that must be provided. These allow the following:

(1) the expression of concurrent activities (threads, tasks or processes);
(2) the provision of synchronization mechanisms between concurrent activities;
(3) primitives that support communication between concurrent activities.

In considering the interaction of tasks, it is possible to distinguish between three types of behaviour:

- independent

- cooperating
- competing

Independent tasks do not communicate or synchronize with each other. Cooperating tasks, by comparison, regularly communicate and synchronize their activities in order to perform some common operation. For example, a component of an embedded computer system may have several tasks involved in keeping the temperature and humidity of a gas in a vessel within certain defined limits. This may require frequent interactions.

A computer system has a finite number of resources which may be shared between processes and tasks; for example, peripheral devices, memory, and processor power. In order for tasks to obtain their fair share of these resources, they must compete with each other. The act of resource allocation inevitably requires communication and synchronization between the tasks in the system. But although these tasks communicate and synchronize in order to obtain resources, they are, essentially, independent.

Discussion of the facilities which support tasks creation and task interaction is the focus of this and the next two chapters.

10.3 Concurrent execution

Although the notion of tasks or threads is common to all concurrent programming languages, there are considerable variations in the models of concurrency adopted. These variations appertain to:

- Structure
- Level
- Granularity
- Initialization
- Termination
- Representation

The *structure* of a task may be classified as follows.

- Static: the number of tasks is fixed and known at compile-time. This is required for most hard real-time systems.
- Dynamic: tasks are created at any time. The number of extant tasks is determined only at run-time. Open systems often utilize a dynamic number of tasks.

Another distinction between languages comes from the *level* of parallelism supported. Again, two distinct cases can be identified.

(1) Nested: tasks are defined at any level of the program text; in particular, tasks are allowed to be defined within other tasks.
(2) Flat: tasks are defined only at the outermost level of the program text.

Language	Structure	Level
Concurrent Pascal	static	flat
occam2	static	nested
Modula-1	dynamic	flat
C/POSIX	dynamic	flat
C11	dynamic	flat
Ada	dynamic	nested
Java	dynamic	nested
C#	dynamic	nested

Table 10.1: The structure and level characteristics of several concurrent programming languages.

Table 10.1 gives the structure and level characteristics for a number of concurrent programming languages. In this table, the language C is considered to be the original C language used in collaboration with the Real-Time POSIX pthread mechanisms, whereas C11 is the more recent version of the language with built-in threading support.

Within languages that support nested constructs, there is also an interesting distinction between what may be called **coarse** and **fine grain** parallelism. A coarse grain concurrent program contains relatively few tasks, each with a significant life history. By comparison, programs with a fine grain of parallelism will have a large number of simple tasks, some of which will exist for only a single action. Most concurrent programming languages, typified by Ada, display coarse grain parallelism. Occam2 is a good example of a concurrent language with fine grain parallelism.

When a task is created, it may need to be supplied with information pertinent to its execution (much as a procedure may need to be supplied with information when it is called). There are two ways of performing this **initialization**. The first is to pass the information in the form of parameters to the task; the second is to communicate explicitly with the task after it has commenced its execution. Most modern concurrent languages allow parameters to be passed at task creation time.

Task **termination** can be accomplished in a variety of ways. The circumstances under which tasks are allowed to terminate can be summarised as follows:

(1) completion of execution of the task's body;
(2) suicide, by execution of a 'self-terminate' statement;
(3) abortion, through the explicit action of another task;
(4) occurrence of an untrapped error condition;
(5) never: tasks are assumed to execute non-terminating loops;
(6) when no longer needed.

With nested levels, hierarchies of tasks can be created and intertask relationships formed. For any task, it is useful to distinguish between the task (or block) that is responsible for its creation and the task (or block) which is affected by its termination. The former relationship is know as **parent/child** and has the attribute that the parent may be

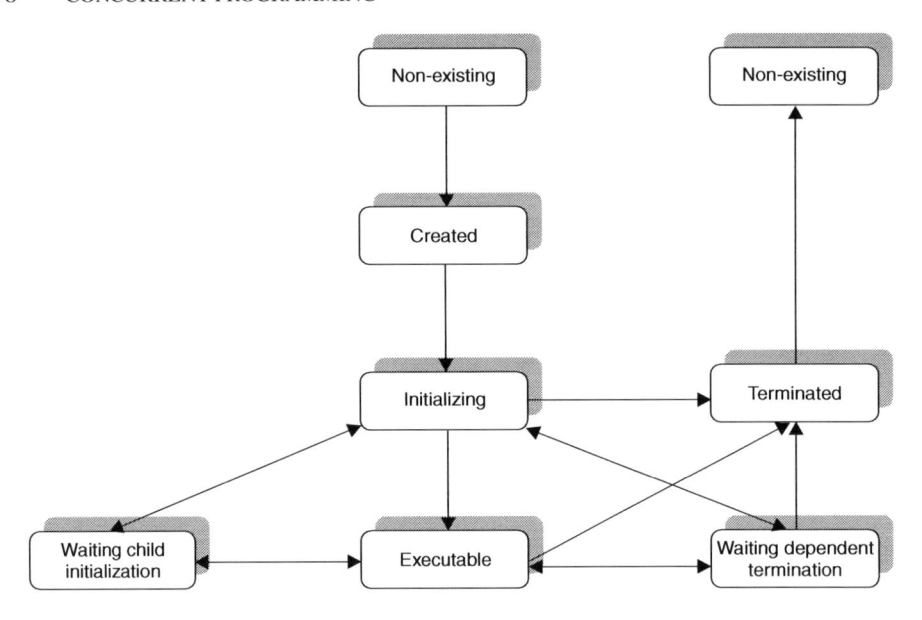

Figure 10.3: State diagram for a task.

delayed while the child is being created and initialised. The latter relationship is termed **guardian/dependant**. A task may be dependent on the guardian task itself or on an inner block of the guardian. The guardian is not allowed to exit from a block until all dependent tasks of that block have terminated (that is, a task cannot exist outside its scope). It follows that a guardian cannot terminate until all its dependants have also terminated. This rule has the particular consequence that a program itself will not be able to terminate until all tasks created within it have also terminated.

In some situations, the parent of a task will also be its guardian. This will be the case when using languages which allow only static task structures. With dynamic task structures (that are also nested), the parent and guardian may or may not be identical (for example with Ada). Figure 10.3 includes the new states that have been introduced in the above discussion.

One of the ways a task may terminate (point (3) in the above list) is by the application of an abort statement. The existence of abort in a concurrent programming language is a question of some contention and is considered in Chapter 12 within the context of resource control. For a hierarchy of tasks, it is usually necessary for the abort of a guardian to imply the abort of all dependants (and their dependants and so on).

The final circumstance for termination, in the above list, can be programmed in Ada using the "select" statement but this is not discussed in this book. In essence, it allows a server task to terminate if all other tasks that could communicate with it have already terminated.

10.3.1 Tasks and objects

The object-oriented programming paradigm encourages system (and program) builders to consider the artifact under construction as a collection of cooperating objects (or, to use a more neutral term, *entities*). Within this paradigm, it is constructive to consider two kinds of object – active and reactive. **Active** objects undertake spontaneous actions (with the help of a processor): they enable the computation to proceed. **Reactive** objects, by comparison, only perform actions when 'invoked' by an active object. Other programming paradigms, such as data-flow or real-time networks, also identify active agents and passive data.

Only active entities give rise to spontaneous actions. Resources are reactive but can control access to their internal states (and any real resources they control). Some resources can only be used by one agent at a time; in other cases the operations that can be carried out at a given time depend on the resources' current states. A common example of the latter is a data buffer whose elements cannot be extracted if it is empty. The term **passive** will be used to indicate a reactive entity that can allow open access.

The implementation of resource entities requires some form of control agent. If the control agent is itself passive (such as a semaphore), then the resource is said to be **protected** (or **synchronized**). Alternatively, if an active agent is required to program the correct level of control, then the resource is in some sense active. The term **server** will be used to identify this type of entity, and the term **protected resource** to indicate the passive kind. These, together with **active** and **passive**, are the four abstract program entities used in this book.

In a concurrent programming language, active entities are represented by tasks/threads. Passive entities can be represented either directly as data variables or they can be encapsulated by some module/package/class construct that provides a procedural interface. Protected resources may also be encapsulated in a module-like construct and require the availability of a low-level synchronization facility. Servers, because they need to program the control agent, require a task.

From an object-oriented programming perspective four types of objects can be identified:

passive object – a reactive entity with no synchronization constraints, it needs an external thread of control for its methods to be executed;

protected object – a reactive entity with synchronization constraints, it is typically shared between many tasks and it needs an external thread of control for its methods to be executed;

active object – an object with an explicit or implicit internal task;

server object – an active object with synchronization constraints, it is typically shared between many tasks.

A key question for language designers is whether to support primitives for both protected resources and servers. Resources, because they typically use a low-level control agent (for example, a semaphore), are normally implemented efficiently (at least on single-processor systems). But they can be inflexible and lead to poor program structures for some classes of problems (this is discussed further in Chapter 11). Servers, because the control agent is programmed using a task, are eminently flexible. The drawback of this approach is that it can lead to a proliferation of tasks, with a resulting high number of context switches during execution. This is particularly problematic if the language does not support protected resources and hence servers must be used for all such entities. As will be illustrated in this chapter and Chapters 11, Ada, supports the full range of entities.

10.4 Task representation

There are three basic mechanisms for representing concurrent execution: fork and join, cobegin and explicit task declaration.

10.4.1 Fork and join

This simple approach does not provide a visible entity for a task but merely supports two statements. The fork statement specifies that a designated routine should start executing concurrently with the invoker of the fork. The join statement allows the invoker to synchronize with the completion of the invoked routine. For example:

```
function F return ... is
begin
  ...
end F;

procedure P is
begin
  ...
  C:= fork F;
  .
  .
  .
  J:= join C;
  ...
end P;
```

Between the execution of the fork and the join, procedure P and function F will be executing concurrently. At the point of the join, the procedure will wait until the function has finished (if it has not already done so). Figure 10.4 illustrates the execution of fork and join.

The use of fork and join primitives are most prevalent in parallel programming languages (and are also called spawn and join). The Linux operating system provides the clone system call that allows a new process to be created that shares the same address space as the parent process. The wait and waitpid system calls provide the join mechanism.

A version of fork and join can also be found in the Real-Time POSIX standard; here fork and vfork are used to create a copy of the invoker, and are used with the wait and waitpid system calls.

Fork and join allow for dynamic process/task creation and provide a means of passing information to the child via parameters. Usually only a single value is returned by the

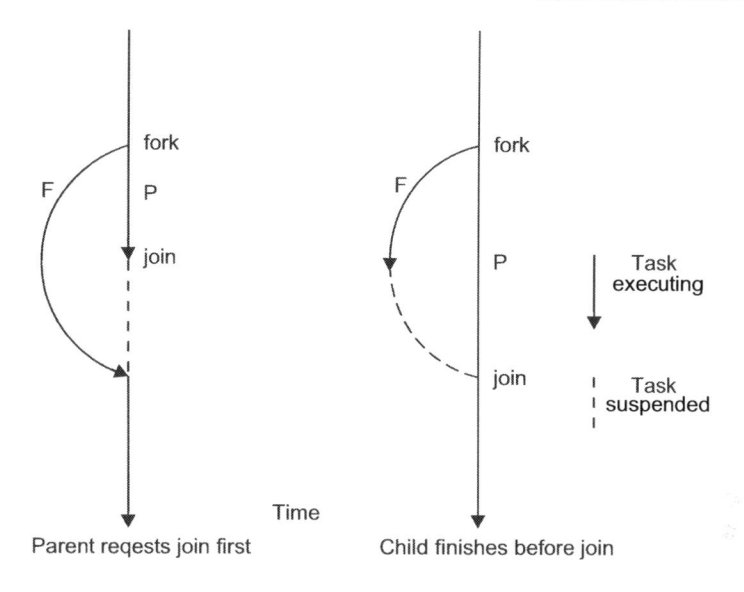

Figure 10.4: Fork and join.

child on its termination. Although flexible, fork and join do not provide a structured approach to process/task creation and can be error prone in use. For example, in some systems a guardian must explicitly 'rejoin' all dependants rather than merely wait for their completion.

10.4.2 Cobegin

The cobegin (or parbegin or par) is a structured way of denoting the concurrent execution of a collection of statements:

```
cobegin
  S1;
  S2;
  S3;
  ...
  Sn
coend
```

This code causes the statements S1, S2 and so on to be executed concurrently. The cobegin statement terminates when all the concurrent statements have terminated. Each of the Si statements may be any construct allowed within the language, including simple assignments or procedure calls. If procedure calls are used, data can be passed to the invoked task via the parameters of the call. A cobegin statement could even include a sequence of statements that itself has a cobegin within it. In this way, a hierarchy of tasks can be supported. Figure 10.5 illustrates the execution of the cobegin statement.

Cobegin can be found in early concurrent languages (like Concurrent Pascal and occam2) but like "fork and join" it has fallen from favour in modern real-time languages.

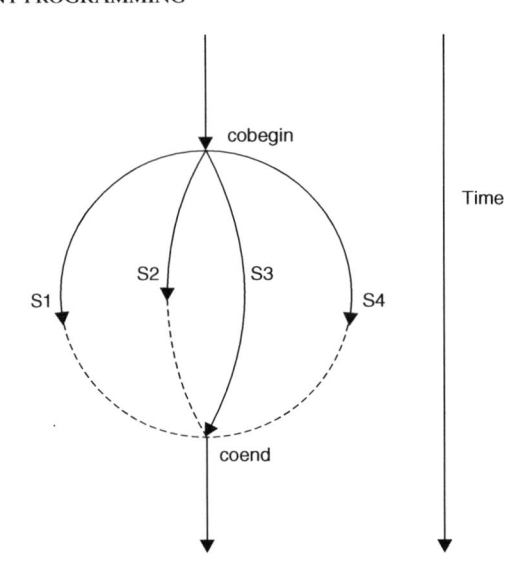

Figure 10.5: Cobegin.

10.4.3 Explicit task declaration

Although sequential routines may be executed concurrently by means of the cobegin or fork, the structure of a concurrent program can be made much clearer if the routines themselves state whether they will be executed concurrently. Explicit task declaration provides such a facility, and has become the standard way of expressing concurrency in concurrent real-time languages. The following section considers the mechanisms provided by Ada.

10.5 Concurrent execution in Ada

The conventional unit of parallelism is called a **task** in Ada. Tasks may be declared at any program level; they are created implicitly upon entry to the scope of their declaration. The following example illustrates a procedure containing two tasks (A and B).

```
procedure Example1 is
  task A;
  task B;

  task body A is
  -- local declarations for task A
  begin
  -- sequence of statement for task A
  end A;

  task body B is
  -- local declarations for task B
  begin
  -- sequence of statements for task B
  end B;
```

```ada
begin
  -- tasks A and B start their executions before
  -- the first statement of the sequence of
  -- statements belonging to the procedure
  ...
end Example1;  -- the procedure does not terminate
               -- until tasks A and B have terminated.
```

Tasks consist of a specification and a body. They can be passed initialization data upon creation.

In the above, tasks A and B (which are created when the procedure is called) are said to have anonymous types, as they do not have types declared for them. Types could easily have been given for A and B:

```ada
task type A_Type;
task type B_Type;
A : A_Type;
B : B_Type;

task body A_Type is
  -- as before for task body A
task body B_Type is
  -- as before for task body B
```

With task types, a number of instances of the same task can easily be declared:

```ada
task type T;
A,B : T;

type Long is array (1..100) of T;
type Mixture is record
  Index : Integer;
  Action : T;
end record;

L : Long;
M : Mixture;

task body T is ...
```

To give a more concrete example of the use of tasks in an Ada program consider the implementation of a robot arm system. The arm can move in three dimensions. The movement in each dimension is powered by a separate motor that is controlled by a distinct Ada task. These tasks loop around, each reading a new relative setting for its dimension and then calling a low-level procedure Move_Arm to cause the arm to move.

First a package is declared that provides the necessary support types and subprograms.

```ada
package Arm_Support is
  type Dimension is (Xplane, Yplane, Zplane);
  type Coordinate is new Integer range ...;

  procedure Move_Arm(D: Dimension; C: Coordinate);
    -- Moves the arm to C
```

```ada
   function New_Setting(D: Dimension) return Coordinate;
     -- Returns a new required relative position
end Arm_Support;
```

Now the main program can be presented.

```ada
with Arm_Support; use Arm_Support;
procedure Main is
  task type Control(Dim : Dimension);

  C1 : Control(Xplane);
  C2 : Control(Yplane);
  C3 : Control(Zplane);

  task body Control is
     Position : Coordinate;     -- current position
     Setting  : Coordinate;     -- required relative movement
  begin
     Position := Coordinate'First;  -- rest position
     loop
        Move_Arm(Dim, Position);
        Setting := New_Setting(Dim);
        Position := Position + Setting;
     end loop;
  end Control;
begin
  null;
end Main;
```

By giving non-static values to the bounds of an array (of tasks), a dynamic number of tasks is created. Dynamic task creation can also be obtained explicitly using the 'new' operator on an access type (of a task type):

```ada
procedure Example2 is
  task type T;
  type A is access T;
  P : A;
  Q : A:= new T;
begin
  ...
  P := new T;
  Q := new T;
  ...
end Example2;
```

Q is declared to be of type A and is given a 'value' of a new allocation of T. This creates a task that immediately starts its initialization and execution; the task is designated Q.all (all is an Ada naming convention used to indicate the task itself, not the access pointer). During execution of the procedure, P is allocated a task (P.all) followed by a further allocation to Q. There are now three tasks active within the procedure; P.all, Q.all and the task that was created first. This first task is now anonymous as Q is no longer pointing to it. In addition to these three tasks, there is the task that is executing the main procedure code itself (called the **environment task** in Ada); in total, therefore, there are four distinct threads of control.

Tasks created by the operation of an allocator ('new') have the important property that the block that acts as its guardian (or **master** as Ada calls it) is not the block in which it is created but the one that contains the declaration of the access type. To illustrate this point, consider the following:

```
declare
  task type T;
  type A is access T;
begin
  .
  .
  .
  declare              -- inner block
    X : T;
    Y : A:= new T;
  begin
    -- sequence of statements
  end;   -- must wait for X to terminate but not Y.all
  .
  .      -- Y.all could still be active although the name Y is
         -- out of scope
  .
end;     -- must wait for Y.all to terminate
```

Although both X and Y.all are created within the inner block, only X has this block as its master. Task Y.all is considered to be a dependent of the outer block, and it therefore does not affect the termination of the inner block.

If a task fails while it is being initialised (an exercise called **activation** in Ada) then the parent of that task has the exception Tasking_Error raised. This could occur, for example, if an inappropriate initial value is given to a variable. Once a task has started its true execution, it can catch any raised exceptions itself. A full description of Ada's support for exception handling is given in Chapter 17.

10.5.1 Task discriminants

Task types may have special components called discriminants which parameterize the type. Discriminants are constrained to be of either a discrete type or access (pointer) type. They provide a mechanisms for passing limited parameters to the task at its creation time. For example, the following

```
task type Multiple(Id : Integer := 1);

task body Multiple is
begin
   -- Id is in scope during the body
   -- and is set to the value passed at creation time ;
end Multiple;
```

```
M1  : Multiple;
M3  : Multiple(3);
M22 : Multiple(22);
```

declares a task type with an integer discriminant. Instances of the task then have an integer passed when they are created. It is possible to set a default value of the discriminant – in this case the value 1.

10.5.2 Task representation aspects

Ada allows the programmer some control over how types are mapped to the underlying hardware resources. These are called **representation aspects**. There are several aspects that are relevant to the Ada tasking model:

- CPU – this allows the program to specify on which CPU the task should be scheduled to execute; Section 10.6.2 will consider this in detail.
- Dispatching_Domain – this allows the program to set a group of processors on which the task can be scheduled; Section 10.6.2 will also consider this in detail;
- priority – this allows the priority of the task to be set; Section 15.3 will consider this in detail;
- deadline – this allows the initial deadline of a task to be set; Section 15.5.1 will consider this in detail.

10.5.3 Task identification

One of the main uses of access variables is in providing another means of naming tasks. All task types in Ada are considered to be limited private. It is therefore not possible to pass a task by assignment to another data structure or program unit. For example, if Robot_Arm and New_Arm are two variables of the same access type (the access type being obtained from a task type) then the following is illegal:

```
Robot_Arm.all := New_Arm.all;   -- not legal Ada
```

However,

```
Robot_Arm := New_Arm;
```

is quite legal and means that Robot_Arm is now designating the same task as New_Arm. Care must be exercised here, as duplicated names can cause confusion and lead to programs that are difficult to understand. Furthermore, tasks may be left without any access pointers; such tasks are, as noted earlier, said to be **anonymous**. For example, if Robot_Arm pointed to a task, when it was overwritten with New_Arm, the previous task will have become anonymous if there were no other pointers to it. The task does, however, still exist and may be executing.

In some circumstances it is useful for a task to have a unique identifier (rather than a name) For example, a server task is not usually concerned with the type of the client tasks. Indeed, when communication and synchronization are discussed in the next chapter,

```
package Ada.Task_Identification is
  type Task_Id is private;
  Null_Task_Id : constant Task_Id;

  function "=" (Left, Right : Task_Id) return Boolean;

  function Current_Task return Task_Id;
    -- returns unique id of calling task

    -- other functions not relevant to this discussion
private
  ...
end Ada.Task_Identification;
```

Program 10.1: The `Ada.Task_Identification` package.

it will be seen that the server has no direct knowledge of who its clients are. However, there are occasions when a server needs to know that the client task it is communicating with is the same client task that it previously communicated with. Although the core Ada language supports no such facility, the Systems Programming Annex provides a mechanism by which a task can obtain its own unique identification. This can then be passed to other tasks. An abridged version of the associated package is shown in Program 10.1.

As well as this package, the Annex supports two attributes:

(1) For any prefix T of a task type, T'Identity returns a value of type Task_Id that equals the unique identifier of the task denoted by T.

(2) For any prefix E that denotes an entry declaration, E'Caller returns a value of type Task_Id that equals the unique identifier of the task whose entry call is being serviced. The attribute is only allowed inside an entry body (or an accept statement) – see Chapter 11.

Care must be taken when using task identifiers since there is no guarantee that, at some later time, the task will still be active or even in scope.

10.5.4 Task termination

Having considered creation and representation, one is left with task termination. Ada provides a range of options; a task will terminate if

(1) it completes execution of its body (either normally or as the result of an unhandled exception);

(2) it executes a 'terminate' alternative of a select statement (this is part of Ada's support for server tasks and the rendezvous; it is not considered in this book) thereby implying that it is no longer required;

(3) it is aborted.

```ada
with Ada.Task_Identification; with Ada.Exceptions;

package Ada.Task_Termination is
  ...
  type Cause_Of_Termination is (Normal, Abnormal,
                                Unhandled_Exception);

  type Termination_Handler is access protected procedure
     (Cause : in Cause_Of_Termination;
      T     : in Ada.Task_Identification.Task_Id;
      X     : in Ada.Exceptions.Exception_Occurrence);

  procedure Set_Specific_Handler
     (T       : in Ada.Task_Identification.Task_Id;
      Handler : in Termination_Handler);

  function Specific_Handler (T : Ada.Task_Identification.Task_Id)
     return Termination_Handler;
end Ada.Task_Termination;
```

Program 10.2: The Ada.Task_Termination package.

If an unhandled exception has caused the task's demise then the effect of the error is isolated to just that task.

Another task can enquire (by the use of an attribute) if a task has terminated:

```ada
if T'Terminated then    -- for some task T
  -- error recovery action
end if;
```

However using this mechanism, the enquiring task cannot differentiate between normal or error termination of the other task; and, of course, the task could terminate just after the test has been performed.

In Ada, extra support is available to help the program manage task termination, in particular unexpected termination due to error conditions. An abridged version of the package is shown in Program 10.2. Essentially, a task can have an associated access variable to a protected procedure[1]. The Ada run-time support system will call this procedure when the task terminates. A parameter to the call gives the cause of the termination.

10.5.5 Task abortion

Any task can abort any other task whose name is in scope. When a task is aborted, all its dependants are also aborted. The abort facility allows wayward tasks to be removed. It is, of course, a vary dangerous mechanism and should only be used when there is no alternative course of action (see Section 18.5.1).

---

[1] A protected procedure in Ada is a procedure that is declared within a monitor-like object, see Section 11.8.

10.5.6 OOP and concurrency

Although Ada has always been a concurrent programming language, early versions of the language, did not support the object-oriented programming model. When OOP was introduced (in Ada 95), the language did not attempt to integrate its support for concurrent programming directly into the OOP model. Instead, the models were orthogonal and paradigms had to be created to allow the benefits of OOP to be available in a concurrent environment. Since Ada 95, object-oriented programming techniques have advanced and the notion of an *interface* has emerged as the preferred mechanism for acquiring many of the benefits of multiple inheritance without most of the problems (see Section 9.4.5). The introduction of this mechanism into current Ada allows tasks to support interfaces. Whilst this does not give the full power of extensible tasks, it does give much of the functionality.

The interface facility provided by Ada 2005 is related to inter-task communication, and will be considered in detail in Section 11.8.5.

10.6 Multiprocessor and distributed systems

Most concurrent programming languages usually attempt to define their semantics so that that they can be implemented on single processor or multiprocessor platform where there is access to global shared memory. The term *processor* is used in this book to indicate a Central Processing Unit (CPU) that is only capable of physically executing a single thread of control at any point in time. Hence, multicore platforms constitute multiprocessors; platforms that support hyper-threading also constitute multiprocessors.

In the multiple processor case, it is usual to assume that all processors in the system can execute all tasks. Hence, when a task is dispatched it can be dispatched to any of the available processors. This is sometimes called **global dispatching**. As a result, during its lifetime, a task may migrate from processor to processor. On multiprocessor platforms, it is also assumed that all processors can access all shared data and shared resources, although not necessarily with uniform access times.

From a real-time perspective, predictability is a major concern. Fixing tasks to processors and not allowing them to migrate, often results in more predictable response times (see Section 8.3). Hence, some operating systems (for example Linux) provide an API that allows threads to be constrained to execute on a limited set of processors. This is usually called **processor affinity**.

Whilst tasks can be mapped to different processors in a distributed system, it is more usual to provide some other form of encapsulation method to represent the "unit" of distribution. For example, processes, objects, partitions, agents and guardians have all been proposed as units of distribution. All these constructs provide well-defined interfaces that allow them to encapsulate local resources and provide remote access.

Hence, the production of an application to execute on a distributed system involves several steps which are not required when programs are produced for a single or multiprocessor platform:

- **Partitioning** is the activity of dividing the system into parts (units of distribution)

210 CONCURRENT PROGRAMMING

suitable for placement onto the processing nodes of the target system.
- **Configuration** takes place when the partitioned parts of the program are associated with particular processing elements in the target system.
- **Allocation** covers the actual activity of turning the configured system into a collection of executable modules and downloading these to the processing elements of the target system.
- **Transparent execution** is the execution of the distributed software so that remote resources can be accessed in a manner which is independent of their location – usually using some form of message passing.
- **Reconfiguration** is the dynamic change to the location of a software component or resource.

Languages which have been designed explicitly to address distributed programming will provide linguistic support for at least the partitioning stage of system development. Some approaches will allow configuration information to be included in the program source, whereas others will provide a separate **configuration** language. Allocation and reconfiguration, typically, require support from the programming support environment and operating system.

This book does not focus on distributed systems, and consequently, this topic is not discussed further. The support that Ada provides for multiprocessor is, however, considered.

The Ada Reference Manual (ARM) allows a program's implementation to be on a multiprocessor system and provides direct support that allows programmers to partition their tasks onto the processors in the given system.

The following ARM quotes illustrate the freedom that Ada allows implementations.

"NOTES 1 Concurrent task execution may be implemented on multicomputers, multiprocessors, or with interleaved execution on a single physical processor. On the other hand, whenever an implementation can determine that the required semantic effects can be achieved when parts of the execution of a given task are performed by different physical processors acting in parallel, it may choose to perform them in this way" ARM Section 9 par 11.

This simply allows multiprocessor execution and also allows parallel execution of a single task if it can be achieved, in effect, "as if executed sequentially".

"In a multiprocessor system, a task can be on the ready queues of more than one processor. At the extreme, if several processors share the same set of ready tasks, the contents of their ready queues is identical, and so they can be viewed as sharing one ready queue, and can be implemented that way. Thus, the dispatching model covers multiprocessors where dispatching is implemented using a single ready queue, as well as those with separate dispatching domains." ARM Section D.2.1 par 11.

As of Ada 2012, the language allows the programmer to directly control the placement of tasks to processors.

MULTIPROCESSOR AND DISTRIBUTED SYSTEMS 211

10.6.1 Multiprocessors and real-time

Section 8.3 considered the underlying schedulability analysis techniques for multiprocessor systems. It made a distinction between systems that are

(1) Fully Partitioned – each task is allocated to a single processor on which all its jobs must run; and
(2) Global – all tasks can run on all processors, tasks may migrate during execution.

There are many motivation for choosing either global or partitioned allocation, some of these motivations come from issues of scheduling. These details are not significant here, what is important is that the Ada language is able to support both schemes. From these schemes, two further variants are commonly discussed: for global scheduling, tasks are restricted to a subset of the available processors; and for partitioned scheduling, the program can explicitly change a task's affinity and hence cause it to be moved at run-time.

Restricting the set of processors on which a task can be globally scheduled supports scalability – as platforms move to contain hundreds of processors, the overheads of allowing full task migration become excessive and outweighs any advantage that might accrue from global scheduling. Controlled changing of a task's affinity has been shown to lead to improved schedulability for certain types of application (see discussion in Section 8.3 on semi-partitioned execution).

10.6.2 Dispatching Domains and Ada

The package shown in Program 10.4 allows the system's CPUs to be partitioned into a group of non-overlapping **dispatching domains**. A dispatching domain represents a set of processors (`CPU_Set`) on which a task may execute. Each processor is contained within exactly one dispatching domain.

One dispatching domain is defined to be the *System* dispatching domain; the Ada environment task and any created from that task are allocated (by default) to the *System* dispatching domain. All CPUs allocated by the environment to the Ada program are initially placed in this domain.

Subprograms are defined to allow new dispatching domains to be created. CPUs allocated in new domains are automatically removed from the *System* dispatching domain. Tasks can be assigned to a dispatching domain and be globally scheduled within that dispatching domain; alternatively they can be assigned to a dispatching domain and restricted to executing on a specific CPU within that dispatching domain. Tasks cannot be assigned to more than one dispatching domain, or restricted to more than one CPU (within a dispatching domain).

Package 10.3 just defines a parent unit for all multiprocessor facilities, and gives a range for an integer representation of each CPU. Note the value 0 is used to indicate `Not_A_Specific_CPU`; so the CPUs are actually numbered from one. The function `Number_Of_CPUs` will, for any execution of the program, always return the same value. In effect the number of CPUs is a constant and reflects the number of available processors at system start up.

```ada
package System.Multiprocessors is
  pragma Preelaborate(Multiprocessors);
  type CPU_Range is range 0 .. implementation-defined;
  Not_A_Specific_CPU : constant CPU_Range := 0;
  subtype CPU is CPU_Range range 1 .. CPU_Range'Last;
  function Number_Of_CPUs return CPU;
end System.Multiprocessors;
```

Program 10.3: The `System.Multiprocessors` package.

```ada
with Ada.Real_Time;
with Ada.Task_Identification;
package System.Multiprocessors.Dispatching_Domains is
  Dispatching_Domain_Error : exception;
  type Dispatching_Domain (<>) is limited private;
  System_Dispatching_Domain : constant Dispatching_Domain;
  function Create (First : CPU; Last : CPU_Range)
            return Dispatching_Domain;
  function Get_First_CPU (Domain : Dispatching_Domain)
            return CPU;
  function Get_Last_CPU (Domain : Dispatching_Domain)
            return CPU_Range;

  type CPU_Set is array(CPU range <>) of Boolean;
  function Create (Set : CPU_Set) return Dispatching_Domain;
  function Get_CPU_Set (Domain : Dispatching_Domain) return CPU_Set;

  function Get_Dispatching_Domain
      (T : Ada.Task_Identification.Task_Id :=
       Ada.Task_Identification.Current_Task)
         return Dispatching_Domain;
  procedure Assign_Task(Domain : in out Dispatching_Domain;
                CPU : in CPU_Range := Not_A_Specific_CPU;
                T : in Ada.Task_Identification.Task_Id :=
                Ada.Task_Identification.Current_Task);
  procedure Set_CPU(CPU : in CPU_Range;
              T : in Ada.Task_Identification.Task_Id :=
              Ada.Task_Identification.Current_Task);
  function Get_CPU(T : Ada.Task_Identification.Task_Id :=
              Ada.Task_Identification.Current_Task)
                return CPU_Range;
  procedure Delay_Until_And_Set_CPU
      (Delay_Until_Time : in Ada.Real_Time.Time;
       CPU : in CPU_Range);
private
  ... -- not specified by the language
end System.Multiprocessors.Dispatching_Domains;
```

Program 10.4: The `System.Multiprocessor.Dispatching_Domains` package.

As well as being able to call the subprograms in Program 10.4, a task can have its CPU and dispatching domain set using language-defined representation aspects at the task's declaration time. For example:

```
task type Fixed(Proc : CPU_Range) with CPU => Proc;

task body Fixed is
begin
  ...
end Fixed;
```

declares a task type, an instance of which will be restricted to run on the CPU passed as a discriminant when it is created. Similarly,

```
Domain : Dispatching_Domain := Dispatching_Domains.create(1,3);

task type Fixed with Dispatching_Domain => Domain;
task body Fixed is
begin
  ..
end Fixed;
```

would declare a task type, whose instances may only execute on a dispatching domain that consists of CPUs 1, 2 and 3.

10.7 A simple embedded system

In order to illustrate some of the advantages and disadvantages of concurrent programming, a simple embedded system will now be considered. Figure 10.6 outlines this simple system. A task T takes readings from a set of thermocouples (via an analogue to digital converter, ADC) and makes appropriate changes to a heater (via a digitally controlled switch). Task P has a similar function, but for pressure (it uses a digital to analogue converter, DAC). Both T and P must communicate data to S, which presents measurements to an operator via a display. Note that P and T are active; S is a resource (it just responds to requests from T and P): it may be implemented as a protected resource or a server if it interacts more extensively with the user.

The overall objective of this embedded system is to keep the temperature and pressure of some chemical process within defined limits. A real system of this type would clearly be more complex – allowing, for example, the operator to change the limits. However, even for this simple system, the implementation could take one of three forms:

(1) A single program is used which ignores the logical concurrency of T, P and S. No operating system support is required.

(2) T, P and S are written in a sequential programming language (either as separate programs or distinct procedures in the same program) and operating system primitives are used for program/process creation and interaction.

(3) A single concurrent program is used which retains the logical structure of T, P and S. No direct operating system support is required by the program although a run-time support system is needed.

214   CONCURRENT PROGRAMMING

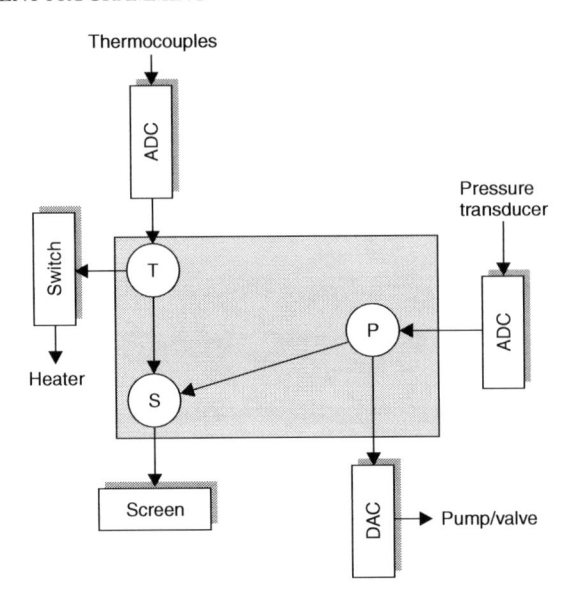

Figure 10.6: A simple embedded system.

To illustrate these solutions, consider the Ada code to implement the simple embedded system. In order to simplify the structure of the control software, the following passive packages will be assumed to have been implemented:

```
package Data_Types is

  -- necessary type definitions
  type Temp_Reading is new Integer range 10..500;
  type Pressure_Reading is new Integer range 0..750;
  type Heater_Setting is (On, Off);
  type Pressure_Setting is new Integer range 0..9;

end Data_Types;

with Data_Types; use Data_Types;
package IO is
  -- procedures for data exchange with the environment
  procedure Read(TR : out Temp_Reading);     -- from ADC
  procedure Read(PR : out Pressure_Reading);
    -- note, this is an example of overloading; two reads
    -- are defined but they have a different parameter type;
    -- this is also the case with the following writes

  procedure Write(HS : Heater_Setting);      -- to switch.
  procedure Write(PS : Pressure_Setting);    -- to DAC
  procedure Write(TR : Temp_Reading);        -- to console
  procedure Write(PR : Pressure_Reading);    -- to console

end IO;
```

A SIMPLE EMBEDDED SYSTEM

```ada
with Data_Types; use Data_Types;
package Control_Procedures is

   -- procedures for converting a reading into
   -- an appropriate setting for output to
   procedure Temp_Convert(TR : Temp_Reading;
                          HS : out Heater_Setting);
   procedure Pressure_Convert(PR : Pressure_Reading;
                              PS : out Pressure_Setting);

end Control_Procedures;
```

Sequential solution

A simple sequential control program could have the following structure:

```ada
with Data_Types, IO, Control_Procedures;
use Data_Types, IO, Control_Procedures;
procedure Controller is
   TR : Temp_Reading;
   PR : Pressure_Reading;
   HS : Heater_Setting;
   PS : Pressure_Setting;
begin
   loop
      Read(TR);         -- from ADC
      Temp_Convert(TR,HS);  -- convert reading to setting
      Write(HS);        -- to switch
      Write(TR);        -- to console
      Read(PR);         -- as above for pressure
      Pressure_Convert(PR,PS);
      Write(PS);
      Write(PR);
   end loop; -- infinite loop, common in embedded software
end Controller;
```

This code has the immediate handicap that temperature and pressure readings must be taken at the same rate, which may not be in accordance with requirements. The use of counters and appropriate **if** statements will improve the situation, but it may still be necessary to split the computationally intensive sections (the conversion procedures `Temp_Convert` and `Pressure_Convert`) into a number of distinct actions, and interleave these actions so as to meet a required balance of work. Even if this were done, there remains a serious drawback with this program structure: while waiting to read a temperature no attention can be given to pressure (and vice versa). Moreover, if there is a system failure that results in, say, control never returning from the temperature `Read`, then in addition to this problem, no further pressure `Read`s would be taken.

An improvement on this sequential program can be made by including two boolean functions in the package `IO`, `Ready_Temp` and `Ready_Pres`, to indicate the availability of an item to read. The control program then becomes

216   CONCURRENT PROGRAMMING

```ada
with Data_Types, IO, Control_Procedures;
use Data_Types, IO, Control_Procedures;
procedure Controller is
  TR : Temp_Reading;
  PR : Pressure_Reading;
  HS : Heater_Setting;
  PS : Pressure_Setting;
  Ready_Temp, Ready_Pres : Boolean;
begin
  loop
    ...
    if Ready_Temp then
      Read(TR);
      Temp_Convert(TR,HS);
      Write(HS);    -- assuming write to be reliable
      Write(TR);
    end if;
    if Ready_Pres then
      Read(PR);
      Pressure_Convert(PR,PS);
      Write(PS);
      Write(PR);
    end if;
  end loop;
end Controller;
```

This solution is more reliable; unfortunately the program now spends a high proportion of its time in a 'busy loop' polling the input devices to see if they are ready. Busy-waits are, in general, unacceptably inefficient. They tie up the processor and make it difficult to impose a queue discipline on waiting requests. Moreover, programs that rely on busy waiting are difficult to design, understand or prove correct.

The major criticism that can be levelled at the sequential program is that no recognition is given to the fact that the pressure and temperature cycles are entirely independent subsystems. In a concurrent programming environment, this can be rectified by coding each system as a task.

Using operating system primitives

Consider an operating system which allows a new task/thread to be created and started by calling the following Ada subprogram:

```ada
package Operating_System_Interface is
  type Thread_ID is private;
  type Thread is access procedure;  -- a pointer type

  function Create_Thread(Code : Thread) return Thread_ID;
  -- other subprograms for thread interaction
private
  type Thread_ID is ...;
end Operating_System_Interface;
```

A SIMPLE EMBEDDED SYSTEM   217

The simple embedded system can now be implemented as follows. First, the two controller procedures are placed in a package:

```ada
package Processes is
  procedure Pressure_Controller;
  procedure Temp_Controller;
end Processes;

with Data_Types, IO, Control_Procedures;
use Data_Types, IO, Control_Procedures;
package body Processes is
  procedure Temp_Controller is
    TR : Temp_Reading;
    HS : Heater_Setting;
  begin
    loop
      Read(TR);
      Temp_Convert(TR,HS);
      Write(HS);
      Write(TR);
    end loop;
  end Temp_Controller;

  procedure Pressure_Controller is
    PR : Pressure_Reading;
    PS : Pressure_Setting;
  begin
    loop
      Read(PR);
      Pressure_Convert(PR,PS);
      Write(PS);
      Write(PR);
    end loop;
  end Pressure_Controller;
end Processes;
```

Now the `Controller` procedure can be given:

```ada
with Operating_System_Interface; use Operating_System_Interface;
with Processes; use Processes;
procedure Controller is
  Tc, Pc: Thread_Id;
begin
  -- create the threads
  -- 'Access returns a pointer to the procedure
  Tc := Create_Thread(Temp_Controller'Access);
  Pc := Create_Thread(Pressure_Controller'Access);
end Controller;
```

Procedures `Temp_Controller` and `Pressure_Controller` execute concurrently and each contains an infinite loop within which the control cycle is defined. While one thread is suspended waiting for a read, the other may be executing; if they are both suspended a busy loop is not executed.

Although this solution does have advantages over the sequential solution, the lack

218   CONCURRENT PROGRAMMING

of language support for expressing concurrency means that the program can become difficult to write and maintain. For the simple example given above, the added complexity is manageable. However, for large systems with many concurrent tasks and potentially complex interactions between them, having a procedural interface obscures the structure of the program. For example, it is not obvious which procedures are really procedures or which ones are intended to be concurrent activities.

Using a concurrent programming language

In a concurrent programming language, concurrent activities can be identified explicitly in the code; for example in Ada:

```ada
package Embedded_System is
   task Temp_Controller;
   task Pressure_Controller;
end Embedded_System;

with Data_Types; use Data_Types;
with IO; use IO;
with Control_Procedures; use Control_Procedures;
package body Embedded_System is

   task body Temp_Controller is
      TR : Temp_Reading; HS : Heater_Setting;
   begin
     loop
        Read(TR);
        Temp_Convert(TR,HS);
        Write(HS);
        Write(TR);
     end loop;
   end Temp_Controller;

   task body Pressure_Controller is
      PR : Pressure_Reading; PS : Pressure_Setting;
   begin
     loop
        Read(PR);
        Pressure_Convert(PR,PS);
        Write(PS);
        Write(PR);
     end loop;
   end Pressure_Controller;
end Embedded_System;

with Embedded_System;
procedure Controller is
begin
   null;    -- Temp_Controller and Pressure_Controller
            -- have started their executions
end Controller;
```

LANGUAGE-SUPPORTED VERSUS OPERATING-SYSTEM-SUPPORTED CONCURRENCY   219

The logic of the application is now reflected in the code; the inherent parallelism of the domain is represented by concurrently executing tasks in the program.

Although an improvement, one major problem remains with this two-task solution. Both `Temp_Controller` and `Pressure_Controller` send data to the console, but the console is a resource that can only sensibly be accessed by one task at a time. In Figure 10.6, control over the console was given to a third entity (S) which will need a representation in the program – `Screen_Controller`. This entity may be a server or a protected resource (depending on the complete definition of the required behaviour of `Screen_Controller`). This has transposed the problem from one of concurrent access to a passive resource to one of inter-task communication, or at least communication between a task and some other concurrency primitive. It is necessary for tasks `Temp_Controller` and `Pressure_Controller` to pass data to `Screen_Controller`. Moreover, `Screen_Controller` must ensure that it deals with only one request at a time. These requirements and difficulties are of primary importance in the design of concurrent programming languages, and are considered in the following chapters.

The concurrent version of this simple embedded system has a structure that follows that which is outlined in Chapter 2. Each task is iterative, it gets its data at the start of each iteration, it processes the data and it writes its results at the end of each iteration. This example will be revisited throughout this book as various aspects of real-time systems are discussed. In particular, extra control variables will be added to define the rate of execution of the tasks.

10.8 Language-supported versus operating-system-supported concurrency

Although this book is focusing on Ada, it is clear that an alternative approach is to use a language, like C, and a real-time operating system (such as one that conforms to the POSIX API).

There has been a long debate among programmers, language designers and operating system designers as to whether it is appropriate to provide support for concurrency in a language or whether this should be provided by the operating system only. Arguments in favour of including concurrency in the programming languages include the following:

(1) It leads to more readable and maintainable programs.

(2) There are many different types of operating system; defining the concurrency in the language makes the program more portable.

(3) An embedded computer may not have any resident operating system available.

These arguments were clearly the ones which held the most weight with the designers of Ada. Arguments against concurrency in a language include the following:

(1) Different languages have different models of concurrency; it is easier to compose programs from different languages if they all use the same operating system model

of concurrency.

(2) It may be difficult to implement a language's model of concurrency efficiently on top of an operating system's model.

(3) Operating system API standards, such as POSIX, have emerged and therefore programs are more portable.

The need to support multiple languages was one of the main reasons why the civil aircraft industry when developing its Integrated Modular Avionics programme opted for a standard applications–kernel interface (called APEX) supporting concurrency rather than adopting the Ada model of concurrency [4]. However, it should be noted that certain compiler optimisations may lead to race conditions if the compiler does not take into account potential concurrent execution of the program [20, 16]. This is particularly true for multiprocessor systems. As a consequence of this, C and C++ have added language-defined support for multithreading into the most recent version of their international standards.

Summary

The application domains of most real-time systems are inherently parallel. It follows that the inclusion of the notion of task/thread within a real-time programming language makes an enormous difference to the expressive power and ease of use of the language. These factors in turn contribute significantly to reducing the software construction costs whilst improving the reliability of the final system.

Without concurrency, the software must be constructed as a single control loop. The structure of this loop cannot retain the logical distinction between system components. It is particularly difficult to give task-oriented timing and reliability requirements without the notion of a task being visible in the code.

The use of a concurrent programming language is not, however, without its costs. In particular, it becomes necessary to use a run-time support system (or operating system) to manage the execution of the system tasks.

The behaviour of a task is best described in terms of states. In this chapter, the following states are discussed:

- non-existing
- created
- initialised
- executable
- waiting dependent termination
- waiting child initialization
- terminated

Within concurrent programming languages, there are a number of variations in the task model adopted. These variations can be analysed under six headings.

(1) structure – static or dynamic task model
(2) level – top-level tasks only (flat) or multilevel (nested)
(3) initialization – with or without parameter passing
(4) granularity – fine or coarse grain
(5) termination –
   - natural
   - suicide
   - aborted
   - untrapped error
   - never
   - when no longer needed
(6) representation – coroutines, fork/join, cobegin; explicit task declarations

Ada provides a dynamic model with support for nested tasks and a range of termination options. The most recent version of the language supports program-control over the placement of tasks onto CPUs.

Chapter 11
Shared variable-based synchronization and communication

11.1 Mutual exclusion and condition synchronization
11.2 Coordinated sections
11.3 Busy waiting
11.4 Suspend and resume
11.5 Semaphores
11.6 Conditional critical regions
11.7 Monitors
11.8 Protected objects in Ada
11.9 Shared memory multiprocessor
11.10 Simple embedded system revisited
Summary

The major difficulties associated with concurrent programming arise from task interactions. Rarely are tasks as independent of one another as they were in the simple example at the end of Chapter 10. The correct behaviour of a concurrent program is critically dependent on synchronization and communication between tasks. In its widest sense, synchronization is the satisfaction of constraints on the interleaving of the actions of different tasks (for example, a particular action by one task only occurring after a specific action by another task). The term is also used in the narrower sense of bringing two tasks simultaneously into predefined states. Communication is the passing of information from one task to another. The two concepts are linked, since some forms of communication require synchronization, and synchronization can be considered as contentless communication.

Inter-task communication is usually based upon either **shared variables** or **message passing**. Shared variables are objects to which more than one task has access; communication can therefore proceed by each task referencing these variables when appropriate. Message passing involves the explicit exchange of data between two tasks by means of a message that passes from one task to another via some agency. Note that the choice between shared variables and message passing is one for the language or operating systems designers; it does not imply that any particular implementation method should be used. Shared variables are easy to support if there is shared memory between the tasks and, hence, they are an ideal mechanisms for communication between tasks in a shared memory multiprocessor system. However, they can still be used even if the hardware incorporates a communication medium. Similarly, a message-passing primitive is an ideal abstraction for a distributed system where there is potentially no shared physical memory. But again, it can also be supported via shared memory.

This book is mainly concerned with single and multiprocessor systems. Message-passing systems tend to complicate schedulability analysis as the receiver task has to wait for the sender task. This increases the difficulty in determining how long the receiver will block. For this reason, only shared-variable communication is considered in this book.

This chapter will focus first on the general issues of shared variable-based communication and synchronization primitives. In particular, busy waiting, semaphores, conditional critical regions, monitors and protected types are discussed. The topic of shared memory multiprocessors is also considered.

11.1 Mutual exclusion and condition synchronization

Although shared variables appear to be a straightforward way of passing information between tasks, their unrestricted use is unreliable and unsafe due to multiple update problems. Consider two tasks updating a shared variable, X, with the assignment:

```
X:= X+1
```

On most hardware this will not be executed as an **indivisible** (atomic) operation, but will be implemented in three distinct instructions:

(1) load the value of X into some register (or to the top of the stack);
(2) increment the value in the register by 1; and
(3) store the value in the register back to X.

As the three operations are not indivisible, two tasks simultaneously updating the variable could follow an interleaving that would produce an incorrect result. For example, if X was originally 5, the two tasks could each load 5 into their registers, increment and then store 6.

A sequence of statements that must appear to be executed indivisibly is called a **critical section**. The synchronization required to protect a critical section is known as **mutual exclusion**. Atomicity, although absent from the assignment operation, is assumed to be present at the memory level. Thus, if one task is executing X := 5, simultaneously with another executing X := 6, the result will be either 5 or 6 (not some other value). If this were not true, it would be difficult to reason about concurrent programs or implement higher levels of atomicity, such as mutual exclusion synchronization. Clearly, however, if two tasks are updating a structured object, this atomicity will only apply at the single word element level.

The mutual exclusion problem itself was first described by Dijkstra [31]. It lies at the heart of most concurrent task synchronizations and is of great theoretical as well as practical interest. Mutual exclusion is not, however, the only synchronization of importance; indeed, if two tasks do not share variables then there is no need for mutual exclusion. Condition synchronization is another significant requirement and is needed when a task wishes to perform an operation that can only sensibly, or safely, be performed if another task has itself taken some action or is in some defined state.

An example of condition synchronization comes with the use of buffers. Two tasks that exchange data may perform better if communication is not direct but via a buffer. This has the advantage of de-coupling the tasks and allows for small fluctuations in the speed at which the two tasks are working. For example, an input task may receive data in bursts that must be buffered for the appropriate user task. The use of a buffer to link two tasks is common in concurrent programs and is known as a **producer–consumer** system.

Two condition synchronizations are necessary if a finite (bounded) buffer is used. Firstly, the producer task must not attempt to deposit data into the buffer if the buffer is full. Secondly, the consumer task cannot be allowed to extract objects from the buffer if the buffer is empty. Moreover, if simultaneous deposits or extractions are possible, mutual exclusion must be ensured so that two producers, for example, do not corrupt the 'next free slot' pointer of the buffer.

The implementation of any form of synchronization implies that tasks must at times be held back until it is appropriate for them to proceed. In Section 11.2, the general problem of coordinating tasks is considered before considering the synchronization mechanisms that have been developed over the years to help with this coordination. In Section 11.3, mutual exclusion and condition synchronization will be programmed (in pseudo code with explicit task declaration) using **busy-wait** loops and **flags**. From this analysis, it should be clear that further primitives are needed to ease the coding of algorithms that require synchronization.

11.2 Coordinated sections

The previous section introduced the notion of a critical section. This is a section of code that accesses data that is to be shared between multiple tasks and that must be executed under mutual exclusion. Of course, tasks may want to perform different operations on the shared data so, in practice, there may be several related critical sections. Each critical section must be executed indivisibly with respect to itself and the other related critical section. Critical sections reduce the amount of concurrency in a system and, hence, must only be used where necessary. Too many critical sections will add implementation overheads, and remove the option of the parallel execution of tasks in a multiprocessor system.

More generally, the sections of code may not require such strong synchronization constraints but, nevertheless, they are some constraints of their execution order and interleaving. These are call **coordinated sections** in this book. Where the coordination constraints require indivisibility then coordinated sections are equivalent to critical sections. In the producer-consumer problem, access to the bounded buffer is usually performed in related critical sections (one depositing data into the buffer and one for extracting data from the buffer).

Other coordination problems are not so constrained. One of the standard task coordination problems is the **readers–writers** problem. In this problem, many reader and many writer tasks are attempting to access a large data structure. Readers can read concurrently, as they do not alter the data; however, writers require mutual exclusion over the data both from other writers and from readers. Allowing readers to read concurrently increases the

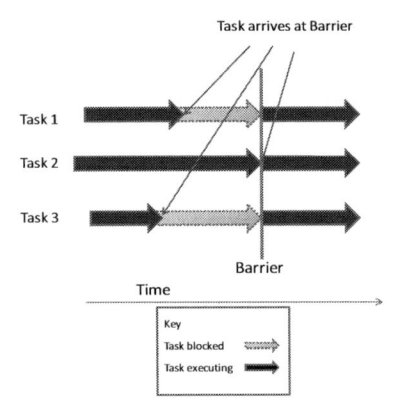

Figure 11.1: Task coordination using a Barrier (Bar).

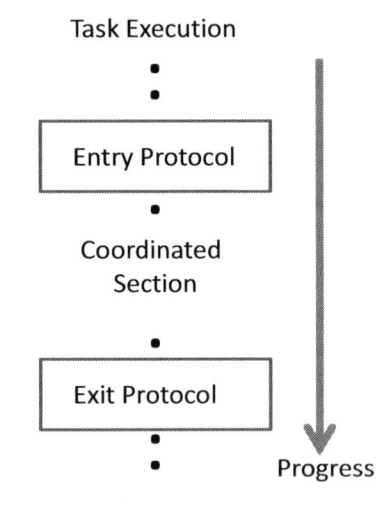

Figure 11.2: Task coordination using entry and exit protocols.

overall performance of the system if the time spent reading is greater than the overhead of implementing more complex task coordination. There are different variations on this scheme; the one considered here is where preference is always given to waiting writers. Hence, as soon as a writer is available, all new readers will be blocked until all writers have finished (or all current readers have finished). Of course, in extreme situations, this may lead to starvation of readers.

Another, common coordination problem is that of a **bar** (or a **barrier**) – illustrated in Figure 11.1. Here, several tasks must wait at the barrier (bar) until all tasks have arrived. Only when all tasks are present can they proceed. Ada uses the term *barrier* to mean a

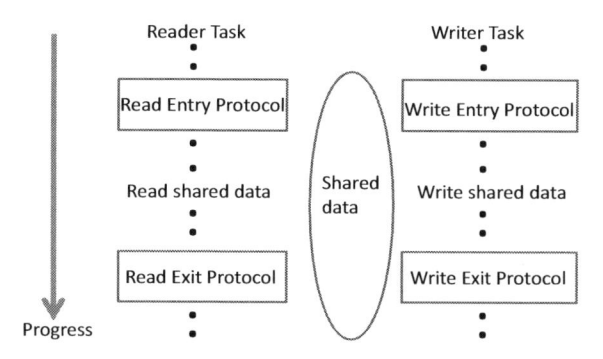

Figure 11.3: The readers-writers task coordination.

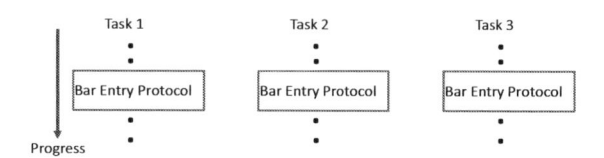

Figure 11.4: Task coordination using a Bar.

guard (see Section 11.8), so this book will refer to this type of coordination as a **bar**.

The key to solving most task coordination problems is to surround each coordinated section with an entry and an exit protocol. The entry protocol determines if the conditions for the operation to proceed are right, and if not, blocks the calling task until they are right. The exit protocol determines whether any blocked operations can now proceed. Data may be needed to keep track of the current state of the requested coordination. This data must be accessed under mutual exclusion. Figure 11.2 illustrates this.

The design of the solution to the readers-writers coordination problem is illustrated in Figure 11.3, and the bar coordination problem in Figure 11.4. Note in the latter case, there is only an entry protocol and no exit protocol.

The following sections will now focus on the synchronization mechanisms that can be used to program the entry and exit protocols.

11.3 Busy waiting

One way to implement synchronization is to have tasks set and check shared variables that are acting as flags. This approach works reasonably well for implementing condition synchronization, but (as will be illustrated shortly) no simple method for mutual exclusion exists. To signal a condition, a task sets the value of a flag; to wait for this condition, another task checks this flag and proceeds only when the appropriate value is read:

```
task T1;   -- pseudo code for waiting task
  ...
  while flag = down do
    null
  end;
  ...
end T1;

task T2;   -- signalling task
  ...
  flag := up;
  ...
end T2;
```

If the condition is not yet set (that is, flag is still down) then `T1` has no choice but to loop round and recheck the flag. This is **busy waiting**; also known as **spinning** (with the flag variables called **spin locks**).

Busy-wait algorithms are in general inefficient; they involve tasks using up processing cycles when they cannot perform useful work. Even on a multiprocessor system, they can give rise to excessive traffic on the memory bus or network (if distributed). Moreover, it is not possible to impose queuing disciplines easily if there is more than one task waiting on a condition (that is, checking the value of a flag). More seriously, they can leave to **livelock**. This is an error condition where tasks get stuck in their busy-wait loops and are unable to make progress.

Mutual exclusion presents even more difficulties as the algorithms required are more complex. Consider two tasks (`T1` and `T2` again) that have mutual critical sections. In order to protect access to these critical sections, it is again assumed that each task executes an entry protocol before the critical section and an exit protocol afterwards. Each task can therefore be considered to have the following form:

```
task T; -- pseudo code
  loop
    entry protocol
      critical section
    exit protocol
    non-critical section
  end
end T;
```

An algorithm is presented below that provides mutual exclusion and absence of livelock. It was first presented by Peterson [64]. The approach of Peterson is to have two flags (`flag1` and `flag2`) that are manipulated by the task that 'owns' them and a `turn` variable that is only used if there is contention for entry to the critical sections:

```
task T1; -- pseudo code
  loop
    flag1:= up;      -- announce intent to enter
    turn:= 2;        -- give priority to other task
    while flag2 = up and turn = 2 do
```

```
        null;
      end;
      <critical section>
      flag1:= down;
      <non-critical section>
  end
end T1;

task T2;
  loop
    flag2:= up;      -- announce intent to enter
    turn:= 1;        -- give priority to other task
    while flag1 = up and turn = 1 do
      null;
    end;
    <critical section>
    flag2:= down;
    <non-critical section>
  end
end T2;
```

If only one task wishes to enter its critical section then the other task's flag will be down and entry will be immediate. However, if both flags have been raised then the value of turn becomes significant. Let us say that it has the initial value 1; then there are four possible interleavings, depending on the order in which each task assigns a value to turn and then checks its value in the while statement:

```
First Possibility -- T1 first then T2
T1 sets turn to 2
T1 checks turn and enters busy loop
T2 sets turn to 1 (turn will now stay with that value)
T2 checks turn and enters busy loop
T1 loops around rechecks turn and enters critical section


Second Possibility -- T2 first then T1
T2 sets turn to 1
T2 checks turn and enters busy loop
T1 sets turn to 2 (turn will now stay with that value)
T1 checks turn and enters busy loop
T2 loops around rechecks turn and enters critical section


Third Possibility -- interleaved T1 and T2
T1 sets turn to 2
T2 sets turn to 1 (turn will stay with this value)
T2 enters busy loop
T1 enters critical section


Fourth Possibility -- interleaved T2 and T1
T2 sets turn to 1
T1 sets turn to 2 (turn will stay with this value)
```

```
T1 enters busy loop
T2 enters critical section
```

All four possibilities lead to one task in its critical section and one task in a busy loop.

In general, although a single interleaving can only illustrate the failure of a system to meet its specification, it is not possible to show easily that all possible interleavings lead to compliance with the specification. Normally, proof methods (including model checking) are needed to show such compliance.

Interestingly, the above algorithm is fair in the sense that if there is contention for access (to their critical sections) and, say, `T1` was successful (via either the first or third possible interleaving) then `T2` is bound to enter next. When `T1` exits its critical section, it lowers `flag1`. This could let `T2` into its critical section, but even if it does not (because `T2` was not actually executing at that time) then `T1` would proceed, enter and leave its non-critical section, raise `flag1`, set `turn` to 2 and then be placed in a busy loop. There it would remain until `T2` had entered and left its critical section and reset `flag2` as its exit protocol.

In terms of reliability, the failure of a task in its non-critical section will not affect the other task. This is not the case with failure in the protocols or critical section. Here, premature termination of a task would lead to livelock difficulties for the remaining program.

This discussion has been given at length to illustrate the difficulties of implementing synchronization between tasks with only shared variables and no additional primitives other than those found in sequential languages. These difficulties can be summarised as follows:

- Protocols that use busy loops are difficult to design, understand and prove correct. (The reader might like to consider generalizing Peterson's algorithm for *n* tasks.)

- Testing programs may not examine rare interleavings that break mutual exclusion or lead to livelock.

- Busy-wait loops are inefficient.

- An unreliable (rogue) task that misuses shared variables will corrupt the entire system.

The above problems are exacerbated when the algorithms are implemented in a multiprocessor environment. Here weak memory models may imply that flags are not updated in the expected order.

No concurrent programming language relies entirely on busy waiting and shared variables; other methods and primitives have been introduced. For shared-variable systems, semaphores and monitors are the most significant constructs and are described in Sections 11.5 and 11.7.

11.4 Suspend and resume

One of the problems with busy-wait loops is that they waste valuable processor time. An alternative approach is to suspend (that is, remove from the set of runnable tasks) the calling task if the condition for which it is waiting does not hold. Consider, for example, simple condition synchronization using a `flag`. One task sets the flag, and another task waits until the flag is set and then clears it. A simple suspend and resume mechanism could be used as follows:

```
task T1;  -- pseudo code for waiting task
  ...
  if flag = down do
    suspend;
  end;
  flag := down;
  ...
end T1;

task T2;  -- signalling task
  ...
  flag := up;
  resume T1; -- has no effect, if T1 is not suspended
  ...
end T2;
```

Unfortunately, this approach suffers from what is called a **data race condition**, which is defined below.

> *A data race condition is a fault in the design of the interactions between two or more tasks whereby the result is unexpected and critically dependent on the sequence or timing of accesses to shared data.*

In this case, task `T1` could test the `flag`, and then the underlying run-time support system (or operating system) could decide to preempt it and run `T2`. `T2` sets the `flag` and `resumes T1`. `T1` is, of course, not suspended, so the `resume` has no effect. Now, when `T1` next runs, it thinks the `flag` is `down` and therefore suspends itself.

The reason for this problem is that the `flag` is a shared resource which is being tested and an action is being taken which depends on its status (the task is suspending itself). This testing and suspending is not an atomic operation, and therefore interference can occur from other tasks.

There are several well-known solutions to this race condition problem, all of which provide a form of **two-stage suspend** operation. `T1` essentially has to announce that it is planning to suspend in the near future; any resume operation which finds that `T1` is not suspended will have a deferred effect. When `T1` does suspend, it will immediately be resumed; that is, the suspend operation itself will have no effect.

Although suspend and resume is a low-level facility, which can be error-prone in its use, it is an efficient mechanism which can be used to construct higher-level synchronization primitives. For this reason, Ada provides, as part of its Real-Time Annex, a safe version of this mechanism. It is based around the concept of a **suspension** object, which

```ada
package Ada.Synchronous_Task_Control is
   type Suspension_Object is limited private;
   procedure Set_True(S : in out Suspension_Object);
   procedure Set_False(S : in out Suspension_Object);
   function Current_State(S : Suspension_Object) return Boolean;
   procedure Suspend_Until_True(S: in out Suspension_Object);
     -- raises Program_Error if more than one task tries
     -- to suspend on S at once.
private
   -- not specified by the language
end Ada.Synchronous_Task_Control;
```

Program 11.1: The `Ada.Synchronous_Task_Control` package.

can hold the value `True` or `False`. Program 11.1 gives the package specification.

All four subprograms defined by the package are atomic with respect to each other. On return from the `Suspend_Until_True` procedure, the referenced suspension object is reset to `False`.

The simple condition synchronization problem, given earlier in this section, can, therefore, be easily solved.

```ada
with Ada.Synchronous_Task_Control;
use Ada.Synchronous_Task_Control;

...
Flag : Suspension_Object;
...
task body T1 is
begin
   ...
   Suspend_Until_True(Flag);
   ...
end T1;

task body T2 is
begin
   ...
   Set_True(Flag);
   ...
end T2;
```

Suspension objects only provide condition synchronization – as only one task can be suspended at any one time. Hence they cannot be used to provide higher level mechanisms such as semaphores (see following section).

Suspend and resume are useful low-level primitives, however, no operating system or language relies solely on these mechanisms for mutual exclusion and condition synchronization. If present, they clearly introduce a new state into the state transition diagram introduced in Chapter 10. The general state diagram for a task, therefore, is extended in Figure 11.5.

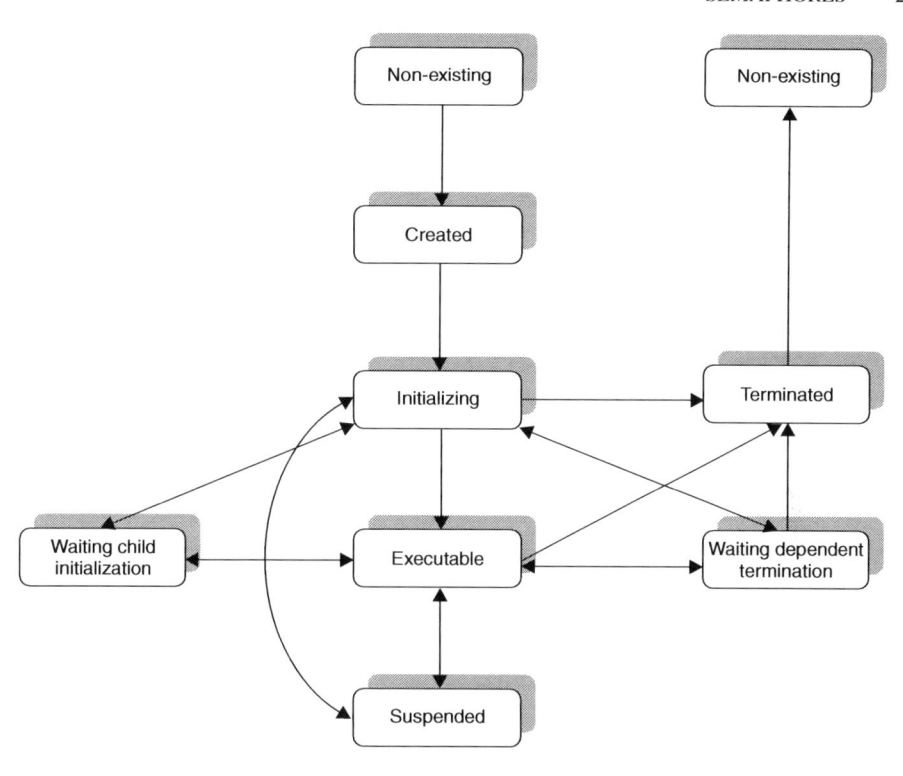

Figure 11.5: State diagram for a task.

11.5 Semaphores

Semaphores are a simple mechanism for programming mutual exclusion and condition synchronization. They were originally designed by Dijkstra [32] and have the two following benefits:

(1) They simplify the protocols for synchronization.
(2) They remove the need for busy-wait loops.

A **semaphore** is a non-negative integer variable that, apart from initialisation, can only be acted upon by two procedures. These procedures are called `wait` and `signal` in this book. The semantics of `wait` and `signal` are as follows:

(1) `wait(S)` – If the value of the semaphore, S, is greater than zero then decrement its value by one; otherwise delay the task until S is greater than zero (and then decrement its value).
(2) `signal(S)` – Increment the value of the semaphore, S, by one.

General semaphores are often called **counting semaphores**, as their operations increment and decrement an integer count. The additional important property of `wait` and `signal` is that their actions are atomic (indivisible). Two tasks, both executing `wait` operations on the same semaphore, cannot interfere with each other. Moreover, a task cannot fail during the execution of a semaphore operation.

Condition synchronization and mutual exclusion can be programmed easily with semaphores. First, consider condition synchronization:

```
-- pseudo code for condition synchronization
consyn : semaphore; -- initially 0
task T1; -- waiting task
  ...
  wait(consyn);
  ...
end T1;

task T2; -- signalling task
  ...
  signal(consyn);
  ...
end T2;
```

When T1 executes the `wait` on a 0 semaphore, it will be delayed until T2 executes the `signal`. This will set `consyn` to 1 and hence the `wait` can now succeed; T1 will continue and `consyn` will be decremented to 0. Note that if T2 executes the `signal` first, the semaphore will be set to 1, so T1 will not be delayed by the action of the `wait`.

Mutual exclusion is similarly straightforward:

```
-- pseudo code for mutual exclusion

mutex : semaphore; -- initially 1
task T1;
  loop
    wait(mutex);
      <critical section>
    signal(mutex);
    <non-critical section>
  end
end T1;


task T2;
  loop
    wait (mutex);
      <critical section>
    signal (mutex);
    <non-critical section>
  end
end T2;
```

If T1 and T2 are in contention then they will execute their `wait` statements simultaneously. However, as `wait` is atomic, one task will complete execution of this statement before the other begins. One task will execute a `wait(mutex)` with mutex=1, which will allow the task to proceed into its critical section and set `mutex` to 0; the other task will execute `wait(mutex)` with `mutex=0`, and be delayed. Once the first task has exited its critical section, it will `signal(mutex)`. This will cause the semaphore to become 1 again and allow the second task to enter its critical section (and set `mutex` to 0 again).

With a wait/signal bracket around a section of code, the initial value of the semaphore will restrict the maximum amount of concurrent execution of the code. If the initial value is 0, no task will ever enter; if it is 1 then a single task may enter (that is, mutual exclusion); for values greater than one, the given number of concurrent executions of the code are allowed.

11.5.1 Suspended tasks

In the definition of `wait` it is clear that if the semaphore is zero then the calling task is delayed. One method of delay (busy waiting) has already been introduced and criticised. A more efficient mechanism, that of suspending the task, was introduced in Section 11.4. In fact, all synchronization primitives deal with delay by some form of suspension; the task is removed from the set of executable tasks.

When a task executes a `wait` on a zero semaphore, the RTSS (run-time support system) is invoked, the task is removed from the processor, and placed in a queue of suspended tasks (that is a queue of tasks suspended on that particular semaphore). The RTSS must then select another task to run. Eventually, if the program is correct, another task will execute a signal on that semaphore. As a result, the RTSS will pick out one of the suspended tasks awaiting a signal on that semaphore and make it executable again.

From these considerations, a slightly different definition of `wait` and `signal` can be given. This definition is closer to what an implementation would do:

```
-- pseudo code for wait(S)
if S > 0 then
  S:= S-1;
else
  number_suspended := number_suspended + 1
  suspend_calling_task;

-- pseudo code signal(S)
if number_suspended > 0 then
  number_suspended := number_suspended - 1;
  make_one_suspended_task_executable_again;
else
  S:= S+1;
end if;
```

With this definition, the increment of a semaphore immediately followed by its decrement is avoided.

Note that the above algorithm does not define the order in which tasks are released from the suspended state. Usually, they are released in a FIFO order, although arguably with a true concurrent language, the programmer should assume a non-deterministic order. However, for a real-time programming language, the priority of the tasks has an important role to play (see Chapter 4).

11.5.2 Implementation

The above algorithm for implementing a semaphore is quite straightforward, although it involves the support of a queue mechanism. Where difficulty could arise is in the requirement for indivisibility in the execution of the `wait` and `signal` operations. Indivisibility means that once a task has started to execute one of these procedures it will continue to execute until the operation has been completed. With the aid of the RTSS, this is easily achieved; the scheduler is programmed so that it does not swap out a task while it is executing a `wait` or a `signal`; they are **non-preemptible** operations.

Unfortunately, the RTSS is not always in full control of scheduling events. Although all internal actions are under its influence, external actions happen asynchronously and could disturb the atomicity of the semaphore operations. To prohibit this, the RTSS will typically disable interrupts for the duration of the execution of the indivisible sequence of statements. In this way, no external events can interfere.

This disabling of interrupts is adequate for a single processor system but not for a multiprocessor one. With a shared-memory system, two parallel tasks may be executing a `wait` or `signal` (on the same semaphore) and the RTSS is powerless to prevent it. In these circumstances, a 'lock' mechanism is needed to protect access to the operations. Two such mechanisms are used.

On some processors, a 'test and set' instruction is provided. This allows a task to access a bit in the following way.

(1) If the bit is zero then set it to one and return zero.

(2) If the bit is one return one.

These actions are themselves indivisible. Two parallel tasks, both wishing to operate a `wait` (for example), will do a test and set operation on the same lock bit (which is initially zero). One task will succeed and set the bit to one; the other task will have returned a one and will, therefore, have to loop round and retest the lock. When the first task has completed the wait operation, it will assign the bit to zero (that is, unlock the semaphore) and the other task will proceed to execute its `wait` operation.

If no test and set instruction is available then a similar effect can be obtained by a swap instruction. Again, the lock is associated with a bit that is initially zero. A task wishing to execute a semaphore operation will swap a one with the lock bit. If it gets a zero back from the lock then it can proceed; if it gets back a one then some other task is active with the semaphore and it must retest.

As indicated in Section 11.1, a primitive such as a semaphore cannot conjure up mutual exclusion out of 'fresh air'. It is necessary for memory locations to exhibit the essence of atomicity in order for higher-level structures to be built. Similarly, although busy-wait loops are removed from the programmer's domain by the use of semaphores, it may be necessary to use busy waits (as above) to implement the wait and signal operations. *It should be noted, however, that the latter use of busy waits is only short-lived (the time it takes to execute a wait or signal operation), whereas their use for delaying access to the program's critical sections could involve many milliseconds of looping.*

A final point to note with 'test and set' and swap instructions, their use must not be undermined by the caching of the memory location.

11.5.3 Liveness provision

In Section 11.3, the error condition livelock was illustrated. Unfortunately (but inevitably), the use of synchronization primitives introduces other error conditions. **Deadlock** is the most serious such condition and entails a set of tasks being in a state from which it is impossible for any of them to proceed. This is similar to livelock but the tasks are suspended. To illustrate this condition, consider two tasks T1 and T2 wishing to gain access to two non-concurrent resources (that is, resources that can only be accessed by one task at a time) that are protected by two semaphores S1 and S2. If both tasks access the resource in the same order then no problem arises:

```
    T1                          T2
wait (S1);                  wait (S1);
  wait (S2);                  wait (S2);
  .                           .
  .                           .
  .                           .
  signal (S2);                signal (S2);
signal (S1);                signal (S1);
```

The first task to execute the wait on S1 successfully will also successfully undertake the wait on S2 and subsequently signal the two semaphores and allow the other task in. A problem occurs, however, if one of the tasks wishes to use the resources in the reverse order, for example:

```
    T1                          T2
wait (S1);                  wait (S2);
  wait (S2);                  wait (S1);
  .                           .
  .                           .
  .                           .
  signal (S2);                signal (S1);
signal (S1);                signal (S2);
```

In this case, an interleaving could allow T1 and T2 to execute successfully the wait on S1 and S2, respectively, but then inevitably both tasks will be suspended waiting on the other semaphore which is now zero.

It is in the nature of an interdependent concurrent program that usually once a subset of the tasks becomes deadlocked all the other tasks will eventually become part of the deadlocked set.

The testing of software rarely removes other than the most obvious deadlocks; they can occur infrequently but with devastating results. This error is not isolated to the use of semaphores and is possible in all concurrent programming languages. The design of languages that prohibit the programming of deadlocks is a desirable, but not yet fully attainable, goal. However, as discussed in Section 5.5 it can de avoided with a carefully chosen resource synchronization policy. Further issues relating to deadlock avoidance, detection and recovery will be considered in Chapters 12.

Indefinite postponement (sometimes called **lockout** or **starvation**) is a less severe error condition whereby a task that wishes to gain access to a resource, via a critical section, is never allowed to do so because there are always other tasks gaining access before it. With a semaphore system, a task may remain indefinitely suspended (that is, queued on the semaphore) due to the way the RTSS picks tasks from this queue when a signal arrives. Even if the delay is not in fact indefinite, but merely open ended (indeterminate), this may give rise to an error in a real-time system.

If a task is free from livelocks, deadlocks and indefinite postponements then it is said to possess **liveness**. Informally, the liveness property implies that if a task wishes to perform some action then it will, eventually, be allowed to do so. In particular, if a task requests access to a critical section it will gain access within a finite time. For a real-time system, liveness itself is not sufficient. It must be possible to give an upper bound on how long it takes for access to be granted.

11.5.4 Binary and quantity semaphores

The definition of a (general) semaphore is a non-negative integer; by implication its actual value can rise to any supported positive number. But in all the examples given so far in this chapter (that is, for condition synchronization and mutual exclusion), only the values 0 and 1 have been used. A simple form of semaphore, known as a **binary semaphore**, can be implemented that takes only these values; that is, the signalling of a semaphore which has the value 1 has no effect – the semaphore retains the value 1. The construction of a general semaphore from two binary semaphores and an integer can then be achieved, if the general form is required.

Another variation on the normal definition of a semaphore is the **quantity semaphore**. With this structure, the amount to be decremented by the `wait` (and incremented by the `signal`) is not fixed as 1, but is given as a parameter to the procedures:

```
wait(S, i) :-   if S >= i then
                    S := S-i
                else
                    delay
                    S := S-i
signal(S, i) :- S := S+i
```

11.5.5 Example semaphore program in Ada

To illustrate a simple program that uses semaphores, an abstract data type for semaphores will be used.

```
package Semaphores is
  type Semaphore(Initial : Natural := 1) is limited private;
  procedure Wait (S : in out Semaphore);
  procedure Signal (S : in out Semaphore);
private
  -- full definition of Semaphore not shown
end Semaphores;
```

SEMAPHORES

Ada does not directly support semaphores, but the `Wait` and `Signal` procedures can, however, be constructed from the Ada synchronization primitives; these have not yet been discussed, so the full definition of the type semaphore and the body of the package will not be given here (see Section 11.8). The essence of abstract data types is, however, that they can be used without knowledge of their implementation.

An example of the use of this package is the producer/consumer system that requires a bounded buffer to pass integers between the two tasks:

```ada
with Semaphores; use Semaphores;
procedure Main is
  package Buffer is
    procedure Append (I : Integer);
    procedure Take (I : out Integer);
  end Buffer;
  task Producer;
  task Consumer;

  package body Buffer is separate;  -- see below
  use Buffer;

  task body Producer is
    Item : Integer;
  begin
    loop
      -- produce item
      Append (Item);
    end loop;
  end Producer;

  task body Consumer is
    Item : Integer;
  begin
    loop
      Take (Item);
      -- consume item
    end loop;
  end Consumer;
begin
  null;
end Main;
```

The buffer itself must protect against concurrent access, appending to a full buffer and taking from an empty one. This it does by the use of three semaphores:

```ada
separate (Main)
package body Buffer is
  Size : constant Natural := 32;
  type Buffer_Range is mod Size;
  Buf : array (Buffer_Range) of Integer;
  Top, Base : Buffer_Range := 0;

  Mutex : Semaphore;  -- default is 1
  Item_Available : Semaphore(0);
```

```ada
   Space_Available : Semaphore(Initial => Size);

   procedure Append (I : Integer) is
   begin
     Wait(Space_Available);
     Wait(Mutex);
       Buf(Top) := I;
       Top := Top + 1;
     Signal(Mutex);
     Signal(Item_Available);
   end Append;

   procedure Take (I : out Integer) is
   begin
     Wait(Item_Available);
     Wait(Mutex);
       I := Buf(Base);
       Base := Base + 1;
     Signal(Mutex);
     Signal(Space_Available);
   end Take;
end Buffer;
```

The initial values of the three semaphores are different. `Mutex` is an ordinary mutual exclusion semaphore and is given the default initial value of 1; `Item_Available` protects against taking from an empty buffer and has the initial value 0; and `Space_Available` (initially `Size`) is used to prevent `Append` operations to a full buffer.

When the program starts, any consumer task that calls `Take` will be suspended on `Wait(Item_Available)`; only after a producer task has called `Append`, and in doing so `Signal(Item_Available)`, will the consumer task continue.

11.5.6 Criticisms of semaphores

Although the semaphore is an elegant low-level synchronization primitive, a real-time program built only upon the use of semaphores is again error-prone. It needs just one occurrence of a semaphore to be omitted or misplaced for the entire program to collapse at run-time. Mutual exclusion may not be assured and deadlock may appear just when the software is dealing with a rare but critical event. What is required is a more structured synchronization primitive.

What the semaphore provides is a means to program mutual exclusion over a critical section. A more structured approach would give mutual exclusion directly. This is precisely what is provided for by the constructs discussed in Sections 11.6 to 11.8.

The example shown in Section 11.5.5 demonstrated that an abstract data type for semaphores can be constructed in Ada. However, no high-level concurrent programming language relies entirely on semaphores. They are important historically but are arguably not adequate for the real-time domain.

11.6 Conditional critical regions

Conditional critical regions (CCRs) are an attempt to overcome some of the problems associated with semaphores. A critical region is a section of code that is guaranteed to be executed in mutual exclusion. This must be compared with the concept of a critical section that should be executed under mutual exclusion (but in error may not be). Clearly, the programming of a critical section as a critical region immediately meets the requirement for mutual exclusion.

Variables that must be protected from concurrent usage are grouped together into named regions and are tagged as being resources. Tasks are prohibited from entering a region in which another task is already active. Condition synchronization is provided by guards on the regions. When a task wishes to enter a critical region, it evaluates the guard (under mutual exclusion); if the guard evaluates true, it may enter, but if it is false, the task is delayed. As with semaphores, the programmer should not assume any order of access if more than one task is delayed attempting to enter the same critical region (for whatever reason).

To illustrate the use of CCRs, an outline of the bounded buffer program is given below.

```
-- pseudo code
program buffer_eg;
  type buffer_t is record
    slots      : array(1..N) of Integer;
    size       : integer range 0..N;
    head, tail : integer range 1..N;
  end record;

  buffer : buffer_t;

  resource buf : buffer;

  task producer;
    ...
    loop
      region buf when buffer.size < N do
        -- place integer in buffer etc
      end region;
      ...
    end loop;
  end,

  task consumer;
    ...
    loop
      region buf when buffer.size > 0 do
        -- take integer from buffer etc
      end region
      ...
    end loop;
  end;
end;
```

242 SHARED VARIABLE-BASED SYNCHRONIZATION AND COMMUNICATION

One potential performance problem with CCRs is that tasks must re-evaluate their guards every time a CCR naming that resource is left. A suspended task must become executable again in order to test the guard; if it is still false, it must return to the suspended state.

A version of CCRs has been implemented in Edison [19], a language intended for embedded applications, implemented on multiprocessor systems. Each processor only executes a single task so that it may continually evaluate its guards if necessary. However, this may cause excess traffic on the network/bus.

11.7 Monitors

The main problem with conditional regions is that they can be dispersed throughout the program. Monitors are intended to alleviate this problem by providing more structured control regions. They also use a form of condition synchronization that is more efficient to implement.

The intended critical regions are written as procedures and are encapsulated together into a single module called a monitor. As a module, all variables that must be accessed under mutual exclusion are hidden; additionally, as a monitor, all procedure calls into the module are guaranteed to execute with mutual exclusion. Hence a monitor provides two important properties:

- automatic mutual exclusion over its operations, and
- encapsulation of the shared data.

Monitors appeared as a refinement of conditional critical regions. They can be found in numerous programming languages including Modula-1, Concurrent Pascal and Mesa.

To continue, for comparison, with the bounded buffer example, a buffer monitor would have the following structure:

```
monitor buffer;  -- pseudo code
  export append, take;
  -- declaration of necessary variables

  procedure append (I : integer);
    ...
  end;

  procedure take (I : integer);
    ...
  end;
begin
  -- initialization of monitor variables
end
```

With languages that support monitors, concurrent calls to append and/or take (in the above example) are serialised – by definition. No mutual exclusion semaphore needs be provided by the programmer. The languages run-time support system will implement the appropriate entry and exit protocols.

Although providing for mutual exclusion, there is still a need for condition synchronization within the monitor. In theory, semaphores could still be used but normally a simpler synchronization primitive is introduced. In Hoare's monitors [44], this primitive is called a **condition variable** and is acted upon by two operators which, because of similarities with the semaphore structure, will again be called wait and signal. When a task issues a wait operation, it is blocked (suspended) and placed on a queue associated with that condition variable (this can be compared with a wait on a semaphore with a value of zero; however, note that a wait on a condition variable *always* blocks unlike a wait on a semaphore). A blocked task then releases its mutually exclusive hold on the monitor, allowing another task to enter. When a task executes a signal operation, it will release one blocked task. If no task is blocked on the specified variable then the *signal has no effect*. (Again note the contrast with signal on a semaphore, which always has an effect on the semaphore. Indeed, wait and signal for monitors are more akin to suspend and resume in their semantics.) The bounded buffer example can now be given in full:

```
monitor buffer;  -- pseudo code
  export append, take;
  constant size = 32;
  buf : array[0...size-1] of integer;
  top, base : 0..size-1;
  spaceAvailable, itemAvailable : condition;
  numberInBuffer : integer;

  procedure append (I : integer);
  begin
    if numberInBuffer = size then
      wait(spaceAvailable);
    buf[top] := I;
    numberInBuffer := numberInBuffer+1;
    top := (top+1) mod size;
    signal(itemAvailable);
  end append;

  procedure take (I : out integer);
  begin
    if numberInBuffer = 0 then
      wait(itemAvailable);
    I := buf[base];
    base := (base+1) mod size;
    numberInBuffer := numberInBuffer-1;
    signal(spaceAvailable);
  end take;

begin  -- initialization
  numberInBuffer := 0;
  top := 0;
  base := 0;
end;
```

If a task calls (for example) take when there is nothing in the buffer, then it will become suspended on `itemAvailable`. A task appending an item will, however, signal this suspended task when an item does becomes available.

The semantics for `wait` and `signal`, given above, are not complete; as they stand, two or more tasks could become active within a monitor. This would occur following a signal operation in which a blocked task was freed. The freed task and the one that freed it are then both executing inside the monitor. To prohibit this clearly undesirable activity, the semantics of `signal` must be modified. Four different approaches are used in languages:

(1) A signal is allowed only as the last action of a task before it leaves the monitor (this is the case with the buffer example above).

(2) A signal operation has the side-effect of executing a return statement; that is, the task is forced to leave the monitor.

(3) A signal operation which unblocks another task has the effect of blocking itself; this task will only execute again when the monitor is free.

(4) A signal operation which unblocks another task does not block and the freed task must compete for access to the monitor once the signalling task exits.

In case (3), which was proposed by Hoare in his original paper on monitors, the tasks that are blocked because of a signal action are placed on a 'ready queue' and are chosen, when the monitor is free, in preference to tasks blocked on entry. In case (4), it is the freed task which is placed on the 'ready queue'.

11.7.1 Conditional waiting

With monitors, once a task has exclusive access to the monitor it executes the called monitor procedure. If additional synchronization constraints are needed, they must be explicitly programmed using condition variables. The key to understanding how to use condition variables with monitors is that the program has to specify the condition(s) that will cause a *task to have to wait* (once it has obtained exclusive access) and the name of the condition that must occur (be notified) for it to continue. So with the bounded buffer, the producer must *wait* for *space to become available*, The consumer must *wait* for an *item to become available*. It is not possible with monitors for the program to indicate, for example, that the `append` procedure needs exclusive access to the buffer BUT only when there is space available. This synchronization model for supporting critical sections is called the **conditional waiting** model, as the program has to specify the condition that will cause the critical section to have to delay its execution. A delay in execution implies that the task gives up its exclusive access to the monitor and is suspended on an internal queue. Once it is notified, it will reacquire exclusive access and continue. This relinquishing and reacquiring exclusivity, along with the task's suspension and resumption, occurs automatically and is implemented by the run-time support system for monitors.

The **conditional waiting** synchronization model can be compared with the **avoidance synchronization** synchronization model supported by Ada and discussed in Section 11.8.

11.7.2 Nested monitor calls

A nested monitor call occurs where a monitor procedure calls a procedure defined within another monitor. This can cause problems when the nested procedure suspends on a condition variable. The mutual exclusion in the last monitor call will be relinquished by the task, due to the semantics of the wait and equivalent operations. However, mutual exclusion will not be relinquished in the monitors from which the nested calls have been made. Tasks that attempt to invoke procedures in these monitors will become blocked. This can have performance implications, since blockage will decrease the amount of concurrency exhibited by the system.

Various approaches to the nested monitor problem have been suggested. The most popular one is to maintain the lock. Other approaches include prohibiting nested procedure calls altogether and providing constructs which specify that certain monitor procedures may release their mutual exclusion lock during remote calls.

11.7.3 Criticisms of monitors

The monitor gives a structured and elegant solution to mutual exclusion problems such as the bounded buffer. It does not, however, deal well with condition synchronization, resorting to low-level condition variables which are semaphore-like primitives. All the criticisms surrounding the use of semaphores apply equally (if not more so) to condition variables.

In addition, although monitors encapsulate all the entities concerned with a resource, and provide the important mutual exclusion, their internal structure may still be difficult to understand due to the use of condition variables.

11.8 Protected objects in Ada

The criticism of monitors centres on their use of condition variables. By replacing this approach to synchronisation by the use of guards, a more structured abstraction is obtained. This form of monitor will be termed a **protected object**.

With monitors and condition variables, the program has to specified the conditions that will cause a task to wait once it has exclusive access to the monitor. Hence, this is why the synchronisation model is called the conditional waiting model (see Section 11.7.1). With protected objects, a different approach is taken. The operations of a protected object are *never* allowed to block once they have started. The model is called **avoidance synchronisation**, as an operation is avoided until it can be completed without further blocking. Ada is the only major language that provides this mechanism.

A protected object in Ada encapsulates data items and allows access to them only via **protected actions**. A protected action is either a protected subprogram or protected entry. The language guarantees that these subprograms and entries will be executed in a manner that ensures that the data is updated under mutual exclusion. Condition synchronisation is provided by having boolean expressions on entries (these are guards but are termed **barriers** in Ada) that must evaluate to true before a task is allowed entry. Consequently, protected objects are rather like monitors and conditional critical regions. They provide the structuring facility of monitors with the high-level synchronisation mechanism of conditional critical regions.

A protected unit may be declared as a type or as a single instance; it has a specification and a body (hence it is declared in a similar way to a task). Its specification may contain functions, procedures and entries.

The following declaration illustrates how protected types can be used to provide simple mutual exclusion over a shared integer:

```
protected type Shared_Integer(Initial_Value : Integer) is
  function Read return  Integer;
  procedure Write(New_Value : Integer);
  procedure Increment(By : Integer);
private
  The_Data : Integer := Initial_Value;
end Shared_Integer;

My_Data : Shared_Integer(42);
```

The above protected type encapsulates a shared integer. The object declaration `My_Data` declares an instance of the protected type and passes the initial value for the encapsulated data. The encapsulated data can now only be accessed by the three subprograms: `Read`, `Write` and `Increment`.

A protected procedure provides mutually exclusive read/write access to the data encapsulated. In this case, concurrent calls to the procedure `Write` or `Increment` will be executed in mutual exclusion; that is, only one can be executing at any one time.

Protected functions provide concurrent read-only access to the encapsulated data. In the above example, this means that many calls to `Read` can be executed simultaneously. However, calls to a protected function are still executed mutually exclusively with calls to a protected procedure. A `Read` call cannot be executed if there is a currently executing procedure call; a procedure call cannot be executed if there are one or more concurrently executing function calls. In the most recent version of Ada, the program can specify (with the `Exclusive_Functions` aspect) that a particular protected object's functions should be treated the same as its protected procedures and executed in mutual exclusion.

The body of the `Shared_Integer` is simply

```
protected body Shared_Integer is
  function Read return Integer is
  begin
    return The_Data;
  end Read;

  procedure Write(New_Value : Integer) is
  begin
    The_Data := New_Value;
  end Write;

  procedure Increment(By : Integer) is
  begin
    The_Data := The_Data + By;
  end Increment;
end Shared_Integer;
```

PROTECTED OBJECTS IN ADA

A protected entry is similar to a protected procedure in that it is guaranteed to execute in mutual exclusion and has read/write access to the encapsulated data. However, a protected entry is guarded by a boolean expression (the barrier) inside the body of the protected object; if this barrier evaluates to false when the entry call is made, the calling task is suspended until the barrier evaluates to true and no other tasks are currently active inside the protected object. Hence protected entry calls can be used to implement condition synchronisation.

Consider a bounded buffer shared between several tasks. The specification of the buffer is shown below (where `Data_Item` is some type in scope).

```ada
-- a bounded buffer

Buffer_Size : constant Integer := 10;
type Index is mod Buffer_Size;
subtype Count is Natural range 0 .. Buffer_Size;
type Buffer is array (Index) of Data_Item;

protected type Bounded_Buffer is
   entry Get(Item : out Data_Item);
   entry Put(Item : in Data_Item);
private
   First : Index := Index'First;
   Last : Index := Index'Last;
   Number_In_Buffer : Count := 0;
   Buf : Buffer;
end Bounded_Buffer;

My_Buffer : Bounded_Buffer;
```

Two entries have been declared; these represent the public interface of the buffer. The data items declared in the private part are those items which must be accessed under mutual exclusion. In this case, the buffer is an array and is accessed via two indices; there is also a count indicating the number of items in the buffer. The body of this protected type is given below.

```ada
protected body Bounded_Buffer is
   entry Get(Item : out Data_Item)
        when Number_In_Buffer /= 0 is
   begin
     Item := Buf(First);
     First := First + 1; -- mod types wrap around
     Number_In_Buffer := Number_In_Buffer - 1;
   end Get;

   entry Put(Item : in Data_Item)
        when Number_In_Buffer /= Buffer_Size is
   begin
     Last := Last + 1;
     Buf(Last) := Item;
     Number_In_Buffer := Number_In_Buffer + 1;
   end Put;
end Bounded_Buffer;
```

248 SHARED VARIABLE-BASED SYNCHRONIZATION AND COMMUNICATION

The Get entry is guarded by the barrier 'when Number_In_Buffer /= 0'; only when this evaluates to true can a task execute the Get entry; similarly with the Put entry. Barriers define a precondition; only when they evaluate to true can the entry be accepted.

Although calls to a protected object can be delayed because the object is in use (that is, they cannot be executed with the requested read or read/write access), Ada does not view the call as being suspended. Calls which are delayed due to an entry barrier being false are, however, considered suspended and placed on a queue. The reasons for this are:

- it is assumed that protected operations are short-lived, and
- once started a protected operation cannot suspend its execution – all calls which are potentially suspending are prohibitive and raise exceptions – it can only requeue (see Section 12.3.2).

Hence a task should not be delayed for a significant period while attempting to access the protected object – other than for reasons associated with the order of scheduling. Once a procedure (or function) call has gained access it will immediately start to execute the subprogram; an entry call will evaluate the barrier and will, of course, be blocked if the barrier is false. In Section 15.3, the implementation strategy required by the Real-Time Systems Annex is considered which guarantees that a task is never delayed when trying to gain access to a protected object.

The following summarises the restrictions that Ada places on the code inside a protected action in order to ensure that it is non-blocking:

- no entry call statements
- no delay statements
- no task creation or activation
- no calls to a subprogram which contains a potentially blocking operation
- no accept statements – part of the message-passing facilities of Ada
- no select statements.

The exception Program_Error is raised if a blocking operation is called. A call to an external protected procedure/function is not considered potentially blocking.

11.8.1 Entry calls and barriers

To issue a call to a protected object, a task simply names the object and the required subprogram or entry. For example, to place some data into the above bounded buffer requires the following call

```
My_Buffer.Put(Some_Item);
```

At any instant in time, a protected entry is either open or closed. It is open if, when checked, the boolean expression evaluates to true; otherwise it is closed.

When closed, the task is queued until boolean expression evaluates to true. To avoid this potentially unbounded delay, the entry call can be placed inside a select statement and a timeout can be given, as illustrated below:

```
select
   Protected_Object.The_Entry();
or
   delay 0.01;
end select;
```

The above will cancel the entry call to the protected object if the code does not start executing within 0.01 seconds of the calling task being queue. Note an absolute time can also be given (see Section 13.3);

Generally, the protected entry barriers of a protected object are evaluated when:

(a) a task calls one of its protected entries and the associated barrier references a variable or an attribute which might have changed since the barrier was last evaluated;

(b) a task leaves a protected procedure or protected entry and there are tasks queued on entries whose barriers reference variables or attributes which might have changed since the barriers were last evaluated.

Barriers are not evaluated as a result of a protected function call. Note that it is not possible for two tasks to be active within a protected entry or procedure as the barriers are only evaluated when a task leaves the object.

When a task calls a protected entry or a protected subprogram, the protected object may already be locked: if one or more tasks are executing protected functions inside the protected object, the object is said to have an active **read lock**; if a task is executing a protected procedure or a protected entry, the object is said to have an active **read/write lock**.

If more than one task calls the same closed barrier then the calls are queued, by default, in a first-come, first-served fashion. However, this default can be changed (see Section 15.3).

Two more examples will now be given. Consider first a simple resource controller. When only a single resource is requested (by a call to the entry Allocate) and released (by a call to the procedure Deallocate), the code is straightforward:

```
protected Resource_Control is
   entry Allocate;
   procedure Deallocate;
private
   Free : Boolean := True;
end Resource_Control;

protected body Resource_Control is
   entry Allocate when Free is
   begin
      Free := False;
   end Allocate;
```

```
  procedure Deallocate is
  begin
    Free := True;
  end Deallocate;
end Resource_Control;
```

The resource is initially available and hence the Free flag is true. A call to Allocate changes the flag, and therefore closes the barrier; all subsequent calls to Allocate will be blocked. When Deallocate is called, the barrier is opened. This will allow one of the waiting tasks to proceed by executing the body of Allocate. The effect of this execution is to close the barrier again, and hence no further executions of the entry body will be possible (until there is a further call of Deallocate).

Interestingly, the general resource controller (where groups of resources are requested and released) is not easy to program using just guards. The reasons for this will be explained in Chapter 12, where resource control is considered in some detail.

Each entry queue has an attribute associated with it that indicates how many tasks are currently queued. This is used in the following example. Assume that a task wishes to broadcast a value (of type Message) to a number of waiting tasks. The waiting tasks will call a Receive entry which is only open when a new message has arrived. At that time, all waiting tasks are released.

Although all tasks can now proceed, they must pass through the protected object in strict sequence (as only one can ever be active in the object). The last task out must then set the barrier to false again so that subsequent calls to Receive are blocked until a new message is broadcast. This explicit setting of the barriers can be compared with the use of condition variables which have no lasting effect (within the monitor) once all tasks have exited. The code for the broadcast example is as follows (note that the attribute Count indicates the number of tasks queued on an entry, and that Message is a type in scope.):

```
protected type Broadcast is
   entry Receive(M : out Message);
   procedure Send(M : Message);
private
   New_Message : Message;
   Message_Arrived : Boolean := False;
end Broadcast;

protected body Broadcast is
   entry Receive(M : out Message) when Message_Arrived is
   begin
     M := New_Message;
     if Receive'Count = 0 then Message_Arrived := False; end if;
   end Receive;

   procedure Send(M : Message) is
   begin
     if Receive'Count > 0 then
       Message_Arrived := True;
       New_Message := M;
     end if;
   end Send;
end Broadcast;
```

As there may be no tasks waiting for the message, the `send` procedure has to check the `count` attribute. Only if it is greater than zero will it set the barrier to true (and record the new message).

Finally, this section gives a full Ada implementation of the semaphores package given in Section 11.5.5. This shows that protected objects are not only an excellent structuring abstraction but have the same expressive power as semaphores. Note that, here, the type `Semaphore` is declared to be "limited private" as the type is implemented using protected objects, which are themselves, by definition, limited private.

```ada
package Semaphores is
  type Semaphore(Initial : Natural := 1) is limited private;
  procedure Wait (S : in out Semaphore);
  procedure Signal (S : in out Semaphore);
private
  protected type Semaphore(Initial : Natural := 1) is
    entry Wait_Imp;
    procedure Signal_Imp;
  private
    Value : Natural := Initial;
  end Semaphore;
end Semaphores;

package body Semaphores is
  protected body Semaphore is
    entry Wait_Imp when Value > 0 is
    begin
      Value := Value - 1;
    end Wait_Imp;

    procedure Signal_Imp is
    begin
      Value := Value + 1;
    end Signal_Imp;
  end Semaphore;

  procedure Wait(S : in out Semaphore) is
  begin
    S.Wait_Imp;
  end Wait;

  procedure Signal(S : in out Semaphore) is
  begin
    S.Signal_Imp;
  end Signal;
end Semaphores;
```

11.8.2 Private entries and entry families

So far this chapter has considered the basic protected type. As with tasks, protected objects may have private entries. These are not directly visible to users of the protected object. But they may be used during requeue operations (see Section 12.3.2).

A protected type can also declare a family of entries by placing a discrete subtype definition in the specification of the entry declaration. The barrier associated with the entry can use the index of the family (usually to index into an array of booleans). Consider the following:

```
type Family is Integer range 1 .. 3;

protected Controller is
  entry Request(Family)(...);
end Controller;
```

For the protected body, it is not necessary to enumerate all the members of the family (indeed, the programmer is not allowed to do so). Instead, a shorthand notation is provided:

```
protected body Controller is
  entry Request(for I in Family)(...)
     when Some_Barrier_Using(I) is
  begin
     ...
  end Request;
end Controller;
```

This is notionally equivalent to

```
-- Not Valid Ada
protected body Controller is
  entry Request(1)(...) when Some_Barrier_Using(1) is
  begin
     ...
  end Request;

  entry Request(2)(...) when Some_Barrier_Using(2) is
  begin
     ...
  end Request;

  entry Request(3)(...) when Some_Barrier_Using(3) is
  begin
     ...
  end Request;
end Controller;
```

For example, the following defines a protected type which provides a group communication facility. The type Group defines several communications groups. The protected procedure Send transmits a Data_Item to a particular group. The family of entries Receive allows a task to wait for a Data_Item on a particular group:

```
type Group is range 1 .. 10;
type Group_Data_Arrived is array(Group) of Boolean;

protected type Group_Controller is
  procedure Send(To_Group : Group;
                 This_Data : Data_Item);
  entry Receive(Group)(Data : out Data_Item);
private
```

```ada
      Arrived : Group_Data_Arrived := (others => False);
      The_Data : Data_Item;
   end Group_Controller;

   My_Controller : Group_Controller;

   protected body Group_Controller is
      procedure Send(To_Group : Group; This_Data : Data_Item) is
      begin
         if Receive(To_Group)'Count > 0 then
            Arrived(To_Group) := True;
            The_Data := This_Data;
         end if;
      end Send;

      entry Receive(for From in Group)(Data : out Data_Item)
                   when Arrived(From) is
         -- this is a family of entries
      begin
         if Receive(From)'Count = 0 then
            Arrived(From) := False;
         end if;
         Data := The_Data;
      end Receive;
   end Group_Controller;
```

When a task sends data to a particular group, the Send procedure looks to see if any tasks are waiting on the Receive entry for that particular member of the family. If tasks are waiting, it sets a boolean flag associated with the member to true.[1] On exit from the procedure, the barriers associated with the Receive family entries are re-evaluated. The appropriate group's boolean evaluates to true and so that entry of the family is open. The entry body is executed and, if only one task is waiting, the boolean is set to false; in all cases the data is sent to the first queued task. If the guard is still open, the entry body is executed again, and so on until all tasks queued for the group are released with the multi-cast value. Note that, once a task is executing inside the protected object, no other task can join an entry queue or be removed from an entry queue.

There are other ways of manipulating the barrier on the entry family (for example saving the identifier of the group during the Send operation and comparing the family index with the group identifier). However, the given solution is easily extendible if the message is to be sent to more than one group.

It is useful to dwell on one further feature of the above code. In general, a call of Send may release blocked tasks on Receive. But it cannot just set the barrier to true on Receive: it must first check to see if any task is blocked (using the 'Count attribute). Moreover, the last task to be released must set the barrier again to false. These checks must be made, as a change to a barrier value is persistent. This can be compared with a signal on a monitor's condition variable (see Section 11.7), which has either an immediate effect or no effect at all.

---

[1] Note that the Count attribute can only be applied to a specific family member.

11.8.3 The readers and writers problem

One of the motivations for the notion of a protected object is that a single mechanism provides both mutual exclusion and condition synchronisation. As indicated in Section 11.2, critical sections with mutual exclusion give too strong a constraint for many synchronisation protocols. Hence, the notion of coordinated sections. A commonly used example of such protocols is the readers and writers problem. Consider a (non-sharable) resource such as a file. Because of multiple update difficulties, the necessary synchronisation are such that if one task is writing to the file, then no other task should be either writing or reading. If, however, there is no writer task, then any number of tasks can have read access.

Although a standard protected object can implement the readers/writers algorithm (if the read operation is encoded as a function and the write as a procedure), there are two drawbacks with this simple approach:

(1) The programmer cannot easily control the order of access to the protected object; specifically, it is not possible to give preference to write operations over reads.
(2) If the read or write operations are potentially blocking, then they cannot be made from within a protected object.

To overcome these difficulties, the reading and writing are viewed as coordinated sections. Recall from Figure 11.2 the sections are bracketed by entry and exit protocols. The entry protocol ensures that the conditions are right for the operation to be performed. The exit protocol ensures that any used variables are left in an appropriate state to allow the next operation to proceed.

The reading and writing operations are first encapsulated in a package.

```
with Data_Items; use Data_Items;
package Readers_Writers is
  procedure Read (I : out Item);   -- for some type Item
  procedure Write (I : Item);
end Readers_Writers;
```

The body of the package implements the entry and exit protocols. Here, preference is given to writes over reads:

```
package body Readers_Writers is
  procedure Read_File(I : out Item)
         is separate;  -- details not important
  procedure Write_File(I : Item)
         is separate;  -- details not important

  protected Control is
    entry Start_Read;
    procedure Stop_Read;
    entry Start_Write;
    procedure Stop_Write;
  private
    Readers : Natural := 0;   -- Number of current readers
    Writers : Boolean := False;  -- Writers present
  end Control;
```

```ada
   procedure Read (I : out Item) is
   begin
      Control.Start_Read;  -- entry protocol
        Read_File(I);      -- coordinated section
      Control.Stop_Read;   -- exit protocol
   end Read;

   procedure Write (I : Item) is
   begin
      Control.Start_Write;  -- entry protocol
        Write_File(I);      -- coordinated section
      Control.Stop_Write;   -- exit protocol
   end Write;

   protected body Control is
      entry Start_Read when not Writers and
                 Start_Write'Count = 0 is
      begin
         Readers := Readers + 1;
      end Start_Read;

      procedure Stop_Read is
      begin
         Readers := Readers - 1;
      end Stop_Read;

      entry Start_Write when not Writers and Readers = 0 is
      begin
         Writers := True;
      end Start_Write;

      procedure Stop_Write is
      begin
         Writers := False;
      end Stop_Write;
   end Control;
end Readers_Writers;
```

The entry protocol for a writer ensures that a writer can only begin writing if there is no writer currently writing and there are no current readers. The use of 'Count on the Start_Read barrier ensures that waiting writers are given preference. The exit protocol for both readers and writers is a non-blocking call to announce the termination of that operation.

11.8.4 The Bar (Barrier) Problem

One of the standard synchronization problems introduced in Section 11.2 was the Barrier or Bar. A simple bar blocks several tasks, until all have arrived. In this case, no data is passed but a form of multicast could be programmed that passes data as well. Either is trivial to implement with protected objects, as shown below.

```ada
package Barriers is
  Max_Capacity : constant Positive := ...;
    -- set to an appropriate value
  type Capacity_Range is range 1 .. Max_Capacity;

  protected type Barrier(Needed : Capacity_Range) is
    entry Wait;
    function Capacity return Capacity_Range;
    function Value return Capacity_Range;
  private
    Release_All : Boolean := False;
  end Barrier;
end Barriers;

package body Barriers is
  protected body Barrier is
    entry Wait when Barrier.Wait'Count = Needed or
                      Release_All is
    begin
       Release_All :=  Barrier.Wait'Count > 0;
    end Wait;

    function Capacity return Capacity_Range is
    begin
       return Needed;
    end Capacity;

    function Value return Capacity_Range is
    begin
       return Needed - Barrier.Wait'Count;
    end Value;
  end Barrier;
end Barriers;
```

Tasks wishing to block at a barrier simply call the Wait subprogram; the two functions return information about the barrier.

Barrier/Bars are commonly used in multiprocessor applications and may have direct hardware support on some processors. For this reason, Ada provides a standard package in the Real-Time Annex to support them. This is shown in Program 11.2. Here one of the waiting tasks is singled out to be notified (has a returned Notified value set to true) during the releasing phase of the barrier. All other tasks have Notified set to false.

11.8.5 Protected objects and object-oriented programming

Interfaces in Ada are classified according to the type of object that can be supported. For the purpose of this book the following interfaces are relevant:

- protected interface – this specifies a collection of functions and procedures that can

```ada
package Ada.Synchronous_Barriers is
  pragma Preelaborate(Synchronous_Barriers);

  subtype Barrier_Limit is Positive
          range 1 .. implemtation-defined;
  type Synchronous_Barrier (Release_Threshold : Barrier_Limit)
          is limited private;

  procedure Wait_For_Release (
                  The_Barrier : in out Synchronous_Barrier;
                  Notified : out Boolean);
private
  -- not specified by the language
end Ada.Synchronous_Barriers;
```

Program 11.2: The `Ada.Synchronous_Barriers` package.

only be implemented by a protected type;

- task interface – this specifies a collection of functions and procedures that can only be implemented by a task type;

- synchronized interface – this specifies a collection of functions and procedures that can be implemented by a task type or a protected type.

Synchronized and protected interfaces will be considered in this section; discussion of task interfaces are not included in this book as they are associated with direct communication between tasks (the Ada rendezvous), and this form of communication is not considered ideal for real-time systems.

The key idea of a synchronized interface is that there is some implied synchronization between the task that calls an operation from an interface and the object that implements the interface. Synchronization in Ada is achieved via two main mechanisms: a protected action (call of an entry or protected subprogram – a shared variable-based communication mechanism) or the rendezvous (a message-based communication mechanisms). Hence, a task type or a protected type can implement a synchronized interface. Both protected entries and procedures can implement a synchronized interface procedure. A protected function can implement a synchronized interface function.

Where the programmer is not concerned with the form of synchronization, a synchronized interface is the appropriate abstraction. For situations where the programmer requires a particular form of synchronisation, protected interfaces or task interfaces should be used explicitly. For example, there are various communication paradigms that all have at their heart some form of buffer. They, therefore, all have buffer-like operations in common. Some programs will use these paradigms and will not care whether the implementation uses a mailbox, a link or whatever. Some will require a task in the implementations (i.e. a server), others will just need a protected object (a passive resource). Synchronized interfaces allow the programmer to defer the commitment to a particular paradigm and its implementation approach.

Consider, the operations that can be performed on all integer buffers:

```ada
package Integer_Buffers is
  type Buffer is synchronized interface;
  procedure Put(Buf : in out Buffer; Item : in Integer)
           is abstract;
  procedure Get(Buf : in out Buffer; Item : out Integer)
           is abstract;
end Integer_Buffers;
```

In the above code, the `Buffer` type declaration indicates that it is a synchronized interface, which supports the `Put` and `Get` procedures.

Now consider a protected type that can implement this interface.

```ada
with Integer_Buffers;
package Integer_Buffers.MailBoxes is
  subtype Capacity_Range is range ...;
  subtype Count is Integer range ...;
  type Buffer_Store is array(Capacity_Range) of Integer;

  protected type Mailbox is new Buffer with
    overriding entry Put(Item : in Integer);
    overriding entry Get(Item : out Integer);
  private
    First : Capacity_Range := Capacity_Range'first;
    Last : Capacity_Range := Capacity_Range'last;
    Number_In_Buffer : Count := 0;
    Box_Store : Buffer_Store;
  end Mailbox;
end Integer_Buffers.Mailboxes;
```

Here, the declaration of the `Mailbox` protected type indicates that it implements the `Buffer` interface by being derived from that type. The 'overriding' keyword on the entries indicate that these entries are the entries that implement the interface's procedures. The name of the entry and its parameter type must match the interface's. Note, however, because of the way OOP is supported in Ada, the `Buf` parameter is not required as its type is the same as the type that the `Mailbox` is derived from. Hence, it is an implicit parameter that is generated when an instance of the mailbox is used. For example, in

```ada
with Integer_Buffers.Mailboxes;
use Integer_Buffers.Mailboxes;
...
Mail : Mailbox;
...
Mail.Put(42);
```

the `Mail` object provides the implicit first parameter.

Rules for overriding subprograms in a synchronized and protected interfaces

Interfaces can contain abstract procedure and function declarations. A protected object (or protected type) declaration can have functions, procedures and entries. It is, therefore, necessary to have some simple rules that determine which protected actions override (implement) which interface subprograms. These rules are:

- a function that is defined in a synchronized or protected interface can only be overridden (implemented) by a function in a protected object (or protected type) declaration;
- a procedure that is defined in a synchronized or protected interface can be overridden (implemented) by a procedure *OR* an entry in a protected object (or protected type) declaration.

Synchronized interfaces and timeouts

Consider a revised version of the `Integer_Buffer` package,

```
package Integer_Buffers is
  type Buffer is synchronized interface;
  procedure Put(Buf : in out Buffer; Item : in Integer)
          is abstract with Synchronization => Optional;
  procedure Get(Buf : in out Buffer; Item : out Integer)
          is abstract;

  type Any_Buffer is access all Buffer'Class;
end Integer_Buffers;
```

Here, the definition of `Any_Buffer` type allows variables to be declared that can reference any protected (or task type) that is derived from this interface. A user that is given such a reference can call `Put` and `Get` without being aware of how it is implemented. Given that `Put` or `Get` could be implemented by an entry, the calling task can be indefinitely delayed waiting for the guard to become true. Ada allows timed entry calls to be used in this situation so that the caller can timeout if necessary. However, in this instance, the caller does not know that an indefinite delay can occur. If, for example, `Put` is implemented by a protected procedure then no timeout will be necessary. For this reason, Ada allows a call to a procedure via an interface to be placed in a select statement. For example:

```
  B : Any_Buffer;
  ...
  select
    B.Put(3);
  or
    delay 10.0;
  end select;
```

If the resulting call is to a procedure, then the timeout is ignored.

If the designer of the interface intends that one of its abstract procedures be implemented by an entry then (since Ada 2012) it can use an aspect. Similarly, if a protected procedure implementation is required, an aspect can be used. The following examples specified that `Put` must be implemented by a procedure, and `Get` by an entry.

260 SHARED VARIABLE-BASED SYNCHRONIZATION AND COMMUNICATION

```
package Integer_Buffers is
  type Buffer is synchronized interface;

  procedure Put(Buf : in out Buffer; Item : in Integer)
      is abstract with Synchronisation => By_Protected_Procedure;
  procedure Get(Buf : in out Buffer; Item : out Integer)
      is abstract with Synchronisation => By_Entry;

  type Any_Buffer is access all Buffer'Class;
end Integer_Buffers;
```

For completeness, Ada allows **with** Synchronization => Optional, which is the default, to be specified explicitly.

11.9 Shared memory multiprocessors

Multiprocessor systems are becoming more prevalent. In particular symmetric multiprocessor (SMP) systems, where processors have shared access to the main memory, are often the default platform for large real-time systems rather than a single processor system. Although multiprocessors present challenges for the timing analysis needed for real-time systems (see Section 8.2), from a theoretical concurrent programming viewpoint, a program that is properly synchronized and executes successfully on a single processor systems will execute successfully on a SMP system. Programs that are not properly synchronized may suffer from data race conditions (see Section 11.4). Even properly synchronized programs can suffer from deadlocks. Consequently, a program that *appears* to execute correctly on a single processor cannot be guaranteed to work correctly on a multiprocessor as it is doubtful that all possible interleaving of task executions will have been exercised on the single processor system. As a result, concurrency-related faults/bugs will remain dormant.

In order to understand how a concurrent program executes on a SMP system it is necessary to understand the memory consistency model provided by the machine. The simplest model is **sequential consistency**. An SMP system is sequentially consistent if the result of any execution of a program is the same as if the instructions of all the processors are executed in some sequential order, and the instructions of any task within the sequence is the same as that specified by its program logic [50]. Hence, both atomicity of instructions and the maintenance of task instruction sequences are required.

Sequential consistency is a very restrictive property, and if rigidly supported would disallow many optimisation that are typically performed by compilers and modern multiprocessors. For example, a compiler would not be able to reorder the instructions and the hardware would not be able to execute instructions out of order. The presence of hardware caches exacerbates these problems.

To overcome the severe constraints imposed by the requirement of sequential consistency, **relaxed (weaker) memory models** can be used. These either relax the instruction order or the atomicity requirements. Different SMP architectures adopt different approaches – see Adve [1] for a classification.

From the programmer's perspective, it is crucial to understand what guarantees a programming language provides when a shared variable is updated. In particular, when that update becomes visible to other tasks potentially executing on other processors. The remainder of this section considers the guarantees provided by Ada. It is the compiler and the run-time systems that must implement these guarantees on the underlying architecture's memory model irrespective of the memory model it provides.

Ada and shared variables

Ada has no explicit memory model, however, the Ada language defines the conditions under which it is safe to read and write to shared variables outside the rendezvous or protected objects. Hence, the model is implicit.

The safe conditions are as follows.

- Where one task writes a variable before activating another task that reads the variable.
- Where the activation of one task writes the variable and the task awaiting completion of the activation reads the variable.
- Where one task writes the variable and another task waits for the termination of the task and then reads the variable.
- Where one task writes the variable before making an entry call on another task, and the other task reads the variable during the corresponding entry body or accept statement.
- Where one task writes a shared variable during an accept statement and the calling task reads the variable after the corresponding entry call has returned.
- Where one task writes a variable whilst executing a protected procedure body or entry, and the other task reads the variable, for example as part of a later execution of an entry body of the same protected body.

If the Systems Programming Annex is supported, there are extra facilities that can be used to control shared variables between *unsynchronized* tasks. They come in the form of extra representation aspects (see Section 9.5) that can be applied to certain objects or type declarations. They include the following.

- Volatile – the Volatile representation aspect ensures that all tasks of the program (on all processors) that read or update volatile variables see the same order of updates to the variables.
- Independent – the Independent representation aspect ensures that the associated object is independently addressable; this means that it can be accessed without the surrounding memory locations being touched.
- Atomic – Whilst Volatile indicates that all reads and writes must be be seen in the same order, Atomic imposes the further restriction that they must be indivisible. That is, if two tasks attempt to read and write the shared variable at the same time, then the result must be internally consistent. An implementation is not required to support atomic operations for all types of variable; however, if not supported for a particular object, the representation aspect (and hence the program) must be rejected by the compiler.

262   SHARED VARIABLE-BASED SYNCHRONIZATION AND COMMUNICATION

The language defines accesses to volatile and atomic variables to be interactions with the external environment, and hence compilers must ensure that no reordering of instructions occur across their use.

11.10 Simple embedded system revisited

In Section 10.7, a simple embedded system was introduced and a concurrent solution was proposed. The solution is now updated to illustrate communication with the operator console. Recall that the structure of the controller is as below:

```
package Embedded_System is
  task Temp_Controller;
  task Pressure_Controller;
end Embedded_System;

with Data_Types; use Data_Types;
with IO; use IO;
with Control_Procedures; use Control_Procedures;
package body Embedded_System is

  task body Temp_Controller is
    TR : Temp_Reading; HS : Heater_Setting;
  begin
    loop
      Read(TR);
      Temp_Convert(TR,HS);
      Write(HS);
      Write(TR);
    end loop;
  end Temp_Controller;

  task body Pressure_Controller is
    PR : Pressure_Reading; PS : Pressure_Setting;
  begin
    loop
      Read(PR);
      Pressure_Convert(PR,PS);
      Write(PS);
      Write(PR);
    end loop;
  end Pressure_Controller;

end Embedded_System;
```

and that the interfaces to the I/O routines were:

```
with Data_Types; use Data_Types;
package IO is
    -- procedures for data exchange with the environment
  procedure Read(TR : out Temp_Reading);     -- from DAC
  procedure Read(PR : out Pressure_Reading); -- from DAC
```

SIMPLE EMBEDDED SYSTEM REVISITED   263

```ada
    procedure Write(HS : Heater_Setting);    -- to switch.
    procedure Write(PS : Pressure_Setting);  -- to DAC
    procedure Write(TR : Temp_Reading);      -- to console
    procedure Write(PR : Pressure_Reading);  -- to console
end IO;
```

The body of the I/O routines can now be completed. The data to be sent to the console is stored in a monitor (in this case using a protected object). The console task will call the entry to get the new data.

```ada
package body IO is
  task Console;
  protected Console_Data is
    procedure Write(R : Temp_Reading);
    procedure Write(R : Pressure_Reading);
    entry Read(TR : out Temp_Reading;
               PR : out Pressure_Reading);
  private
    Last_Temperature : Temp_Reading;
    Last_Pressure :Pressure_Reading;
    New_Reading : Boolean := False;
  end Console_Data;

  -- procedures for data exchange with the environment
  procedure Read(TR : out Temp_Reading) is separate;
  procedure Read(PR : out Pressure_Reading) is separate;
  procedure Write(HS : Heater_Setting) is separate;
  procedure Write(PS : Pressure_Setting) is separate;

  task body Console is
    TR : Temp_Reading;
    PR : Pressure_Reading;
  begin
    loop
       ...
      Console_Data.Read(TR, PR);
      -- Display new readings
    end loop;
  end Console;

  protected body Console_Data is
    procedure Write(R : Temp_Reading) is
    begin
      Last_Temperature := R;
      New_Reading := True;
    end Write;

    procedure Write(R : Pressure_Reading) is
    begin
      Last_Pressure := R;
      New_Reading := True;
    end Write;
```

```
    entry Read(TR : out Temp_Reading;
              PR : out Pressure_Reading)
        when New_Reading is
    begin
      TR := Last_Temperature;
      PR := Last_Pressure;
      New_Reading := False;
    end Read;
  end Console_Data;

  procedure Write(TR : Temp_Reading) is
  begin
    Console_Data.Write(TR);
  end Write;      -- to screen

  procedure Write(PR : Pressure_Reading)   is
  begin
    Console_Data.Write(PR);
  end Write; -- to screen
end IO;
```

Summary

Tasks interactions require operating systems and concurrent programming languages to support synchronization and inter-task communication. Communication can be based on either shared variables or message passing. This chapter has been concerned with shared variables, the multiple update difficulties they present and the mutual exclusion synchronization needed to counter these difficulties. In this discussion, the following terms were introduced:

- critical section – code that must be executed under mutual exclusion;
- producer–consumer system – two or more tasks exchanging data via a finite buffer;
- busy waiting – a task continually checking a condition to see if it is now able to proceed;
- livelock – an error condition in which one or more tasks are prohibited from progressing whilst using up processing cycles.

Examples were used to show how difficult it is to program mutual exclusion using only shared variables. Semaphores were introduced to simplify these algorithms and to remove busy waiting. A semaphore is a non-negative integer that can only be acted upon by `wait` and `signal` procedures. The executions of these procedures are atomic.

The provision of a semaphore primitive has the consequence of introducing a new state for a task; namely, suspended. It also introduces two new error conditions:

- deadlock – a collection of suspended tasks that cannot proceed;
- indefinite postponement – a task being unable to proceed as resources are not made available for it (also called lockout or starvation).

Semaphores can be criticised as being too low-level and error-prone in use. Following their development, several more structured primitives were introduced:

- conditional critical regions
- monitors
- protected objects.

Monitors are an important language feature. They consist of a module, entry to which is assured (by definition) to be under mutual exclusion. Within the body of a monitor, a task can suspend itself if the conditions are not appropriate for it to proceed. This suspension is achieved using a condition variable. When a suspended task is awoken (by a `signal` operation on the condition variable), it is imperative that this does not result in two tasks being active in the module at the same time.

Although monitors provide a high-level structure for mutual exclusion, other types of synchronization must be programmed using very low-level condition variables. The synchronization model uses *conditional waiting*. Ada's protected objects give the structuring advantages of monitors and the high-level synchronization mechanisms of conditional critical regions. The synchronization model uses *avoidance synchronization*. A protected object encapsulates data items and allows access to them only via protected actions. A protected action is either a protected subprogram (procedure or function) or protected entry.

A protected procedure provides mutually exclusive read/write access to the data encapsulated. Protected functions provide concurrent read-only access to the encapsulated data. A protected entry, like a protected procedure, is guaranteed to execute in mutual exclusion and has read/write access to the encapsulated data. However, a protected entry is guarded by a boolean expression (the barrier) inside the body of the protected object; if this barrier evaluates to false when the entry call is made, the calling task is suspended until the barrier evaluates to true and no other tasks are currently active inside the protected object. Calls to entries can have timeouts associated with them to prevent indefinite blocking.

Integrating concurrency and OOP is fraught with difficulties. Ada tries to simplify the problem by supporting interfaces but not inheritance with protected types.

The next chapter considers how the shared variable-based communication and synchronization mechanisms can be used to implement general resource controllers.

Chapter 12
Resource control

12.1 Resource management
12.2 Expressive power and ease of use
12.3 The requeue facility
12.4 Real-time solutions to the resource control problem
12.5 Resource control and security
12.6 Resource usage
12.7 Deadlock
Summary

Section 10.2.1 introduced the mechanisms that are needed to facilities concurrent programming. In considering the interaction of tasks, that section distinguished between three types of behaviour:

- independent
- cooperating
- competing

Independent tasks do not communicate or synchronize with each other. Cooperating tasks, by comparison, regularly communicate and synchronize their activities in order to perform some common operation – they have coordinated sections of code. The mechanism described in Chapter 11 can be used to aid this coordination.

Section 10.2.1 pointed out that coordination between tasks is also required if they are to share access to scarce resources such as external devices, files, shared data fields, buffers and encoded algorithms. These tasks were termed **competing** tasks. Much of the logical (that is, non-temporal) behaviour of real-time software is concerned with the allocation of resources between competing tasks. Although the tasks do not communicate directly with each other to pass information concerning their own activities, they may communicate to coordinate access to the shared resources. A few resources are amenable to unlimited concurrent access, most however are in some way restricted in their usage.

As noted in Chapter 10, the implementation of resource entities requires some form of control agent. If the control agent is passive then the resource is said

268   RESOURCE CONTROL

to be **protected** (or **synchronized**). Alternatively, if an active agent is required to program the correct level of control, the resource controller is called a **server**.

This chapter discusses the problem of reliable resource control. The general allocation of resources between competing tasks is considered. Although such tasks are independent of each other, the act of resource allocation has implications for reliability. In particular, failure of a task could result in an allocated resource becoming unavailable to other tasks. Tasks may be starved of resources if other tasks are allowed to monopolise them. Furthermore, tasks can become deadlocked by holding resources that other tasks require while at the same time requesting more resources.

12.1   Resource management

Concerns of modularity (in particular information hiding) dictate that resources must be encapsulated and be accessed only through a high-level procedural interface; for example, a package should, wherever possible, be used. Note in all of the following examples, the details of the actual resource are omitted.

```
package Resources is
  type Resource is ...;

  type Resource_Control is synchronized interface;
  procedure Allocate(RC: in out Resource_Control;
                     R : out Resource) is abstract;
  procedure Free(RC: in out Resource_Control;
                 R : in out Resource) is abstract;
end Resources;
```

The use of a synchronized interface allows both active and passive resource controllers to be represented. If the resource manager is a server, then the body of `Resource_Control` will contain a task (or an access object to a task type). A protected resource will use a protected object within the package body. This book is only considering passive resource managers using Ada protected objects as these have simpler timing properties. Active resource managers use message-passing, which tend to complicate schedulability analysis as the receiver task has to wait for the sender task. This increases the difficulty in determining how long the receiver will block. Of course, this does not rule out a server task using a passive resource manager to actively manage the resource if necessary.

The next section discusses the expressive power and ease of use (usability) of Ada's protected objects for resource management. After this discussion, a further section on security will look at how a resource controller can protect itself against misuse.

12.2   Expressive power and ease of use

Bloom [15], in 1979, suggested criteria for evaluating synchronization primitives in the context of resource management. This analysis forms the basis of this section, which looks at the expressive power and ease of use of synchronization primitives for resource control. The primitives to be evaluated are monitors (with their use of condition variables) and protected resources (implemented as protected objects). The latter uses guards for synchronization, and hence one aspect of this analysis is a comparison between **conditional waiting** and **avoidance synchronization** (as introduced in Section 11.8).

Bloom uses the term 'expressive power' to mean the ability of a language to express required constraints on synchronization. Ease of use of a synchronization primitive encompasses:

- the ease with which it expresses each of these synchronization constraints, and
- the ease with which it allows the constraints to be combined to achieve more complex synchronization schemes.

In the context of resource control, the information needed to express these constraints can be categorized (following Bloom) as follows:

- the type of service request;
- the order in which requests arrive;
- the state of the server and any objects it manages; and
- the parameters of a request.

Bloom's original set of constraints included 'the history of the object' (that is, the sequence of all previous service requests). It is assumed here that the state of the object can be extended to include whatever historical information is needed. An addition to the list is however made, as Bloom did not include:

- the priority of the client.

As indicated above, there are in general two linguistic approaches to constrain access to a service. The first is the **conditional waiting**: all requests are accepted, but any task whose request cannot currently be met is suspended on a queue. The conventional monitor typifies this approach: a task whose request cannot be met is queued on a condition variable, and resumed when the request can be serviced. The second approach is **avoidance**: requests are not accepted unless they can be met. The conditions under which a request can safely be accepted are expressed as a guard on the action of acceptance.

It should be clear that the Ada model described so far deals adequately with the first three constraints in the above list. A full discussion of task priority is given in Chapter 15. For the purpose of this chapter, the priority of a task is taken to be a measure of the task's urgency. Here, attention is focused on the fourth issue, which causes some difficulties for avoidance synchronization mechanisms.

12.2.1 The resource allocation problem

Resource allocation is a fundamental problem in all aspects of concurrent programming. Its consideration exercises all Bloom's criteria and forms an appropriate basis for assessing

270   RESOURCE CONTROL

the synchronization mechanisms of concurrent languages.

Consider the problem of constructing a resource controller that allocates some resource to a group of client agents. There are a number of instances of the resource but the number is bounded; contention is possible and must be catered for in the design of the program. If the client tasks only require a single instance of the resource, then the problem is straightforward. For example, in the following, the resource (although not directly represented) can be encoded as a protected object:

```
protected Resource_Controller is
   entry Allocate(R : out Resource);
   procedure Release(R : Resource);
private
   Free : Natural := Max;
   ...
end Resource_Controller;

protected body Resource_Controller is
   entry Allocate(R : out Resource) when Free > 0 is
   begin
      Free := Free - 1;
      ...
   end Allocate;
   procedure Release(R : Resource) is
   begin
      Free := Free + 1;
      ...
   end Release;
end Resource_Controller;
```

To generalise this code requires the caller to state how many resources are required (up to some maximum). The semantics required (to help avoid deadlocks) are that either all requested resources are assigned to the caller or none are (and the caller blocks until the resources are free).

This resource allocation problem is difficult to program with avoidance synchronization. In order to determine the size of the request, the communication must be accepted and the parameter read. But if, having read the parameter, the internal state of the resource controller is such that there are currently not enough resources available, then the communication must be terminated and the client must try again. To prevent polling, a different entry must be tried. A detailed examination of this problem has shown that an acceptable solution is not available if avoidance synchronization only is used. Note that a solution is possible, so the issue is one of ease of use rather than expressive power. Nevertheless, the elegance of this solution is poor when compared with a standard solution that utilizes monitors. A monitor uses condition synchronization (not avoidance synchronization) and it is therefore trivially easy to block the caller after the parameter has been read but before it leaves the monitor.

Using entry families

A possible solution in Ada (without any additional language feature) to the resource allocation problem assumes that the number of distinct requests is relatively small and can be represented by a family of entries. Each entry in the family is guarded by the boolean expression F <= Free, where F is the family index:

```
type Request_Range is range 1..Max;

protected Resource_Controller is
  entry Allocate(Request_Range)(R : out Resource);
  procedure Release(R : Resource; Amount : Request_Range);
private
  Free : Request_Range := Request_Range'Last;
  ...
end Resource_Controller;

protected body Resource_Controller is
  entry Allocate(for F in Request_Range)(R : out Resource)
                when F <= Free is
  begin
    Free := Free - F;
    ...
  end Allocate;

  procedure Release(R : Resource; Amount : Request_Range) is
  begin
    ...
    Free := Free + Amount;
  end Release;
end Resource_Controller;
```

Although this solution is concise, there are two potential problems:

(1) This may not be practical for a large number of resources, as there needs to be Max entry queues; these must be serviced individually, which could be inefficient.

(2) It is difficult to allocate the resources selectively – when several requests can be serviced, an arbitrary choice between them is made (note that if the Real-Time Systems Annex is supported, the request can be serviced in a priority order; if all calling tasks have the same priority, then the family is serviced from the smallest index to the largest).

The latter problem can be ameliorated by having each entry in the family guarded by its own boolean, and then selectively setting the booleans to True. For example, if on freeing new resources it is required to service the largest request first, the following algorithm can be used. Note that a request to Allocate that can be satisfied immediately is always accepted. Hence a boolean variable (Normal) is needed to distinguish between a normal allocation and a phase of allocations following a Release:

```
type Request_Range is range 1..Max;
type Bools is array(Request_Range) of Boolean;
```

```ada
protected Resource_Controller is
  entry Allocate(Request_Range)(R : out Resource);
  procedure Release(R : Resource; Amount : Request_Range);
private
  Free : Request_Range := Request_Range'Last;
  Barrier : Bools := (others => False);
  Normal : Boolean := True;
end Resource_Controller;

protected body Resource_Controller is
  entry Allocate(for F in Request_Range)(R : out Resource)
        when F <= Free and (Normal or Barrier(F)) is
  begin
    Free := Free - F;
    if not Normal then
      Barrier(F) := False;
      Normal := True;
      for I in reverse 1 .. F loop
        if Allocate(I)'Count /= 0 and I <= Free then
          Barrier(I) := True;
          Normal := False;
          exit;
        end if;
      end loop;
    end if;
    ...
  end Allocate;

  procedure Release(R : Resource;
                    Amount : Request_Range) is
  begin
    Free := Free + Amount;
    for I in reverse 1 .. Free loop
      if Allocate(I)'Count /= 0 then
        Barrier(I) := True;
        Normal := False;
        exit;
      end if;
    end loop;
    ...
  end Release;
end Resource_Controller;
```

Note that the loop bound in entry Allocate is F not Free as there cannot be a task queued on Allocate requiring more than F instances of the resource.

The correctness of this algorithm relies on the property that requests already queued upon Allocate (when resources are released) are serviced before any new call to Allocate (from outside the resources controller). It also relies on tasks not removing themselves from entry queues, that is, after the count attribute has been read (and the associated barrier raised) but before the released task actually executes Allocate. Furthermore, it assumes that tasks only ever release resources that they have acquired.

The double interaction solution

One possible solution to the resource allocation problem, which does not rely on a family of entries, is for the resource controller to reject calls that cannot be satisfied. In this approach, the client must first request resources and, if refused, try again. To avoid continuously requesting resources when no new resources are available, the client calls a different entry from the original request entry:

```ada
type Request_Range is range 1..Max;

protected Resource_Controller is
   entry Allocate(R : out Resource; Amount : Request_Range;
                  Ok : out Boolean);
   entry Try_Again(R : out Resource; Amount : Request_Range;
                   Ok : out Boolean);
   procedure Release(R : Resource; Amount : Request_Range);
private
   Free : Request_Range := Request_Range'Last;
   New_Resources_Released : Boolean := False;
   ...
end Resource_Controller;

protected body Resource_Controller is
   entry Allocate(R : out Resource; Amount : Request_Range;
                  Ok : out Boolean) when Free > 0 is
   begin
      if Amount <= Free then
         Free := Free - Amount;
         Ok := True;
         -- allocate
      else
         Ok := False;
      end if;
   end Allocate;

   entry Try_Again(R : out Resource; Amount : Request_Range;
         Ok : out Boolean) when New_Resources_Released is
   begin
      if Try_Again'Count = 0 then
         New_Resources_Released := False;
      end if;
      if Amount <= Free then
         Free := Free - Amount;
         Ok := True;
         -- allocate
      else
         Ok := False;
      end if;
   end Try_Again;

   procedure Release(R : Resource; Amount : Request_Range) is
   begin
      Free := Free + Amount;
```

274   RESOURCE CONTROL

```ada
      -- free resources
      if Try_Again'Count > 0 then
        New_Resources_Released := True;
      end if;
    end Release;
end Resource_Controller;
```

To use this controller, each client must then make the following calls:

```ada
Resource_Controller.Allocate(Res,N,Done);
while not Done loop
  Resource_Controller.Try_Again(Res,N,Done);
end loop;
```

Even this code is not entirely satisfactory, for the following reasons:

(1) The clients must `Try_Again` for their resources each time any resources are released; this is inefficient.

(2) If a client is tardy in calling `Try_Again`, it may miss the opportunity to acquire its resources (as only those tasks queued on `Try_Again`, at the point when new resources become available, are considered).

(3) It is difficult to allocate the resources selectively – when several requests can be serviced, then they are serviced in a FIFO order.

An alternative approach is to require the resource controller to record outstanding requests:

```ada
type Request_Range is range 1..Max;

protected Resource_Controller is
   entry Allocate(R : out Resource; Amount : Request_Range;
                  Ok : out Boolean);
   entry Try_Again(R : out Resource; Amount : Request_Range;
                   Ok : out Boolean);
   procedure Release(R : Resource; Amount : Request_Range);
private
   Free : Request_Range := Request_Range'Last;
   New_Resources_Released : Boolean := False;
   ...
end Resource_Controller;

protected body Resource_Controller is

   procedure Log_Request(Amount : Request_Range) is
   begin
      -- store details of request
   end Log_Request;

   procedure Done_Request(Amount : Request_Range) is
   begin
      -- remove details of request
   end Done_Request;
```

```ada
function Outstanding_Requests return Boolean is
begin
  -- returns True if there are outstanding requests to
  -- be serviced
end Outstanding_Requests;

procedure Seen_Request(Amount : Request_Range) is
begin
  -- log details of failed request
end Seen_Request;

function More_Outstanding_Requests return Boolean is
begin
  -- returns True if there are outstanding requests
  -- to be serviced which have not been considered
  -- this time around
end More_Outstanding_Requests;

entry Allocate(R : out Resource; Amount : Request_Range;
               Ok : out Boolean)
      when Free > 0 and not New_Resources_Released is
begin
  if Amount <= Free then
    Free := Free - Amount;
    Ok := True;
    -- allocate
  else
    Ok := False;
    Log_Request(Amount);
  end if;
end Allocate;

entry Try_Again(R : out Resource; Amount : Request_Range;
      Ok : out Boolean) when New_Resources_Released is
begin
  if Amount <= Free then
    Free := Free - Amount;
    Ok := True;
    Done_Request(Amount);
    -- allocate
  else
    Ok := False;
    Seen_Request(Amount);
  end if;
  if not More_Outstanding_Requests then
    New_Resources_Released := False;
  end if;
end Try_Again;

procedure Release(R : Resource; Amount : Request_Range) is
begin
  Free := Free + Amount;
  -- free resources
```

```ada
   if Outstanding_Requests then
     New_Resources_Released := True;
   end if;
 end Release;
end Resource_Controller;
```

In order to ensure that tasks waiting on the `Try_Again` entry are serviced before new requests, it is necessary to guard the `Allocate` entry. Unfortunately, this algorithm then breaks down if the client does not make the call to `Try_Again` (due, for example, to being aborted or suffering an asynchronous transfer of control – see Section 18.5.1). To solve this problem, it is necessary to encapsulate the double interaction in a procedure and provide a controlled variable (see Section 9.4.4) that, during finalisations, informs the resource controller (via a new protected procedure `Done_Waiting`) that it is no longer interested:

```ada
type Resource_Recovery is new
       Finalization.Limited_Controlled with null record;

procedure Finalize(Rr : in out Resource_Recovery) is
begin
  Resource_Controller.Done_Waiting;
end Finalize;

procedure Allocate(R : out Resource; Amount : Request_Range) is
  Got : Boolean;
  Protection : Resource_Recovery;
begin
  Resource_Controller.Allocate(R, Amount, Got);
  while not Got loop
    Resource_Controller.Try_Again(R, Amount, Got);
  end loop;
end Allocate;
```

Note that with this solution, the `Done_Waiting` routine will be called *every time* the procedure `Allocate` is left (either normally or because of task abortion). The resource controller will therefore have to keep track of the actual client tasks rather than just the requests. It can do this by using task identifiers provided by the Systems Programming Annex. The controller can then determine if a task executing `Done_Waiting` has an outstanding request.

Even with this solution, the controller still has difficulty in allocating resources selectively. However, the fundamental problem with this approach is that the task must make a double interaction with the resource controller even though only a single logical action is being undertaken.

12.2.2 Solutions using language support

Two methods have been proposed to increase the effectiveness of avoidance synchronization. One of these, requeue, has been incorporated into Ada. The other approach, which is less general purpose, is to allow the guard/barrier to have access to 'in' parameters. This approach is adopted in the language SR. The resource control problem is easily coded with this approach; for example, using Ada-like syntax:

```ada
type Request_Range is range 1..Max;

protected Resource_Controller is
  entry Allocate(R : out Resource; Amount : Request_Range);
  procedure Release(R : Resource; Amount : Request_Range);
private
  Free : Request_Range := Request_Range'Last;
  ...
end Resource_Controller;

protected body Resource_Controller is
  entry Allocate(R : out Resource; Amount : Request_Range)
       when Amount <= Free is   -- Not Legal Ada
  begin
    Free := Free - Amount;
  end Allocate;

  procedure Release(R : Resource; Amount : Request_Range) is
  begin
    Free := Free + Amount;
  end Release;
end Resource_Controller;
```

The main drawback with this approach is implementation efficiency. It is no longer possible to evaluate a barrier once per entry; each task's placement on the entry queue will lead to a barrier evaluation. However, optimisations are possible that would allow a compiler to recognise when 'in' parameters were not being used; efficient code could then be produced.

The second solution to this problem is to provide a requeue facility.

12.3 The requeue facility

The key notion behind requeue is to move the task (which has been through one guard or barrier – we shall use the term 'guard' in this discussion) to 'beyond' another guard.

For an analogy, consider a person (task) waiting to enter a room (protected object) which has one or more doors (guarded entries) giving access to the room. Once inside, the person can be ejected (requeued) from the room and once again be placed behind a (potentially closed) door.

Ada allows requeues between task entries and protected object entries. A requeue can be to the same entry, to another entry in the same unit, or to another unit altogether. Requeues from task entries to protected object entries (and vice versa) are allowed. However, the main use of requeue is to send the calling task to a different entry of the same unit from which the requeue was executed.

The resource control problem provides illustrative examples of the application of requeue. One solution is given now; some variations are considered later in this chapter (Section 12.4).

278   RESOURCE CONTROL

12.3.1 Requeue example – concurrent solution to the resource control problem

One of the problems with the double interaction solution was that a task could be delayed (say, due to preemption) before it could requeue on the `Try_Again` entry. Consequently, when new resources became available it was not in a position to have them allocated. Requeue allows a task to be ejected from a protected object and placed back on an entry queue as an atomic operation. It is therefore not possible for the task to miss the newly available resources.

In the following algorithm, an unsuccessful request is now requeued to a private entry (called `Assign`) of the protected object. The caller of this protected object now makes a single call on `Allocate`. Whenever resources are released, a note is taken of how many tasks are on the `Assign` entry. This number of tasks can then retry to either obtain their allocations or be requeued back onto the same `Assign` entry. The last task to retry closes the barrier:

```ada
type Request_Range is range 1..Max;

protected Resource_Controller is
   entry Allocate(R: out Resource; Amount: Request_Range);
   procedure Release(R: Resource; Amount: Request_Range);
private
   entry Assign(R: out Resource; Amount: Request_Range);
   Free : Request_Range := Request_Range'Last;
   New_Resources_Released : Boolean := False;
   To_Try : Natural := 0;
   ...
end Resource_Controller;

protected body Resource_Controller is
   entry Allocate(R : out Resource; Amount : Request_Range)
         when Free > 0 is
   begin
     if Amount <= Free then
       Free := Free - Amount;
       -- allocate
     else
       requeue Assign;
     end if;
   end Allocate;

   entry Assign(R : out Resource; Amount : Request_Range)
     when New_Resources_Released is
   begin
     To_Try := To_Try - 1;
     if To_Try = 0 then
       New_Resources_Released := False;
     end if;
     if Amount <= Free then
       Free := Free - Amount;
       -- allocate
```

```ada
    else
      requeue Assign;
    end if;
  end Assign;

  procedure Release(R: Resource; Amount: Request_Range) is
  begin
    Free := Free + Amount;
    -- free resources
    if Assign'Count > 0 then
      To_Try := Assign'Count;
      New_Resources_Released := True;
    end if;
  end Release;
end Resource_Controller;
```

Note that this will only work if the `Assign` entry queuing discipline is FIFO. When priorities are used, two entry queues are needed. Tasks must requeue from one entry to the other (and back again after the next release). This is illustrated in the example given in Section 12.4.

Finally, it should be observed that a more efficient algorithm can be derived if the protected object records the smallest outstanding request. The barrier should then only be set to true in `Release` (or remain true in `Assign`) if `Free >= Smallest`.

Even with this style of solution, it is difficult to give priority to certain requests other than in FIFO or task priority order. As indicated earlier, to program this level of control requires a family of entries. However, with requeue, a more straightforward solution can be given (as compared with the earlier code that did not use requeue):

```ada
type Request_Range is range 1..Max;
type Bools is array(Request_Range) of Boolean;

protected Resource_Controller is
  entry Allocate(Request_Range)(R: out Resource);
  procedure Release(R: Resource; Amount: Request_Range);
private
  entry Assign(Request_Range)(R: out Resource);
  Free : Request_Range := Request_Range'Last;
  Barrier : Bools := (others => False);
  ...
end Resource_Controller;

protected body Resource_Controller is
  entry Allocate(for F in Request_Range)(R: out Resource)
                when True is
  begin
    if F <= Free then
      Free := Free - F;
      ...
    else
      requeue Assign(F);
    end if;
  end Allocate;
```

```ada
   entry Assign(for F in Request_Range)(R: out Resource)
                when Barrier(F) is
   begin
      Free := Free - F;
      Barrier(F) := False;
      for I in reverse 1 .. F loop
         if Allocate(I)'Count /= 0 and I <= Free then
            Barrier(I) := True;
            exit;
         end if;
      end loop;
      ...
   end Assign;

   procedure Release(R: Resource; Amount: Request_Range) is
   begin
      Free := Free + Amount;
      for I in reverse 1 .. Free loop
         if Assign(I)'Count /= 0 then
            Barrier(I) := True;
            exit;
         end if;
      end loop;
      ...
   end Release;
end Resource_Controller;
```

This algorithm not only is more straightforward than the one given earlier, but also has the advantage that it is resilient to a task removing itself from an entry queue (after the count attribute has acknowledged its presence). Once a task has been requeued it cannot be aborted or subject to a time-out on the entry call – see following discussion.

12.3.2 Semantics of requeue

It is important to appreciate that requeue is not a simple call. If procedure P calls procedure Q, then, after Q has finished, control is passed back to P. But if entry X requeues on entry Y, control is not passed back to X. After Y has completed, control passes back to the object that called X. Hence, when an entry executes a requeue, that entry is completed.

One consequence of this is that when a requeue is from one protected object to another then mutual exclusion on the original object is given up once the task is queued. Other tasks waiting to enter the first object will be able to do so. However, a requeue to the same protected object will retain the mutual exclusion lock (if the target entry is open).

The entry named in a requeue statement (called the **target** entry) has no parameters. For example, in the resource control program, the parameter definition of Assign are identical to those of Allocate. Because of this rule, it is not necessary to give the actual parameters with the call; indeed, it is forbidden to do so (in case the programmer tries to change them). Hence if the target entry has no parameters, no information is passed;

if it has parameters, then the corresponding parameters in the entity that is executing the requeue are mapped across.

An optional 'with abort' clause can be used with the requeue statement. Usually when a task is on an entry queue, it will remain there until serviced unless it made a timed entry call (see Section 11.8.1) or is removed due to the use of asynchronous transfer of control or abort (see Section 18.5.1). Once the task starts to execute the entry of a protected object, the timeout is cancelled and the effect of any abort attempt is postponed until the task comes out of the entry. There is, however, a question as to what should happen with requeue. Consider the abort issue; clearly two views can be taken:

- As the first call has been accepted, the abort should now remain postponed so that the protected object can be assured that the second call is there.
- If the requeue puts the calling task back onto an entry queue, then abort should again be possible.

A similar argument can be made with timeouts. The requeue statement allows both views to be programmed; the default does not allow further timeouts or aborts, the addition of the 'with abort' clause enables the task to be removed from the second entry. For example:

```
requeue Assign with abort;
```

The real issue (in deciding whether to use 'with abort' or not) is whether the protected object having requeued the client task expects it to be there when the barrier is opened. If the correct behaviour of the object requires the task's presence, then 'with abort' should *not* be used.

12.4 Real-time solutions to the resource control problem

Consider again the resource control problem in the case where entry queues are ordered by priority. The top priority task will now be put back at the front of the queue and other tasks will not be able to proceed. To allow other tasks to still make progress in this situation requires two queues. Whenever resources are released, unsuccessful tasks are moved from one queue to the other. A family of two is used in the following code:

```
type Request_Range is range 1..Max;
type Family is range 1..2;
type Bools is array(Family) of Boolean;

protected Resource_Controller is
  entry Allocate(R: out Resource; Amount: Request_Range);
  procedure Release(R: Resource; Amount: Request_Range);
private
  entry Assign(Family)(R: out Resource; Amount: Request_Range);
  Free : Request_Range := Request_Range'Last;
  New_Resources_Released : Bools := (others => False);
  Queue_At : Family := 1;
  ...
end Resource_Controller;
```

282 RESOURCE CONTROL

```ada
protected body Resource_Controller is

   entry Allocate(R: out Resource; Amount: Request_Range)
         when Free > 0 is
   begin
     if Amount <= Free then
       Free := Free - Amount;
       -- allocate resources
     else
       requeue Assign(Queue_At);
     end if;
   end Allocate;

   entry Assign(for F in Family)
              (R: out Resource; Amount: Request_Range)
         when New_Resources_Released(F) is
   begin
     -- for this code to execute F
     -- must not equal Queue_At
     if Assign(F)'Count = 0 then
       New_Resources_Released(F) := False;
     end if;
     if Amount <= Free then
       Free := Free - Amount;
       -- allocate resources
     else
       requeue Assign(Queue_At);
     end if;
   end Assign;

   procedure Release(R: Resource; Amount: Request_Range) is
   begin
     Free := Free + Amount;
     -- free resources
     if Assign(Queue_At)'Count > 0 then
       New_Resources_Released(Queue_At) := True;
       if Queue_At = 1 then
         Queue_At := 2;
       else
         Queue_At := 1;
       end if;
     end if;
   end;
end Resource_Controller;
```

An alternative real-time model is that the highest priority tasks receives the resource as soon as possible and, consequently, is blocked for a bounded minimum time. Here, resources are not given to lower priority waiting tasks, even though there are enough resources to satisfy their requests. The solution to this problem is not immediately obvious. Consider first a flawed attempt; it assumes that the entry queues are ordered according to the priority of the queued tasks:

```ada
-- Flawed priority-driven resource allocation algorithm
type Request_Range is range 1..Max;

protected Resource_Controller is
  entry Allocate(R: out Resource; Amount: Request_Range);
  procedure Release(R: Resource; Amount: Request_Range);
private
  entry Assign(R: out Resource; Amount: Request_Range);
  Free : Request_Range := Request_Range'Last;
  New_Resources_Released : Boolean := False;
end Resource_Controller;

protected body Resource_Controller is

  entry Allocate(R: out Resource; Amount: Request_Range)
                when Free > 0 is
  begin
    if Amount <= Free then
      Free := Free - Amount;
      -- allocate
    else
      New_Resources_Released := False;
      requeue Assign;
    end if;
  end Allocate;

  entry Assign(R: out Resource; Amount: Request_Range)
                when New_Resources_Released is
  begin
    if Amount <= Free then
      Free := Free - Amount;
      -- allocate
    else
      New_Resources_Released := False;
      requeue Assign;
    end if;
  end Assign;

  procedure Release(R: Resource; Amount: Request_Range) is
  begin
     Free := Free + Amount;
     -- free resources
     New_Resources_Released := True;
  end Release;
end Resource_Controller;
```

The problem with this 'solution' is that a low priority task could be given some free resources (when it calls `Allocate`) when a higher priority task is queued on `Assign` (because there are not enough resources to satisfy its request). This breaks our requirement that the highest priority task must be serviced first. An alternative approach would be to have only a single entry for `Allocate` and `Assign`. Consider the following algorithm:

284 RESOURCE CONTROL

```ada
type Request_Range is range 1..Max;

protected Resource_Controller is
  entry Allocate(R: out Resource; Amount: Request_Range);
  procedure Release(R: Resource; Amount: Request_Range);
private
  Free : Request_Range := Request_Range'Last;
  Blocked : Natural := 0;
  ...
end Resource_Controller;

protected body Resource_Controller is
  entry Allocate(R: out Resource; Amount: Request_Range)
        when Free > 0 and Blocked /= Allocate'Count is
  begin
    if Amount <= Free then
      Free := Free - Amount;
      -- allocate
    else
      Blocked := Allocate'Count + 1;
      requeue Allocate with abort;
    end if;
  end Allocate;

  procedure Release(R: Resource; Amount: Request_Range) is
  begin
    Free := Free + Amount;
    -- free resources
    Blocked := 0;
  end Release;
end Resource_Controller;
```

Here, a note is taken (in `Blocked`) by the controller of the number of tasks on the `Allocate` entry. This is then used as part of the barrier. When the number queued (given by `'Count`) changes (either because new tasks arrive or because currently queued tasks time-out or are aborted), the barrier becomes open and the controller checks again to see if it can service the highest priority task.

The above algorithm makes use of the `Count` attribute within the barrier of an entry. This is a powerful programming technique; and a number of examples of its use are given elsewhere in this book. However, it should be noted that such usage will usually lead to the barrier expression being evaluated twice. Once as the call arrives, and (if the barrier evaluates to false) again when it is queued (as `'Count` has now increased).

12.5   Resource control and security

In all the examples so far given in this chapter, it has been assumed that any task allocated resources returns them. In general, a resource manager may wish to know the identity of the calling client so that

- a request can be refused on the grounds of deadlock prevention (see Section 12.7) or fairness (that is, to grant the request would be unfair to other clients), or
- it can be guaranteed that resources are released only by the task that earlier obtained them.

In Ada it is possible for a protected object to know the identity of its clients by using task identification (see Section 10.5). Consider the simple resource controller that only manages one resource.

```ada
protected Controller is
  entry Allocate;
  procedure Free;
private
  Allocated : Boolean := False;
  Current_Owner : Task_Id := Null_Task_Id;
end Controller;

protected body Controller is

  entry Allocate when not Allocated is
  begin
    Allocated := True;
    Current_Owner := Allocated'Caller;
  end Allocate;

  procedure Free is
  begin
    if Current_Task /= Current_Owner then
      raise Invalid_Caller; -- an appropriate exception
    end if;
    Allocated := False;
    Current_Owner := Null_Task_Id;
  end Free;

end Controller;
```

Note that with this facility, the caller of an entry is identified by the Caller attribute, whereas the caller of a procedure is obtained from the function Current_Task. The reasons for this difference are not important here.

12.6 Resource usage

When competing or cooperating tasks require resources, the normal mode of operation is for them to: request the resource (waiting if necessary), use the resource, and then release it. A resource is normally requested for use in one of two modes of access. These are shared access or exclusive access. Shared access is where the resource can be used concurrently by more than one task: for example a read-only file. Exclusive access requires that only one task is allowed access to the resource at any one time: for example, a physical resource like a 3D printer. Some resources can be used in either mode. In this case, if a task requests access to the resource in sharable mode while it is being accessed in exclusive mode, then that task must wait. If the resource was already being accessed in sharable mode then the task can continue. Similarly, if exclusive access to a resource is requested then the task making the request must wait for the tasks currently accessing the resource in sharable mode to finish.

As tasks may be blocked when requesting resources, it is imperative that they do not request resources until they need them. Furthermore, once allocated they should release them as soon as possible. If this is not done then the performance of the system can drop dramatically as tasks continually wait for their share of a scarce resource. Unfortunately, if tasks release resources too soon and then fail, they may have passed on erroneous information through the resource. For this reason, a *two-phased* resource usage pattern is employed (see Section 18.1.1).

12.7 Deadlock

In was noted in Chapter 11 that when many tasks compete for a finite number of resources, a situation may occur where one task, T_1, has sole access to a resource, R_1, while waiting for access to another resource, R_2. If task T_2 already has sole access to R_2 and is waiting for access to R_1, then deadlock has occurred because both tasks are waiting for each other to release a resource. With deadlock, all affected tasks are suspended indefinitely. A similar acute condition is where a collection of tasks are inhibited from proceeding but are still executing. As noted earlier, this situation is known as livelock. A typical example would be a collection of interacting tasks stuck in loops from which they cannot proceed but in which they are doing no useful work.

There are in general four necessary conditions that must hold if deadlock is to occur:

- **mutual exclusion** – only one task can use a resource at once (that is, the resource is non-sharable or at least limited in its concurrent access);
- **hold and wait** – there must exist tasks which are holding resources while waiting for others;
- **no preemption** – a resource can only be released voluntarily by a task; and
- **circular wait** – a circular chain of tasks must exist such that each task holds resources which are being requested by the next task in the chain.

If a real-time system is to be reliable, it must address the issue of deadlock. There are three possible approaches:

- deadlock prevention
- deadlock avoidance
- deadlock detection and recovery.

These strategies are not discussed further in this book as they are adequately dealt with in most Operating Systems textbooks. In Chapter 4 it was shown how a particular method of scheduling tasks and resources (the Priority Ceiling Protocol) avoids deadlock in single processor systems.

Summary

In every computer system, there are many tasks competing for a limited set of resources. Algorithms are required which both manage the resource allocation/deallocation procedures (the mechanism of resource allocation) and which guarantee that resources are allocated to tasks according to a predefined behaviour (the policy of resource allocation). These algorithms are also responsible for ensuring that tasks cannot deadlock while waiting for resource allocation requests to be fulfilled.

Sharing resources between tasks requires those tasks to communicate and synchronize. Therefore it is essential that the synchronization facilities provided by a real-time language have sufficient expressive power to allow a wide range of synchronization constraints to be specified. These constraints can be categorized as follows: resource scheduling must take account of

- the type of service request;
- the order in which requests arrive;
- the state of the server and any objects it manages;
- the parameters of a request;
- the priority of the client.

Where there is insufficient expressive power, tasks are often forced into a double interaction with a resource manager. This must be performed as an atomic action; otherwise it is possible for the client task to be aborted after the first interaction but before the second. If this possibility does exist then it is very difficult to program reliable resource managers. One means of extending the expressive power of guards is to allow requeuing. This facility enables avoidance synchronization to be as effective as condition synchronization. This chapter has discussed, in detail, Ada's support for 'requeue' and how it can be used in resource allocation. A task that calls an entry can be requeued to the same entry, or another entry in the same protected object, or an entry in another protected object. The requeue can have a "with abort" option that reinstates any timeout associated with the call and allows the calling task (and hence the entry call) to be aborted. Without this option, all timeouts are cancelled and the task becomes abort-deferred until the requeued call is serviced.

It has also looked at issues such as deadlock prevention.

Chapter 13
Real-time facilities

13.1 The notion of time
13.2 Access to a clock
13.3 Delaying a task
13.4 Programming timeouts
Summary

In Chapter 1, it was noted that a language for programming embedded systems requires facilities for real-time control. Indeed, the term 'real-time' has been used as a synonym for this class of system. Facilities for real-time control are generally built upon the concurrency model within the language.

The introduction of the notion of time into a programming language can best be described in terms of three largely independent topics:

(1) Interfacing with 'Time'; for example, accessing clocks so that the passage of time can be measured, delaying tasks until some future time, and programming timeouts so that the non-occurrence of some event can be recognised and dealt with.

(2) Representing timing requirements; for example, specifying rates of execution and deadlines.

(3) Satisfying timing requirements.

This chapter is largely concerned with the first two of these topics, although it will commence with some discussion of the notion of time itself. Chapters 4 – 8 consider ways of implementing systems such that the worst-case temporal behaviour can be predicted, and hence timing requirements ratified.

13.1 The notion of time

Our everyday experiences are so intrinsically linked to notions of past, present and future that it is surprising that the question 'What is time?' is still largely unresolved. Philosophers, mathematicians, physicists and, more recently, engineers have all studied 'time' in minute detail, but there is still no consensus on a definitive theory of time. As St Augustine stated:

> What, then, is time? If no one asks me, I know what it is. If I wish to explain it to him who asks me, I do not know.

A key question in the philosophical discussions of time can be stated succinctly as 'do we exist in time, or is time part of our existence?'. The two mainstream schools of thought are Reductionism and Platonism. All agree that human (and biological) history is made up of events, and that these events are ordered. Platonists believe that time is a fundamental property of nature; it is continuous, non-ending and non-beginning, 'and possesses these properties as a matter of necessity'. Our notion of time is derived from a mapping of historical events onto this external time reference.

Reductionists, by comparison, do without this external reference. Historical time, as made up of historical events, is the only meaningful notion of time. By assuming that certain events are 'regular' (for example, sunrise, winter solstice, vibrations of atoms, and so on), they can invent a useful time reference that enables the passage of time to be measured. But this time reference is a construction, not a given.

A consequence of the Reductionists view is that time cannot progress without change occurring. If the universe started with a 'Big Bang' then this represents the very first historical event and hence time itself started with 'space' at this first epoch. For Platonists, the Big Bang is just one event on an unbounded time line.

Over large distances, Einstein showed that relativity effects impinge not only on time directly but also on the temporal ordering of events. Within the special theory of relativity, the observer of events imposes a frame of reference. One observer may place event A before event B; another observer (in a different frame of reference) may reverse the order. Due to such difficulties with temporal ordering, Einstein introduced **causal ordering**. Event A may cause event B if all possible observers see event A occurring first. Another way of defining such causality is to postulate the existence of a signal that travels, at a speed no greater than the speed of light, from event A to event B.

These different themes of time are well illustrated by the notion of simultaneous events. To Platonists, the events are simultaneous if they occur 'at the same time'. For Reductionists, simultaneous events 'happen together'. With Special Relativity, simultaneous events are those for which a causal relationship does not exist.

From a mathematical point of view, there are many different topologies for time. The most common one comes from equating the passage of time with a 'real' line. Hence time is linear, transitive, irreflective and dense:

- Linearity: $\forall x, y : x < y \; or \; y < x \; or \; x = y$
- Transitivity: $\forall x, y, z : (x < y \; and \; y < z) \Rightarrow x < z$
- Irreflexivity: $\forall x : not \; (x < x)$
- Density: $\forall x, y : x < y \Rightarrow \exists z : (x < z < y)$

The engineering perspective can largely ignore the philosopher's issue of time. An embedded real-time computer system needs to coordinate its execution with the 'time' of its environment. The term 'real' is used to draw a distinction with the computer's time. It is real because it is external. Whether this external frame of reference is a Reductionist's construction or an approximative for the Platonists' 'absolute' time frame is not significant. Moreover, for most applications, relativistic effects can also be ignored. In terms of the mathematical topology of real-time systems, there are conflicting opinions as to whether time should be viewed as dense or discrete. Because computers work in discrete time, there is some advantage in constructing computational models based upon discrete time. The significant experience that other branches of engineering have in using, to good effect, dense time models argues the other way. A third approach, hybrid systems, attempts to integrate continuous and discrete time, and is essential for use within cyber-physical systems.

If, by general consensus, a series of events is deemed to be regular then it is possible to define a standard measurement of time. Many such standards have existed in the past. Table 13.1 gives a brief description of some of the more significant ones. This description is taken from Hoogeboom and Halang [45].

13.2 Access to a clock

If a program is going to interact in any meaningful way with the time frame of its environment then it must have access to some method of 'telling the time' or, at least, have some way of measuring the passage of time. This can be done in two distinct ways:

- by having direct access to the environment's time frame,
- by using an internal hardware clock that gives an adequate approximation to the passage of time in the environment.

The first approach is becoming more common and can be achieved in a number of ways. The simplest is for the environment to supply a regular interrupt that is clocked internally. Alternatively the system can be fitted with radio receivers and use one of the international time signals. UTC signals are broadcast by land-based radio stations (on shortwave frequencies) and satellites. For example, GPS (Global Positioning System) incorporates a time signal. Radio signals typically have an accuracy of 0.1-10 milliseconds; GPS provides a much better service with an accuracy of about 1 microsecond. If the system is linked to its environment via a telephone line or a network then these may also provide a time service (with an accuracy of perhaps a few milliseconds). With the Internet, NTP (Network Time Protocol) does indeed provide such a service.

Internal hardware clocks are devices that count the number of oscillations that occur in a quartz crystal. They typically divide this count by a fixed number and store the result in a register (counter) that the system's software can access. Inevitable this 'time' count is not always in perfect synchronization with the external time reference. The error is called **clock drift**. Clock drift may occur due, for example, to temperature changes within the system. A standard quartz crystal may draft by perhaps 10^{-6} seconds per second, i.e., one second in 11.6 days. A high precision clock may have drift values of 10^{-7} or 10^{-8}.

In distributed systems there is not only the drift between internal and external time that must be allowed for but also the **skew** between any of the clocks within the systems.

292 REAL-TIME FACILITIES

Name	Description	Note
True solar day	Time between two successive culminations (highest point of the Sun)	Varies through the year by 15 minutes (approx.)
Temporal hour	One-twelfth part of the time between sunrise and sunset	Varies considerably through the year
Universal Time (UT0)	Mean solar time at Greenwich meridian	Defined in 1884
Second (1)	1/86 400 of a mean solar day	
Second (2)	1/31 566 925.9747 of the tropical year for 1900	Ephemeris Time defined in 1955
UT1	Correction to UT0 because of polar motion	
UT2	Correction of UT1 because of variation in the speed of rotation of the Earth	
Second (3)	Duration of 9 192 631 770 periods of the radiation corresponding to the transition between two hyperfine levels of the ground state of the Caesium 133 atom	Accuracy of current Caesium atomic clocks deemed to be one part in 10^{13} (that is, one clock error per 300 000 years)
International Atomic Time (IAT)	Based upon Caesium atomic clock	
Coordinated Universal Time (UTC)	An IAT clock synchronized to UT2 by the addition of occasional leap ticks	Maximum difference between UT2 (which is based on astronomical measurement) and UTC (which is based upon atomic measurement) is kept to below 0.5 seconds

Table 13.1: Time standards.

If each node in the distributed system has its own clock then they will not provide a perfect source of time. If a *global time* services is needed then some form of clock synchronization protocol is needed. Many such protocols exist; they differ in how they deal with node and network failure. Further details on these protocols can be found in the literature on distributed systems.

From the programmer's perspective, access to time can either be provided by a clock primitive in the language or via a device driver for the internal clock, external clock or radio receiver. The programming of device drivers is the topic of Chapter 16; the following subsections illustrate how Ada provides clock abstractions. In general Ada is silent about how these abstractions should be interpreted in distributed systems.

13.2.1 The clock packages in Ada

Access to a clock in Ada is provided by a predefined (compulsory) library package called Calendar and an optional real-time facility. The Calendar package (see Program 13.1) implements an abstract data type for Time. It provides a function Clock for reading the time and various subprograms for converting between Time and humanly understandable units, such as Years, Months, Days and Seconds. The first three of these are given as integer subtypes. Seconds are, however, defined as a subtype of the primitive type Duration.

Type Duration is a predefined fixed-point real that represents an interval of time (relative time). Both its accuracy and its range are implementation-dependent, although its range must be at least –86 400.0 .. 86 400.0, which covers the number of seconds in a day. Its granularity must be no greater than 20 milliseconds. In essence, a value of type Duration should be interpreted as a value in seconds. Note that in addition to the above subprograms, the Calendar package defines arithmetic operators for combinations of Duration and Time parameters and comparative operations for Time values.

The code required to measure the time taken to perform a computation is quite straightforward. Note the use of the "-" operator, which takes two Time values but returns a value of type Duration.

```
declare
   Old_Time, New_Time : Time;
   Interval : Duration;
begin
   Old_Time := Clock;
   -- other computations
   New_Time := Clock;
   Interval := New_Time - Old_Time;
end;
```

From Ada 2005 some additional packages were provided that help with:

- constructing code that manipulates time values (including days that may have leap seconds included/excluded),
- formatting time values for input and output, and
- provide rudimentary support for time zones.

The other language clock is provided by the optional package Real_Time. This has a similar form to Calendar but is intended to give a finer granularity. The constant Time_Unit is the smallest amount of time representable by the Time type. The value of Tick must be no greater than one millisecond; the range of Time (from the epoch that represents the program's start-up) must be at least fifty years.

As well as providing a finer granularity, the Clock of Real_Time is defined to be **monotonic**. The Calendar clock is intended to provide an abstraction for a 'wall clock' and is, therefore, subject to leap years, leap seconds and other adjustments. A monotonic clock has *no* such adjustments. The Real_Time package is outlined in Program 13.2.

In addition to these real-time clocks, Ada also provides clocks that measure the execution times of tasks. These facilities are discussed in Chapter 15.

```ada
package Ada.Calendar is

  type Time is private;

  subtype Year_Number is Integer range 1901..2099;
  subtype Month_Number is Integer range 1..12;
  subtype Day_Number is Integer range 1..31;
  subtype Day_Duration is Duration range 0.0..86400.0;

  function Clock return Time;

  function Year(Date:Time) return Year_Number;
  function Month(Date:Time) return Month_Number;
  function Day(Date:Time) return Day_Number;
  function Seconds(Date:Time) return Day_Duration;

  procedure Split(Date:in Time; Year:out Year_Number;
                  Month:out Month_Number; Day:out Day_Number;
                  Seconds:out Day_Duration);

  function Time_Of(Year:Year_Number; Month:Month_Number;
                   Day:Day_Number; Seconds:Day_Duration := 0.0)
                   return Time;

  function "+"(Left:Time;Right:Duration) return Time;
  function "+"(Left:Duration;Right:Time) return Time;
  function "-"(Left:Time;Right:Duration) return Time;
  function "-"(Left:Time;Right:Time) return Duration;

  function "<"(Left,Right:Time) return Boolean;
  function "<="(Left,Right:Time) return Boolean;
  function ">"(Left,Right:Time) return Boolean;
  function ">="(Left,Right:Time) return Boolean;

  Time_Error:exception;
  -- Time_Error is raised by Time_Of, Split,"+",and "-"

private
  -- implementation dependent
end Ada.Calendar;
```

Program 13.1: The Ada.Calendar package.

```ada
package Ada.Real_Time is
  type Time is private;
  Time_First: constant Time;
  Time_Last: constant Time;
  Time_Unit: constant :=  -- implementation-defined-real-number;

  type Time_Span is private;
  Time_Span_First: constant Time_Span;
  Time_Span_Last: constant Time_Span;
  Time_Span_Zero: constant Time_Span;
  Time_Span_Unit: constant Time_Span;

  Tick: constant Time_Span;
  function Clock return Time;

  function "+" (Left: Time; Right: Time_Span) return Time;
  ...

  function "<" (Left, Right: Time) return Boolean;
  ...

  function "+" (Left, Right: Time_Span) return Time_Span;
  ...

  function "<" (Left, Right: Time_Span) return Boolean;
  ...

  function "abs"(Right : Time_Span) return Time_Span;

  function To_Duration (Ts : Time_Span) return Duration;
  function To_Time_Span (D : Duration) return Time_Span;

  function Nanoseconds  (Ns: Integer) return Time_Span;
  function Microseconds (Us: Integer) return Time_Span;
  function Milliseconds (Ms: Integer) return Time_Span;

  type Seconds_Count is range -- implementation-defined

  procedure Split(T : in Time; Sc: out Seconds_Count;
                  Ts : out Time_Span);
  function Time_Of(Sc: Seconds_Count; Ts: Time_Span) return Time;

private
  -- not specified by the language
end Ada.Real_Time;
```

Program 13.2: The Ada.Real_Time package

13.3 Delaying a task

In addition to having access to a clock, tasks must also be able to delay their execution either for a relative period of time or until some absolute time in the future.

13.3.1 Relative delays

A relative delay enables a task to queue on a future event rather than busy-wait on calls to the clock. For example, the following code shows how a task can loop waiting for 10 seconds to pass:

```
Start := Clock;  -- from calendar
loop
  exit when (Clock - Start) > 10.0;
end loop;
```

To eliminate the need for these busy-waits, most languages and operating systems provide some form of delay primitive. In Ada, this is a delay statement.

```
delay 10.0;
```

The value after **delay** (of type Duration) is relative (that is, the above statement means delay 10 seconds from the current time – a negative value is treated as zero).

It is important to appreciate that a 'delay' only guarantees that the task is made runnable after the period has expired. The actual delay before the task begins executing is, of course, dependent on the other tasks which are competing for the processor. It should also be noted that the granularity of the delay and the granularity of the clock are not necessarily the same. Moreover, the internal clock may be implemented using an interrupt which could be inhibited for short periods. Figure 13.1 illustrates the factors affecting the delay.

13.3.2 Absolute delays

The use of **delay** in Ada supports a relative time period (for example, 10 seconds from now). If a delay to an absolute time is required, then either the programmer must calculate the period to delay or an additional primitive is required. For example, if an action should take place 10 seconds after the start of some other action, then the following Ada code could be used (with Calendar):

```
Start := Clock;
First_Action;
delay 10.0 - (Clock - Start);
Second_Action;
```

Unfortunately, this might not achieve the desired result. In order for this formulation to have the required behaviour, then

```
delay 10.0 - (Clock - Start);
```

would have to be an uninterruptible (atomic) action, which it is not. For example, if First_Action took two seconds to complete then

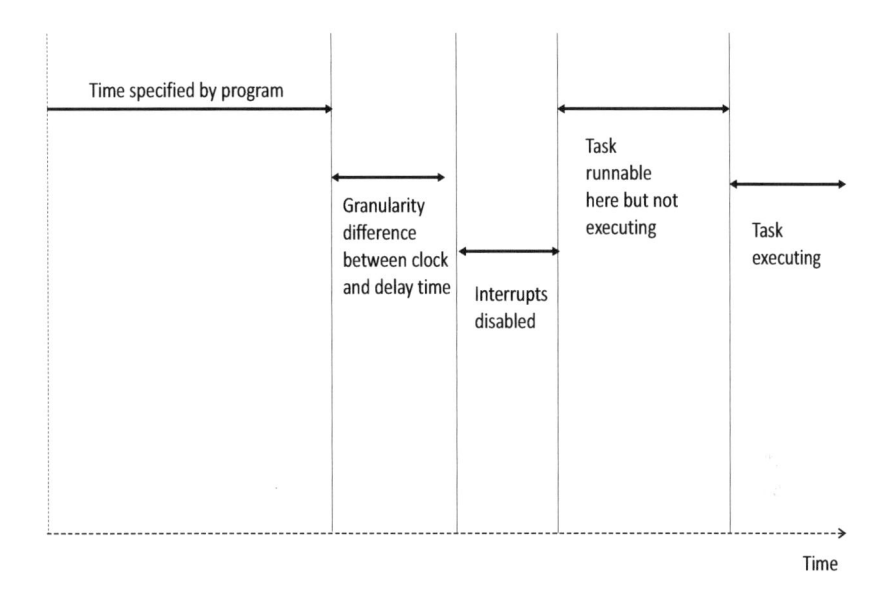

Figure 13.1: Delay times.

```
10.0 - (Clock - Start);
```

would equate to eight seconds. But after having calculated this value, if the task involved is preempted by some other task it could be three seconds (say) before it next executes. At that time it will delay for eight seconds rather than five. To solve this problem, Ada introduces the **delay until** statement:

```
Start := Clock;
First_Action;
```
delay until `Start + 10.0;`
```
Second_Action;
```

As with delay, **delay until** is accurate only in its lower bound. The task involved will not be released before the current time has reached that specified in the statement but it may be released later.

The time overrun associated with both relative and absolute delays is called the **local drift** and it it cannot be eliminated. It is possible, however, to eliminate the **cumulative drift** that could arise if local drifts were allowed to superimpose. The following code shows how the computation Action is programmed to be executed, on average, every 7 seconds. This code will compensate for any local drift. For example, if two consecutive calls to Action were actually 7.4 seconds apart then the subsequent delay would be for only 6.6 seconds (approximately).

```
declare
   Next : Time;
   Interval : constant Duration := 7.0;
begin
```

```
  Next := Clock + Interval;
  loop
    Action;
    delay until Next;
    Next := Next + Interval;
  end loop;
end;
```

13.4 Programming timeouts

Perhaps the simplest time constraint that an embedded system can have is the requirement to recognise, and act upon, the non-occurrence of some external event. For example, a temperature sensor may be required to log a new reading every second, the failure to give a reading within 10 seconds being defined as a fault. In general, a **timeout** is a restriction on the time a task is prepared to wait for a communication.

As well as waiting for communication, timeouts are also required on the execution of actions. For example, a programmer might require that a section of code be executed within a certain time. If this does not happen at run-time, then some error recovery might be required.

Shared variable communication and timeouts

In Chapter 11, various communication and synchronization mechanisms based on shared variables were discussed. Both mutual exclusive access to a critical section and condition synchronization were seen as being important requirements. When a task attempts to gain access to a critical section, it is blocked if another task is already active in the section. This blocking, however, is bounded by the time taken to execute the code of the section and the number of other tasks that also wish to execute the critical section. For this reason, it is not usually deemed necessary to have a timeout associated with attempting entry. In Section 5.4, the issue of analysing this blocking time was considered in detail.

In contrast, the blocking associated with condition synchronization is not so easily bounded and depends on the application. For example, a producer task attempting to place data in a full buffer must wait for a consumer task to take data out. The consumer tasks might not be prepared to do this for a significant period of time. For this reason, it is important to allow tasks the option of timing out while waiting for condition synchronizations.

With Ada's protected objects, avoidance synchronization is used and, therefore, it is at the point of the protected entry call that the timeout must be applied. To illustrate this, consider a task that wants to read some data that is stored in a protected object. The data is only available under certain conditions; and hence the data is accessed via an entry. The calling task does not want to be indefinitely held if no data is available within a certain duration. This is achieved by placing the entry call in a "select statement" where a timeout can be added.

```
select
  P.E ;  -- E is an entry in Protected Object P
or
```

```
   delay 0.5;
   null;
end select;
```

The **null** is not strictly needed but shows that the delay can have arbitrary statements following, that are executed if the delay expires before the entry call is serviced. This form of the select statement cannot have more than one entry call. The action it invokes is called a **timed entry call**. It must be emphasized that the time period specified in the call is a timeout value for the call starting to be be serviced; *it is not a timeout on the termination of the associated entry call.*

When a task wishes only to make an entry call if the called protected object is immediately prepared to service the call, then rather than make a timed entry call with time zero, a **conditional entry call** can be made:

```
select
   P.E    -- entry E in Protected Object P
else
   -- other actions
end select;
```

Timeouts on actions

In Section 18.4, mechanisms will be discussed that allowed tasks to have their control flows altered by asynchronous notifications. A timeout can be considered such a notification, and therefore if asynchronous notifications are supported, timeouts can also be used. Both a resumption (asynchronous events) and a termination (asynchronous transfer of control) model can be augmented by timeouts. Although for timeouts on actions, it is the termination model that is needed.

For example, in Section 18.5.1, the Ada asynchronous transfer of control (ATC) facility will be introduced. With this, an action can be aborted if a 'triggering event' occurs before the action has completed. One of the allowed triggering events is the passage of time. To illustrate this, consider a task that contains an action that must be completed within 100 milliseconds. The following code supports this requirement directly:

```
select
   delay 0.1;
then abort
   -- action
end select;
```

If the action takes too long, the triggering event will be taken and the action will be aborted. This is clearly an effective way of catching code that is stuck in a non-terminating loop or has some other program error.

Timeouts are thus usually associated with error conditions; if a communication has not occurred within X milliseconds then something unfortunate has happened and corrective action must be taken. This is, however, not their only use. Further uses of timeout will be considered in Chapter 19.

Summary

The management of time presents a number of difficulties that set embedded systems apart from other computing applications. Current real-time languages are often inadequate in their provisions for this vital area.

The introduction of the notion of time into real-time programming languages has been described in terms of three requirements:

- access to a clock,
- delaying,
- timeouts.

Ada provide two abstract data types for time and a collection of time-related operators.

If a task wishes to pause for a period of time, a delay primitive is needed to prevent the task having to busy wait. Such a primitive always guarantees to suspend the task for at least the designated time, but it cannot force the scheduler to run the task immediately the delay has expired. It is not possible, therefore, to avoid local drift, although it is possible to limit the cumulative drift that could arise from repeated execution of delays.

Ada allows timeouts to be set using the "select statement". This allows a task to timeout while waiting for an entry to become open, and an action to be aborted if it has been not completed within a specified time.

Chapter 14
Programming real-time abstractions

14.1 Real-time tasks
14.2 Programming periodic activities
14.3 Programming aperiodic and sporadic activities
14.4 The role of real-time events and their handlers
14.5 Controlling input and output jitter
14.6 The Ravenscar profile
14.7 Simple embedded system revisited Summary

One of the main factors that differentiate a real-time system from other computer systems is the need to specify timing requirements arising from within the application. The notion of a *temporal scope* was introduced in Chapter 2. This led to the development of the real-time programming model presented in Sections 2.4 and 3.8.

This chapter illustrates how this model can be represented in Ada. In particular, how Ada supports the representation of:

- periodic tasks,
- sporadic and aperiodic tasks, and
- input and output jitter control.

Tasks that have any of the above attributes are termed **real-time tasks**.

In general, languages can support the programming of real-time tasks at various levels of abstraction. Ada provides relatively low-level abstractions that the programmer can combine to implement various real-time models. In contrast, other languages (e.g. Real-Time Java) provide a combination of low and high level abstraction.

This chapter first considers the relationship between a real-time task and the typical task representation techniques that were considered in Chapter 10. It then illustrates how periodic activities can be programmed in Ada. This is followed by a discussion on how event-triggered sporadic and aperiodic activities can be implemented. After this, the chapter turns its attention to the control of input and output jitter. Finally the chapter shows how real-time tasks can be represented in a dedicated language profile.

14.1 Real-time tasks

In theory any concurrent activity (be it a result of explicit task creation or the execution of a fork or a cobegin statement) can be considered real-time if real-time attributes are associated with it, and it is scheduled for execution by a real-time scheduler. However, in practice, real-time tasks often have constraints placed on the programming style to ensure that their execution is predictable – if not deterministic. For example, a hard real-time task might be prohibited from executing an unbounded loop statement. Ada does not syntactically distinguish between a concurrent task and a real-time task. Instead, programming guidelines are applied and tools in the development environment are used to check conformance.

14.2 Programming periodic activities

In keeping with many real-time languages, Ada does not support the explicit specification of periodic or sporadic tasks with deadlines; rather low-level mechanisms are provided that can be used for a variety of purposes – e.g. a delay primitive, timers and so on. These can be used within a looping task to provide the same functionality as a periodic activity.

For example, in Ada, a periodic task that has an iteration rate of 50 times a second might take the following form:

```
task type Periodic_T;
task body Periodic_T is
   Next_Release     : Time;
   Release_Interval : constant Time_Span := Milliseconds (20);
begin
   Next_Release := Clock + Release_Interval;
   loop
      -- sample data (for example) or
      -- calculate and send a control signal
      delay until Next_Release;
      Next_Release := Next_Release + Release_Interval;
   end loop;
end Periodic_T;
```

Note that in the above case, the task starts immediately it is created. Section 4.2.4 has discussed that from a schedulability analysis perspective, the worst case response times come when all tasks are release at the critical instant. Hence, in order to facilitate testing, it may be appropriate to ensure that all tasks are released at the same time. Also, in Section 7.5, it was shown that improved schedulability can be obtained when periodic tasks releases are offset against each other. For these reasons, it might be more appropriate for a periodic task to have the following structure.

```ada
task type Periodic_T(Start : access Time);

task body Periodic_T is
   Next_Release      : Time;
   Release_Interval  : constant Time_Span := Milliseconds (20);
begin
   Next_Release := Start.all;
   loop
      delay until Next_Release;
      -- sample data (for example) or
      -- calculate and send a control signal
      Next_Release := Next_Release + Release_Interval;
   end loop;
end Periodic_T;
```

In the above example, the start time for the task is passed as a parameter to the task when it is created. This allows multiple tasks to have their start times coordinate, if that is appropriate.

As an aside: Ada tasks can only have discrete or access types passed as parameters. Hence, in this example, it is necessary for the start time (time is a private type) to be passed indirectly.

14.3 Programming aperiodic and sporadic activities

As indicated in Section 2.2, the main difference between aperiodic and sporadic activities is that the latter have a defined minimum inter-arrival time (MIT), whereas the former do not. From a programming point of view, the main issues are:

- for aperiodic activities: how is the amount of time that is spent in their execution bounded;
- for sporadic activities: whether the language/operating system supports the detection of MIT violations.

In common with Ada's approach to supporting periodic task, the language provides no direct abstractions to support sporadic or aperiodic tasks. Instead, the lower-level mechanisms can be used to program the precise model required. Consider, for example, an aperiodic/sporadic Ada task that is released by an interrupt. Typically, it is necessary to use a protected object to handle the interrupt and release the task for execution:

```ada
protected Aperiodic_Controller is
  procedure Interrupt_Handler; -- mapped to interrupt
  entry Wait_For_Next_Interrupt;
private
  Call_Outstanding : Boolean := False;
end Aperiodic_Controller;

protected body Aperiodic_Controller is
  procedure Interrupt_Handler is
  begin
```

```ada
      Call_Outstanding := True;
   end Interrupt_Handler;

   entry Wait_For_Next_Interrupt when Call_Outstanding is
   begin
      Call_Outstanding := False;
   end Wait_For_Next_Interrupt;
end Aperiodic_Controller;


task body Aperiodic_T is
begin
   loop
      Aperiodic_Controller.Wait_For_Next_Interrupt;
      -- action
   end loop;
end Aperiodic_T;
```

The details of the Ada model of interrupt handling will be considered in Section 16.3. Here it is assumed that the occurrence of an interrupt results in a call to the procedure Interrupt_Handler. This simply sets the boolean variable to true, thereby opening the barrier and allowing the task to be released. As with periodic tasks, a loop must be used to get repeated releases.

The structure of the above code is agnostic on whether the frequency of the release event is controlled by the environment, or whether the program itself imposes constraints on how much CPU time it will allow for the processing of such events. If the external environment does not constrain the rate of interrupts, there are two approach that can be used to enforce a minimum separation between the releases of task. The first is illustrated below. The controller now allows a minimum inter-arrival time (MIT) to be set. When a sporadic task is released, it is informed of the earliest time that it can make another Wait_For_Next_Interrupt entry call. The task then will delay until this time arrives before making the call.

```ada
protected Sporadic_Controller is
   procedure Set_MIT(T: Time_Span);
   procedure Interrupt_Handler;
   entry Wait_For_Next_Interrupt(Next_Time : out Time);
private
   Available : Boolean := False;
   MIT : Time_Span := some_default;
end Sporadic_Controller;

protected body Sporadic_Controller is
   procedure Set_MIT(T: Time_Span) is
   begin
      MIT := T;
   end Set_MIT;

   procedure Interrupt_Handler is
   begin
      Available := True;
   end Interrupt_Handler;
```

```ada
  entry Wait_For_Next_Interrupt(
        Next_Time : out Time)
        when Available is
  begin
    Available := False;
    Next_Time := Clock + MIT;
  end Wait_For_Next_Interrupt;
end Sporadic_Controller;

task body Sporadic_T is
  Next : Time;
begin
  Sporadic_Controller.Set_MIT(...);
  loop
    Sporadic_Controller.Wait_For_Next_Interrupt(Next);
    -- action
    delay until Next;
  end loop;
end Aperiodic_T;
```

Of course, the above code will not stop the code executing within the interrupt handler executing. To achieve this, it will be necessary to disable interrupts from the device when an interrupt occurs and then enable them again after the MIT has passed. In order to encapsulate this code within the controller, it is necessary to use Ada's requeue facility. This is illustrated below.

```ada
protected Sporadic_Controller is
  procedure Set_MIT(T: Time_Span);
  procedure Interrupt_Handler;
  entry Wait_For_Next_Interrupt(Next_Time : out Time);
private
  entry Wait_Interrupt(Next_Time : out Time);
  Available : Boolean := False;
  MIT : Time_Span; -- := some_default;
end Sporadic_Controller;

protected body Sporadic_Controller is
  procedure Set_MIT(T: Time_Span) is
  begin
    MIT := T;
  end Set_MIT;

  procedure Interrupt_Handler is
  begin
    Available := True;
    -- disable interrupts
  end Interrupt_Handler;

  entry Wait_For_Next_Interrupt(
        Next_Time : out Time) when True is
  begin
    -- enable interrupts
```

```
      requeue Wait_Interrupt with abort;
   end Wait_For_Next_Interrupt;

   entry Wait_Interrupt(Next_Time : out Time) when Available is
   begin
      Available := False;
      Next_Time := Clock + MIT;
   end Wait_Interrupt;
end Sporadic_Controller;
```

The second approach to constrain the amount of execution time consumed by an aperiodic/sporadic tasks is to use execution-time servers (as introduced in Section 7.7). This topic will be dealt with again, in detail, in Section 19.6 from within a context of fault-tolerance.

14.4 The role of real-time events and their handlers

It is useful in real-time systems to distinguish between two forms of computation that occur at run-time: tasks and event handlers. A real-time task is a long-lived entity with state and intervals of activity and inactivity. While active, it competes with other tasks for the available resources – the rules of this competition are captured in a scheduling or dispatching policy (for example, fixed priority or EDF). A real-time task can be released by the passage of time or by an event, examples of which have been given in the previous sections.

Events handlers can similarly be released by the passage of time or be event triggered. However, in comparison with real-time tasks, an event handler is usually a short-lived, stateless, one-shot or periodic computation. Its execution is, at least conceptually, immediate; and having completed it has no lasting direct effect other than by means of changes it has made to the permanent state of the system. For example, if a central heating system must come on at 7.00am then the control system needs a clock and a way of postponing execution until that clock says 7.00am. Using tasks, the only way to deliver this coordination is to have the task delay until 7.00am and then turn the heating on. In this and other situations, this concurrency overhead is unnecessary and inefficient. Hence events and event handlers have an important role to play in reducing this overhead.

When an event occurs, it is said to be *triggered*; other terms used are *fired*, *invoked* or *delivered*. The event handling code normally does not contain any synchronization calls that could lead to it becoming suspended; the handler runs to completion. Where these requirements can not be guaranteed, it is necessary to schedule the event handlers rather than execute them immediately their corresponding events occur. Events can also be used as an asynchronous notification techniques as will be described in Section 18.4.

This section focuses on time-triggered events and their handlers. Events that are triggered by the environment or other tasks are also considered in Section 18.4.

Ada 2005 introduced a low-level mechanism that allows a handler to be associated with a *timing event*. When the event's time is due (as determined by the real-time clock), the handler code is executed. Timing Events are supported by a child package of `Ada.Real_Time` (see Program 14.1).

```ada
package Ada.Real_Time.Timing_Events is
  type Timing_Event is tagged limited private;
  type Timing_Event_Handler is access protected
          procedure(Event : in out Timing_Event);
  procedure Set_Handler(Event : in out Timing_Event;
       At_Time : Time; Handler: Timing_Event_Handler);
  procedure Set_Handler(Event : in out Timing_Event;
       In_Time: Time_Span; Handler: Timing_Event_Handler);
  function Is_Handler_Set(Event : Timing_Event)
         return Boolean;
  function Current_Handler(Event : Timing_Event)
           return Timing_Event_Handler;
  procedure Cancel_Handler(Event : in out Timing_Event;
         Cancelled : out Boolean);
  function Time_Of_Event(Event : Timing_Event) return Time;
private
  -- Not specified by the language.
end Ada.Real_Time.Timing_Events;
```

Program 14.1: The `Ada.Real_Time.Timing_Events` package.

The handler type is an access to a protected procedure with the timing event itself been passed back to the handler when the event is triggered. The event is *set* by the attachment of a handler. Two Set_Handler procedures are defined, one using absolute time the other relative time. If a **null** handler is passed the event is *cleared*, this can also be achieved by calling Cancel_Handler. With this routine the boolean flag indicates if the event was actually set before it was cleared. If Set_Handler is called on an event that is already set then a new time is posted for the event with the original time and handler being lost. As a handler is called by a clock, it must be accessible for the lifetime of the program. Consequently, only library-level handlers can be used.

As soon as possible after the time defined for the event, the handler is executed; this clears the event. It will not be triggered again unless it is reset. The most effective way for an implementation to support timing events is to execute the handlers directly from the interrupt handler of the clock. For example, consider a clock that interrupts every 10ms. On each occurrence, the clock handler will check the system's delay queue to see if any tasks need to be made runnable or if any timing events need to be triggered. Tasks are moved to ready queues, handlers are executed directly[1]. As the clock interrupt is typically the highest priority interrupt in the system, the application code's protected object (that embodies the handler procedure) must have a ceiling of Interrupt_Priority'Last – see Section 15.3.

Two further subprograms are defined in the support package. One allows the current handler to be obtained while the other allows the current time of the event to be requested. Both return with appropriate values if the event is not set (**null** and Ada.Real_Time.Time_First respectively).

---

[1] The scheduling analysis developed in Section 7.9.3 to account for clock overheads can easily be extended to accommodate timing events

As the handlers for timing events are executed directly by the Ada run-time system they suffer little release jitter. Consequently, they are ideal for controlling input and output jitter. An example of this will be given in the next section.

14.5 Controlling input and output jitter

As discussed in Chapter 2, in many application areas, particularly control systems, real-time tasks have a simple structure. They are typically periodic and read their sensor inputs at the start of each release, perform some computation, and produce output for actuators within some deadline. There are also usually some requirements on the minimum and maximum latency of the task. In these applications, significant variations in the timing of the input and output operations during each period has to be avoided. The variation is called **input and output jitter**. The latter being the variation in the actual latency of the task. In many applications, controlling jitter is performed by the I/O device itself. These "smart" sensors and actuators can perform their I/O operations at particular points in time with minimum latency. However where these are not available, the application must implement the necessary requirements.

Few programming real-time languages explicitly have facilities to directly specify jitter requirements. There are, however, several ways by which the programmer can use other real-time mechanisms to meet the requirements. Sections 2.2 and 2.4 showed how a jitter-constrained task could be transformed into two or three tasks each with its own deadline. Then by judicial use of scheduling parameters or temporal scopes, the required behavior could be achieved. However, in situations where it is necessary to undertake a small computation periodically (and with minimum jitter), a time-triggered event can be used and is more efficient. These approaches will be illustrated in the following subsections.

14.5.1 Controlling I/O jitter with timing events

The input and output from and to sensors and actuators is a good example of where small amounts of computation are constrained by jitter requirements. Consider for example a periodic control activity. It reads a sensor, performs some computation based on the sensor value and writes a result to an actuator. In order to ensure that the environment does not become unstable, the control algorithms require that the sensor be read every 40 milliseconds (for example); the variation in the time at which the sensor is read each cycle (input jitter) is 2 millisecond. The output should be written to the actuator within a deadline of 30 milliseconds, and the output jitter must be no more than 4 milliseconds. Figure 14.1 illustrates these timing constraints.

One way to get the tight time constraints is to use two timing events in conjunction with a task. First, the time constraint on the input can be implemented by the following protected type:

```
protected type Sensor_Reader
  with Interrupt_Priority => Interrupt_Priority'Last is
  procedure Start;
```

CONTROLLING INPUT AND OUTPUT JITTER

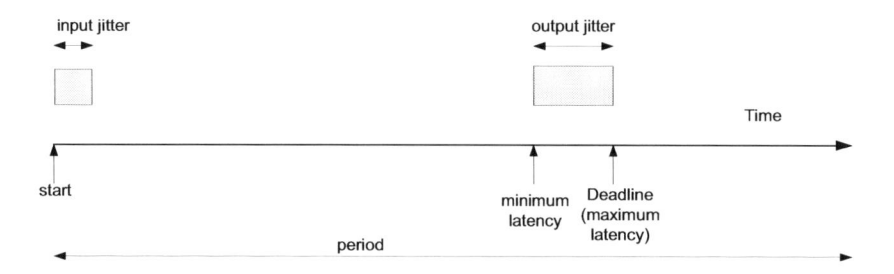

Figure 14.1: A simple task with input and output jitter constraints.

```
  entry Read(Data : out Sensor_Data);
  procedure Timer(Event : in out Timing_Event);
private
  Next_Time : Time;
  Reading : Sensor_Data;
  Data_Available : Boolean := True;
end Sensor_Reader;

Input_Jitter_Control : Timing_Event;
Input_Period : Time_Span := Milliseconds(40);
```

The procedure `Start` is used to initiate the first sensor reading. The routine then sets up the next reading using the `Input_Jitter_Control` timing event. The timer will call the `Timer` procedure at the appropriate time. This will take the next sensor reading, and set up the next event. The control algorithm simply calls the `Read` entry, which becomes open every time new data is available. The body of the protected type is given below.

```
protected body Sensor_Reader is
  procedure Start is
  begin
    Reading := Read_Sensor;  -- obtain Reading from sensor interface
    Next_Time := Clock + Input_Period;
    Data_Available := True;
    Set_Handler(Input_Jitter_Control, Next_Time, Timer'Access);
  end Start;

  entry Read(Data : out Sensor_Data) when Data_Available is
  begin
    Data := Reading;
    Data_Available := False;
  end Read;

  procedure Timer(Event : in out Timing_Event) is
  begin
    Reading := Read_Sensor;
    Data_Available := True;
```

```ada
      Next_Time := Next_Time + Input_Period;
      Set_Handler(Input_Jitter_Control, Next_Time, Timer'Access);
   end Timer;
end Sensor_Reader;
```

The repetitive use of timing events is an effective solution for this type of requirement. A similar approach can be used for control of the output.

```ada
protected type Actuator_Writer with
   Interrupt_Priority => Interrupt_Priority'Last is
   procedure Start;
   procedure Write(Data : Actuator_Data);
   procedure Timer(Event : in out Timing_Event);
private
   Next_Time : Time;
   Value : Actuator_Data;
end Actuator_Writer;

Output_Jitter_Control : Timing_Event;
Output_Period : Time_Span := Milliseconds(40);

with Ada.Integer_text_IO; use Ada.Integer_text_IO;
protected body Actuator_Writer is
   procedure Start is
   begin
      Actual_Write(Value); -- initial value
      Next_Time := Clock + Output_Period;
      Set_Handler(Output_Jitter_Control, Next_Time, Timer'Access);
   end Start;

   procedure Write(Data : Actuator_Data) is
   begin
       Value := Data;
   end Write;

   procedure Timer(Event : in out Timing_Event) is
   begin
      Actual_Write(Value);
      Next_Time := Next_Time + Output_Period;
      Set_Handler(Output_Jitter_Control, Next_Time, Timer'Access);
   end Timer;
end Actuator_Writer;
```

Now, the actuator Start routine is called 26 milliseconds (that is, 30 - 4 milliseconds) after starting the sensor data collection timer (assuming the code does not suffer from preemptions):

```ada
procedure Main is
   ...
   SR : Sensor_Reader;
   AW : Actuator_Writer;
begin
   ...
   SR.start;
```

```
   delay 0.026;
   AW.start;
   ...
end Main;
```

Finally, the control algorithm task can be given. Note that it contains no 'delay until' statement. The rate is controlled by the opening and closing of the Read entry.

The full main program is given below.

```
with Actuator_Writers, Sensor_Readers;
use Actuator_Writers, Sensor_Readers;
procedure Main is

   SR : aliased Sensor_Reader;
   AW : aliased Actuator_Writer;

   task type Control_Algorithm (Input  : access Sensor_Reader;
                                Output : access Actuator_Writer);

   Control : Control_Algorithm(SR'access, AW'access);

   task body Control_Algorithm is
      Input_Data  : Sensor_Data;
      Output_Data : Actuator_Data;
   begin
     loop
        Input.Read(Input_Data);
        -- process data;
        Output_Data := ...;
        Output.Write(Output_Data);
     end loop;
   end Control_Algorithm;
begin
   SR.start;
   delay 0.026;
   AW.start;
end Main;
```

The use of timing events to represent a periodic activity is appropriate for small execution times or when minimum jitter on the periodic activity is required. But it has the disadvantage that the code is always executed at interrupt priority level and hence has a temporal interference on the rest of the program. Furthermore, all input and output is treated with the same urgency. To have more control it is necessary to create three tasks: one for input, one for processing and one for output. Each can be given its own deadline and scheduled so that they start at different offsets from one and other. This approach is illustrated next.

14.5.2 Controlling I/O jitter with multiple tasks

With the multiple task approach, the sensor reader and sensor write are also tasks. Each task is given an offset and an appropriate priority in order to meet its deadline. The example

312   PROGRAMMING REAL-TIME ABSTRACTIONS

presented in Section 14.5.1 is now re-factored as illustrated below.

```ada
Start : aliased Time := ....;
Control_Offset : aliased Time := Start + Milliseconds(2);
Actuator_Offset : aliased Time := Start + Milliseconds(26);

Sensor_Priority : Priority := ...;
Control_Priority : Priority := ...;
Actuator_Priority : Priority := ...;
Release_Interval : constant Time_Span := Milliseconds (40);

task type Sensor_Reader(Start_At : access Time; Pri : Priority)
    with Priority => Pri;

task type Actuator_Writer(Start_At : access Time; Pri : Priority)
    with Priority => Pri;

task type Control_Algorithm(Start_At : access Time; Pri : Priority)
    with Priority => Pri;

SR : Sensor_Reader(Start'access, Sensor_Priority );
CA : Control_Algorithm(Control_Offset'access, Control_Priority);
AW : Actuator_Writer(Actuator_Offset'access, Actuator_Priority);
```

Where the bodies of the tasks are structured as follows.

```ada
task body Sensor_Reader is
  Next_Release : Time;
begin
  Next_Release := Start_At.all;
  loop
    delay until Next_Release;
    -- read sensor and store result in
    -- an atomic variable or in a protected object
    Next_Release := Next_Release + Release_Interval;
  end loop;
end Sensor_Reader;

task body Actuator_Writer is
  Next_Release : Time;
begin
  Next_Release := Start_At.all;
  loop
    delay until Next_Release;
    -- get value from atomic variable or protected object and
    -- output to actuator
    Next_Release := Next_Release + Release_Interval;
  end loop;
end Actuator_Writer;

task body Control_Algorithm is
  Next_Release : Time;
begin
```

CONTROLLING INPUT AND OUTPUT JITTER 313

```ada
   Next_Release := Start_At.all;
   loop
     delay until Next_Release;
     -- get value from atomic variable or protected object
     -- process and write
     -- output to atomic variable or protected object
     Next_Release := Next_Release + Release_Interval;
   end loop;
end Control_Algorithm;
```

14.5.3 Controlling I/O jitter with dynamic priorities

Although the three tasks solution is the most flexible structure and is easily analysed by schedulability analysis, it is resource expensive requiring three tasks along with their associated stacks etc.

An alternative approach that maintains the flexibility but reduces the overhead is to use dynamic priorities (see Section 15.4), as illustrated below.

```ada
Start : aliased Time := ....;

Sensor_Priority : Priority := ...;
Control_Priority : Priority := ...;
Actuator_Priority : Priority := ...;
Release_Interval : constant Time_Span := Milliseconds (40);
Offset_1 : aliased Time_Span :=  Milliseconds(2);
Offset_2 : aliased Time_Span :=  Milliseconds(26);


task type New_Control_Algorithm (
     St : access Time; Off1 : access Time_Span;
     Off2 : access Time_Span; Priority1 : Priority;
     Priority2 : Priority; Priority3 : Priority);

Dynamic_Controller : New_Control_Algorithm(
    Start'access, Offset_1'access, Offset_2'access,
    Sensor_Priority, Control_Priority, Actuator_Priority);
```

Where the body of `Dynamic_Controller` is

```ada
task body New_Control_Algorithm is
  Next_Release    : Time;
  Sensor_Value : Sensor_Data;
  Actuator_Value : Actuator_Data;
begin
  Next_Release := St.all;
  Dynamic_Priorities.Set_Priority(Priority1);
  loop
    delay until Next_Release;
    -- read sensor and store result in Sensor_Value
    Dynamic_Priorities.Set_Priority(Priority2);
```

```
      delay until (Next_Release + Off1.all);
      -- process sensor reading and write Actuator_Value
      Dynamic_Priorities.Set_Priority(Priority3);
      delay until (Next_Release + Off2.all);
      -- output Actuator_Value to actuator
      Next_Release := Next_Release + Release_Interval;
      Dynamic_Priorities.Set_Priority(Priority1);
   end loop;
end New_Control_Algorithm;
```

This code can be viewed as if it were three separate tasks on a single processor; but as was noted in Section 7.5, tasks with offsets can be difficult to analyse.

14.6 The Ravenscar profile

The last four chapters have presented the wide variations that are available in concurrency models. They have also shown that the Ada model is very flexible allowing dynamic task creation, nested task hierarchies, a variety of mechanisms for terminating tasks, and a variety of synchronisation schemes. But in this chapter it has been demonstrated that many of the requirements for programming predictable real-time systems can be met by a relatively simple concurrency model. In recognition of the fact that only a subset of language features are needed for many real-time applications, Ada defines a profile that has just these features. The profile is named after the small Yorkshire coastal village of Ravenscar where the workshop at which the profile was defined took place.

The profile focusses on the tasking features of Ada and aims to:

- provide the minimum features needed to program basic real-time abstractions,
- be implementable with a small and efficient run-time support system, and
- be implementable with a sufficiently simple run-time support system that it could be verified to the level required for safety-critical applications.

Rather than define what the Ravensacr profile contains, it is actually specified by noting what parts of the full Ada language are not available in the profile. For example, the Ravenscar profile specifies the following restrictions on the way Ada tasks are declared.

- Task hierarchies are prohibited – all tasks must be declared at library level;
- The dynamic creation of tasks is prohibited – all task instances must be created at the library level without using an allocator;
- The use of task entries is prohibited – task entries are used in Ada to support synchronous communication (the Ada rendezvous) between tasks, they are not considered in this book and are not part of the Ravenscar profile.

These restrictions imply that a Ravenscar program has a static number of independent tasks that only communicate via protected objects. As will be described in the next chapter, fixed priorities can be assigned to such tasks and protected objects, and as a result the fixed priority scheduling scheme defined in Part II can be applied. Note the code presented earlier in this chapter for periodic and sporadic tasks is Ravenscar compliant.

Using a subset of a programming language is common in many application domains. For example, developers of safety-critical systems often use a subset to avoid complicated or unsafe language features: e.g. the use of MISRA C in the automobile domain. In many cases, conformance to a subset must be checked by tools in the program development environment. In contrast, the Ada language definition of a profile allows subsets to be specified and checked by the compiler. The Ada language conveys programmer directives to the compiler via pragmas. One such pragma is named **Restrictions** and it expresses the programmer's intent to abide by certain restrictions. A pragma **Profile** expresses the programs's intent to abide by a set of restrictions. The language supports the Ravenscar profile:

```
pragma Profile(Ravenscar);
```

that can be used as the first line of the file containing the main Ada program. It is known as a **configuration pragma**.

In full, the Ravenscar profile is equivalent to the following

```
pragma Task_Dispatching_Policy (FIFO_Within_Priorities);
pragma Locking_Policy (Ceiling_Locking);
pragma Detect_Blocking;
pragma Restrictions (
No_Abort_Statements,
No_Dynamic_Attachment,
No_Dynamic_CPU_Assignment,
No_Dynamic_Priorities,
No_Implicit_Heap_Allocations,
No_Local_Protected_Objects,
No_Local_Timing_Events,
No_Protected_Type_Allocators,
No_Relative_Delay,
No_Requeue_Statements,
No_Select_Statements,
No_Specific_Termination_Handlers,
No_Task_Allocators,
No_Task_Hierarchy,
No_Task_Termination,
Simple_Barriers,
Max_Entry_Queue_Length => 1,
Max_Protected_Entries => 1,
Max_Task_Entries => 0,
No_Dependence => Ada.Asynchronous_Task_Control,
No_Dependence => Ada.Calendar,
No_Dependence => Ada.Execution_Time.Group_Budgets,
No_Dependence => Ada.Execution_Time.Timers,
No_Dependence => Ada.Synchronization_Barriers,
No_Dependence => Ada.Task_Attributes,
No_Dependence => System.Multiprocessors.Dispatching_Domains);
```

The No_Dependence entries imply that the associated library package cannot be included ('withed') in any part of the program.

316 PROGRAMMING REAL-TIME ABSTRACTIONS

The Ravenscar profile forms the basis of the real-time programming model that was defined in Section 2.4. Not all restricted language features have been introduced in this book, but the above list is included to show that the profile is very constrained and prohibits features, such as 'no requeue statements', that have been used in earlier chapters to provide necessary primitives for some real-time requirements. Hence Ravenscar has an important role in providing a profile that leads to simple analysable real-time systems; but for the complete set of real-time abstractions many more features of the full Ada tasking model are required.

One aspect of Ravenscar that is particularly restrictive is its support for shared variable-based communication. The following restrictions are imposed.

(1) All protected objects must appear in library level packages.

(2) The dynamic creation of protected objects is prohibited – there must be no protected object creation using the new constructor.

(3) Entry families are prohibited.

(4) Private entries are prohibited.

(5) There must only be one entry per protected type and only a maximum of one task queued at any time.

(6) An entry barrier shall only be a single boolean variable (or literal).

(7) The use of Count in barriers is prohibited.

Restrictions (1) .. (4) are primarily to facilitate the implementation of an efficient run-time support system that potentially could be certified for use in safety-critical systems. Restrictions (5) .. (7) are primarily to simplify timing analysis.

The above restrictions do have a major impact on how programs are written. For example, consider the bounded buffer presented in Section 11.8, whose specification is repeated below:

```ada
-- a bounded buffer

Buffer_Size : constant Integer := 10;
type Index is mod Buffer_Size ;
subtype Count is Natural range 0 .. Buffer_Size;
type Buffer is array (Index) of Data_Item;

protected type Bounded_Buffer is
   entry Get(Item: out Data_Item);
   entry Put(Item: in Data_Item);
private
   First : Index := Index'First;
   Last : Index := Index'Last;
   Number_In_Buffer : Count := 0;
   Buf : Buffer;
end Bounded_Buffer;

My_Buffer : Bounded_Buffer;
```

This code is not Ravenscar compliant because there are two declared entries, and Ravenscar requires only one. Hence, it is necessary to change the abstraction slightly. There are several possibilities. One or both entries could be changed to procedures, with a boolean out parameter indicating whether the operations was successful. For example, trying to Get from an empty buffer instead of blocking returns false. Often an aperiodic thread uses the presence of data in a buffer as its release condition. Consequently, here Put is made a procedure.

```
protected type Bounded_Buffer is
  entry Get (Item : out Data_Item);
  procedure Put (Item : in Data_Item; Ok : out Boolean);
private
  First : Index := Index'First;
  Last : Index := Index'Last;
  Num : Count := 0;
  Buf : Buffer;
end Bounded_Buffer;
```

The original barrier on the Get entry was ;

```
entry Get(Item: out Data_Item)
    when Number_In_Buffer /= 0 is
```

This barrier is not Ravenscar complaint as Ravenscar requires that an entry barrier shall only be a single boolean variable (or literal). Hence, the body of the protected object is refactored to be:

```
protected body Bounded_Buffer is
  entry Get (Item : out Data_Item) when Not_Empty is
  begin
    Item := Buf(First);
    First := First + 1;
    Num := Num - 1;
    if Num = 0 then Not_Empty := False; end if;
  end Get;

  procedure Put (Item : in Data_Item;
                 Ok : out Boolean) is
  begin
    if Num = Buffer_Size then
       Ok := False;
    else
       Last := Last + 1;
       Num := Num + 1;
       Buf(Last) := Item;
       Ok := True;
       Not_Empty := True;
    end if;
  end Put;
end Bounded_Buffer;
```

where Not_Empty is a boolean variable that must be added to the protected type's specification.

The final consideration is whether more than one task can be queued waiting for data on the `Get` entry. If this is possible, then more significant changes are required. Consider the following.

```ada
package Multicasts is
  protected Multicast is
    entry Receive(Data : out Integer);
    procedure Send(Data : in Integer);
  private
    Go : Boolean := False;
    The_Data : Integer;
  end Multicast;
end Multicasts;
```

Here the intention is that data can be send to several waiting receivers:

```ada
package body Multicasts is
  protected body Multicast is
    entry Receive(Data : out Integer) when Go is
    begin
      Data := The_Data;
      if Receive'Count = 0 then
        Go := False;
      end if;
    end Receive;

    procedure Send(Data : in Integer) is
    begin
      The_Data := Data;
      Go := True;
    end Send;
  end Multicast;
end Multicasts;
```

Having multiple receivers queued on the `Receive` entry violates the Ravenscar restrictions. Yet, this seems to be what is required by the communication abstraction.

The use of the Ravenscar Profile requires the programmer to be more explicit in their requirements. In this case, the programmer must decide exactly how many tasks will be queued up on the `Receive` entry, and make this more explicit in the code. Suppose that there are three tasks that need to received the data. Each of these tasks must wait on its own entry in a separate protected object. Hence, the package specification becomes:

```ada
pragma Profile(Ravenscar);
package Multicasts_R is

  protected Multicast_Sender is
    procedure Send(Data : in Integer);
  end Multicast_Sender;

  protected type Multicast_Receiver is
    entry Receive(Data : out Integer);
    procedure Send(Data : in Integer);
  private
    Go : Boolean := False;
```

```
      The_Data : Integer;
   end Multicast_Receiver;

   MR1: Multicast_Receiver;
   MR2: Multicast_Receiver;
   MR3: Multicast_Receiver;
end Multicasts_R;
```

and the body:

```
package body Multicasts_R is

   protected body Multicast_Sender is
      procedure Send(Data : in Integer) is
      begin
         MR1.Send(Data);
         MR2.Send(Data);
         MR3.Send(Data);
      end Send;
   end Multicast_Sender;

   protected body Multicast_Receiver is
      entry Receive(Data : out Integer) when Go is
      begin
         Data := The_Data;
         Go := False;
      end Receive;

      procedure Send(Data : in Integer) is
      begin
         The_Data := Data;
         Go := True;
      end Send;
   end Multicast_Receiver;
end Multicasts_R;
```

It is clear from this section that conforming to the Ravenscar Profile makes the programming of some algorithms requiring task communication more difficult. This is the trade-off when restricting the use of the Ada language so that it only supports the real-time programming model outlined in Sections 2.4 and 3.8. The restrictions allow the worst-case timing properties of programs to be predicted using the techniques discussed in Part II of this book.

14.7 Simple embedded system revisited

In Section 10.7, a simple embedded system was introduced. The solution is now updated to illustrate the periodic nature of the control tasks.

```
with IO, Data_Types, Control_Procedures, Ada.Real_Time;
use IO, Data_Types, Control_Procedures, Ada.Real_Time;
package body Embedded_System is
```

```ada
task body Temp_Controller is
   TR : Temp_Reading;
   HS : Heater_Setting;
   Next_Release : Time;
   Release_Interval : constant Time_Span := Milliseconds(20);
begin
   Next_Release := Clock + Release_Interval;
   loop
      Read(TR);
      Temp_Convert(TR,HS);
      Write(HS);
      Write(TR);
      delay until Next_Release;
      Next_Release := Next_Release + Release_Interval;
   end loop;
end Temp_Controller;

task body Pressure_Controller is
   PR : Pressure_Reading;
   PS : Pressure_Setting;
   Next_Release : Time;
   Release_Interval : constant Time_Span := Milliseconds(30);
begin
   Next_Release := Clock + Release_Interval;
   loop
      Read(PR);
      Pressure_Convert(PR,PS);
      Write(PS);
      Write(PR);
      delay until Next_Release;
      Next_Release := Next_Release + Release_Interval;
   end loop;
end Pressure_Controller;
end Embedded_System;
```

Of course, the above code assumes that there are no input and output jitter control requirements. If there are, then the techniques given in Section 14.5 can be applied.

Summary

The provision of abstractions that match the typical requirements found in an application domain makes an enormous difference to the ease with which a language can be used in that domain. However, there is a tradeoff. Too many domain-specific programming languages leads to development problems, as the more esoteric the language the more difficult it is to find programmers. Ada walks a tightrope trying to be generic and yet relevant to the real-time and embedded systems domains.

This chapter has introduced some of the common abstractions for representing typical temporal scopes, and shown how they are explicitly supported or how they can be programmed. In particular, the ability to

- program periodic/sporadic and aperiodic tasks, and
- control input and latency (output) jitter

have been examined.

Ada is a comprehensive language with many feature. Some of these features make the timing analysis of programs more difficult. For this reason, the language allows the program to restrict the use of certain language features. The Ravenscar Profile is a set of restrictions that simplify the Ada concurrency so that timing analysis of programs is facilitated. In terms of tasks, these restrictions are that task can be only created at the library level and task hierarchies are prohibited. Tasks can only communicate via protected objects, which have also been created at the library level.

Chapter 15
Programming schedulable systems

15.1 Programming cyclic executives
15.2 Programming preemptive priority-based systems
15.3 Ada and fixed priority scheduling
15.4 Dynamic priorities and other Ada facilities
15.5 Programming EDF systems
15.6 Mixed scheduling
15.7 Scheduling and the Ravenscar profile
15.8 Simple embedded system revisited
Summary

In Part II of this book, a number of approaches to scheduling were introduced. These approaches were chosen partly due to their inherent value and maturity, but also because it is possible to use these techniques in programming real systems with current languages and operating systems. This chapter starts by looking briefly at the programming of cyclic executives. This scheduling approach is particularly suitable for small single processor systems. Larger systems nowadays more commonly use fixed priority-based scheduling, which is supported by all real-time operating systems. Ada has comprehensive support for this approach and this is discussed in detail. More flexible scheduling can be obtained by allowing the program to change task priorities dynamically. This is also essential if applications have different modes of operation where tasks operating in more than one mode have different timing requirements.

EDF scheduling has been growing in importance over the last few years, and its support is becoming more widely available. As from Ada 2005, it is available to programs through a different dispatching policy. EDF is particularly suitable for soft real-time systems. Modern real-time systems have both hard and soft components, and it is beneficial to schedule the hard tasks using fixed priorities and the soft tasks using EDF. Ada allows the use of such mixed scheduling schemes within a priority based framework.

323

15.1 Programming cyclic executives

To implement a simple cyclic executive requires no special language support. None of the temporal or scheduling information needs to be represented in the application's code. Rather, a series of procedure calls are linked together with a simple hardware interrupt that is configured to occur at regular intervals. For instance, the code for the example given in Section 4.1 would have the following simple form in Ada (with the interrupt occurring every 25ms):

```
with Ada.Real_Time; use Ada.Real_Time;

procedure Cyclic_Executive is
  procedure Procedure_For_A is separate;
  procedure Procedure_For_B is separate;
  procedure Procedure_For_C is separate;
  procedure Procedure_For_D is separate;
  procedure Procedure_For_E is separate;
  Minor_Cycle : constant Time_Span := Milliseconds(25);
  Next : Time := Clock + Minor_Cycle;
begin
  loop -- MAJOR CYCLE
    delay until Next;
    Next := Next + Minor_Cycle;
    -- minor cycle 1
    Procedure_For_A;
    Procedure_For_B;
    Procedure_For_C;
    delay until Next;
    Next := Next + Minor_Cycle;
    -- minor cycle 2
    Procedure_For_A;
    Procedure_For_B;
    Procedure_For_D;
    Procedure_For_E;
    delay until Next;
    Next := Next + Minor_Cycle;
    -- minor cycle 3
    Procedure_For_A;
    Procedure_For_B;
    Procedure_For_C;
    delay until Next;
    Next := Next + Minor_Cycle;
    -- minor cycle 4
    Procedure_For_A;
    Procedure_For_B;
    Procedure_For_D;
  end loop;
end Cyclic_Executive;
```

Some protection can be added to this structure to identify an execution time overrun. Before each "delay until" statement, the clock can be read and a check performed to ensure there is no overrun in the current minor cycle. If there is a minor cycle overflow then recovery can be attempted or the system restarted. Of course the recovery code cannot know which procedure in the minor cycle caused the overflow. There is no firewall protection between the procedures.

15.2 Programming preemptive priority-based systems

Few programming languages explicitly define priorities as part of their concurrency facilities. Those that do, often provide only a rudimentary model. Ada does provide a comprehensive model. What is minimally required is:

- an effective range of priorities,
- immediate preemptive switching to higher priority tasks when they become runnable, and
- support for at least priority inheritance, but ideally some form of priority ceiling protocol.

15.3 Ada and fixed priority scheduling

As indicated in the Section 9.2, Ada is defined as a core language plus a number of annexes for specialized application domains. These annexes do not contain any new language features (in the way of new syntax) but define pragmas, aspects and library packages that must be supported if that particular annex is to be adhered to. This section considers some of the provisions of the Real-Time Systems Annex. In particular, those that allow priorities to be assigned to tasks (and protected objects).

To indicate that priority-based scheduling is required of the run-time implementation of the application's Ada program, the dispatching policy must be defined. This is done using a configuration pragma:

pragma Task_Dispatching_Policy(FIFO_Within_Priorities);

Where tasks share the same priority, then they are queued in FIFO order. Hence, as tasks become runnable, they are placed at the back of a notional **ready queue** for that priority level. One exception to this case is when a task is preempted; here the task is placed at the front of the ready queue for that priority level. On a multiprocessor system, it is implementation defined whether this policy is on a per-processor basis or across the entire processor cluster.

To allocate a priority to a task there are, within package System, the following declarations:

```
subtype Any_Priority is Integer range
        {<implementation-defined>};
subtype Priority is Any_Priority range
        Any_Priority'First .. {<implementation-defined>};
subtype Interrupt_Priority is Any_Priority range
        Priority'Last+1 .. Any_Priority'Last;

Default_Priority : constant Priority :=
                   (Priority'First + Priority'Last)/2;
```

An integer range is split between standard priorities and (the higher) interrupt priority range. An implementation must support a range for `System.Priority` of at least 30 values and at least one distinct `System.Interrupt_Priority` value. (See Section 7.6 for a discussion on the impact of limited priority ranges.)

A task has its initial priority set by including a representation aspect in its specification:

```
task Controller with Priority => 10;
```

If a task-type definition contains such an aspect, then all tasks of that type will have the same priority unless a discriminant is used:

```
task type  Controllers(Task_Priority : System.Priority)
    with Priority => Task_Priority;
```

For protected objects acting as interrupt handlers, a special aspect is defined:

```
with Interrupt_Priority => Expression;
```

The definition, and use, of a different aspect for interrupt levels improves the readability of programs and helps to remove errors that can occur if task and interrupt priority levels are confused.

A priority assigned using one of these aspects is called a **base priority**. A task may also have an **active priority** that may be higher where the `FIFO_Within_Priorities` dispatching policy is being used – this will be explained in due course.

The main program, which is executed by a notional environmental task, can have its priority set by placing the `Priority` aspect in the main subprogram.

```
procedure Main with Priority => 7 is -- for example
begin
   ...
end Main;
```

If this is not done, the default value, defined in `System`, is used. Any other task that fails to use the aspect has a default base priority equal to the base priority of the task that created it.

In order to make use of the immediate ceiling priority protocol (ICPP), an Ada program must include the following configuration pragma (see Section 14.6)

```
pragma Locking_Policy(Ceiling_Locking);
procedure Main with Priority => 7 is
begin
   ...
end Main
```

An implementation may define other locking policies; only `Ceiling_Locking` is required by the Real-Time Systems Annex. The default policy, if the pragma is missing, is implementation defined. To specify the ceiling priority for each protected object, the `Priority` and `Interrupt_Priority` aspects defined earlier are used. If the aspect is missing, a ceiling of `System.Priority'Last` is assumed.

The exception `Program_Error` is raised if a task calls a protected object with an active priority greater than the defined ceiling. If such a call were allowed, then this could result in the mutually exclusive protection of the object being violated. If it is an interrupt

ADA AND FIXED PRIORITY SCHEDULING

handler that calls in with an inappropriate priority, then the program becomes erroneous. This must ultimately be prevented through adequate testing and/or static analysis of the program.

With `Ceiling_Locking`, an effective implementation will use the thread of the calling task to execute not only the code of the protected call, but also the code of any other task that happens to have been released by the actions of the original call. For example, consider the following simple protected object:

```
protected Gate_Control with Priority => 28 is
  entry Stop_And_Close;
  procedure Open;
private
  Gate: Boolean := False;
end Gate_Control;

protected body Gate_Control is
  entry Stop_And_Close when Gate is
  begin
    Gate := False;
  end Stop_And_Close;

  procedure Open is
  begin
    Gate := True;
  end Open;
end Gate_Control;
```

Assume a task T, priority 20, calls `Stop_And_Close` and is blocked. Later, task S (priority 27) calls `Open`. The thread that implements S will undertake the following actions (at priority 28):

(1) Execute the code of `Open` for S.
(2) Evaluate the barrier on the entry and note that T can now proceed.
(3) Execute the code of `Stop_And_Close` for T.
(4) Evaluate the barrier again.
(5) Continue with the execution of S after its call on the protected object (at priority 27).

As a result, there has been no context switch. The alternative is for S to make T runnable at point (2); T now has a higher priority (28) than S (27) and hence the system must switch to T to complete its execution within `Gate_Control`. As T leaves, a switch back to S is required. This is much more expensive.

As a task enters a protected object, its active priority may rise above the base priority level defined by the `Priority` or `Interrupt_Priority` aspect. The priority used to determine the order of dispatching is the active priority of a task. This active priority is, when the dispatching policy is `FIFO_Within_Priorities`, the maximum of the task's base priority and any priority it has inherited.

The use of a protected object is one way in which a task can inherit a higher active priority. There are others, for example during task activation, a task will inherit the active priority of the parent task that created it; remember (from Section 10.5) the parent task

```ada
with Ada.Task_Identification;
with System;
package Ada.Dynamic_Priorities is
  procedure Set_Priority(Priority : System.Any_Priority;
            T : Task_Identification.Task_Id :=
            Task_Identification.Current_Task);
    -- raises Program_Error if T is the Null_Task_Id
    -- has no effect if the task has terminated

  function Get_Priority(T : Task_Identification.Task_Id :=
          Task_Identification.Current_Task)
          return System.Any_Priority;
    -- raises Tasking_Error if the task has terminated
    -- or Program_Error if T is the Null_Task_Id
private
  -- not specified by the language
end Ada.Dynamic_Priorities;
```

Program 15.1: The Ada.Dynamic_Priorities package.

is blocked waiting for its child task to complete, and this could be a source of priority inversion without this inheritance rule.

15.4 Dynamic priorities and other Ada facilities

The above discussions have assumed that the base priority of a task remains constant during the entire existence of the task. This is an adequate model for many scheduling approaches. There are, however, situations in which it is necessary to alter base priorities. For example:

- to implement mode changes;
- to implement application specific scheduling schemes.

In the first example, base priority changes are infrequent and correspond to changes in the relative temporal properties of the tasks after a mode change (for example, a task running more frequently in the new mode). The second use of dynamic priorities allows programmers to construct their own schedulers. An example of this is the programming of execution-time servers that will be illustrated in the Section 19.6.1.

To support dynamic priorities, the language provides a library package – see Program 15.1. The function Get_Priority returns the current base priority of the task; this can be changed by the use of Set_Priority. A change of base priority takes effect immediately the task is outside a protected object.

Ada also allows the ceiling priority of a protected object to be changed at run-time. For any protected object, P, the attribute P'Priority represents a component of P of type System.Any_Priority. References to the Priority attribute can only occur from within the body of the associated protected body. Such references can be read or write. If the locking policy Ceiling_Locking is in effect then a change to the Priority

```ada
with Ada.Task_Identification;
package Ada.Asynchronous_Task_Control is
  procedure Hold(T : Task_Identification.Task_Id);
  procedure Continue(T : Task_Identification.Task_Id);
  function Is_Held(T : Task_Identification.Task_Id)
           return Boolean;
end Ada.Asynchronous_Task_Control;
```

Program 15.2: The Ada.Asynchronous_Task_Control package.

attribute results in the ceiling value changing to this new value – but only at the end of the protected action that resulted in the change.

As well as changing the priority of a task, which obviously effects it likelihood of being scheduling, Ada also allows a task to suspend itself and to suspend other tasks. These two facilities are call *synchronous task control* (see Program 11.1) and *asynchronous task control*. The latter is supported by Program 15.2.

For each processor, there is a conceptual idle task which can always run (but has a priority below any application task). A call of Hold lowers the *base priority* of the designated task to below that of the idle task. It is said to be *held*. If the designated task is not executing with an inherited priority, it will be suspended immediately. A call of Continue restores the task's base priority. This facility will be used in Section 19.6.1 to program a type of execution-time server.

Ada also provides other facilities which are useful for programming a wide variety of real-time systems that are scheduled using fixed priorities. For example, prioritised entry queues, task attributes, and so on. There are also a number of other dispatching policies. One for EDF scheduling is defined later in this chapter (Section 15.5). Another defines non-preemptive scheduling: Non_Preemptive_FIFO_Within_Priorities. This has similar properties to the preemptive version other than the obvious requirement for a task to continue executing even when a higher priority tasks becomes runnable. Interrupts can still occur, but task switching is postponed until the task itself executes a blocking operation such as a delay statement. Note the execution of 'delay 0.0' is sufficient to end a period of non-preemptive execution. A further dispatching policy defined in the real-time annex is Round-Robin scheduling. This is the usual algorithm where tasks of the same priority are allocated a quantum of execution time before they are suspended and return to the back of the queue for that priority level. To ensure that the integrity of protected objects is not compromised by this policy then suspension is itself suspended whilst a task executes within such objects.

As well as supporting a number of distinct dispatching policies Ada also allows mixed systems to be specified. This is described later in this chapter once EDF scheduling has been defined (see Section 15.6).

15.5 Programming EDF systems

To support the programming of applications that wish to make use of EDF scheduling, three language features are required:

330   PROGRAMMING SCHEDULABLE SYSTEMS

```ada
with Ada.Real_Time; with Ada.Task_Identification;

package Ada.Dispatching.EDF is
  subtype Deadline is Ada.Real_Time.Time;
  Default_Deadline : constant Deadline :=
            Ada.Real_Time.Time_Last;
  procedure Set_Deadline(D : in Deadline;
          T : in Ada.Task_Identification.Task_ID :=
          Ada.Task_Identification.Current_Task);
  procedure Delay_Until_And_Set_Deadline(
          Delay_Until_Time : in Ada.Real_Time.Time;
          TS : in Ada.Real_Time.Time_Span);
  function Get_Deadline(T : in Ada.Task_Identification.Task_ID :=
          Ada.Task_Identification.Current_Task) return Deadline;
end Ada.Dispatching.EDF;
```

Program 15.3: The `Ada.Dispatching.EDF` package.

- a formal representation of the deadline of a task,
- use of deadlines to control dispatching, and
- a means of sharing data between tasks that is compatible with EDF.

Of all the mainstream engineering languages only Ada gives direct support to EDF scheduling.

15.5.1 Representing deadlines in Ada

A task's deadline can be set using the facilities defined in Program 15.3.
The identifier `Deadline` is explicitly introduced even though it is a direct subtype of the time type from `Ada.Real_Time`. The `Set` and `Get` subprograms have obvious utility. A call of `Delay_Until_And_Set_Deadline` delays the calling task until time `Delay_Until_Time`. When the task becomes runnable again it will have a deadline of `Delay_Until_Time + TS`. The inclusion of this procedure reflects a common task structure for periodic activity. Consider the example of a periodic task; now assume it has a deadline at the end of its execution (i.e. every time it executes is should finish before its next release):

```ada
with Ada.Real_Time; use Ada.Real_Time;
with Ada.Dispatching.EDF; use Ada.Dispatching.EDF;

...

  task Periodic_Task;

  task body Periodic_Task is
    Interval : Time_Span := Milliseconds(30);
    -- define the period of the task, 30ms in this example
```

```
   Next : Time;
begin
   Next := Clock;   -- start time
   Set_Deadline(Clock+Interval);
   loop
      -- undertake the work of the task
      Next := Next + Interval;
      Delay_Until_And_Set_Deadline(Next,Interval);
   end loop;
end Periodic_Task;
```

...

If, rather than use just this one procedure call, the task had a set deadline call and a delay until statement then this would most likely result in an extra unwanted task switch (first the deadline is extended and hence a more urgent task will preempt, later the task will execute again just to put itself on the delay queue).

With EDF, all dispatching decision are based on deadlines, and hence it is necessary for a task to always have a deadline[1]. However, a task must progress though activation before it can get to a position to call Set_Deadline and hence a default deadline value is given to all tasks (Default_Deadline defined in Ada.Dispatching.EDF). But this default value is well into the future and hence activation will take place with very low urgency (all other task executions will occur before this task's activation). If more urgency is required, the following language defined aspect is available for inclusion in a task's specification:

```
Relative_Deadline => Relative_Deadline_Expression
```

where the type of the parameter is Ada.Real_Time.Time_Span. The initial absolute deadline of a task containing this pragma is the value of Ada.Real_ Time.Clock + Relative_Deadline_Expression. The call of the clock being made between task creation and the start of its activation.

So the example above should use this aspect rather than include the first call of Set_Deadline:

```
task Periodic_Task with Relative_Deadline => Milliseconds(30);
```

A final point to note with the deadline assignment routine concerns when it will take effect. The usual result of a call to Set_Deadline is for the associated deadline to be increased into the future and that a task switch is then likely (if EDF dispatching is in force). As this would not be appropriate if the task is currently executing within a protected object the setting of a task's deadline to the new value takes place as soon as is practical but not while the task is performing a protected action. This is similar to the rule that applies to changes to the base priority of a task using the dynamic priority facility.

Once a deadline is set then it becomes possible to check at runtime that the program's execution does indeed meet its deadlines. This is easily accommodated by the asynchronous transfer of control (select-then-abort) feature (see Section 18.5.1):

---

[1] This is one of the criticisms of EDF - even tasks that have no actual deadline must be given an artificial one so that it will be scheduled.

```
loop
  select
    delay until Ada.Dispatching.EDF.Get_Deadline;
    -- action to be take when deadline missed
  then abort
    -- code
  end select;
end loop;
```

A fuller description of the options available to the programmer when a deadline is missed is given in Chapter 19.

15.5.2 Dispatching

To request EDF dispatching, the following use of the dispatching policy pragma is supported:

```
pragma Task_Dispatching_Policy(EDF_Across_Priorities);
```

The main result of employing this policy is that the ready queues are now ordered according to deadline (not FIFO). Each ready queue is still associated with a single priority but at the head of any ready queue is the runnable task with the earliest deadline. Whenever a task is added to a ready queue for its priority it is placed in the position dictated by its current absolute deadline.

The active priority of a task, under EDF dispatching, is no longer directly linked to the base priority of the task. The rules for computing the active priority of a task are somewhat complex and are covered in the next section – they are derived from consideration of each task's use of protected objects. For a simple program with no protected objects the following straightforward rules apply:

- any priorities set by the tasks are ignored
- all tasks are always placed on the ready queue for priority value System.Priority'First[2].

Hence only one ready queue is used (and that queue is ordered by deadline).

Of course real programs require task interactions, and for Ada real-time programs this usually means the use of protected objects. To complete the definition of the EDF dispatching policy the rules for using protected objects must be considered. This is outlined below.

15.5.3 EDF and Baker's algorithm

In Section 6.5, Baker's algorithm was introduced as a means of controlling access to shared objects when EDF scheduling was in force. Ada supports Baker's approach by:

---

[2] If EDF dispatching is defined just for a range of priorities then this priority value is the initial (lowest) value in that range – see Section 15.6.

- using deadline to represent urgency
- using base priority to represent each task's preemption level
- using ceiling priorities to represent preemption levels for protected objects
- using standard `Ceiling_Locking` for access to protected objects.

So tasks have a base priority but this is not used directly to control dispatching, EDF controls dispatching; the base priority only defines a preemption level.

Baker's algorithm states that a newly released task, T1 say, preempts the currently running task, T2, if and only if:

- the deadline of T1 is earlier than the deadline of T2, and
- the preemption level of T1 is higher than the preemption of any locked protected object (i.e. protected objects that are currently in use by any other task).

To keep track of all locked protected objects is an implementation overhead and hence the rules defined for Ada have the following form. Remember that if `EDF_Across_Priorities` is defined then all ready queues within the range `Priority'First .. Priority'Last` are ordered by deadline. Now rather than always place tasks in the queue for `Priority'First` the following rules apply:

- Whenever a task T is added to a ready queue, other than when it is preempted, it is placed on the ready queue with the highest priority R, if one exists, such that:
  - another task, S, is executing within a protected object with ceiling priority R; and
  - task T has an earlier deadline than task S; and
  - the base priority (preemption level) of task T is greater than R.

  If no such ready queue exists the task is added to the ready queue for `Priority'First`.

- When a task is chosen for execution it runs with the active priority of the ready queue from which the task was taken. If it inherits a higher active priority it will return to its original active priority when it no longer inherits the higher level.

It follows that if no protected objects are in use at the time of the release of T then T will be placed in the ready queue at level `Priority'First` at the position dictated by its deadline.

A potential task switch occurs for the currently running task T whenever:

- a change to the deadline of T takes effect; or
- a decrease to the deadline of any task on a ready queue for that processor takes effect and the new deadline is earlier than that of the running task; or
- there is a non-empty ready queue for that processor with a higher priority than the priority of the running task.

334   PROGRAMMING SCHEDULABLE SYSTEMS

So dispatching is preemptive, but it may not be clear that the above rules implement Baker's algorithm. Consider four scenarios. Remember in all of these behaviours, the running task is always returned to its ready queue whenever a task arrives. A task (possible the same task) is then chosen to become the running task following the rules defined above.

The system contains four tasks: T1, T2, T3 and T4 and three resources that are implemented as protected objects: R1, R2 and R3. Table 15.1 defines the parameters of these entities.

Task	Relative Deadline D	Preemption Level L	Uses Resources	Arrives at time	Absolute Deadline A
T1	100	1	R1,R3	0	100
T2	80	2	R2,R3	2	82
T3	60	3	R2	4	64
T4	40	4	R1	8	48

Table 15.1: A task set (time attributes in milliseconds.)

Consider just a single invocation of each task. The arrival times have been chosen so that the tasks arrive in order of lowest preemption level task first etc. Assume all computation times are sufficient to cause the executions to overlap.

The resources are all used by more than one task, but only one at a time and hence the ceiling values of the resources are straightforward to calculate. For R1, it is used by T1 and T4; hence the ceiling preemption level is 4. For R2, it is used by T2 and T3; hence the ceiling value is 3. Finally R3, it is used by T1 and T2; the ceiling equals 2 (see Table 15.2).

Protected Object	Ceiling Value
R1	4
R2	3
R3	2

Table 15.2: Ceiling Values.

To implement this set of tasks and resources will require ready queues at level 0 (value of `Priority'First` in this example) and values 2, 3 and 4.

Scenario 1

At time 0, T1 arrives. All ready queues are empty and all resources are free so T1 is placed in queue 0. It becomes the running/executing task. This is illustrated in the following where 'Level' is the priority level, 'executing' is the name of the task that is currently executing, and 'Ready Queue' shows the other executable tasks in the system. Again remember that the executing task is not on a ready queue, but is returned to a ready queue before any dispatching decision is taken.

```
            Level      Executing      Ready Queue

              0          [ T1 ]
```

At time 2, T2 arrives and is added to ready queue 0 in front of T1 as it has a shorter absolute deadline. Now T2 is chosen for execution.

```
              0          [ T2 ]         [ T1 ]
```

Assume at time 3, T2 calls R3. Its active priority will raise to 2.

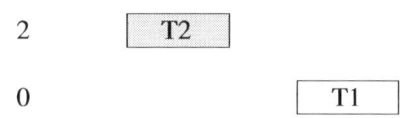

```
              2          [ T2 ]

              0                         [ T1 ]
```

At time 4, T3 arrives. Task T2 is joined by T3 on queue 2, as T3 has an earlier deadline and a higher preemption level; T3 is at the head of this queue and becomes the running task.

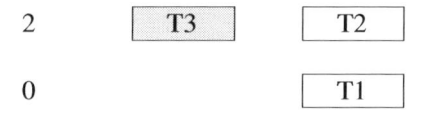

```
              2          [ T3 ]         [ T2 ]

              0                         [ T1 ]
```

At time 8, T4 arrives. Tasks T3 and T2 are now joined by T4 as it has a deadline earlier that T3 and a higher preemption level (than 2). Task T4 now becomes the running task, and will execute until it completes; any calls it makes on resources R1 will be allowed immediately as this resource is free.

```
              2          [ T4 ]      [ T3 ]──▶[ T2 ]

              0                         [ T1 ]
```

At some time later, T4 will complete then T3 will execute (at priority 2, or 4 if it locks R2) then when it completes, T2 will execute (also at priority 2) until it releases resource R3, at which point its priority will drop to 0 but it will continue to execute. Eventually when T2 completes, T1 will resume (initially at priority 0 – but this will rise if it accesses either of the resources it uses).

Scenario 2

Here we make the simple change that, at time 3, T2 calls R2 instead of R3. Its active priority will raise to 3. Now when T3 arrives at time 4, it will not have a high enough preemption level to join ready queue 3 and will be placed on the lowest queue at level 0 (but ahead of T1). Task T2 continues to execute.

336   PROGRAMMING SCHEDULABLE SYSTEMS

At time 8, T4 arrives. It passes both elements of the test and is placed on the queue at level 3 ahead of T2 and therefore preempts it.

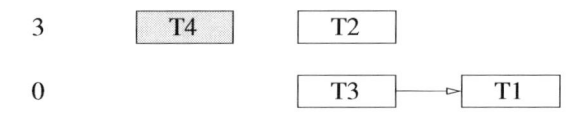

```
3            | T4 |          | T2 |

0                             | T3 |---▷| T1 |
```

At some time later, T4 will complete then T2 will execute (at priority 3) until it releases resource R2, at which point its priority will drop to 0. Now T3 will preempt and becomes the running task.

Scenario 3

For another example, return to the first scenario but assume T3 makes use of resource R2 before T4 arrives:

- At time 0, T1 arrives. All ready queues are empty and all resources are free so T1 is placed in queue 0. It becomes the running task.
- At time 2, T2 arrives and is added to ready queue 0 in front of T1.
- Assume at time 3, T2 calls R3. Its active priority will raise to 2.
- At time 4, T3 arrives and becomes the running task at priority level 2.
- At time 5, T3 calls R2 (note all resource requests are always to resources that are currently free) and thus its active priority raises to 3.

```
3            | T3 |

2                             | T2 |

0                             | T1 |
```

- At time 8, T4 arrives. There is now one task on queue 0; one on queue 2 (T2 holding resource R3) and one task on queue 3 (T3 holding R2). The highest ready queue that the dispatch rules determines is that at level 3, and hence T4 joins T3 on this queue – but at the head and hence becomes the running task.

```
3            | T4 |    | T3 |

2                      | T2 |

0                      | T1 |
```

Scenario 4

Now consider a simple change to the parameters – let the relative deadline of T4 be 58 so thats its absolute deadline is 66 which is later than T3's absolute deadline. At time 3, T2 calls R2. Its active priority will rise to 3. Now when T3 arrives at time 4, it will not have a high enough preemption level to join ready queue 3 and will be placed on the lowest queue at level 0 (but ahead of T1). Task T2 continues to execute. At time 8, T4 arrives but will fail the preemption rule as its deadline is not earlier than T3's. T4 will be placed on the level 0 queue between T3 and T1.

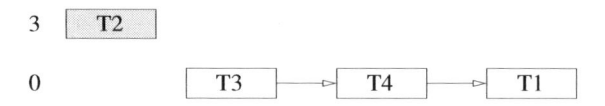

```
3   [ T2 ]

0              [ T3 ]──▷[ T4 ]──▷[ T1 ]
```

Task T2 will continue until it completes its execution in the protected object. Its priority will then fall to 0 and T3 will preempt it. All tasks now execute in deadline order.

Final note

The above rules and descriptions are, unfortunately, not quite complete. The ready queue for `Priority'First` plays a central role in the model as it is, in some senses, the default queue. If a task is not entitled to be put in a higher queue, or if no protected objects are in use, then it is placed in this base queue. Indeed during the execution of a typical program most runnable tasks will be in the `Priority'First` ready queue most of the time. However the protocol only works if there are no protected objects with a ceiling at the `Priority'First` level. Such ceiling values must be prohibited but this is not a significant constraint.

15.5.4 Example of an EDF program

Recap what the programmer needs to do to use EDF. First preemption levels are chosen for each task based on the temporal properties of the task. Optimally, preemption levels will be assigned in reverse (relative) deadline order. Preemption levels are assigned to tasks using the 'priority' attribute of each task. These will be *exactly* the same assignments that would be needed with fixed priority assignment and the deadline-monotonic priority algorithm. Next, shared protected objects are identified and ceiling values assigned. Again this is identical in the fixed priority and EDF schemes. Finally, the required dispatching policy is asserted.

To illustrate the minimal changes that have to be made to the application code to move form one scheduling paradigm to another consider a simple periodic task scheduled according to the standard fixed priority method. This task has a period and deadline of 10ms.

```
task Example
   with Priority => 5 is
end Example;
```

338 PROGRAMMING SCHEDULABLE SYSTEMS

```ada
task body Example is
  Next_Release : Ada.Real_Time.Time;
  Period : Ada.Real_Time.Time_Span
    := Ada.Real_Time.Milliseconds(10);
begin
  Next_Release := Ada.Real_Time.Clock;
  loop
    -- code
    Next_Release := Next_Release + Period;
    delay until Next_Release;
  end loop;
end Example;
```

If EDF dispatching is required (perhaps to make the system schedulable) then very little change is needed. The priority levels of the task remains exactly the same. The task's code must, however, now explicitly refer to deadlines (the implicit deadline was always there as it was used to derive the value 5 for the task's priority):

```ada
task Example is
  with Priority => 5, Relative_Deadline => 10 is
    -- gives an initial relative deadline of 10 milliseconds
end Example;

task body Example is
  Next_Release: Ada.Real_Time.Time;
  Period : Ada.Real_Time.Time_Span
    := Ada.Real_Time.Milliseconds(10);
begin
  Next_Release := Ada.Real_Time.Clock;
  loop
    -- code
    Next_Release := Next_Release + Period;
    Delay_Until_and_Set_Deadline(Next_Release, Period);
  end loop;
end Example;
```

Finally the dispatching policy must be changed from

```ada
pragma Task_Dispatching_Policy(FIFO_Within_Priorities);
```

to

```ada
pragma Task_Dispatching_Policy(EDF_Across_Priorities);
```

No other changes are needed – any protected objects used by this or other tasks in the program retain their assigned ceilings.

15.6 Mixed scheduling

As was noted earlier, Ada allows a system with a combination of dispatching policies to be utilised. To accomplish this, the system's priority range is split into a number of distinct non-overlapping bands. In each band, a specified dispatching policy is in effect. The bands themselves are ordered by priority. So a runnable task in a high priority band will take precedence over any other runnable task in a lower priority band. For example, there could be a band of fixed priorities on top of a band of EDF with a single round robin level for non-real-time tasks at the bottom. To illustrate this assume a priority range of 1..16, the following configuration pragmas can be used to partition this range as follows

pragma Priority_Specific_Dispatching
             (FIFO_Within_Priorities, 10, 16);

pragma Priority_Specific_Dispatching
             (EDF_Across_Priorities, 2, 9);

pragma Priority_Specific_Dispatching
             (Round_Robin_Within_Priorities, 1, 1);

Any task is assigned a dispatching policy by virtue of its base priority. If a task has base priority 12 it will be dispatched according to the fixed priority rules, if it has base priority 8 then it is under the control of the EDF rules. In a mixed system all tasks have a preemption level (it is just its base priority) and all tasks have a deadline (it will be Default_Deadline if none is assigned in the program). But this deadline will have no effect if the task in not in an EDF band. With this example a runnable task with priority 14 will always execute before an 'EDF task' even if the 'EDF task' has an earlier deadline.

To achieve any mixture including one or more EDF bands, the properties assigned in the definition of EDF dispatching to level Priority'First need to be redefined to use the minimum value of whatever range is used for the EDF tasks. Also note that two adjacent EDF bands are not equivalent to one complete band. Runnable tasks in the upper bands will always take precedence over runnable tasks in the lower bands.

For completeness any priority value not includes in the pragma is assumed to be FIFO_Within_Priorities. Any of the predefined policies can be mixed apart from the non-preemptive one. It is deemed incompatible to mix non-preemption with any other scheme as non-preemption is a system-wide property, a low priority preemptive task would impact on a higher priority task in another band.

Tasks within different bands can communicate using protected objects. The use of Ceiling_Locking ensures that protected objects behave as required. For example an 'EDF task' (priority level 7) could share data with a 'round robin' task (priority level 1) and a 'fixed priority' task (priority 12). The protected object would have a ceiling value of (at least) 12. When the EDF task accesses the object its active priority will rise from 7 to 12, and while executing this protected action it will prevent any other task executing from within the EDF band. The 'round robin' task will similarly execute with priority 12 – if its quantum is exhausted inside the object it will continue to execute until it has completed the protected action.

If a task changes its base priority at run-time (using the Set_Priority routine) then it may also change its dispatching group. For example, a task in the above illustration with base priority 7 that is changed to have priority 12 will move from EDF to fixed priority scheduling.

Perhaps one minor weaknesses of Ada's support for mixed dispatching rules is that a task cannot directly ask under what policy it is being scheduled. However, a task can always find out its own priority (using Get_Priority) and from that use program constants to

340   PROGRAMMING SCHEDULABLE SYSTEMS

ascertain under which policy it is executing.

This ability to mix dispatching policies is unique to Ada. Experience will show whether this level of support for real-time programs proves to be useful, and if implementations are able to deliver this flexibility in an efficient manner.

15.7 Scheduling and the Ravenscar profile

In section 14.6, the Ravenscar configuration pragma was introduced. This pragma informs the compiler that the program uses a restricted subset of the Ada tasking model. This chapter has discussed the support that Ada provides for real-time scheduling. With the Ravenscar Profile:

- the use of the package `Ada.Dynamic_Priorities` is prohibited; and
- the following configuration pragmas are automatically introduced:
    - `Task_Dispatching_Policy(FIFO_Within_Priorities)`
    - `Locking_Policy(Ceiling_Locking)`.

15.8 Simple embedded system revisited

In Section 10.7, a simple embedded system was introduced. The solution is now updated to illustrate the setting of priorities.

```
package Embedded_System is
  task Temp_Controller with Priority => 5;  -- for example
  task Pressure_Controller with Priority => 4;
end Embedded_System;
```

Of course, it is also necessary to assign a ceiling priority to the protected object contained in the `IO` package body:

```
protected Console_Data
     with Priority => 5 is
  procedure Write(R : Temp_Reading);
  procedure Write(R : Pressure_Reading);
  entry Read(TR : out Temp_Reading;
          PR : out Pressure_Reading);
 private
    Last_Temperature : Temp_Reading;
    Last_Pressure :Pressure_Reading;
    New_Reading : Boolean := False;
end Console_Data;
```

and select the appropriate scheduler:

```
pragma Profile(Ravenscar);
with Embedded_System;
procedure Control is
begin
  null;
end;
```

Summary

For scheduling theory to be employed in real applications it must be accessible from the programming languages used to implement the applications. Either the languages must directly support the scheduling schemes or it must provide a means by which the application can access these schemes as they are supported by the underlying operating system.

The most mature scheduling theory is based upon preemptive fixed priority dispatching. In this chapter the means by which Ada supports this dispatching scheme has been described.

However, fixed priority dispatching is not the only scheduling scheme available. Earliest Deadline First (EDF) is one of a number of alternative schemes that are, theoretically, at least as important. Unfortunately EDF is not as easily available to application programmers. Unless a bespoke EDF-oriented operating system is constructed, the only way to make use of EDF is via the provisions now available in Ada. This chapter has therefore also described Ada's support for EDF scheduling. This has included discussions of its use of a variation of Baker's algorithms for controlling access to protected objects. Finally in this chapter the means by which mixed dispatching schemes (e.g. fixed priority, EDF and round robin) can be programmed in Ada has been included.

Chapter 16
Low-level programming

16.1 Hardware input/output mechanisms
16.2 Language requirements
16.3 Programming devices in Ada
16.4 Scheduling device drivers
16.5 Memory management
Summary

One of the main characteristics of an embedded system is the requirement that it interacts with special-purpose input and output (I/O) devices. Unfortunately, there are many different types of device interfaces and control mechanisms. This is mainly because: different computers provide different methods of interfacing with devices; different devices have separate requirements for their control; and similar devices from different manufacturers have different interfaces and control requirements.

To provide a rationale for the high-level language facilities needed to program low-level devices, one must understand the basic hardware I/O functions. Therefore this chapter considers these mechanisms first, then deals with language features in general, and finally gives details for Ada.

Embedded systems often have limited memory capacity. Consequently, the programmer must ensure that the compiler allocates only the memory needed for the job in hand. Furthermore, dynamic memory allocation must be carefully controlled to ensure the absence of any memory leaks.

16.1 Hardware input/output mechanisms

As far as input and output devices are concerned, there are two general classes of computer architecture: one with a logically separate bus for memory and I/O and the other with memory and I/O devices on the same logical bus. These are represented diagrammatically in Figures 16.1 and 16.2.

The interface to a device is normally through a set of **device registers**. With logically separate buses for memory and I/O devices, the computer must have two sets of assembly instructions: one for accessing memory and one for accessing device registers. The latter is sometimes called **port-mapped** IO and normally take the form of:

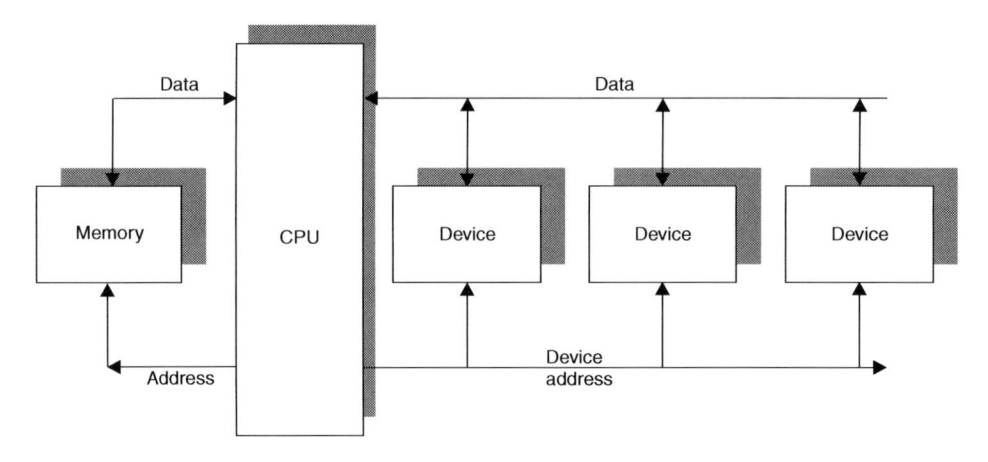

Figure 16.1: Architecture with separate buses.

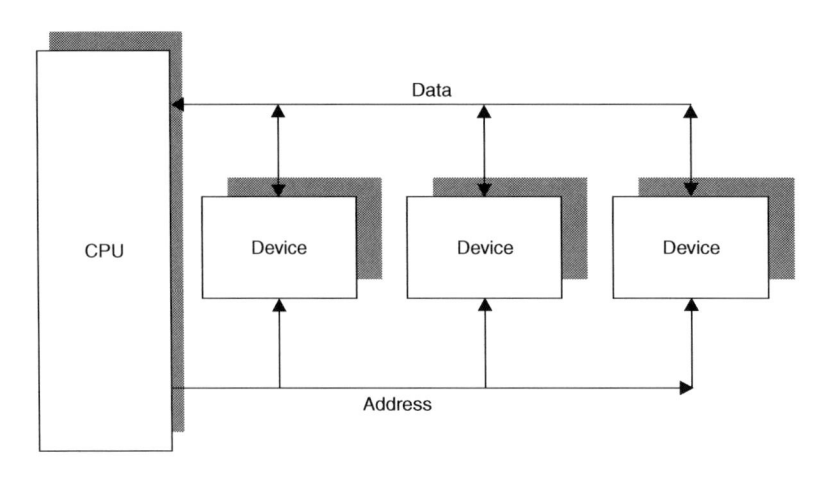

Figure 16.2: Memory-mapped architecture.

```
IN    AC, PORT
OUT   AC, PORT
```

Where IN reads the contents of the device register identified by PORT into the accumulator AC, and OUT writes the contents of the accumulator to the device register. (The term PORT is used here to indicate an address on the I/O device bus.) There may also be other instructions for reading a device's status. The Intel 486 and the Pentium are examples of an architecture which allows devices to be accessed via special instructions.

With devices on the same logical bus, certain addresses will access a memory location and others will access a device. This approach is called **memory-mapped I/O**. The Motorola M68000, ARM and PowerPC range of computers had/have memory mapped I/O.

It is necessary to interface with a device in order to control the device's operations (for example, initializing the device and preparing the device for the transfer of data) and to control the data transfer (for example, initiating or performing the data transfer). It is possible to describe two general mechanisms for performing and controlling input/output; these are status-driven control mechanisms and interrupt-driven control mechanisms.

16.1.1 Status driven

With this type of control mechanism, a program performs explicit tests in order to determine the status of a given device. Once the status of the device has been determined, the program is able to carry out the appropriate actions. Typically there are three kinds of hardware instruction supporting this type of mechanism. These are:

- test operations that enable the program to determine the status of the given device;
- control operations that direct the device to perform non-transfer device-dependent actions such as positioning disk read heads;
- I/O operations that perform the actual transfer of data between the device and the CPU.

Although historically devices with status-driven I/O were common, as they were inexpensive, nowadays, because of the continuing decrease in hardware cost, most devices are interrupt-driven. However, interrupts can of course be turned off and polling of device status used instead. Interrupts also add to the non-deterministic behaviour of real-time systems and are sometimes prohibited on safety grounds – for example if it is not possible to bound the number of interrupts.

16.1.2 Interrupt-driven

Even with the interrupt-driven mechanism, there are many possible variations depending on how the transfers need to be initiated and controlled. Three of these variations are: interrupt-driven program-controlled, interrupt-driven program-initiated, and interrupt-driven channel-program controlled.

Interrupt-driven program-controlled

Here, a device requests an interrupt as a result of encountering certain events, for example the arrival of data. When the request is acknowledged, the processor suspends the executing task and invokes a designated interrupt-handling task which performs appropriate actions in response to the interrupt. When the interrupt-handling task has performed its function, the state of the processor is restored to its state prior to the interrupt, and control of the processor is returned to the suspended task.

Interrupt-driven program-initiated

This type of input/output mechanism is often referred to as an **I/O Controller** or **Direct Memory Access Controller** (or DMA). A DMA device is positioned between the input/output device and main memory. The DMA device takes the place of the processor in the transfer of data between the I/O device and memory. Although the I/O is initiated by the program, the DMA device controls the actual transfers of data (one block at a time). For each piece of data to be transferred, a request is made by the DMA device for a memory cycle and the transfer is made when the request is granted. When the transfer of the entire block is completed, a *transfer complete* interrupt is generated by the device. This is handled by the interrupt-driven program-controlled mechanism.

The term **cycle stealing** is often used to refer to the impact that DMA devices have on the access to memory. It can lead to non-deterministic behaviour and makes it very difficult to calculate the worst-case execution time of a program (see Section 4.5). Where possible its use in real-time systems should be minimised.

Interrupt-driven channel-program controlled

Channel-program controlled input/output extends the concept of program-initiated input-output by eliminating as much as possible the involvement of the central processor in the handling of input/output devices. The mechanism consists of three major components: the hardware channel and connected devices, the channel program (often called a 'script') and the input/output instructions.

The hardware channel's operations include those of the DMA devices given above. In addition, the channel directs device control operations as instructed by the channel program. The execution of channel programs is initiated from within the application. Once a channel has been instructed to execute a channel program, the selected channel and device proceed independent of the central processor until the specified channel program has been completed or some exceptional condition has occurred. Channel programs normally consist of one or more channel control words which are decoded and executed one at a time by the channel.

In many respects, a hardware channel can be viewed as an autonomous processor sharing memory with the central processor; hence it is often called an I/O coprocessor. Its impact on memory access times of the central processor can be unpredictable (as with DMA devices).

16.1.3 Elements required for interrupt-driven devices

As can be seen from the previous section, the role of interrupts in controlling input/output is an important one. They allow input/output to be performed asynchronously and so avoid the 'busy waiting' or constant status checking that is necessary if a purely status-controlled mechanism is used.

In order to support interrupt-driven input and output, the following mechanisms are required.

Context-switching mechanisms

When an interrupt occurs, the current processor state must be preserved and the appropriate service routine activated. Once the interrupt has been serviced, the original task is resumed and execution continues. Alternatively, a new task may be selected by the scheduler as a consequence of the interrupt. This whole task is known as **context switching** and its actions can be summarized as follows:

- preserving the state of the processor immediately prior to the occurrence of the interrupt;
- placing the processor in the required state for processing the interrupt;
- restoring the suspended task state after the interrupt tasking has been completed.

The state of the task executing on a processor consists of:

- the memory address of the current (or next) instruction in the execution sequence;
- the program status information (this may contain information concerning the mode of processing, current priority, memory protection, allowed interrupts, and so on);
- the contents of the programmable registers.

The type of context switching provided can be characterized by the extent of the task state preservation, and restoration, that is performed by the hardware. Three levels of context switching can be distinguished:

- basic – just the program counter is saved and a new one loaded;
- partial – the program counter and the program status registers are saved and new ones loaded;
- complete – the full context of the task is saved and a new context loaded.

Depending on the degree of processor state preservation required, it may be necessary to supplement the actions of the hardware by explicit software support. For example, a partial context switch may be adequate for an interrupt-handling model which views the handler as a procedure or subroutine. However, if the handler is viewed as being a separate task with its own stack and data areas, there will need to be a low-level handler which does a full context switch between the interrupted task and the handling task. If, on the other hand, the hardware undertakes a full context switch, no such low-level handler is required. Most processors provide only a partial context switch. The ARM processor, for example, supplies a fast interrupt where some of the general-purpose registers are also saved.

It should be noted that some modern processors allow instructions to be fetched, decoded and executed in parallel. Some also allow instructions to be executed out of order from that specified in the program. This chapter will assume that interrupts are **precise** [79] in that, when an interrupt handler executes:

- all instructions issued before the interrupted instruction have finished executing and have modified the program state correctly;

- instructions issued after the interrupted instruction have not been executed and no program state has been modified;

- if the interrupted instruction itself caused the interrupt (for example, an instruction which causes memory violation) then either the instruction has been completely executed or not executed at all.

If an interrupt is not precise, it is assumed that the recovery is transparent to the interrupt handling software. See Walker and Cragon [79] for a taxonomy of interrupt handling.

Interrupting device identification

Devices differ in the way they must be controlled; consequently, they will require different interrupt-handling routines. In order to invoke the appropriate handler, some means of identifying the interrupting device must exist. Four interrupting device identification mechanisms can be distinguished: vectored, status, polling and high-level language primitive.

A **vectored** mechanism for identifying the interrupting device consists of a set of dedicated (and usually contiguous) memory locations called an **interrupt vector table** and a hardware mapping of device addresses onto the interrupt vector. An interrupt vector may be used by one particular device or may be shared by several devices. The programmer must associate a particular interrupt vector location explicitly with an interrupt-service routine. This may be done either by setting the vector location to the address of the service routine, or by setting it to an instruction that causes a branch to occur to the required routine. In this way, the service routine is directly tied to an interrupt vector location, which in turn is indirectly tied to a device or set of devices. Therefore, when a particular service routine is invoked and executed, the interrupting device has been implicitly identified.

A **status** mechanism for identifying an interrupting device is used for machine configurations on which several devices are connected to a device controller and they do not have unique interrupt vectors. It is also used in the case where a generalized service routine will initially handle all interrupts. With this mechanism, each interrupt has an associated status word which specifies the device causing the interrupt and the reason for the interrupt (among other things). The status information may be provided automatically by the hardware in a dedicated memory location for a given interrupt or class of interrupts, or it may need to be retrieved by means of some appropriate instruction.

The **polling** device identification mechanism is the simplest of all. When an interrupt occurs, a general interrupt-service routine is invoked to handle the interrupt. The status of each device is interrogated in order to determine which device has requested the interrupt. When the interrupting device has been identified, the interrupt is serviced in the appropriate manner.

With some computer architectures, interrupt handling is directly associated with a **high-level language primitive**. With these systems, an interrupt is often viewed as a synchronization message down an associated channel. In this case, the device is identified by the channel which becomes active.

Interrupt identification

Once the device has been identified, the appropriate interrupt-handling routine must determine why it generated the interrupt. In general, this can be supplied either by status information provided by the device or by having different interrupts from the same device occurring through different vectored locations or channels.

Interrupt control

Once a device is switched on and has been initialized, although it may be able to produce interrupts, they will be ignored unless the device has had its interrupts enabled. This control (enabling/disabling) of interrupts may be performed by means of the following interrupt control mechanisms.

Status interrupt control mechanisms provide flags, either in an interrupt state table or via device and program status words, to enable and disable the interrupts. The flags are accessible (and may be modified) by normal bit-oriented instructions or special bit-testing/setting instructions.

Mask interrupt control mechanisms associate each device interrupt with a particular bit position in a word. If the bit is set to one the interrupt will be blocked; if it is set to zero then it will be allowed. The interrupt mask word may be addressable by normal bit-oriented (or word-oriented) instructions or may be accessible only through special interrupt-masking instructions.

Level interrupt control mechanisms have devices associated with certain levels. The current level of the processor determines which devices may or may not interrupt. Only those devices with a higher logical level may interrupt. When the highest logical level is active, only those interrupts which cannot be disabled (for example, power fail) are allowed. This does not explicitly disable interrupts, so interrupts at a lower logical level than the current processor level will still be generated, and will not need to be re-enabled when the processor level falls appropriately.

Priority control

Some devices have higher urgency than others, and therefore a priority facility is often associated with interrupts. This mechanism may be static or dynamic and is usually related to the device interrupt control facility and the priority levels of the processor.

16.1.4 A simple example I/O system

In order to illustrate the various components of an I/O system, a simple machine is described.

Each device supported on the machine has as many different types of register as are necessary for its operation. These registers are memory-mapped. The most common types used are **control and status** registers which contain all the information on a device's status, and allow the device's interrupts to be enabled and disabled. **Data buffer** registers act as

350 LOW-LEVEL PROGRAMMING

buffer registers for temporarily storing data to be transferred into or out of the machine via the device.

A typical control and status register for the computer has the following structure:

```
bits
 15 - 12    : Errors             -- set when device errors occur
 11         : Busy               -- set when the device is busy
 10 -  8    : Unit select        -- where more than one device is
                                 -- being controlled
  7         : Done/ready         -- I/O completed or device ready
  6         : Interrupt enable   -- when set enables interrupts
  5 -  3    : reserved           -- reserved for future use
  2 -  1    : Device function    -- set to indicate required function
  0         : Device enable      -- set to enable the device
```

The typical structure of a data buffer register used for a character-orientated device is:

```
bits
 15 - 8     : Unused
  7 - 0     : Data
```

Bit 0 is the least significant bit of the register.

A device may have more than one of each of these registers, the exact number being dependent on the nature of the device. For example, one particular Motorola parallel interface and timer device has 14 registers.

Interrupts allow devices to notify the processor when they require service; they are vectored. When an interrupt occurs, the processor stores the current program counter (PC) and the current processor status word (PSW) on the system stack. The PSW will contain, among other things, the processor priority. Its actual layout is given below:

```
bits
 15 - 11    : Mode information
 10 -  8    : Unused
  7 -  5    : Priority
  4 -  0    : Condition codes
```

The condition codes contain information on the result of the last processor operation.

The new PC and PSW are loaded from two preassigned consecutive memory locations (the interrupt vector). The first word contains the address of the interrupt service routine and the second contains the PSW, including the priority at which the interrupt is to be handled. A low-priority interrupt handler can be interrupted by a higher-priority interrupt.

This example I/O system will be returned to later.

16.2 Language requirements

As noted above, one of the main characteristics of an embedded system is the need to interact with input and output devices, all of which have their particular characteristics. The programming of such devices has traditionally been the stronghold of the assembly language programmer, but languages like C and Ada have now attempted to provide progressively higher-level mechanisms for these low-level functions. This makes device-driving and interrupt-handling routines easier to read, write and maintain. The support can be partitioned into two components: **modularity and encapsulation facilities** and an **abstract model** of device handling.

16.2.1 Modularity and encapsulation facilities

Low-level device interfacing is necessarily machine-dependent, and therefore in general it is not portable.

In any software system, it is important to separate the non-portable sections of code from the portable ones. Wherever possible, it is advisable to encapsulate all the machine-dependent code into units which are clearly identifiable. In Ada, the package and protected type facilities are used.

16.2.2 Abstract models of device handling

A device can be considered to be a processor performing a fixed task. A computer system can, therefore, be considered to be a collection of parallel tasks. There are several models by which the device 'task' can communicate and synchronize with the tasks executing inside the main processor. All models must provide:

(1) **Facilities for representing, addressing and manipulating device registers**

A device register may be represented as a program variable, an object, or even a communication channel.

(2) **A suitable representation of interrupts**

The following representations are possible:

(a) **Procedure**

The interrupt is viewed as a procedure call (in a sense, it is a remote procedure call coming from the device task). Any communication and synchronization required must be programmed in the interrupt handler procedure. The procedure is non-nested: only global state or state local to the handler can be accessed.

(b) **Sporadic task**

The interrupt is viewed as a request to execute a task. The handler is a sporadic task and it can access both local persistent data and global data (if shared-variable communication is available in the concurrency model).

(c) **Asynchronous notification**

The interrupt is viewed as an asynchronous notification directed at a task. The handler can access both the local state of the task and the global state. Both the resumption model and the termination are possible (see the next Chapter).

352 LOW-LEVEL PROGRAMMING

(d) **Shared-variable condition synchronization**

The interrupt is viewed as a condition synchronization within a shared-variable synchronization mechanism; for example, a signal operation on a semaphore or a send operation on a condition variable in a monitor. The handler can access both the local state of the task/monitor and the global state.

(e) **Message-based synchronization**

The interrupt is viewed as a content-less message sent down a communication channel. The receiving task can access the local state of the task.

All of the above approaches, except the procedural approach, require a full context switch as the handler executes in the scope of a task. Optimizations are possible if the handlers are restricted. For example, if the handler in the asynchronous notification model has resumption semantics and it does not access any data local to the task, then the interrupt can be handled with only a partial context switch.

Not all these models can be found in real-time languages and operating systems. The most popular one is the procedural model as this requires little support. Usually, real-time systems implemented in C and C++ adopt this model with device registers represented as program variables. For sequential systems, the asynchronous event model is identical in effect to the procedural model, as there is only one task to interrupt and therefore there is no need to identify the task or the event. The Ada model is a hybrid between a procedure model and a shared-variable condition synchronization model. The interrupt is mapped to a protected procedure call and registers are accessed via program variables. Real-Time Java views an interrupt as an asynchronous event where the handler is a schedulable object. Older languages supported other models. For example, Modula-1 and Real-Time Euclid mapped interrupts to condition variables and semaphores respectively (again registers are represented as program variables) and are, therefore, pure shared-variable models. Occam2 viewed an interrupt as a message down a channel, with device registers also represented as channels.

16.3 Programming devices in Ada

In Ada, there are three ways in which tasks can synchronize and communicate with each other:

- through the rendezvous;
- using protected units; and
- via shared variables.

In general, Ada assumes that the device and the program have access to shared memory device registers which can be specified using its representation specification techniques.

The preferred method of device driving is to encapsulate the device operations in a protected object. An interrupt is handled by a protected procedure call.

PROGRAMMING DEVICES IN ADA   353

16.3.1 Addressing and manipulating device registers

Ada presents the programmer with a comprehensive set of facilities for specifying the implementation of data types. These are collectively known as **representation aspects**, and they indicate how the types of the language are to be mapped onto the underlying hardware. A type can only have a single representation. The representation is specified separately from the logical structure of the type. Of course, the specification of the representation of a type is optional and can be left to the compiler.

Representation aspects are a compromise between abstract and concrete structures. Three distinct specifications are available:

(1) **Attribute definition clause** – allows various attributes of an object, task or subprogram to be set; for example, the size (in bits) of objects, the storage alignment, the maximum storage space for a task, the address of an object.

(2) **Enumeration representation clause** – the literals of an enumeration type may be given specific internal values.

(3) **Record representation clause** – record components can be assigned offsets and lengths within single storage units.

If an implementation cannot obey a specification request then the compiler must either reject the program or raise an exception at run-time.

In order to illustrate the use of these mechanisms, consider the following type declarations which represent a typical control and status register of the simple machine defined earlier.

```
type Error_T is (None, Read_Error, Write_Error,
                 Power_Fail, Other);
type Function_T is (Read, Write, Seek);
type Unit_T is new Integer range 0 .. 7;

type Csr_T is record
  Errors   : Error_T;
  Busy     : Boolean;
  Unit     : Unit_T;
  Done     : Boolean;
  Ienable  : Boolean;
  Dfun     : Function_T;
  Denable  : Boolean;
end record;
```

An enumeration representation clause specifies the internal codes for the literals of the enumeration type. For example, the internal codes for the function required by the device above may be:

```
01  --  READ
10  --  WRITE
11  --  SEEK
```

In Ada, this is specified by:

354 LOW-LEVEL PROGRAMMING

```ada
type Function_T is (Read, Write, Seek);
for Function_T use (Read => 1, Write => 2, Seek => 3);
```

Similarly, for `Error_t`:

```ada
type Error_T is (None, Read_Error, Write_Error, Power_Fail, Other);
for Error_T use (None => 0, Read_Error => 1, Write_Error => 2,
                 Power_Fail => 3, Other => 4);
-- note, this is in fact the default assignment
```

A record representation clause specifies the storage representation of records; that is, the order, position and size of its components. The bits in the record are numbered from 0; the range in the component clause specifies the number of bits to be allocated.

For example, the control status register is given by:

```ada
Word : constant := 2;  -- number of storage units in a word
Bits_In_Word : constant := 16;  -- bits in word
for Csr_T use record
   Denable  at 0*Word range 0..0;    -- at word 0 bit 0
   Dfun     at 0*Word range 1..2;
   Ienable  at 0*Word range 6..6;
   Done     at 0*Word range 7..7;
   Unit     at 0*Word range 8 .. 10;
   Busy     at 0*Word range 11 .. 11;
   Errors   at 0*Word range 12 .. 15;
end record;

for Csr_T'Size use Bits_In_Word;  -- the size of object of Csr type
for Csr_T'Alignment use Word;  -- object should be word aligned
for Csr_T'Bit_order use Low_Order_First;
   -- first bit is least significant bit of byte
```

A size attribute specifies the amount of storage that is to be associated with a type. In this example, the register is a single 16-bit word. The alignment attribute specifies that the compiler should always place objects on an integral number of storage units boundary, in this case a word boundary. The bit-ordering attribute specifies whether the machine numbers the most significant bit as 0 (big endian) or the least significant bit (little endian). Note that bits 3, 4 and 5 (which were reserved for future use) have not been specified.

Finally, an actual register needs to be declared and placed at the required location in memory. In Ada, `Address` is an implementation-defined type defined in package `System`. A child package (`System.Storage_Elements.To_Address`) provides a function for converting an integer value into the address type.

```ada
Tcsr : Csr_T;
for Tcsr'Address use System.Storage_Elements.To_Address(8#177566#);
```

Having now constructed the abstract data representation of the register, and placed an appropriately defined variable at the correct address, the hardware register can be manipulated by assignments to this variable:

```ada
Tcsr := (Denable => True, Dfun => Read,
         Ienable => True, Done => False,
         Unit => 4, Errors => None);
```

The use of this record aggregate assumes that the entire register will be assigned values at the same time. To ensure that Dfun is not set before the other fields of the record it may be necessary to use a temporary (shadow) control register:

```
Temp_Cr : Csr_T;
```

This temporary register is then assigned control values and copied into the real register variable:

```
Tcsr := Temp_Cr;
```

The code for this assignment will in most cases ensure that the entire control register is updated in a single action. If any doubt still remains, then the pragma Atomic can be used (which instructs the compiler to generate the update as a simple operation or produce an error message).

After the completion of the I/O operation, the device itself may alter the values on the register; this is recognized in the program as changes in the values of the record components:

```
if Tcsr.Errors = Read_Error then
  raise Disk_Error;
end if;
```

The object Tcsr is therefore a collection of shared variables, which are shared between the device control task and the device itself. Mutual exclusion between these two concurrent (and parallel) tasks is necessary to give reliability and performance. This is achieved in Ada by using a protected object.

16.3.2 Interrupt handling

Ada defines the following model of an interrupt:

- An interrupt represents a class of events that are detected by the hardware or the system software.
- The **occurrence** of an interrupt consists of its **generation** and its **delivery**.
- The generation of an interrupt is the event in the underlying hardware or system which makes the interrupt available to the program.
- Delivery is the action which invokes a part of the program (called the interrupt handler) in response to the interrupt occurrence. In between the generation of the interrupt and its delivery, the interrupt is said to be **pending**. The handler is invoked once for each delivery of the interrupt. The **latency** of an interrupt is the time spent while in the pending state.
- While an interrupt is being handled, further interrupts from the same source are **blocked**; all future occurrences of the interrupt are prevented from being delivered. It is usually device-dependent as to whether a blocked interrupt remains pending or is lost.

356   LOW-LEVEL PROGRAMMING

- Certain interrupts are **reserved**. The programmer is not allowed to provide a handler for a reserved interrupt. Usually, a reserved interrupt is handled directly by the run-time support system of Ada (for example, a clock interrupt used to implement the delay statement).
- Each non-reserved interrupt has a default handler that is assigned by the run-time support system.

Handling interrupts using protected procedures

The main representation of an interrupt handler in Ada is a parameterless protected procedure. Each interrupt has a unique discrete identifier which is supported by the system. How this unique identifier is represented is implementation-defined; it might, for example, be the address of the hardware interrupt vector associated with the interrupt. Where Ada is implemented on top of an operating system that supports signals, each signal may be mapped to a particular interrupt identifier. Thus allowing signal handlers to be programmed in the language.

Up until Ada 2012, identifying interrupt-handling protected procedures was done using one of two pragmas:

```
pragma Attach_Handler(Handler_Name, Expression);
  -- This can appear in the specification of a library-level
  -- protected object and allows the static association of a
  -- named handler with the interrupt identified by the
  -- expression; the handler becomes attached when the
  -- protected object is created.
  -- Raises Program_Error:
  --     (a) when the protected object is created and
  --         the interrupt is reserved,
  --     (b) if the interrupt already has a
  --         user-defined handler, or
  --     (c) if any ceiling priority defined is
  --         not in the range Ada.Interrupt_Priority.

pragma Interrupt_Handler(Handler_Name);
  -- This can appear in the specification of a library-level
  -- protected object and allows the dynamic association of
  -- the named parameterless procedure as an interrupt
  -- handler for one or more interrupts. Objects created
  -- from such a protected type must be library level.
```

In Ada 2012, these have now become aspect specifications attached to the related protected procedures:

```
procedure IRQ_1 with Attach_Handler => Interrupt_Identifier;

procedure IRQ_2 with Interrupt_Handler;
```

Although, identification using pragmas is still allowed.

Program 16.1 defines the Systems Programming Annex's support for interrupt identification and the dynamic attachment of handlers. In all cases where `Program_Error` is raised, the currently attached handler is not changed.

All protected objects that have interrupt-handling procedures also have a ceiling priority that falls within the `System.Interrupt_Priority` range; for example:

```ada
protected Handler is
  pragma Interrupt_Priority(Interrupt_Priority'First);
  procedure IH;
  pragma Interrupt_Handler(IH);
end Handler;
```

or from Ada 2012:

```ada
protected Handler
      with Interrupt_Priority => Interrupt_Priority'First is
  procedure IH with Interrupt_Handler;
end Handler;
```

It is also possible that an implementation will allow the association of names with interrupts via the package `Ada.Interrupts.Names` (see Program 16.2). This will be used in the examples in the remainder of this chapter.

16.3.3 A simple driver example

A common class of equipment to be attached to an embedded computer system is the analogue to digital converter (ADC). The converter samples some environmental factors, such as temperature or pressure; it translates the measurements it receives, which are usually in millivolts, and provides scaled integer values on a hardware register. Consider a single converter that has a 16-bit result register at hardware address 8#150000# and a control register at 8#150002#. The computer is a 16-bit machine and the control register is structured as follows:

Bit	Name	Meaning
0	A/D Start	Set to 1 to start a conversion.
6	Interrupt Enable/Disable	Set to 1 to enable interrupts
7	Done	Set to 1 when conversion is complete.
8–13	Channel	The converter has 64 analogue inputs, the particular one required is indicated by the value of the channel.
15	Error	Set to 1 by the converter if device malfunctions.

The driver for this ADC will be structured as a protected type within a package body, so that the interrupt it generates can be processed as a protected procedure call, and so that more than one ADC can be catered for:

```ada
package Adc_Device_Driver is
  Max_Measure : constant := (2**16)-1;
  type Channel is range 0..63;
  subtype Measurement is Integer range 0..Max_Measure;
  procedure Read(Ch: Channel; M : out Measurement);
    -- potentially blocking
  Conversion_Error : exception;
```

358 LOW-LEVEL PROGRAMMING

```ada
package Ada.Interrupts is
  type Interrupt_Id is implementation_defined; -- must be discrete
  type Parameterless_Handler is access protected procedure;

  function Is_Reserved(Interrupt : Interrupt_Id) return Boolean;
    -- Returns True if the interrupt is reserved,
    -- returns False otherwise.
  function Is_Attached(Interrupt : Interrupt_Id) return Boolean;
    -- Returns True if the interrupt is attached to a
    -- handler, returns False otherwise.
    -- Raises Program_Error if the interrupt is reserved.
  function Current_Handler(Interrupt : Interrupt_Id)
                            return Parameterless_Handler;
    -- Returns an access variable to the current handler for
    -- the interrupt. If no user handler has been attached, a
    -- value is returned which represents the default handler.
    -- Raises Program_Error if the interrupt is reserved.
  procedure Attach_Handler(New_Handler : Parameterless_Handler;
                           Interrupt : Interrupt_Id);
    -- Assigns New_Handler as the current handler.
    -- If New_Handler is null, the default handler is restored.
    -- Raises Program_Error:
    --      (a) if the protected object associated with the
    --          New_Handler has not been identified with a
    --          aspect Interrupt_Handler,
    --      (b) if the interrupt is reserved,
    --      (c) if the current handler was attached statically
    --          using aspect Attach_Handler.
  procedure Exchange_Handler(
          Old_Handler : out Parameterless_Handler;
          New_Handler : Parameterless_Handler;
          Interrupt : Interrupt_Id);
    -- Assigns New_Handler as the current handler for the
    -- Interrupt and returns the previous handler in
    -- Old_Handler.
    -- If New_Handler is null, the default handler is restored.
    -- Raises Program_Error:
    --      (a) if the protected object associated with the
    --          New_Handler has not been identified with a
    --          aspect Interrupt_Handler,
    --      (b) if the interrupt is reserved,
    --      (c) if the current handler was attached statically
    --          using aspect Attach_Handler.
  procedure Detach_Handler(Interrupt : Interrupt_Id);
    -- Restores the default handler for the specified interrupt.
    -- Raises Program_Error:
    --      (a) if the interrupt is reserved,
    --      (b) if the current handler was attached statically
    --          using aspect Attach_Handler.
private
  ... -- not specified by the language
end Ada.Interrupts;
```

Program 16.1: The Ada.Interrupts package.

```ada
package Ada.Interrupts.Names is
  implementation_defined : constant Interrupt_Id :=
                                        implementation_defined;
  ...
  implementation_defined : constant Interrupt_Id :=
                                        implementation_defined;
private
  ... -- not specified by the language
end Ada.Interrupts.Names;
```

Program 16.2: The `Ada.Interrupts.Names` package.

```ada
private
  for Channel'Size use 6;
  -- indicates that six bits only must be used
end Adc_Device_Driver;
```

For any request, the driver will make three attempts before raising the exception. The package body follows:

```ada
with Ada.Interrupts.Names; use Ada.Interrupts;
with System; use System;
with System.Storage_Elements; use System.Storage_Elements;
package body Adc_Device_Driver is
  Bits_In_Word : constant := 16;
  Word : constant := 2; -- bytes in word
  type Flag is (Down, Set);

  type Control_Register is
  record
    Ad_Start : Flag;
    Ienable  : Flag;
    Done     : Flag;
    Ch       : Channel;
    Error    : Flag;
  end record;

  for Control_Register use
    -- specifies the layout of the control register
  record
      Ad_Start at 0*Word range 0..0;
      Ienable  at 0*Word range 6..6;
      Done     at 0*Word range 7..7;
      Ch       at 0*Word range 8..13;
      Error    at 0*Word range 15..15;
  end record;

  for Control_Register'Size use Bits_In_Word;
    -- the register is 16-bits long
  for Control_Register'Alignment use Word;
    -- on a word boundary
  for Control_Register'Bit_order use Low_Order_First;
```

360 LOW-LEVEL PROGRAMMING

```ada
type Data_Register is range 0 .. Max_Measure;
for Data_Register'Size use Bits_In_Word;
  -- the register is 16-bits long

Contr_Reg_Addr : constant Address := To_Address(8#150002#);
Data_Reg_Addr  : constant Address := To_Address(8#150000#);
Adc_Priority   : constant Interrupt_Priority := 63;
Control_Reg : aliased Control_Register;
    -- aliased indicates that pointers are used to access it
for Control_Reg'Address use Contr_Reg_Addr;
    -- specifies the address of the control register
Data_Reg : aliased Data_Register;
for Data_Reg'Address use Data_Reg_Addr;
    -- specifies the address of the data register

protected type Interrupt_Interface(Int_Id : Interrupt_Id;
              Cr : access Control_Register;
              Dr : access Data_Register)
              with Interrupt_Priority => Adc_Priority is
  entry Read(Chan : Channel; M : out Measurement);
private
  entry Done(Chan : Channel; M : out Measurement);
  procedure Handler with Attach_Handler => Int_Id;
  Interrupt_Occurred : Boolean := False;
  Next_Request : Boolean := True;
end Interrupt_Interface;

Adc_Interface : Interrupt_Interface(Names.Adc,
              Control_Reg'Access,
              Data_Reg'Access);
  -- this assumes that 'Adc' is registered as an
  -- Interrupt_Id in Ada.Interrupts.Names
  -- 'Access gives the address of the object

protected body Interrupt_Interface is

  entry Read(Chan : Channel; M : out Measurement)
        when Next_Request is
    Shadow_Register : Control_Register;
  begin
    Shadow_Register := (Ad_Start => Set, Ienable => Set,
        Done => Down, Ch  => Chan, Error => Down);
    Cr.all := Shadow_Register;
    Interrupt_Occurred := False;
    Next_Request := False;
    requeue Done;
  end Read;

  procedure Handler is
  begin
    Interrupt_Occurred := True;
  end Handler;
```

```ada
   entry Done(Chan : Channel; M : out Measurement)
                            when Interrupt_Occurred is
   begin
      Next_Request := True;
      if Cr.Done = Set and Cr. Error = Down then
           M := Measurement(Dr.all);
      else
         raise Conversion_Error;
      end if;
   end Done;
end Interrupt_Interface;

procedure Read(Ch : Channel; M : out Measurement) is
begin
   for I in 1..3 loop
      begin
         Adc_Interface.Read(Ch,M);
         return;
      exception
         when Conversion_Error => null;
      end;
   end loop;
   raise Conversion_Error;
end Read;
end Adc_Device_Driver;
```

The client tasks simply call the Read procedure indicating the channel number from which to read, and an output variable for the actual value read. Inside the procedure, an inner loop attempts three conversions by calling the Read entry in the protected object associated with the converter. Inside this entry, the control register, Cr, is set up with appropriate values. Once the control register has been assigned, the client task is requeued on a private entry to await the interrupt (see Section 12.3.2 for a discussion on requeue). The Next_Request flag is used to ensure only one call to Read is outstanding.

Once the interrupt has arrived (as a parameterless protected procedure call), the barrier on the Done entry is set to true; this results in the Done entry being executed (as part of the interrupt handler), which ensures that Cr.Done has been set and that the error flag has not been raised. If this is the case, the out parameter M is constructed, using a type conversion, from the value on the buffer register. (Note that this value cannot be out of range for the subtype Measurement.) If the conversion has not been successful, the exception Conversion_Error is raised; this is trapped by the Read procedure, which makes three attempts in total at a conversion before allowing the exception to propagate.

The above example illustrates that it is often necessary when writing device drivers to convert objects from one type to another. In these circumstances the strong typing features of Ada can be an irritant. It is, however, possible to circumvent this difficulty by using a generic function that is provided as a predefined library unit:

```ada
generic
   type Source (<>) is limited private;
   type Target (<>) is limited private;
function Ada.Unchecked_Conversion(S : Source) return Target
   with Convention => Intrinsic;
```

362 LOW-LEVEL PROGRAMMING

```ada
pragma Pure(Ada.Unchecked_Conversion);
```

The effect of unchecked conversion is to copy the bit pattern of the source over to the target. The programmer must make sure that the conversion is sensible and that all possible patterns are acceptable (i.e. legal) for the target.

16.3.4 Accessing I/O devices through special instructions

If special instructions are required, assembler code may have to be integrated with Ada code. The machine code insertion mechanism enables programmers to write Ada code which contains visible non-Ada objects. This is achieved in a controlled way by only allowing machine code instructions to operate within the context of a subprogram body. Moreover, if a subprogram contains code statements then it can contain only code statements and 'use' clauses (comments and pragmas being allowed as usual).

As would be expected, the details and characteristics of using code inserts are largely implementation dependent; implementation-specific pragmas and attributes may be used to impose particular restrictions and calling conventions on the use of objects defining code instructions. A code statement has the following structure:

```ada
code_statement ::= qualified_expression
```

The qualified expression should be of a type declared within a predefined library package called `System.Machine_Code`. It is this package that provides record declarations (in standard Ada) to represent the instructions of the target machine. The following example illustrates the approach:

```ada
D : Data; -- to be input

procedure In_Op with Inline;

procedure In_Op is
  use System.Machine_Code;
begin
  My_Machine_Format'(Code => In_Instruction, Reg => 1, Port => 1);
  My_Machine_Format'(CODE => SAVE, REG => 1, D'Address);
end;
```

The aspect `Inline` instructs the compiler to include inline code, rather than a procedure call, whenever the subprogram is used.

Even though this code insertion method is defined in Ada, the language makes it quite clear (ARM 13.8.4) that an implementation need not provide a `Machine_Code` package unless the Systems Programming Annex is supported. If it does not, the use of machine code inserts is prohibited.

16.4 Scheduling device drivers

As many real-time systems have I/O components, it is important that the scheduling analysis incorporates any features which are particular to this low-level programming. It has

SCHEDULING DEVICE DRIVERS

already been noted that DMA and channel-program controlled techniques are often too unpredictable (in their temporal behaviour) to be analysed. Attention in this section is therefore focused upon the interrupt-driven program-controlled and status driven approaches.

Where an interrupt releases a sporadic task for execution, there is a cost that must be allocated to the interrupt handler itself. The priority of the handler is likely to be greater than that of the sporadic task, which means that tasks with priorities greater than the sporadic task (but less than the interrupt handler) will suffer an interference. Indeed, this is an example of priority inversion, as the handler's only job is to release the sporadic task – its priority should ideally be the same as the sporadic task. Unfortunately, most hardware platforms require the interrupt priorities to be higher than the ordinary software priorities. To model the interrupt handler, an extra 'task' is included in the schedulability test (see Section 7.9). It has a 'period' equal to the sporadic task, a priority equal to the interrupt priority level and an execution time equal to its own worst-case behaviour.

With status-driven devices, the control code can be analysed in the usual way. Such devices, however, do introduce a particular difficulty. Often the protocol for using an input device is as follows: ask for a reading, wait for the reading to be taken by the hardware, and then access a register to bring the reading into the program. The problem is how to manage the delay while the reading is being taken. Depending on the likely duration of the delay, three approaches are possible:

- busy wait on the 'done' flag
- reschedule the task to some future time
- for periodic tasks, split the action between periods.

With small delays, a busy wait is acceptable. From a scheduling point of view, the 'delay' is all computation time and hence as long as the 'delay' is bounded, there is no change to the analysis approach. To protect against a failure in the device (that is, it never sets the done bit), a timeout algorithm can be used.

If the delay is sizable, it is more effective to suspend the task, execute other work and then return to the I/O task at some future time when the value should be available. So if the reading time was 30 ms, the code would be:

```
begin
  --set up reading
  delay Milliseconds(30);
  -- take reading and use
end;
```

From a scheduling perspective, this structure has three significant implications. Firstly, the response times are not as easy to calculate. Each half of the task must be analysed separately. The total response time is obtained by adding together both sub-response times, and the 30 ms delay. Although there is a delay in the task, this is ignored when considering the impact that this task has on lower-priority tasks. Secondly, the extra computation time involved in delaying and being rescheduled again must be added to the worst-case execution time of the task (see Section 7.9 for a discussion on how to include system overheads). Thirdly, there is an impact on blocking. Recall that the simple equation for calculating the response time of a task is (see Section 5.1):

$$R_i = C_i + B_i + I_i$$

B_i is the blocking time (that is, the maximum time the task can be delayed by the actions of a lower-priority task). Various protocols for resource sharing were considered in Section 5.4. The effective ones all had the property that B_i consisted of just one block. However, when a task delays (and lets lower priority tasks execute), it can be blocked again when it is released from the delay queue. Hence the response time equation becomes:

$$R_i = C_i + (N+1)B_i + I_i$$

where N is the number of internal delays.

With periodic tasks, there is another way of managing this explicit delay. This method is called **period displacement** and involves initiating the reading in one period but taking the reading in the next. For example:

```
-- set up first reading
loop
  delay until Next_Release;
  -- check done flag set
  -- take reading and use
  -- set up for next reading
  Next_Release := Next_Release + Period;
end loop;
```

This is a straightforward approach with no impact on scheduling. Of course, the reading is one period old, which may not be acceptable to the application. To ensure that there is sufficient gap between the end of one execution and the start of the next, the deadline of the task can be adjusted. So, if S is the settling time for the device the required constraint is $D \leq T - S$. Note that the maximum staleness of the reading is bounded by $T + D$ (or $T + R$ once the worst-case response time is calculated).

16.5 Memory management

Embedded real-time systems often have only a limited amount of memory available; this is either because of the cost or because of other constraints associated with the surrounding system (for example, size, power or weight constraints). It may, therefore, be necessary to control how this memory is allocated so that it can be used effectively. Furthermore, where there is more than one type of memory (with different access characteristics) within the system, it may be necessary to instruct the compiler to place certain data types at certain locations. By doing this, the program is able to increase performance and predictability as well as interact with the outside world.

This chapter has already considered how data items can be allocated to particular memory locations, and how certain fields within storage units can be used to represent specific data types. This section considers the more general issues of storage management. Attention is focused on management of the two basic components that compilers use to manage data at run-time: the heap and the stack.

16.5.1 Heap management

The run-time implementations of most programming languages provide a large amount of memory (called the **heap**) so that the programmer can make run-time requests for chunks to be allocated (for example, to contain an array whose bounds were not known at compile time). An allocator (usually the **new** operator) is used for this purpose. It returns a pointer to memory within the heap of adequate size for the program's data structure. The run-time support system is responsible for managing the heap. Key problems are deciding how much space is required and when allocated space can be released. The first of these problems, in general, requires application knowledge. The second can be handled in several ways, including:

- require the programmer to return the memory explicitly – this is error-prone but is easy to implement; it is the approach taken by the C programming language where the functions `malloc` and `free` are used – the function `sizeof` allows the size of data types in bytes to be obtained (from the compiler);

- require the run-time support system to monitor the memory and determine when it can logically no longer be accessed – the scope rules of Ada allows an implementation to adopt this approach; when an access type goes out of scope, all the memory associated with that access type can be freed;

- require the run-time support system to monitor the memory, and release chunks which are no longer being used (**garbage collection**) – this is, perhaps, the most general approach, as it allows memory to be freed even though its associated access type is still in scope.

From a real-time perspective, the above approaches have an increasing impact on the ability to analyse the timing properties of the program. In particular, garbage collection may be performed either when the heap is full or by an asynchronous activity (incremental garbage collection). In either case, running the garbage collector may have a significant impact on the response time of a time-critical task. Although there has been much work on real-time garbage collection and progress continues to be made, there is still a reluctance to rely on these techniques in time-critical systems.

In Ada, the heap is represented by one or more **storage pools**. Storage pools are associated with a particular Ada partition (for a non-distributable Ada system this is simply the whole program). Each object which is of an access type has an associated storage pool. The allocator ('new') takes its memory from the target pool. The `Ada.Unchecked_Deallocation` facility returns data to the pool. An implementation may support a single global pool which will be reclaimed when the partition terminates, or it may support pools defined at different accessibility levels which will be reclaimed when the associated scope is exited. By default, the implementation chooses a standard storage pool per access type. Note that all objects accessed directly (not via an access pointer) are placed on the stack, not the heap.

To give more user control over storage management, Ada defines a package called `System.Storage_Pools` which is given in Program 16.3.

Programmers can implement their own storage pools by extending the `Root_Storage_Pool` type and providing concrete implementations for the sub-

```ada
with Ada.Finalization; with System.Storage_Elements;
package System.Storage_Pools is
  pragma Preelaborate(System.Storage_Pools);

  type Root_Storage_Pool is abstract new
       Ada.Finalization.Limited_Controlled with private;

  procedure Allocate(Pool : in out Root_Storage_Pool;
           Storage_Address : out Address;
           Size_In_Storage_Elements : in System.
                Storage_Elements.Storage_Count;
           Alignment : in System.Storage_Elements.Storage_Count)
       is abstract;

  procedure Deallocate(Pool : in out Root_Storage_Pool;
           Storage_Address : in Address;
           Size_In_Storage_Elements : in System.
                Storage_Elements.Storage_Count;
           Alignment : in System.Storage_Elements.Storage_Count)
       is abstract;

  function Storage_Size(Pool : Root_Storage_Pool) return
           System.Storage_Elements.Storage_Count is abstract;
private
  ...
end System.Storage_Pools;
```

Program 16.3: The `System.Storage_Pools` package.

program bodies. To associate an access type with a storage pool, the pool is first declared and then the `Storage_Pool` attribute is used:

```ada
My_Pool : Some_Storage_Pool_Type;

type A is access Some_Object;
for A'Storage_Pool use My_Pool;
```

Now all calls to 'new' using A will automatically call `Allocate`; calls to `Ada.Unchecked_Deallocation` will call `Deallocate`; both referring to `My_Pool`. Furthermore, the implementation is allowed (but not required) to call `Deallocate` when the access type goes out of scope. Finally, it should be noted that Ada does not require an implementation to support more general garbage collection.

16.5.2 Stack management

As well as managing the heap, embedded programmers also have to be concerned with stack size. While specifying the stack size of a task requires trivial support (for example, in Ada it is via the `Storage_Size` attribute applied to a task), calculating the required stack size is more difficult. As tasks enter blocks and execute procedures their stacks grow. To accurately estimate the maximum extent of this growth requires knowledge of the execution behaviour of each task. This knowledge is similar to that required to undertake worst-case execution time (WCET) analysis (see Section 4.5). Hence both WCET and worst-case stack usage bounds can be obtained from a single tool performing control flow analysis of the task's code.

Summary

One of the main characteristics of an embedded system is the requirement that it interacts with special-purpose input and output devices. To program device drivers in high-level languages requires:

- the ability to pass data and control information to and from the device;
- the ability to handle interrupts.

Normally control and data information is passed to devices through device registers. These registers are either accessed by special addresses in a memory-mapped I/O architecture, or via special machine instructions. Interrupt handling requires context switching, device and interrupt identification, interrupt control, and device prioritization.

The programming of devices has traditionally been the stronghold of the assembly language programmer, but languages like C and Ada have progressively attempted to provide high-level mechanisms for these low-level functions. This makes device driver and interrupt-handling routines easier to read, write and maintain. The main requirement on a high-level language is that it provides an abstract model of device handling. Encapsulation facilities are also required so that the non-portable code of the program can be separated from the portable part.

The model of device handling is built on top of the language's model of concurrency. A device can be considered to be a processor performing a fixed task. A computer system can therefore be modelled as several parallel tasks which need to communicate and synchronize. There are several ways in which interrupts can be modelled. They must all have:

(1) Facilities for addressing and manipulating device registers.
(2) A suitable representation of interrupts.

In Ada, device registers can be defined as scalars and user-defined record types, with a comprehensive set of facilities for mapping types onto the underlying hardware. Interrupts are viewed as hardware-generated procedure calls to a protected object.

Interaction with devices has implications for timing analysis. This chapter has also considered how the schedulability analysis presented in Part II can be used to analyse programs that contain interrupt handlers and accesses to device registers. Finally, this Chapter has briefly considered how memory can be managed by the embedded system programmer. Both heap and stack management have been covered.

Chapter 17
Exceptions and exception handling

17.1 Exception handling in older real-time languages
17.2 Modern exception handling
17.3 Exception handling in Ada
17.4 Recovery blocks and exceptions
17.5 The real-time impact of exception handling
Summary

Chapter 3 considered how systems can be made more reliable and introduced exceptions as a framework for implementing software fault tolerance. In this chapter, exceptions and exception handling are considered in more detail and their provision in Ada is discussed.

There are a number of general requirements for an exception handling facility:

(R1) As with all language features, the facility must be simple to understand and use.

(R2) The code for exception handling should not be so obtrusive as to obscure understanding of the program's normal error-free operation. A mechanism which intermingles code for normal processing and exceptional processing will prove difficult to understand and maintain. It may well lead to a less reliable system.

(R3) The mechanism should be designed so that run-time overheads are incurred only when handling an exception. Although the majority of applications require that the performance of a program that uses exceptions is not adversely affected under normal operating conditions, this may not always be the case. Under some circumstances, in particular where speed of recovery is of prime importance, an application may be prepared to tolerate a little overhead on the normal error-free operation.

(R4) The mechanism should allow the uniform treatment of exceptions detected both by the environment and by the program. For example, an exception such as **arithmetic overflow**, which is detected by the hardware, should be handled in exactly the same manner as an exception raised by the program

370 EXCEPTIONS AND EXCEPTION HANDLING

as a result of an assertion failure.

(R5) As already mentioned in Chapter 3, the exception mechanism should allow recovery actions to be programmed.

17.1 Exception handling in older real-time languages

Although the terms 'exception' and 'exception handling' are relatively new, they simply express an approach to programming which attempts to contain and handle error situations. Consequently, most programming languages have facilities which enable at least some exceptions to be handled. This section briefly appraises these facilities in terms of the requirements set out above.

17.1.1 Unusual return value and status flags

One of the most primitive forms of an exception handling mechanism is the *unusual return value* or *error return* from a procedure or a function. Its main advantage is that it is simple and does not require any new language mechanism for its implementation. C supports this approach, and typically it would be used as follows:

```
if(function_call(parameters) == AN_ERROR) {
  /* error handling code */
} else {
  /* normal return code */
};
```

Where a function already returns a value and it is not possible to partition the range of values to indicate an error, then *status flags* are used. These are atomic shared variables which can be set and tested. For example, C when used with Real-Time POSIX has a shared integer variable called `errno` that is set by the system to the most recent detected error condition[1]. Using this approach, the above code can be rewritten:

```
#include <errno.h>
 ...
 ret = function_call(parameters);
 if (errno == AN_ERROR) {
  /* error handling code */
 } else {
  /* normal return code */
 };
```

As can be seen, although this meets the simplicity requirement R1 and allows recovery actions to be programmed (R5), it fails to satisfy R2, R3 and R4. The code is obtrusive, it entails overheads every time it is used, and it is not clear how to handle errors detected by the environment. Furthermore, if the error is not checked for, the program can fail in an unpredictable manner.

---
[1] In a multithread environment, `errno` is a function that returns a thread-specific error code.

17.1.2 Forced branch

In assembly languages, the typical mechanism for exception handling is for subroutines to *skip return*. In other words, the instruction immediately following the subroutine call is skipped to indicate the presence (or the absence) of an error. This is achieved by the subroutine incrementing its return address (program counter) by the length of a simple jump instruction to indicate an error-free (or error) return. In the case where more than one exceptional return is possible, the subroutine will assume that the caller has more than one jump instruction after the call, and will manipulate the program counter accordingly.

For example, assuming two possible error conditions, the following might be used to call a subroutine which outputs a character to a device.

```
jsr pc, PRINT_CHAR
jmp IO_ERROR
jmp DEVICE_NOT_ENABLED
# normal processing
```

The subroutine, for a normal return, would increment the return address by two `jmp` instructions.

Although this approach incurs little overhead (R3) and enables recovery actions to be programmed (R5), it can lead to obscure program structures, and therefore violates requirements R1 and R2. R4 also cannot be satisfied.

17.1.3 Non-local `goto` and error procedures

A high-level language version of a forced branch might require different labels to be passed as parameters to procedures or to have standard label variables (a label variable is an object to which a program address can be assigned and which can be used to transfer control). RTL/2 is an example of an early real-time language which provides the latter facility in the form of a non-local `goto`.

Notice that, when used in this way, the `goto` is more than just a jump; it implies an abnormal return from a procedure. Consequently, the stack must be unwound until the environment restored is that of the procedure containing the declaration of the label. The equivalent result can be obtained in the C language by using the `setjmp` and `longjmp` facility. The `setjmp` establishes the label and the `longjmp` performs the goto.

With this approach, the penalty of unwinding the stack is only incurred when an error has occurred, so requirement R3 has been satisfied. Although the use of `goto`s is very flexible (satisfying R4 and R5), they can lead to very obscure programs. They therefore fail to satisfy the requirements R1 and R2.

Using a non-local goto, the control flow of the program has been broken. This is appropriate for unrecoverable errors. For recoverable errors an **error procedure variable** can be used. Again, the main criticism of this approach is that programs can become very difficult to understand and maintain.

17.2 Modern exception handling

It has been shown that the traditional approaches to exception handling often result in the handling code being intermingled with the program's normal flow of execution. The modern approach is to introduce exception-handling facilities directly into the language and thereby provide a more structured exception handling mechanism. The exact nature of these facilities varies from language to language; however, there are several common threads that can be identified. These are discussed in the following subsections.

17.2.1 Exceptions and their representation

In Section 3.5.1, it was noted that there are two types of error detection: environmental detection and application detection. Also, depending on the delay in detecting the error, it may be necessary to raise the exception synchronously or asynchronously. A synchronous exception is raised as an immediate result of a section of code attempting an inappropriate operation. An asynchronous exception is raised some time after the operation that resulted in the error occurring. It may be raised in the task that originally executed the operation or in another task. There are therefore four classes of exceptions:

(1) Detected by the environment and raised synchronously – an array bounds violation or divide by zero are examples of such exceptions.

(2) Detected by the application and raised synchronously – for example, the failure of a program-defined assertion check.

(3) Detected by the environment and raised asynchronously – an exception raised as the result of power failure or the failure of some health monitoring mechanism.

(4) Detected by the application and raised asynchronously – for example, one task may recognize that an error condition has occurred that will result in another task not meeting its deadline or not terminating correctly.

Asynchronous exceptions are often called asynchronous notifications or signals . This chapter will focus on synchronous exception handling and leave the topic of asynchronous exception handling until Chapter 18.

With synchronous exceptions, there are several models for their declaration. For example, they can be viewed as:

- a constant name which needs to be explicitly declared, or
- an object of a particular type which may or may not need to be explicitly declared.

Ada requires exceptions to be declared like constants; for example, the exceptions that can be raised by the run-time environment are declared in package Standard - see Program 17.1 . This package is visible to all Ada programs.

MODERN EXCEPTION HANDLING

```
package Standard is
  ...
  Constraint_Error : exception;
  Program_Error    : exception;
  Storage_Error    : exception;
  Tasking_Error    : exception;
  ...
end Standard;
```

Program 17.1: The `Standard` package.

17.2.2 The domain of an exception handler

Within a program, there may be several handlers for a particular exception. Associated with each handler is a **domain** which specifies the region of computation during which, if an exception occurs, the handler will be activated. The accuracy with which a domain can be specified will determine how precisely the source of the exception can be located. In a block structured language, like Ada, the domain is normally the block. For example, consider a temperature sensor whose value should fall in the range 0 to 100 °C. The following Ada block defines temperature to be an integer between 0 and 100. If the calculated value falls outside that range, the run-time support system for Ada raises a Constraint_Error exception. The invocation of the associated handler enables any necessary corrective action to be performed.

```
declare
  subtype Temperature is Integer range 0 .. 100;
begin
  -- read temperature sensor and calculate its value
exception
  -- handler for Constraint_Error
end;
```

The details will be filled in shortly.

Where blocks form the basis of other units, such as procedures and functions, the domain of an exception handler is usually that unit.

As the domain of the exception handler specifies how precisely the error can be located, it can be argued that the granularity of the block is inadequate. For example consider the following sequence of calculations, each of which possibly could cause Constraint_Error to be raised.

```
declare
  subtype Temperature is Integer range 0 .. 100;
  subtype Pressure is Integer range 0 .. 50;
  subtype Flow is Integer range 0 .. 200;
begin
  -- read temperature sensor and calculate its value
  -- read pressure sensor and calculate its value
  -- read flow sensor and calculate its value

  -- adjust temperature, pressure and flow
  -- according to requirements
```

374 EXCEPTIONS AND EXCEPTION HANDLING

```ada
exception
   -- handler for Constraint_Error
end;
```

The problem for the handler is to decide which calculation caused the exception to be raised. Further difficulties arise when arithmetic overflow and underflow can occur.

With exception handler domains based on blocks, one solution to this problem is to decrease the size of the block and/or nest them. Using the sensor example:

```ada
declare
   subtype Temperature is Integer range 0 .. 100;
   subtype Pressure is Integer range 0 .. 50;
   subtype Flow is Integer range 0 .. 200;
begin
   begin
      -- read temperature sensor and calculate its value
   exception
      -- handler for Constraint_Error for temperature
   end;
   begin
      -- read pressure sensor and calculate its value
   exception
      -- handler for Constraint_Error for pressure
   end;
   begin
      -- read flow sensor and calculate its value
   exception
      -- handler for Constraint_Error for flow
   end;
   -- adjust temperature, pressure and flow according
   -- to requirements
exception
   -- handler for other possible exceptions
end;
```

Alternatively, procedures containing handlers could be created for each of the nested blocks. However, in either case this can become long-winded and tedious. A different solution is to allow exceptions to be handled at the statement level. Using such an approach the above example would be rewritten thus:

```ada
-- NOT VALID Ada
declare
   subtype Temperature is Integer range 0 .. 100;
   subtype Pressure is Integer range 0 .. 50;
   subtype Flow is Integer range 0 .. 200;
begin
   Read_Temperature_Sensor;
       exception -- handler for Constraint_Error;
   Read_Pressure_Sensor;
       exception -- handler for Constraint_Error;
   Read_Flow_Sensor;
       exception -- handler for Constraint_Error;
   -- adjust temperature, pressure and flow as required
end;
```

The CHILL programming language [27], for example, has such a facility. Although this enables the cause of the exception to be located more precisely, it intermingles the exception handling code with the normal flow of operation, which may result in less clear programs and violate Requirement R2 (given at the beginning of this chapter).

The preferred approach to this problem is to allow parameters to be passed with the exceptions. With some object-oriented languages (like Java) this is automatic, as the exception is represented as an object, and therefore can contain as much information as the programmer wishes. In contrast, Ada provides a predefined procedure Exception_Information that returns implementation-defined details on the occurrence of the exception.

17.2.3 Exception propagation

Closely related to the concept of an exception domain is the notion of exception propagation. So far it has been implied that if a block or procedure raises an exception, then there is a handler associated with that block or procedure. However, this may not be the case, and there are two possible methods for dealing with a situation where no immediate exception handler can be found.

The first approach is to regard the absence of a handler as a programmer error which should be reported at compile time. However, it is often the case that an exception raised in a procedure can only be handled within the context from which the procedure was called. In this situation, it is not possible to have the handler local to the procedure. For example, an exception raised in a procedure as a result of a failed assertion involving the parameters can only be handled in the calling context. Unfortunately, it is not always possible for the compiler to check whether the calling context includes the appropriate exception handlers, as this may require complex flow control analysis. This is particularly difficult when the procedure calls other procedures which may also raise exceptions. Consequently, languages which require compile-time error generation for such situations require that a procedure specifies which exceptions it may raise (that is, not handle locally). The compiler can then check the calling context for an appropriate handler and if necessary generate the required error message. This is the approach taken by the CHILL language. Java and C++ also allow a function to define which exceptions it can raise. However, unlike CHILL, they do not require a handler to be available in the calling context.

The second approach, which can be adopted when no local handler for an exception can be found, is to look for handlers up the chain of invokers at run-time; this is called **propagating** the exception. Ada (along with Java and C++) allows exception propagation.

A potential problem with exception propagation occurs when the language requires exceptions to be declared and given scope. Under some circumstances it is possible for an exception to be propagated outside its scope, thereby making it impossible for a handler to be found. To cope with this, most languages provide a 'catch all' exception handler. This handler is also used to save the programmer enumerating many exception names.

An unhandled exception causes a sequential program to be aborted. If the program contains more than one task and a particular task does not handle an exception it has raised, then usually that task is aborted. However, it is not clear whether the exception should be propagated to any other task. Exceptions in multi-tasking programs will be considered in detail in Chapter 18.

17.2.4 Resumption versus termination model

A crucial consideration in any exception-handling facility is whether the invoker of the exception should continue its execution after the exception has been handled. If the invoker can continue, then it may be possible for the handler to cure the problem that caused the exception to be raised and for the invoker to resume as if nothing has happened. This is referred to as the **resumption** or **notify** model. The model where control is not returned to the invoker is called **termination** or **escape**. Clearly it is possible to have a model in which the handler can decide whether to resume the operation which caused the exception, or to terminate the operation. This is called the **hybrid** model.

The resumption model

To illustrate the resumption model, consider three procedures P, Q and R. Procedure P invokes Q which in turn invokes R. Procedure R raises an exception r which is handled by Q, assuming there is no local handler in R. The handler for r is Hr. In the course of handling r, Hr raises exception q which is handled by Hq in procedure P (the caller of Q). Once this has been handled Hr continues its execution and when finished R continues. Figure 17.1 represents this sequence of events diagrammatically by arcs numbered 1 to 6.

The resumption model is most easily understood by viewing the handler as an implicit procedure which is called when the exception is raised.

The problem with this approach is that it is often difficult to repair errors which are raised by the run-time environment. For example, an arithmetic overflow occurring in the middle of a sequence of complex expressions may result in several registers containing partial evaluations. As a consequence of calling the handler, these registers may be overwritten.

The languages Pearl and Mesa both provide a mechanism whereby a handler can return to the context from which the exception was raised. Both languages also support the termination model.

Although implementing a strict resumption model is difficult, a compromise is to re-execute the block associated with the exception handler. The Eiffel language provides such a facility, called **retry**, as part of its exception handling model. The handler is able to set a local flag to indicate that an error has occurred and the block is able to test that flag. Note that for such a scheme to work, the local variables of the block must not be re-initialized on a retry.

The advantage of the resumption model comes when the exception has been raised asynchronously, and therefore has little to do with the current task's execution. Asynchronous event handling is discusses in detail in Section 18.4.

The termination model

In the termination model, when an exception has been raised and the handler has been called, control does not return to the point where the exception occurred. Instead, the block or procedure containing the handler is terminated, and control passed to the calling block or procedure. An invoked procedure may therefore terminate in one of a number of conditions. One of these is the **normal condition**, while the others are **exception conditions**.

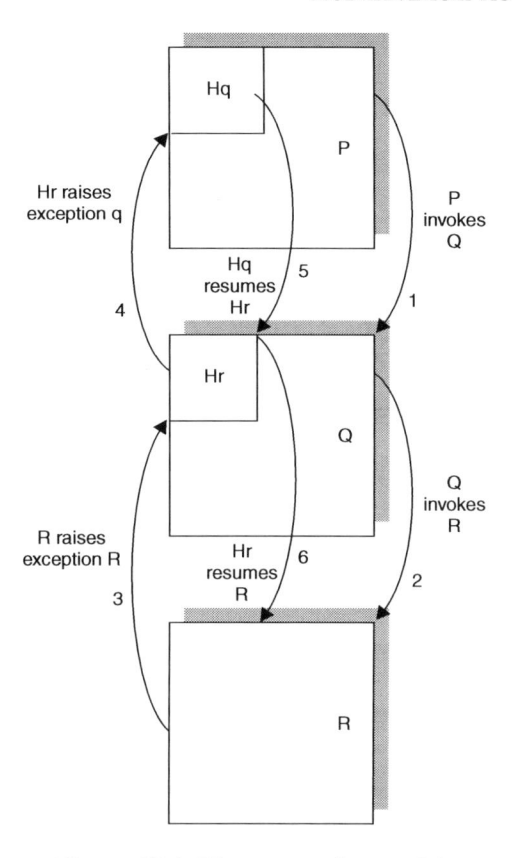

Figure 17.1: The resumption model.

When the handler is inside a block, control is given to the first statement following the block after the exception has been handled; as the following example shows.

```
declare
  subtype Temperature is Integer range 0 .. 100;
begin
  ...
  begin
    -- read temperature sensor and calculate its value,
    -- may result in an exception being raised
  exception
    -- handler for Constraint_Error for temperature,
    -- once handled this block terminates
  end;
  -- code here executed when block exits normally
  -- or when an exception has been raised and handled.
exception
  -- handler for other possible exceptions
end;
```

With procedures, as opposed to blocks, the flow of control can change quite dramatically,

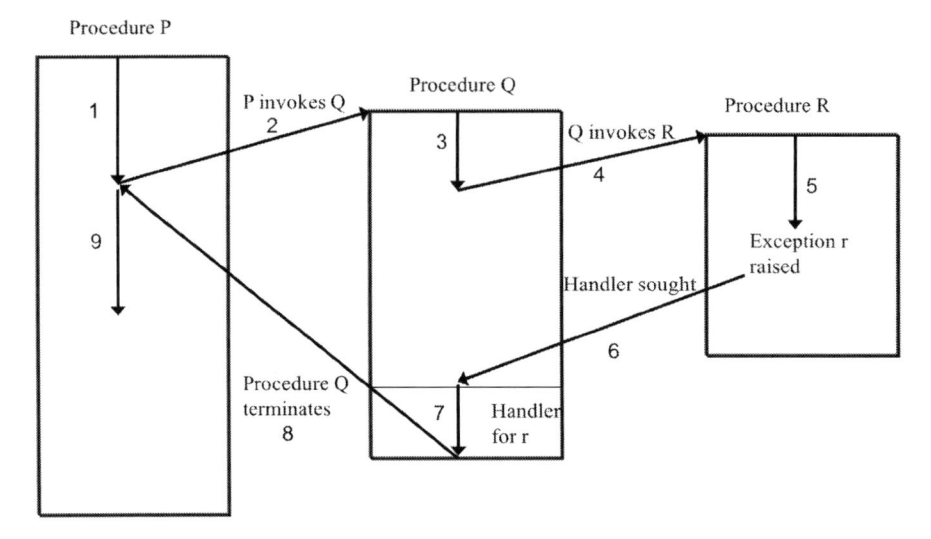

Figure 17.2: The termination model.

as Figure 17.2 illustrates. Again procedure P has invoked procedure Q, which has in turn called procedure R. An exception is raised in R and handled in Q.

Ada (and, for example, Java) supports the termination model of exception handling.

The hybrid model

With the hybrid model, it is up to the handler to decide whether the error is recoverable. If it is, the handler can return a value and the semantics are the same as in the resumption model. If the error is not recoverable, the invoker is terminated. The signal mechanisms of Mesa and Real-Time Basic provide such a facility. As noted before, Eiffel also supports the restricted 'retry' model.

Exception handling and operating systems

In many cases, a program in a language like Ada will be executed on top of an operating system such as Linux or Windows. These systems will detect certain synchronous error conditions; for example, memory violation or illegal instruction. Typically, this will result in the executing task being terminated. However, many systems allow the programmer to attempt error recovery. The recovery model supported by Linux, for instance, allows the programmer to handle these synchronous exceptions (via *signals*) by associating a handler with the exception. This handler is called by the system when the error condition is detected. Once the handler is finished, the task is resumed at the point where it was 'interrupted' – hence Linux supports the resumption model.

If a language supports the termination model, it is the responsibility of the run-time support system for that language to catch the error and undertake the necessary manipulation of program state so that the programmer can use the termination model.

17.3 Exception handling in Ada

The Ada language supports explicit exception declaration, the termination model of exception handling with propagation of unhandled exceptions, and a limited form of exception parameters.

Exception declaration

Exceptions in Ada are declared in the same fashion as constants; the type of constant being defined by the keyword **exception**. The following example declares an exception called Stuck_Valve.

```
Stuck_Valve : exception;
```

Every exception declared using the keyword **exception** has an associated Exception_Id that is supported by the predefined package Ada.Exceptions (see Program 17.2). This identity can be obtained using the pre-defined attribute Identity. The identity of the Stuck_Valve exception, given above, can be found by:

```
with Ada.Exceptions; use Ada;
with Valves;  -- for example
package My_Exceptions is
   Id : Exceptions.Exception_Id := Valves.Stuck_Valve'Identity;
end My_Exceptions;
```

assuming that Stuck_Valve is declared in package Valves.

An exception can be declared in the same place as any other declaration and, like every other declaration, it has scope.

The language has several standard exceptions whose scopes are the whole program. These exceptions may be raised by the language's run-time support system in response to certain error conditions. They include:

- Constraint_Error
  This is raised, for example, when an attempt is made to assign a value to an object which is outside its declared range, when an access to an array is outside the array bounds, or when access using a null pointer is attempted. It is also raised by the execution of a predefined numeric operation that cannot deliver a correct result within the declared accuracy for real types. This includes the familiar divide by zero error.
- Storage_Error
  This is raised when the dynamic storage allocator is unable to fulfil a demand for storage because the physical limitations of the machine have been exhausted.

Raising an exception

As well as exceptions being raised by the environment in which the program executes, they may also be raised explicitly by the program using the **raise** statement. The following

```ada
package Ada.Exceptions is
  type Exception_Id is private;
    -- each exception has an associated identifier
  Null_Id : constant Exception_Id;
  function Exception_Name(Id : Exception_Id) return String;

  type Exception_Occurrence is limited private;
    -- each exception occurrence has an associated identifier
  type Exception_Occurrence_Access is
       access all Exception_Occurrence;
  Null_Occurrence : constant Exception_Occurrence;

  procedure Raise_Exception(E : in Exception_Id;
            Message : in String := "");
    -- raises the exception E and associates Message with
    -- the exception occurrence

  function Exception_Message(X : Exception_Occurrence)
           return String;
    -- allows the string passed by Raise_Exception to be accessed
    -- in the handler

  procedure Reraise_Occurrence(X : in Exception_Occurrence);
    -- re-raises the exception

  function Exception_Identity(X : Exception_Occurrence)
           return Exception_Id;
    -- returns the exception identifier of the exception

  function Exception_Name(X : Exception_Occurrence) return String;
    -- same as Exception_Name(Exception_Identity(X)).

  function Exception_Information(X : Exception_Occurrence)
           return String;
    -- the same as Exception_Message(X) but contains more details
    -- if the message comes from the implementation

  procedure Save_Occurrence(Target : out Exception_Occurrence;
                            Source : in Exception_Occurrence);
    -- allows assignment to objects of type Exception_Occurrence

  function Save_Occurrence(Source : Exception_Occurrence)
                    return Exception_Occurrence_Access;
    -- allows assignment to objects of type Exception_Occurrence
private
  ... -- not specified by the language
end Ada.Exceptions;
```

Program 17.2: The `Ada.Exceptions` pacakge.

example raises the exception `Io_Error` (which must have been previously declared and be in scope) if an I/O request produces device errors.

```
begin
  ...
  -- statements that request a device to perform some I/O
  if Io_Device_In_Error then
    raise Io_Error;
  end if;
  ...
end;
```

Notice that no `else` part of the `if` statement is required because control is *not* returned to the statement following the raise.

If `Io_Error` had been declared as an `Exception_Id`, it would have been necessary to raise the exception using the procedure `Ada.Exceptions.Raise_Exception`. This would also have allowed a textual string to be passed as a parameter to the exception.

Each individual raising of an exception is called an exception **occurrence** and is represented by a value of type `Ada.Exceptions.Exception_Occurrence`. When an exception is handled, the value of the `Exception_Occurrence` can be found and used to determine more information about the cause of the exception.

Exception handling

Every block in Ada (and every subprogram and task) can contain an optional collection of exception handlers. These are declared at the end of the block (or subprogram or task). Each handler is a sequence of statements. Preceding the sequence are: the keyword **when**, an optional parameter (to which the identity of the exception occurrence will be assigned), the names of the exceptions which are to be serviced by the handler, and the symbol =>. For example, the following block declares three exceptions and provides two handlers.

```
declare
  Sensor_High, Sensor_Low, Sensor_Dead : exception;
  -- other declarations
begin
  -- statements that may cause the above exceptions
  -- to be raised
exception
  when E: Sensor_High | Sensor_Low =>
    -- Take some corrective action
    -- if either Sensor_High or Sensor_Low is raised.
    -- E contains the exception occurrence
  when Sensor_Dead =>
    -- sound an alarm if the exception
    -- Sensor_Dead is raised
end;
```

To avoid enumerating all possible exception names, Ada provides a **when others** handler name. This is only allowed as the last exception-handling choice and stands for all exceptions not previously listed in the current collection of handlers. For example, the

382 EXCEPTIONS AND EXCEPTION HANDLING

following block prints out information about the exception, and sounds an alarm when any exception except `Sensor_Low` or `Sensor_High` is raised (including `Sensor_Dead`).

```
declare
   Sensor_High, Sensor_Low, Sensor_Dead : exception;
   -- other declarations
   use Text_Io;
begin
   -- statements that may cause the above exceptions
   -- to be raised
exception
   when Sensor_High | Sensor_Low =>
     -- take some corrective action
   when E: others  =>
     Put(Exception_Name(E));
     Put_Line(" caught. The following information is available ");
     Put_Line(Exception_Information(E));
     -- sound an alarm
end;
```

An exception raised in an exception handler cannot be handled by that handler or other handlers in the same block (or procedure). Instead, the block is terminated and a handler sought in the surrounding block or at the point of call for a subprogram.

Exception propagation

If there is no exception handler in the enclosing block (or subprogram), the exception is raised again. Ada thus **propagates** exceptions. In the case of a block, this results in the exception being raised in the enclosing block, or subprogram. In the case of a subprogram, the exception is raised at its point of call.

A common misconception with Ada is that exception handlers can be provided in the initialization section of packages to handle exceptions that are raised in the execution of their nested subprograms. An exception raised and *not* handled by a subprogram is propagated to the *caller* of the subprogram. Therefore, such an exception will only be handled by the initialization code if it itself called the subprogram. The following example illustrates this point.

```
package Temperature_Control is
   subtype Temperature is Integer range 0 .. 100;
   Sensor_Dead, Actuator_Dead : exception;

   procedure Set_Temperature(New_Temp : in Temperature);
      -- raises Actuator_Dead
   function Read_Temperature return Temperature;
      -- raises Sensor_Dead
end Temperature_Control;

package body Temperature_Control is
   procedure Set_Temperature(New_Temp : in Temperature) is
   begin
      -- inform actuator of new temperature
```

```ada
      if No_Response then
         raise Actuator_Dead;
      end if;
   end Set_Temperature;

   function Read_Temperature return Temperature is
   begin
      -- read sensor
      if No_Response then
         raise Sensor_Dead;
      end if;
      -- calculate temperature
      return Reading;
   exception
      when Constraint_Error =>
         -- the temperature has gone outside
         -- its expected range;
         -- take some appropriate action
   end Read_Temperature;
begin
   -- initialization of package
   Set_Temperature(Initial_Reading);
exception
   when Actuator_Dead =>
      -- take some corrective action
end Temperature_Control;
```

In this example, the procedure Set_Temperature, which can be called from outside the package, is also called during the initialization of the package. This procedure may raise the exception Actuator_Dead. The handler for Actuator_Dead given in the initialization section of the package *will only catch the exception when the procedure is called from the initialization code*. It will not catch the exception when the procedure is called from outside the package.

If the code which initialized a package body itself raises an exception which is not handled locally, the exception is propagated to the point where the package came into scope.

Last wishes

An exception can also be propagated by a program re-raising the exception in the local handler. The statement **raise** (or the procedure Ada.Exceptions.Reraise_Occurrence) has the effect of re-raising the last exception (or the specific exception occurrence). This facility is useful in the programming of **last wishes**. Here it is often the case that the significance of an exception is unknown to the local handler, but must be handled in order to clean up any partial resource allocation that may have occurred previous to the exception being raised. For example, consider a procedure that allocates several devices. Any exception raised during the allocation routine, which is propagated directly to the caller, may leave some devices allocated. The allocator, therefore, wishes to deallocate the associated devices if it has not been possible to allocate the full request. The following illustrates this approach.

```ada
subtype Devices is Integer range 1 .. Max;

procedure Allocate (Number :  Devices) is
begin
  -- request each device be allocated in turn
  -- noting which requests are granted
exception
  when others   =>
    -- deallocate those devices allocated
    raise; -- re-raise the exception
end Allocate;
```

Used in this way, the procedure can be considered to implement the failure atomicity property of an atomic action; all the resources are allocated or none are (see Chapter 18).

As a further illustration, consider a procedure which sets the positions of slats and flaps on the wings of a fly-by-wire aircraft during its landing phase. These alter the amount of lift on the plane; asymmetrical wing settings on landing (or take-off) will cause the plane to become unstable. Assuming that the initial settings are symmetrical, the following procedure ensures that they remain symmetrical, even if an exception is raised – either as a result of a failure of the physical system or because of a program error [2].

```ada
procedure Wing_Settings ( -- relevant parameters) is
begin
  -- carry out the required setting
  -- of slats and flaps;
  -- exceptions may be raised
exception
  when others   =>
    -- ensure the settings are symmetrical
    -- re-raise exception to indicate
    -- a slatless and flapless landing
    raise;
end Wing_Settings;
```

Ada allows an alternative mechanism for programming last wishes using controlled types (see Section 9.4.4). With these types, it is possible to define subprograms that are called (automatically) when objects of the type:

- are created – *initialize*;
- cease to exist – *finalize*;
- are assigned a new value – *adjust*.

To gain access to these features, the type must be derived from Controlled, a predefined type declared in the library package Ada.Finalization. The package defines procedures for Initialize, Finalize and Adjust. When a type is derived from controlled, these procedures may be overridden.

---

[2] This, of course, is a crude example used to illustrate an approach; it is not necessarily the approach that would be taken in practice.

To use controlled types to support last wishes requires a dummy controlled variable to be declared in the procedure. The finalization procedure can then be used to ensure a termination condition in the presence of exceptions. In the above example, it would ensure that the slats and flaps have a symmetrical setting. Note that the `Finalize` procedure is executed in both normal and exceptional terminations.

Suppressing exceptions

There is an aphorism which has become popular with programmers; it normally takes the form: 'there is no such thing as a free lunch!'. One of the requirements for exception handling facilities was that they should not incur run-time overheads unless exceptions were raised (R3). The facilities provided by Ada have been described, and on the surface they appear to meet this requirement. However, there will always be some overhead associated with detecting possible error conditions.

For example, Ada provides a standard exception called `Constraint_Error` that is raised when a null pointer is used, or where there is an array bound error, or where an object is assigned a value outside its permissible range. In order to catch these error conditions, a compiler must generate appropriate code. For instance, when an object is being accessed through a pointer, a compiler will, in the absence of any global flow control analysis (or hardware support), insert code which tests to see if the pointer is null before accessing the object. Although hidden from the programmer, this code will be executed even when no exception is to be raised. If a program uses many pointers, this can result in a significant overhead both in terms of execution time and code size. Furthermore, the presence of the code may require it to be tested during any validation process, and this may be difficult to do.

The Ada language does recognize that the standard exceptions raised by the run-time environment may be too costly for a particular application. Consequently, it provides a facility by which these checks can be suppressed. This is achieved by use of the `Suppress` pragma which eliminates a whole range of run-time checks. The pragma affects only the compilation unit in which it appears. Of course, if a run-time error check is suppressed and subsequently the error occurs, then the language considers the program to be 'erroneous' and the subsequent behaviour of the program is undefined.

A full example

The following package illustrates the use of exceptions in an abstract data type which implements a single `Stack`. This example was chosen as it enables the full specification and body to be given without leaving anything to the reader's imagination. The package is generic and, therefore, can be instantiated for different types.

```
generic
  Size : Natural := 100;
  type Item is private;
package Stack is
  Stack_Full, Stack_Empty : exception;
```

386 EXCEPTIONS AND EXCEPTION HANDLING

```ada
  procedure Push(X:in Item);
  procedure Pop(X:out Item);

end Stack;

package body Stack is
  type Stack_Index is new Integer range 0 .. Size-1;
  type Stack_Array is array(Stack_Index) of Item;
  type Stack is
    record
      S : Stack_Array;
      Sp : Stack_Index := 0;
    end record;
  Stk : Stack;

  procedure Push(X:in Item) is
  begin
    if Stk.Sp = Stack_Index'Last then
      raise Stack_Full;
    end if;
    Stk.Sp :=Stk.Sp + 1;
    Stk.S(Stk.Sp) := X;
  end Push;

  procedure Pop(X:out Item) is
  begin
    if Stk.Sp = Stack_Index'First then
      raise Stack_Empty;
    end if;
    X := Stk.S(Stk.Sp);
    Stk.Sp := Stk.Sp - 1;
  end Pop;
end Stack;
```

It may be used as follows:

```ada
with Stack;
with Text_Io;
procedure Use_Stack is
  package Integer_Stack is new Stack(Item => Integer);
  X : Integer;
  use Integer_Stack;
begin
  ...
  Push(X);
  ...
  Pop(X);
  ...
exception
  when Stack_Full =>
    Text_Io.Put_Line("stack overflow!");
  when Stack_Empty =>
    Text_Io.Put_Line("stack empty!");
end Use_Stack;
```

Difficulties with the Ada model of exceptions

Although the Ada language provides a comprehensive set of facilities for exception handling, there are some difficulties with its ease of use.

(1) **Exceptions and packages**. Exceptions that can be raised by the use of a package are declared in the package specification along with any subprograms that can be called. Unfortunately, it is not obvious which subprograms can raise which exceptions. If the users of the package are unaware of its implementation, they must attempt to associate the names of exceptions with the subprogram names. In the stack example given above, the user could assume that the exception Stack_Full is raised by the procedure Pop and not Push! For large packages, it may not be obvious which exceptions can be raised by which subprograms. The programmer in this case must resort to either enumerating all possible exceptions every time a subprogram is called, or to the use of **when others**. Writers of packages should therefore indicate which subprograms can raise which exceptions using comments.

(2) **Parameter passing**. Ada does not allow a full range of parameters to be passed to handlers only a character string. This can be inconvenient if an object of a particular type needs to be passed.

(3) **Scope and propagation**. It is possible for exceptions to be propagated outside the scope of their declaration. Such exceptions can only be trapped by **when others**. However, they may go back into scope again when propagated further up the dynamic chain. This is disconcerting, although probably inevitable when using a block structured language and exception propagation.

17.4 Recovery blocks and exceptions

In Chapter 3, the notion of recovery blocks was introduced as a mechanism for fault-tolerant programming. Its main advantage over forward error recovery mechanisms is that it can be used to recover from unanticipated errors, particularly from errors in the design of software components. So far in this chapter, only anticipated errors have been considered, although catch-all exception handlers can be used to trap unknown exceptions. In this section, the implementation of recovery blocks using exceptions and exception handlers is described.

As a reminder, the structure of a recovery block is shown below:

```
ensure <acceptance test>
by
  <primary module>
else by
  <alternative module>
else by
  <alternative module>
  ...
else by
  <alternative module>
else error
```

388 EXCEPTIONS AND EXCEPTION HANDLING

The error detection facility is provided by the acceptance test. This test is simply the negation of a test which would raise an exception using forward error recovery. The only problem is the implementation of state saving and state restoration. In the example below, this is shown as an Ada package which implements a recovery cache. The procedure `Save` stores the state of the global and local variables of the program in the recovery cache; this does not include the values of the program counter, stack pointer and so on. A call of `Restore` will reset the program variables to the states saved. A call to `Discard` will delete the saved values.

```ada
package Recovery_Cache is
  procedure Save;
  procedure Restore;
  procedure Discard;
end Recovery_Cache;
```

Clearly, there is some magic going on inside the package which will require support from the run-time system and possibly even hardware support for the recovery cache. Also, this may not be the most efficient way to perform state restoration. It may be more desirable to provide more basic primitives, and to allow the program to use its knowledge of the application to optimize the amount of information saved [71].

The purpose of the next example is to show that given recovery cache implementation techniques, recovery blocks can be used in an exception handling environment. Notice also that by using exception handlers, forward error recovery can be achieved before restoring the state. This overcomes a criticism of recovery blocks: that it is difficult to reset the environment.

The recovery block scheme can, therefore, be implemented using a language with exceptions plus a bit of help from the underlying run-time support system. For example, in Ada the structure for a triple redundant recovery block would be:

```ada
procedure Recovery_Block is
  Primary_Failure, Secondary_Failure,
        Tertiary_Failure: exception;
  Recovery_Block_Failure : exception;
  type Module is (Primary, Secondary, Tertiary);
  function Acceptance_Test return Boolean is
  begin
     -- code for the acceptance test
  end Acceptance_Test;

  procedure Primary is
  begin
    -- code for primary algorithm
    if not Acceptance_Test then
      raise Primary_Failure;
    end if;
  exception
    when Primary_Failure   =>
      -- forward recovery code here to return environment
      -- to the required state
      raise;
    when others   =>
```

```ada
      -- unexpected error
      -- forward recovery code here to return environment
      -- to the required state
      raise Primary_Failure;
end Primary;

procedure Secondary is
begin
  -- code for secondary algorithm
  if not Acceptance_Test then
    raise Secondary_Failure;
  end if;
exception
  when Secondary_Failure =>
    -- forward recovery code here
    raise;
  when others =>
    -- unexpected error
    -- forward recovery code here
    raise Secondary_Failure;
end Secondary;

procedure Tertiary is
begin
  -- code for tertiary algorithm
  if not Acceptance_Test then
    raise Tertiary_Failure;
  end if;
exception
  when Tertiary_Failure =>
    -- forward recovery to return environment
    -- to the required state
    raise;
  when others =>
    -- unexpected error
    -- forward recovery to return environment
    -- to the required state
    raise Tertiary_Failure;
end Tertiary;

begin
  Recovery_Cache.Save;
  for Try in Module loop
    begin
      case Try is
        when Primary => Primary; exit;
        when Secondary => Secondary; exit;
        when Tertiary => Tertiary;
      end case;
    exception
      when Primary_Failure =>
        Recovery_Cache.Restore;
      when Secondary_Failure =>
```

```
            Recovery_Cache.Restore;
      when Tertiary_Failure =>
            Recovery_Cache.Restore;
            raise Recovery_Block_Failure;
      when others =>
            Recovery_Cache.Restore;
            raise Recovery_Block_Failure;
    end;
  end loop;
  Recovery_Cache.Discard;
end Recovery_Block;
```

17.5 The real-time impact of exception handling

The occurrence of exceptions and the execution of the handlers may increase the worst-case execution time of a task. Where the presence of exception is routinely expected, the worst-case execution time analysis must take into account the additional flow controls than are generated. Thus the worst-case values used in schedulability analysis include provisions for the raising and handling of exceptions.

If the raising of an exception is a rare occurrence then, as indicated in Section 7.4, the handling must be included as part of the fault model that the application assumes. See Section 7.4 for how such a fault model can be incorporated in the schedulability analysis.

Of course, the raising of exception may not impact on the worst-case behaviour but instead decrease the quality of service provided.

Summary

This chapter has studied the various models of exception handling for sequential tasks. Although many different models exist they all address the following issues.

- Exception representation – an exception may, or may not, be explicitly represented in a language.
- The domain of an exception handler – associated with each handler is a domain which specifies the region of computation during which, if an exception occurs, the handler will be activated. The domain is normally associated with a block, subprogram or a statement.
- Exception propagation – this is closely related to the idea of an exception domain. It is possible that when an exception is raised there is no exception handler in the enclosing domain. In this case, either the exception can be propagated to the next outer level enclosing domain, or it can be considered to be a programmer error (which can often be flagged at compilation time).
- Resumption or termination model – this determines the action to be taken after an exception has been handled. With the resumption model, the invoker of the exception is resumed at the statement after the one at which the exception was invoked. With the termination model, the block or procedure containing the handler is terminated, and control is passed to the

Language	Domain	Propagation	Model	Parameters
Ada	Block	Yes	Termination	Limited
Java	Block	Yes	Termination	Yes
C++	Block	Yes	Termination	Yes
CHILL	Statement	No	Termination	No
CLU	Statement	No	Termination	Yes
Mesa	Block	Yes	Hybrid	Yes
Python	Block	Yes	Termination	Yes

Table 17.1: The exception-handling facilities of various languages.

calling block or procedure. The hybrid model enables the handler to choose whether to resume or to terminate.

- Parameter passing to the handler – may or may not be allowed.

The exception handling facilities of various languages are summarized in Table 17.1.

It is not unanimously accepted that exception-handling facilities should be provided in a language. To sceptics, an exception is a `goto` where the destination is undeterminable and the source is unknown. They can, therefore, be considered to be the antithesis of structured programming. This, however, is not the view taken in this book.

Chapter 18
Atomic actions, concurrent processes and reliability

18.1 Atomic actions
18.2 Atomic actions in Ada
18.3 Recoverable atomic actions
18.4 Asynchronous notification
18.5 Asynchronous notification in Ada
18.6 Atomic actions and scheduling analysis
Summary

Chapter 3 considered how reliable software could be produced in the presence of a variety of errors. Modular decomposition and atomic actions were identified as two techniques essential for damage confinement and assessment. Also, the notions of forward and backward error recovery were introduced as approaches to dynamic error recovery. It was shown that where tasks communicate and synchronize their activities, backward error recovery may lead to the domino effect. In Chapter 17, exception handling was discussed as a mechanism for providing both forward and backward error recovery in sequential tasks. This chapter brings together exception handling and concurrency in order to show how tasks can interact reliably in the presence of other tasks and in the presence of faults. The notion of an atomic action is explored in more detail and the concept of asynchronous notification is introduced.

In Chapter 10, the interaction of tasks was described in terms of three types of behaviour:

- independent,
- cooperation, and
- competition.

Independent tasks do not communicate or synchronize with each other. Consequently, if an error occurs within one task, then recovery procedures can be initiated by that task in isolation from the rest of the system. Recovery blocks and exception handling can be used as described in Chapters 3 and 17.

Cooperating tasks, by comparison, regularly communicate and synchronize their activities in order to perform some common operation. If any error condition occurs, it is necessary for all tasks involved to perform error recovery. The programming of such error recovery is the topic of this chapter.

Competing tasks communicate and synchronize in order to obtain resources; they are, however, essentially, independent. An error in one should have no effect on the others. Unfortunately, this is not always the case, particularly if the error occurred while a task was in the act of being allocated a resource. Reliable resource allocation was considered in Chapter 12.

Where cooperating tasks communicate and synchronize through shared resources, recovery may involve the resource itself. This aspect of resource allocation was also considered in Chapter 12.

18.1 Atomic actions

One of the main motivations for introducing concurrent tasks into a language is that they enable parallelism in the real world to be reflected in application programs. This enables such programs to be expressed in a more natural way and leads to the production of more reliable and maintainable systems. Disappointingly, however, concurrent tasks create many new problems which did not exist in the purely sequential program. Consequently, Chapter 11 was dedicated to discussing some of the solutions to these problems: in particular, communication and synchronization between tasks using shared variables (correctly). This was undertaken in a fairly isolated manner and no consideration has yet been given to the way in which groups of concurrent tasks should be structured in order to coordinate their activities.

The interaction between two tasks has, so far, been expressed in terms of a single communication. In reality, this is not always the case. For example, withdrawal from a bank account may involve a ledger task and a payment task in a sequence of communications to authenticate the drawer, check the balance and pay the money. Furthermore, it may be necessary for more than two tasks to interact in this way to perform the required action. In all such situations, it is imperative that the tasks involved see a consistent system state. With concurrent tasks, it is all too easy for groups of tasks to interfere with one other.

What is required is for each group of tasks to execute their joint activity as an **indivisible**, or **atomic**, action. Of course, a single task may also want to protect itself from the interference of other tasks (for example, during resource allocation). It follows that an atomic action may involve one or more tasks. Atomic actions have also been called *multiparty* interactions [36, 83].

There are several almost equivalent ways of expressing the properties of an atomic action [59, 69].

(1) An action is atomic if the tasks performing it are not aware of the existence of any other active task, and no other active task is aware of the activity of the tasks during the time the tasks are performing the action.

(2) An action is atomic if the tasks performing it do not communicate with other tasks while the action is being performed.

(3) An action is atomic if the tasks performing it can detect no state change except those performed by themselves and if they do not reveal their

state changes until the action is complete.
(4) Actions are atomic if they can be considered, so far as other tasks are concerned, to be indivisible and instantaneous, such that the effects on the system are as if they were interleaved as opposed to concurrent.

These are not quite all equivalent. For example, consider the second expression: an action is atomic if the tasks performing it communicate only among themselves and not with other tasks in the system. Unlike the other three, this does not really define the true nature of an atomic action. While it will guarantee that the action is indivisible, it is too strong a constraint on the tasks. Interactions between an atomic action and the rest of the system can be allowed as long as they have no impact on the activity of the atomic action and do not provide the rest of the system with any information concerning the progress of the action [3]. In general, in order to allow such interactions requires detailed knowledge of the atomic action's function and its interface to the rest of the system. As this cannot be supported by a general language implementation, it is tempting, following Anderson and Lee [3], to adopt the more restrictive (second) definition. This can only be done, however, if the resources necessary to complete an atomic action are acquired by the underlying implementation, not by instructions given in the program. If resources are to be acquired and released when the programmer desires, tasks within atomic actions will have to communicate with general-purpose resource managers.

Although an atomic action is viewed as being indivisible, it can have an internal structure. To allow modular decomposition of atomic actions, the notion of a **nested atomic action** is introduced. The tasks involved in a nested action must be a subset of those involved in the outer level of the action. If this were not the case, a nested action could smuggle information concerning the outer level action to an external task. The outer level action would then no longer be indivisible.

18.1.1 Two-phase atomic actions

Ideally, all tasks involved in an atomic action should obtain the resources they require (for the duration of the action) prior to its commencement. These resources could then be released after the atomic action had terminated. If these rules were followed, there would be no need for an atomic action to interact with any external entity and the stricter definition of atomic action could be adopted.

Unfortunately, this ideal can lead to poor resource utilization, and hence a more pragmatic approach is needed. Firstly, it is necessary to allow an atomic action to start without its full complement of resources. At some point, a task within the action will request a resource allocation; the atomic action must then communicate with the resource manager. This manager may be a server task. If a strict definition of atomic action is adhered to, this server would have to form part of the atomic action, with the effect of serializing all actions involving the server. Clearly, this is undesirable, and hence an atomic action is allowed to communicate externally with resource servers.

Within this context, a resource server is defined to be a custodian of non-sharable system utilities. It protects these utilities against inappropriate access, but does not, itself, perform any actions upon them.

A further improvement in resource allocation can be made if a task is allowed to release a resource prior to completion of the associated atomic action. In order for this premature release to make sense, the state of the resource must be identical to that which would appertain if the resource was retained until completion of the atomic action. Its early release will, however, enhance the concurrency of the whole system.

If resources are to be obtained late and released early it could be possible for an external state change to be affected by a released resource and observed by the acquisition of a new resource. This would break the definition of atomic action. It follows that the only safe policy for resource usage is one that has two distinct phases. In the first 'growing' phase, resources can be requested (only); in the following 'shrinking' phase, resources can be released (but no new allocations can be made). With such a structure, the integrity of the atomic action is assured. However, it should be noted that if resources are released early then it will be more difficult to provide recovery if the atomic action fails. This is because the resource has been updated and another task may have observed the new state of the resource. Any attempt to invoke recovery in the other task may lead to the domino effect (see Section 3.5.3).

In all the following discussions, atomic actions are assumed to be two-phased; recoverable actions do not release any resources until the action successfully completes.

18.1.2 Atomic transactions

Within the theories of operating systems and databases, the term **atomic transaction** is often used. An atomic transaction has all the properties of an atomic action plus the added feature that its execution is allowed either to succeed or fail. By failure, it is meant that an error has occurred from which the transaction cannot recover; for example, a processor failure. If an atomic action fails then the components of the system, which are being manipulated by the action, may be left in an inconsistent state. With an atomic transaction, this cannot happen because the components are returned to their original state (that is, the state they were *before* the transaction commenced). Atomic transactions are sometimes called **recoverable actions** and, unfortunately, the terms **atomic action** and **atomic transaction** are often interchanged.

The two distinctive properties of atomic transactions are:

- failure atomicity; meaning that the transaction must either complete successfully or (in the case of failure) have no effect;
- synchronization atomicity (or isolation); meaning that the transaction is indivisible in the sense that its partial execution cannot be observed by any concurrently executing transaction.

Although atomic transactions are useful for those applications which involve the manipulation of databases, they are not suitable for programming fault-tolerant systems *per se*. This is because they imply that some form of recovery mechanism will be supplied by the system. Such a mechanism would be fixed, with the programmer having no control over its operation. Although atomic transactions provide a form of backward error recovery, they do not allow recovery procedures to be performed. Notwithstanding these points, atomic transactions do have a role in protecting the integrity of a real-time database system.

18.1.3 Requirements for atomic actions

If a real-time programming language is to be capable of supporting atomic actions, it must be possible to express the requirements necessary for their implementation. These requirements are independent of the notion of a task and the form of intertask communication provided by a language. They are the following.

- **Well-defined boundaries**

    Each atomic action should have a start, an end and a side boundary. The start boundary is the location in each task involved in the atomic action where the action is deemed to start. The end boundary is the location in each task involved in the atomic action where the action is deemed to end. The side boundary separates those tasks involved in the atomic action from those in the rest of the system.

- **Indivisibility (Isolation)**

    An atomic action must not allow the exchange of any information between the tasks active inside the action and those outside (resource managers excluded). If two atomic actions do share data then the value of that data after the atomic actions is determined by the strict sequencing of the two actions in some order.

    There is no implied synchronization at the start of an atomic action. Tasks can enter at different times. However, there is an implied synchronization at the end of an atomic action; tasks are not allowed to leave the atomic action until all tasks are willing and able to leave.

- **Nesting**

    Atomic actions may be nested as long as they do not overlap with other atomic actions. Consequently, in general, only strict nesting is allowed (two structures are strictly nested if one is completely contained within the other).

- **Concurrency**

    It should be possible to execute different atomic actions concurrently. One way to enforce indivisibility is to run atomic actions sequentially. However, this could seriously impair the performance of the overall system and therefore should be avoided. Nevertheless, the overall effect of running a collection of atomic actions concurrently must be the same as that which would be obtained from serializing their executions.

- As it is the intention that atomic actions should form the basis of damage confinement, they must allow recovery procedures to be programmed.

Figure 18.1 diagrammatically represents the boundaries of a nested atomic action in a system of 6 tasks. Action B involves only tasks T3 and T4, whereas action A also includes T2 and T5. The other tasks (T1 and T6) are outside the boundaries of both atomic actions.

It, perhaps, should be noted at this point, that some definitions of atomic actions require that all tasks be synchronized on *both* entry and exit of the action.

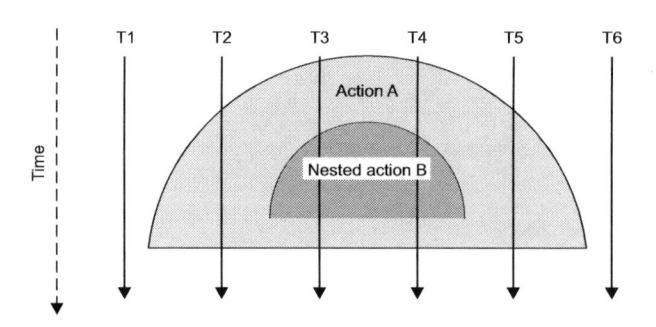

Figure 18.1: Nested atomic actions.

18.2 Atomic actions in Ada

Atomic actions provide structuring support for the software of large embedded systems. To get the full benefit of this aid requires the support of the real-time language. Unfortunately, such support is not directly provided by any of the major languages. This section considers the suitability of Ada for programming atomic actions. Following this, a possible language framework is given, and then this framework is extended to provide forward and backward error recovery.

The problem of resource allocation has already been considered in Chapter 12. Here, it is assumed that resources have two modes of use: sharable and non-sharable, with some resources being amenable to both sharable and non-sharable modes. Furthermore, it is assumed that all actions are two-phased, and that the resource manager will ensure that appropriate usage is made of the resources. Also tasks within an action synchronize their own access to the resource to avoid any interference.

Atomic actions could be encapsulated within Ada's protected objects. However, this would not allow any parallelism within an action. Hence, an alternative approach is adopted. In a similar fashion to the solution to the reader/writers problem presented in Section 11.2, the entry and exit protocols are implemented by a protected object, and then the application code is surrounded by calls to the protected routines. Figure 18.2 illustrates an atomic action that requires three tasks (T1, T2, and T3). Each task has its own role to play in the action. These roles and represented by the action procedures: for example, Task T1 calls `Action Procedure_1` etc. These action procedures then liaise with an action controller to provide the required synchronization. Figure 18.3 shows the structure of the roles.

The Ada approach to implementing an atomic action is illustrated below for a three task system. Here, the action is encapsulated within an Ada package

```
package Action_X is
  procedure Action_Procedure_1(--params);
  procedure Action_Procedure_2(--params);
  procedure Action_Procedure_3(--params);
end Action_X;
```

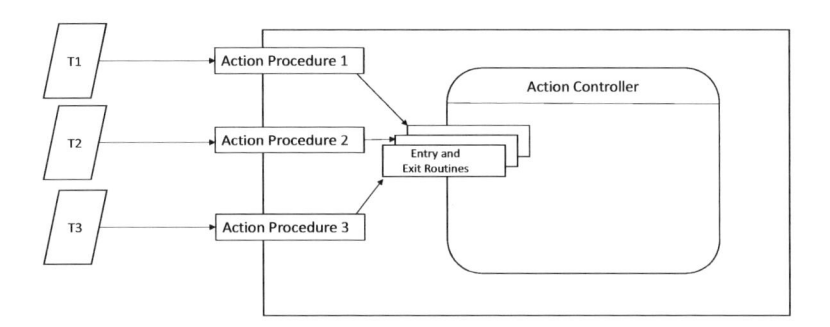

Figure 18.2: The structure of an action controller.

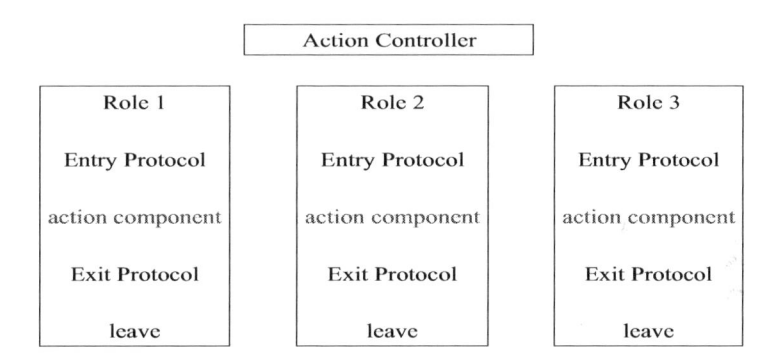

Figure 18.3: Using the action controller.

The body of the package contains the action controller, which is implemented as a protected type.

```
package body Action_X is
  protected Action_Controller is
    entry First;
    entry Second;
    entry Third;
    entry Finished;
  private
    First_Here : Boolean := False;
    Second_Here : Boolean := False;
    Third_Here : Boolean := False;
    Release : Boolean := False;
  end Action_Controller;
```

```ada
protected body Action_Controller is
  entry First when not First_Here is
  begin
    First_Here := True;
  end First;

  entry Second when not Second_Here is
  begin
    Second_Here := True;
  end Second;

  entry Third when not Third_Here is
  begin
    Third_Here := True;
  end Third;

  entry Finished when Release or Finished'Count = 3 is
  begin
    if Finished'Count = 0 then
      Release := False;
      First_Here := False;
      Second_Here := False;
      Third_Here := False;
    else
      Release := True;
    end if;
  end Finished;
end Action_Controller;
```

In the above code, the action is synchronized by the `Action_Controller` protected object. This ensures that only three tasks can be active in the action at any one time and that they are synchronized on exit. The boolean `Release` is used to program the required release conditions on `Finished`. The first two calls on `Finished` will be blocked as both parts of the barrier expression are false. When the third call comes, the `Count` attribute will become three; the barrier becomes open and one task will execute the entry body. The `Release` variable ensures that the other two tasks are both released. The last task to exit must ensure that the barrier is closed again.

The structure of the application code is given below.

```ada
  procedure Action_Procedure_1(--params) is
  begin
    Action_Controller.First;
    -- acquire resources
    -- the action itself, communicates with tasks executing
    -- inside the action via resources
    Action_Controller.Finished;
    -- release resources
  end Action_Procedure_1;

  -- similar for second and third task
begin
  -- any initialization of local resources
end Action_X;
```

More details on how to program atomic actions in Ada can be found in Wellings and Burns [80].

18.3 Recoverable atomic actions

Although the approach described above has enabled a simple atomic action to be expressed, it relies on programmer discipline to ensure that no interactions with external tasks occur (apart from with resource allocators). Moreover, it assumes that no task within an atomic action is aborted; if the real-time language supports an abort facility (as Ada does) then a task could be asynchronously removed from the action leaving the action in an inconsistent state.

In general, none of the mainstream concurrent languages or operating systems directly support backward or forward error recovery facilities in the context of atomic actions. (However, Ada does provide asynchronous notification mechanisms which can be used to help program recovery – see Section 18.5.) Language mechanisms have been proposed in research-oriented systems. In order to discuss these mechanisms, a simple language framework for atomic actions is introduced. The proposed recovery mechanisms are then discussed in the context of this framework.

To simplify the framework, only static tasks will be considered. Also it will be assumed that all the tasks taking part in an atomic action are known at compile time. Each task involved in an action declares an action statement which specifies: the action name, the other tasks taking part in the action, and the code to be executed by the declaring task on entry to the action. For example a task T_1 which wishes to enter into an atomic action A with tasks T_2 and T_3 would declare the following action:

```
action A with (T₂, T₃) do
    -- acquire resources
    -- communicate with T₂ and T₃
    -- release resources
end A;
```

It is assumed that resource allocators are known and that communication inside the action is restricted to the three T tasks (together with external calls to the resource allocators). These restrictions are checked at compile time. All other tasks declare similar actions, and nested actions are allowed as long as strict nesting is observed. Note that if the tasks are not known at compile time, then any communication with a task will be allowed only if both tasks are active in the same atomic action.

The imposed synchronization on the action is as follows. Tasks entering the action are not blocked. A task is blocked inside the action only if it has to wait for a resource to be allocated, or if it attempts to communicate with another task inside the action and that task is either active in the action, but not in a position to accept the communication, or is not as yet active in the action.

Tasks may leave the action only when all tasks active in the action wish to leave. This was not the case in the examples given earlier. There it was assumed that all tasks must enter the action before any could leave. Here it is possible for a subset of the named tasks to enter the action and subsequently leave (without recourse to any interactions with the missing tasks). This facility is deemed to be essential in a real-time system where deadlines are important. It solves the **deserter** problem where all tasks are held in an action because one task has not arrived. This issue will be considered along with error recovery in the next two subsections.

18.3.1 Atomic actions and backward error recovery

Atomic actions are important because they constrain the flow of information around the system to well-defined boundaries and therefore can provide the basis for both damage confinement and error recovery. In this section, backward error recovery between concurrent tasks is described.

In Chapter 3, it was shown that when backward error recovery is applied to groups of communicating tasks, it is possible for all the tasks to be rolled back to the start of their execution. This was the so-called *domino effect*. The problem occurred because there was no consistent set of recovery points or a recovery line. An atomic action provides that recovery line automatically. If an error occurs inside an atomic action then the tasks involved can be rolled back to the start of the action and alternative algorithms executed; the atomic action ensures that tasks have not passed any erroneous values through communication with tasks outside the action. When atomic actions are used in this way they are called **conversations** [66].

With conversations each action statement contains a recovery block. For example:

```
action A with (T₂, T₃) do
   ensure <acceptance test>
   by
      -- primary module
   else by
      -- alternative module
   else by
      -- alternative module
   else error
end A;
```

Other tasks involved in the conversation declare their part in the action similarly. The basic semantics of a conversation can be summarized as follows.

- On entry to the conversation, the state of a task is saved. The set of entry points forms the recovery line.
- While inside the conversation, a task is allowed only to communicate with other tasks active in the conversation and general resource managers. As conversations are built from atomic actions, this property is inherited.
- In order to leave the conversation, all tasks active in the conversation must have passed their acceptance test. If this is the case, then the conversation is finished and all recovery points are discarded.
- *If any task fails its acceptance test, all tasks have their state restored to that saved at the start of the conversation and they execute their alternative modules. It is,*

therefore, assumed that any error recovery to be performed inside a conversation *must* be performed by *all* tasks taking part in the conversation.
- Conversations can be nested, but only strict nesting is allowed.
- If all alternatives in the conversation fail then recovery must be performed at a higher level.

It should be noted that in conversations, as defined by Randell [66], all tasks taking part in the conversation must have entered the conversation before any of the other tasks can leave. This differs from the semantics described here. If a task does not enter into a conversation, either because of tardiness or because it has failed, then as long as the other tasks active in the conversation do not wish to communicate with it, the conversation can complete successfully. If a task does attempt to communicate with a missing task then either it can block and wait for the task to arrive or it can continue. Adopting this approach has two benefits [41].

- It allows conversations to be specified where participation is not compulsory.
- It allows tasks with deadlines to leave the conversation, continue and if necessary take some alternative action.

Although conversations allow groups of tasks to coordinate their recovery, they have been criticized. One important point is that when a conversation fails, all the tasks are restored and all enter their alternative modules. This forces the same tasks to communicate again to achieve the desired effect; a task cannot break out of the conversation. This may be not what is required. Gregory and Knight [41] point out that in practice when one task fails to achieve its goal in a primary module through communication with one group of tasks, it may wish to communicate with a completely new group of tasks in its secondary module. Furthermore, the acceptance test for this secondary module may be quite different. There is no way to express these requirements using conversations.

18.3.2 Atomic actions and forward error recovery

It was pointed out in Chapter 3, that although backward error recovery enables recovery from unanticipated errors, it is difficult to undo any operation that may have been performed in the environment in which the embedded system operates. Consequently forward error recovery and exception handling must be considered. In this section, exception handling between the concurrent tasks involved in an atomic action is discussed.

With backward error recovery, when an error occurs all tasks involved in the atomic action participate in recovery. The same is true with exception handling and forward error recovery. If an exception occurs in one of the tasks active in an atomic action then that exception is raised in *all* tasks active in the action. The exception is said to be **asynchronous** as it originates from another task. The following is a possible Ada-like syntax for an atomic action supporting exception handling.

```
action A with (P2, P3) do
   -- the action
exception
```

```
   when exception_a =>
      -- sequence of statements
   when exception_b =>
      -- sequence of statements
   when others =>
      raise atomic_action_failure;
end A;
```

With the termination model of exception handling, if all tasks active in the action have a handler and all handle the exception without raising any further exception, then the atomic action completes normally. If a resumption model is used, when the exception has been handled, the tasks active in the atomic action resume their execution at the point where the exception was raised.

With either model, if there is no exception handler *in any one of the tasks active in the action* or one of the handlers fails then *the atomic action fails* with a standard exception *atomic_action_failure*. This exception is raised in all the involved tasks.

There are two issues which must be considered when exception handling is added to atomic actions: resolution of concurrently raised exceptions and exceptions in nested actions [26]. These are now briefly reviewed.

Resolution of concurrently raised exceptions

It is possibly for more than one task active in an atomic action to raise different exceptions at the same time. As Campbell and Randell [26] point out, this event is likely if the errors resulting from some fault cannot be uniquely identified by the error detection facility provided by each component of the atomic action. If two exceptions are simultaneously raised in an atomic action, there may be two separate exception handlers in each task. It may be difficult to decide which one should be chosen. Furthermore, the two exceptions in conjunction constitute a third exception which is the exception that indicates that both the other two exceptional conditions have occurred.

In order to resolve concurrently raised exceptions, Campbell and Randell propose the use of an **exception tree**. If several exceptions are raised concurrently then the exception used to identify the handler is that at the root of the smallest subtree that contains all the exceptions (although it is not clear how to combine any parameters associated with this exception). Each atomic action component can declare its own exception tree; the different tasks involved in an atomic action may well have different exception trees.

Exceptions and internal atomic actions

Where atomic actions are nested, it is possible for one task active in an action to raise an exception when other tasks in the same action are involved in a nested action. Figure 18.4 illustrates the problem.

When the exception is raised, all tasks involved must participate in the recovery action. Unfortunately, the internal action, by definition, is indivisible. To raise the exception in that action would potentially compromise that indivisibility. Furthermore, the internal action may have no knowledge of the possible exceptions that can be raised.

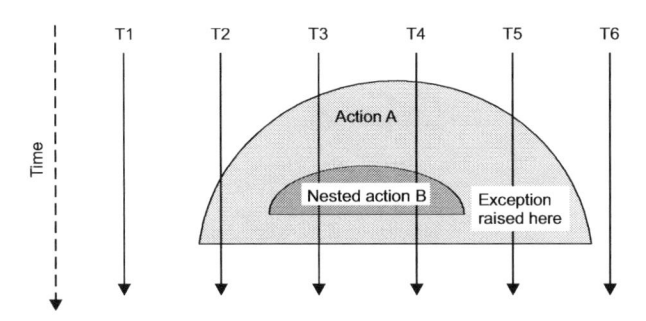

Figure 18.4: An exception in a nested atomic actions.

Campbell and Randell [26] have discussed two possible solutions to this problem. The first solution is to hold back the raising of the exception until the internal action has finished. This they reject because:

- In a real-time system, the exception being raised may be associated with the missing of a deadline. To hold back the recovery procedure may seriously place in jeopardy the action's timely response.
- The error condition detected may indicate that the internal action may never terminate because some deadlock condition has arisen.

For these reasons, Campbell and Randell allow internal actions to have a predefined abortion exception. This exception is raised to indicate to the action that an exception has been raised in a surrounding action and that the assumptions under which the action was invoked are no longer valid. If such an exception is raised, the internal action should invoke fault-tolerant measures to abort itself. Once the action has been aborted, the containing action can handle the original exception.

If the internal action cannot abort itself then it must signal an atomic action failure exception. This then may be combined with the outstanding exception so as to affect the choice of recovery performed by the surrounding action. If no abortion exception is defined, the surrounding action must wait for the internal action to complete. Alternatively, a default handler could be provided which would raise the atomic action failure exception.

18.4 Asynchronous notification

Although forward and backward error recovery have been discussed separately, in reality they may need to be combined in many real-time systems. Backward error recovery is needed to recover from unanticipated errors, and forward error recovery is needed to undo or ameliorate any interaction with the environment. Indeed, forward error handling can be used to implement a backward error recovery scheme – see Section 18.5.3.

As discussed in Section 18.2, none of the major real-time languages support atomic actions, and it is necessary to use more primitive language facilities to achieve the same effect. The same is true for recoverable actions. One of the main requirements for a recoverable action is to be able to gain the attention of a task involved in an action and notify it that an error has occurred in another task. Most languages and operating systems support some form of asynchronous notification mechanism. As with exceptions, there are two basic models: resumption and termination.

The resumption model of asynchronous notification handling (often called **event handling**) behaves like a software interrupt. A task indicates which events it is willing to handle; when the event is signalled, the task is interrupted (unless it has temporally inhibited the event from being delivered) and an event handler is executed. The handler responds to the asynchronous event and then the task continues with its execution from the point at which it was interrupted. This sounds very similar to the resumption model of exception handling given in Section 17.2.4. The main difference is that the event is usually *not* signalled by the affected task (or because of an operation the affected task is performing), but is signalled *asynchronously*. However, many operating systems do not provide a special exception handling facility for synchronous exception handling, but use the asynchronous events mechanisms instead. The C/Real-Time POSIX signal facility is an example of an asynchronous event model with resumption.

Note that, with the resumption model, the flow of control of a task is only temporarily changed; after the event has been handled the task is resumed. In a multithreaded process, it is possible to associate a distinct thread with the event and to schedule the thread when the event is signalled. Real-Time Java provides support for this model.

With the termination model of asynchronous notification, each task specifies a domain of execution during which it is prepared to receive an asynchronous notification that will cause the domain to be terminated. This form is often called **asynchronous transfer of control** or ATC. If an ATC request occurs outside this domain, it may be ignored or queued. After the ATC has been handled, control is returned to the interrupted task at a location different to that where the ATC was delivered. This, of course, is very similar to the termination model of exception handling. Ada supports asynchronous transfer of control mechanisms.

An extreme form of asynchronous notification with termination semantics is to abort the task and allow another task to perform some recovery. All operating systems and most concurrent programming languages provide such a facility. However, aborting an operating system process can be expensive and is often an extreme response to many error conditions. Aborting a operating system thread is less expensive but still potentially dangerous as it can leave resources in an undefined state. Consequently, some form of safe asynchronous notification mechanism is also required.

The inclusion of an asynchronous notification mechanism into a language (or operating system) is controversial, as it complicates the language's semantics and increases the complexity of the run-time support system. This section thus first considers the application requirements which justify the inclusion of such a facility. The Ada model of asynchronous notification is then discussed.

18.4.1 The user need for asynchronous notification

The fundamental requirement for an asynchronous notification facility is to enable a task to respond *quickly* to a condition which has been detected by another task. The emphasis here is on a quick response; clearly a task can always respond to an event by simply polling or waiting for that event. The notification of the event could be mapped onto the task's communication and synchronization mechanism. The handling task, when it is ready to receive the event, simply issues the appropriate request.

Unfortunately, there are occasions when polling for events or waiting for the event to occur is inadequate. These include the following:

- **Error recovery**

  This chapter has already emphasised that when groups of tasks undertake atomic actions, an error detected in one task requires all other tasks to participate in the recovery. For example, a hardware fault may mean that the task will never finish its planned execution because the preconditions under which it started no longer hold; the task may never reach its polling point. Also, a timing fault might have occurred, which means that the task will no longer meet the deadline for the delivery of its service. In both these situations, the task must be informed that an error has been detected and that it must undertake some error recovery as quickly as possible. Recovery from timing faults will be considered in detail in Section 19.2.

- **Mode changes**

  A real-time system often has several modes of operation. For example, a fly-by-wire civil aircraft may have a take-off mode, a cruising mode and a landing mode. On many occasions, changes between modes can be carefully managed and will occur at well-defined points in the system's execution, as in a normal flight plan for a civil aircraft. Unfortunately, in some application areas, mode changes are expected but cannot be planned. For example, a fault may lead to an aircraft abandoning its take-off and entering an emergency mode of operation; or an accident in a manufacturing task may require an immediate mode change to ensure an orderly shutdown of the plant. In these situations, tasks must be quickly and safely informed that the mode in which they are operating has changed, and that they now need to undertake a different set of actions.

- **Scheduling using partial/imprecise computations**

  There are many algorithms where the accuracy of the results depends on how much time can be allocated to their calculation. For example, numerical computations, statistical estimations and heuristic searches may all produce an initial estimation of the required result, and then refine that result to a greater accuracy. At run-time, a certain amount of time can be allocated to an algorithm, and then, when that time has been used, the task must be interrupted to stop further refinement of the result.

- **User interrupts**

  In a general interactive computing environment, users often wish to stop the current processing because they have detected an error condition and wish to start again.

18.5 Asynchronous notification in Ada

The asynchronous notification facilities in Ada allow an application to respond to:

- events being signalled asynchronous from the external environment – this is in support of interrupt handling and was considered in detail in Section 16.3;
- events being triggered by the passage of time – the handling for these events are executed at the priority of the clock device and was considered in detail in Section 14.4;
- asynchronous transfer of control (ATC) requests on a task – supporting a termination model;
- task abortion.

There is no generalised mechanisms for a resumption model of asynchronous notification, hence this section will focus on ATC and task abortion.

18.5.1 Asynchronous transfer of control

Ada provides a structured form of asynchronous notification handling called asynchronous transfer of control (ATC). To emphasize that ATC is a form of communication and synchronization, the mechanism is built on top of the inter-task communication facility.

The Ada `select` statement has the following forms:

- a selective accept (to support the server side of the rendezvous) – this is not discussed in this book,
- a timed and a conditional entry call (to either a task or a protected entry) – this was discussed in Section 11.8.1,
- an asynchronous select – discussed below.

The asynchronous select statement provides an asynchronous notification mechanism with termination semantics.

The execution of the asynchronous select begins with the issuing of the triggering entry call or the issuing of the triggering delay. If the triggering statement is an entry call, the parameters are evaluated as normal and the call issued. If the call is queued, then a sequence of statements in an abortable part is executed.

If the triggering statement completes before the execution of the abortable part completes, the abortable part is aborted. When these activities have finished, the optional sequence of statements following the triggering statement is executed.

If the abortable part completes before the completion of the entry call, an attempt is made to cancel the entry call and, if successful, the execution of the asynchronous select statement is finished. The following illustrates the syntax:

```
select
  Trigger.Event;
  -- optional sequence of statements to be
```

```
  -- executed after the event has been received
then abort
  -- abortable sequence of statements
end select;
```

Note that the triggering statement can be a delay statement and, therefore a timeout can be associated with the abortable part.

If the cancellation of the triggering event fails because the protected action has started, then the asynchronous select statement waits for the triggering statement to complete before executing the optional sequence of statements following the triggering statement.

Clearly, it is possible for the triggering event to occur even before the abortable part has started its execution. In this case the abortable part is not executed and therefore not aborted.

Consider the following example:

```
protected Service is
  entry Atc_Event;
  procedure Set_Available;
private
  Available : Boolean := False;
end Service;

protected body Service is
  entry Atc_Event when Available is
  begin
    Seq2;
  end Atc_Event;

  procedure Set_Available is
  begin
    Available := True;
  end Set_Available;

end Service;

task To_Be_Interrupted;
task body To_Be_Interrupted is
begin
  ...
  select    -- ATC statement
    Service.Atc_Event;
    Seq3;
  then abort
    Seq1;
  end select;
  Seq4;
  ...
end To_Be_Interrupted;
```

When the above ATC statement is executed, the statements which are executed will depend on the order of events that occur:

```
if the entry is available immediately then
   Service.Atc_Event is issued
   Seq2 is executed
   Seq3 is executed
   Seq4 is executed (Seq1 is never started)

elsif no protected action starts before Seq1 finishes then
   Service.Atc_Event is issued
   Seq1 is executed
   Service.Atc_Event is cancelled
   Seq4 is executed

elsif the entry finishes before Seq1 finishes then
   Service.Atc_Event is issued
   partial execution of Seq1 occurs concurrently with Seq2
   Seq1 is aborted and finalised
   Seq3 is executed
   Seq4 is executed

else (the entry finishes after Seq1 finishes)
   Service.Atc_Event is issued
   Seq1 is executed concurrently with partial execution of Seq2
   Service.Atc_Event cancellation is attempted but is unsuccessful
   execution of Seq2 completes
   Seq3 is executed
   Seq4 is executed
end if
```

Note that there is a race condition between Seq1 finishing and the entry call finishing. The situation could occur where Seq1 does finish but is nevertheless aborted.

Ada allows some operations to be **abort deferred**. If Seq1 contains an abort-deferred operation, then its cancellation will not occur until the operation is completed. An example of such an operation is a call on a protected object.

The above discussion has concentrated on the concurrent behaviour of Seq1 and the triggering protected action. Indeed, on a multiprocessor implementation it could be the case that Seq1 and Seq2 are executing in parallel. However, on a single-processor system, the triggering event will only ever occur if the action that causes it has a higher priority than Seq1. The normal behaviour will thus be the preemption of Seq1 by Seq2. When Seq2 (the triggering entry) completes, Seq1 will be aborted before it can execute again. And hence the ATC is 'immediate' (unless an abort-deferred operation is in progress).

Exceptions and ATC

With the asynchronous select statement, potentially two activities occur concurrently: the abortable part may execute concurrently with the triggering action (when the action is an entry call). In either one of these activities, exceptions may be raised and unhandled. Therefore, at first sight it may appear that potentially two exceptions can be propagated simultaneously from the select statement. However, this is not the case: one of the exceptions is deemed to be lost (that raised in the abortable part when it is aborted), and hence only one exception is propagated.

18.5.2 Task abortion

Tasks in Ada can be aborted using an abort statement; any task may abort any other named task by executing this statement.

Once aborted tasks are said to become **abnormal**, and are prevented from interacting with any other task. Ideally, an abnormal task will stop executing immediately. However, some implementations may not be able to facilitate immediate shut down, and hence all Ada requires is that the task terminates before it next interacts with other tasks. Note that the Real-Time Systems Annex does require 'immediate' to be just that on a single processor system.

After a task has been marked as abnormal, execution of its body is aborted. This means that the execution of every construct in the task body is aborted (including any dependent tasks), unless it is involved in the execution of an abort-deferred operation. The execution of an abort-deferred operation is allowed to complete before it is aborted. As noted above, the same rules for aborting a task body also apply to aborting a sequence of statements in the asynchronous select statement discussed earlier.

If a construct, which has been aborted, is blocked outside an abort-deferred operation (other than at an entry call), the construct becomes abnormal and is immediately completed. Other constructs must complete no later than the next **abort completion point** (if any) that occurs outside an abort-deferred operation. Abort completion points include:

- the end of activation of a task;
- the point where the execution initiates the activation of another task;
- the start or end of an entry call, delay statement or abort statement;
- the start of the execution of a select statement, or of the sequence of statements of an exception handler.

The following operations are defined to be abort-deferred:

- a protected action;
- waiting for an entry call to complete;
- waiting for termination of dependent tasks;
- the execution of an 'initialize' procedure, a 'finalize' procedure, or an assignment operation of an object with a controlled part.

18.5.3 Ada and atomic actions

It was shown in Section 17.4 that backward error recovery in a sequential system could be implemented by exception handling. In this section, the Ada ATC facility and exception handling is used to implement backward and forward error recovery. It is assumed that the underlying Ada implementation and run-time are fault free, and therefore the strong typing provided by Ada will ensure that the Ada program itself remains viable.

Backward error recovery

The following package is a generic version of the one was given in Section 17.4 for saving and restoring a task's state.

```
generic
  type Data is private;
package Recovery_Cache is
  procedure Save(D : in Data);
  procedure Restore(D : out Data);
end Recovery_Cache;
```

Consider three Ada tasks which wish to enter into a recoverable atomic action. Each will call their appropriate procedure in the package given below.

```
package Conversation is

  procedure T1(Params : Param);   -- called by task 1
  procedure T2(Params : Param);   -- called by task 2
  procedure T3(Params : Param);   -- called by task 3

  Atomic_Action_Failure : exception;

end Conversation;
```

The body of the package encapsulates the action and ensures that only communication between the three tasks is allowed during the conversation.[1] The `Controller` protected object is responsible for propagating any error condition noticed in one task to all tasks, saving and restoring any persistent data in the recovery cache, and ensuring that all tasks leave the action at the same time. It contains three protected entries and a protected procedure.

- The `Wait_Abort` entry represents the asynchronous event on which the tasks will wait while performing their part of the action.
- Each task calls `Done` if it has finished its component of the action without error. Only when all three tasks have called `Done` will they be allowed to leave.
- Similarly, each task calls `Cleanup` if it has had to perform any recovery.
- If any task recognizes an error condition (either because of a raised exception or the failure of the acceptance test), it will call `Signal_Abort`. This will set the flag `Killed` to true, indicating that the tasks must be recovered.

Note that, as backward error recovery will be performed, the tasks are not concerned with the actual cause of the error. When `Killed` becomes true, all tasks in the action receive the asynchronous event. Once the event has been handled, all tasks must wait on the `Cleanup` entry so that they can all terminate the conversation module together.

---

[1] In practice, this might be difficult to ensure because of Ada's scope rules. One way of increasing the security would be to require that the `Conversation` package is at the library level and its body only references pure (state-free) packages. The solution presented here assumes that the tasks are well behaved. It also assumes, for simplicity, that the correct tasks call `T1`, `T2` and `T3` at the correct times.

```ada
with Recovery_Cache;
package body Conversation is
  Primary_Failure, Secondary_Failure, Tertiary_Failure: exception;
  type Module is (Primary, Secondary, Tertiary);

  protected Controller is
    entry Wait_Abort;
    entry Done;
    entry Cleanup;
    procedure Signal_Abort;
  private
    Killed : Boolean := False;
    Releasing_Done : Boolean := False;
    Releasing_Cleanup : Boolean := False;
    Informed : Integer := 0;
  end Controller;

  -- any local protected objects for communication between actions

  protected body Controller is
    entry Wait_Abort when Killed is
    begin
      Informed := Informed + 1;
      if Informed = 3 then
        Killed := False;
        Informed := 0;
      end if;
    end Wait_Abort;

    procedure Signal_Abort is
    begin
      Killed := True;
    end Signal_Abort;

    entry Done when Done'Count = 3 or Releasing_Done is
    begin
      Releasing_Done := Done'Count > 0;
    end Done;

    entry Cleanup when Cleanup'Count = 3 or Releasing_Cleanup is
    begin
      Releasing_Cleanup := Cleanup'Count > 0;
    end Cleanup;
  end Controller;

  procedure T1(Params : Param) is separate;
  procedure T2(Params : Param) is separate;
  procedure T3(Params : Param) is separate;

end Conversation;
```

The code for each task is contained within a single procedure: e.g. T1. Within such a procedure, three attempts are made to perform the action. If all attempts fail, the exception

Atomic_Action_Failure is raised. Each attempt is surrounded by a call that saves the state and restores the state (if the attempt fails). Each attempt is encapsulated in a separate local procedure (`T1_Primary` etc), which contains a single 'select and then abort' statement to perform the required protocol with the controller. The recovery cache is used by each task to save its local data.

```
separate (Conversation)
procedure T1(Params : Param) is
  procedure T1_Primary is
  begin
    select
      Controller.Wait_Abort;  -- triggering event
      Controller.Cleanup;     -- wait for all to finish
      raise Primary_Failure;
    then abort
      begin
        -- code to implement atomic action,
        -- the acceptance test might raise an exception
        if Accept_Test = Failed then
          Controller.Signal_Abort;
        else
          Controller.Done;  --signal completion
        end if;
      exception
        when others =>
          Controller.Signal_Abort;
      end;
    end select;
  end T1_Primary;

  procedure T1_Secondary is ... ;
  procedure T1_Tertiary is ... ;

  package My_Cache is new Recovery_Cache(..);  -- for local data

begin
  My_Cache.Save(..);

  for Try in Module loop
    begin
      case Try is
        when Primary => T1_Primary; return;
        when Secondary => T1_Secondary; return;
        when Tertiary => T1_Tertiary;
      end case;
    exception
      when Primary_Failure =>
        My_Cache.Restore(..);
      when Secondary_Failure =>
        My_Cache.Restore(..);
      when Tertiary_Failure =>
        My_Cache.Restore(..);
        raise Atomic_Action_Failure;
```

ASYNCHRONOUS NOTIFICATION IN ADA 415

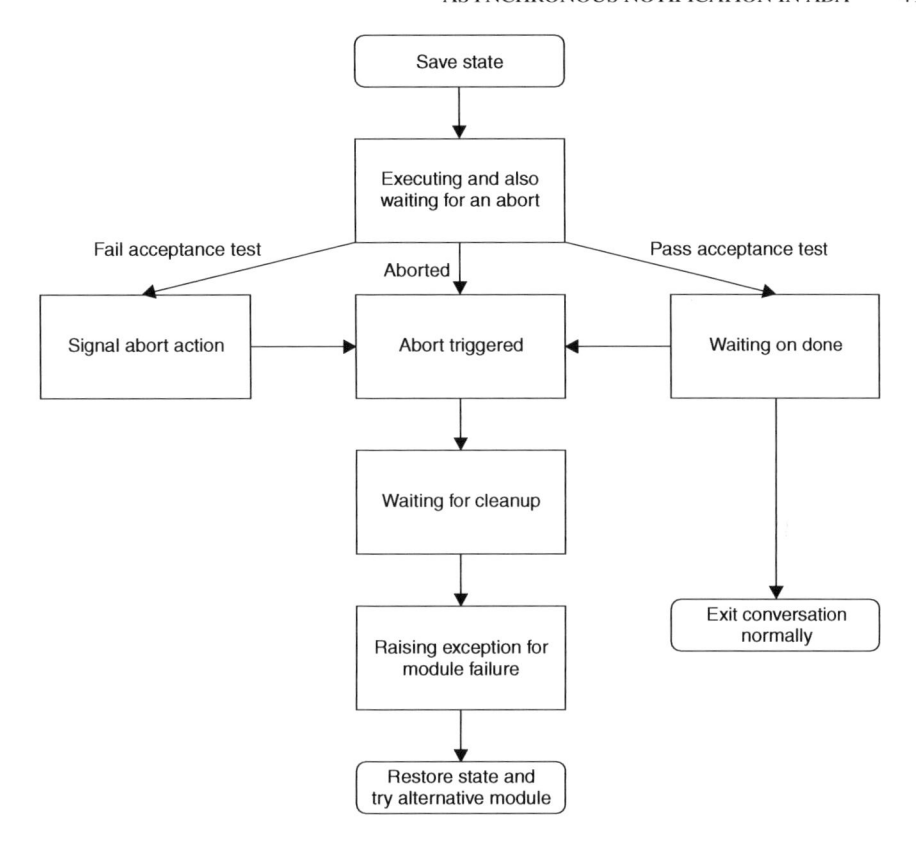

Figure 18.5: Simple state transition diagram for a conversation.

```
      when others =>
         My_Cache.Restore(..);
         raise Atomic_Action_Failure;
      end;
   end loop;

end T1;

-- similarly for T2 and T3
```

Figure 18.5 illustrates a simple state transition diagram for a participating task in a conversation.

Forward error recovery

Ada's ATC facility can be used with exceptions to implement atomic actions with forward error recovery between concurrently executing tasks. Consider again the following package for implementing an atomic action between three tasks.

416 ATOMIC ACTIONS, CONCURRENT PROCESSES AND RELIABILITY

```ada
package Action is
  procedure T1(Params : Param);  -- called by task 1
  procedure T2(Params : Param);  -- called by task 2
  procedure T3(Params : Param);  -- called by task 3

  Atomic_Action_Failure : exception;
end Action;
```

As with backward error recovery, the body of the package encapsulates the action and ensures that only communications between the three tasks are allowed. The `Controller` protected object is responsible for propagating any exception raised in one task to all tasks, and for ensuring that all tasks leave the action at the same time.

```ada
with Ada.Exceptions;
use Ada.Exceptions;
package body Action is
  type Vote_T is (Commit, Aborted);
  protected Controller is
    entry Wait_Abort(E: out Exception_Id);
    entry Done;
    entry Cleanup (Vote: Vote_T; Result : out Vote_T);
    procedure Signal_Abort(E: Exception_Id);
  private
    entry Wait_Cleanup(Vote: Vote_T; Result : out Vote_T);
    Killed : Boolean := False;
    Releasing_Cleanup : Boolean := False;
    Releasing_Done : Boolean := False;
    Reason : Exception_Id;
    Final_Result : Vote_T := Commit;
    Informed : Integer := 0;
  end Controller;

  -- any local protected objects for communication between actions

  protected body Controller is
    entry Wait_Abort(E: out Exception_Id) when Killed is
    begin
      E := Reason;
      Informed := Informed + 1;
      if Informed = 3 then
        Killed := False;
        Informed := 0;
      end if;
    end Wait_Abort;

    entry Done when Done'Count = 3 or Releasing_Done is
    begin
      if Done'Count > 0 then
        Releasing_Done := True;
      else
        Releasing_Done := False;
      end if;
    end Done;
```

```ada
   entry Cleanup (Vote: Vote_T; Result : out Vote_T) when True is
   begin
     if Vote = Aborted then
        Final_Result := Aborted;
     end if;
     requeue Wait_Cleanup with abort;
   end Cleanup;

   procedure Signal_Abort(E: Exception_Id) is
   begin
     Killed := True;
     Reason := E;
   end Signal_Abort;

   entry Wait_Cleanup (Vote: Vote_T; Result: out Vote_T)
       when Wait_Cleanup'Count = 3 or Releasing_Cleanup is
   begin
     Result := Final_Result;
     if Wait_Cleanup'Count > 0 then
        Releasing_Cleanup := True;
     else
        Releasing_Cleanup := False;
        Final_Result := Commit;
     end if;
   end Wait_Cleanup;
end Controller;

procedure T1(Params: Param) is
   X : Exception_Id;
   Handled_Ok : Boolean := False;
   Decision : Vote_T;
begin
   select
     Controller.Wait_Abort(X); -- triggering event
     Raise_Exception(X); -- raise common exception
   then abort
     begin
        -- code to implement atomic action
        Controller.Done; --signal completion
     exception
        when E: others =>
          Controller.Signal_Abort(Exception_Identity(E));
     end;
   end select;
exception
    -- if any exception is raised during the action
    -- all tasks must participate in the recovery
    when E: others =>
      -- Exception_Identity(E) has been raised in all tasks
      if Handled_Ok then
         Controller.Cleanup(Commit, Decision);
      else
```

```
           Controller.Cleanup(Aborted, Decision);
         end if;
         if Decision = Aborted then
            raise Atomic_Action_Failure;
         end if;
   end T1;

   procedure T2(Params : Param) is ...;

   procedure T3(Params : Param) is ...;
end Action;
```

Each component of the action (T1, T2, and T3) has identical structure. The component executes a select statement with an abortable part. The triggering event is signalled by the `Controller` protected object if any component indicates that an exception has been raised and not handled locally in one of the components. The abortable part contains the actual code of the component. If this code executes without incident, the `Controller` is informed that this component is ready to commit the action. If any exceptions are raised during the abortable part, the `Controller` is informed and the identity of the exception passed. Note that, unlike backward error recovery (given earlier), here the cause of the error must be communicated.

If the `Controller` has received notification of an unhandled exception, it releases all tasks waiting on the `Wait_Abort` triggering event (any task late in arriving will receive the event immediately it tries to enter into its select statement). The tasks have their abortable parts aborted (if started), and the exception is raised in each task by the statement after the entry call to the controller. If the exception is successfully handled by the component, the task indicates that it is prepared to commit the action. If not, then it indicates that the action must be aborted. If any task indicates that the action is to be aborted, then all tasks will raise the exception `Atomic_Action_Failure`. Figure 18.6 shows the approach using a simple state transition diagram.

The above example illustrates that it is possible to program atomic actions with forward error recovery in Ada. However, there are two points to note about this example:

- Only the first exception to be passed to the `Controller` will be raised in all tasks. It is not possible to get concurrent raising of exceptions, as any exception raised in an abortable part when it is aborted is lost.

- The approach does not deal with the deserter problem. If one of the participants in the action does not arrive, the others are left waiting at the end of the action. To cope with this situation, it is necessary for each task to log its arrival with the action controller (this is left as an exercise for the reader).

18.5.4 Other examples of using asynchronous transfer of control

The examples presented in this subsection are derived from the application requirements mentioned earlier.

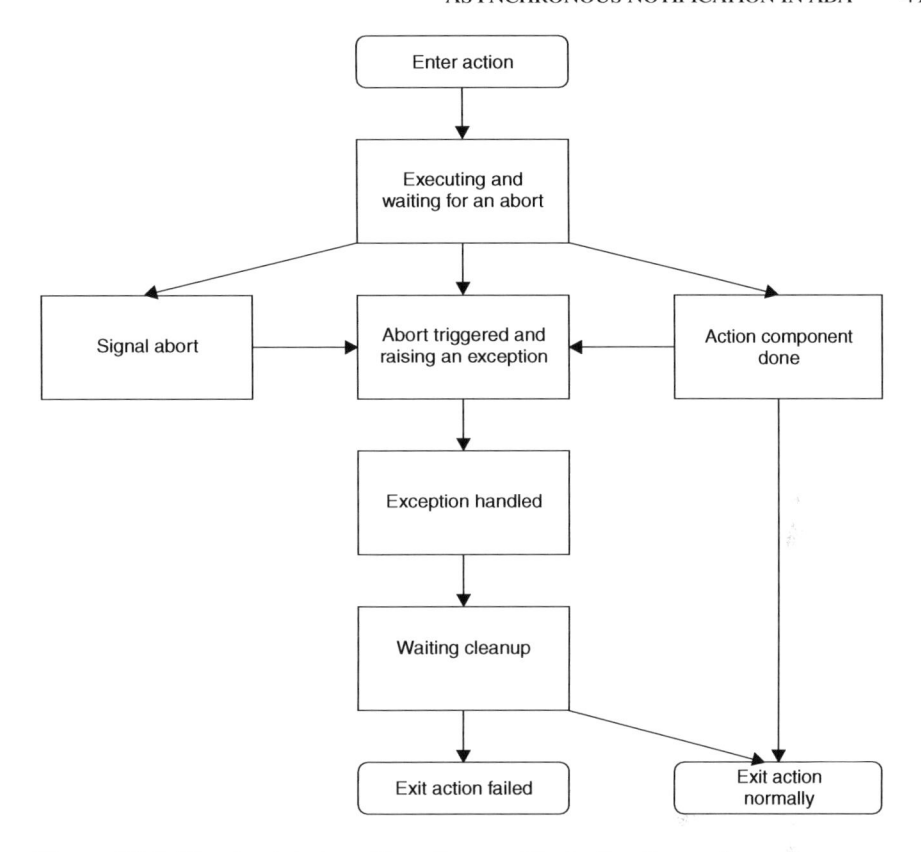

Figure 18.6: Simple state transition diagram illustrating forward error recovery.

Simple Error recovery

Before recovery can be initiated to handle a fault, the fault must cause a detectable error to occur in the system. Once the error has been detected, some form of damage assessment and damage confinement must be undertaken before error recovery can begin. The details of these activities are application dependent; however, typically, a set of tasks might need to be informed of the error. The following code fragment illustrates the approach:

```ada
with Broadcasts; -- see Chapter 11
...
type Error_Id is (Err1, Err2, Err3);
  -- some appropriate identifier

package Error_Notification is new Broadcasts(Error_Id);
Error_Occurred : Error_Notification.Broadcast;
     -- a protected object

task Error_Monitor;

-- all tasks interested in the error have the following structure
task type Interested_Party;
```

```ada
task body Interested_Party is
  Reason : Error_Id;
begin
  loop
    ...
    select
      Error_Occurred.Receive(Reason);
        -- a protected entry call
      case Reason is
        when Err1 =>
          -- appropriate recovery action
        when Err2 =>
          -- appropriate recovery action
        when Err3 =>
          -- appropriate recovery action
      end case;
    then abort
      loop
        -- normal operation
      end loop;
    end select;
  end loop;
end Interested_Party;

task body Error_Monitor is
  Error : Error_Id;
begin
  ...
  -- when error detected
  Error_Occurred.Send(Error);
  -- a protected procedure call
  ...
end Error_Monitor;
```

The above code fragment makes use of a generic package, which provides a general purpose broadcast facility (via a protected object). The Error_Monitoring task detects the error condition and sends the broadcast to all those tasks that are listening. Those tasks executing within the select statement will receive the error notification, but those outside will not (in this case). The use of a different communication abstraction for error notification (such as a persistent signal) would ensure that all interested tasks received notification eventually.

The above example illustrates an interesting compromise between demanding that a task polls for the event or explicitly waits for the event, and forcing the task to respond immediately to the event. In Ada, the task must indicate explicitly that it is prepared to have its flow of control changed by executing the *select then abort* statement; however, once it has done this, it is free to continue executing. Any race conditions that result between the triggering event being signalled and the task issuing the *select then abort* statement must be catered for by the programmer. Furthermore, any section of code that should not be aborted must be encapsulated in a protected object, thus making it an abort-deferred operation.

Deadline overrun detection

If a task has a deadline associated with part of its execution, then the *select then abort* statement can be used to detect a deadline overrun. For example, the following task must undertake some action before a certain time:

```
with Ada.Real_Time; use Ada.Real_Time;
task Critical;

task body Critical is
  Deadline : Real_Time.Time := ...; -- some appropriate value
begin
  ...
  select
    delay until Deadline;
    -- recovery action
  then abort
    -- time-critical section of code
  end select;
  ...
end Critical;
```

Alternatively, the task may wish the action to be performed within a certain interval of time:

```
with Ada.Calendar; use Ada.Calendar;
task Critical;

task body Critical is
  Within_Deadline : Duration := ...; -- some appropriate value
begin
  ...
  select
    delay Within_Deadline;
    -- recovery action
  then abort
    -- time-critical section of code
  end select;
  ...
end Critical;
```

The topic of tolerating timing failures in programs is considered in detail in Chapter 19.

Mode changes

Consider a periodic task in an embedded application which can operate in two modes. In a non-critical mode, the task wishes to read a sensor every ten seconds, perform some exact, but extensive, calculation and output some value to an actuator. However, in a critical mode it is required to read the sensor every second, undertake a simple inexact calculation and then output this value. A mode change is signalled via a persistent signal. The following program fragment illustrates how the periodic task can be structured:

```ada
with Persistent_Signals; use Persistent_Signals;
with Ada.Calendar; use Ada.Calendar;
   ...

type Mode is (Non_Critical, Critical);
Change_Mode : Persistent_Signal;

task Sensor_Monitor;

task body Sensor_Monitor is
  Current_Mode : Mode := Non_Critical;
  Next_Time : Time := Clock;
  Critical_Period : constant Duration := 1.0;
  Non_Critical_Period : constant Duration := 10.0;
  Current_Period : Duration := Non_Critical_Period;
begin
  loop
    select
      Change_Mode.Wait;
      if Current_Mode = Critical then
        Current_Mode := Non_Critical;
        Current_Period := Non_Critical_Period;
      else
        Current_Mode := Critical;
        Current_Period := Critical_Period;
      end if;
    then abort
      loop
        -- read sensor
        -- perform appropriate calculation and
        -- output to actuator
        Next_Time := Next_Time + Current_Period;
        delay until Next_Time;
      end loop;
    end select;
  end loop;
end Sensor_Monitor;
```

If the output to the actuator involves a number of operations (or there is more than one actuator to set), then this action could be encapsulated in a call to a protected object. This would force the action to be an abort-deferred operation.

Partial/imprecise/anytime computations

Partial or imprecise computations are those that can produce intermediate results of varying accuracy. Moreover, the accuracy of these results does not decrease as the execution of the tasks continues. With these tasks, it is usual to define a minimum precision that is needed by the application.

A task which is to perform a partial computation can place its data into a protected object. The client task can retrieve the data from the protected object. Using a protected object to encapsulate the passing of the result ensures that no inconsistent value is returned to the client due to the task receiving an ATC in the middle of the update.

The following illustrates the approach:

```ada
with Persistent_Signals; use Persistent_Signals;
with Ada.Real_Time; use Ada.Real_Time;
   ...
Out_Of_Time : Persistent_Signal;

protected Shared_Data is
   procedure Write(D : Data);
   entry Read(D: out Data);
private
   The_Data : Data;
   Data_Available : Boolean := False;
end Shared_Data;

task Client;
task Imprecise_Server;

protected body Shared_Data is
   procedure Write(D : Data) is
   begin
      The_Data := D;
      Data_Available := True;
   end Write;

   entry Read(D : out Data) when Data_Available is
   begin
      D := The_Data;
      Data_Available := False;
   end Read;
end Shared_Data;

task body Client is
   ...
begin
   loop
      ...
      Out_Of_Time.Send;
      Shared_Data.Read(Result);
   end loop;
end Client;

task body Imprecise_Server is
   -- declaration of Result
begin
   loop
      ...
      -- produce result with minimum required precision
      Shared_Data.Write(Result);
      select
         Out_Of_Time.Wait;
```

424   ATOMIC ACTIONS, CONCURRENT PROCESSES AND RELIABILITY

```
    then abort
      -- iteratively compute a refined Result
      loop
        -- next iteration
        ...
        Shared_Data.Write(Result);
        exit when Best_Possible_Result_Obtained;
      end loop;
    end select;
  end loop;
end Imprecise_Server;
```

Again, note the use of a call on a protected object in the abortable sequence of statements to ensure that a consistent value is written.

18.6 Atomic actions and scheduling analysis

This chapter has focused on the primitives needed for a group of tasks to act in a fault-tolerant manner. To achieve the necessary level of coordination, the tasks involved in, for example, an atomic action must wait for certain conditions to be true and to notify partner tasks when it is appropriate for them to resume their computation. This cooperative behaviour is quite different from the model so far assumed for scheduling analysis. Here tasks are independent, they compete for the processing resources and only interact asynchronously via some form of protected shared state.

To derive scheduling analysis for cooperating real-time tasks is not straightforward. For example, one task could miss its short deadline waiting for another task with a much longer deadline to commit on some joint action. Also if one of a set of cooperating tasks has not yet been released then at some point the other tasks will need to wait for the missing task to 'wake up'.

Atomic actions do however have a useful (and necessary) property that once all involved tasks are runnable then at all times at least one of the tasks must be able to make progress. A number may be suspended waiting for some future event, but at least one must be runnable and will eventually lead to all tasks progressing to the end of the action (either successfully or via some degraded action following either backward or forward error recovery).

This allows a set of real-time tasks to engage in an atomic action, and their worst-case timing behaviour to be predicted, if

- they are released at the same time (either via the same external event, or because they are periodic tasks with the same period and release times),
- they have the same relative deadline (or at least adopt the shortest deadline of the tasks in the set), and thus
- share the same priority (when scheduled using a fixed priority scheme) or deadline (if scheduled using EDF).

So, using fixed priority scheduling on a single processor as an example, the set of cooperating tasks can be analysed as if they are just one (compound) task. If their worst-case computation times are added together then the interference that lower priority tasks suffer from this compound task will be the same as from the individual tasks. And if the set of cooperating tasks access external resources (using, say, the immediately ceiling priority inheritance protocol) then the analysis of the compound task would use a single blocking term. As a result, if the compound task is deemed to meet the shortest deadline of the cooperating tasks then obviously all of these tasks will also meet their deadlines.

In Section 7.4 where the scheduling of individual tasks undertaking forward or backward error recovery was considered, a *fault model* was used to capture the worst-case error condition that the task (and the entire system) should survive. Extra computation time was added into the response-time equation to account for the fault model. If all tasks were still schedulable then the error behaviour as depicted by the fault model could be tolerated without a deadline been missed.

The same approach can be applied to the techniques discussed in this chapter. A number of plausible scenarios can be defined and the 'extra' computation time needed for each of the cooperating tasks for each of these scenarios can be derived. These values are then used to compute the total worst-case execution time of the compound task. If for all plausible scenarios, all tasks (including the compound task) are schedule then the system is guaranteed to be both fault tolerance and real-time.

Summary

Reliable execution of tasks is essential if real-time embedded systems are to be used in critical applications. When tasks interact, it is necessary to constrain their intertask communication so that recovery procedures can be programmed, if required. Atomic actions have been discussed in this chapter as a mechanism by which programs, consisting of many tasks, can be structured to facilitate damage confinement and error recovery.

Actions are atomic if they can be considered, so far as other tasks are concerned, to be indivisible and instantaneous, such that the effects on the system are as if they are interleaved as opposed to concurrent. An atomic action has well-defined boundaries and can be nested. Resources used in an atomic action are allocated during an initial *growing phase*, and released either as part of a subsequent *shrinking phase* or at the end of the action (if the action is to be recoverable).

A **conversation** is an atomic action with backward error recovery facilities (in the form of recovery blocks). On entry to the conversation, the state of the task is saved. While inside the conversation, a task is only allowed to communicate with other tasks active in the conversation and general resource managers. In order to leave the conversation, all tasks active in the conversation must have passed their acceptance test. If any task fails its acceptance test, all tasks have their state restored to that saved at the start of the conversation and they execute their alternative modules. Conversations can be nested and if all alternatives in an inner conversation fail then recovery must be performed at an outer level.

Forward error recovery via exception handlers can also be added to atomic actions. If an exception is raised by one task then all tasks active in the action must handle the exception. Two issues that must be addressed when using this approach are the resolution of concurrently raised exceptions and exceptions in internal actions.

Few mainstream languages or operating systems directly support the notion of an atomic action or a recoverable atomic action. However, most communication and synchronization primitives allow the isolation property of an action to be programmed. To implement a recoverable action requires an asynchronous notification mechanism. This can either have resumption semantics (in which case it is called an asynchronous event handling mechanism) or it can have termination semantics (in which case it is called asynchronous transfer of control).

Ada provides the termination model of asynchronous transfer of control. The Ada mechanism is built on top of the select statement. These termination approaches, in combination with exceptions, allow for an elegant implementation of a recoverable action.

The Ada ATC model is generic and can be used to meet a range of other application requirements in addition to error recovery, such as mode changes and imprecise/anytime computations.

Chapter 19
Tolerating timing faults

19.1 Dynamic redundancy and timing faults
19.2 Deadline miss detection
19.3 Overrun of worst-case execution time
19.4 Overrun of sporadic events
19.5 Overrun of resource usage
19.6 Damage confinement
19.7 Error recovery
Summary

Throughout this book, it has been assumed that real-time systems have high reliability requirements. One method of achieving this reliability is to incorporate fault tolerance into the software. The inclusion of timing constraints introduces the possibility of these constraints being broken at run-time and failures occurring in the time domain. With soft systems, a task may need to know if a timing constraint has been missed, even though it can accommodate this under normal execution. More importantly, in a hard system (or subsystem), where deadlines are critical, a missed deadline needs to trigger some error recovery routine.

If the system has been shown to be schedulable under worst-case execution times then it is arguable that deadlines cannot be missed. However, the discussions of reliability in Chapter 3 indicated strongly the need for a multifaceted approach to reliability; that is, prove that nothing can go wrong and include routines for adequately dealing with the problems that arise when they do.

This chapter considers the causes of timing faults and how they can be tolerated within the context of the dynamic redundancy approach to fault tolerance introduced in Chapter 3.

19.1 Dynamic redundancy and timing faults

In Chapter 3, the four phases of dynamic software fault tolerance were introduce. These are now reviewed in the context of timing faults.

(1) **Error detection** – Most timing faults will eventually manifest themselves in the form of missed deadlines.

428   TOLERATING TIMING FAULTS

(2) **Damage confinement and assessment** – When deadlines have been missed, it must be decided which tasks in the system are at fault. Ideally, confinement techniques should ensure that only faulty tasks miss their deadlines.

(3) **Error recovery** – The response to deadline misses requires that the application undertakes some recovery, perhaps providing a degraded service.

(4) **Fault treatment and continued service** – Timing errors can result from transient overloads. Hence they can often be ignored. However, persistent deadline misses may indicate more serious problems and require some form of maintenance to be undertaken.

In order to understand where timing faults come from, consider the Response-Time Equation 5.5 (from Chapter 5), which is reproduce below.

$$R_i = C_i + B_i + \sum_{j \in hp(i)} \left\lceil \frac{R_i}{T_j} \right\rceil C_j$$

If this has been used as the basis of the schedulability test and the application has been deemed schedulable, then the system may still miss deadlines because:

- worst-case execution time (WCET) calculations were inaccurate (optimistic rather than pessimistic) and hence one or more values of C_i are incorrect;
- blocking times were underestimated and hence one or more values of B_i are incorrect;
- assumptions made in the schedulability checker were not valid, for example the test ignores the cost of context switching (that is, assumes it to be instantaneous) which is invalid for most execution platforms;
- the schedulability checker itself had a design error and hence produced the wrong result;
- the scheduling algorithm could not cope with a load even though it is theoretically schedulable; for example the processor utilisation is less than 100%, which is sufficient for EDF scheduling but may not be adequate if fixed priority scheduling is employed;
- the system is working outside its design parameters, for example sporadic events occurring more frequently than was assumed in the schedulability analysis.

In this latter case (for instance, an information overflow manifesting itself as an unacceptable rate of interrupts), the system designers may still wish for fail-soft or fail-safe behaviour.

Chapter 3 introduced the *fault* → *error* → *failure* chain. Assuming the schedulability analysis is correct, the following chains are possible in the context of priority-based systems [33]:

(1) *Fault* (in task τ_i's WCET calculation or assumptions) → *error* (overrun of τ_i's WCET) → *error propagation* (deadline miss of τ_i) → *failure* (to deliver service in a timely manner);

(2) *Fault* (in task τ_i's WCET calculation or assumptions) → *error* (overrun of τ_i's WCET) → *error propagation* (greater interference on lower priority tasks) → *error propagation* (deadline miss of lower priority tasks) → *failure* (to deliver service in a timely manner);

(3) *Fault* (in task τ_i's minimum inter-arrival time assumptions) → *error* (greater computation requirement for τ_i) → *error propagation* (deadline miss of τ_i) → *failure* (to deliver service in a timely manner);

(4) *Fault* (in task τ_i's minimum inter-arrival time assumptions) → *error* (greater interference on lower priority tasks) → *error propagation* (deadline miss of lower priority tasks) → *failure* (to deliver service in a timely manner);

(5) *Fault* (in task τ_i's WCET calculation or assumptions when using a shared resource) → *error* (overrun of τ_i's resource usage) → *error propagation* (greater blocking time of higher priority tasks sharing the resource) → *error propagation* (deadline miss of higher priority tasks) → *failure* (to deliver service in a timely manner).

Similar chains will exists for other scheduling approaches and faults, where instead of the term "lower/higher priority" the corresponding eligibility criterion can be substituted (e.g. "later/earlier absolute deadline").

To be tolerant of timing faults, it is necessary to be able to detect:

- miss of a deadline – the final error in all the above error propagation chains;
- overrun of a worst-case execution time – potentially causing the task and/or lower eligibility tasks to miss their deadlines (error chains 1 and 2)
- a sporadic event occurring more often than predicted – potentially causing the task and/or lower eligibility tasks to miss their deadlines (error chains 3 and 4)
- overrun in the usage of a resource – potentially causing higher eligibility tasks to miss their deadlines (error chain 5).

Of course the last three error conditions do not necessary indicate that deadlines will be missed; for example, an overrun of WCET in one task might be compensated by a sporadic event occurring less often than the maximum allowed. Hence, the damage confinement and assessment phase of providing fault tolerance (introduced in Section 3.5) must determine what actions to take. Both forward and backward recovery are then possible.

If timing faults are to be handled, their associated error conditions have to be detected first. If the run-time environment or operating system is aware of the salient characteristics of a task, it will be able to detect problems and bring them to the attention of the application. Alternatively, it is necessary to provide primitive facilities that will allow the application to detect its own timing errors. With all error detection mechanisms, the earlier the problem can be detected the more chance there is to pinpoint the problem and the more time there is to recover.

The following sections will discuss error detection mechanisms for the above timing faults, consider possible error confinement approaches, and identify strategies for recovery. Fault treatment typically involves maintenance, which is a topic outside the scope of this book. However, it is noted that for non-stop real-time applications some form of dynamic

430   TOLERATING TIMING FAULTS

change management or mode change is required. The impact of this can has serious real-time implications.

19.2 Deadline miss detection

Deadline miss detection is the minimum that is required if a real-time system is to tolerate timing failures. It is a "catch all" mechanisms that will detect even problems outside the failure hypothesis. For example, it will detect problems resulting from errors in the schedulability analysis. Of course, with all "catch all" mechanisms, it may be difficult to pinpoint the cause of the problem and it leaves little time for recovery.

This section discusses how deadline miss detection is facilitated in Ada. Strategies for dealing with deadline misses are considered in Section 19.7.

Ada allows the deadline of a task to be specified and this parameter can be used to influence scheduling (see Section 15.5). However, the Ada run-time support system does not use this information to detect deadline misses. For this, the language provide primitive mechanisms that the program has to use to detect the missed deadline itself. One way of achieving this is to use the asynchronous transfer of control facility discussed in Section 18.5.1. Hence to detect a deadline overrun of the periodic task given in Section 14.2 requires the main functionality of the task to be embedded in a 'select then abort' statement. For example:

```
task body Periodic_T is
  Next_Release : Time;
  Next_Deadline : Time;
  Release_Interval : constant Time_Span := Milliseconds(...);
  Deadline : constant Time_Span := Milliseconds(...);
begin
  -- read clock and calculate the Next_Release and Next_Deadline
  loop
    select
      delay until Next_Deadline;
      -- deadline miss detected, perform recovery
    then abort
      -- sample data (for example) or
      -- calculate and send a control signal
    end select;
    delay until Next_Release;
    Next_Release := Next_Release + Release_Interval;
    Next_Deadline := Next_Release + Deadline;
  end loop;
end Periodic_T;
```

A similar approach can be used to detect a deadline miss in a sporadic task.

One of the problems with this approach is that it combines detection with a particular recovery strategy, that of stopping the task from what it is doing. This is, clearly, one option. Another is to use a different task to handle the deadline miss. The possible recovery strategies could include extending the deadline, lowering the errant task's priority, or some other action short of terminating it (see Section 19.7).

DEADLINE MISS DETECTION 431

To simply detect a deadline miss, the Ada timing event facility that was discussed in Section 14.4 can be used (see Program 14.1). In Section 3.5.1, the watchdog timer approach to fault detection was presented. This can be easily programmed using Ada's timing events. The essential idea is that on initializing the watchdog with a first deadline and a period, the watchdog sets up a timing event for the first deadline. The task must now call the watchdog to reset the timing event before its deadline has expired. If it does so, the watchdog sets the event to expire at the next deadline, and so on. If the task does not call to reset the event, the event will be triggered. The specification of the watchdog is given first

```ada
protected type Watchdog(Event : access Timing_Event)
    with Interrupt_Priority => Interrupt_Priority'Last;
  procedure Initialize(First_Deadline : Time;
                       Required_Period : Time_Span);
  entry Alarm_Control(T: out Task_Id);
    -- Called by alarm handling task
  procedure Call_In;
    -- Called by application code when it completes.
private
  procedure Timer_Handler(Event : in out Timing_Event);
    -- Timer event code, ie the handler.
  Alarm : Boolean := False;
  Tid : Task_Id;
  Next_Deadline : Time;
  Period : Time_Span;
end Watchdog;
```

This watchdog object has a common structure. An entry with an initially closed barrier holds back a monitoring task that will be released by the handler if the handler executes. In this example the handler is actually never executed unless there is a missed deadline. Each time the monitored task calls `Call_In`, the timing event is reset to a point in the future. Only if another call does not occur before its next deadline will the handler be executed and the barrier opened releasing the monitoring task.

```ada
protected body Watchdog is
  procedure Initialize(First_Deadline : Time;
                       Required_Period : Time_Span) is
  begin
    Next_Deadline := First_Deadline;
    Period := Required_Period;
    Set_Handler(Event.all, Next_Deadline, Timer_Handler'Access);
    Tid := Current_Task;
  end Initialize;

  entry Alarm_Control(T: out Task_Id) when Alarm is
  begin
    T := Tid;
    Alarm := False;
  end Alarm_Control;

  procedure Timer_Handler(Event : in out Timing_Event) is
  begin
```

432 TOLERATING TIMING FAULTS

```ada
      Alarm := True;
      -- Note no use is made of the parameter in this example
   end Timer_Handler;

   procedure Call_In is
   begin
      Next_Deadline := Next_Deadline + Period;
      Set_Handler(Event.all, Next_Deadline, Timer'Access);
      -- Note this call to Set_Handler cancels the previous call
   end Call_In;
end Watchdog;
```

The revised structure of the periodic task is shown below.

```ada
with Watchdogs; use Watchdogs;
...
Watch : Watchdog;
Deadline_Miss_Event : aliased Timing_Event;
Set_Handler(Deadline_Miss_Event, Next_Deadline, Timer'Access);

task body Periodic_T is
   Next_Release : Time;
   Release_Interval : constant Duration := ...; -- or
   Release_Interval : constant Time_Span := Milliseconds(...);
begin
   -- read clock and calculate the Next_Release and First_Deadline
   Watch.Initialize(First_Deadline, Release_Interval);
   loop
      -- sample data (for example) or
      -- calculate and send a control signal
      Watch.Call_In;
      delay until Next_Release;
      Next_Release := Next_Release + Release_Interval;
   end loop;
end Periodic_T;
```

Note that this approach is Ravenscar compliant, whereas the use of the select-then-abort statement is prohibited.

19.3 Overrun of worst-case execution time

Good fault tolerance practices attempt to confine the consequences of an error to a well-defined region of the program. Facilities such as modules, packages and atomic actions help with this goal. However, if a task consumes more of the CPU resource than has been anticipated, then it may not be that task that misses its deadline. For example, consider a high-priority task with a fair amount of slack time that overruns its worst-case execution time. The tasks that will miss their deadlines may be lower priority tasks with less slack available (see Chain 2 in section 19.1). Ideally, it should be possible to catch the timing error in the task that caused it. This implies that it is necessary to be able to detect when a task overruns the worst-case execution time that the implementer has allowed for it. Of

```ada
with Ada.Task_Identification; use Ada;
with Ada.Real_Time; use Ada.Real_Time;
package Ada.Execution_Time is
   type CPU_Time is private;
   CPU_Time_First : constant CPU_Time;
   CPU_Time_Last  : constant CPU_Time;
   CPU_Time_Unit  : constant :=
         <implementation-defined-real-number>;
   CPU_Tick : constant Time_Span;

   function Clock(T : Task_Identification.Task_ID
           := Task_Identification.Current_Task) return CPU_Time;

   function "+"  (Left : CPU_Time; Right : Time_Span)
      return CPU_Time;
   function "+"  (Left : Time_Span; Right : CPU_Time)
      return CPU_Time;
   -- similarly for "-", "<", "<=", ">" and ">="

   procedure Split
       (T : CPU_Time; SC : out Seconds_Count; TS : out Time_Span);
   function Time_Of (SC : Seconds_Count; TS : Time_Span)
           return CPU_Time;
   ...
private
   -- Not specified by the language.
end Ada.Execution_Time;
```

Program 19.1: An abridged version of the `Ada.Execution_Time` package.

course, if a task is non preemptively scheduled (and does not block waiting for resources), its CPU execution time is equal to its elapse time and the same mechanisms that were used to detect deadline overrun can be used. However, tasks are normally preemptively scheduled, and this makes measuring CPU time usage more difficult. It usually has to be supported explicitly in the host operating system.

Ada directly supports execution-time clocks for tasks, and supports timers that can be fired when tasks have used a defined amount of execution time. Indeed it has added a clock per task that measures the task's execution time. A package, `Ada.Execution_Time` – see Program 19.1, is defined that is similar in structure to `Ada.Calendar` and `Ada.Real_Time`.

When a task is created so is an execution-time clock. This clock registers zero at creation and starts recording the task execution time from the point at which the task starts it *activation* (see Section 10.5). To read the value of any task's clock, a `Clock` function is defined. So, in the following, a loop is allocated 7ms of execution time before exiting at the end of its current iteration:

```ada
Start : CPU_Time;
Interval : Time_Span := Milliseconds(7);
...
```

434   TOLERATING TIMING FAULTS

```
Start := Ada.Execution_Time.Clock;
while Ada.Execution_Time.Clock - Start < Interval loop
  --code
end loop;
```

Note the '−' operator returns a value of type `Time_Span` which can then be compared with `Interval`.

To monitor the execution time of each invocation of a periodic task, for example, is simple:

```
Last : CPU_Time;
Exe_Time : Time_Span;
Last := Execution_Time.Clock;
loop
  -- code of task
  Exe_Time := Ada.Execution_Time.Clock - Last;
  Last := Ada.Execution_Time.Clock;
  -- print out or store Exe_Time
 delay until ...
end loop;
...
```

As well as monitoring a task's execution time profile, it is also possible to trigger an event if its execution-time clock gets to some specified value. A child package of `Ada.Execution_Time` provides support for this type of event – see Program 19.2.

Each `Timer` event is directly linked to the task that will trigger it. This static linkage is ensured by the access discriminant for the type that is required to be **constant** and **not null**.

The handler must, as usual, be a protected procedure; but there is now a need to specify the minimum ceiling priority the associated protected object must have (if ceiling violation is to be avoided). This priority will be set by the supporting implementation.

The `Set_Handler` procedures and the other routines all have the same properties as those defined with timing events. However, in recognition that an implementation may have a limited capacity for timers, or that only one timer per task is possible, the exception `Timer_Resource_Error` may be raised when a `Timer` is defined or when a `Set_Handler` procedure is called for the first time with a new `Timer` parameter.

An example of using this Ada facilities will be given in Section 19.7 where strategies for recovery are considered.

19.4   Overrun of sporadic events

A sporadic event firing more frequently than anticipated can have an enormous impact on a system attempting to meet hard deadlines. Here the term **sporadic overrun** is used to denote this fault. Where the event is the result of an interrupt, the consequences can be potentially devastating. For example, during the first landing on the moon, the guidance computer was reset after a CPU on the Lunar Landing Module was flooded with radar data interrupts. The landing was nearly aborted as a result [70].

There are a variety of techniques that have been developed over the years to deal with this situation. The two basic approaches are either to stop the early firing from occurring,

```ada
package Ada.Execution_Time.Timers is
   type Timer(T : not null access constant
         Ada.Task_Identification.Task_ID) is tagged
      limited private;

   type Timer_Handler is access protected
      procedure(TM : in out Timer);

   Min_Handler_Ceiling : constant System.Any_Priority :=
     <Implementation Defined>;

   procedure Set_Handler(TM: in out Timer;
         In_Time : Time_Span; Handler : Timer_Handler);
   procedure Set_Handler(TM: in out Timer;
         At_Time : CPU_Time;  Handler : Timer_Handler);

   procedure Cancel_Handler(TM : in out Timer;
                            Cancelled : in out Boolean);

   function Current_Handler(TM : Timer) return Timer_Handler;

   function Time_Remaining(TM : Timer) return Time_Span;

   Timer_Resource_Error : exception;

private
   -- Not specified by the language.
end Ada.Execution_Time.Timers;
```

Program 19.2: The `Ada.Execution_Time.Timers` package.

or to bound the total amount of the CPU time allocated to all events from the same source. The latter uses 'server' technology which was discussed in Section 7.7.

Here the focus is on what support can be provided to prohibit the firings or to detect them when they occur and take some corrective action. Two types of events are consider: those resulting from hardware interrupts and those resulting from the software firing of an event. In keeping with the overall Ada philosophy, low level mechanisms can be used to handle event overruns.

Hardware interrupts

Where the event is triggered by a hardware interrupt, on most occasions, the interrupt can be inhibited from occurring by manipulating the associated device control registers (see Chapter 16). A simple approach is illustrated below (see Section 14.3 for other approaches). Here, the assumption is that there is a required minimum inter-arrival time (MIT) between interrupt occurrences.

```ada
protected Sporadic_Interrupt_Controller is
  procedure Interrupt; -- mapped onto interrupt
```

```ada
    entry Wait_For_Next_Interrupt;
private
    procedure Timer_Handler(Event : in out Timing_Event);
    Call_Outstanding : Boolean := False;
    MIT : Time_Span := Milliseconds(...);
end Sporadic_Interrupt_Controller;

Event: Timing_Event;

protected body Sporadic_Interrupt_Controller is
    procedure Interrupt is
    begin
        -- turn off interrupts
        Set_Handler(Event, MIT, Timer_Handler'Access);
        Call_Outstanding := True;
    end Interrupt;

    entry Wait_For_Next_Interrupt when Call_Outstanding is
    begin
        Call_Outstanding := False;
    end Wait_For_Next_Interrupt;

    procedure Timer_Handler(Event : in out Timing_Event) is
    begin
        -- Turn interrupts back on
    end Timer_Handler;
end Sporadic_Interrupt_Controller;
```

Once an interrupt from the device occurs, interrupts are disabled and a timing event is set to expire at the required minimum inter-arrival time. When this occurs, the device's interrupts are enabled.

The sporadic task has a familiar structure

```ada
task body Sporadic_T is
begin
    loop
        Sporadic_Interrupt_Controller.Wait_For_Next_Interrupt;
        -- action
    end loop;
end Sporadic_T;
```

Of course, it is device dependent what happens if the device wants to interrupt and is unable to. Usually, the device overruns and any data is lost.

Ada 2012 has provided a new (optional) package to measure the amount of time the system spends handling interrupts including the time spent executing run-time or system services on its behalf – see Program 19.3. For each interrupt, the execution time value is initially set to zero.

If the package is supported, the function Clock returns the current cumulative execution time of the interrupt identified by Interrupt. The function Supported returns True if the implementation is monitoring the execution time of the interrupt identified by Interrupt; otherwise, it returns False. For any interrupt not supported, Clock will return zero.

```ada
with Ada.Interrupts;
package Ada.Execution_Time.Interrupts is
  function Clock (Interrupt : Ada.Interrupts.Interrupt_Id)
    return CPU_Time;
  function Supported (Interrupt : Ada.Interrupts.Interrupt_Id)
    return Boolean;
end Ada.Execution_Time.Interrupts;
```

Program 19.3: The `Ada.Execution_Time.Interrupts` package.

```ada
package Ada.Execution_Time is
   ...
   Interrupt_Clocks_Supported : constant Boolean :=
                 implementation-defined;
   Separate_Interrupt_Clocks_Supported : constant Boolean :=
                 implementation-defined;
   function Clock_For_Interrupts return CPU_Time;
private
   -- Not specified by the language.
end Ada.Execution_Time
```

Program 19.4: The `Ada.Execution_Time` package's support for interrupts.

In addition to this package, the `Ada.Execution_Time` package (see Program 19.1) has some new features, as shown in Program 19.4, that (if supported) allows the total time spent handling all interrupts to be obtained.

Software firing

If the sporadic event is fired from a software task, then the above approach can be modified so that (for example) an exception is raised.

```ada
protected Sporadic_Interrupt_Controller is
  procedure Release;
  entry Wait_For_Next_Release;
private
  Call_Outstanding : Boolean := False;
  MIT : Time_Span := Milliseconds(...);  -- Min. inter-arrive time
  Last_Release : Time;
end Sporadic_Interrupt_Controller;

MIT_VIOLATION : exception;

protected body Sporadic_Interrupt_Controller is
  procedure Release is
    Now : Time := Clock;
  begin
    if Now - Last_Release < MIT then
      raise MIT_VIOLATION;
    else
```

438 TOLERATING TIMING FAULTS

```
      Last_Release := Now;
    end if;
    Call_Outstanding := True;
  end Interrupt;

  entry Wait_For_Next_Release when Call_Outstanding is
  begin
    Call_Outstanding := False;
  end Wait_For_Next_Interrupt;
end Sporadic_Interrupt_Controller;
```

Raising an exception is only one possible approach.

The usual constraint on a sporadic task is that there is a minimum separation between any two releases. A generalisation of this constraint, which allows for bursts of release events, is to set a limit of M release in any length of time L. Although these constraints are a little more complicated to program, the above approaches can be extended to this M in L case.

19.5 Overrun of resource usage

Problems caused by errors in accessing resources are notoriously difficult to handle. At a functional level, they can corrupt shared state and potentially lead to deadlock. From a timing perspective, the whole raison d'etre for priority (or more generally, eligibility) inheritance protocols such as those discussed in Section 5.4 is to avoid timing problems. However, even approaches involving inheritance and ceiling protocols can cause problems if the blocking time assumed by the schedulability analysis is incorrect. There are two main potential causes for this:

- a task may overrun its allotted access time for the resource, or
- unanticipated resource contention that has not been taken into account in the blocking-time analysis.

The latter being possible in large systems with the use of prewritten library code. In Section 13.4 timeouts were introduced as a mechanisms for detecting the absence of some expected communication or event. There are several reasons why these are inadequate in the context of blocking time.

(1) With inheritance protocols, blocking is cumulative. Timeout could be used on entry to critical sections, however the programmer would have to keep a running track of the total blocking time in the current release.

(2) With immediate ceiling protocols, the blocking occurs before execution of the task. Hence a timeout has no use, as there is no contention when accessing the critical section.

(3) Support for critical sections do not always have a timeout mechanisms. For example, Ada protected types have no associated timeout mechanisms.

DAMAGE CONFINEMENT   439

Hence, whilst timeouts have a role to play, their use is limited in this context.

For finer control, it is possible to use detection of WCET overruns at the block level. Hence all resource accesses would have to be policed to ensure that the calling task did not overrun its allotted usage. Of course, as already pointed out in Section 19.1, an overrun in one resource may be compensated by under use of another. Furthermore, detecting overruns on every resource access may be prohibitively expensive.

As a last resort, overruns in blocking times will, if significant, cause tasks to miss their deadlines, which will be detected. Good programming practice dictates that synchronized code is short and of a simple form. Errors are therefore far less likely.

19.6 Damage confinement

The role of damage confinement of time-related faults is to prevent propagation of the resulting errors to other components in the system. There are two aspects of this that can be identified:

- protecting the system from the impact of sporadic task overruns and unbounded aperiodic activities,
- supporting composability and temporal isolations.

The problem of overruns in sporadic objects has already been mentioned in Section 19.4. Aperiodic events also present a similar problem. As they have no well-defined release characteristics, they can impose an unbounded demand on the processor's time. If not handled properly, they can result in periodic or sporadic tasks missing their deadlines, even though those tasks have been 'guaranteed'. In Section 5.2.2, **execution-time servers** were introduced. Execution-time servers protect the processing resources needed by periodic tasks but otherwise allow aperiodic and sporadic tasks to run as soon as possible. Several types of servers were discussed including the Sporadic Server and Deferrable Server.

When composing systems of multiple applications, whether dynamically or statically, it is often required that each application be isolated from one another. Memory management hardware has provided that isolation in the spatial domain for many years. However, the facilities to support temporal isolation, where the applications share the same computing resource, has only recently become available. This has been brought about by **hierarchical schedulers** and **reservation-based systems**. Usually, two levels of scheduling are used. A global (top-level) scheduler and multiple application-level (second-level) scheduler. Typically the application-level scheduler is also called a **Server** or **Execution-time Server** or **Group Server**. The latter term will be used in this book

Although the above confinement techniques are similar, they have slightly different emphasis. For temporal isolation, the key requirement is that the Group Server be *guaranteed its budget each period*; that is it must be possible for the tasks contained within the group to consume all the group's budget on each release (and not be allowed to consume any more). To support aperiodic execution, it is sufficient that the aperiodic server *consumes no more than its budget each period*. Hence schedulability analysis can be undertaken on tasks scheduled within a group. Whereas, the analysis of the impact of an aperiodic server can be bounded, typically no analysis of the tasks contained within the server need be done. If a group contains only sporadic tasks, the budget must be guaranteed. The goal here is to ensure that the sporadic task does not violated the CPU time that has been allocated to it, for example by being released more often than its minimum inter-arrival time and consuming more than its maximum budget on each release.

With group servers, the schedulability analysis is simpler if the associated tasks are 'bound'. The term 'bound' in this context refers to the relationship between the tasks' periods and the period of the group server. A bound relationship is where the periods of the tasks are exact multiples of the period of the group and have arrival times that coincide with its replenishment.

19.6.1 Programming servers in Ada

Although Ada does not directly support servers, it does provide the primitives from which servers can be programmed.

Group budgets allows different group servers to be implemented; consequently the language itself does not have to provide a small number of predefined server types. Note, servers can be constructed for fixed priority or EDF scheduling.

A typical server has a budget and a replenishment period. At the start of each period, the available budget is restored to its maximum amount. Unused budget at this time is discarded. To program a server requires timing events to trigger replenishment and a means of grouping tasks together and allocating them an amount of CPU resource. A standard package (a child of Ada.Execution_Time – see Program 19.5) is defined to accomplish this. The type Group_Budget represents a CPU budget to be used by a group of tasks on a particular processor.

There are a number of routines defined in this package, consider first those concerned with the grouping of tasks. Each Group_Budget has a set of tasks associated with it. Tasks are added to the set by calls of Add_Task, and removed using Remove_Task. Functions are defined to test if a task in a member of any group budget, or one specific group budget. A further function returns the collection of tasks associated with a group budget by returning an unconstrained array type of task IDs.

An important property of these facilities is that a task can be a member of at most one group budget. Attempting to add it to a second group will cause Group_Budget_Error to be raised. When a task terminates, if it is still a member of a group budget, it is automatically removed.

The budget decreases whenever a task from the associated set executes. The accuracy of this accounting is implementation defined. To increase the amount of budget available, two routines are provided. The Replenish procedure sets the budget to the amount of 'real-time' given in the To parameter. It replaces the current value of the budget. By comparison, the Add procedure increases the budget by the Interval amount. But, as this parameter can be negative it can also be used to, in effect, reduce the budget.

To inquire about the state of the budget, two functions are provided. Note that when Budget_Has_Expired returns True then Budget_Remaining will return Time_Span_Zero.

A handler is associated with a group budget by use of the Set_Handler procedure. There is an implicit event associated with a Group_Budget that occurs whenever the

```ada
with System;
with System.Multiprocessorsl
package Ada.Execution_Time.Group_Budgets is
  type Group_Budget(CPU : System.Multiprocessors.CPU :=
System.Multiprocessors.CPU'First) is tagged limited private;

  type Group_Budget_Handler is access
       protected procedure(GB : in out Group_Budget);

  type Task_Array is array(Positive range <>) of
                               Ada.Task_Identification.Task_ID;

  Min_Handler_Ceiling : constant System.Any_Priority :=
    <Implementation Defined>;

  procedure Add_Task(GB: in out Group_Budget;
                     T : Ada.Task_Identification.Task_ID);
  procedure Remove_Task(GB: in out Group_Budget;
                     T : Ada.Task_Identification.Task_ID);
  function Is_Member(GB: Group_Budget;
           T : Ada.Task_Identification.Task_ID) return Boolean;
  function Is_A_Group_Member(
           T : Ada.Task_Identification.Task_ID) return Boolean;
  function Members(GB: Group_Budget) return Task_Array;

  procedure Replenish(GB: in out Group_Budget; To : Time_Span);
  procedure Add(GB: in out Group_Budget; Interval : Time_Span);
  function Budget_Has_Expired(GB: Group_Budget) return Boolean;
  function Budget_Remaining(GB: Group_Budget) return Time_Span;

  procedure Set_Handler(GB: in out Group_Budget;
                        Handler : Group_Budget_Handler);
  function Current_Handler(GB: Group_Budget)
                           return Group_Budget_Handler;
  procedure Cancel_Handler(GB: in out Group_Budget;
             Cancelled : out Boolean);

  Group_Budget_Error : exception;
private
    -- not specified by the language
end Ada.Execution_Time.Group_Budgets;
```

Program 19.5: The Ada.Execution_Time.Group_Budgets package.

budget goes to zero. If at that time there is a non-null handler set for the budget, the handler will be executed.

As with timers, an implementation must define the minimum ceiling priority level for the protected object linked to any group budget handler. Also note there are `Current_Handler` and `Cancel_Handler` subprograms defined.

By comparison with timers and timing events, which are trigger when a certain clock value is reached (but will then never be reached again for monotonic clocks), the group budget event can occur many times - whenever the budget goes to zero. So the handler is permanently associated with the group budget, it is executed every time the budget is exhausted (obviously following replenishment and further usage). The handler can be changed by a further call to `Set_Handler` or removed by using a null parameter to this routine (or by calling `Cancel_Handler`), but for normal execution the same handler is called each time. The better analogy for a group budget event is an interrupt, its handler is called each time the interrupt occurs.

When the budget is zero, the associated tasks *continue* to execute. If action should be taken when there is no budget, this has to be programmed (it must be instigated by the handler). So group budgets are not in themselves a server abstraction - but they allow these abstractions to be constructed.

To give a simple example, consider four aperiodic tasks that should share a budget of 2ms that is replenished every 10ms. The tasks first register with a `Controller1` protected object that will manage the budget. They then loop around waiting for the next invocation event. In all of the examples in this section, fixed priority scheduling on a single processor is assumed.

```
task Aperiodic_Task is
  with Priority => Some_Value;
end Aperiodic_Task;

task body Aperiodic_Task is
  ...
begin
  Controller1.Register;
  loop
    -- wait for next invocation
    -- undertake the work of the task
  end loop;
end Aperiodic_Task;
```

The `Controller1` protected object will use a timing event and a group budget, and hence defines handlers for both.

```
protected Controller1
    with Interrupt_Priority => Interrupt_Priority'Last is
  entry Register;
  procedure Timer_Handler(E : in out Timing_Event);
  procedure Group_Handler(G : in out Group_Budget);
private
  T_Event : Timing_Event;
  G_Budget : Group_Budget;
  For_All : Boolean := False;
end Controller1;
```

```ada
protected body Controller1 is
  entry Register when Register'Count = 4 or For_All is
  begin
    if not For_All then
      For_All := True;
      G_Budget.Add(Milliseconds(2));
      G_Budget.Add_Task(Register'Caller);
      T_Event.Set_Handler(Milliseconds(10),Timer_Handler'Access);
      G_Budget.Set_Handler(Group_Handler'access);
    else
      G_Budget.Add_Task(Register'Caller);
    end if;
  end Register;

  procedure Timer_Handler(E : in out Timing_Event) is
    T_Array : Task_Array := G_Budget.Members;
  begin
    G_Budget.Replenish(Milliseconds(2));
    for ID in T_Array'Range loop
      Asynchronous_Task_Control.Continue(T_Array(ID));
    end loop;
    E.Set_Handler(Milliseconds(10),Timer_Handler'Access);
  end Timer_Handler;

  procedure Group_Handler(G : in out Group_Budget) is
    T_Array : Task_Array := G.Members;
  begin
    for ID in T_Array'Range loop
      Asynchronous_Task_Control.Hold(T_Array(ID));
    end loop;
  end Group_Handler;
end Controller1;
```

The `Register` entry blocks all calls until each of the four 'clients' have called in. The final task to register (which becomes the first task to enter) sets up the group budget and the timing event, adds itself to the group and alters the boolean flag so that the other three tasks will also complete their registration. For these tasks it is straightforward to add themselves to the group budget. Note the tasks in this example may have different priorities.

The two handlers work together to control the tasks. Whenever the group budget handler executes, it stops the tasks from executing by using the `Hold` routine. It always gets a new list of members in case any have terminated. The `Timer_Handler` releases all the tasks using `Continue`, it replenishes the budget and then sets up another timing event for the next period (10ms).

In a less stringent application it may be sufficient to just prevent new invocations of each task if the budget is exhausted. The current execution is allowed to complete and hence tasks are not suspended. The following example implements this simpler scheme, and additionally allows tasks to register dynamically (rather than all together at the beginning). The protected object is made more general purpose by representing it as a type with discriminants for its main parameters (replenishment in terms of milliseconds and budget measured in microseconds):

```ada
protected type Controller2(Period, Bud : Positive)
    with Interrupt_Priority => Interrupt_Priority'Last is
  procedure Register;
  entry Proceed;
  procedure Timer_Handler(E : in out Timing_Event);
  procedure Group_Handler(G : in out Group_Budget);
private
  T_Event : Timing_Event;
  G_Budget : Group_Budget;
  First : Boolean := True;
  Allowed : Boolean := False;
  Req_Budget : Time_Span := Microseconds(Bud);
  Req_Period : Time_Span := Milliseconds(Period);
end Controller2;

Con : Controller2(10, 2000);
```

The client task would now have the following structure:

```ada
task body Aperiodic_Task is
   ...
begin
  Con.Register;
  ...
  loop
    Con.Proceed; -- wait for next invocation
    -- undertake the work of the task
  end loop;
  ...
end Aperiodic_Task;
```

The body of the controller is as follows:

```ada
protected body Controller2 is
  entry Proceed when Allowed is
  begin
    null;
  end Proceed;

  procedure Register is
  begin
    if First then
      First := False;
      Add(G_Budget,Req_Budget);
      T_Event.Set_Handler(Req_Period,Timer_Handler'Access);
      G_Budget.Set_Handler(Group_Handler'Access);
      Allowed := True;
    end if;
    G_Budget.Add_Task(Current_Task);
  end Register;

  procedure Timer_Handler(E : in out Timing_Event) is
  begin
    Allowed := True;
```

```ada
      G_Budget.Replenish(Req_Budget);
      E.Set_Handler(Req_Period,Timer_Handler'Access);
   end Timer_Handler;

   procedure Group_Handler(G : in out Group_Budget) is
   begin
      Allowed := False;
   end Group_Handler;
end Controller2;
```

The next example illustrates a Deferrable Server. Here, the server has a fixed priority, and when the budget is exhausted, the tasks are moved to a background priority Priority'First (using the facilities found in the Ada.Dynamic_Priorities package). This is closer to the first example, but retains some of the properties of the second approach:

```ada
protected type Controller3(Period, Bud : Positive;
                Pri : Priority)
   with Interrupt_Priority => Interrupt_Priority'Last is
   procedure Register;
   procedure Timer_Handler(E : in out Timing_Event);
   procedure Group_Handler(G : in out Group_Budget);
private
   T_Event : Timing_Event;
   G_Budget : Group_Budget;
   First : Boolean := True;
   Req_Budget : Time_Span := Microseconds(Bud);
   Req_Period : Time_Span := Milliseconds(Period);
end Controller3;

Con : Controller3(10, 2000, 12);
-- assume this server has priority 12

protected body Controller3 is
   procedure Register is
   begin
      if First then
         First := False;
         G_Budget.Add(Req_Budget);
         T_Event.Set_Handler(Req_Period,Timer_Handler'Access);
         G_Budget.Set_Handler(Group_Handler'Access);
      end if;
      Add_Task(G_Budget,Current_Task);
      if G_Budget.Budget_Has_Expired then
         Set_Priority(Priority'First); -- background priority
      else
         Set_Priority(Pri); -- servers priority
      end if;
   end Register;

   procedure Timer_Handler(E : in out Timing_Event) is
      T_Array : Task_Array := G_Budget.Members;
   begin
```

```
   G_Budget.Replenish(Req_Budget);
   for ID in T_Array'Range loop
     Set_Priority(Pri,T_Array(ID));
   end loop;
   E.Set_Handler(Req_Period,Timer_Handler'Access);
 end Timer_Handler;

 procedure Group_Handler(G : in out Group_Budget) is
   T_Array : Task_Array := G_Budget.Members;
 begin
   for ID in T_Array'Range loop
     Set_Priority(Priority'First,T_Array(ID));
   end loop;
 end Group_Handler;
end Controller3;
```

When a task registers, it is running outside the budget so it is necessary to check if the budget is exhausted during registration. If it is, the priority of the task must be set to the low value.

19.7 Error recovery

Once timing errors have been detected, strategies for recovery must be developed. Inevitably this is application-dependent, however there are several techniques that can be utilized. This section first considers recovery at the individual task level, and then considers more system-wide responses.

19.7.1 Task-level recovery

The goal of the damage-confinement techniques outlined in the previous section has been to attempt to isolate timing errors to individual tasks or groups of tasks.

Strategies for handling WCET overrun

Monitoring WCET overrun has been suggested as a mechanisms for detecting a common fault before the error propagates outside the errant task. Once detected, the task response will depend on whether it is a hard, soft or firm.

- WCET overrun in hard real-time tasks – Although the error detection techniques introduced in Chapter 3 have detected functional failures that might cause overruns (such as non-terminating loops), WCET overrun can still occur due to inaccuracies in calculating the WCET values. One possibility, is that the WCET values used in the schedulability analysis discussed in Part II of this book consists of the addition of two components. The first is the time allocated for the primary algorithm and the second is the time for recovery (assuming a fault hypothesis of a single failure per task per release). The first time is the time that is used by the system when monitoring. When this time passes, forward or backward error recovery occurs and the alternative algorithm is executed. This can either be within the same task and the budget increased, or by releasing a dedicated recovery task. Typically, these alternative algorithms try to provide a degraded service. Another possibility is simply to do nothing. This assumes that there is enough slack in the system for the task (and other lower priority tasks) to still meet their deadlines.

- WCET overruns in soft/firm real-time tasks – Typically overruns in soft and firm real-time tasks can be ignored if the isolation techniques guarantee the capacity needed for the hard real-time tasks. Alternatively, the tasks priorities can be lowered, or the current releases can be terminated and the tasks re-released when their next release event occurs.

As an example of the later, consider the use of Ada's execution-time timers to lower the priority of a task if it overruns its worst-case execution time. In this example, the task has a worst-case execution time of 1.25ms per invocation. If it executes for more than this value its priority should be lowered from its correct value of 14 to a minimum value of 2. If it is still executing after a further 0.25ms then that invocation of the task must be terminated; this implies the use of an ATC construct. First, the overrun handler protected type is defined

```ada
protected Overrun with Priority => Min_Handler_Ceiling is
  entry Stop_Task;
  procedure Handler(TM : in out Timer);
  procedure Reset(C1 : CPU_Time);
private
  Abandon : Boolean := False;
  First_Occurence : Boolean := True;
  WCET_Overrun : CPU_Time;
end Overrun;

protected body Overrun is

  entry Stop_Task when Abandon is
  begin
    null;
  end Stop_Task;

  procedure Reset(C1 : CPU_Time) is
  begin
    Abandon := False;
    First_Occurence := True;
    WCET_Overrun := C1;
  end Reset;

  procedure Handler(TM : in out Timer) is
  begin
    if First_Occurence then
      Set_Handler(TM,WCET_Overrun,Handler'Access);
      Set_Priority(2, TM.T.all);
      First_Occurence := False;
    else
      Abandon := True;
    end if;
```

448 TOLERATING TIMING FAULTS

```ada
   end Handler;
end Overrun;
```

It may not be immediately clear why a `Reset` routine is required. But without it a race condition may lead to incorrect execution. Consider the code of the task:

```ada
task Hard_Example;
task body Hard_Example is
   ID : aliased Task_ID := Current_Task;
   WCET_Error : Timer(ID'access);
   WCET : CPU_Time := Ada.Execution_Time.Time_Of(0,
                     Microseconds(1250));
   WCET_Overrun : CPU_Time := Time_Of(0,Microseconds(250));
   Bool : Boolean := False;
   ...
begin
   -- initialisation
   loop
      Overrun.Reset(WCET_Overrun);
      Set_Handler(WCET_Error,WCET,Overrun.Handler'Access);
      select
         Overrun.Stop_Task;
         -- handler the error if possible at priority level 2
      then abort
         -- code of the application
      end select;
      Cancel_Handler(WCET_Error, Bool);
      Set_Priority(14);
      delay until ...
   end loop;
   ...
end Hard_Example;
```

It is possible for the timer to trigger (or *expire*) after completion of the select statement but before it can be cancelled. This would leave the state of the boolean variable, `Abandon` with the incorrect value of `True`. Similarly, it is necessary to cancel the timer before changing the priority back to 14 - otherwise the event could trigger just before executing the delay statement and the task would be stuck with the wrong low priority for its next invocation.

Strategies for handling sporadic event overruns

There are several responses to the violation of minimum inter-arrival time of a sporadic task: the release event can be ignore, an exception can be thrown, the last event can be overwritten, (if it has not already been acted upon) or the actual release of the task can be delayed until the MIT has passed. Of course, the task could ignore the violation and executed anyway.

Strategies for handling deadline misses

Although the early identification of potential timing problems facilitate damage assessment, many real-time systems just focus on the recovery from missed deadlines. Again, several strategies are possible.

Deadline miss of hard real-time tasks – It is possible to set two deadlines for each task. An early deadline whose miss will cause the invocation of forward or backward error recovery. A later deadline is the deadline used by the schedulability test. In both cases, the recovery should aim to produce a degraded service for the task.

Deadline miss of soft real-time task – Typically this can be ignored and treated as a transient overload situation. A count of missed deadlines can be maintained, and when it passes a certain threshold a health monitoring system can be informed (see below).

Deadline miss of a firm real-time task – As a firm task produces no value passed its deadline, its current release can be terminated.

As an example of handling a deadline miss, consider a soft real-time system where an application wishes to monitor any deadline misses, but take no action unless a certain threshold is reached. When it is reached, a health monitor task must be released. One approach is to use a variation of the watchdog introduced in Section 19.2. The following code illustrates this approach.

```
with ...; use ...;
package Deadline_Miss_Handlers is
  protected type Deadline_Miss_Handler(Event : access Timing_Event;
                                       Threshhold : Integer) is
    with Interrupt_Priority => Interrupt_Priority'Last;

    procedure Initialize(First_Deadline : Time;
                         Required_Period : Time_Span);
    entry Alarm_Control(T: out Task_Id);
    -- Called by health monitoring task
    procedure Call_In;
    -- Called by application code when it completes.

  private
    procedure Miss_Handler(Event : in out Timing_Event);
    Alarm : Boolean := False;
    Tid : Task_Id;
    Next_Deadline : Time;
    Period : Time_Span;
    Deadlines_Missed : Integer := 0;
    Current_Deadline_Missed : Boolean := False;
  end Deadline_Miss_Handler;
end Deadline_Miss_Handlers;

package body Deadline_Miss_Handlers is
  protected body Deadline_Miss_Handler is
    procedure Initialize(First_Deadline : Time;
                         Required_Period : Time_Span) is
```

```
   begin
     Next_Deadline := First_Deadline;
     Period := Required_Period;
     Set_Handler(Event.all, Next_Deadline, Timer'Access);
     Tid := Current_Task;
   end Initialize;

   entry Alarm_Control(T: out Task_Id) when Alarm is
   begin
     T := Tid;
     Alarm := False;
   end Alarm_Control;

   procedure Miss_Handler(Event : in out Timing_Event) is
   begin
     Current_Deadline_Missed := True;
     Deadlines_Missed := Deadlines_Missed + 1;
     if Deadlines_Missed = Threshhold then
        Alarm := True;
        Deadlines_Missed := 0;
     end if;
   end Miss_Handler;

   procedure Call_In is
   begin
     if not Current_Deadline_Missed and Deadlines_Missed > 0 then
        Deadlines_Missed := Deadlines_Missed - 1;
     end if;
     Next_Deadline := Next_Deadline + Period;
     Set_Handler(Event.all, Next_Deadline, Timer'Access);
     -- Note this call to Set_Handler cancels the previous call
   end Call_In;
  end Deadline_Miss_Handler;
end Deadline_Miss_Handlers;
```

19.7.2 Mode changes and event-based reconfiguration

In the above discussions, it has generally been assumed that a missed deadline and other timing errors can be dealt with by the task that is actually responsible for the problem. This is not always the case. Often the consequences of a timing error are as follows.

- Other tasks must alter their deadlines or even terminate what they are doing.
- New tasks may need to be started.
- Critically important computation may require more processor time than is currently available; to obtain the extra time, other less significant tasks may need to be 'suspended' (See next section).
- Tasks may need to be 'interrupted' in order to undertake one of the following (typically):

– immediately return their best results they have obtained so far;
– change to quicker (but presumably less accurate) algorithms;
– abandon what they are presently doing and become ready to take new instructions: 'restart without reload'.

These actions are sometimes known as **event-based reconfiguration**.

Some systems may additionally enter unanticipated situations in which deadlines are liable to be missed. A good illustration of this is found in systems that experience **unplanned mode changes**. This is where some event in the environment occurs which results in certain computations that have already been initialized, no longer being required. If the system were to complete these computations then other deadlines would be missed; it is thus necessary to terminate prematurely the tasks or temporal scopes that contain the computations.

To perform event-based reconfiguration and mode changes requires communication between the tasks concerned. Due to the asynchronous nature of this communication, it is necessary to use the asynchronous notification mechanisms (see Section 18.4). These mechanisms are low level; arguably what is really required is to be able to tell the scheduler to stop invoking certain threads that are now not required and to begin to invoke other tasks. In Ada, this can be achieved using the `Ada.Asynchronous_Task_Control` package – see Program 15.2.

19.7.3 Mixed criticality systems

Section 8.1 identified an increasingly important trend in the design of real-time and embedded systems that of the integration of components with different levels of criticality onto a common hardware platform. As discussed in that section, a key aspect of these Mixed Criticality Systems (MCS) is that system parameters, such as tasks' worst-case execution times (WCETs), become dependent on the criticality level of the tasks. So the same code will have a higher WCET if it is defined to be safety-critical (as a higher level of assurance is required) than it would if it is just considered to be mission critical or indeed non-critical.

A MCS is therefore composed of a collection of multi-task applications/components running on the same hardware. Each application, and hence each task, is allocated a criticality level, and may have more than one estimate of WCET. The fact that with MCS a task may have more than one WCET parameter significantly alters the approach to scheduling. One such approach was presented in Section 8.1.2. It required that a low criticality task should never execute for more than its WCET when it is interfering with lower priority but higher-integrity tasks. And higher-integrity tasks, if they executed beyond defined bounds, can cause lower-integrity tasks to have their priorities reduced; a form of event-based reconfiguration.

This section sketches an implementation of the priority changing protocol. The code is assumed to execute on a bare machine single processor implementation.

All priorities are changed from within a protected object (`Pri_Changer`). An execution time handler (`Timer`) is defined for each task. For lower criticality tasks this handler is called if and when any invocation of the task executes for more than its defined WCET. For higher criticality tasks the handler is called when the lower bound on its execution time is exceeded. If both situations the priorities of the lower criticality tasks are reduced so that all higher criticality tasks have priorities higher than all lower criticality tasks.

In order for the system to return to the original priority settings, a background (lowest priority) control task is included in the system. This task will only execute if there is no work for the real tasks to undertake (i.e. all system tasks are suspended). At this time it is safe to return the low criticality tasks to their default (higher) priorities.

The `Pri_Changer` object again makes use of the dynamic priorities package. It therefore needs to record the task IDs of the system's tasks, and the specific priorities to be used in the two modes. The priority changer is specified in the following package:

```
with System;
with Ada.Task_Identification; use Ada.Task_Identification;
with Ada.Execution_Time.Timers; use Ada.Execution_Time.Timers;
with Ada.Dynamic_Priorities; use Ada.Dynamic_Priorities;
package Overload_Control is
   Max_Tasks : constant natural := ...;
   type Mode is (Normal, Overload);
   type Task_Ids is array(1..Max_Tasks) of Task_ID;

   protected Pri_Changer is
      with Priority => Min_Handler_Ceiling is
      procedure Change;
        -- called by background task
      procedure Changer(TM : in out Timer);
        -- called by the Timer handlers
      procedure Register(N : Natural);
        -- called once by each system tasks
   private
      Current_Mode : Mode := Normal;
      IDs : Task_Ids;
   end Pri_Changer;
end Overload_Control;
```

The body of this package is as follows:

```
package body Overload_Control is
   Task_Pris : array(1..Max_Tasks, Mode) of positive;
   protected body Pri_Changer is
     procedure Change is
     begin
        if Current_Mode = Overload then
           Current_Mode := Normal;
           for I in 1..Max_Tasks loop
              Set_Priority(Task_Pris(I,Normal),IDs(I));
           end loop;
        end if;
     end Change;
     procedure Changer(TM : in out Timer) is
     begin
        if Current_Mode = Normal then
           Current_Mode := Overload;
           for I in 1..Max_Tasks loop
              Set_Priority(Task_Pris(I,Overload),IDs(I));
```

```
         end loop;
       end if;
    end Changer;
    procedure Register(N : Natural) is
    begin
       IDs(N) := Current_Task;
    end Register;
  end Pri_Changer;
begin
  -- the static values represent the required
  -- priorities in the two modes are assigned to
  -- the Task_Pris array
end Overload_Control;
```

The background task has a low priority and whenever its get to run it calls Change in the protected object Pri_Changer and attempts to return the system to the normal mode. For most executions of the task this will be a 'null op' as the system will be in this mode. However, execution time is not wasted as this task only runs when the system is otherwise idle.

The code for each periodic task has the usual form. Each task uses a Timer, with the handler being assigned to Pri_Changer.Changer'Access.

Summary

This chapter has discussed the toleration of timing faults from with the framework of dynamic software fault tolerance. Timing faults manifest themselves in the following conditions:

- overrun of deadline,
- overrun of worst-case execution time,
- sporadic events occurring more often than predicted,
- overrun of resource usage.

Ada provides low-level mechanisms that the programmer can use to detect these faults:

- overrun of deadline – detected by using of the Ada.Timing_Events package or the select-then-abort statement,
- overrun of worst-case execution time – detected by using the Ada.Execution_Time and the Ada.Execution_Time.Timers packages,
- sporadic events occurring more often than predicted – detected by using the Ada.Timing_Events package in conjunction with protected objects.

Overrun of resource usage is difficult to detect. The amount of execution time consumed in protected operations can be monitored (using Ada.Execution_Time and the `Ada.Execution_Time.Timers` packages) but given that these operations are meant to be short, it is not clear this is worth the resulting overheads.

Execution time and aperiodic servers provide the main mechanisms in support of damage confinement. Ada provides this via the notion of group budgets. It has a flexible set of mechanisms that allow various server approaches to be implemented (using the `Ada.Execution_Time.Group_Budget`, `Ada.Timing_Events` packages and protected objects).

Error recovery strategies depend on an application's context. Many timing errors can be considered transient and can be ignored. Others require a task to stop what it is doing and undertake an alternative action. On occasions, a task in isolation can not deal with the problem and reconfiguration and mode changes may need to be performed. In a mixed criticality system, recovery may involve degraded provisions for the lower criticality tasks (e.g. run them at a lower priority than that required to ensure they meet their deadlines).

In some high-integrity applications, there is little scope for error handling within the program itself. A deadline miss will lead to attempt to recover at the system level. This could involve a switch to another version of the software running on another processor, or the cold restarting of the current program.

Part IV

CONCLUSIONS

Chapter 20
Mine control case study

20.1 Mine drainage
20.2 The HRT-HOOD design method
20.3 The logical architecture design
20.4 The physical architecture design
20.5 Translation to Ada
20.6 Fault tolerance and distribution
Summary

In this chapter, a case study is presented which includes many of the facilities described in this book. A full design is given using the HRT-HOOOD design method and the UML diagrammatical notation. Implementation in Ada is then derived from systematic translations. As the goal of this chapter is to illustrate the real-time programming abstractions, these translations are kept as simply as possible.

A full implementation is shown for the real-time components in Ada with the Ravenscar profile.

20.1 Mine drainage

The example that has been chosen is based on one which commonly appears in the literature. It concerns the software necessary to manage a simplified pump control system for a mining environment [49, 75, 74, 22, 47, 29]; it possesses many of the characteristics which typify embedded real-time systems. It is assumed that the system will be implemented on a single processor with a simple memory-mapped I/O architecture.

The system is used to pump water, which collects in a sump at the bottom of the mine shaft, to the surface. The main safety requirement is that the pump should not be operated when the level of methane gas in the mine reaches a high value due to the risk of explosion. A simple schematic diagram of the system is given in Figure 20.1.

The relationship between the control system and the external devices is shown in Figure 20.2. Note that only the high and low water sensors communicate via interrupts (indicated by dashed arrows); all the other devices are either polled or directly controlled.

458   MINE CONTROL CASE STUDY

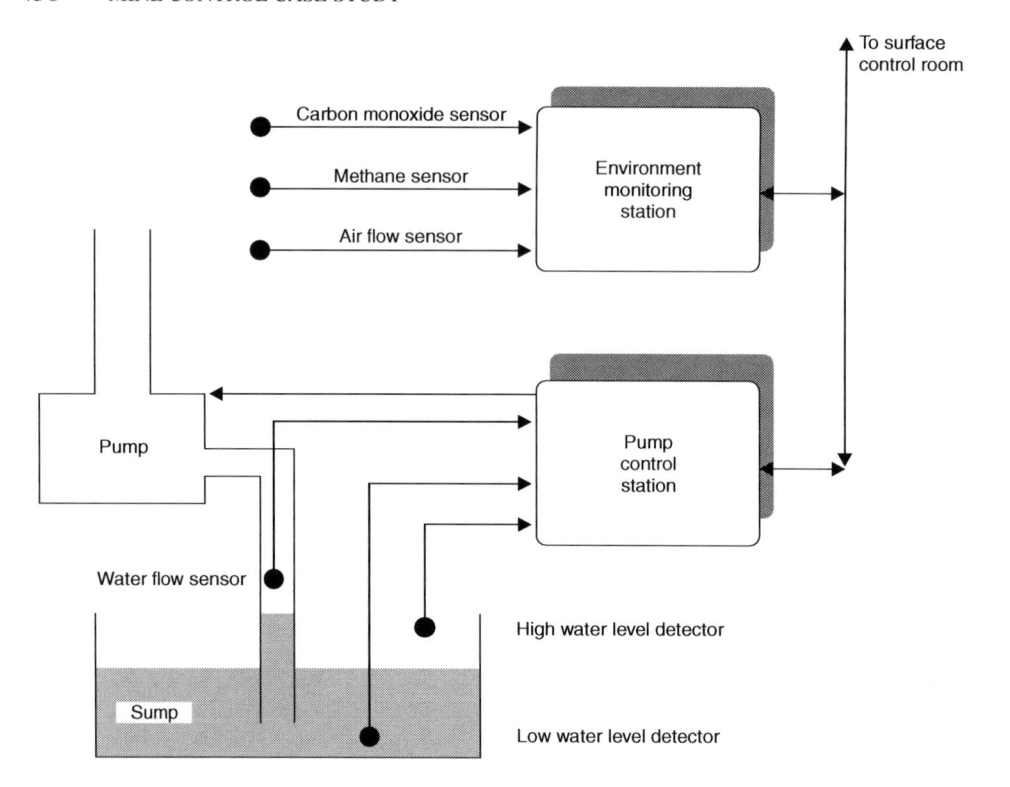

Figure 20.1: A mine drainage control system.

Most traditional software development methods incorporate a life cycle model in which the following activities are recognized:

- requirements specification – during which an authoritative specification of the system's required functional and non-functional behaviour is produced;
- architectural design – during which a top-level description of the proposed system is developed;
- detailed design – during which the complete system design is specified;
- coding – during which the system is implemented;
- testing – during which the efficacy of the system is tested.

For hard real-time systems, this has the significant disadvantage that timing problems will only be recognized during testing, or worse, after deployment. HRT-HOOD [24] is different from traditional design methods in that it directly addresses the concerns of hard real-time systems. It views the design process as a progression of increasingly specific *commitments* [22]. These commitments define properties of the system design which designers operating at a more detailed level are not at liberty to change. Those aspects of a design to which no commitment is made at some particular level in the design hierarchy are effectively the subject of *obligations* that lower levels of design must address. Early

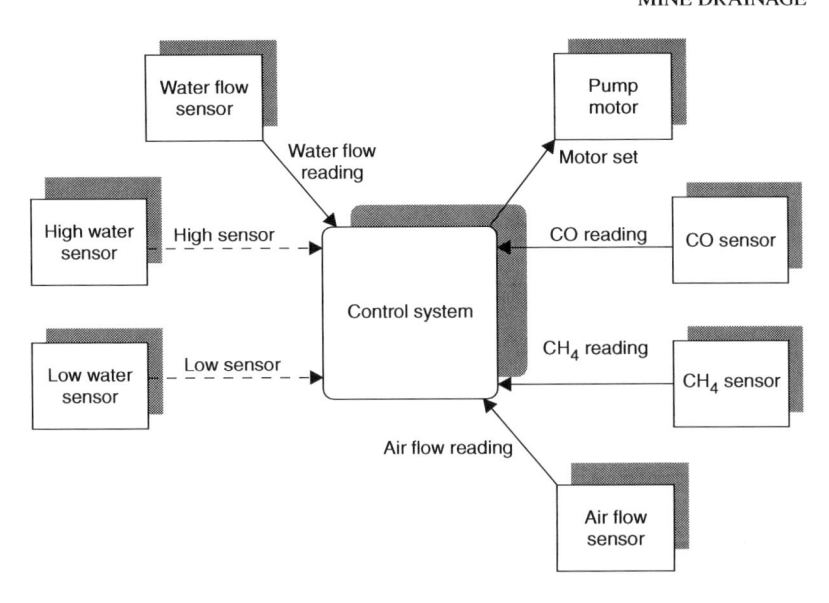

Figure 20.2: Graph showing external devices.

in design there may already be commitments to the architectural structure of a system, in terms of object definitions and relationships. However, the detailed behaviour of the defined objects remains the subject of obligations which must be met during further design and implementation.

The process of refining a design – transforming obligations into commitments – is often subject to *constraints* imposed primarily by the execution environment. The execution environment is the set of hardware and software components (for example, processors, task dispatchers, device drivers) on top of which the system is built. It may impose both resource constraints (for example, processor speed, communication bandwidth) and constraints of mechanism (for example, interrupt priorities, task dispatching, data locking). To the extent that the execution environment is immutable, these constraints are fixed.

Obligations, commitments and constraints have an important influence on the architectural design of any application. Therefore HRT-HOOD defines two activities of the architectural design:

- the logical architecture design activity;
- the physical architecture design activity.

The logical architecture embodies commitments which can be made independently of the constraints imposed by the execution environment, and is primarily aimed at satisfying the functional requirements (although the existence of timing requirements, such as end-to-end deadlines, will strongly influence the decomposition of the logical architecture). The physical architecture takes these functional requirements and other constraints into account, and embraces the non-functional requirements. The physical architecture forms the basis for asserting that the application's non-functional requirements will be met once the detailed design and implementation have taken place. It addresses timing and dependability requirements, and the necessary schedulability analysis that will ensure (guarantee) that the system, once built, will function correctly in both the value and time domains.

Although the physical architecture is a refinement of the logical architecture, its development will usually be an iterative and concurrent process in which both models are developed/modified. The analysis techniques embodied in the physical architecture can, and should, be applied as early as possible. Initial resource budgets can be defined that are then subject to modification and revision as the logical architecture is refined. In this way a 'feasible' design is tracked from requirements through to deployment.

In this Chapter, the HRT-HOOD method is followed but UML is used to represent the logical and physical architectures.

20.1.1 Functional requirements

The functional specification of the system may be divided into four components: the pump operation, the environment monitoring, the operator interaction, and system monitoring.

Pump operation

The required behaviour of the pump controller is that it monitors the water levels in the sump. When the water reaches a high level (or when requested by the operator), the pump is turned on and the sump is drained until the water reaches the low level. At this point (or when requested by the operator), the pump is turned off. A flow of water in the pipes can be detected if required.

The pump should only be allowed to operate if the methane level in the mine is below a critical level. An alarm should be signalled if the pump cannot operate or if there is no water flow when there should be.

Environment monitoring

The environment must be monitored to detect the level of methane in the air; there is a level beyond which it is not safe to cut coal or operate the pump. The monitoring also measures the level of carbon monoxide in the mine and detects whether there is an adequate flow of air. Alarms must be signalled if gas levels or air-flow become critical.

Operator interaction

The system is controlled from the surface via an operator's console. The operator is informed of all critical events.

System monitoring

All the system events are to be stored in an archival database, and may be retrieved and displayed upon request.

MINE DRAINAGE 461

20.1.2 Non-functional requirements

The non-functional requirements can be divided into three components: timing, dependability, and security. This case study is mainly concerned with the timing requirements and consequently dependability and security will not be addressed (see Burns and Lister [22] for a full consideration of dependability and security aspects).

There are several requirements which relate to the timeliness of system actions. The following list is adapted from Burns and Lister [22]:

(i) Monitoring periods

The maximum periods for reading the environment sensors may be dictated by legislation. For the purpose of this example, it is assumed that these periods are the same for all sensors, namely 100 ms. In the case of methane, there may be a more stringent requirement based on the proximity of the pump and the need to ensure that it never operates when the methane level is critically high. This is discussed in (ii) below. In Section 16.4, it was described how a device driver can be analysed. In the case study, the 'period displacement' approach will be used for the CH_4 and CO sensors. These environmental sensors each require 40 ms in order for a reading to become available. Hence they require a deadline of 60 ms.

The water flow object executes periodically and has two roles. While the pump is operational it checks that there is a water flow; but while the pump is off (or disabled) it also checks that the water has stopped flowing. This latter check is used as confirmation that the pump has indeed been stopped. Due to a time lag in the flow of water, this object is given a period of 1 second, and it uses the results of two consecutive readings to determine the actual state of the pump. To make sure that two consecutive readings are actually one second apart (approximately), the object is given a tight deadline of 40 ms (that is, two readings will be at least 960 ms, but no more than 1040 ms, apart).

It is assumed that the water level detectors are event-driven and that the system should respond within 200 ms. The physics of the application indicates that there must be at least 6 seconds between interrupts from the two water level indicators.

(ii) Shut-down deadline

To avoid explosions, there is a deadline within which the pump must be switched off once the methane level exceeds a critical threshold. This deadline is related to the methane-sampling period, to the rate at which methane can accumulate, and to the margin of safety between the level of methane regarded as critical and the level at which it explodes. With a direct reading of the sensor, the relationship can be expressed by the inequality:

R(T + D) < M

where
    R is the rate at which methane can accumulate
    T is the sampling period
    D is the shut-down deadline
    M is the safety margin.

If 'period displacement' is used then a further period of time is needed:

	Periodic/sporadic	Period	Deadline
CH$_4$ sensor	P	80	30
CO sensor	P	100	60
Air flow	P	100	100
Water flow	P	1000	40
High water level detector	S	6000	200
Low water level detector	S	6000	200

Table 20.1: Attributes of periodic and sporadic entities.

```
R(2T + D) < M
```

Note that the period T and the deadline D can be traded off against each other, and both can be traded off against the safety margin M. The longer the period or the deadline, the more conservative must be the safety margin; the shorter the period or deadline, the closer to its safety limits the mine can operate. The designer may therefore vary any of D, T or M in satisfying the deadline and periodicity requirements.

In this example, it is assumed that the presence of methane pockets may cause levels to rise rapidly, and therefore a deadline requirement (from methane going high to the pump been disabled) of 200 ms is assumed. This can be met by setting the rate for the methane sensor at 80 ms, with a deadline of 30 ms. Note that this level will ensure that correct readings are taken from the sensor (that is, the displacement between two readings is at least 50 ms).

(iii) Operator information deadline

The operator must be informed within 1 second of detection of critically high methane or carbon monoxide readings, within 2 seconds of a critically low air-flow reading, and within 3 seconds of a failure in the operation of the pump. These requirements are easily met when compared with the other timing requirements.

In summary, Table 20.1 defines the periods, or minimum inter-arrival times ('period') and deadlines (in milliseconds) for the sensors.

20.2 The HRT-HOOD design method

HRT-HOOD facilitates the logical architectural design of a system by providing different object types. They are:

- **Passive** – reentrant objects which have no control over when invocations of their operations are executed, and do not spontaneously invoke operations in other objects.
- **Active** – objects which may control when invocations of their operations are executed, and may spontaneously invoke operations in other objects. Active objects are the most general class of objects and have no restrictions placed on them.

- **Protected** – objects which may control when invocations of their operations are executed, but do not spontaneously invoke operations in other objects; in general protected objects may **not** have arbitrary synchronisation constraints and must be analysable for the blocking times they impose on their callers.
- **Cyclic** – objects which represent periodic activities, they may spontaneously invoke operations in other objects and only have very restrictive interfaces.
- **Sporadic** – objects which represent sporadic activities; sporadic objects may spontaneously invoke operations in other objects; each sporadic has a **single** operation which is called to invoke the sporadic.

A hard real-time program designed using HRT-HOOD will contain at the terminal level (that is, after full design decomposition) only cyclic, sporadic, protected and passive objects. Active objects, because they cannot be fully analysed, are only allowed for background activity. Active object types may be used during decomposition of the main system but must be transformed into one of the other types before reaching the terminal level. HRT-HOOD supports the hierarchical decomposition of a *parent* object into *child* objects.

Within each cyclic and sporadic object, there will be a single task that is the entity subject to schedulability analysis as part of the verification of the physical architecture.

20.3 The logical architecture design

The logical architecture addresses those requirements which are independent of the physical constraints (for example, processor speed) imposed by the execution environment. The functional requirements identified in Section 20.1.1 fall into this category. Consideration of the other system requirements is deferred until the design of the physical architecture, described later.

20.3.1 First level decomposition

The first step in developing the logical architecture is the identification of appropriate subsystems from which the system can be built. The functional requirements of the system suggest four distinct components:

(1) pump controller component – responsible for operating the pump;
(2) environment monitor component – responsible for monitoring the environment;
(3) operator console component – responsible for the interface to the operators;
(4) data logger component – responsible for logging operational and environmental data.

Figure 20.3 illustrates this decomposition. Each component has a number of provided and required interfaces.

- The `PumpController` provides one interface to the system (`PumpOperations`) which exports all the operations that are available on the pump. Both the

464   MINE CONTROL CASE STUDY

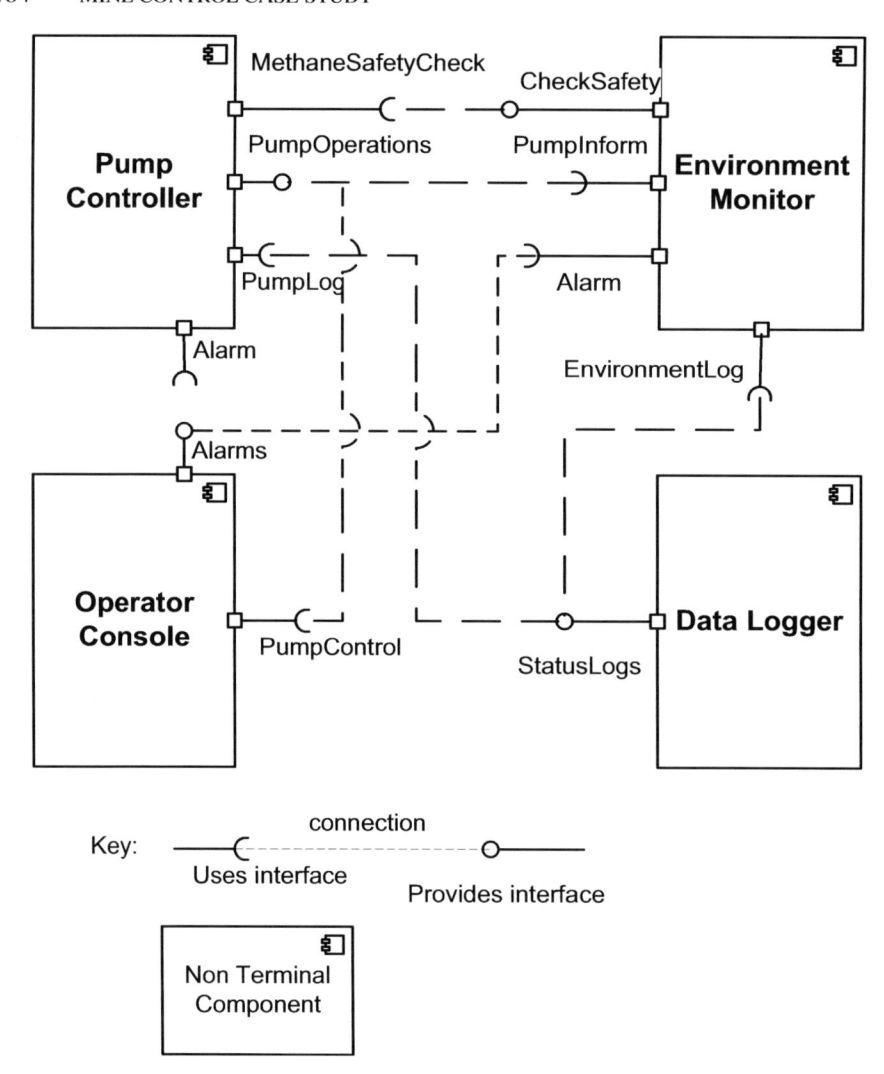

Figure 20.3: First-level component decomposition of the control system.

`OperatorConsole` and the `EnvironmentMonitor` make use of these operations through their respective required interfaces. Figures 20.4 shows the relationship between these interfaces. The operations 'not safe' and 'is safe' are called by the `EnvironmentMonitor` to inform the `PumpController` whether it is safe to operate the pump (due to the level of methane in the environment). The 'request status' and 'set pump' operations are called by the `OperatorConsole`.

- The `PumpController` makes use of the services provided by the others components via its `MethaneSafetyCheck`, `PumpLog`, and `Alarm` required interfaces (see Figure 20.5 where all the other relationship between the various interfaces are shown.). As an additional reliability feature, the pump controller will always check

THE LOGICAL ARCHITECTURE DESIGN

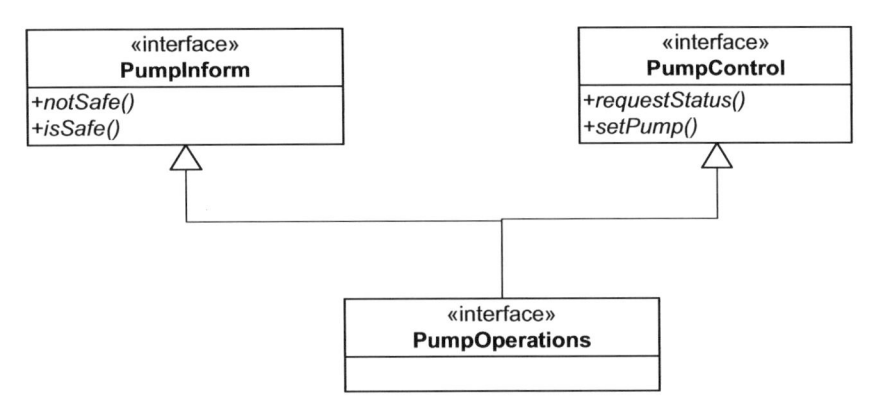

Figure 20.4: `PumpController` related interfaces.

that the methane level is low before starting the pump (by calling 'check safe' operation via the `MethaneSafetyCheck` interface). If the pump controller finds that the pump cannot be started (or that the water does not appear to be flowing when the pump is notionally on) then it raises an alarm through the `Alarm` interface. The pump reports its state changes via the `PumpLog` interface.

- The `EnvironmentMonitor` has the single operation 'check safe' which it provides via the `CheckSafety` interface.

- The `OperatorConsole` provides the alarm operation via the `Alarms` interface, which as well as being called by the `PumpController`, is also called by the `EnvironmentalMonitor` if any of its readings are too high. As well as receiving the alarm calls, the `OperatorConsole` can request the status of the pump and attempt to override the high and low water sensors by directly operating the pump. However, in the latter case the methane check is still made, with an exception being used to inform the operator that the pump cannot be turned on.

- The `DataLogger` support six operations which are merely data logging actions that are called by the pump controller and the environment monitor.

20.3.2 Pump controller

The decomposition appropriate to the pump controller is shown in Figure 20.6. The pump controller is decomposed into three objects. The first object controls the pump motor. As this object simply responds to commands, requires mutual exclusion for its operations, and does not spontaneously call other objects, it is a *protected* object. All of the pump controller's operations are implemented by the motor object. As the system is real-time, none of the operations can be arbitrarily blocked (although they require mutual exclusion).

The other two objects control the water sensors. The flow sensor object is a *cyclic* object which continually monitors the flow of water from the mine. The high–low water sensor is an *active* object which handles the interrupts from the high and low water sensors. It decomposes into two *sporadic* objects, as shown in Figure 20.7.

466   MINE CONTROL CASE STUDY

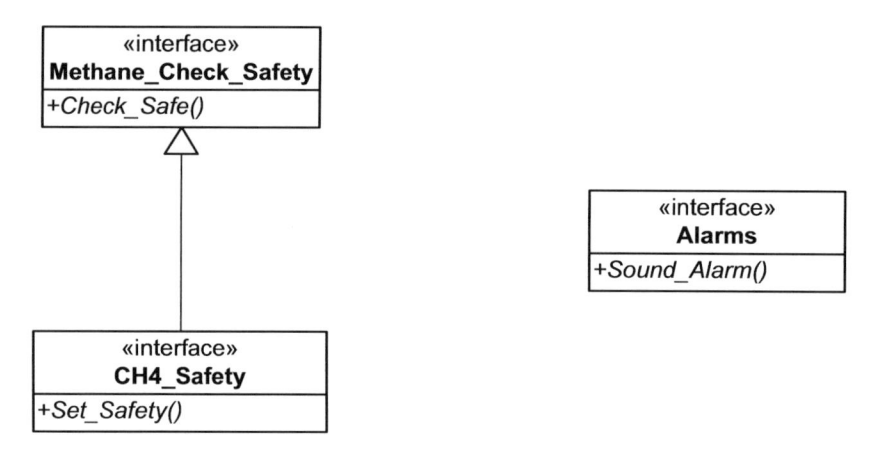

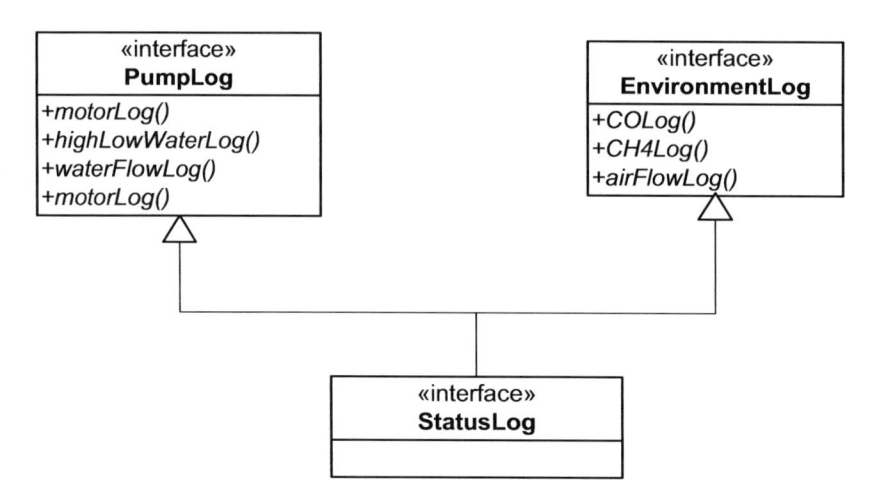

```
«interface»
Methane_Check_Safety
+Check_Safe()
        △
        |
«interface»
CH4_Safety
+Set_Safety()

«interface»
Alarms
+Sound_Alarm()

«interface»
PumpLog
+motorLog()
+highLowWaterLog()
+waterFlowLog()
+motorLog()

«interface»
EnvironmentLog
+COLog()
+CH4Log()
+airFlowLog()

«interface»
StatusLog
```

Figure 20.5: Other defined interfaces.

20.3.3   The environment monitor

The environment monitor decomposes into four terminal objects, as shown in Figure 20.8. Three of the objects are *cyclic* objects which monitor the CH_4 level, CO level and the air flow in the mine environment. Only the CH_4 level is requested by other objects in the system; consequently a *protected* object is used to control access to the current value.

20.3.4   The data logger and the operator console

This case study is not concerned with the details of the data logger or the operator console. However, it is a requirement that they only delay the real-time tasks for a bounded time. It is assumed, therefore, that their interfaces contain protected objects.

THE PHYSICAL ARCHITECTURE DESIGN   467

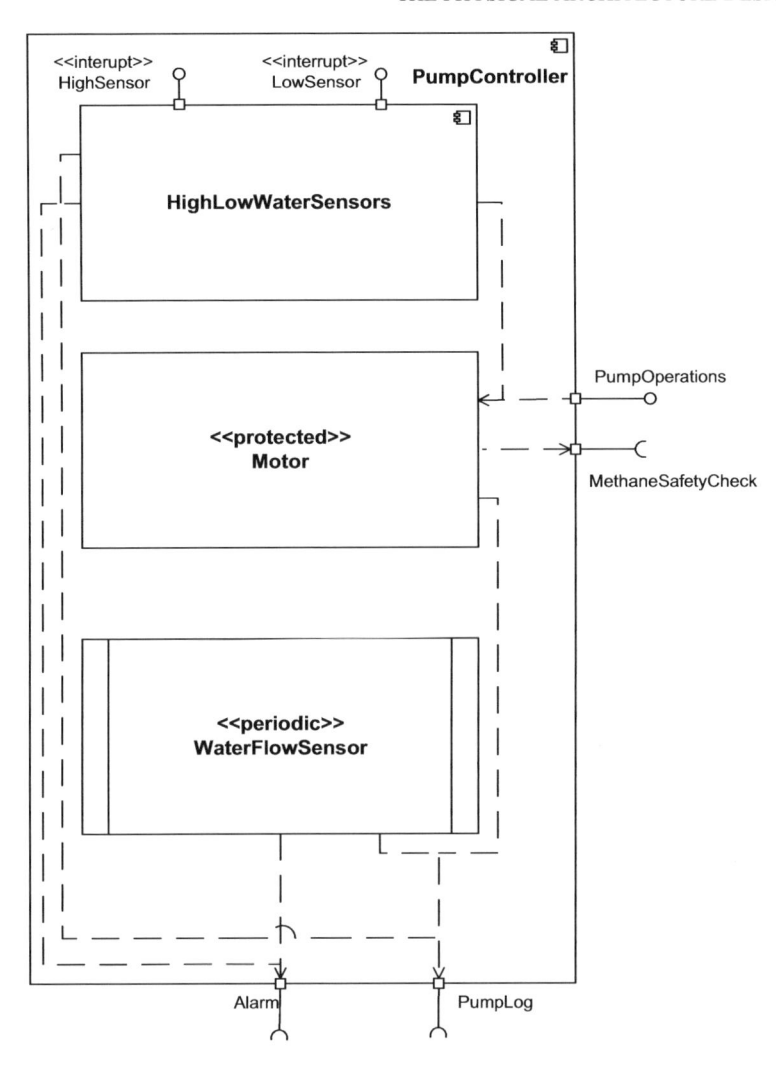

Figure 20.6: Hierarchical decomposition of the `PumpController` object.

20.4 The physical architecture design

HRT-HOOD supports the design of a physical architecture by:

- allowing timing attributes to be associated with objects,
- providing a framework from within which a schedulability approach can be defined and the analysis of the terminal objects undertaken, and
- providing the abstractions with which the designer can express the handling of timing errors.

To illustrate the analysis described in Chapter 5, fixed priority scheduling will be used and

468   MINE CONTROL CASE STUDY

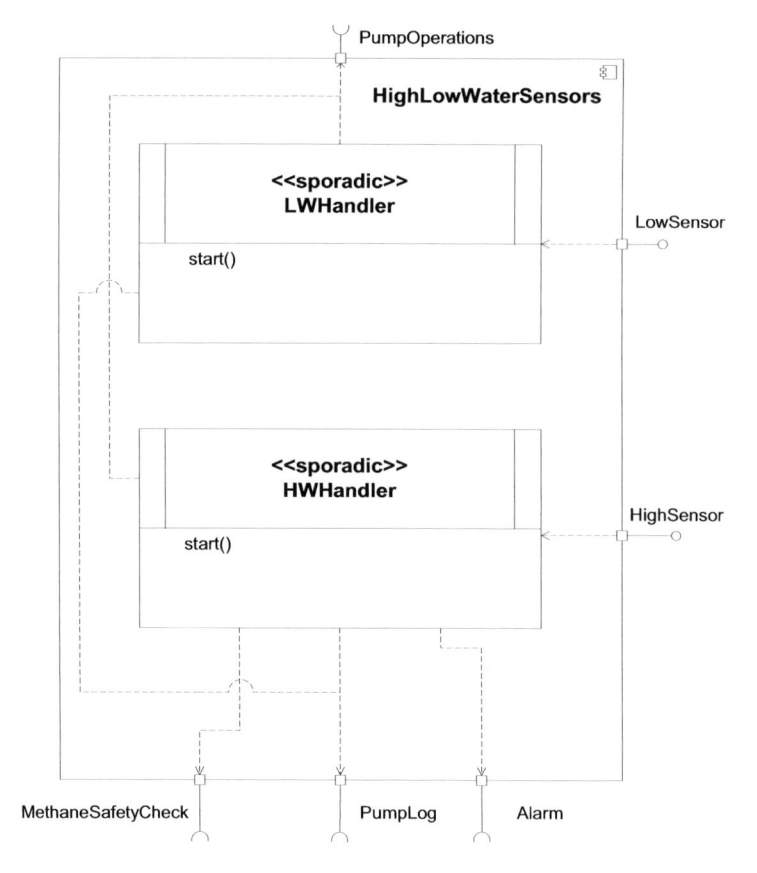

Figure 20.7: Decomposition of the `HighLowWaterSensors`.

the response-time form of analysis will be undertaken. Table 20.2 summarizes the timing attributes of the objects introduced in the logical architecture.

20.4.1 Scheduling analysis

Once the code has been developed, it must be analysed to obtain its worst-case execution times. As indicated in Section 4.5, these values can be obtained via either direct measurement or by modelling the hardware. None of the code derived is particularly extensive, so it is reasonable to assume that a low speed processor is adequate. Table 20.3 contains some representative values for the worst-case execution times (in milliseconds) for each object in the design. Note the times for each task include time spent executing within other objects, the time spent executing exception handlers and the associated context switch times. To model the effect of the interrupt handlers 'pseudo' sporadic objects are introduced (the maximum handler execution time is 2ms).

THE PHYSICAL ARCHITECTURE DESIGN   469

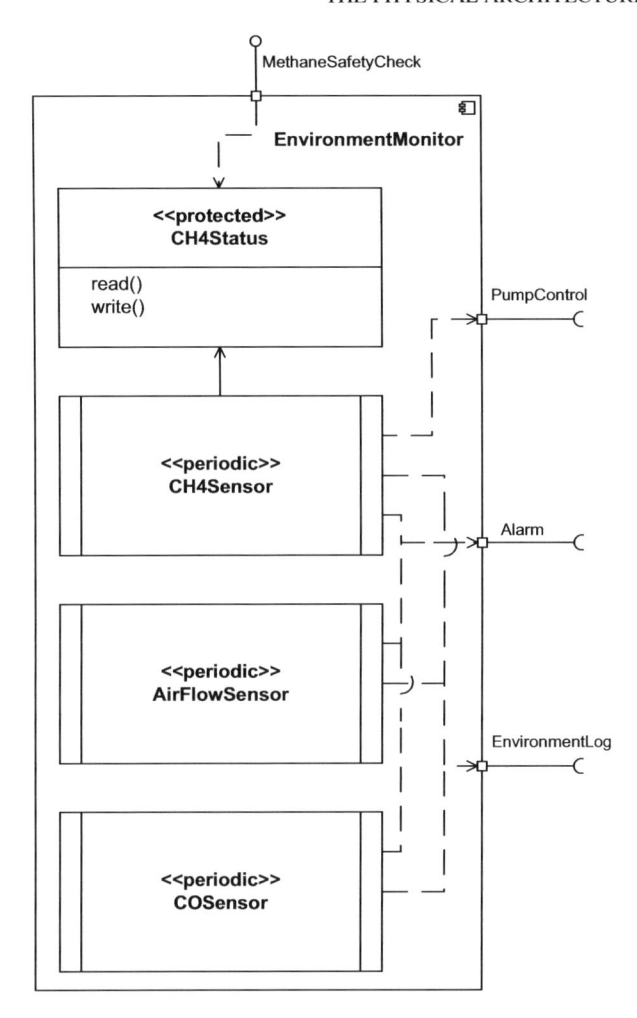

Figure 20.8: Hierarchical decomposition of the `EnvironmentMonitor`.

The execution environment imposes its own set of important parameters – these are given in Table 20.4. Note that the clock interrupt is of sufficient granularity to ensure no release jitter for the periodic tasks.

The maximum blocking time, for all tasks, occurs when the operator console makes a call upon the motor object. It can be assumed that the task that makes the call is of low priority. The worst-case execution time for this protected operation is assumed to be 3 ms.

The above information can now be synthesised to provide a comprehensive analysis of the response times of all tasks in the system. This analysis is given in Table 20.5. The conclusion of the analysis is that all deadlines are met. Note the two sporadic tasks are computed to have the same response times, as the interrupts that release the tasks are separated by at least 6 seconds. Hence, the sporadic tasks can never execute concurrently.

MINE CONTROL CASE STUDY

	Type	Period	Deadline	Priority
CH_4 sensor	Periodic	80	30	10
CO sensor	Periodic	100	60	8
Air-flow sensor	Periodic	100	100	7
Water-flow sensor	Periodic	1000	40	9
HW handler	Sporadic	6000	200	6
LW handler	Sporadic	6000	200	6
Motor	Protected			10
CH_4 status	Protected			10
Operator console	Protected			10
Data logger	Protected			10

Table 20.2: Attributes of design objects.

	Type	WCET
CH_4 sensor	Periodic	12
CO sensor	Periodic	10
Air flow sensor	Periodic	10
Water flow sensor	Periodic	10
HW handler	Sporadic	20
LW handler	Sporadic	20
InterruptLW	Sporadic	2
InterruptHW	Sporadic	2

Table 20.3: Worst-case execution times.

	Symbol	Time
Clock period	T_{CLK}	20
Clock overhead	CT^c	2
Cost of single task move	CT^s	1

Table 20.4: Overheads.

	Type	T	B	C	D	P	R
CH_4 sensor	Periodic	80	3	12	30	10	25
CO sensor	Periodic	100	3	10	60	8	47
Air flow sensor	Periodic	100	3	10	100	7	57
Water flow sensor	Periodic	1000	3	10	40	9	35
HW handler	Sporadic	6000	3	20	200	6	79
LW handler	Sporadic	6000	3	20	200	6	79

Table 20.5: Analysis results.

20.5 Translation to Ada

HRT-HOOD supports a systematic translation to Ada. For each non-terminal object, two packages are generated. The first contains all the types that are used for communication between its child objects. The second contains all the interfaces provided by that object. For each terminal object, two child packages are also generated: the first simply contains a collection of data types and variables defining the object's real-time attributes; the second contains the code for the object itself (including a single task for cyclic and sporadic).

To ease the translation, two standard templates are used: one for a cyclic (periodic) task and one for a sporadic task. The periodic template is defined as a task type that takes an access discriminant to an extensible type. The application extends this type to provide the state and code for the task.

```ada
with System; use System;
with Ada.Real_Time; use Ada.Real_Time;
package Cyclics is
  type Cyclic_State is abstract tagged
    record
      Pri : Priority;
      Period_In_Milli : Time_Span;
    end record;
  procedure Initialize_Code(S: in out Cyclic_State)
            is abstract;
  procedure Periodic_Code(S: in out Cyclic_State)
            is abstract;
  type Any_Cyclic_State is access all Cyclic_State'Class;

  task type Cyclic (S : Any_Cyclic_State) is
    with Priority => S.Pri;
  end Cyclic;
end Cyclics;
```

The body of the package contains the body of the task, which has the standard structure for a periodic task that was introduced in Section 14.2. Note the calls to `Initialize_Code` and `Periodic_Code` are dispatching operations to the application code associated with the template during instantiation.

```ada
package body Cyclics is
  task body Cyclic is
    T: Time;
  begin
    S.Initialize_Code;
    T:= Clock + S.Period_In_Milli;
    loop
      delay until T;
      S.Periodic_Code;
      T := T + S.Period_In_Milli;
    end loop;
  end Cyclic;
end Cyclics;
```

In the case of the sporadic task template, two interfaces are used to ensure that the application calls the correct operation. Following the structure given in Section 14.3 a task and a protected type is needed:

```ada
with System; use System;
with Ada.Real_Time; use Ada.Real_Time;
package Sporadics is

  type Sporadic_Invoke_Interface is synchronized interface;
  procedure Start(S: in out Sporadic_Invoke_Interface)
          is abstract;
  type Any_Sporadic_Invoke_Interface is access all
          Sporadic_Invoke_Interface'Class;

  type Sporadic_Thread_Interface is synchronized interface;
  procedure Wait_Start(S: in out Sporadic_Thread_Interface)
          is abstract;
  type Any_Sporadic_Thread_Interface is access all
          Sporadic_Thread_Interface'Class;

  type Sporadic_State is abstract tagged
    record
      Pri : Priority;
      Ceiling_Priority : Priority;
      MIT_In_Milli : Time_Span;
    end record;
  procedure Initialize_Code(S: in out Sporadic_State)
          is abstract;
  procedure Sporadic_Code(S: in out Sporadic_State)
          is abstract;
  type Any_Sporadic_State is access all Sporadic_State'Class;

  protected type Sporadic_Agent(S: Any_Sporadic_State)
        with Priority => S.Ceiling_Priority is
        new Sporadic_Invoke_Interface and
            Sporadic_Thread_Interface
  with
    -- for the Start operation
    overriding procedure Start;
    overriding entry Wait_Start;
  private
    Start_Open : Boolean := False;
  end Sporadic_Agent;

  task type Sporadic (S : Any_Sporadic_State;
                      A : Any_Sporadic_Thread_Interface) is
    with Priority => S.Pri;
  end Sporadic;
end Sporadics;
```

For simplicity the body of the package does not enforce minimum inter-arrival time separation. (A more sophisticated mapping would enable overruns on the interrupting device to be detected and handled – see Section 19.4.)

```ada
package body Sporadics is
  protected body Sporadic_Agent is
```

```ada
   procedure Start is
   begin
      Start_Open := True;
   end Start;

   entry Wait_Start
           when Start_Open is
   begin
      Start_Open := False;
   end Wait_Start;
end Sporadic_Agent;

task body Sporadic is
begin
   S.Initialize_Code;
   loop
      A.Wait_Start;
      S.Sporadic_Code;
   end loop;
end Sporadic;
end Sporadics;
```

Finally, the translations assume a package called `Device_Register_Types` that defines the control registers for the devices (using the approach given in Chapter 16).

```ada
with System; use System;
package Device_Register_Types is
   Word : constant := 2;       -- two bytes in a word
   One_Word : constant := 16;  -- 16 bits in a word
   -- register field types
   type Device_Error is (Clear, Set);
   type Device_Operation is (Clear, Set);
   type Interrupt_Status is (I_Disabled, I_Enabled);
   type Device_Status is (D_Disabled, D_Enabled);

   -- register type itself
   type Csr is
     record
        Error_Bit  : Device_Error;
        Operation  : Device_Operation;
        Done       : Boolean;
        Interrupt  : Interrupt_Status;
        Device     : Device_Status;
     end record;
   -- bit representation of the register field
   for Device_Error use (Clear => 0, Set => 1);
   for Device_Operation use (Clear => 0, Set => 1);
   for Interrupt_Status use (I_Disabled => 0,
                             I_Enabled => 1);
   for Device_Status use (D_Disabled => 0,
                          D_Enabled => 1);
   for Csr use
     record at mod Word;
        Error_Bit  at 0 range 15 ..15;
```

```
      Operation  at 0 range 10 ..10;
      Done       at 0 range  7 .. 7;
      Interrupt  at 0 range  6 .. 6;
      Device     at 0 range  0 .. 0;
   end record;
   for Csr'Size use One_Word;
   for Csr'Alignment use Word;
   for Csr'Bit_Order use Low_Order_First;
end Device_Register_Types;
```

20.5.1 The mine control system object

The top level object in the system is the "mine control object": it as no operations but does define several types that are used by its child objects. These are, therefore, declared in the following package specification.

```
package Mine_Control_System_Types is
   -- types used in communications between the
   -- Pump_Controller and the Environment_Monitor
   type Methane_Status is (Motor_Safe, Motor_Unsafe);

   -- types used in communications between the
   -- Pump_Controller and the Data_Logger
   type Motor_State_Changes is (Motor_Started,
        Motor_Stopped, Motor_Safe, Motor_Unsafe);
   type Water_Flow is (Yes, No);
   type Water_Mark is (High, Low);

   -- types used in communications between the
   -- Pump_Controller and the Operator_Console
   type Pump_Status is (On, Off);
   type Pump_Condition is (Enabled, Disabled);
   type Operational_Status is record
      Ps : Pump_Status;
      Pc : Pump_Condition;
   end record;
   type Alarm_Reason is (High_Methane, High_Co, No_Air_Flow,
        Ch4_Device_Error, Co_Device_Error,
        Pump_Fault, Pump_Unsafe_To_Operate, Unknown_Error);

   -- types used in communications between the
   -- Environment_Monitor and the Data_Logger
   type Air_Flow_Status is (Air_Flow, No_Air_Flow);
   type Ch4_Reading is new Integer range 0 .. 1023;
   type Co_Reading is new Integer range 0 .. 1023;
   Co_High  : constant Co_Reading  := 600;
   Ch4_High : constant Ch4_Reading := 400;

   -- there are no new types needed for communications between the
   -- Environment_Monitor and the Operator_Console
end Mine_Control_System_Types;
```

Figure 20.3 shows the first level of decomposition of the system. Each of these objects can potentially be implemented on a separate processor. However, for the purpose of this example, a single-processor implementation is considered.

Each of the mine control system children objects are now taken in turn and decomposed.

20.5.2 The pump controller object

The pump controller object is a non-terminal object. It introduces no new types but does provide interfaces illustrated in Figure 20.5; these are specified in the following package. To allow different views on the pump controller, three interfaces are provided.

```ada
with Mine_Control_System_Types;
use Mine_Control_System_Types;
package Pump_Controller is

  Pump_Not_Safe : exception;  -- raised by Set_Pump

  type Pump_Control is synchronized interface;
  function Request_Status(PC : Pump_Control)
    return Operational_Status is abstract;
  procedure Set_Pump(PC: in out Pump_Control;
                     To : Pump_Status) is abstract;
  type Any_Pump_Control is access all Pump_Control'Class;

  type Pump_Inform is synchronized interface;
  procedure Not_Safe(PI: in out Pump_Inform) is abstract;
  procedure Is_Safe (PI: in out Pump_Inform) is abstract;
  type Any_Pump_Inform is access all Pump_Inform'Class;

  type Pump_Operations is synchronized interface and
       Pump_Control and Pump_Inform;
  type Any_Pump_Operations is access all
     Pump_Operations'Class;
end Pump_Controller;
```

As a non-terminal object, objects providing operations for these interfaces must be implemented by child objects. For traceability, each child object of the objects in the top-level are viewed as child packages in Ada.

The decomposition appropriate to the pump controller was shown in Figure 20.6. It consists of one non-terminal object (the high-low water sensors object) and two terminal objects (the motor and the water-flow sensor). The figure also showed which pump controller operation was implemented by which child object operation.

It is now possible to give the code for these child objects.

The motor

The real-time attributes for the motor object are given first. As a protected object, only a ceiling priority attribute is needed.

476 MINE CONTROL CASE STUDY

```ada
package Pump_Controller.Motor_Rtatt is
  Ceiling_Priority: constant := 10;
end Pump_Controller.Motor_Rtatt;
```

The package specification for the implementation of the motor object is given next. It defines a protected type that implements all the interfaces provided by the pump controller. In this chapter, all protected objects generated to implement synchronization constraints are tagged as `Agent`. The type is parameterised so that (if necessary) multiple motors can be defined. An access reference to the device's control register is provided, along with references to the interfaces that allow the agent to communicate with other objects in the system, and its ceiling priority.

```ada
with Device_Register_Types, Environment_Monitor;
use Device_Register_Types, Environment_Monitor;
with Data_Logger, System;
use Data_Logger, System;
package Pump_Controller.Motor is -- PROTECTED
  protected type Motor_Agent(Pcsr : access Csr;
            Safety : Any_Methane_Check_Safety;
            Log : Any_Pump_Log; Ceiling: Priority)
      with Priority => Ceiling is new Pump_Operations
    with
      overriding function Request_Status return Operational_Status;
      overriding procedure Set_Pump(To : Pump_Status);
      overriding procedure Not_Safe;
      overriding procedure Is_Safe;
    private
      Motor_Status : Pump_Status := Off;
      Motor_Condition : Pump_Condition := Disabled;
    end Motor_Agent;
end Pump_Controller.Motor;
```

The state of the motor is defined by two variables. One which indicates whether the pump should be on or off, and the other whether the pump is enabled or disabled. The pump is disabled when it is unsafe to operate. A state transition diagram for the motor is shown in Figure 20.9. Only in the 'On-Enabled' state will the pump actually be operating.

The body of the `Motor` package contains the body of the `Motor_Agent` protected type, which implements the state transitions and their assocaited actions.

```ada
with Data_Logger;
with Environment_Monitor; use  Environment_Monitor;
with System; use System;
with System.Storage_Elements; use System.Storage_Elements;
package body Pump_Controller.Motor is

  protected body Motor_Agent is
    procedure Not_Safe is
    begin
      if Motor_Status = On then
        Pcsr.Operation := Clear; -- turn off motor
        Log.Motor_Log(Motor_Stopped);
      end if;
      Motor_Condition := Disabled;
```

TRANSLATION TO ADA 477

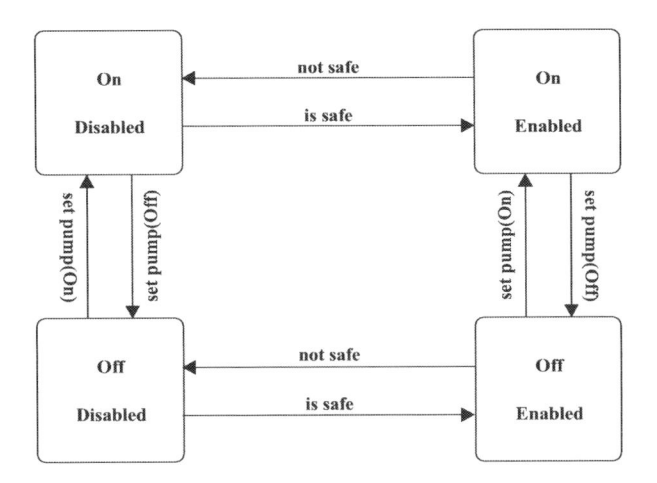

Figure 20.9: State transition diagram for the motor.

```
   Log.Motor_Log(Motor_Unsafe);
end Not_Safe;

procedure Is_Safe is
begin
   if Motor_Status = On then
      Pcsr.Operation := Set;  -- start motor
      Log.Motor_Log(Motor_Started);
   end if;
   Motor_Condition := Enabled;
   Log.Motor_Log(Motor_Safe);
end Is_Safe;

function Request_Status return Operational_Status is
begin
   return (Ps => Motor_Status, Pc => Motor_Condition);
end Request_Status;

procedure Set_Pump(To : Pump_Status) is
begin
   if To = On then
      if Motor_Status = Off then
         if Motor_Condition = Disabled then
            raise Pump_Not_Safe;
         end if;
         if Safety.Check_Safe  = Motor_Safe then
            Motor_Status := On;
            Pcsr.Operation := Set;  -- turn on motor
            Log.Motor_Log(Motor_Started);
         else
            raise Pump_Not_Safe;
         end if;
```

478   MINE CONTROL CASE STUDY

```ada
         end if;
      else
         if Motor_Status = On then
            Motor_Status := Off;
            if Motor_Condition = Enabled then
               Pcsr.Operation := Clear;  -- turn off motor
               Log.Motor_Log(Motor_Stopped);
            end if;
         end if;
      end if;
   end Set_Pump;
 end Motor_Agent;
end Pump_Controller.Motor;
```

Water flow sensor handling object

The water-flow sensor is a cyclic object, and therefore has the following real-time attributes.

```ada
with System; use System;
with Ada.Real_Time; use Ada.Real_Time;
package Pump_Controller.Water_Flow_Sensor_Rtatt is
   Period : Time_Span := Milliseconds(1000);
   Thread_Priority : constant Priority := 9;
end Pump_Controller.Water_Flow_Sensor_Rtatt;
```

In order to instantiated the periodic task template, it is first necessary to extend the `Cyclic_State` to contain the state needed for the sensor, and to override the operations. The actual sensor object will be created when the architecture itself is instantiated.

```ada
with Cyclics; use Cyclics;
with Device_Register_Types; use Device_Register_Types;
with Operator_Console; use Operator_Console;
with Data_Logger; use Data_Logger;
package Pump_Controller.Water_Flow_Sensor is  -- CYCLIC
   -- calls Operator_Console.Alarm
   -- calls Data_Logger.Water_Flow_Log
   -- calls Motor.Request_Status

   type Sensor_State(
        Wfcsr : access Csr;   Motor: Any_Pump_Control;
        Operator : Any_Alarms;
        Logger : Any_Pump_Log) is new Cyclic_State with
   record
      Flow : Water_Flow := No;
      Current_Pump_Status,
      Last_Pump_Status : Pump_Status := Off;
   end record;
   overriding procedure Initialize_Code(
                       S : in out Sensor_State);
   overriding procedure Periodic_Code(
                       S : in out Sensor_State);
end Pump_Controller.Water_Flow_Sensor;
```

The body contains two subprograms: one for initializing the sensor (`Initialize`), and the other for the code to be executed each period (`Periodic_Code`). Every invocation, the task simply checks that if the pump is on, water is flowing and if the pump is off, no water flows. Alarms are sounded if these two invariants are violated.

```ada
with Pump_Controller.Motor; use Pump_Controller.Motor;
with Mine_Control_System_Types;
use Mine_Control_System_Types;
package body Pump_Controller.Water_Flow_Sensor is
   procedure Initialize_Code(S : in out Sensor_State) is
   begin
      -- enable device
      S.Wfcsr.Device := D_Enabled;
   end Initialize_Code;

   procedure Periodic_Code(S : in out Sensor_State) is
   begin
      S.Current_Pump_Status := S.Motor.Request_Status.Ps;
      if (S.Wfcsr.Operation = Set) then
         S.Flow :=  Yes;
      else
         S.Flow := No;
      end if;
      if S.Current_Pump_Status = On and
          S.Last_Pump_Status = On and S.Flow = No then
         S.Operator.Sound_Alarm(Pump_Fault);
      elsif S.Current_Pump_Status = Off and
          S.Last_Pump_Status = Off and S.Flow = Yes then
         S.Operator.Sound_Alarm(Pump_Fault);
      end if;
      S.Last_Pump_Status := S.Current_Pump_Status;
      S.Logger.Water_Flow_Log(S.Flow);
   end Periodic_Code;
end Pump_Controller.Water_Flow_Sensor;
```

The High-Low Water Sensors object

This object is an active (non-terminal) object. Both of its provided operations are called from interrupts, and are therefore defined to be operations in a protected type. As the interrupts are mutually exclusive, the same protected object is used for both interrupts.

```ada
with System; use System;
with Ada.Interrupts; use Ada.Interrupts;
with Sporadics; use Sporadics;
package Pump_Controller.High_Low_Water_Sensors is
   -- Operations called from interrupt handlers
   -- No public interface

   type High_Sensor is protected interface;
   procedure Sensor_High_Ih(HS : in out High_Sensor)
            is abstract;
```

```ada
   type Low_Sensor is protected interface;
   procedure Sensor_Low_Ih(LS : in out Low_Sensor)
             is abstract;

   protected type HLW_Agent(Waterh_Interrupt: Interrupt_Id;
              Waterl_Interrupt: Interrupt_Id;
              HW : Any_Sporadic_Invoke_Interface;
              LW : Any_Sporadic_Invoke_Interface;
              Ceiling : Priority)
       with Priority => Ceiling is new High_Sensor and Low_Sensor
   with
      overriding procedure Sensor_High_Ih
         with Attach_Handler => Waterh_Interrupt;
         -- assigns interrupt handler
      overriding procedure Sensor_Low_Ih
         with Attach_Handler => Waterl_Interrupt;
         -- assigns interrupt handler
   end HLW_Agent;
end Pump_Controller.High_Low_Water_Sensors;
```

The decomposition of the high-low water sensors is given in Figure 20.7. It consists of two sporadic objects: one to handle the high water interrupt and the other to handle the low water interrupt. Hence, the body of the high-low water sensors object simply calls the start method to release the tasks.

```ada
package body Pump_Controller.High_Low_Water_Sensors is
   protected body HLW_Agent is
      procedure Sensor_High_Ih is
      begin
         HW.Start;
      end Sensor_High_Ih;

      procedure Sensor_Low_Ih is
      begin
         LW.Start;
      end Sensor_Low_Ih;
   end HLW_Agent;
end Pump_Controller.High_Low_Water_Sensors;
```

The HW Handler and the LW Handler objects

The two sporadic objects responsible for responding to the high and low water interrupts are considered next. The generated code for the two objects are identical in structure. Here only the high water handler is given. First its real-time attributes are defined:

```ada
with System; use System;
package Pump_Controller.High_Low_Water_Sensors.
        Hw_Handler_Rtatt is
   Ceiling_Priority :  constant Priority := Priority'Last;
   Thread_Priority  :  constant Priority := 6;
end Pump_Controller.High_Low_Water_Sensors.Hw_Handler_Rtatt;
```

Note that as the sporadic object will be invoked from a interrupt handler, it must have the maximum ceiling priority. The code for the object's operations is straightforward, and given below.

```ada
with Sporadics; use Sporadics;
with Device_Register_Types; use Device_Register_Types;
with Pump_Controller; use Pump_Controller;
with Data_logger; use Data_Logger;
with Operator_Console; use Operator_Console;
package Pump_Controller.High_Low_Water_Sensors.Hw_Handler is
  -- SPORADIC
  type HW_Sensor_State(
          Hwcsr : access Csr; Operator : Any_Alarms;
          Motor: Any_Pump_Control; Logger : Any_Pump_Log)
       is new Sporadic_State with null record;
  overriding procedure Initialize_Code(
                      S : in out HW_Sensor_State);
  overriding procedure Sporadic_Code(
                      S : in out HW_Sensor_State);
end Pump_Controller.High_Low_Water_Sensors.Hw_Handler;

package body Pump_Controller.High_Low_Water_Sensors.
             Hw_Handler is
  procedure Sporadic_Code(S : in out HW_Sensor_State) is
  begin
    S.Motor.Set_Pump(On);
    S.Logger.High_Low_Water_Log(High);
    S.Hwcsr.Interrupt := I_Disabled;
  exception
    when Pump_Not_Safe =>
      S.Operator.Sound_Alarm(Pump_Unsafe_To_Operate);
  end Sporadic_Code;

  procedure Initialize_Code(S : in out HW_Sensor_State) is
  begin
    S.Hwcsr.Device := D_Enabled;
    S.Hwcsr.Interrupt := I_Enabled;
  end Initialize_Code;
end Pump_Controller.High_Low_Water_Sensors.Hw_Handler;
```

The low-water handler object code is similarly structured.

20.5.3 Environment monitoring

The environment monitor subsystem's goal is to monitor the mine to ensure that it is safe for the work force. It is an active object with two interfaces: one used by the pump controller to determine if the methane level is currently safe or not. The other is used by the internal objects to set the status.

```ada
with Mine_Control_System_Types;
use Mine_Control_System_Types;
package Environment_Monitor is
  type Methane_Check_Safety is synchronized interface;
```

482 MINE CONTROL CASE STUDY

```ada
  function Check_Safe(S : in Methane_Check_Safety)
    return Methane_Status is abstract;
  type Any_Methane_Check_Safety is access all
       Methane_Check_Safety'Class;

  type CH4_Safety is synchronized interface and
    Methane_Check_Safety;
  procedure Set_Safety(S: in out CH4_Safety;
                       M : Methane_Status) is abstract;
  type Any_CH4_Safety is access all CH4_Safety'Class;
end Environment_Monitor;
```

The decomposition of the environment monitor subsystem is shown in Figure 20.8. Note that the `Check_Safe` subprogram allows the pump controller to observe the current state of the methane level without blocking, via the CH_4 status protected object. All other components are periodic activities.

The following subsections illustrate the decomposition. The real-time attributes are not shown.

CH4 status object

The CH4 status object simply contains data which indicates whether it is safe to operate the pump. The code for the operations is straightforward.

```ada
with Mine_Control_System_Types;
use Mine_Control_system_Types;
with System; use System;
package Environment_Monitor.Ch4_Status is  -- PROTECTED
  protected type Methane_Agent(Ceiling : Priority)
        with Priority => Ceiling is new CH4_Safety
  with
      overriding function Check_Safe return Methane_Status;
      overriding procedure Set_Safety(M : Methane_Status);
  private
      Current_Status : Methane_Status := Motor_Unsafe;
  end Methane_Agent;
end Environment_Monitor.Ch4_Status;

package body Environment_Monitor.Ch4_Status is
  protected body Methane_Agent is
    function Check_Safe return Methane_Status is
    begin
      return Current_Status;
    end Check_Safe;

    procedure Set_Safety(M : Methane_Status) is
    begin
      Current_Status := M;
    end Set_Safety;
  end Methane_Agent;
end Environment_Monitor.Ch4_Status;
```

CH4 sensor handling object

The function of the CH4 sensor is to measure the level of methane in the environment. As with the previous water flow sensor object, the approach is to extend the `Cyclic_State` type and override the operations.

```ada
with Cyclics; use Cyclics;
with Device_Register_Types; use Device_Register_Types;
with Operator_Console; use Operator_Console;
with Data_Logger; use Data_Logger;
with Pump_Controller; use Pump_Controller;
package Environment_Monitor.Ch4_Sensor is -- CYCLIC
   -- calls Pump_Controller.Is_Safe
   -- calls Pump_Controller.Not_Safe
   -- calls Operator_Console.Alarm
   -- calls Data_Logger.Ch4_Log

   type CH4_Sensor_State(
      Ch4csr : access Csr;
      Ch4dbr : access Ch4_Reading;
      CH4_Status : Any_CH4_Safety;
      Motor: Any_Pump_Inform;
      Operator : Any_Alarms;
      Logger : Any_Environment_Log)
      is new Cyclic_State with
   record
      Ch4_Present : Ch4_Reading;
   end record;
   overriding procedure Initialize_Code(
                    S : in out CH4_Sensor_State);
   overriding procedure Periodic_Code(
                    S : in out CH4_Sensor_State);
end Environment_Monitor.Ch4_Sensor;
```

The requirement is that the methane level should not rise above a threshold. Inevitably, around this threshold the sensor will continually signal safe and unsafe. To avoid this jitter, lower and upper bounds on the threshold are used. Note that, as the ADC takes some time to produce its result, the conversion is requested at the end of one period to be used at the start of the next.

```ada
package body Environment_Monitor.Ch4_Sensor is
   Jitter_Range : constant Ch4_Reading := 40;

   procedure Initialize_Code(S : in out Ch4_Sensor_State) is
   begin
      -- enable device
      S.Ch4csr.Device := D_Enabled;
      S.Ch4csr.Operation := Set;
   end Initialize_Code;

   procedure Periodic_Code(S : in out Ch4_Sensor_State) is
      Methane : Methane_Status;
   begin
      if not S.Ch4csr.Done then
```

```ada
          S.Operator.Sound_Alarm(Ch4_Device_Error);
       else
          -- read device register for sensor value
          S.Ch4_Present := S.Ch4dbr.all;
          Methane := S.CH4_Status.Check_Safe;
          if S.Ch4_Present > Ch4_High then
            if Methane = Motor_Safe then
               S.Motor.Not_Safe;
               S.Ch4_Status.Set_Safety(Motor_Unsafe);
               S.Operator.Sound_Alarm(High_Methane);
            end if;
          elsif (S.Ch4_Present < (Ch4_High - Jitter_Range)) and
                (Methane = Motor_Unsafe) then
            S.Motor.Is_Safe;
            S.Ch4_Status.Set_Safety(Motor_Safe);
          end if;
          S.Logger.Ch4_Log(S.Ch4_Present);
       end if;
       S.Ch4csr.Operation := Set;
          -- start conversion for next iteration
   end Periodic_Code;
end Environment_Monitor.Ch4_Sensor;
```

20.5.4 Air flow sensor handling object

The air flow sensor is another periodic object which simply monitors the flow of air in the mine.

```ada
with Cyclics; use Cyclics;
with Device_Register_Types; use Device_Register_Types;
with Operator_Console; use Operator_Console;
with Data_Logger; use Data_Logger;
package Environment_Monitor.Air_Flow_Sensor is -- CYCLIC
   -- calls Data_Logger.Air_Flow_Log
   -- calls Operator_Console.Alarm
   type AF_Sensor_State(Afcsr : access Csr;
        Operator : Any_Alarms; Logger : Any_Environment_Log)
        is new Cyclic_State with
   record
      Air_Flow_Reading : Boolean := True;
   end record;
   overriding procedure Initialize_Code(S : in out AF_Sensor_State);
   overriding procedure Periodic_Code(S : in out AF_Sensor_State);
end Environment_Monitor.Air_Flow_Sensor;

package body Environment_Monitor.Air_Flow_Sensor is
   procedure Initialize_Code(S : in out AF_Sensor_State) is
   begin
      -- enable device
      S.Afcsr.Device := D_Enabled;
   end Initialize_Code;
```

```ada
  procedure Periodic_Code(S : in out AF_Sensor_State) is
  begin
    -- read device register for flow indication
    -- (operation bit set to 1);
    S.Air_Flow_Reading := S.Afcsr.Operation = Set;
    if not S.Air_Flow_Reading then
      S.Operator.Sound_Alarm(No_Air_Flow);
      S.Logger.Air_Flow_Log(No_Air_Flow);
    else
      S.Logger.Air_Flow_Log(Air_Flow);
    end if;
  end Periodic_Code;
end Environment_Monitor.Air_Flow_Sensor;
```

20.5.5 CO sensor handling object

The CO sensor is, again, straightforward in its implementation.

```ada
with Cyclics; use Cyclics;
with Device_Register_Types; use Device_Register_Types;
with Operator_Console; use Operator_Console;
with Data_Logger; use Data_Logger;
package Environment_Monitor.Co_Sensor is   -- CYCLIC
  -- calls Data_Logger.Co_log
  -- calls Operator_Console.Alarm
  type CO_Sensor_State(Cocsr : access Csr;
       Codbr : access CO_Reading; Operator : Any_Alarms;
       Logger : Any_Environment_Log) is
       new Cyclic_State with
  record
    Co_Present : Co_Reading;
  end record;
  overriding procedure Initialize_Code(S : in out CO_Sensor_State);
  overriding procedure Periodic_Code(S : in out CO_Sensor_State);
end Environment_Monitor.Co_Sensor;

package body Environment_Monitor.Co_Sensor is
  procedure Initialize_Code(S : in out CO_Sensor_State) is
  begin
    -- enable device
    S.Cocsr.Device := D_Enabled;
    S.Cocsr.Operation := Set;  -- start conversion
  end Initialize_Code;

  procedure Periodic_Code(S : in out CO_Sensor_State) is
  begin
    if not S.Cocsr.Done then
      S.Operator.Sound_Alarm(Co_Device_Error);
    else
      -- read device register for sensor value
      S.Co_Present := S.Codbr.all;
      if S.Co_Present > Co_High then
```

486 MINE CONTROL CASE STUDY

```ada
         S.Operator.Sound_Alarm(High_Co);
       end if;
       S.Logger.Co_Log(S.Co_Present);
     end if;
     S.Cocsr.Operation := Set;  -- start conversion
   end Periodic_Code;
end Environment_Monitor.Co_Sensor;
```

20.5.6 Data logger

Only the interface to the Data logger object is shown.

```ada
with Mine_Control_System_Types;
use Mine_Control_System_Types;
package Data_Logger is  -- ACTIVE
  type Pump_Log is interface;
  procedure High_Low_Water_Log(Pump: in out Pump_Log;
             Mark : Water_Mark) is abstract;
  procedure Water_Flow_Log(Pump: in out Pump_Log;
             Reading : Water_Flow) is abstract;
  procedure Motor_Log(Pump: in out Pump_Log;
             State : Motor_State_Changes) is abstract;
  type Any_Pump_Log is access all Pump_Log'Class;

  type Environment_Log is interface;
  procedure Co_Log(Envir: in out Environment_Log;
                   Reading : Co_Reading) is abstract;
  procedure Ch4_Log(Envir: in out Environment_Log;
                    Reading : Ch4_Reading) is abstract;
  procedure Air_Flow_Log(Envir: in out Environment_Log;
                         Reading : Air_Flow_Status) is abstract;
  type Any_Environment_Log is access all Environment_Log'Class;

  type Status_Log is interface and Pump_Log
      and Environment_Log;

  type Logger is new Status_log with null record;
  procedure High_Low_Water_Log(Pump: in out Logger;
           Mark : Water_Mark);
  procedure Water_Flow_Log(Pump: in out Logger;
           Reading : Water_Flow);
  procedure Motor_Log(Pump: in out Logger;
           State : Motor_State_Changes);
  procedure Co_Log(Envir: in out Logger;
                   Reading : Co_Reading);
  procedure Ch4_Log(Envir: in out Logger;
                    Reading : Ch4_Reading);
  procedure Air_Flow_Log(Envir: in out Logger;
                         Reading : Air_Flow_Status);
end Data_Logger;
```

20.5.7 Operator console

Only the interface to the Operator console object is shown.

```ada
with Mine_Control_System_Types;
use Mine_Control_System_Types;
package Operator_Console is -- ACTIVE
   type Alarms is interface;
   procedure Sound_Alarm(A: Alarms; Reason : Alarm_Reason)
            is abstract;
   type Any_Alarms is access all Alarms'Class;

   type Console is new Alarms with null record;
   procedure Sound_Alarm(C: Console; Reason : Alarm_Reason);
end Operator_Console;
```

20.5.8 Configuring the system

Having defined all the types representing the needed objects, it is now possible to consider the instances to instantiate the software architecture. The configuration is illustrated below.

```ada
-- with and use clauses omitted
package Mine_Control_System is
  -- The Data_Logger
  The_Logger : aliased Logger;

  -- The Operators Console
  The_Console : aliased Console;

  -- CH4 status
  CH4_Status_Agent : aliased Methane_Agent(
                     CH4_Status_Rtatt.Ceiling_Priority);

  -- The Motor
  Ctrl_Reg_Addr1 : constant Address := To_Address(16#Aa14#);
  Pcsr : aliased Device_Register_Types.Csr :=
     (Error_Bit => Clear, Operation => Set,
      Done => False, Interrupt => I_Enabled,
      Device => D_Enabled);
  for Pcsr'Address use Ctrl_Reg_Addr1;

  Pump_Motor : aliased Pump_Controller.Motor.Motor_Agent(
     Pcsr'Access, CH4_Status_Agent'Access,
     The_Logger'Access, Motor_Rtatt.Ceiling_Priority);

  -- The Waterflow Sensor
  Ctrl_Reg_Addr2 : constant Address := To_Address(16#Aa14#);
  Wfcsr : aliased Device_Register_Types.Csr;
  for Wfcsr'Address use Ctrl_Reg_Addr2;
  Water_Flow_Sensor_State: aliased Pump_Controller.
     Water_Flow_Sensor.Sensor_State := (
        Wfcsr => Wfcsr'Access,
```

```ada
            Motor => Pump_Motor'Access,
            Operator => The_Console'Access,
            Logger => The_Logger'Access,
            Flow => No,
            Current_Pump_Status => Off,
            Last_Pump_Status => Off,
            Period_In_Milli => Water_Flow_Sensor_Rtatt.Period,
            Pri => Water_Flow_Sensor_Rtatt.Thread_Priority);
   Water_Flow_Thread : Cyclic(Water_Flow_Sensor_State'Access);

   -- HW Handler
   Hw_Cntrl_Reg_Addr : constant Address :=
                       To_Address(16#Aa10#);
   Hwcsr : aliased Device_Register_Types.Csr;
   for Hwcsr'Address use Hw_Cntrl_Reg_Addr;
   High_Water_State : aliased Pump_Controller.
   High_Low_Water_Sensors.HW_Handler.HW_Sensor_State(
         Hwcsr'Access,
         The_Console'Access,
         Pump_Motor'Access,
         The_Logger'Access);
   HW_Agent : aliased Sporadic_Agent(High_Water_State'Access);
   HW_Thread : Sporadic(High_Water_State'Access,
                        HW_Agent'Access);

   -- LW Handler
   Lw_Cntrl_Reg_Addr : constant Address :=
                       To_Address(16#Aa12#);
   Lwcsr : aliased Device_Register_Types.Csr;
   for Hwcsr'Address use Hw_Cntrl_Reg_Addr;
   Low_Water_State : aliased Pump_Controller.
     High_Low_Water_Sensors.LW_Handler.LW_Sensor_State(
         Lwcsr'Access,
         The_Console'Access,
         Pump_Motor'Access,
         The_Logger'Access);
   LW_Agent : aliased Sporadic_Agent(Low_Water_State'Access);
   LW_Thread : Sporadic(Low_Water_State'Access,
                        LW_Agent'Access);

   -- The High Low Water Sensor
   HLW_Interrupt_Handler : Agent(Ada.Interrupts.Names.HW,
      Ada.Interrupts.Names.LW,
      HW_Agent'Access, LW_Agent'Access,
      High_Low_Water_Sensors_Rtatt.Ceiling_Priority);

   -- CO Sensor, air flow sensor, and CH4 sensor
   -- are similar to airflow sensor

end Mine_Control_System;
```

Once configured, the Ada main program simply selects the appropriate scheduling regime and profile.

```ada
pragma Task_Dispatching_Policy(FIFO_Within_Priorities);
pragma Locking_Policy(Ceiling_Locking);
pragma Profile(Ravenscar);
with Pump_Controller, Pump_Controller.Water_Flow_Sensor;
with Environment_Monitor, Environment_Monitor.Ch4_Sensor,
     Environment_Monitor.Air_Flow_Sensor,
     Environment_Monitor.Co_Sensor;
with Operator_Console;
with Data_Logger;
with Mine_Control_System;
procedure Main is
begin
  null;
end Main;
```

20.6 Fault tolerance and distribution

Chapter 3 identified four sources of faults which can result in an embedded system software failure.

(1) Inadequate specification.
(2) Faults introduced from design errors in software components.
(3) Faults introduced by failure of one or more processor components of the embedded system.
(4) Faults introduced by transient or permanent interference in the supporting communication subsystem.

It is these last three on which this book has concentrated. They are now discussed in turn in relation to the case study. Ada's approach to software fault tolerance is to use exception handling as a framework from which error recovery can be built.

20.6.1 Design errors

As this case study is necessarily simplified, the scope for fault tolerance of software design errors is small. In the example, the HRT-HOOD design methodology, in conjunction with the languages data abstraction facilities, has been used in an attempt to prevent faults from entering the system during the design and implementation phases. In a real application, this would then be followed by a comprehensive testing phase to remove any faults that had, nevertheless, been introduced. Simulations and model checking techniques may also be used.

Any residual design faults in the program will cause unanticipated errors to occur. Although backward error recovery or *N*-version programming is ideal for recovering from these types of errors, there is little scope in the example for design diversity. Although a two version system, one in Ada and the other in, say, Real-Time Java could be used.

490   MINE CONTROL CASE STUDY

If within the case study it is assumed that all unanticipated errors result in exceptions being raised, each operation could be protected by a "catch all" exception handler. For example, the Ch4 sensor object could be modified to inform the operator if an unexpected error occurs. For safety, in this situation, an attempt is made to turn off the motor. In Ada, this would take the following form.

```
procedure Periodic_Code(S : in out Sensor_State) is
begin
   ...
exception
   when others =>
     S.Operator.Sound_Alarm(Unknown_Error);
     S.Ch4_Status.Set_Safety(Motor_Unsafe);
     S.Motor.Not_Safe;
end Periodic_Code;
```

Although mine flooding is serious, the application's requirements dictate that fire is more dangerous; therefore error handling always attempts to ensure that the pump is turned off (fail safe).

It should be noted that all interactions which manipulate the pump and the status of methane should be in the form of atomic actions. The code given in the case study allows another task to determine that the motor is in an unsafe position, even though the methane status might indicate that the pump is safe to operate. This might lead to a race condition.

20.6.2   Processor and communication failure

In general, if the mine control system was implemented on a single processor computer and any part of the processor failed then the whole system would be in jeopardy. Consequently, either some form of hardware redundancy must be applied or distribution is required. Control systems of the kind found in mines are naturally distributed. The top level decomposition illustrated in Figure 20.3 shows four components that could clearly execute on distinct processes.

Ada does not define failure semantics for partially failed programs. However, an exception is raised by the underlying implementation when it is unable to make contact with a remote node.

It has been assumed that all transient communication failures will be masked by the underlying distributed system's implementation. If a more permanent failure occurs then an appropriate exception should be raised by the implementation, which the application can then handle. For example, if the remote call to `Is_Safe` generates an exception, the pump should be disabled.

20.6.3   Other hardware failures

The above assumes that only the processor and the communications subsystem can fail. Clearly, it is equally likely that the sensors may fail either through deterioration or through damage. In the example presented in this chapter, no attempt has been made to increase the reliability of the sensors as this book has only touched upon hardware redundancy techniques. One approach would be to replicate each sensor and have each replica controlled by a different task. The tasks would then have to communicate in order to compare results. These results would inevitably be slightly different, and therefore some form of matching algorithm would be required.

Summary

This case study has been included to illustrate some of the issues discussed in this book. Unfortunately a single, relatively small, application cannot exercise all the important concepts that have been covered. In particular, issues of size and complexity are clearly not addressable within this context.

Nevertheless, it is hoped that the case study has helped to consolidate the reader's understanding of a number of topics, for example.

- top-down design and decomposition
- concurrency and models of interprocess communication
- forward error recovery techniques and fault tolerant design
- periodic and sporadic processes
- priority assignment and scheduling analysis
- distributed programming.

Chapter 21
Conclusions

The distinguishing characteristic of real-time systems is that correctness is not just a function of the logical results of program execution but of the time at which these results are produced. This one characteristic makes the study of real-time systems quite separate from other areas of computing. The importance of many real-time systems also places unique responsibilities on the practitioner. As more and more computers are being embedded in engineering applications, the greater is the risk of human, ecological or economic catastrophe. These risks arise from the problem of not being able to prove (or at least convincingly demonstrate) that all temporal and functional constraints will be met in all situations.

Real-time systems can be classified in a number of ways. First is the degree to which the application can tolerate tardiness in the system's responses. Those which have some flexibility are termed *soft* real-time systems; those with temporal rigidity are called *hard*. A deadline of three hours may be hard but easily attainable; one of three microseconds (hard or soft) presents the developer with considerable difficulty. Where deadlines, or response times, are very short the system is often called *real* real-time.

A non-real-time system can wait almost indefinitely for processors and other system resources. As long as such a system possesses *liveness* then it will execute appropriately. This is not the case with a real-time system. Because time is bounded and processors are not infinitely fast, a real-time program must be seen to be executing on a system with limited resources. It becomes necessary, therefore, to schedule the use of these resources between competing requests from different parts of the same program; a far from trivial endeavour.

Other characteristics of a typical modern real-time system are:

- they are often geographically distributed;
- they may contain a very large and complex software component;
- they may contain subsystems of different criticality;
- they must interact with concurrent real-world entities;
- they may contain processing elements which are subject to cost, power, size or weight constraints.

It follows from the very nature of most real-time applications that there is a stringent requirement for high reliability. This can also be formulated as a need for dependability and safety. Often, there is an almost symbiotic relationship between the computer system and its immediate environment. One cannot function without the other, as in a fly-by-wire aircraft. To give high levels of reliability requires fault-tolerant hardware and software. There is a need for tolerance of loss of functionality and missed deadlines (even for hard real-time systems).

The combination of temporal requirements, limited resources, concurrent environmental entities and high reliability requirements (together with distributed processing) presents the system engineer with unique problems. Real-time embedded systems engineering, with its central role in the emerging field of cyber-physical systems, is now recognised as a distinct discipline. It has its own body of knowledge and theoretical foundation. From an understanding of the science of large real-time systems, the following are emerging:

- specification techniques that can capture temporal and fault tolerance requirements;
- design methods that have at their heart temporal requirements, and that can deal with methods of providing fault tolerance and distribution;
- programming languages and operating systems that can be used to implement these designs.

This book has been concerned with the theory and practice of implementing real-time Ada systems. Both have to take into account the characteristics and requirements of such systems, fault tolerance techniques, models of concurrency, time-related language features, resource control and low-level programming techniques. The goal has been to discuss the techniques that allow the production of analysable real-time applications. The focus has been has been on the ability to analyse application for their timing properties. To this end, Part I of this book has presented a real-time programming model along with the schedulability analysis techniques (in Part II) that can be used to predict the response times of applications that conform to that model. Part III has then discussed, in detail, the facilities provided by Ada that directly support the model; these are summarised in Table 21.1.

Ada is still the most appropriate language for high-integrity system and those systems that have hard real-time constraints. Of course some systems will be written in more than one language. This is a result of the requirement to use legacy code, and the recognition that it is not appropriate to use the same language for all classes of applications. For example, a real-time application with a significant user interface component might be written in a mixture of Ada and Java. An 'intelligent' real-time systems might require a rule-based component for which the most appropriate language might be Prolog.

21.1 Future challenges

Many of the challenges facing real-time computing are, however, manifest only in large complex applications. For example, consider the International Space Station. The primary function of its computer systems is mission and life support. Other activities include flight control (particularly of the orbital transfer vehicle), external monitoring, the control and

	Ada
Support for programming in the large	Packages; Generics; Tagged types
Support for concurrent programming	Tasks; Protected types
Facilities for fault-tolerant	Exceptions; ATC Execution-time clocks and timers
Real-time facilities	Clocks; Timing events and delays
Scheduling facilities	Coherent priority model Dynamic priorities; Group budgets EDF
Model of device handling	Shared memory; Representation aspects
Profiles	Restricted tasking Ravenscar

Table 21.1: Summary of the facilities provided by Ada.

coordination of experiments, and the management of the mission database. A particularly important aspect of the on-board software is the interface it presents to the flight personnel.

The on-board execution environment for the space station has the following pertinent characteristics:

- It is large and complex (that is, there are a large variety of activities to be computerised).
- It has non-stop execution.
- It has a long operational life (perhaps over 30 years).
- It will experience evolutionary software changes (without stopping).
- It must have highly dependable execution.
- It has components with hard and soft real-time deadlines.
- The distributed system contains heterogeneous processors.

To meet the challenges of this kind of application, the science of real-time systems must continue to develop. There are still many research themes to explore. Even the current state of understanding, which has been the focus of attention in this book, is rarely put into practice. In a search for the 'next generation' of real-time systems, Stankovic identified several research issues [76]. Although much progress has been made since 1988, the following research topics are still crucial to the development of the discipline.

- Specification and verification techniques that can handle the needs of real-time systems with a large number of interacting components of different criticality.
- Design methodologies that consider timing properties from the very beginning of the design process.
- Programming languages with explicit constructs to express time-related behaviour (in particular, relating to distributed computation).
- Scheduling algorithms that can handle complex task structures and resource constraints, timing requirements of varying granularity, and probabilistic guarantees.
- Real-time queuing models.
- Run-time support, or operating system functions, designed to deal with fault tolerant resource usage.
- Tool support for predicting the worst-case and average execution times for software on complex modern multicore processors.
- The integration of worst-case and average case performance metrics.
- Communication architectures and protocols for efficiently dealing with messages that require timely delivery across the Internet.
- Architecture support for fault tolerance and dynamic reconfiguration.
- Integrated support for Artificial Intelligence (for example, machine learning) components.
- Programming language and operating system support for atomic actions, recovery blocks, conversations or group communication protocols.
- Programming languages with explicit support for change management (i.e. the ability to do software upgrades to non-stop systems).
- Real-time virtual machines to support 'write once run anywhere' real-time applications with stringent timing constraints.
- Real-time reflective (self-modifying) architectures allowing applications to adapt their behaviour in response to changing environments.

It is to be hoped that some readers of this book will be able to contribute to these research themes.

References

[1] S. V. Adve and K. Gharachorloo. Shared memory consistency models: A tutorial. *IEEE Computer*, 29(12):66–76, 1996.

[2] S.T. Allworth and R.N. Zobel. *Introduction to Real-Time Software Design*. MacMillan, 1987.

[3] T. Anderson and P.A. Lee. *Fault Tolerance Principles and Practice:*. Prentice-Hall International, 2nd edition, 1990.

[4] ARINC AEE Committee. Avionics application software standard interface, 1999.

[5] N. Audsley et al. Applying new scheduling theory to static priority pre-emptive scheduling. *Software Engineering Journal*, 8(5):284–292, 1993.

[6] N.C. Audsley. On priority assignment in fixed priority scheduling. *Information Processing Letters*, 79(1):39–44, 2001.

[7] A. Avizienis and D.E. Ball. On the achievement of a highly dependable and fault-tolerant air traffic control system. *Computer*, 20(2):84–90, 1987.

[8] A. Avizienis, J.-C. Laprie, B. Randell, and C. Landwehr. Basic concepts and taxonomy of dependable and secure computing. *EEE Transactions on Dependable and Secure Computing*, 1(1):11–33, Jan-March 2004.

[9] A. Avizienis, M. Lyu, and W. Schutz. Multi-version software developmnt: A UCLA/Honeywell joint project for fault-tolerant flight control systems. CSD-880034, Department of Computer Science, University of California, Los Angeles, 1988.

[10] T. P. Baker. Stack-based scheduling of realtime processes. *Real Time Systems*, 3(1), 1991.

[11] S. Baruah. Optimal utilization bounds for the fixed-priority scheduling of periodic task systems on identical multiprocessors. *IEEE Transactions on Computers*, 53(6), 2004.

[12] S. Baruah, N. Cohen, G. Plaxton, and D. Varvel. Proportionate progress: A notion of fairness in resource allocation. *Algorithmica*, 15(6):600–625, June 1996.

[13] I.J. Bate and A. Burns. Timing analysis of fixed priority real-time systems with offsets. In *9th Euromicro Workshop on Real-Time Systems*, pages 153–160, 1997.

[14] E. Bini, G.C. Buttazzo, and G.M. Buttazzo. Rate monotonic scheduling: The hyperbolic bound. *IEEE Transaction in Computer Systems*, 52(7):933–942, 2007.

[15] T. Bloom. Evaluating synchronisation mechanisms. In *Proceedings of the Seventh ACM Symposium on Operating System Principles*, pages 24–32, Pacific Grove, 1979.

[16] H-J. Boehm. Threads cannot be implemented as a library. In *PLDI '05: Proceedings of the 2005 ACM SIGPLAN conference on Programming language design and implementation*, pages 261–268, New York, NY, USA, 2005. ACM.

[17] S.S. Brilliant, J.C. Knight, and N.G. Leveson. The consistent comparison problem in N-version software. *ACM Software Engineering Notes*, 12(1):29–34, 1987.

[18] S.S. Brilliant, J.C. Knight, and N.G. Leveson. Analysis of faults in an N-version software experiment. *IEEE Transactions on Software Engineering*, 16(2):238–47, 1990.

[19] P. Brinch-Hansen. Edison: A multiprocessor language. *Software-Practice and Experience*, 11(4):325–361, 1981.

[20] P. A. Buhr. Are safe concurrency libraries possible? *Communications of the ACM*, 38(2):117–120, 1995.

[21] A. Burns, M. GutiÃl'rrez, M. Aldea Rivas, and M. G. Harbour. A deadline-floor inheritance protocol for edf scheduled embedded real-time systems with resource sharing. *IEEE Transactions on Computers*, 64(5):1241–1253, May 2015.

[22] A. Burns and A. M. Lister. A framework for building dependable systems. *Computer Journal*, 34(2):173–181, 1991.

[23] A. Burns, D. Prasad, A. Bondavalli, F. Di Giandomenico, K. Ramamritham, J. Stankovic, and L. Stringini. The meaning and role of value in scheduling flexible real-time systems. *Journal of Systems Architecture",*, 46:305–325, 2000.

[24] A. Burns and A. J. Wellings. *Hard Real-Time HOOD: A Structured Design Method for Hard Real-Time Ada Systems*. Elsevier, 1995.

[25] G.C. Buttazzo. *Hard Real-Time Computing Systems*. Springer, 2005.

[26] R.H. Campbell and B. Randell. Error recovery in asynchronous systems. *IEEE Transactions on Software Engineering*, 1(8):811–826, 1986.

[27] CCITT. CCITT high level language (CHILL) recommendation Z.200, 1980.

[28] L. Chen and A. Avizienis. N-version programming: A fault-tolerance approach to reliability of software operation. In *Digest of Papers, The Eighth Annual International Conference on Fault-Tolerant Computing*, pages 3–9, Toulouse, France, 1978.

[29] J. de la Puente, A. Alonso, and A. Alvarez. Mapping HRT-HOOD designs to Ada 95 hierarchical libraries. In *Ada-Europe'96 Conference, Springer-Verlag*, 1996.

[30] S. K. Dhall and C. L. Liu. On a real-time scheduling problem. *Operations Research*, 26(1):127–140, Feb. 1978.

[31] E.W. Dijkstra. Solution of a problem in concurrent program control. *Communications of the ACM*, 8(9):569–, 1965.

[32] E.W. Dijkstra. Cooperating sequential processes. In F. Genuys, editor, *Programming Languages*. Academic Press, London, 1968.

[33] O. Marchi dos Santos and A.J. Wellings. Run time detection of blocking time violations in real-time systems. *Proceedings of the 14th IEEE International Conference on Embedded and Real-Time Computing Systems and Applications*, 2008.

[34] B.P. Douglass. *Doing Hard Time: Developing Real-Time Systems with UML, Objects Frameworks and Patterns*. Addison Wesley, 1999.

[35] D.E. Eckhardt, A.K. Caglayan, J.C. Knight, J.D. Lee, D.F. McAllister, M.A. Vouk, and J.P.J. Kelly. An experimental evaluation of software redundancy as a strategy for improving reliability. *IEEE Transactions on Software Engineering*, 17(7):692–702, 1991.

[36] M. Evangelist, M. Francez, and S. Katz. Multiparty interactions for interprocess communication and synchronization. *IEEE Transactions on Software Engineering*, 15(11):1417–26, 1989.

[37] J.R. Garman. The bug heard round the world. *Software Engineering Notes*, 6(3):3–10, 1981.

[38] A.L. Goel and F.B. Bastani. Software reliability. *IEEE Transactions on Software Engineering*, SE-11(12):1409–1410, 1985.

[39] J. Goossens, S. Funk, and S. Baruah. Priority-driven scheduling of periodic task systems on multiprocessors. *Real Time Systems: The International Journal of Time-Critical Computing*, 25(2–3):187–205, 2003.

[40] J. Gray. Why do computers stop and what can be done about it? In *Proceedings on the 5th Symposium on Reliability in Distributed Software and Database Systems*, pages 3–12, 1986.

[41] S.T. Gregory and J.C. Knight. A new linguistic approach to backward error recovery. In *The Fifteenth Annual International Symposium on Fault-Tolerant Computing Digest of Papers*, pages 404–409, 1985.

[42] L. Hatton. N-version design versus one good version. *IEEE Software*, 14(6):71–6, 1997.

[43] H. Hecht and M. Hecht. Fault-tolerant software. In D.K. Pradhan, editor, *Fault-Tolerant Computing Theory and Techniques Volume II*, pages 659–685. Prentice-Hall, 1986.

[44] C.A.R. Hoare. Monitors - an operating system structuring concept. *CACM*, 17(10):549–557, 1974.

[45] B. Hoogeboom and W.A. Halang. The concept of time in the specification of real-time systems. In K.M. Kavi, editor, *Real-Time Systems: Abstractions, Languages and desihn Methodologies*, pages 19–38. IEEE Computer Society Press, 1992.

[46] J. J. Horning, H. C. Lauer, P. M. Melliar-Smith, and B. Randell. A program structure for error detection and recovery. In E. Gelenbe and C. Kaiser, editors, *Lecture Notes in Computer Science 16*, pages 171 – 187. Springer-Verlag, 1974.

[47] M. Joseph, editor. *Real-Time Systems: Specification, Verification and Analysis*. Prentice-Hall, 1996.

[48] J.C. Knight, N.G. Leveson, and L.D. St.Jean. A large scale experiment in N-version programming. In *Digest of Papers, The Fifteenth Annual International Symposium on Fault-Tolerant Computing*, pages 135–139, Nichigan, USA, 1985.

[49] J. Kramer, J. Magee, M.S. Sloman, and A.M. Lister. CONIC: an integrated approach to distributed computer control systems. In *IEE Proceedings (Part E)*, pages 1–10, 1983.

[50] L. Lamport. How to make a correct multiprocess program execute correctly on a multiprocessor. *IEEE Transactions on Computers*, 46(7):779–782, 1997.

[51] J.C. Laprie. Dependable - its attributes, impairments and means. In B. Randell et al., editors, *Predictable Dependable Computig Systems*. Springer, 1995.

[52] P.A. Lee, N. Ghani, and K. Heron. A recovery cache for the PDP-11. *IEEE Transactions on Computers*, C-29(6):546–549, 1980.

[53] M.M. Lehman and L.A. Belady. The characteristics of large systems. In *Program Evolution - Processes of Software Change, APIC Studies in Data processing No. 27*, pages 289–329. Academic Press, 1985.

[54] N.G. Leveson. Software safety: Why, what and how. *ACM Computing Surveys*, 18(2):125–163, 1986.

[55] B. Littlewood, P. Popov, and L. Strigini. Modelling software design diversity - a review. *ACM Computing Surveys*, 33(2):177–208, 2001.

[56] B. Littlewood and L. Strigini. Validation of ultrahigh dependability for software-based systems. *Communications of the ACM*, 36(11):69–80, 1993.

[57] C.L. Liu and J.W. Layland. Scheduling algorithms for multiprogramming in a hard real-time environment. *JACM*, 20(1):46–61, 1973.

[58] J.W.S. Liu. *Real-Time Systems*. Prentice Hall, 2000.

[59] D.B. Lomet. Process structuring, synchronisation and recovery using atomic actions. In *Proceedings ACM Conference Language Design for Reliable Software SIGPLAN*, pages 128–137, 1977.

[60] J. M. Lopez, J. L. Diaz, and D. F. Garcia. Utilization bounds for EDF scheduling on real-time multiprocessor systems. *Real-Time Systems Journal*, 28(1):39–68, 2004.

[61] D.J. Martin. Dissimilar software in high integrity applications in flight controls. In *AGARD Symposium on Software for Avionics*, page 36:1, 1982.

[62] D.-I. Oh and T. P. Baker. Utilization bounds for N-processor rate monotone scheduling with static processor assignment. *Real-Time Systems Journal*, 15:183–192, 1998.

[63] D.L. Parnas. Software aging. In *Proceedings of the 16th international conference on Software engineering*, pages 279 – 287, 1994.

[64] G.L. Peterson. Myths about the mutual exclusion problem. *Information Processing Letters*, 12(3):115–16, 1981.

[65] J.M. Purtilo and P. Jalote. An environment for developing fault-tolerant software. *IEEE Transactions on Software Engineering*, 17(2):153–9, 1991.

[66] B. Randell. System structure for software fault tolerance. *IEEE Transactions on Software Engineering*, SE-1(2):220–232, 1975.

[67] B. Randell. *The Origins of Digital Computers: selected papers*. Springer Verlag, 1982.

[68] B. Randell, J-C. Laprie, H. Kopetz, and B. Littlewood(Eds.). *Predictably Dependable Computing Systems*. Springer, 1995.

[69] B. Randell, P.A. Lee, and P.C. Treleaven. Reliability issues in computing system design. *ACM Computing Surveys*, 10(2):123–165, 1978.

[70] J. Regehr. Safe and structured use of interrupts in real-time and embedded software. In Insup Lee, Joseph Y-T. Leug, and Sang H. Son, editors, *Handbook of Real-Time and Embedded Systems*, pages 16–1–16–12. Chapman and Hall/CRC, 2007.

[71] P. Rogers and A. J. Wellings. An incremental recovery cache supporting software fault tolerance mechanisms. *Computer Systems Science and Engineering*, 15(1):33–48, January 2000.

[72] L. Sha, R. Rajkumar, and J. P. Lehoczky. Priority inheritance protocols: An approach to real-time synchronisation. *IEEE Transactions on Computers*, 39(9):1175–1185, 1990.

[73] S.K. Shrivastava. Sequential Pascal with recovery blocks. *Software - Practice and Experience*, 8(2):177–186, 1978.

[74] S.K. Shrivastava, L. Mancini, and B. Randell. On the duality of fault tolerant structures. In *Lecture Notes in Computer Science*, volume 309, pages 19 – 37. Springer-Verlag, 1987.

[75] M. Sloman and J. Kramer. *Distributed Systems and Computer Networks*. Prentice-Hall, 1987.

[76] J.A. Stankovic. Misconceptions about real-time computing: A serious problem for next generation systems. *IEEE Computer*, 21(10):10–19, 1988.

[77] K. Tindell, A. Burns, and A. J. Wellings. An extendible approach for analysing fixed priority hard real-time tasks. *Real-Time Systems*, 6(2):133–151, 1994.

[78] S. Vestal. Preemptive scheduling of multi-criticality systems with varying degrees of execution time assurance. In *Proc. of the IEEE Real-Time Systems Symposium (RTSS)*, pages 239–243, 2007.

[79] W. Walker and H.G. Cragon. Interrupt processing in concurrent processors. *Computer*, 28(6):36–46, 1995.

[80] A. J. Wellings and A. Burns. Implementing atomic actions in Ada 95. *IEEE Transactions on Software Engineering*, 23(2):107–123, 1997.

[81] Xerox Corporation. Mesa language manual verson 5.0, 1985.

[82] S.J. Young. *Real Time Languages: Design and Development*. Ellis Horwood Publishers, Chichester, 1982.

[83] J. Yuh-Jzer and S. A. Smolka. A comprehensive study of the complexity of multiparty interaction. *Journal of the ACM*, 43(1):75–115, 1996.

[84] F. Zhang and A. Burns. Schedulability analysis for real-time systems with EDF scheduling. *IEEE Transaction on Computers*, 58(9):1250–1258, 2008.

Index

'Count, 253, 272, 274, 279
'Storage_Pool, 366

abort completion point, 411
abort-deferred operation, 410, 411
abortion, 197
absolute delay, 296
absolute error, 160
abstract data types, 171, 174
acceptance test, 55, 57
access permissions, 52
access variables, 162
active object, 199, 462
active priority, 327
actuator, 4
Ada
    'Caller, 207
    'Count, 250
    abstract data types, 175
    anonymous tasks, 206
    Atomic, 261
    Atomic_Components, 261
    barrier, 246
    concurrent execution, 202
    dynamic task creation, 204
    entry call, 248
    generics, 184
    interfaces, 256
    package, 171
        Ada.Asynchronous_Task_Control, 329
        Ada.Calendar, 294
        Ada.Dispatching.EDF, 330
        Ada.Exceptions, 380
        Ada.Execution_Time, 433
        Ada.Execution_Time.Group_Budgets, 441
        Ada.Execution_Time.Interrupts, 437
        Ada.Execution_Time.Timers, 435, 437
        Ada.Interrupts, 358
        Ada.Interrupts.Names, 359
        Ada.Real_Time, 295
        Ada.Real_Time.Timing_Events, 307
        Ada.Synchronous_Barriers, 257
        Ada.Task_Identification, 207
        Ada.Task_Termination, 208
        Standard, 373
        System.Storage_Pools, 366
    protected interfaces, 256
    protected objects, 245
    semaphores, 238
    synchronized interfaces, 256
    task, 202
        termination, 207
    task identifiers, 206
    task interfaces, 256
    Task_Id, 207
    Tasking_Error, 205
    terminate alternative, 207
    unhandled exception, 207
allocation, 210
alternative module, 55
Amdahl's Law, 192
Annexes, 156
anytime algorithms, 422

INDEX

aperiodic activities, 3, 29, 303
aperiodic servers, 439
aperiodic task, 26, 87, 303
application error detection, 50
arbitrary deadlines, 28, 113
architectural design, 17, 458
arrays, 161
aspect, 187
    Attach_Handler, 356
    Interrupt_Priority, 326
    Priority, 326
assembly language, 154
assertions, 51
asynchronous events, 405
asynchronous exceptions, 372
asynchronous notification, 372, 405, 407
asynchronous select statement, 408
asynchronous transfer of control, *see* ATC
ATC, 299, 405, 408
    exceptions, 410
atomic actions, 52, 393, 394
    Ada, 398
    ATC, 411
    backward error recovery, 402
    concurrent languages, 398
    exceptions, 404
    forward error recovery, 403
    requirements, 397
atomic data, 261
atomic operation, 224
atomic transactions, 52, 396
atomicity, 58
Attach_Handler, 356
attaching an interrupt handler, 356
attribute, 187
    Count, 253, 272, 274, 279
attribute definition clause, 353
avoidance synchronization, 245, 269

backward error recovery, 53
    atomic actions, 402
    concurrent tasks, 412
Baker's algorithm, 108, 332
bar, 225, 226
barrier, 225, 226, 245, 247, 255

evaluation, 248
    protected entry call, 248
base priority, 326
basic block, 79
best-effort, 146
binary semaphores, 238
block structure, 157
blocking
    response time analysis, 95
blocking analysis, 91
Bloom's criteria, 269
Bohrbugs, 38
bounded buffer, 225
    Ada, 247
    conditional critical regions, 241
    monitors, 242, 243
bounded liveliness, 24
broadcast, 419
bugs, 38
busy period, 85
busy waiting, 216, 225, 227

C
    exception handling, 370
C++, 375
C/Real-Time POSIX
    exception handling, 378
    vfork, 200
Calendar, 293
CAN, 142
case statement, 165
catch all, 375
causal ordering, 290
ceiling function, 84
ceiling protocols
    deadlock, 99
    mutual exclusion, 99
channel programs, 346
child packages, 178
child task, 197
CHILL, 155, 375
circular wait, 286
class hierarchy, 177
class-wide types, 178
client/server model, 207
clock drift, 291

INDEX

clock skew, 292
clocks, 293
    access to, 291
    modelling, 126
cluster-based, 142
coarse grain parallelism, 197
cobegin, 201
coding, 17, 458
coding checks, 51
commitments, 458
communication, command and control, 6
comparison points, 46
comparison status indicators, 46
comparison vectors, 46
competing tasks, 196, 267, 393
concurrency
    granularity, 196
    initialization, 196
    level, 196
    representation, 196
    structure, 196
    termination, 196
concurrent control, 11
concurrent exceptions, 404
Concurrent Pascal, 242
concurrent programming, 191
condition synchronisation, 247
    Ada, 248
condition synchronization, 224
    semaphores, 234
condition variables, 243
conditional critical regions, 241
conditional entry call, 299
conditional waiting, 244, 269
configuration, 210
configuration pragma, 315
consistent comparison problem, 47
constrained deadlines, 28, 89
constraint error, 373
Constraint_Error, 373
constraints, 459
constructors, 176
context switching, 347
    overheads, 124
continuous, 15
controlled types, 179, 276, 384, 411

controlled variables, 385
conversation, 425
conversations, 402
cooperating tasks, 196, 267, 393
cooperative dispatching, 73
cooperative scheduling, 114
coordinated sections, 225
count attribute, 253, 272, 274, 279
counting semaphores, 233
critical instant, 74
critical section, 224
criticality, 132
cumulative drift, 297
cyber-physical systems, 8, 291
cycle stealing, 346
cyclic executive, 70, 324
cyclic object, 463

damage confinement, 439
damage confinement and assessment, 49, 52, 428
data logging, 7
data retrieval, 7
data types, 158
deadline, 31
deadline less than period, 87
deadline miss
    recovery, 449
deadline miss detection, 430
deadline monotonic, 89
deadline monotonic priority ordering, 90
deadline overrun detection, 421
deadline primitive, 31
deadline scheduling, 26
Deadline-Floor Protocol, 108
deadlock, 95, 99, 237, 286
    avoidance, 286
    detection and recovery, 286
    prevention, 286
deferrable server, 88, 121, 439, 445
deferred preemption, 73, 115, 116
delay, 31, 296
    absolute, 296
    relative, 296
delay primitive, 31
delta, 161

dense time, 290
dependability, 64
dependant, 198
derived deadline, 33
derived types, 159, 177
design diversity, 45, 58
destructors, 176
detailed design, 17, 458
device driving, 343, 352
    scheduling, 362
device handling models, 351
device identification, 348
device polling, 348
devices, 11
Dhall effect, 139
digital control, 7
discrete time, 83
discrete types, 158
dispatching domain, 211
distributed systems, 194, 209
DMA, 346
dominate schedulability tests, 73
domino effect, 53, 402
driver task, 45
dual-priority scheduling, 89
dynamic reasonableness checks, 51
dynamic redundancy, 44, 58, 59
dynamic scheduling, 70

Earliest Deadline First, 72, *see* EDF
ease of use, 268
EDF, 72, 102, 103, 329
    blocking, 108
    execution-time servers, 109
    QPA, 107
    utilization-based schedulability test, 101
EDF_Across_Priorities, 332
Edison, 242
efficiency, 153
Eiffel, 376, 378
embedded systems, 1, 3
encapsulation, 171, 351
entry
    family, 251, 271
entry barriers, 248

entry call, 248, 411
    conditional, 299
    timed, 299
enumeration representation clause, 353
enumeration types, 158
environemnt task, 205
environmental error detection, 50
error, 36
    detection, 44, 49, 50, 58, 427
    diagnosis, 49
    recovery, 50, 52, 428
error diagnosis, 49
error recovery, 419, 446
event handler, 28
event-triggered systems, 3, 28
exact schedulability tests, 73
exception catching, 59
exception handler, 157
exception handling, 36, 59, 369, 381
    hybrid model, 376, 378
    notify model, 376
    requirements, 369
    resumption model, 376
    termination model, 376
    when others, 381
exception propagation, 382
exceptions, 59, 379, 410
    ATC, 410
    atomic actions, 404
    classes, 372
    domains, 373
    identifiers, 379
    propagation, 375
    recovery blocks, 387
    reraising, 383
    suppression, 385
exclusive functions, 246
execution environment, 459
execution-time clocks, 433
    timers, 434, 436, 437
execution-time servers, 88, 121, 439, 440
expressive power, 153, 268
external state, 37

fail controlled, 41
fail late, 40

INDEX 507

fail never, 41
fail safe, 26, 43
fail silent, 40
fail soft, 43
fail stop, 41
fail uncontrolled, 40
failure, 36, 39
failure modes, 39
fault, 37
    active, 37
    avoidance, 41
    domant, 37
    intermittent, 37
    location, 55
    permanent, 37
    prevention, 41
    removal, 41, 42
    software bugs, 38
    sources, 35
    transient, 37
    treatment and continued service, 50, 54, 428
fault model, 61, 117
fault tolerance, 26, 36, 41, 42, 116, 427, 489
    real-time, 427
fault, error, failure chain, 37
feed-forward controller, 14
feedback controller, 14
finalisation, 276
fine grain parallelism, 197
firewalling, 52
firm real-time, 3, 26
Fixed Priority Scheduling, *see* FPS
fixed-point types, 161
flexibility, 153
flits, 143
float, 160
for loop, 166
fork and join, 200
forward error recovery, 53, 59, 427
    atomic actions, 403
    concurrent tasks, 415
FPS, 72, 74, 75, 83
fully partitioned, 211
functions, 169

garbage collection, 365
global dispatching, 209
global placement, 138
global time, 292
GPS, 291
graceful degradation, 43
group budgets, 440
group communication protocol, 252
guardian, 198

hard real-time, 2, 26, 88
hardware input/output mechanisms, 343
hardware interfaces, 12
heap management, 365
    Ada, 365
Heisenbugs, 38
high availability, 43
hold and wait, 286
HRT-HOOD, 457
hybrid model of exception handling, 376, 378
hybrid systems, 146, 291

ICPP, 95, 97, 326
ideal fault-tolerant component, 60
identifiers, 157
if statement, 164
immediate ceiling priority inheritance, 95, 97
implicit deadlines, 28
imprecise computations, 407, 422
incremental checkpointing, 53
indefinite postponement, 237
independent, 261
independent tasks, 195, 267, 393
indivisible action, 394
indivisible operation, 224
inexact voting, 47, 58
information hiding, 171
inheritance, 176, 177
initialization, 196
inline expansion, 170
input jitter, 3, 25, 27
input/output jitter, 308, 311
    Ada, 308, 313
insufficient priorities, 120

508　INDEX

interactive system, 26
interface, 181, 182
 limited, 184
interference, 83
intermittent fault, 37
internal state, 37
interrupt
 identification, 356
 latency, 355
 priority control, 349
interrupt control, 349
interrupt handling
 Ada model, 355
 attaching an Ada handler, 356
 dynamic attaching in Ada, 356
 model, 355
 protected procedure, 356
interrupt identification, 349
interrupt masks, 349
interrupt-driven device control, 345
interrupt-driven program-controlled device control, 345
intertask communication, 195
iteration, 165

job, 74

kernel-level threads, 193

last wishes, 383
Least Laxity First, 72, 103
library-level threads, 193
limited interface, 184
limited private, 175
linear time, 290
Linux, 200
Liu and Layland utilization bound, 75
livelock, 228
liveness, 237, 238
LLF, 72
 utilization-based schedulability test, 103
local drift, 297
Locking_Policy, 326
lockout, 237
logical architecture, 459, 463
long integer, 158

low-level programming, 12

major cycle, 70
manufacturing control system, 5
Mars Pathfinder, 93
masking redundancy, 44
memory management, 364
memory-mapped I/O, 343
Mesa, 155, 242, 376, 378
message passing, 223
mine drainage, 457
minimum inter-arrival time, 87
minor cycle, 70
mishaps, 63
MIT, 435
mixed scheduling, 338
mixed-criticality system, 451
mixed-criticality systems, 26, 132
mode changes, 407, 421, 450
model checking, 24
Modula-1, 242
modular decomposition, 52
modularity, 351
modules, 170
 Ada, 171
monitors, 242
 criticisms, 245
multi-media systems, 7
multiprocessor system, 194
 mutual exclusion, 143
 schedulability analysis, 138
multiprocessors, 209
 shared memory, 260
mutual exclusion, 96, 99, 224, 286
 Peterson's algorithm, 228
 protected objects, 245
 semaphores, 234

N Modular Redundancy, 44
N-version programming, 45, 53
 recovery blocks, 58
name notation, 162
necessary conditions for schedulability, 72
necessary schedulability tests, 73
nested atomic actions, 395

INDEX

nested monitor calls, 245
network-on-chip, 143
NMR, 44
no preemption, 286
non-local goto, 371
non-preemptive scheduling, 73, 115
notify model, 376
NTP, 291
NUMA, 194
numerical computation, 13

object-oriented abstraction, 19
object-oriented programming, 176, 199
obligations, 458
OCPP, 95, 98
OCPP versus ICPP, 98
offset analysis, 117
omission failure, 40
OOP, 176
    interfaces, 182
OOP and concurrency, 209
open systems, 144
operating systems, 192
operating systems vs language concurrency, 219
ordinal scale, 145
original ceiling priority protocol, 95
output jitter, 3, 25

package, 171
    System, 325
    Ada.Asynchronous_Task_Control, 329
    Ada.Calendar, 294
    Ada.Dispatching.EDF, 330
    Ada.Dynamic_Priorities, 328
    Ada.Exceptions, 380
    Ada.Execution_Time, 433
    Ada.Execution_Time.Group_Budgets, 440, 441
    Ada.Execution_Time.Interrupts, 437
    Ada.Execution_Time.Timers, 435, 437
    Ada.Interrupts, 358
    Ada.Interrupts.Names, 359
    Ada.Real_Time, 295
    Ada.Real_Time.Timing_Events, 307
    Ada.Synchronous_Barriers, 257
    Ada.Task_Identification, 207
    Ada.Task_Termination, 208
    Calendar, 294
    Exceptions, 379
    Standard, 372, 373
    System, 354
    System.Machine_Code, 362
    System.Multiprocessors, 212
    System.Storage_Elements, 354, 365
    System.Storage_Pools, 366
package body, 171
package specification, 171
parallelism, 194
parameter passing, 167
parent task, 197
partial computations, 422
partitioned placement, 138
partitioning, 210
passive, 199
passive object, 462
Patriot missile defence system, 38
PDCS, 2
Pearl, 376
period, 29
period displacement, 364, 461
periodic, 25
periodic activities, 3
periodic server, 121
periodic task, 302
    release jitter, 113
permanent fault, 37
persistent signal, 421, 423
Peterson's mutual exclusion algorithm, 228
physical architecture, 459, 467
pointers, 162
polymorphism, 176
portability, 153
power-aware systems, 122
preemption levels, 332
preemptive scheduling, 73

prefix notation, 180
primary module, 55
priority, 72, 269, 283, 325
    assignment
        deadline monotonic, 89
        optimal, 119
        rate monotonic, 74
    ceiling protocol, 95
    ceiling protocol emulation, 98
    inheritance, 93
    interrupt, 325
    inversion, 91
priority-based scheduling, 325
priority-based systems, 325
Priority_Specific_Dispatching, 339
private entries, 251
procedures, 168
process, 192
process control, 4
processor affinity, 209
processor demand function, 103
producer–consumer, 225
progenitors, 184
Program_Error, 327
programming in the large, 156, 170
programming in the small, 156
protected, 199, 268
protected action, 245
protected entry, 245, 247
    barriers, 248
protected function, 246
protected objects, 245, 303, 327
    device driving, 352
    entry family, 251
    HRT-HOOD, 463
    interfaces, 256
    private entry, 251
    readers/writers problem, 254
protected procedure, 246
    interrupt handling, 356
protected resource, 199
protected subprogram, 245
protection mechanisms, 52

quantity semaphores, 238
Quick Processor Demand Analysis, 107

race condition, 231
raising an exception, 59
rate monotonic, 74
Ravenscar, 314
    scheduling, 340
reactive objects, 199
reactive system, 3
read lock, 249
read/write locks, 249
readability, 152
readers-writers, 227
readers/writers problem, 254
ready queue, 210, 325
real numbers, 13, 159
real-time
    definition of, 2
    programming model, 30
Real-Time Basic, 378
real-time clock, 293
real-time control, 10
real-time events, 306
Real-Time Systems Annex, 326
real-time task, 302
reasonableness checks, 51
reconfiguration, 210, 450
record aggregates, 161
record representation clause, 353
records, 161
recoverable action, 396
recoverable atomic actions, 401
recovery blocks, 55
    exceptions, 387
    N-version programming, 58
recovery cache, 53
recovery lines, 54
recovery point, 53, 55
recurrence relationship, 84
recursion, 165
redundancy, 44
relative delay, 296
relative error, 160
release, 74
release jitter, 111
reliability, 11
    definition, 36
    metrics, 62

INDEX 511

prediction, 62
safety, 63
remote monitoring, 7
rendezvous, 352
replication checks, 50
representation aspect
    Priority, 326
representation aspects, 206, 353
request order, 269
request parameters, 269
request priority, 269
request type, 269
requeue
    semantics, 280
    with abort, 281
requirement specification, 18, 458
resource, 199
resource allocation, 269
resource control, 267, 281
resource management, 268
resource usage, 285
    overruns, 429
resource usage overruns, 438
response failure, 2
response time, 10, 36
response time analysis, 83, 362
    arbitrary deadlines, 113
    blocking, 95
    cooperative scheduling, 115
    iterative solution, 85
    release jitter, 112
resumption model, 376, 406
reusability, 184
reversal checks, 51
robot arm, 203
    Ada, 203
RTL/2, 371
RTSS, 235
run-time dispatching, 176, 178
run-time support system, 194

safety, 11, 63
safety integrity levels(SIL), 132
schedulability analysis
    notation, 74
schedulability test, 72

scheduling, 69, 362, 407
    cooperative, 73
    kernel models, 123
    non-preemptive, 73
    preemptive, 73
    response time analysis, 83
    utilization-based analysis, 75
security, 64, 152, 284
select-then-abort, 299, 331
semaphores, 233
    Ada, 238
    criticisms, 240
    implementation, 235
sensor, 4
separate compilation, 171, 173
sequence, 164
server, 88
server state, 269
servers, 199, 268
shared variables, 223
short integer, 158
signals, 378, 405
    monitor, 243
    on a semaphore, 233
simple embedded system, 262, 319, 340
simple task model, 73
simplicity, 153
simulators, 20
single processor, 194
SMP, 194, 260
soft real-time, 2, 26, 88
software aging, 38
software architecture, 30
software bugs, 38
software dynamic redundancy, 49
software reliability growth models, 63
special instructions, 343
specification, 48
specifying timing requirements, 23
sporadic, 3, 25, 26
sporadic activities, 303
sporadic activity, 31
sporadic event
    overruns, 429
sporadic event overrun
    recovery, 448

sporadic events overruns, 434, 435
sporadic object, 463
sporadic overrun, 434
Sporadic Server, 88
sporadic server, 121, 439
sporadic task, 71, 87, 126
    release jitter, 111
Stack Resource Policy, 108
stack resource policy, 108
standard time, 291
starvation, 237
static redundancy, 44, 58
static scheduling, 70
status driven device control mechanisms, 345
storage pools, 365, 366
structural checks, 51
stubs, 174
subprograms, 167
subtypes, 159
sufficient conditions for schedulability, 72
sufficient schedulability tests, 73
suspend and resume, 231
suspended tasks, 235
suspension object, 232
sustainable schedulability tests, 73
swap instruction, 236
synchronized interface, 258
    timeouts, 259
synchronous exceptions, 372
system overheads, 74, 123
system repair, 55

tagged types, 177
task, 192
    abortion, 197, 208, 276
    activation, 328
    blocking, 91
    declaration, 202
    discriminant, 326
    identification, 206
    identifiers, 206
    interaction, 91
    representation, 200
    states, 71, 194, 198
    termination, 197, 207, 411
    types, 326
task discriminants, 205
task-based scheduling, 71
TDMA, 142
temporal scopes, 24, 27
termination, 196
    Ada, 207
termination model, 376, 406
test and set, 236
testing, 17, 20, 458
the barrier problem, 255
thread, 192
    synchronization, 195
threads, 193
threshold value, 47
throwing an exception, 59
time, 289, 293
    continuous, 291
    discrete, 291
    standard, 291
time failure, 39
time triggered events, 306
time-aware system, 3
time-line, 76
time-triggered system, 3
time-triggered systems, 28
timed entry call, 299
timeouts, 298
timing checks, 50
timing errors, 427
timing events, 306
timing faults, 427
TMR, 44
transactions, 52
transducer, 4
transient blocking, 95
transient fault, 37
transient overload, 88
transparent execution, 210
triggering event, 408
    cancellation, 409
triple modular redundancy, 44
two-phase actions, 395
two-stage suspend, 231
type extensibility, 176

type security, 158
typedef, 158

UAV, 133
unanticipated errors, 36
unchecked conversion, 362
unchecked deallocation, 163
unhandled exception, 375
Universal time, 291
user interrupts, 407
UTC, 291
utilization-based schedulability tests, 75

value failure, 39
Value-Based Scheduling, 72
VBS, 72
vectored interrupts, 348
virtual links, 143
volatile data, 261
vote comparison, 47

wait
    monitor, 243
    on a semaphore, 233
watchdog timer, 50, 431
WCET, 79, 126, 132
    overrun, 432, 433
        recovery, 446
while loop, 166
wormhole routing, 142
worst-case behaviour, 10, 69
worst-case execution time, 28
    overruns, 429
worst-case execution time analysis, 79

Printed in Poland
by Amazon Fulfillment
Poland Sp. z o.o., Wrocław